SEEDS OF DISASTER, ROOTS OF RESPONSE

HOW PRIVATE ACTION CAN REDUCE PUBLIC VULNERABILITY

In the wake of 9/11 and Hurricane Katrina, executives and policymakers are more motivated than ever to reduce the vulnerability of social and economic systems to disasters. Most prior work on "critical infrastructure protection" has focused on the responsibilities and actions of government rather than on those of the private-sector firms that provide most vital services. *Seeds of Disaster, Roots of Response* is the first systematic attempt to understand how private decisions and operations affect public vulnerability. It describes effective and sustainable approaches – both business strategies and public policies – to ensure provision of critical services in the event of disaster. The authors are business leaders from multiple industries and experts in fields as diverse as risk analysis, economics, engineering, organization theory, and public policy. The book shows the necessity of deeply rooted collaboration between private and public institutions, and the accountability and leadership required to go from words to action.

Philip E. Auerswald, PhD, is director of the Center for Science and Technology Policy and an assistant professor at the School of Public Policy, George Mason University. Professor Auerswald's work focuses on linked processes of technological and organizational change in the contexts of policy, economics, and strategy. He is the co-editor of *Innovations: Technology | Governance | Globalization,* a quarterly journal from MIT Press about people using technology to address global challenges.

Lewis M. Branscomb, PhD, is professor of Public Policy and Corporate Management, Emeritus, at Harvard University's Kennedy School of Government. He also holds faculty appointments at the University of California, San Diego. Branscomb was the co-chairman of the project of the National Academies of Science and of Engineering and the Institute of Medicine, which authored the 2002 report *Making the Nation Safer: Science and Technology for Countering Terrorism.*

Todd M. La Porte, PhD, is an associate professor at George Mason University. He was a member of the Faculty of Technology, Policy and Management at the Delft University of Technology in The Netherlands. He also served for six years as an analyst in the information technology and the international security programs at the Office of Technology Assessment (OTA), a research office of the U.S. Congress.

Erwann O. Michel-Kerjan, PhD, is managing director of the Center for Risk Management and Decision Processes at the University of Pennsylvania's Wharton School. His work focuses on financing extreme events, with a prime interest in the creation and implementation of private–public collaboration among top decision makers of organizations or countries in America and Europe. He is a member of the Global Risk Network of the World Economic Forum.

Seeds of Disaster, Roots of Response

How Private Action Can Reduce Public Vulnerability

Edited by

PHILIP E. AUERSWALD
School of Public Policy, George Mason University

LEWIS M. BRANSCOMB
Kennedy School of Government, Harvard University

TODD M. LA PORTE
School of Public Policy, George Mason University

ERWANN O. MICHEL-KERJAN
The Wharton School, University of Pennsylvania

CAMBRIDGE
UNIVERSITY PRESS

CAMBRIDGE UNIVERSITY PRESS
Cambridge, New York, Melbourne, Madrid, Cape Town, Singapore, São Paulo

Cambridge University Press
32 Avenue of the Americas, New York, NY 10013-2473, USA

www.cambridge.org
Information on this title: www.cambridge.org/9780521857963

First published 2006

Printed in the United States of America

A catalog record for this publication is available from the British Library.

Library of Congress Cataloging in Publication Data

Seeds of disaster, roots of response : how private action can reduce public
vulnerability / edited by Philip E. Auerswald ... [et al.].
    p.   cm.
Includes bibliographical references and index.
ISBN-13: 978-0-521-85796-3 (hardback)
ISBN-10: 0-521-85796-1 (hardback)
ISBN-13: 978-0-521-68572-6 (pbk.)
ISBN-10: 0-521-68572-9 (pbk.)
1. Emergency management.   2. Infrastructure (Economics) – Security measures.
3. Public-private sector cooperation.   4. Crisis management.   5. Risk management.
6. Preparedness.   I. Auerswald, Philip E.   II. Title.
HV551.2.S44   2006
363.34′60973 – dc22   2006015888

ISBN-13   978-0-521-85796-3 hardback
ISBN-10   0-521-85796-1 hardback

ISBN-13   978-0-521-68572-6 paperback
ISBN-10   0-521-68572-9 paperback

CONTENTS

v

LIST OF CONTRIBUTORS

Philip E. Auerswald, School of Public Policy, George Mason University

Lewis M. Branscomb, John F. Kennedy School of Government, Harvard University

Todd M. La Porte, School of Public Policy, George Mason University

Erwann O. Michel-Kerjan, The Wharton School, University of Pennsylvania

Jay Apt, Carnegie Mellon University

Thomas Bowe, PJM Interconnect

Lloyd Dixon, RAND Corporation

John D. Donahue, Kennedy School of Government, Harvard University

Jacob Feinstein, Consolidated Edison (ret.)

Stephen E. Flynn, Council on Foreign Relations

Robert Allan Frosch, Kennedy School of Government, Harvard University

Sean P. Gorman, FortiusOne

Geoffrey Heal, Columbia Business School

Michael Kearns, The Wharton School, University of Pennsylvania

Paul Kleindorfer, The Wharton School, University of Pennsylvania

Michael Kormos, PJM Interconnect

Howard Kunreuther, The Wharton School, University of Pennsylvania

List of Contributors

Patrick Lagadec, École Polytechnique in Paris

Todd R. LaPorte, University of California, Berkeley

Lester B. Lave, Carnegie Mellon University

Brian D. Lopez, Lawrence Livermore National Laboratories

James W. MacDonald, ACE USA

M. Granger Morgan, Carnegie Mellon University

Franklin W. Nutter, Reinsurance Association of American

Daniel B. Prieto, Reform Institute

Robert Reville, RAND Corporation

Emery Roe, California State University, East Bay

Paul R. Schulman, Mills College

Richard J. Zeckhauser, Kennedy School of Government, Harvard University

See author biographies on page 531.

FOREWORD

The nation's critical infrastructures are the great underlying strength of our country. In a word, things work. We take it for granted that when we throw the switch, the lights come on; when we turn the faucet, water flows; when we pick up the phone, we get a dial tone; when we dial 911, help arrives; and when necessary, we can confidently dispatch goods for overnight delivery to any location in the nation. These infrastructures underpin our economic strength, our national security, and our society's welfare – in simple terms, they are our nation's life support systems. It is the ready availability of reliable telecommunications, transportation, electrical power, fuel, financial, and emergency services that constitutes the solid foundation of our economy. Without ever-reliable telecommunications, power, and transportation infrastructures, our ability to mobilize and deploy the armed forces would be crippled. And finally, our modern society has become vitally dependent on these infrastructures for our most basic activities of subsistence, work, entertainment, transportation, and communications. Denial of any one of these services would cause widespread discomfort and discontent.

However, these infrastructures are not as robust as we might believe. Under continuing pressure to improve services, these systems' owners and operators eagerly pursued and incorporated the latest and best of information-age technology – computers to replace manual control, software to autonomously analyze and manipulate operations, higher communications speed and bandwidth to quickly move vast amounts of data, use of the Internet for commercial transactions and critical system control, and satellites to provide precision timing and location information for all the foregoing, to name a few. And in the rush to incorporate the latest technology, scant attention has been paid to resilience, survivability, and security. The modern information and communication technology incorporated in the late decades of the last century contained early indications of increasing reliability problems and vulnerabilities. Widespread electric power outages appeared. Computer networks were invaded by unauthorized intruders. Thousands of computers were rendered inoperative by viruses. And cyber crime emerged as a serious law-enforcement challenge.

In recognition of these happenings and following a growing concern with domestic and foreign terrorism, a governmental interagency working group was formed to assess the magnitude of the emerging problems and to recommend a course of action to address them. After a year of deliberation, the working group concluded that the problems were of such importance, magnitude, and complexity that they warranted a concerted, high-level deliberative effort by a Presidential commission. Because of the preponderant ownership of the infrastructures by the private sector, the working group recommended that the commission comprise representatives from both the private and public sectors. Such a commission was directed by President Clinton by Executive Order 13010 on July 15, 1996. The resulting President's Commission on Critical Infrastructure Protection was charged with identifying the threats to the United States' critical infrastructures, assessing their vulnerabilities, and devising a strategy and plan for their protection. I had the pleasure of chairing that effort.

The commission was uniquely tailored for its task. As envisioned by the working group, the commission comprised representatives from federal departments and agencies and from the private sector; a steering committee of senior government officials helped us weave our way through the tangled web of government equities, and an advisory committee of key industry leaders (appointed by President Clinton) provided advice from the perspective of infrastructure owners, operators, and consumers. The commission deliberated full time over a period of 15 months and rendered its report in October 1997.

Much of the Commission's 15-month effort was devoted to researching and characterizing the infrastructures. They were then subjected to detailed analyses to identify their principal vulnerabilities. These analyses were conducted on a sector-by-sector basis. We found that networks of computers, databases, and communications (which can be called the cyber infrastructure) underpin each of the critical infrastructures. In other words, we found that every infrastructure relies on a cyber infrastructure to provide the communications and data handling necessary for its functioning. And we found that the critical infrastructures are interdependent – they are linked in a mutually supportive web that is not well understood. In addition, increasing the network linkage is creating unknown intersections and dependencies among infrastructures. This linkage increases the likelihood that a major disruption in one infrastructure will cascade into another. The bottom line is that the complexity of our systems, the almost frenetic manner in which they have evolved with little or no attention to security, has created a seemingly endless range of vulnerabilities.

As to the threat, we did not find a "smoking keyboard" – we found no evidence that our nation's infrastructures were in immediate danger of a devastating cyber attack. Essentially, we found no credible information that a nation-state or international terrorist organization was prepared and poised to launch a debilitating cyber assault. However, we did learn that the capability to do serious damage to these systems was widely available. All it would take were the right skills and the right tools – skills that most teenagers have already mastered and dangerous tools that are readily available on the Internet. In short, we found that the capability to do harm was widespread and growing. Our conclusion, reached early in our deliberations, was that waiting for a serious threat to develop was a dangerous strategy. We needed to act immediately to protect our future.

I do not intend to recount all of the findings and recommendations of the commission. The reader can review them in the published commission report "Critical Foundations – Protecting America's Infrastructures." However, several key conclusions and recommendations warrant discussion here because of their special relevance to the writings in this book.

Having concluded that our infrastructures were highly vulnerable and that a serious threat was sure to emerge, the central question before the commission was how to apportion responsibility for fixing the problem. As one would expect, there was lively debate regarding the many possible options. They ranged from government-centric solutions involving legislation and regulation prescribing mandatory remedial actions by industry and government, to the opposite extreme of voluntary actions prompted by political leaders' urgings through stressing patriotic duty and the national interest. After much deliberation, we concluded that the private sector has a clear responsibility to protect itself from the lesser threats, such as individual hackers and criminals, and the government has the larger responsibility to protect citizens from national security threats. In short, we found that infrastructure protection is a shared responsibility. A complicating factor, however, is that the tools or weapons that hackers and criminals use are in many cases the same weapons used by terrorists and information warriors, albeit for more dangerous purposes. Therefore the sharing of responsibility for protection is somewhat blurred. Further exploration and discussion of this concept of shared responsibility is woven throughout the chapters of this book.

A second basic question faced by the commission involved what specific measures were required to "harden" the infrastructures in order to withstand a debilitating attack. Again, the solutions discussed ranged from issuing government-mandated standards on protection – involving such things as firewalls, access control, system administration, redundancy, and back-up – to leaving the matter entirely in the hands of the owners and operators who have unique understanding of the operations and vulnerabilities of their systems. In this case, we opted for putting the matter primarily in the hands of the owners and operators, but strengthened by strong information-sharing mechanisms among owners and operators and between them and the government. The chapters in Parts III, IV, and VI of this book explore this matter in considerable detail.

Finally, a key challenge faced by the commission was determining what, if any, restructuring of the government bureaucracy was needed to implement the resulting strategy and plans for securing the nation's critical infrastructures. Underlying all of our deliberations in this area was the conviction that top-level political leadership was essential to fostering the unprecedented public–private partnership so essential to carrying out the plan. We made a series of recommendations of how the government should be organized to address this challenge. Many of the distinguished contributors to this book place special emphasis on the role of leadership in addressing this problem.

The efforts of the President's Commission on Critical Infrastructure Protection were only a beginning. But they were the beginning of a broader government-wide effort to deal with the nation's homeland security, a central feature of which was the protection of its critical infrastructures. A decade later, we have tragic evidence of the criticality of our infrastructures, our dependencies on them, and their vulnerabilities. Their physical vulnerability is clear, and we have ample evidence of their vulnerability to cyber attack, demonstrated by the many virus and denial-of-service attacks capturing the headlines over recent years. As analyzed in detail in Part V of this book, there is also clear evidence of the potential for major economic losses. That questions the financial vulnerability of our infrastructures as well, and it calls for the development of effective risk-transfer mechanisms to ensure prompt recovery of our nation after a disaster.

With the structuring of the new Department of Homeland Security, we now see organizational emphasis on the mission of protecting our critical infrastructures. We see physical and cyber security being stressed throughout government and even more generally in commerce, education, and industry. And finally, we see a surge of financial resources for both development and investment being devoted to this vital area.

Perhaps most important in the critical infrastructure area, we recognize the need for complementary, focused public and private action. Various councils, agencies, committees, and task forces have been spawned and are actively addressing a wide range of critical infrastructure security topics. Still, this is a relatively new mission area for our government, and we are defining new relationships between levels of government and public and private infrastructure institutions. No doubt, we should expect a few missteps as we plot a course toward safety in a world of new threats, vulnerabilities, interdependencies, and an unprecedented pace of change. But we now need to get it right – 10 years have elapsed with too little progress in this vital area.

A specific challenge that still eludes us is defining an effective relationship between the public and private sectors. Effective sharing of threat, vulnerability, and incident information – essential to the protection of our infrastructures – has advanced little in spite of the rhetoric, commissions, councils, and strategies that dot the critical infrastructure landscape. Effective frameworks for working together, schemas for information sharing, and incentive mechanisms, here and abroad, still have not emerged.

The faltering steps of the new Department of Homeland Security – especially those elements charged with critical infrastructure protection – to assume the leadership role envisioned by the commission has delayed progress. State and local governments, which have been collectively patient for the last four years, have little tolerance left for promises of leadership in protecting our infrastructures. Private-sector companies – infrastructure and security providers alike – are concluding they can no longer afford to wait for leadership and are stepping out on their own. These companies are simply hoping that they are picking the right solutions and making the right investments in the absence of leadership.

I regret ending on a negative note. But I remain convinced, as my colleagues and I wrote 10 years ago, that waiting for a serious threat to develop is a dangerous and ineffective strategy for protecting the nation's critical infrastructures. It is in this light that I urge you to read the words of the distinguished authors in this book. They make an important contribution to the future security of our nation by carrying the exploration of this vitally important matter forward.

General Robert T. Marsh, USAF (Retired)

PREFACE

Shortly after the September 11, 2001, attacks, the presidents of the National Academy of Sciences, the National Academy of Engineering, and the Institute of Medicine in the United States initiated a study of science and technology for countering terrorism. Lewis Branscomb, a co-editor of this book, and Richard Klausner were appointed co-chairs of the committee. The study team included more than 100 scientific and technical authors and 46 reviewers. Within seven months, the committee produced *Making the Nation Safer: Science and Technology for Countering Terrorism*, a report that focused on research and development strategies, describing actions to reduce immediate risks using existing knowledge and technologies and research to reduce future risks through the development of new capabilities. Many of the report's recommendations for research and development priorities were later incorporated into the science and technology strategy for the Department of Homeland Security.

Making the Nation Safer also highlighted a number of policy issues to be addressed for the nation's safety and security to benefit fully from any technical successes. Foremost among these policy issues was the role of private action in reducing public vulnerability. Then as now, most of the likely targets of terrorist attack are owned by private-sector firms. Furthermore, the severity of any attack (or, for that matter, of any major natural disaster) may be seriously aggravated by the disruption of critical services such as energy and water – services that are also mostly provided by private-sector firms. *Making the Nation Safer* addresses this concern in the following terms:

> Economic systems, like ecological systems, tend to become less resilient (more prone to failure when strongly perturbed) as they become more efficient, so our infrastructures are vulnerable to local disruptions, which could lead to widespread or catastrophic failures. In addition, the high level of

inter-connectedness of these systems means that the abuse, destruction, or inter-ruption of any one of them quickly affects the others. As a result, the whole society is vulnerable, with the welfare and even lives of significant portions of the population placed at risk.

While the U.S. government has, in the past five years, advanced an agenda to promote science and technology for counterterrorism, it has done little to provide the firms that ultimately assure the delivery of critical services with incentives to invest in reducing public vulnerability.

This book represents an attempt to seriously address the private role in public security. In particular, what factors affect the investment decisions of the firms that provide critical infrastructure services – those that assure the social and economic continuity of nations and groups of nations?

The work in this volume draws from the efforts by more than half a dozen research teams, each of which has long been active in research on risks and consequences of terrorism and other disasters – particularly as they affect the continuity of the critical infrastructure services. Among these teams are those represented by the editors: George Mason University's School of Public Policy, Harvard's John F. Kennedy School of Government, and the Wharton School at the University of Pennsylvania. Researchers at George Mason's Critical Infras-tructure Protection Program have since 2003 advanced policy-relevant work concerning infrastructure vulnerabilities and strategies to ensure the provision of critical services. The Belfer Center for Science and International Affairs at Harvard's Kennedy School has also applied longstanding contributions to the study of terrorism and national security to the study of public–private part-nerships in homeland security. For more than 20 years, the Risk Management and Decision Processes Center at the Wharton School has also been furthering knowledge about the nature of extreme events from terrorism, technological failure, or natural hazards and the contribution that markets and governments can make to address the new large-scale dimension associated with these emerg-ing catastrophic risks.

The efforts of these research teams complemented those of other leading teams at a variety of institutions in the United States and abroad, notably Carnegie Mellon University, Columbia University, the Lawrence Livermore National Laboratory, Mills College, RAND Corporation, the University of Cal-ifornia at Berkeley, and the École Polytechnique in Paris.

In the winter of 2004, George Mason University's Critical Infrastructure Pro-tection Project funded a project titled "Private Efficiency, Public Vulnerability: Developing Sustainable Strategies for Protecting Critical Infrastructure." Philip Auerswald from George Mason and Lewis Branscomb from Harvard served as lead investigators of the project. Its centerpiece was a workshop held at

Harvard's Kennedy School, May 27–28, 2004. A premise of the project was that the threat to critical infrastructure from terrorist attacks is best addressed as part of an overall strategy for national safety and security. While each category of risk has specific characteristics, the mitigation of risk from terrorist attack is inherently linked to the mitigation of risk from natural and technological disasters, and from service failures due to human error.

Following the workshop, the lead investigators undertook to produce a research volume that would organize the multiple perspectives offered at the workshop. The goal was to provide senior executives, policymakers, and citizens with a systematic analysis of issues and potential actions. Erwann Michel-Kerjan from the Wharton School and Todd M. La Porte of George Mason joined Auerswald and Branscomb as author-editors of the volume. To provide additional balance and depth to the collection of papers, the author-editors soon broadened the list of invited contributors to include academics and private-sector leaders who had not originally participated in the May 2004 workshop.

The contributors to this volume are among the most respected individuals in this field. Each draws on his own experience from business, government, and research institutions (responsibility for the content of this book, of course, lies with them, not with the institutions with which they are identified). While the contributed chapters represent the disparate views of the individual expert authors, all advance the collective objective of providing readers with a comprehensive and thoughtful analysis of the role of private firms in ensuring public security. Despite the complexity of the subject matter, a surprising degree of consensus emerged among the authors and editors concerning core policy-relevant issues. These are summarized in the book's conclusion.

In addition to being of immediate policy relevance, we believe this book will contribute to establishing a new field of interdisciplinary study on the topic of "security externalities," addressing, among other topics, the risks, physical and financial vulnerability, and organizational resilience of critical infrastructure services in times of disaster. Indeed, as events in this young century have regrettably illustrated, the experience of disaster in various forms may become more the rule that guides public policy and business strategy than the exception that is ignored. To the extent that this is the case, understanding of security externalities may emerge in this century as a major domain of study, just as environmental externalities did in the previous century.

The book is divided into six parts. The first and last parts comprise an introduction to the issues and a summary of its conclusions, both authored by the four editors. The parts in between address five linked challenges, each necessary but not sufficient in the overall effort to mobilize private action to reduce public vulnerability: (1) recognizing infrastructure vulnerability, (2) managing high reliability organizations, (3) securing interdependent networks, (4) creating markets, and (5) building trust. Each of these sections is introduced by a chapter, written by the editors, that places the rest of the chapters in the section in the context of the overall analytic flow of the book.

This volume at once addresses a vitally important policy issue and contributes to developing a fundamentally new domain of academic inquiry. We hope readers will appreciate the various but complementary perspectives offered and will be prompted to further consider how routine private decisions can represent not only the seeds of disaster, but also the roots of response.

ACKNOWLEDGMENTS

This volume is a product of the "Private Efficiency, Public Vulnerability" project, supported primarily by grant #60NANB2D0108 from the National Institute of Standards and Technology (NIST) through the Critical Infrastructure Protection Program (CIPP) at George Mason University. Any opinions, findings, or recommendations expressed in this material are those of the authors and do not necessarily reflect the views of NIST or CIPP.

Beyond the project's sponsor, our first thanks goes to the authors of the chapters contributed to this volume and to the other participants in the May 2004 workshop that laid the groundwork for the book. We have greatly appreciated the dedication all have shown to the shared objective of advancing scholarship, improving policy, and increasing public awareness concerning the vital issues we have together sought to address.

We secondly would like to recognize the sustained support of CIPP director John McCarthy and the valuable assistance of staff members Kevin Thomas, Kathleen Emmons, and Christine Pommerening. We are also pleased to acknowledge the support of the Belfer Center for Science and International Affairs at Harvard's Kennedy School of Government, which hosted the May 2004 workshop that laid the groundwork for this book. Professor John Holdren, director of the Science, Technology and Public Policy Program in the Belfer Center, sponsored the event, and his assistants Patricia McLaughlin and Robert Stowe helped in many ways to make the workshop both productive and enjoyable. We are also pleased to acknowledge the support of the Risk Management and Decision Processes Center at the Wharton School of the University of Pennsylvania in helping to bring this project to fruition.

We want to express our special appreciation for the encouragement and guidance of John Berger, a Senior Editor at Cambridge University Press. He saw the promise of this volume and contributed substantially to realizing the final product.

We save our most heartfelt thanks for last: to Bonnie Nevel, who edited every chapter in the book and prepared the volume for production. Much more than a copy editor, she helped create a book with a coherence of style and an organized flow of material that at the same time conveys the individual personality of each contributor. Her efforts were not only highly professional but reflected an exceptional commitment to a task whose complexity none of the editors fully foresaw at the outset.

> – Philip E. Auerswald, Lewis M. Branscomb, Todd M. La Porte,
> and Erwann O. Michel-Kerjan
> July, 2006

PART I

Seeds of Disaster

1

WHERE PRIVATE EFFICIENCY MEETS PUBLIC VULNERABILITY

The Critical Infrastructure Challenge

Philip E. Auerswald, Lewis M. Branscomb, Todd M. La Porte, and Erwann O. Michel-Kerjan

2001: September 11 attacks. The theoretical vulnerability of the United States to a major terrorist strike is suddenly a stark reality. Impacts are global and enduring.

2003: U.S.–Canada blackout. A massive failure of the electric power distribution system demonstrates how human error can jeopardize vital public services.

2004: Indian Ocean tsunami. A deadly wave travels through Southeast Asian waters more quickly than potentially life-saving warnings through airwaves. Nearly 300,000 lose their lives.

2005: Hurricane Katrina. Four years after the 9/11 attacks, a violent but long-anticipated hurricane overwhelms a vulnerable coastline, meets an unprepared government, and inflicts lasting damage on a population. A superpower fails to meet the most basic needs of its citizens in crisis.

Are these recent disasters related? Will coming years bring ones even more severe? Is our modern, highly interconnected, global economy creating new types of vulnerabilities and worsening old ones? Who can act to reduce these vulnerabilities – in particular, to prevent terrorist attacks and natural disasters from having catastrophic consequences? More to the point, who *will* act?

This book contributes to the current and long-overdue debate on these questions. A series of important recent reports and studies sound the alarm on the inadequate preparedness of government at all levels to cope with the new generation of challenges evidenced by the crises listed above; the reports of the 9/11 Commission and of the congressional committee investigating the government's actions during and shortly after Hurricane Katrina are particularly notable.[1] This book focuses on the private sector's role, will, and capacity in reducing public vulnerability to disasters. The book addresses public policies that would make the impacts of extreme events less severe and that would facilitate recovery after they occur. We do not offer definitive answers. We do show, however, that on many critical points relating to extreme event preparedness and recovery, conventional wisdom is wrong.

Conventional wisdom holds that, in the aftermath of the 9/11 terrorist attacks and the Madrid terrorist bombings on March 11, 2004, among numerous others, national governments around the world are working closely and effectively with relevant private enterprises to minimize the probability and impact of future attacks. They are not.

Conventional wisdom holds that federally backed insurance markets for catastrophic risks currently help induce private firms and households to invest in reducing the public's vulnerability from high-impact events. They do not.

Conventional wisdom holds that people base their decisions on how to prepare for extreme events on rational expectations regarding relevant probabilities. They do not.

Conventional wisdom holds that catastrophic terrorism, natural disasters, or inadvertent failures of large-scale public services are so distinct from each other that they should be addressed and managed separately. They are not.

Conventional wisdom holds that federal, regional, and municipal governments are able to reduce the likelihood of catastrophic events, and that the power to ensure recovery from such events occurs rapidly. They have neither.

The twenty-first century is not the twentieth. In almost every part of the world, economic life today is far more institutionally decentralized than it was 50 years ago, at the height of the industrial age. In developed countries, the infrastructure that provides essential services to citizens is more complex and interconnected by orders of magnitude than it was even a generation ago. In the United States, more than 80 percent of the shopping malls, office buildings, theaters, factories, energy installations, and airlines – all of which are potentially the subject of attack or natural disaster – are owned by private businesses.[2] Even though transportation facilities, such as airports, bridges, dams, and tunnels, are typically owned by municipal, state, or federal authorities, the planes, trucks, railcars, and ships that use these facilities are privately held.

Private actors seeking to increase competitiveness through greater operational efficiency will normally outsource, automate, or eliminate tasks viewed as peripheral to their core business competency, and they will avoid investing in equipment viewed as redundant. To reduce costs, managers may seek ways to make use of external infrastructures for which others bear the cost – as in the case of any firm using the Internet as the backbone of internal corporate communications. They may undertake to reduce redundancy in internal systems, and decrease depths of protective "fire walls" to levels consistent with "normal" levels of risk.[3] Other actions, including mergers and acquisitions, may be aimed at realizing economies of scale and scope – improving corporate performance by embracing a wider range of functions and opportunities.

Distributed efforts to improve productive efficiency at the firm level have yielded countless improvements, the cumulative effect of which over past decades has resulted in staggering reductions in costs. Yet competitive pressures do not allow firms to make large investments aimed at reducing vulnerability to disasters that are highly unlikely and nearly impossible to predict. Just as the industrial age exposed environmental vulnerabilities as an economic and social reality, so the post-industrial age in which we now live is in the process of exposing a different set of vulnerabilities: the "endogenous" security vulnerabilities of civil society.

FACING A NEW ERA OF ENDOGENOUS VULNERABILITIES

What makes a public vulnerability endogenous? Simply put, an endogenous event is one for which the outcome is at least in part the result of human actions. Hurricane Katrina is a good example. The hurricane damage was magnified first by the failure of the system of levees and barriers protecting the city of New Orleans, and second by the failure of the public officials responsible for protecting its people – for example, the collapse of communications systems and the absence of security protocols enabling infrastructure-service providers to reach affected areas. An "exogenous" counter-example is a meteor strike: This event is completely the result of actions beyond human control.[4] Until recently, hurricanes and other extreme weather events were similarly viewed as exogenous events (described, in the language of faith rather than of economics, as "acts of God"). However, we increasingly understand that not only the impacts of extreme events, but actually the probability of their occurrence, are affected by human actions – cumulative decisions that weaken natural barriers to storm surges, place human populations in vulnerable areas, and change environmental and climate patterns on a global scale. In millennia of human history, this is new.

The abstract concept of an "endogenous security vulnerability" is thus everywhere present today in the brick-and-mortar world of everyday business decision making. Moreover, the increasing race for competitiveness and economies of scale calls for the development of larger systems, with larger potential associated risks. Many examples exist of large-scale and/or highly connected infrastructures vulnerable to events in which the probability of occurrence is low, but consequences when they do take place are severe: athletic facilities holding

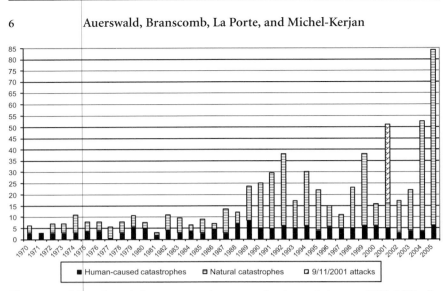

Figure 1.1. Natural and human-caused catastrophe insured losses, 1970–2005 (in US$ billions).

100,000 persons, aircraft like the new Airbus 380 seating up to 850 passengers; food processing and distribution firms serving ever increasing shares of the national market; power distribution networks serving a third of the nation's population; and a new Royal Caribbean cruise liner that will carry 6,400 vacationers. In each of these examples, the quest for economies of scale induced by a highly competitive market economy has potential to amplify the consequences of a catastrophic failure in an infrastructure system. At the same time, as was evidenced in the aftermath of Hurricane Katrina, the efficient practices of private firms subject to market discipline have the potential to be significant assets in a time of crisis.[5] Both increased vulnerability and a potentially increased capacity to respond are natural outcomes of the competitive process in decentralized market economies.

Of course, this business reality does not explain everything. The nature and spectra of potential risks have evolved as well. The recent occurrence of particularly destructive natural disasters raises the question as to whether there are now more natural catastrophes than before. Figure 1.1 illustrates that economic losses due to natural disasters worldwide have increased significantly over the past 25 years. Adjusted for inflation, the combined natural and human-caused insured losses were $5 billion annually in the 1950s, $8 billion in the 1960s, $16 billion in the 1970s, $22 billion in the 1980s, and on average $70 billion annually in the 1990s.[6] The annual increases continue to accelerate. In 2004, the total financial losses attributed to natural disasters around the world were

$120 billion. In 2005, Hurricane Katrina alone caused even higher losses, with the exact total still unknown as we go to press. Population growth and its rapidly increasing urban concentration (both in absolute and relative terms),[7] the increasing value of assets,[8] and the lack of adequate mitigation measures in hazard-prone areas have largely contributed to this totally new level of economic loss. Whether the natural phenomena in such highly exposed areas are becoming more intense is also an open question.[9]

In contrast with natural disasters, both the impacts of a terrorist attack and the probability of one occurring are directly affected by the actions of governments, businesses, and citizens. As the report by the 9/11 Commission documents, prior to the 9/11 attacks, the U.S. government did not adequately respond to repeated warnings or implement indicated policies to reduce the hazard.[10] Government action occurs in a context where the nature of terrorism itself has also dramatically changed over the past 20 years. While the total number of international terrorist attacks worldwide has been significantly decreasing on average during the 1990s compared with the 1980s,[11] the number of terrorist attacks by extremist religious-based organizations has increased. Such terrorist groups have demonstrated a willingness to inflict massive casualties and to view civilians as legitimate targets. That focus has led over the past years to fewer attacks inflicting a considerably higher number of casualties.[12] The 15 terrorist attacks that inflicted the greatest number of casualties (fatalities and injuries combined) occurred after 1982, with two-thirds of them occurring between 1995 and 2005 (Table 1.1).

Terrorist groups such as Al Qaeda have publicly called for attacks that not only inflict massive casualties, but also create major economic disruptions. Thus, the nature of the target has also evolved over time. Traditionally, attacks have been aimed at government, military, and diplomatic targets. Today, most terrorist attacks worldwide are directed against private entities (80 percent of attacks against U.S. interests in 2000, 90 percent in 2001).[13]

As concerns about terrorist attacks have grown, private-sector executives and policymakers have grappled with far greater uncertainties than ever before. The uncertainties are compounded by the fact that potential attackers can engage in "adaptive predation," in which they purposefully adapt their strategies to take advantage of weaknesses in prevention efforts. In contrast, actions can be taken to reduce damage from future natural disasters with the knowledge that only the consequences, but not the probability, of natural disasters will be affected by the adoption of protective measures. The likelihood of an earthquake of a given intensity in Los Angeles will not change if property owners design more quake-resistant structures. The likelihood and consequences of a terrorist attack, however, change over time and are determined by a mix of strategies

Table 1.1. The 15 worst terrorist acts since 1983, in terms of casualties

Date	Location	Event	Fatalities	Injuries
07 Aug 98	Nairobi, Kenya	Bomb attacks on U.S. embassy complex	253	5,075
11 Sep 01	New York, Virginia, and Pennsylvania, USA	Terrorist attacks using aircraft	3,000	2,250
11 Mar 04	Madrid, Spain	Bomb attacks on trains	192	1,500
31 Jan 96	Colombo, Sri Lanka	Bomb attack on Ceylinco House	100	1,500
12 Mar 93	Bombay, India	Series of 13 bomb attacks	300	1,100
26 Feb 93	New York, USA	Bomb attack in the World Trade Center	6	1,000
7 July 05	London, UK	Bomb attacks in trains and bus	57	700
19 Apr 95	Oklahoma City, USA	Truck bomb attack on government building	166	467
12 Oct 02	Bali, Indonesia	Bomb attack in a nightclub	190	300
23 Oct 83	Beirut, Lebanon	Bomb attack on U.S. Marine barracks and French paratrooper base	300	100
03 Sept 04	Beslan, Russia	Hostages killed	360	NA
21 Dec 88	Lockerbie, UK	Explosion of U.S. PanAm B-747	270	NA
18 Jul 94	Buenos Aires, Argentina	Bomb attack	95	147
23 Nov 96	Comoros, Indian Ocean	Hijacked Ethiopian aircraft ditched at sea	127	NA
13 Sep 99	Moscow, Russia	Bomb destroys apartment building	118	NA

and counter-strategies developed by a range of stakeholders. This "dynamic uncertainty" makes the likelihood of future terrorist events against specific targets all but impossible to estimate, increases the difficulty of measuring the effectiveness of public policies and private strategies, and severely complicates efforts to allocate resources.

NO CORPORATION IS AN ISLAND: BUSINESS STRATEGY AND THE ECONOMICS OF SECURITY EXTERNALITIES

Businesses may not always realize how their failure to operate could affect a large number of agents, often rippling far beyond their direct influence. This effect is partially because business entities responsible for initiating a cascading failure across multiple economic sectors are not likely to be held accountable for negligence. As a consequence, there is divergence between what economists refer to as "private costs" and "social costs" of the firms' actions.

Private costs are privately borne; social costs are borne by the community. When both the costs and benefits of an action are privately borne, then there is every reason to believe that investment decisions to mitigate such costs will be privately optimal. However, when a private decision has social impacts, either costs or benefits, that are not taken into account by the private actor, then it is more likely that the outcome will not be optimal from a societal standpoint.

The classic example is environmental pollution. Factories have smokestacks to remove smoke from the workplace. Unless compelled (e.g., by government) to take into account the damage to people by the smoke emitted outside the plant, the manager of the factory will treat the cost to the community of emission to be zero. Smoke in this instance is an example of a negative "environmental externality" resulting from a private decision – the smoke is sent outside the factory, and thereafter is no longer considered to be the manager's problem.

This book develops broadly, and in new contexts, the concept of a "security externality."[14] In the case of a security externality, a private firm undertakes an action that creates a vulnerability (or possibly an uncompensated benefit) elsewhere in the economy. For example, if an electric power distribution firm buys only one very large, ultra-high voltage transformer, it minimizes its own expenses, but it also increases overall vulnerability. If that transformer has no replacement, and if it is attacked, the cost of service interruption will be distributed to all segments of society. On the other hand, if the firm provides technology that allows the damaged transformer to be replaced quickly, the increased assurance of reliable power, even in a terrorist attack, represents a positive security externality.[15] The trade-off between private efficiency and public vulnerability emerges from the existence of security externalities (see Box 1.1). The challenge for public policy is to find a way for the government to provide incentives to the private sector to invest adequately in security (including both technical designs and management practices).

ENSURING THE DELIVERY OF CRITICAL INFRASTRUCTURE SERVICES: EMPHASIS AND ORGANIZATION OF THE VOLUME

The influence of private action on public vulnerability is a broad issue. This book focuses on concrete ways that highly industrialized democracies can better face future disasters or avoid them. Indeed, in a world of limited resources, not everything can be protected. To illustrate the broader concepts, as well as to contribute to a particular policy debate of vital importance, we concentrate on the challenges associated with the protection of society's critical infrastructure of economic networks and public services whose continuity in times of disaster

BOX 1.1 CSX RAILROAD AND THE DISTRICT OF COLUMBIA

Less than a month after a January 2004 train crash in South Carolina resulted in the release of deadly chlorine gas that killed 9 people and hospitalized 58 others, the district's City Council passed an act banning the transportation of hazardous materials within a 2.2-mile radius of the U. S. Capitol without a permit. The act cited the failure of the federal government "to prevent the terrorist threat." Subsequently, CSX petitioned the U.S. Surface Transportation Board (USSTP) to invalidate the legislation, claiming that it would "add hundreds of miles and days of transit time to hazardous materials shipments" and adversely affect rail service around the country. USSTP ruled in CSX's favor in March 2005, putting an end to the district's efforts.

Shortly after the decision, Richard Falkenrath, President Bush's former deputy homeland security advisor, highlighted in congressional testimony the severity of the threat that the act was intended to address: "Of all the various remaining civilian vulnerabilities in America today, one stands alone as uniquely deadly, pervasive, and susceptible to terrorist attack: toxic-inhalation hazard (TIH) of industrial chemicals, such as chlorine, ammonia, phosgene, methylbromide, hydrochloric and various other acids."

The case of CSX Railroad and the District of Columbia illustrates the tensions that have emerged recently between two potentially competing imperatives: corporate efficiency and public security. Despite the urgency created by terrorist threats, as well as the ongoing challenges of dealing with natural disasters, a public–private consensus on how best to address these tensions has not emerged.

is critical to the economic and social continuity of a region, a country, or even a continent.

For at least as long as roads, bridges, and cities have existed, the reliable operation of infrastructure has been a concern of both rulers and merchants. Yet the infrastructure challenges faced by government and business leaders a hundred or even fifty years ago are primitive in comparison with those we must address today. Public policy must address three sources of low-frequency, high-consequence disasters: natural disasters such as hurricanes, floods, and earthquakes; "technogenic" disasters resulting from bad system design, inappropriate regulatory frameworks, and political and managerial failure; and disasters created by terrorists (domestic or foreign) and any other malevolent actors who can purposefully adapt their strategies depending on the security measures we take. The long-established but non-rationalized system of regulatory agencies intended to protect public safety in food, transportation, nuclear energy, oil and gas, and chemical plants, among others, today must function alongside new tools for protecting those same assets from terrorism. The failure of all levels of the U.S. government to properly prepare to mitigate the damage and manage the crisis in a timely fashion during and following Hurricane

Katrina has demonstrated in stark terms how far the United States still has to go in meeting these challenges.

How did the United States get to where it is today? Approaches toward "infrastructure" policy have evolved over the past century, from an initial emphasis on infrastructure adequacy, through deregulation with the aim of increasing efficiency through competition, to a recent focus on infrastructure protection. At the beginning of the 1980s, the national debate was driven by concern over the poor physical condition of public works infrastructure. In a report to Congress on the condition of national infrastructures released in 1983, the Congressional Budget Office focused on seven infrastructures that "share the common characteristics of capital intensiveness and high public investment at all levels of government. They are, moreover, directly critical to activity in the nation's economy."[16] These seven infrastructures were highways, public transit systems, wastewater treatment works, water resources, air traffic control, airports, and municipal water supply. In its 1988 report to the President and Congress, the National Council on Public Works Improvement (created in 1984) defined infrastructure as systems providing services that "form the underpinnings of the nation's defense, a strong economy and our health and safety" (see Box 1.2).[17]

By the early 1990s, policymakers' attentions had largely moved away from broad infrastructure issues. Instead, legislative proposals tended to address the economic needs of individual infrastructure sectors, reducing regulatory

---

BOX 1.2 CRITICAL INFRASTRUCTURE SECTORS

The President's National Strategy for Homeland Security issued on July 16, 2002, identified 13 sectors of the economy as comprising the "critical infrastructure" of the United States:
   Agriculture
   Food
   Water
   Public Health
   Emergency services
   Government
   Defense Industrial Base
   Information and telecommunications
   Energy
   Transportation (people and product)
   Banking and Finance
   Chemical Industry
   Postal and Shipping

constraints to allow infrastructures to increase their efficiency and lower the cost of service through more open competition.

An important turn was made in 1996, however, with the establishment by President Clinton of the President's Commission on Critical Infrastructure Protection, chaired by General Robert Marsh (the author of the foreword to this book). With the work of the commission, the security dimensions of public policies relating to infrastructure began to gain a weight equal to efficiency conditions. During the decade that has elapsed between the publication of the recommendations by the Marsh commission on critical infrastructure protection and the publication of this book, a series of government-commissioned studies have called attention, in tones of accelerating urgency, to the threat of terrorism and the necessity of government action to forestall it. These studies, and the government actions in both statute and executive orders, are detailed by authors in Part II.

Each time the government has attempted to redefine a complete list of critical infrastructures, the list has grown longer.[18] At present, it includes not only operational public service networks such as energy, agriculture, transportation, and communications, but also a collection of "framing services" such as the defense industrial base and public health. This increase in the number of critical infrastructures suggests that a thoughtfully constructed model of the U.S. economy – or that of any technologically sophisticated, free-market democracy – comprises a network of enterprises providing products and services that are highly interdependent. To the extent these interdependencies look like externalities to the managers of each enterprise, and are not fully under their control, the function of this network becomes an unavoidable concern of collective institutions, of which the most comprehensive in its coverage is government. Government regulatory agencies find themselves engaged with almost all the nodes of this largely private interlocking network of infrastructure service providers.

The broader list of interdependent infrastructures also illustrates the range of relationships that exist between governments at different levels and firms engaged in critical service provision – from government corporations such as the U.S. Postal Service to self-regulated sectors such as the chemical industry. In open, democratic societies, protection from the most severe impacts of rare but high-consequence disasters is not the responsibility of government alone. Indeed, the greatest cost of an excessive focus on failures by government entities may be the missed opportunity to encourage more effective action and engagement by private entities.

In this volume, we explore four categories of action toward the aim of ensuring the delivery of critical services: managing organizations, securing networks, creating markets, and building trust.

MANAGING ORGANIZATIONS

In protecting against massive disruptions of critical services, the responsibility for setting goals rests primarily with the government, but the implementation of steps to reduce the vulnerability of privately owned and corporate assets depends primarily on private-sector knowledge and action. Although private firms uniquely understand their operations and the hazards they entail, they currently do not have adequate commercial incentive to fund vulnerability reduction. A few industries, notably nuclear power generation and air traffic control systems, succeed in operating complex and hazardous systems with extraordinarily high levels of reliability, even in the face of extreme stress or system turbulence. These organizations fail so much less often than their normal counterparts that they serve as potential models for all critical infrastructure systems, where society requires services, to the extent possible, to remain functioning against a very wide range of threats and disruptive conditions. To the extent that effective response capabilities can be transferred, or learned, they may prove invaluable to other industries facing disaster risks. However, for reasons stated above, private firms will resist making changes for security reasons that will deeply affect organizational practices. These issues are discussed in Part III.

SECURING NETWORKS

In the presence of interdependencies, even if each firm is resilient, the system may still be vulnerable due to lack of coordination among, and communication between, different industry sectors. As companies build and manage systems with greater reach and higher capacity, they find that those systems are also increasingly linked to other large, technical systems. The use of large-sized networks and their interconnections allow firms to reduce their operating cost, thanks to economies of scale. System engineers have made considerable progress in increasing the reliability and robustness of large service networks at the same time that they have increased their efficiency. The ability of Toyota not only to build and deliver a new car of a particular configuration requested by a customer, but to do so in two weeks, provides additional customer value and attests to the efficiency of Toyota's supply chain. But if parts supply is interrupted, there is very little buffer to sustain production. The complexity and global reach of supply chain networks make them vulnerable to disruption. When the large-scale networks provide critical services, the impacts of their failure are felt widely and immediately. "Cascading" effects may result in the failure of other systems. All of these impacts may be rendered particularly severe if damage is due to deliberate destruction. These issues are discussed in Part IV.

CREATING MARKETS

Various informational and coordination problems have led many to believe that the best solutions are market based. Yet little evidence exists to support the claim that market forces alone are sufficient to induce needed investments in protection. Over the past few years, senior executives and federal officials have begun to view insurance as a market-based tool to address public vulnerabilities. The fact that insurers are private-sector actors tends to facilitate communication with other private firms, avoiding concerns about relationships with federal agencies. Insurers are recognized as risk management experts, and it is in their own interest to limit the exposure of their clients. In theory, the pricing of insurance coverage can be used to induce investments in vulnerability reduction. Yet serious questions exist regarding the extent to which insurance (including reinsurance and access to new financial instruments to cover catastrophic risks) and other market-design mechanisms can actually prove to be a significant tool in ensuring the provision of critical services. Private capital alone may not be able to cover large-scale risks that may reach into the tens – if not hundreds – of billions of dollars, while continuing to provide coverage for more traditional risks we all face in our day-to-day life. Firms – both insurance firms and the businesses they protect – face increasing difficulties estimating the probability of an attack occurring tomorrow and evaluating the consequences. And being insured might also induce private actors to reduce, rather than increase, investments in vulnerability reduction. How might firms at risk assess their vulnerability and identify the technical and managerial measures to mitigate that risk? These issues are discussed in Part V.

BUILDING TRUST

The challenge facing both business and government leaders is not only to balance public and private interests, but to understand the way in which these interests are intertwined. As the number of identifiable infrastructure sectors continues to rise, and their interdependencies evolve in a mesh network of relationships, the public interest takes on a large number of varied forms. How, then, can a collaboration between private interests and government be characterized as a balance to be struck across a single political table? Indeed, how can such a model be applicable to the international cooperation that is also required? A new model of joint public–private collaboration must evolve if there is to be a sustainable, efficient, and robust economy in the face of threats of many kinds. Every catastrophe threatens to destroy the one element most required for response and recovery: trust. These issues are discussed in Part VI.

"We reflect on the 9/11 Commission's finding that the most important failure was one of imagination," wrote the members of the House Committee investigating the response to Hurricane Katrina in their final report. "The Select Committee believes Katrina was primarily a failure of initiative. But there is, of course, a nexus between the two. Both imagination and initiative require good information. And a coordinated process for sharing it. And a willingness to use information – however imperfect or incomplete – to fuel action."

This volume offers an array of insights into how, in a competitive market economy, operational practice, business strategy and public policy can jointly ensure the reliable provision of infrastructure services. Together, these insights serve to direct attention away from the infrastructure itself, and toward the institutions, incentives, and behaviors that have created – and are constantly re-creating – that infrastructure. While there are no easy solutions to the challenges we describe, our final chapter addresses the unavoidable necessity for a more effective public and private collaboration on the provision of critical services and the reduction of public vulnerability. Just as a previous generation of policymakers adapted to the emergence of environmental externalities, policymakers today must adapt to a world in which security externalities are suddenly ubiquitous. Yet to address the new challenges that we highlighted at the outset, improved public policy and business strategies will not be enough. Action requires imagination and initiative – in other words, leadership.

NOTES

1. The National Commission on Terrorist Attacks Upon the United States 2004; Select Bipartisan Committee to Investigate the Preparation for and Response to Hurricane Katrina 2006.
2. President's Council of Science and Technology Advisors 2003, p. 15.
3. Many examples are cited in National Research Council 2002b on the structure of networks and their vulnerability to attack, see Albert et al. 2000.
4. Posner (2005) discusses a variety of catastrophes, including the one that would be caused by a large meteor hitting the earth. That case illustrates a catastrophe in which human actions could mitigate impact, but not the probability of an event occurring.
5. For illustrations, see testimony provided to the U.S. Senate Committee on Homeland Security and Governmental Affairs in November 16, 2005, hearing titled "Hurricane Katrina: What Can Government Learn from the Private Sector's Response?"
6. Data from Munich Re.
7. In 1950, about 30 percent of the world's population – 2.5 billion people – lived in cities. In 2000, about 50 percent of the world's population (6 billion) lived in cities. Projections by the United Nations show that by 2025, that figure will have increased up to 60 percent of a total 2025-population of 8.3 billion people. This results in the increasing number of "mega-cities," with populations above 10 million. In 1950, New York City was the only

such mega-city. In 1990, there were twelve such cities. By 2015, there would be twenty-six, including Tokyo (29 million), Shanghai (18 million), New York (17.6 million), and Los Angeles (14.2 million), just to name a few located in hazard-prone areas.

8. For example, if Hurricane Andrew had occurred in 2002 rather than 1992, it would have inflected double the economic loss, mainly due to increased coastal development and rising asset values located on the coasts of Florida.

9. See Michel-Kerjan et al. 2006. The 2005 hurricane season exceeded the 1933 record for the busiest season since hurricane counting started in 1851 (23). Evidence suggests that the Atlantic Ocean may be entering a cyclical period of more intense storms, and it possible that ocean warming associated with climate change may exacerbate this trend.

10. See, for instance, Enders and Sandler 2000, pp. 307–332; Sandler and Enders 2004, pp. 301–316; Hoffman 1998; Chalk et al. 2005.

11. U.S. Department of State 2004.

12. Pillar 2001; Wedgwood 2002; Stern 2003.

13. U.S. Department of State 2004.

14. The concept of security externalities as employed by the editors of this book is a generalization of the concept of interdependent security discussed by Heal et al. in Part IV of the book on securing networks.

15. This example is discussed in National Research Council 2002b, pp. 180–195.

16. U.S. Congressional Budget Office 1983, p. 1.

17. National Council on Public Works Improvement 1988, p. 33.

18. In the 2003 *National Strategy for the Physical Protection of Critical Infrastructures and Key Assets*, Office of the President, 2003, p. 7, the notion of "key assets" was introduced. Among these are "national monuments, symbols, and icons that represent our nation's heritage, traditions, and values and political power. . . ." These are doubtless important targets for terrorists, but are not addressed in this book because they do not constitute elements of critical infrastructure. The Homeland Security Presidential Directive 7 issued on December 17, 2003, adopts the same critical infrastructure and key assets that are in the 2003 National Strategy.

PART II

A Critical Challenge

2

A NATION FOREWARNED

Vulnerability of Critical Infrastructure in the Twenty-First Century

Lewis M. Branscomb

In the previous chapter, we have seen that social and economic activities depend more and more on large-scale services, that many of the industries providing these services tend to face increasing vulnerability to disasters, and the very competitive pressures that give rise to higher risks also reduce incentives for firms to invest in measures to mitigate those risks. At the same time, the nature of risks has evolved, not only with the threat of international terrorism but with population growth and concentration, giving rise to more devastating consequences from natural disasters as well.

In that global new world, all elements of society – firms, industries, individual citizens, governments at all levels – are both subject to expanded risk and also bear growing responsibility for its mitigation. Against this background, the absence of a clear consensus regarding which groups are accountable for addressing these threats, and what authority and resources they can be expected to mobilize, together contribute to the seeds of disaster.

Part II of this book addresses how the debate is currently framed between the responsibilities and capabilities of the public and private sectors in the United States. We first must appreciate that the debate has not yet been truly joined. The U.S. federal government's perspective seems to be based on seriously unrealistic assumptions about the capabilities and motivations of the private managers of critical infrastructure facilities and services.

ARE CRITICAL INFRASTRUCTURE SERVICES PROTECTED BY THE GOVERNMENT'S "WAR ON TERROR"?

Stephen Flynn sets the U.S. response to the September 11, 2001, attack in its proper context. The administration chose to harken back to World War II to find its metaphor ("the war on terror") to characterize this catastrophic terrorist attack. In American political discourse, the word "war" has been commonly used as a euphemism for a high priority national endeavor. Society has seen officials given responsibility for "wars" on cancer, drugs, poverty, illiteracy, and many other intractable social problems. But the Bush administration took the euphemism literally; it placed its priority on military actions overseas. This led not only to a half-hearted domestic effort in homeland security, but may also have led many private-sector executives to conclude that, just as in the case of a "real" war, the federal government would, in the event, assume responsibility for domestic security as well. So while the U.S. government chose to characterize the terrorist threat in terms of a traditional war in Afghanistan and Iraq, it chose the euphemistic meaning for war in its approach to critical infrastructure. It has assumed, with little evidence to justify it, that market forces would be sufficient motivation for the needed investments in mitigating vulnerabilities in the critical infrastructure industries, despite (or perhaps because of) the evidence that the facilities and services owned by these industries are in most cases the terrorists' targets.

It might be argued that the 9/11 attacks were so sudden and unexpected that they caught the government – and industry – unaware of the likelihood of disasters to come. The largely unsuccessful 1993 Al Qaeda attack on the World Trade Center, followed by the domestic truck bomb two years later outside the Alfred Murrah Federal Building in Oklahoma City should have been warning enough. But the political difficulties of persuading a complacent electorate that major changes would be required to keep the nation safe and secure were daunting. As a result, the government chartered one distinguished commission after another to evaluate the problem and recommend appropriate steps to prepare for it, but went no further.

As discussed in Chapter 3, the first major presidential commission on terrorism focused on critical infrastructure. Chaired by General Robert T. Marsh, (author of the foreword to this book), the President's Commission on Critical Infrastructure Protection produced a report in October 1997, titled *Critical Foundations.*[1] General Marsh, in presenting the report to Congress the following month, said, "In many respects, our most important finding is the need to think differently about infrastructure protection. Today's approach was designed to deal with the Industrial Revolution, then was adjusted to address the stabilization of America after the Civil War, the Depression, World War II, and finally the nuclear stand-off of the Cold War. None of those approaches is particularly applicable to the world as it looks through the lens of information technology in the third millennium."

PRESIDENTIAL COMMISSIONS AND LAWS ON TERRORISM THREATS SINCE 1993

One commission followed another. In 1999, the Hart-Rudman Commission concluded that "America will become increasingly vulnerable to hostile attack on our homeland, and our military superiority will not entirely protect us."[2] The National Commission on Terrorism, chaired by L. Paul Bremer III, reported in September 2000 that "countering the growing danger of the terrorist threat requires significantly stepping up U.S. efforts."[3] It recommended a strong research and design program to build technologies useful in defending against terrorism. Three months later, the second annual report of the Gilmore Commission concluded that the United States "had no coherent functional national strategy for combating terrorism."[4] All of these studies were commissioned by the White House. All were staffed by influential, politically experienced people. It took the successful coordinated attacks on the World Trade Center and the Pentagon and the aborted hijacking that ended with a plane crash in rural Pennsylvania to galvanize the government into action. But what form did that action take?

In Chapter 4, Brian Lopez reviews the history of presidential actions, starting in 1993 and bringing it up to the current time, four years after the 9/11 attacks. Lopez focuses this 12-year history on the role that concern about critical infrastructure has played in the new laws and executive orders that were promulgated both before and after 9/11. Complementing these formal government actions, a team of scientists and engineers at the Lawrence Livermore National Laboratory began to tackle the difficult task of developing the tools needed for a reliable assessment of the vulnerability to terrorism of critical infrastructures in industry.

DEVELOPMENT OF TOOLS FOR VULNERABILITY AND RISK ANALYSIS

Lopez, a leader of this work, describes in Chapter 5 the laboratory's approach to this difficult but very important task. The Livermore Laboratory experts combined their empirical experience in the field, offering to analyze the vulnerabilities of firms that volunteered for this work, with the development and testing of analytical models and tools. The absence of serious dialog between industry and the political and regulatory sides of government followed, at least in part, from the lack of well-established and common tools for assessing the risks, or even the vulnerabilities and means for their mitigation. The Lawrence

Livermore National Laboratory is creating a sophisticated set of tools for this task, but experience with them is still developing and few firms have mastered them for their own purposes.

Firms find the analysis of vulnerability very difficult, for understandable reasons. While competitiveness and vulnerability are produced through the same decisions and processes, they are normally assessed independently. A market economy routinely accounts for improved efficiency, but vulnerability may be assessed only after it has been exposed by active study or system failure. Organizations are most likely to account for only those vulnerabilities that are linked to their core activities. Airlines, for example, have a strong incentive to become intimately familiar with the factors that determine the risk of a crash; oil companies similarly must be well acquainted with factors affecting the probability of an oil spill or refinery fire. In the car industry, safety has even become a marketing feature.

In contrast, accountability for, and accounting of, vulnerabilities distant from core business activities are relatively uncommon – particularly when perceived probabilities of occurrence are very low, and even when potential consequences are disastrous.[5] Thus, while economic incentives and legal and regulatory constraints drive the accounting of core business vulnerabilities, they are less likely to drive the accounting of, and accountability for, vulnerabilities that lie outside the core business concerns of any single firm or industry.

SUSTAINING PUBLIC SUPPORT FOR THE COSTS OF SAFETY AND SERVICES

There are some important constraints on these strategies and policies for disaster mitigation if they are to serve society effectively. First, the public policies for mitigating potential disasters must be sustainable in the face of extended periods of time between rare but high-consequence events.[6] Because the costs of minimizing these events and their consequences will be significant, and returns to the firm will be difficult to assess, businesses will surely resist government regulatory proposals requiring disaster mitigation. If regulations are adopted that drive up the costs of infrastructure services, voting publics as well as firms may well grow weary of the price penalties, absent visible evidence of rewards.

Sustainability of government policies that require mitigation of vulnerability to catastrophic service interruptions can be improved by encouraging firms to increase public safety and convenience by providing more resilient and reliable services and seeking to minimize costs passed through to the public from investments in disaster mitigation. This approach is called a "dual-benefit" strategy – mitigating or possibly reducing costs while increasing the value, reliability, and resilience of services. Such public policies take an "all hazards" approach, including policies to mitigate disasters and service interruptions that result from poor management, inappropriate regulation, and human error.

System failures from accident, inappropriate design, or human error are not only more common than terrorism or natural disasters, but if they are more effectively addressed by service industries, they could provide better service to the public in the absence of war or terrorism. Let us consider four examples: the U.S. and Canada blackout in August 2003, food-borne disease, cyber attacks on the Internet, and railroad tank cars carrying hazardous materials.

The 2003 power failure, which is analyzed in detail in Part IV of this book, was only the latest in a long series of linked power system failures, exacerbated by a lack of intersystem coordination due to deregulation of the power industry. Such failures, which may be called "technogenic," are not only likely to be more frequent than earthquakes or major terror attacks, but they also cause publics to insist on increased accountability in industry and government when they occur. The public will be highly vocal when – as in Hurricane Katrina – failures to plan, mitigate, and respond result in much greater loss of life and property than would have been inevitable under the best of circumstances.

There have been many examples of contamination of food, some of which were deliberate, although almost all were due to poor food management. The U.S. Public Health Service estimates that 76 million people in the United States acquire food-borne diseases annually, with 300,000 hospitalizations and 5,000 deaths.[7] Deliberate efforts to kill or disable people have occurred in the United States, however. In 1984 in Dalles, Oregon, salad bars were deliberately contaminated with *Salmonella typhimurium*, causing 751 cases of salmonellosis. This attack appeared to be a trial run for a more extensive attack intended to disrupt local elections. In 1996, a disgruntled laboratory worker deliberately infected food to be consumed by colleagues with *Shigella dysenteria* Type 2, causing illness in 12 people.[8] Increasing effective measures to reduce food contamination caused by poor food management would also contribute to a better defense against toxicity in food following a natural disaster or deliberate contamination by terrorists – a dual benefit to society.

"Denial of service" attacks on the Internet that saturate all the communications channels, and hacking attacks to gain control of critical computer systems to change what they do or destroy valuable data are examples of what might be experienced in terrorist attack, disrupting response and amplifying consequences from an attack with explosives, chemical, or biological weapons.

Tank cars containing chlorine or other toxic gases under high pressure have ruptured in rail accidents, causing death and injury. The National Transportation Safety Board catalogs 16 rail accidents that released toxic or highly flammable contents from compressed gas cars since 1990.[9] In the rupture of a tank car containing chlorine gas in the town of Graniteville, South Carolina, on January 6, 2005, nine people were killed.[10]

All four of these examples represent public services at the core of the infrastructure businesses providing them. Market forces do, indeed, provide incentive to the firms to provide better core services at a minimum cost. But in each of these cases, the risk in everyday life represents safety and security externalities, which are amplified by the potential of each to become a terrorist weapon. There are many other examples of disasters that represent models, typically on a much smaller scale, of how a critical infrastructure service might become a weapon in a terrorist attack.

Addressing these kinds of disasters through public–private collaboration could, over time, assure that the technologies that provide ever more efficient infrastructure services also keep pace with the need to enhance public safety and security. Such public–private collaboration could include incentives such as better regulation for safety provided by government and improved service offered by the industry. This dual-benefit strategy would be more widely accepted by the public and industry than is a strategy based on response to the threat of terrorism alone.

To what extent should the government rely on individual firms and their associations to address the heightened risks to society resulting from both efficiencies and vulnerabilities, especially in the face of emerging terrorist threats? To what extent does government have both responsibility and unique access to information, facilities, and resources to preserve a healthy and equitable competitive environment for industry while addressing the nation's homeland security needs? This book explores the dynamics of this balance, concluding with suggestions of the appropriate public–private relationship that balances needs of the economy with the requirement of public safety and security.

The challenge to public policy is to structure an incentive system that provides for adequate robust internal operations, functional decentralization, system redundancy, and public–private and private–private coordination, even at the cost of higher prices, while leaving a level playing field for competing firms. Among the policy options available to government are (1) extension of current safety regulations to cover security exposures (often requiring new legislation); (2) research and development subsidies and partnerships with government's technical resources; (3) tax or financial benefits to reduce the economic impact of required capital investments; (4) facilitation of secured information sharing between private firms and government agencies and departments that respects privacy issues; (5) public provision of information on private vulnerabilities for which firms may consequently be held financially accountable by courts; (6) provision of publicly funded terrorism (re)insurance and incentives to insurance and reinsurance firms to offer rates scaled to risk reduction;

(7) encouragement of voluntary collective actions through trade associations; and (8) antitrust protection for such collective action. Some combination of these tools must be deployed in a way that is both politically and economically sustainable.

NOTES

1. Marsh 1997.
2. U.S. Commission on National Security/21st Century 2001.
3. National Commission on Terrorism 2000.
4. Advisory Panel to Assess Domestic Response Capabilities for Terrorism Involving Weapons of Mass Destruction 2000.
5. An example of a core vulnerability for the chemical sector is the flammability of a liquefied natural gas storage tank or a train transporting tank cars filled with liquefied chlorine gas. An out-of-core vulnerability would be a Sarin attack on a crowded theater.
6. Branscomb 2006.
7. Sood 2004.
8. Institute of Medicine of the National Academies 2005.
9. National Transportation Safety Board 2006a.
10. National Transportation Safety Board 2006b.

3

THE BRITTLE SUPERPOWER

Stephen E. Flynn

The United States has been living on borrowed time – and squandering it. In the four years since the September 11, 2001, attacks on the World Trade Center towers and the Pentagon, the Bush administration has chosen to emphasize the use of military operations overseas over an effort to reduce America's vulnerability to catastrophic terrorist attacks at home. While the administration has acknowledged in principle the need to improve critical infrastructure protection, in practice it has placed the burden for doing so primarily on the private sector that owns and operates much of that infrastructure. But this delegation of responsibility fails to acknowledge the practical limits of the marketplace to agree upon common protocols and to make investments to bolster security. As a result, the transportation, energy, information, financial, chemical, food, and logistical networks that underpin U.S. economic power and the American way of life remain virtually unprotected. The tragic loss of life in the aftermath of Hurricane Katrina in 2005 exposed Washington's shocking lack of preparedness to respond to large-scale disasters on American soil. The United States may be the world's sole superpower, but it is showing ominous signs of being a brittle one. If the federal government does not provide meaningful incentives to make U.S. infrastructure more resilient and create workable frameworks for ongoing public and private partnerships to advance security, future terrorist attacks and natural disasters with profound economic and societal disruption are inevitable.

It does not have to be this way. Given the wealth of the United States, it can clearly afford to invest in measures that will make America a more resilient society in the face of human-caused and natural disasters. But critical

This chapter is adapted from Flynn 2004. The author retains the copyright for this chapter.

infrastructure protection and emergency preparedness will not happen if left solely to the marketplace. Nor can they be accomplished solely at the local and state levels. Instead, the federal government should be taking the lead in engaging the private sector in a collective effort to confront the threat of catastrophic acts of terror and natural disasters at home. Unfortunately, while the post-9/11 case for homeland security is seemingly a straightforward one, Washington has demonstrated an extraordinary degree of ambivalence about making any serious effort to tackle this mission. Instead, the White House has favored muscular efforts abroad to combat terrorism and has passed along the emergency preparedness mission to governors, county commissioners, and mayors. The premise behind the Bush administration's strategy of preemptive use of force is that as long as the United States is willing to show sufficient grit, it can successfully hold its enemies at bay. Throughout the 2004 presidential campaign, the President and Vice President asserted that the war on terror had to be waged at its source. In the words of Vice President Dick Cheney, "Wars are not won on the defensive. To fully and finally remove this danger [of terrorism], we have only one option – and that's to take the fight to the enemy."[1] On July 4, 2004, President Bush made the point this way: "We will engage these enemies in these countries [Iraq and Afghanistan] and around the world so we do not have to face them here at home."[2]

Targeting terrorism at its source is an appealing notion. Unfortunately, the enemy is not cooperating. As the March 2004 attacks in Madrid, July 2005 attacks in London, August 2005 attacks in Sharm el Sheikh, Egypt, and October 2005 attacks in Bali, Indonesia, have made clear, there is no central front on which Al Qaeda and its radical jihadist imitators can be cornered and destroyed. Terrorist organizations are living and operating within jurisdictions of U.S. allies and do not need to receive aid and comfort from rogue states. According to the U.S. Department of State's annual global terrorism report, the number of terrorist incidents was at a record high in 2004, despite the U.S.-led invasions of Afghanistan and Iraq.[3] There is mounting evidence that the invasion of Iraq is fueling both the number of recruits and the capabilities of radical jihadist groups.[4]

The reluctance of the White House and the national security community to adapt to the shifting nature of the terrorist threat bears a disturbing resemblance to the opening chapter of World War II. In September 1939, the German army rolled eastward into Poland and unleashed a new form of combat known as "blitzkrieg." When Poland became a victim of the Third Reich, London and Paris finally abandoned their policies of appeasement and declared war. The British and French high commands then began to execute war plans that relied on assumptions drawn from their experiences in World War I. They activated their reserves and reinforced the Maginot Line – defenses of mounted cannons stretching for 250 miles along the Franco–German border. Then they waited for Hitler's next move.

The eight-month period before the fall of Paris came to be known as "the phony war." During this relatively quiet time, France and the United Kingdom were convinced they were deterring the Germans by mobilizing their more plentiful military assets in an updated version of trench warfare. But they did not alter their tactics to respond to the new offensive warfare that the Germans had executed with such lethal results in eastern Europe. In May 1940, France and the United Kingdom paid a heavy price for their complacency: Panzer units raced into the lowlands, circumvented the Maginot Line, and conquered France shortly thereafter. The British expeditionary forces narrowly escaped by fleeing across the English Channel aboard a makeshift armada, leaving much of their armament behind on the beaches of Dunkirk.

Instead of a Maginot Line, the Pentagon is executing its long-standing forward defense strategy, which involves leapfrogging ahead of U.S. borders and waging combat on the turfs of U.S. enemies and allies. Meanwhile, protection of the rear – the American nation itself – remains largely outside the scope of national security, even though the 9/11 attacks were launched from within the United States against targets on American soil.

Al Qaeda has demonstrated that by directing terrorist attacks on major urban areas and the critical foundations of modern life, it can generate a very "big bang for their buck." Al Qaeda also placed the United States at the top of its target list and made clear that it wants to carry out a more devastating attack than those on New York and Washington.[5]

Defenders of the Bush administration's war on terrorism are quick to point to the absence of another 9/11-style attack on U.S. soil as vindication for placing overwhelming emphasis on an offense-oriented strategy. To be sure, there is ample evidence that the war in Iraq has been attracting foreign insurgents and Al Qaeda sympathizers to Baghdad versus to Main Street. However, this is likely to prove to be a short-term reprieve that poses a longer-term danger. Beginning in June 2003, Iraq's energy sector became a primary target for insurgents. By mid-July 2005, nearly 250 attacks on oil and gas pipelines had cost Iraq more than $10 billion in lost oil revenue. Successful attacks on the electrical grid have kept average daily output at 5 to 10 percent below the pre-war level, despite the $1.2 billion the United States has spent to improve Iraqi electrical production.[6]

In some ways, the situation in Iraq is analogous to what happened during the decade-long conflict from 1970 to 1989 against the Soviet occupation of Afghanistan. The foreign participants who joined the mujahideen in that conflict became the hardened foot-soldiers who would ultimately transform themselves into Al Qaeda. But unlike Afghanistan, where the combatants waged war in a pre-modern society, insurgents in Iraq are refining their skills to sabotage critical infrastructures. Accordingly, when these foreign insurgents eventually return to their native lands, they will do so with the experience of successfully targeting complex systems that support economic and daily life within advanced societies.

Even if the United States had not chosen to invade Iraq, an alternative scenario explains why there has not been another attack on American soil. As a practical matter, sophisticated terrorist operations on the scale of the 9/11 attacks take time. Because Al Qaeda has proclaimed that it wants to surpass the destruction and disruption associated with toppling the World Trade Center towers, the current period of quiet may indicate a lull during which the organization is focusing on meticulously planning its next large-scale operation. Deploying the complex organizational structure to carry out those plans could take several years. This is because such an attack typically involves deploying a three-cell structure in which the members of each cell are isolated from one another to ensure the greatest chance of survival if any one cell is compromised.

An Al Qaeda–style operation involves a "logistics" cell to attend to such things as locating safe houses, providing identity documents, and finding jobs for the operatives so they can blend into the civilian population. In addition, a "surveillance" cell is charged with scoping out potential targets, probing security measures, and conducting dry runs. Finally, an "attack" cell may include suicide bombers who are charged with executing the attack.[7]

Establishing extensive organizational capacity is a painstaking process, particularly within the United States, where Al Qaeda must work from a much smaller footprint of operatives and sympathizers than it has in Western Europe or countries like Indonesia. Terrorist cells are also a resource that must be carefully husbanded, because using them will likely translate into losing them. This is because it is impossible to carry out an attack without leaving some forensic clues that expose the cells to enforcement action. Accordingly, cells that go after what would seem to be a plentiful menu of soft targets such as shopping malls or sporting events can generate plenty of short-term media attention. But if these attacks cannot be sustained over time (because the authorities are able to track down and destroy the terrorists' organization), the long-term economic consequences are likely to be modest. As a result, terrorists will want to make sure that they pick meaningful targets where the attack proves to be worth all the organizational effort to carry it out.

In short, it would be foolhardy to act as though the 9/11 attacks were an aberrant event in which Al Qaeda got lucky because America's guard was temporarily down. The sad truth is that America's guard was never really up, and despite all the political rhetoric, little has changed in recent years. The most tempting targets for terrorists remain those that can produce widespread economic and social disruption. However, the White House has declared that safeguarding the nation's critical infrastructure is not really a federal responsibility. According to President Bush's 2002 National Homeland Security Strategy, "The government should only address those activities that the market does not adequately provide – for example, national defense or border security. . . . For other aspects of homeland security, sufficient incentives exist in the private market to supply protection."[8] This expression of faith, however, has not borne out. According to a survey commissioned by the Washington-based Council on Competitiveness just one year after the 9/11 attacks, 92 percent of executives did not believe that terrorists would target their companies, and only 53 percent of the respondents indicated that their companies had increased security spending between 2001 and 2002.[9] With the passing of each month without a new attack, the reluctance of companies to invest in security has only grown.

The lack of enthusiasm among company executives to provide leadership when it comes to developing the means to safeguard critical infrastructures should not be surprising. This is because survival in the marketplace has required that they be responsive to four globalization imperatives for making critical infrastructures (1) as open to as many users as possible; (2) as efficient as possible; (3) as reliable as possible; and (4) as low cost as possible to use. Because the conventional view of security is that it raises costs, undermines efficiency, is at odds with assuring reliability, and constrains access, there has been a clear disincentive for the private sector to make it a priority. As a result, the United States entered the twenty-first century with networks that have an extraordinary capacity to generate wealth but with few meaningful safeguards in the event of an attack.

The challenge of elevating the critical infrastructure protection priority and crafting a tidy security division of labor between the private and public sectors is complicated by two additional factors. First, safeguards that only apply within U.S. borders will not work because the United States' critical infrastructures depend on their links to the rest of North America and the world. Second, the United States competes in a global marketplace, and it must be mindful of not unilaterally incurring costs that place U.S. companies and the U.S. economy at a competitive disadvantage.

Private sector concerns about maintaining competitiveness in the face of the growing security imperative are legitimate. Security is not free. A company incurs costs when it invests in measures to protect the portion of infrastructure it controls. If a company does not believe other companies are willing or able to make a similar investment, then it faces the likelihood of losing market share while simply shifting the infrastructure's vulnerability elsewhere. If terrorists strike, the company still suffers the disruptive consequences of an attack right alongside those who did nothing to prevent it. Those consequences are likely to include the cost of implementing new government requirements. Therefore, infrastructure security suffers from a dilemma commonly referred to as the "tragedy of the commons."

Take the case of the chemical industry. By and large, chemical manufacturers have a good safety record. But security is another matter. Operating on thin profit margins and faced with growing overseas competition, most companies have been reluctant to incur the additional costs associated with improving their security. One plausible scenario is that the manager of a chemical plant will look around his facility and gets squeamish about the many security lapses he finds. After a fitful night's sleep, he will wake up and decides to invest in protective measures that raise the cost to his customers by $50 per shipment. A competitor who does not make that investment will be able to attract business away from the security-conscious plant because his handling costs will be lower. Capable terrorists and criminals will then target this lower-cost operation because it is an easier target. In the event of an attack, particularly one that is catastrophic, two consequences are likely. First, government officials will not discriminate between the more security-conscious and the less security-conscious companies. All chemical plants are likely to be shut down while the authorities try to sort things out. Second, once the dust clears, elected and regulatory officials will scramble to impose new security requirements that could nullify the proactive plant owner's earlier investments. Given this scenario, the most rational behavior of the nervous manager would appear to be to keep tossing and turning at night while focusing on short-term profitability during the day.

The only way to prevent the tragedy of the commons is to convince all the private participants to abide by the same security requirements. When standards are universal, their cost is borne equally across a sector. As taxpayers or as consumers, Americans will end up bankrolling these measures, but what they will be paying for is insurance against the loss of innocent lives and a profound disruption to their society and the economy.

The problem boils down to this: the design, ownership, and day-to-day operational knowledge of critical systems rest almost exclusively with the private sector. But security and safety are public goods whose provision is a core responsibility of government at all levels. The government is unable to protect things that it has only a peripheral understanding and limited jurisdictional reach, and the market will resist providing public goods if doing so puts them at a competitive disadvantage by eroding their profits or sacrificing their market share.

Certainly, the 9/11 attacks created a general sense among public and private sector players that the security imperative requires far more attention than it had been receiving. But the reality is that there still remain disincentives for the private sector to cooperate with government entities on this agenda. Some of the structures in place, such as the laws and regulations that guide the interaction within and among these sectors, remain static. For instance, anti-trust laws severely constrain the ability of industry leaders to come together and agree to common protocols. Also, companies that make a good faith effort to undertake industry-generated anti-terrorist measures potentially risk open-ended liability issues should terrorists succeed in defeating those measures. After the post-mortem, public officials are likely to be the first at the head of the queue insisting that private sector entities be held accountable for not having done enough.

While there are practical barriers to having the private sector assume the bulk of the responsibility for the post-9/11 security mandate, leaving it to the public sector alone to map the path ahead holds little promise as an alternative. When the government announces requirements or "best practices" after a lengthy deliberative process with nominal industry input, it almost always misses the mark. More often than not, the proposed or mandated safeguards reflect a poor understanding of the design and operation of critical infrastructures and the real versus perceived vulnerabilities. This disconnect is because many of the most critical issues span multiple agency jurisdictions, and these agencies rarely work well together. The results end up being a mix of unacknowledged gaps and redundant requirements.

If improving homeland security requires that the U.S. government reconsider many of its assumptions and priorities, it also requires a population that acknowledges that security must become everyone's business. The starting point for engaging civil society in this enterprise is a willingness to accept that there will never be a permanent victory in a war on terrorism by overseas military campaigns. Terrorism is simply too cheap, too available, and too tempting to ever be totally eradicated. And U.S. borders will never serve as a last line of defense against a determined terrorist. What is required is that everyday citizens develop both the maturity to live with the risk of future attacks and the willingness to invest in reasonable measures to mitigate that risk.

This is not a defeatist position. Improving the United States' protections and its resilience to withstand acts of catastrophic terrorism has both tactical value in preventing these attacks and strategic value in deterring them in the first place. Radical jihadist groups do not have unlimited resources. When they strike, they want to be reasonably confident that they will be successful. They also want to inflict real damage that will generate political pressure to adopt draconian measures in response to a traumatized public.

Today's terrorist masterminds know that the main benefit of attacks on critical infrastructure is not the immediate damage they inflict, but the collateral consequences of eroding the public's trust in services on which it depends.

Certainly this lesson has not been lost on Osama bin Laden. In a video tape broadcast on *Aljazeera* on November 1, 2004, bin Laden claims: "for example, Al Qaeda spent $500,000 on the event, while America, in the incident and its aftermath, lost – according to the lowest estimate – more than $500 billion. Meaning that every dollar of Al Qaeda defeated a million dollars by the permission of Allah, besides the loss of a huge number of jobs."[10]

What if the next terrorist strike were on the American food supply system? The attack itself might kill only a handful of people, but without measures in place to reassure the public that follow-on attacks could be prevented or at least contained, consumers at home and abroad would become distrustful of a sector that accounts for more than 10 percent of U.S. gross domestic product. Similarly, a dirty bomb smuggled in a container and set off in a seaport would likely kill only a few unfortunate longshoremen and contaminate several acres of valuable waterfront property. But if there is no credible security system to restore the public's confidence that other containers are safe, mayors and governors throughout the country, as well as the President, will come under withering political pressure to order the shutdown of the intermodal transportation system. Examining cargo in tens of thousands of trucks, trains, and ships to ensure it poses no threat would have devastating economic consequences. When containers stop moving, assembly plants go idle, retail shelves go bare, and workers end up in unemployment lines. A three-week shutdown could spawn a global recession.

As long as catastrophic terrorism is assured of generating a huge bang for the buck, current and future U.S. adversaries will make it the first arrow they reach for in attacking the country. Their confidence in their ability to inflict real damage on the world's sole superpower will be directly proportional to the unwillingness of private and public leaders to acknowledge the risk of market failures associated with excessive reliance on unprotected networks that are sophisticated, concentrated, and interdependent. Given the futility of terrorists taking on U.S. military forces directly, attacking these networks is not irrational. In warfare, combatants always seek to exploit their adversary's weaknesses.

However, if terrorist attacks were likely to be detected, intercepted, contained, and managed without doing any measurable damage to the American way of life or quality of life, their value as a means of warfare would be depreciated. Because such acts violate widely accepted norms, they will almost certainly invite not just American, but also international, retribution. Most adversaries would probably judge this too high a price to pay if striking civilian targets holds out little chance of causing the desired mass disruption.

A focus on critical infrastructure protection can also improve the effectiveness of more conventional counterterrorism measures. By bolstering the security of critical networks in advance of possible attacks, adversaries must put together more complex operations to target them successfully. The resultant need for terrorists to raise more money, recruit expertise, and lengthen planning cycles and rehearsals would be a boon for intelligence services and law enforcement officials. This is because such pre-execution activities elevate the opportunities for infiltration and raise the odds that terrorist groups will attract attention.

There is an added bit of good news that comes from placing greater emphasis on homeland security. The most effective measures for protecting potential targets or making them more resilient in the face of successful attacks almost always have derivative benefits for other public and private goods. For instance, bolstering the tools to detect and intercept terrorists will enhance the means available to authorities for combating criminal acts such as narcotics trafficking, migrant smuggling, cargo theft, and violations of export controls. The risk of an avian flu pandemic and outbreaks such as SARS, AIDS, West Nile virus, foot-and-mouth disease, and mad cow disease have highlighted the challenges of managing deadly pathogens in a shrinking world. Public health investments to deal with biological agents or attacks on food and water supplies will provide U.S. authorities with more effective tools to manage these global threats. Measures adopted to protect infrastructure make it more resilient not only to terrorist attacks, but also to "acts of God" or human and mechanical error. They also invariably reinforce U.S. values that are respected around the world, whereas reliance on aggressive military measures invariably puts those values at risk.

How much security is enough? Answering that question requires identifying both the threat a security measure is designed to counter and the appropriate point at which an additional investment in a security measure yields only a marginal return. Asking members of the private sector to decide independently where this line should be drawn is impractical because they lack access to intelligence and because they need good-Samaritan safeguards should their efforts fall short of deterring every terrorist incident. Only the federal government has access to threat information, and only the federal government can establish liability limits.

In the end, the threshold for success will be met when the American people can conclude that a future attack on U.S. soil will be an exceptional event that does not require wholesale changes in how they go about their lives. This means that they should be confident that there are adequate private and public measures in place to confront the danger and manage its aftermath. In other words, homeland security should strive to achieve what the aviation industry has done with safety. It has been the aviation industry's long-standing and ongoing investments that have sustained air travel (despite the periodic horror of airplanes falling out of the sky) and have convinced the public that it is safe to fly. Public confidence can never be taken for granted after a major jet crash, but private and public aviation officials start from a credible foundation built upon a cooperative effort to incorporate safety into every part of the industry. In the immediate aftermath of airline disasters, the public is reassured by the fact that the lessons learned are quickly compiled and released and that the government and the industry seem willing to take whatever corrective actions are required.

Ongoing and credible efforts to confront risk are essential to the viability of any complex modern enterprise. Aviation safety provides helpful reference points for how to pursue security without turning the United States into a national gated community. First, it demonstrates that Americans do not expect their lives to be risk-free; they just rightfully expect that reasonable measures be in place to manage that risk. Second, managing risk works best if safeguards are integrated as an organic part of a sector's environment and if they are dynamic in adapting to changes in that environment. Third, government plays an essential role in providing incentives and disincentives for people and industry to meet minimum standards. Security simply will not happen by itself.

When it comes to critical infrastructure protection, the issue, then, is to engage the private sector to develop standards and create effective mechanisms for their uniform enforcement. This is a task that necessitates a much different kind of institutional framework than setting up a new federal department of homeland security. What it requires is the creation of a structure that allows the private sector and civil society to participate as equal partners in the process of designing and implementing security for the U.S. homeland.

Admittedly, it will not be easy to muster the political will to admit the post-9/11 error of placing so much emphasis on projecting military might abroad while neglecting efforts to build greater U.S. resilience at home. But now is not a time for timidity. Americans and private sector leaders must demand that Washington make homeland security generally and critical infrastructure specifically a priority. And the entire nation, not just the national security establishment, must be organized for the long struggle against terrorism.

NOTES

1. Remarks by the Vice President at the 123rd Coast Guard Academy Commencement (White House 2004b).
2. White House 2004a.
3. U.S. Department of State 2005. The report does not include the specific figures but states in its overview: "Despite ongoing improvements in U.S. homeland security, military campaigns against insurgents and terrorists in Iraq and Afghanistan, and deepening counterterrorism cooperation among the nations of the world, international terrorism

continued to pose a significant threat to the United States and its partners in 2004." However, the *Washington Post* reports that congressional aides briefed on the U.S. Department of State statistics confirmed that the number of serious terrorist incidents tripled in 2004 (Glasser 2005).

4. Clarke 2004.
5. CNN 2002.
6. See Benjamin and Simon 2005.
7. Flynn 2005c.
8. White House 2005b.
9. Council on Competitiveness 2002.
10. Aljazeera 2004.

4

CRITICAL INFRASTRUCTURE PROTECTION IN THE UNITED STATES SINCE 1993

Brian Lopez

The American public's sense of domestic security, of being safely removed from a turbulent world, was overturned on September 11, 2001. What is less widely recognized is that terrorism has a long history, and in the decade prior to 9/11 the leaders of government were well aware of the growing threat of terrorism to our homeland, as well as U.S. interests abroad. This awareness was documented by a succession of high-level task forces, charged by the White House with evaluation of the terrorist threat and recommendations for mitigating that threat. Through this process, critical infrastructure was identified as a key issue, and the view within the government of its role grew in both scope and importance.

This chapter provides a chronology of U.S. government responses to terrorism from 1993–2005, with a specific focus on critical infrastructure protection. The chapter highlights the key organizations and efforts created to address the emerging area of critical infrastructure protection and the response of infrastructure providers to those efforts. Important excerpts from primary sources are provided. The evolving definitions of "critical infrastructure" and related concepts are tracked via those sources, and the discussion is signposted by capsule summaries of significant indicators of threat and vulnerability to terrorism during each time period.

A NEW THREAT EMERGES: 1993–1995

A series of events and responses from 1993 to 1995 began to make concrete that there was a new world of threat emerging and that it would involve new

The author presents this summary from the perspective of the Lawrence Livermore National Laboratory's Vulnerability and Risk Assessment Program (VRAP), of which the author is the leader.

actors and attack vectors. During this period, the United States had inspectors on the ground in Iraq searching for weapons of mass destruction, and the World Trade Center in New York was bombed for the first time. As the U.S. government processed and reacted to these events, they were followed in 1995 by the Oklahoma City bombing and a Sarin gas attack in the Japanese subway system.

BOX 4.1 EXCERPTS OF "U.S. POLICY ON COUNTER TERRORISM" FROM
PRESIDENTIAL DECISION DIRECTIVE 39 *

The United States shall reduce its vulnerabilities to terrorism, at home and abroad. It shall be the responsibility of all Department and Agency heads to ensure that their personnel and facilities, and the people and facilities under their jurisdiction, are fully protected against terrorism. With regard to ensuring security:

The Attorney General, as the chief law enforcement officer, shall chair a Cabinet Committee to review the vulnerability to terrorism of government facilities in the United States and critical national infrastructure and make recommendations to me and the appropriate Cabinet member or Agency head;

The Director, FBI, as head of the investigative agency for terrorism, shall reduce vulnerabilities by an expanded program of counterterrorism;

The Secretary of Transportation shall reduce vulnerabilities affecting the security of all airports in the United States and all aircraft and passengers and all maritime shipping under U.S. flag or registration or operating within the territory of the United States and shall coordinate security measures for rail, highway, mass transit and pipeline facilities;

The Secretary of State shall reduce vulnerabilities affecting the security of all personnel and facilities at non-military U.S. Government installations abroad and affecting the general safety of American citizens abroad;

The United States shall give the highest priority to developing effective capabilities to detect, prevent, defeat and manage the consequences of nuclear, biological or chemical materials or weapons use by terrorists.

The acquisition of weapons of mass destruction by a terrorist group, through theft or manufacture, is unacceptable. There is no higher priority than preventing the acquisition of this capability or removing this capability from terrorist groups potentially opposed to the United States.

* Clinton, William J. "U.S. Policy on Counter Terrorism" *Presidential Decision Directive 39.* June 21, 1995.

In June of 1995, the White House released Presidential Decision Directive (PDD) 39 defining U.S. policy on counterterrorism. PDD 39 spoke directly to reducing U.S. vulnerabilities to terrorism, including critical infrastructure and several areas that later would be included in critical infrastructure such as government facilities, airports, maritime systems, railways, highways, and pipelines. Box 4.1 highlights the sections of the policy that established the foundation for the involvement and roles of various agencies in future critical infrastructure efforts.[1]

While the elements of what we now refer to as "critical infrastructure" were mentioned in several places in the policy directive, a priority was put on weapons of mass destruction and the protection of government agencies, personnel, and facilities.

THE EMERGING FIELD OF CRITICAL INFRASTRUCTURE PROTECTION: 1996–1998

Continuing threat and vulnerability indicators (domestic and foreign) were apparent with bombings in 1996 of the Summer Olympics in Atlanta and the Khobar Towers in Saudi Arabia, followed in 1998 by bombings of the U.S. embassies in Kenya and Tanzania.

The analysis and defense of critical infrastructure, as an area of open government attention, began to crystallize with the formation of the President's Commission on Critical Infrastructure Protection (PCCIP) in July 1996.[2] Executive Order (EO) 13010 established the PCCIP and also traced the emerging outline for the U.S. government's view of this topic by providing a definition of critical infrastructure, listing specific infrastructures of interest, introducing the physical/cyber divide, and the complication of private ownership.

EO 13010 defined critical infrastructure as national infrastructures so vital that their "incapacity or destruction would have a debilitating impact on the defense or economic security of the United States." The specific critical infrastructures highlighted were "telecommunications, electrical power systems, gas and oil storage and transportation, banking and finance, transportation, water supply systems, emergency services (including medical, police, fire, and rescue), and continuity of government." The vulnerabilities of these infrastructures were divided into two categories: "physical vulnerabilities to tangible property; and cyber vulnerabilities of electronic, radio-frequency, or computer-based attacks on the information or communications components that control critical infrastructures." The executive order also recognized the additional complexity introduced by the extent to which critical infrastructure is privately owned, stating that "because many of these critical infrastructures are owned and operated by the private sector, it is essential that the government and private sector work together to develop a strategy for protecting them and assuring their continued operation."[3]

The PCCIP was composed of representatives from the U.S. Departments of Treasury, Justice, Defense, Commerce, Transportation, and Energy; the Federal Emergency Management Agency, Federal Bureau of Investigation, Central Intelligence Agency, and National Security Agency. The inclusion of representation from the Department of Energy (DOE) on the PCCIP laid the groundwork for the early involvement of the DOE National Laboratory complex in the nation's future critical infrastructure protection activities. Several National Laboratories relocated technical staff to Washington, D.C. to support the PCCIP.

The PCCIP report in October 1997, *Critical Foundations: Protecting America's Infrastructures,* was followed in May 1998 by PDD 63. The directive set a goal of ensuring the country's capability of protecting critical infrastructure from intentional acts by 2003. It maintained the physical and cyber categories of vulnerability suggested by EO 13010, as well as its sensitivity to the complexity of working the private ownership issues. The EO also added the following institutional elements to the nation's efforts in protecting critical infrastructure:

A National Coordinator whose scope will include not only critical infrastructure but also foreign terrorism and threats of domestic mass destruction (including biological weapons) because attacks on the United States may not come labeled in neat jurisdictional boxes;

The National Infrastructure Protection Center (NIPC) at the FBI, which will fuse representatives from FBI, DOD, USSS, Energy, Transportation, the Intelligence Community, and the private sector in an unprecedented attempt at information sharing among agencies in collaboration with the private sector. The NIPC will also provide the principal means of facilitating and coordinating the federal government's response to an incident, mitigating attacks, investigating threats, and monitoring reconstitution efforts;

Information Sharing and Analysis Centers (ISACs) are encouraged to be set up by the private sector in cooperation with the federal government and modeled on the Centers for Disease Control and Prevention;

A National Infrastructure Assurance Council drawn from private sector leaders and state/local officials to provide guidance to the policy formulation of a National Plan;

The Critical Infrastructure Assurance Office (CIAO) will provide support to the National Coordinator's work with government agencies and the private sector in developing a national plan. The office will also help coordinate a national education and awareness program, and legislative and public affairs.[4]

Table 4.1. PDD 63 lead agency assignments

Critical infrastructure sector	Lead agency
Information and communications	Department of Commerce
Banking and finance	Department of the Treasury
Water supply	Environmental Protection Agency
Aviation	Department of Transportation
Highways (including trucking)	
Mass transit	
Pipelines	
Rail	
Waterborne commerce	
Emergency law enforcement services	Department of Justice/Federal Bureau of Investigation
Emergency fire services and continuity of government	Federal Emergency Management Agency
Public health services	Department of Health and Human Services
Electric power oil and gas production and storage	Department of Energy

PDD 63 also identified lead agencies for each of the critical infrastructure sectors to be focal point liaisons with the private sector and to have accountability within the federal government for specific sectors and roles (Table 4.1). One of these roles was to perform initial vulnerability assessments of each sector and develop remediation plans. These initial assessments were to be followed by periodic re-assessments.[5]

With DOE designated as the lead agency for electric power as well as oil and gas production and storage (pipeline security was assigned to the Department of Transportation), the DOE National Laboratory complex was engaged to develop a response to PDD 63. Several National Laboratories relocated technical staff to Washington, D.C. to develop the plan for protecting DOE's portion of the critical infrastructure, to work on an effort across the lead agencies to create a research plan, and to identify and provide teams to begin to assess the vulnerabilities of those infrastructures and suggest mitigation measures. These assessments were to be coordinated by DOE's Office of Energy Assurance.

By late 1998, the office had developed a list of infrastructure providers to be assessed. The waiting list for assessments grew quite rapidly to more than 15. The initial participants in the assessment program were motivated by several factors. Foremost was a sense of stewardship for their piece of the infrastructure. Typically, these executives had worked in their industry for their entire careers, rising from technical positions through management and into the executive ranks. They understood their infrastructure at both a business and a technical level and often had personal concerns and insights into facets of its security. These executives were also interested in their companies being industry leaders in a variety of areas, including emerging ones such as security, and were committed to funding that leadership. They fundamentally understood that their industry was about to undergo an unprecedented evolution driven by deregulation, changes in technology, and increasing threats.

With the advent of deregulation, new competitive pressures were introduced, stock-exchange-like markets were created for electric power, and utilities began to move into new (and often unrelated) business areas. These trends were coupled with the migration of Supervisory Control and Data Acquisition systems[6] from proprietary to commodity hardware, software, and protocols; the increasing interconnection and interdependence of these systems (both internally and externally – with the rapid penetration of the Internet); and an aging workforce that needed to rapidly transition knowledge to the next generation of utility workers. In all, the industry faced a very challenging environment coming over the horizon.

ASSESSMENT AND SELF-REGULATION: 1999–2000

The vulnerability of the nation's electric power infrastructure became apparent to the general public as the "California Energy Crisis" began, resulting in rolling blackouts. Threat indicators continued with the bombing of the *U.S.S. Cole* in 2000 and ultimately with the 9/11 attacks in September 2001.

The national laboratory team (working for the Office of Energy Assurance) focused initially on the electric power sector. The team worked top down from the Independent System Operator and Regional Transmission Organization level to major generators, transmission companies, and multi-state utilities, and eventually to representative state utilities. Initially, the team members, capabilities, and methodologies were leveraged from existing programs within the DOE National Laboratories. Eventually the Office of Energy Assurance team became a more permanent, self-standing team, and it was able to develop and evolve specific methodology and capabilities for the assessments. The electric power sector assessments were followed by assessments of gas and then oil assets across the United States.

The response to these initial assessments was rapid, positive, and proactive. The Office of Energy Assurance team's demonstrations of the susceptibility of an organization to high-consequence vulnerabilities were taken seriously. Both short-term fixes and deeper architectural, procedural, and process improvements were funded by industry. Security became a new executive-level focus for many of the assessed organizations, and several organizations, in the wake of an assessment, actually funded and built internal security programs. Others engaged commercial providers to assist with mitigation, to develop secure designs for current and future systems, and to provide periodic assessments to ensure that the holes that had been uncovered were plugged and that new vulnerabilities had not been introduced.

In addition to previously mentioned motivations for being assessed, a new theme was emerging. Companies were beginning to view their willingness to be assessed by the DOE teams and their subsequent responsiveness to the department's recommendations as a potential bulwark against regulation. The industry's approach was to open themselves to scrutiny and be responsive to assessment findings, thereby providing a strong argument for the legitimacy and effectiveness of self-regulation.

The White House continued to focus on infrastructure protection during this period, directing the formation of the National Infrastructure Assurance Council in July of 1999. Established by Executive Order 13130, the council was given three main missions:

(1) enhance the partnership of the public and private sectors in protecting our critical infrastructure and provide reports on this issue to the President as appropriate;
(2) propose and develop ways to encourage private industry to perform periodic risk assessments of critical processes, including information and telecommunications systems; and
(3) monitor the development of Private Sector Information Sharing and Analysis Centers (PSISACs) and provide recommendations to the National Coordinator and the National Economic Council on how these organizations can best foster improved cooperation among the PSISACs, the National Infrastructure Protection Center (NIPC), and other Federal Government entities.[7]

In response to PDD 63, the Department of Commerce established the Critical Infrastructure Assurance Office and began Project Matrix – an initial effort to analyze the U.S. government's dependency on critical infrastructure.

RESPONDING TO 9/11: 2001–2002

The California energy crisis continued with a series of rolling blackouts in northern and central California, and eventually an unprecedented statewide rolling blackout in March 2001, reacquainting the nation with the vulnerability of the U.S. power grid. Then on 9/11, the terrorist attacks on the World Trade Centers, the Pentagon, and one other target assigned to the hijacked airplane that crashed in Pennsylvania, brought an entirely new level of urgency to the task of protection against terrror attacks. This urgency was further magnified by a series of anthrax attacks later in 2001.

In the wake of 9/11, the pace and intensity of the assessment and mitigation work accelerated markedly. DOE dispatched teams to perform rapid "vulnerability surveys" (stripped-down versions of the full-blown assessment methodology) of 25 critical energy assets across the United States. National Laboratory teams were deployed to analyze critical infrastructure security in preparation for the 2002 Winter Olympics in Salt Lake City.

In response to 9/11, the industry motivation for being assessed shifted from internal (stewardship, industry leadership) and self-interest (staving off regulation) to external. Foremost on the mind of industry executives was deterring and mitigating potential attacks on their infrastructure and personnel. Cost became far less of an issue, and significant short- and medium-term expenditures were approved. Security work was prioritized and fast-tracked. Critical infrastructure providers began to feel public, political, and financial world pressure as the media began a long series of reports and investigations into every facet of homeland security. Wall Street became interested in the state of security of publicly traded infrastructure providers, further accelerating security improvements. Insurance was not generally considered an acceptable mitigation solution in the solemn light of the 9/11 death toll. After 9/11, homeland security became an omnipresent topic.

In October 2001, EO 13228 established an "Office of Homeland Security" at the White House and significantly expanded the list of what the government was now considering as critical infrastructure – adding nuclear sites, the agriculture sector, and special events. The protection section of the order focused on a variety of critical infrastructure issues. Key features of the Executive Order are shown in Box 4.2.

Eight days later, the White House issued EO 13231, "Critical Infrastructure Protection in the Information Age," highlighting the dependence of U.S. economic, government, and defense functions on critical infrastructure. The order stated:

> The information technology revolution has changed the way business is transacted, government operates, and national defense is conducted. Those three functions now depend on an interdependent network of critical information infrastructures. The protection program authorized by this order shall consist of continuous efforts to secure information systems for critical infrastructure, including emergency preparedness communications, and the physical assets that support such systems. Protection of these systems is essential to the telecommunications, energy, financial services, manufacturing, water, transportation, health care, and emergency services sectors.[8]

BOX 4.2 "ESTABLISHING THE OFFICE OF HOMELAND SECURITY,"
FROM *EXECUTIVE ORDER 13228* *

The Office shall coordinate efforts to protect the United States and its critical infrastructure from the consequences of terrorist attacks. In performing this function, the Office shall work with Federal, State, and local agencies, and private entities, as appropriate, to:

(i)   strengthen measures for protecting energy production, transmission, and distribution services and critical facilities; other utilities; telecommunications; facilities that produce, use, store, or dispose of nuclear material; and other critical infrastructure services and critical facilities within the United States from terrorist attack;

(ii)   coordinate efforts to protect critical public and privately owned information systems within the United States from terrorist attack;

(iii)   develop criteria for reviewing whether appropriate security measures are in place at major public and privately owned facilities within the United States;

(iv)   coordinate domestic efforts to ensure that special events determined by appropriate senior officials to have national significance are protected from terrorist attack;

(v)   coordinate efforts to protect transportation systems within the United States, including railways, highways, shipping, ports and waterways, and airports and civilian aircraft, from terrorist attack;

(vi)   coordinate efforts to protect United States livestock, agriculture, and systems for the provision of water and food for human use and consumption from terrorist attack; and

(vii)   coordinate efforts to prevent unauthorized access to, development of, and unlawful importation into the United States of, chemical, biological, radiological, nuclear, explosive, or other related materials that have the potential to be used in terrorist attacks.

* Bush, George W. "Establishing the Office of Homeland Security." *Executive Order 13228.* October 8, 2001, p. 3.

The order also established another new organization: the "President's Critical Infrastructure Protection Board."

During this period, critical infrastructure protection issues were featured in the national media on a regular basis, driving interest and concern across a variety of new sectors. National Laboratory teams, having been involved with critical infrastructure protection issues since 1996, and having protection-focused teams with three to four years of field experience, began to cover a much broader range of critical infrastructure. Again, the teams leveraged the multidisciplinary expertise from existing programs at the National Laboratories and the methodology and field experience gained working in the energy sector, to expand into new sectors and perform assessments of non-energy-related critical infrastructure.

In June 2002, President Bush announced his legislative proposal to create the Department of Homeland Security (DHS), and he established a Transition Planning Office to organize the creation of the new department. That same month, the National Academy of Sciences issued a report entitled *Making the Nation Safer*, which highlighted the importance and vulnerability of critical infrastructure. States were directed to perform vulnerability analyses of their water systems under the Public Health Security and Bioterrorism Preparedness statutes.

The President's National Strategy for Homeland Security was issued in July 2002, by the recently created White House Office of Homeland Security. The national strategy defined "protecting critical infrastructures and key assets" as one of six critical mission areas. It added chemical, postal and shipping, and the public-sector defense industrial base to the list of critical infrastructures and designated DOE as the lead agency for the entire energy sector. The strategy also introduced the concept of "key assets," which it defined in a very broad way, covering everything from targets to icons to events:

> In addition to our critical infrastructure, our country must also protect a number of key assets – individual targets whose destruction would not endanger vital systems, but could create local disaster or profoundly damage our Nation's morale or confidence. Key assets include symbols or historical attractions, such as prominent national, state, or local monuments and icons. In some cases, these include quasi-public symbols that are identified strongly with the United States as a Nation, and fall completely under the jurisdiction of state and local officials or even private foundations. ... Key assets also include individual or localized facilities that deserve special protection because of their destructive potential or their value to the local community. Finally, certain high-profile events are strongly coupled to our national symbols or national morale and deserve special protective efforts by the federal government.[9]

THE DHS ERA: 2003–2005

The vulnerability of the nation's electric power infrastructure became apparent once again to the general public on August 14, 2003, as more than 50 million people were left without power when a blackout cascaded across the Midwest, Northeast, and Canada. SARS, avian flu, mad cow disease outbreaks, and a series of coordinated bombings of the London transit system in July 2005 continued to remind governments and the general public of the nation's vulnerability to critical infrastructure attack. Hurricanes Katrina and Rita demonstrated the crippling impact the wholesale loss of infrastructure can have on a region and caused a renewed examination of the preparedness on all levels of government to meet challenges of this scale and complexity.

In February 2003, the White House issued the National Strategy for the Physical Protection of Critical Infrastructures and Key Assets. It held constant the expanded definition of critical infrastructure sectors (as described in the National Strategy for Homeland Security), while significantly refining the concept of "key assets":

> Key assets represent a broad array of unique facilities, sites, and structures whose disruption or destruction could have significant consequences across multiple dimensions.
>
> One category of key assets comprises the diverse array of national monuments, symbols, and icons that represent our nation's heritage, traditions and values, and political power. They include a wide variety of sites and structures, such as prominent historical attractions, monuments, cultural icons, and centers of government and commerce. The sites and structures that make up this key asset category typically draw large amounts of tourism and frequent media attention factors that impose additional protection challenges.
>
> Another category of key assets includes facilities and structures that represent our national economic power and technological advancement. Many of them house significant amounts of hazardous materials, fuels, and chemical catalysts that enable important production and processing functions. Disruption of these facilities could have significant impact on public health and safety, public confidence, and the economy.
>
> A third category of key assets includes such structures as prominent commercial centers, office buildings, and sports stadiums, where large numbers of people regularly congregate to conduct business or personal transactions, shop, or enjoy a recreational pastime. Given the national-level fame of these sites and facilities and the potential human consequences that could result from their attack, protecting them is important in terms of both preventing fatalities and preserving public confidence.[10]

In March 2003, the Department of Homeland Security (DHS) came into existence, and critical infrastructure protection was identified as a critical mission area, being named as one of the four main directorates of DHS: Information Analysis and Infrastructure Protection, Science and Technology, Border and Transportation Security, and Emergency Preparedness and Response.

In addition to the focus of the department's Information Analysis and Infrastructure Protection directorate on critical infrastructure protection, a critical infrastructure protection research and development portfolio was created within the Science and Technology directorate. The creation of DHS was a massive undertaking, merging 22 agencies, 180,000 employees, and a $40 billion budget. As part of the reorganization, DOE's Office of Energy Assurance was moved to the DHS Information Analysis and Infrastructure Protection directorate. The DOE National Laboratories staffed the new department and executed work on critical infrastructure protection across the directorates.

In December 2003, Homeland Security Presidential Directives (HSPD) 7 and 8 were issued. HSPD 7 superseded PDD 63 and consolidated the expansion of critical infrastructure categories introduced in the National Strategy for Homeland Security. It also instructed the DHS secretary to "evaluate the need for and coordinate the coverage of additional critical infrastructure and key resources categories over time, as appropriate."[11] HSPD 8 directed DHS to establish "National Performance Goals" for a variety of issues, to "strengthen the preparedness of the United States to prevent and respond to threatened or actual domestic terrorist attacks, major disasters, and other emergencies by requiring a national domestic all-hazards preparedness goal."[12] Slated to be operational in 2005, HSPD 8 defines specific National Performance Goals for a variety of preparedness areas, including the protection of critical infrastructure. Critical infrastructure was also identified as one of the key factors for funding allocation: HSPD 8 states that allocations of federal preparedness assistance to the states will be based on "assessments of population concentrations, critical infrastructures, and other significant risk factors, particularly terrorism threats...."[13]

In July 2005, DHS Secretary Michael Chertoff, five months into his tenure, reorganized DHS. Activities related to critical infrastructure protection fared well in this reorganization, with the creation of an assistant secretary position dedicated solely to infrastructure protection and another focused specifically on cyber and telecommunications security. Both of these positions reported to the newly created Under Secretary for Preparedness. In his remarks introducing the reorganization, Secretary Chertoff led off with a discussion of preparedness focused on critical infrastructure. He reiterated the challenge of securing an asset that is owned and operated by private industry. He introduced his risk-based approach, explaining that "for example, some infrastructure is quite vulnerable, but the consequences of an attack are relatively small; other infrastructure may be much less vulnerable, but the consequences of a successful attack are very high, even catastrophic."[14] And he recommitted DHS to HSPD 8's National Performance Goals.

Despite all of this activity on the government side, from late 2003 forward, industry-driven critical infrastructure security efforts began to wane. Funding and priority lessened as the distance from 9/11 increased and many of the stewards retired. In a very bottom-line focused environment, security was viewed as a cost without an immediately calculable return. Several security programs that had been created at companies in the wake of the DOE assessments had their budgets curtailed, and a few were eliminated altogether. These reductions occurred despite the continuing trend of increasing vulnerability due to the nearly wholesale conversion (across sectors) to a very concentrated number of control hardware, software, and system providers (the majority of which are foreign owned); the emergence of new wireless vulnerabilities; and the phasing out of many two-man rule jobs. Critical infrastructure protection was falling out of favor.

What lies ahead for critical infrastructure protection? Possibly a newly reorganized and focused DHS will return critical infrastructure to the fore. Events such as the London train bombings, Hurricane Katrina, and future attacks and natural disasters may refocus government, public, and industry attention on the vulnerabilities of critical infrastructure. Insurance products may emerge that establish minimum standards for infrastructure security. Or regulation may finally come – there is discussion of including provisions in the next energy bill that would begin to set cyber security standards for utilities. Beginning in 2007, DHS funding to the states will be contingent on their meeting the National Performance Goal standards, which in turn should drive infrastructure protection at the state and regional levels. How this will play out with private infrastructure owners in those regions may bring to a head many of the issues with which this book attempts to grapple.

The history of the U.S. government's engagement with the threat of catastrophic terrorism between 1993 and 2006 illustrates both the foresight in identifying critical issues and the difficulty of sustaining focus and creating enduring programs, strategies, and institutions to face those challenges. When 9/11 clarified the urgency, the government was faced with the daunting complexity associated with assembling a new department for homeland security in a nearly instantaneous timeframe. Fortunately, the technical resources of the Department of Energy laboratories already had been engaged, starting back in 1998. Due to the experience and expertise developed prior to 9/11, the laboratories were available to support DHS immediately and make significant progress toward the development of methods of vulnerability assessment and risk evaluation. Some of these capabilities are discussed in the next chapter.

NOTES

1. Clinton 1995.
2. Also referred to as the "Marsh Commission" (led by General Robert T. Marsh).

3. Clinton 1996, p. 1.
4. White House 1998, pp. 1–2.
5. Clinton 1998, p. 7.
6. Supervisory Control and Data Acquisition systems are used in a wide variety of critical infrastructure sectors to remotely monitor and control the infrastructure (which is typically distributed across a large geographical area such as a city, state, or multiple states).
7. Clinton 1999, p. 1.
8. Bush 2001, p. 1.
9. Bush 2002, p. 2.
10. Bush 2003c, Protecting Key Assets, p. 2.
11. Bush 2003a, Critical Infrastructure Identification, Prioritization, and Protection, p. 2.
12. Bush 2003b, Purpose, p. 1.
13. Bush 2003b, Federal Preparedness Assistance, p. 3.
14. Chertoff 2005, p. 2.

5

EVOLUTION OF VULNERABILITY ASSESSMENT METHODS

Brian Lopez

A central theme of this book is the critical role that assessments of vulnerability and risk play in justifying both private and public investments to mitigate them. The challenge of setting priorities, whether in the corporate board room or in government, comes down to the capability of estimating vulnerabilities of critical services and the risks that these vulnerabilities might be exploited to generate consequences. Assessment methods for threat, vulnerability, consequence, and overall risk thus must have a very high priority in a national strategy for critical infrastructure protection. As noted in the previous chapter, as early as 1998 the Department of Energy began investing the talents of its national laboratories in the development and fielding of such methods. This chapter explores some of the progress that has been made in the quest for useful assessment methods through the eyes of one such laboratory.

Presidential Decision Directive (PDD) 63, discussed in the previous chapter, identified the Department of Energy (DOE) as the lead agency for security in the electric power and oil and gas production and storage sectors. In response to the directive, the DOE Office of Energy Assurance established a vulnerability assessment program in 1998. This program was staffed by technical experts from DOE's National Laboratory complex and tasked with following up on the work the laboratories had done over the previous two years in support of the President's Commission on Critical Infrastructure Protection and PDD 63, with field assessments in the assigned sectors. The DOE Office of Energy Assurance program was the genesis of much of the specialized critical infrastructure protection capability, methodology, and expertise base utilized today

The author presents this summary from the perspective of the Lawrence Livermore National Laboratory's Vulnerability and Risk Assessment Program (VRAP), of which the author is the leader.

by the Department of Homeland Security (DHS), DOE, and other U.S. government departments with critical infrastructure protection responsibilities. This chapter discusses the evolution of assessment methodology developed for that and subsequent programs from the perspective of Lawrence Livermore National Laboratory, which supported and then led DOE's multi-laboratory assessment team for several years and subsequent successor efforts for DHS and other federal agencies.

INITIAL EVOLUTION OF THE ASSESSMENT METHODOLOGY

Lawrence Livermore National Laboratory's (LLNL's) initial assessments of the electric power infrastructure (in 1998 and early 1999) emphasized cyber security, with a particular focus on Supervisory Control and Data Acquisition systems[1] vulnerabilities and security. It soon became apparent that a more robust methodology was required.

From 1998 to 2002, the assessment methodology (see Box 5.1) evolved to encompass and improve on a number of security tasks.

The "physical security" task was expanded to cover physical pathways to cyber assets and control centers, related site security, and the physical protection of key assets in the field. Eventually this evolved into a comprehensive review of the entire physical security program of each client.

The "cyber security" task added penetration capabilities very early on. Initially, these capabilities were used to provide real-world demonstrations of the "on paper" vulnerabilities discovered by the team's cyber security analysts – who developed their findings by reviewing network architecture diagrams and security equipment settings, interviewing personnel, and related activities. Over time, these penetration capabilities were expanded at Lawrence Livermore National Laboratory to include purpose-built fixed and mobile penetration capabilities focused on critical infrastructure attack and defense. These two flavors of cyber security assessment (on-paper architecture analysis and real-live penetration) would later be separated into two tasks in order for the cyber penetration team to be able to replicate true "zero-knowledge" attack and compromise of the infrastructure providers.[2]

In a similar vein, a "physical penetration" task was added to demonstrate and validate vulnerabilities identified by the physical assessment team and to help construct credible attack scenarios. Later, physical penetration would often be used to front-end various cyber penetration scenarios (allowing the assessment team to demonstrate a diversity of pathways to critical assets) and ultimately to execute its own zero-knowledge physical penetrations of the infrastructure provider's facilities and physical security systems.

BOX 5.1 OUTLINE OF A TYPICAL LLNL VULNERABILITY AND RISK ASSESSMENT PROGRAM METHODOLOGY FOR DOE'S OFFICE OF ENERGY ASSURANCE (CIRCA 2002, PRE-DHS)

Phase I: Pre-assessment
   Project Scoping and Planning
   Critical Asset Workshop
   Structured Information Request

Phase II: Assessment
   Threat (internal/external, domestic/foreign)
      Capability
      Intent
      Motivation
   Vulnerability
      External Reconnaissance
      Cyber Architecture
      Cyber Penetration
      Physical Security
      Physical Penetration
      Operations Security
      Interdependencies
      Policies and Procedures
   Consequence
      Impact Analysis
   Risk Characterization

Phase III: Post-assessment
   Provide Report, Presentations, Implementation Assistance
   Refine Methodology
   Capture Lessons Learned and Best Practices
   Build Awareness (closed forums and workshops)

A typical VRAP assessment is a 12–14-month effort, conducted by a multi-disciplinary team and consisting of interviews, tours and inspections, reconnaissance, remote/local penetration, and liaison with local/state/federal law enforcement, intelligence, and emergency response organizations.*

* Lopez, Brian. "VRAP Methodology Introductory Slides." Lawrence Livermore National Laboratory, Vulnerability and Risk Assessment Program, Internal document, 2002.

"Operations security" – a standard military and DOE practice that concerns itself with the knowledge an adversary can gain by observing a target's operations, in order to compromise it[3] – was added initially as a piece of the physical security task. Later the operations security portion was broken out into its own distinct task because this was a novel area of particular interest to most critical infrastructure companies.

As our depth of understanding of the various critical infrastructure domains increased, "interdependencies" became a very important area of analysis. Initially this work was paired with the "consequence analysis" task and focused on the interdependencies of the infrastructure being assessed with other infrastructures. For example: If the infrastructure being assessed is incapacitated, what else in the region will be impacted? To what degree? For how long? It also asks the corollary: What dependencies does this infrastructure have that make it vulnerable to unintentional failure and indirect attack? Eventually interdependency analysis became a quite involved effort and was awarded a task of its own as the list of infrastructures considered critical increased and as the team began to untangle the complexity, cascading effects, and dense interdependence of U.S. infrastructure.

The "external reconnaissance" task, initially part of the "cyber architecture" analysis, became a full-fledged task in response to an increasing threat picture. A portion of the cyber penetration and external reconnaissance teams were transitioned to focus on simulating zero-knowledge outsiders. This allowed for the construction of credible scenarios independent of the "inside" knowledge being acquired by the rest of the team. Operations security and physical penetration work further strengthened these scenarios.

As the scope and depth of the assessments grew, it became clear that neither the assessed organizations, assessment teams nor nation as a whole could afford to assess everything. This led to the creation of a "critical assets workshop," which eventually evolved to have several purposes. The two initial goals were to help the assessed organizations identify the assets that were truly critical and build rationale for those decisions; and to help the assessment team down-select the number of facilities, systems, and organizations they needed to evaluate.

The critical assets workshop brings together a broad cross-section of individuals from infrastructure providers that have responsibility for, perspective on, or knowledge about critical assets. Typically this group includes representatives from cyber systems and security, physical security, operations, infrastructure, field personnel, unions, management, public relations, internal communications, risk management, training, emergency response, threat/intelligence, legal, human resources, procurement, contracting, and finance. The group is led through a facilitated process to rank assets across a number of consequence dimensions (such as economic, loss of life, environmental, legal, regulatory, public image) and reaches consensus on an organization-wide ranking. The final product is a rank-ordered list of critical assets to be used by the assessment team.[4] An asset is considered critical if its destruction, incapacitation, or compromise would jeopardize the infrastructure's long-term survival; have a serious, harmful effect on the infrastructure's operations; or require near-term, if not immediate, mitigation.[5]

As the depth and complexity of the assessments grew, the pre-assessment phase became more important to the overall success of each assessment. An advance team was created to work all management, legal, and logistical issues with the infrastructure provider in preparation for engagement with the assessment team. This pre-assessment team worked with the infrastructure organization to develop optimal breadth and depth of interviews and effective sequencing for geographic and system understanding. An initially simple request for data in advance of the on-the-ground assessment grew into a much more structured process, refined periodically by the task leaders to maximize the amount of analysis that could be done prior to the on-site assessment.

The most difficult and constantly evolving portion of analysis has been the risk analysis portion. In this section, assessors trade off the variety of vulnerabilities and mitigation recommendations against the critical assets and threats. I affectionately refer to this as the "apples versus oranges versus Volkswagens" problem – it gets to the root of creating actionable findings for the clients, who want answers to questions like: "What are the top 10 things we can do that will give us the most decreased risk for least investment?" and "If money were no object, what are the top 3 things we should do to decrease our overall risk? Our risk to this specific critical assets? Our risk against this particular attack path, scenario, or vulnerability?"

Consequence assessment has been a relatively stable section of the methodology. This stability can be attributed to the fact that critical infrastructure industries have a long history of safety modeling and analysis. What our assessment teams brought to the table was an ability to discover vulnerabilities not covered by their traditional safety analysis – which, confusingly, most critical infrastructure sectors refer to as "security analysis."

The policies and procedures section of the methodology has also been a stable section. It has deepened over time as we learned more about the typical policies and procedures present in each domain. An additional role added to this task has been to do more root cause analysis. The team's role has transitioned from merely assessing the policies and procedures in a vacuum to following up on the vulnerabilities being generated by the other tasks to determine which are local to various pieces of the organization and which are systemic.

The final piece added to the methodology has been threat analysis. Initially threat was assessed in general terms of insider/outsider, foreign/domestic, and communicated threats to sites or employees. As the domestic and foreign threat picture has ratcheted up, specific analysis of who may be interested in attacking critical infrastructure, what capability they have to execute those attacks, and which targets and attack paths they may prefer, has become much more integral to the assessment process.

INCREASING BREADTH OF DOMAINS

As national awareness of critical infrastructure protection issues increased from 2000 to 2003, demand grew for vulnerability and risk assessments across a variety of critical infrastructures. The National Laboratory teams were well situated to perform this task, having been involved with these issues since 1996 and possessing significant field experience and extant capabilities, teams, and methodologies. The laboratories were asked to complete assessments across a broad array of individual critical infrastructures, and this eventually led to providing "all infrastructure" assessments of entire regions of the country.

CRITICAL INFRASTRUCTURE PROTECTION IN THE GREATER CONTEXT

As DHS came into existence in 2003, there were two major impacts to the DOE teams working in critical infrastructure protection. First, the shifting of responsibility for critical infrastructure protection to a variety of new departments in DHS caused discontinuities in funding and strategy, and hence the demise of the multi-laboratory DOE team and any unified national effort to develop assessment methodology. Second, critical infrastructure began to find its place in the overall cosmology of threats, vulnerabilities, and consequences under consideration by the department. Initial critical infrastructure protection efforts in the department were focused on the development of national lists of critical infrastructure assets across various sectors. In the Information Analysis and Infrastructure Protection directorate of DHS, this was accomplished via a program of Site Assistance Visits – one-day visits to critical infrastructure owners to collect data on their facilities. Often these Site Assistance Visit teams were accompanied by Buffer Zone Protection Plan teams, which assisted the facilities with physical security issues. In other elements of DHS, critical infrastructure protection began to be integrated into large, in-depth, all-hazard assessments of various regions across the country. Developing methodologies for these assessments was challenging. For the first time, critical infrastructure assessment was being integrated with assessments of chemical, biological, nuclear, high-explosive, and other threats across large regions with a variety of key assets. DOE's National Laboratory complex provided a unique resource to DHS for this effort – with its ability to assemble interdisciplinary teams with deep experience in each of these areas, to fuse classified intelligence and other threat information, and to provide the methodological and analytic capacity to assess and integrate the variety of threats, vulnerabilities, and consequences.

WHAT TO DEFEND, WHAT TO DEFEND AGAINST, AND WHY

As LLNL embarked on large regional and national assessments for DHS, it quickly became clear that the methodologies we had developed for assessing individual infrastructures – and even the work done on large multi-state infrastructures and metropolitan-level assessments across all infrastructures – would not scale to meet the challenges posed by DHS. DHS wanted to know, at a national level, what assets to protect in each region, what to protect those assets against, and how to support those decisions within a rational system that would be quantifiable (where possible), would allow for the analysis of tradeoffs, and yet would be creative enough to avoid surprise from novel attacks.

NEW APPROACHES

While the ultimate deliverable remained the same (a matrix of the highest-consequence vulnerabilities versus the most important key assets in each region), the assessment approach needed to encompass the breadth of threats, vulnerabilities, and consequences of interest to DHS across wide swaths of geography, and it needed to provide ways to synthesize the findings into an integrated assessment. The approach had to be plastic enough to represent the variety of the ways that, for example, critical infrastructure would appear at this level of assessment – as an asset, target, weapon, carrier, part of the detection and response systems, and interdependent with many other functions and services in the region.

It was important for the teams to free themselves of our previous vulnerability assessment mindset and attempt to address this larger challenge. We embarked on this process with the following guidance in mind:

1. Understand the problem space fully; start by exploring the overall problem with which DHS is struggling, rather than starting with a particular assessment type or methodology in mind.
2. Build a conceptual foundation for grappling with this class of problem; instead of constructing a specific assessment methodology, attempt to build a more high-level model within which we can discover questions, relationships, and rules; and be able to both generate and test answers.

3. Generate ways of seeing with the model by creating different conceptual lenses that make different things pop out or recede; change what is important, not important, and why; fundamentally change the way our teams see, hear, and experience the region.

4. Architect knowledge structures which we can populate with field data and that generate new thinking.

5. Discover and apply patterns across the variety of assessment domains.

6. Draw distinctions that are as clear and powerful as possible (powerful in the sense of heuristic or generative).

7. Identify key concepts, issues, questions, relationships, rules, and metrics.

8. Analyze and flesh out with examples, definitions, taxonomies, ontologies.

9. Abandon the idea of one perfect assessment process: instead, explore and analyze the array of possible processes and characterize each.

10. Be agnostic; determine the strengths, power, weaknesses, and blind spots of each approach.

11. Ultimately, synthesize, distill, and refine into a conceptual system that captures all aspects of the problem space.[6]

KEY PIECES ON THE BOARD

In reviewing the variety of approaches LLNL had been taking on assessments across a number of domains and scales, and with differing goals, methodology, and terminology, I distilled five key pieces that would likely need to be "on the game board" for any assessment of the scope and complexity required by DHS.[7] These core pieces (or concepts) can be combined in a number of ways to assess a region.

KEY ASSETS AND OPERATIONS

Key assets and operations are specific sites, operations, services, populations, information, and infrastructure to be defended. Each asset is viewed from four perspectives: as a target, as a weapon, as a consequence transmitter or multiplier, and as a detection or response element. Elements can be dynamic – for example, populations have daily and seasonal patterns.

For example, people can be viewed as targets (when having attributes attractive to the adversary or concentrated in groups), as weapons (as suicide bombers, unwitting carriers of biological threats, or providers of concealment), as consequence multipliers (as chaotic masses impeding ingress/egress), and as part of the response structure (people make up and operate the majority of the response structure for a high-consequence event). Critical infrastructure, similarly, could be a target of attack, a weapon for attack (most critical infrastructures can be weaponized), a consequence transmitter (e.g., using the water distribution system as a carrier), and it both supports and in many cases *is* the response infrastructure for high-consequence events. Assets can be defended differently from each of these four perspectives.

THREAT, VULNERABILITY, CONSEQUENCE

Threats, vulnerabilities, and consequences are what need to be defended against. Threats are individuals with the capability and intent to exploit vulnerabilities in order to generate consequences. Threats are also analyzed for the underlying motivations of individuals and groups. This threat analysis consists of three parts:

- Adversary capability – For example, do the adversaries have knowledge about, access to, and ability to deploy chemical or biological weapons? What cyber capabilities do they have? What is their knowledge regarding critical infrastructure? Could they use it as a weapon or otherwise leverage it?
- Adversary intent – Do the adversaries have specific targets in mind? Are they planning to attack icons or other symbolic targets? Are the adversaries interested in generating casualties or economic impact? Or are they aiming to sow fear, uncertainty, and doubt? From the perspective of each critical infrastructure, how could each be used to generate these impacts? How could infrastructure be used to attack or support an attack against a specific target?
- Adversary motivation – What are the underlying motivations and mindsets (e.g., organizational, cultural, religious, personal) of the adversaries?

In assessing a region's vulnerabilities, the team asks the question where and how is the region most vulnerable to the array of possible adversary attacks (for example, chemical, explosives, cyber, or critical infrastructure). Red teaming is employed to generate novel vulnerabilities. The region is also analyzed with regards to its vulnerability to natural (e.g., earthquake, flood) and accidental (e.g., chemical spill) events, and the ways in which critical infrastructure can mitigate or exacerbate those vulnerabilities.

Consequences are assessed by taxonomizing and ranking all consequences on the basis of casualties, economic impact, iconic rank, and the ability to create fear–uncertainty–doubt. These consequences can be generated via a variety of attack vectors (discussed next) or combinations of those vectors.

ATTACK VECTORS

Adversaries can use a variety of attack mechanisms, including chemical, biological, radiological, nuclear, high explosives (commonly referred to as CBRNE), cyber, and as yet unknown attacks. CBRNE vectors encompass well-known ways to generate large consequences in a region. Cyber attacks are a topic around which there is considerable discussion and interest (especially with respect to critical infrastructure) regarding the ways in which these attacks could be employed to generate large consequences. Typically, assessment of attack vectors includes a seventh element, which represents lesser-known and unknown ways to generate large consequences.

CRITICAL INFRASTRUCTURE

As discussed in the previous chapter, the current definition of critical infrastructure encompasses a vast array of infrastructures. Many of these infrastructures have similar structures and vulnerabilities, and these vulnerabilities can be used to generate large consequences.

COMMON DIMENSIONS

Casualties (injuries and fatalities), along with economic, iconic, and "fear–uncertainty–doubt" impacts provide four common dimensions across a number of assessment tasks such as defining consequences, analyzing threat intent and motivation, and categorizing assets in a region. Thinking in terms of these dimensions allows the team to "see" a region as a composition of specific adversary attractors – population concentrations (stadiums, public transportation), economic centers (financial and business sectors), symbolic targets (names and images associated in the mind of adversaries with American power and way of life), fear–uncertainty–doubt hubs (schools, food supply).

COVERING

The insufficient time and resources available to individually assess each potential threat, vulnerability, and consequence is an enormous constraint. On the other hand, defending against only a handful of scenarios, such as the 15 DHS reference scenarios (only one of which is critical infrastructure), places one in the position of defending only a few branches of a 10,000-branch tree. And while the probability that a particular one of those branches will be exercised is low, the collective probability that one of them will be exercised is quite high. The object, therefore, is to cut down the overall number of threats, vulnerabilities, and consequences in such a way as to select threat–vulnerability–consequence combinations that "cover" the space of attacks of the greatest concern, while not overwhelming the ability to assess or defend the region. Ideally, if a region prepares and defends adequately against a well-selected set of threat–vulnerability–consequence triplets, it should be prepared for and able to defend against other triplets of similar consequence level (including those unknown or unexplored at the time of assessment).

CUTDOWN STRATEGIES

In complex regions, one needs to employ triage strategies in order to have a manageable number of things to assess and ultimately defend. Below are a few of the basic variations of "cutdown strategies" we have used and their evolution over the past decade.

Vulnerability–Consequence–Threat. Our initial approach was to lead with our strength (finding vulnerabilities), and then use the level of consequence generated by each vulnerability to cut down the list of vulnerabilities. Then we would apply whatever level of threat we could obtain as a finishing cutdown. We then worked with the infrastructure providers to strictly mitigate vulnerabilities.

Consequence–Vulnerability–Threat. As we began to understand the consequences within each sector better, we began to work the problem backwards, taking the largest consequences and then hunting for all the vulnerabilities that would generate those consequences. Our mitigation strategy also shifted, and we began to add consequence mitigation strategies in addition to mitigating vulnerabilities.

Critical Assets–Consequence–Vulnerability–Threat. The addition of the Critical Assets Workshop (discussed above) to our methodology helped us to focus our assessment of consequences and vulnerabilities onto the most important assets. We continued to mitigate vulnerabilities and more consequences.

Critical Assets–(Threat)–Consequence–Vulnerability. In a perfect world, the threat–consequence–vulnerability sequence would provide the most efficient and effective sequencing, allowing one to focus on the capabilities and intent held by the adversaries, the consequences they can generate, and then working out which vulnerabilities enable those consequences. One could then work to neutralize threats and mitigate consequences in addition to eliminating vulnerabilities. However, this requires high confidence in the threat data. For example, is the U.S. intelligence community tracking every adversary? How certain is the threat assessor in knowing every capability that each adversary has or can obtain? In practice, we must use as much available threat data as there are, weigh it using a confidence level scheme, and use threat and consequence calculations to cut down and focus the vulnerability work.

COMPLICATING FACTORS

The very dynamic and uncertain nature of both threats and vulnerabilities (especially terrorist threats and cyber vulnerabilities) creates further complications. This uncertainty is compounded by the fact that reducing one attack path (through, for example, mitigation, hardening, or redesign), if detected by the adversary, increases the likelihood of alternative attack paths. Although we have been able to successfully apply game theory approaches to this challenge, these models depend on the accuracy of our view of the values, motivations, capabilities, intentions, rationales, and strategies of various adversaries.

ULTIMATELY IT IS ABOUT REDUCING CONSEQUENCES

Whether assessing a single infrastructure provider, a region, or the nation as a whole, ultimately it comes down to reducing consequences – and within that list of consequences, mitigating the ones that generate the greatest impact. Before investing in the effort to find 200 vulnerabilities in any one infrastructure, however, it makes sense to determine first how important that infrastructure really is. And before plugging each and every vulnerability, it makes sense to determine how many of those vulnerabilities generate consequences that can be mitigated, perhaps even on the consequence side (enhancements to consequence mitigation are often preferred because they are more likely to reduce the consequences across a broad set of vulnerabilities, whereas specific vulnerability reductions, by and large, only eliminate that particular vulnerability). Starting with consequences is an effective approach; however, analyzing consequences is becoming more complex as the steadily increasing interdependencies between and within infrastructure sectors adds to the likelihood of unaccounted-for consequences. This complexity is compounded by our reliance on critical infrastructure for almost every phase and aspect of our prevention, detection, response, and recovery efforts.

FROM CONSEQUENCES TO PREPAREDNESS

Having performed consequence-centric assessments (i.e., consequence–vulnerability–threat assessments) across a number of domains over the years, eventually it became apparent to the team that there was a way to take a further step backward in the chain – moving from consequences to preparedness. Inasmuch as security is about consequence mitigation, that mitigation is achieved, in the broad sense, via preparedness. To that end, for our current work we developed an abstract model comprising 18 threat types, 14 classes of consequence at 4 levels of size and complexity, which generate impacts in 6 phases (planning, prevention, detection, notification, response, and recovery) across 22 critical infrastructures and 13 key asset types. For each region assessed, we generate the minimum number of strategically spanning scenarios that allow us to fully exercise the preparedness functions of that region. By running these scenarios against representative groups from approximately 30 distinct constituencies within a region, we are able to generate the most effective overall mitigation measures, pre-tuned by the constituents to the specific context of that region.

While there are downsides to consequence-centric assessment models (the most glaring being that they bias you toward potentially lower-likelihood attacks), defending against terrorism is ultimately a game of resilience. By improving the overall preparedness of a region, constituencies may not prevent every incident (an unrealistic goal), but they will improve the response and recovery to the majority of low- and mid-consequence attacks while significantly mitigating the most high-consequence attacks.

A VARIETY OF "CENTRICS"

The concepts discussed in this chapter provide assessors with multiple starting places and ways of "seeing" a region. For example, assessors may choose to work from the outside-in by developing a threat capabilities list for a particular adversary and using those capabilities to access as many vulnerabilities as possible that will in turn generate the most significant consequences. Another approach would be to view a region as being full of "adversary attractors" such as population concentrations or "fear–uncertainty–doubt" hubs (such as schools, water and food supplies). Assessors can identify these attractors and then build a defense from the inside out against particular consequence–vulnerability–threat pairings that generate pathways to those adversary attractors. One could instead identify all the highest-consequences response assets and harden them against various attack scenarios or choose to focus on devising strategies to protect the detection elements (e.g., sensors, cameras) in a region from critical infrastructure-based incapacitation or spoofing. Still another possible way to see a region is to start from the underlying threat motivation and determine how that motivation focuses an adversary's intent and leads the adversary in turn to seek specific capabilities. One can then develop signatures to detect the various steps in the postulated progression. Thinking from an infrastructure point of view, assessors could determine how to weaponize all of the critical infrastructure in the region. Or if they wanted to think outside the box a little, they could think about how to create a consequence without a current vulnerability and brainstorm an unknown vulnerability that leads to that consequence.

Whether threat-centric, vulnerability-centric, critical infrastructure-centric, or even data-centric (starting from whatever data are available), each of these "centrics" provide unique starting places and pathways to lead the assessor through the analysis and piece together an overall mosaic of the risk to a region.

HYPER-INTERDEPENDENCE TO INTER-SUPPORT

Fundamentally, what has caused (or at least significantly multiplied) many of the critical infrastructure security issues is interdependence. This interdependence is being driven by the increasing interconnection between and within infrastructure sectors. In the future, an inflection point of hyper-interdependence may come, after which this increasing interconnection (if strategically managed) could begin to actually mitigate infrastructure failure. Antecedents of this exist in, for example, the way we currently defend water supply to a critical infrastructure control center. These control centers have gone from relying on a single city water main to redundant mains, onsite wells, large capacity water storage, filtration, and pre-contracted water delivery. Similarly, the more advanced of these control centers can "hot swap" their functions to control centers in other states and countries. In some of our recent work, we have been exploring ways in which control signals and other critical communication could be rerouted via satellite TV channels, broadband cable infrastructure, and paging, cell phone, and digital radio pathways. Distributed power generation, the increasing diversity of power sources and distribution methods, multi-modal transportation, advances in local water filtration, self-directed airspace, the infrastructure being built to support outsourcing, and other similar trends may be leading to a hyper-interdependent world that could be interconnected in such a way as to be able to dynamically manage failure as a single connected meta-system. The necker cube flips. Interdependency becomes inter-support. Cascading failure is replaced by cascading support.

If we wish to leverage the same trend that is working against us, to work for us at this coming point of hyper-interdependence, we must begin now to invest heavily in understanding the complex universe of critical infrastructure, how it operates as a meta-system, and how to secure that meta-system. We must diligently educate the public, government, and the business world regarding the extent to which critical infrastructure is intertwined in the fabric of our lives – in both times of normal operation and in crisis. We must begin to design in security, reliability, and redundancy at the ground level, not just at specific technology levels (e.g., improving SCADA security or general cyber security) or just at an individual company, region, or sector level, but at cross-sector, meta-system, national, and international levels.

CONCLUSIONS

The U.S. government deserves credit for having identified critical infrastructure protection as an important national issue in the mid-1990s. Over the past decade, a variety of efforts across a number of agencies have responded to White House attention on critical infrastructure protection. This high-level attention has been sustained across administrations from both parties (not atypical for matters of national security).

How have we done?

We have made progress. A decade ago you could walk from the street to the internal control room of almost any infrastructure provider in America (except a nuclear power plant). Similarly, five years ago you could have hacked into almost any infrastructure provider with very little skill. There was limited awareness of security issues. Over the past decade, there has been significant improvement in the areas of physical and cyber security, as well as in the general awareness and understanding throughout the infrastructure provider community of threats, vulnerabilities, consequences, critical asset identification, risk frameworks, tradeoff analysis, and mitigation measures. The national laboratories have built a deep knowledge and skill base of experts across sectors; they have developed and honed methodology, tools, and capabilities against real-world infrastructures; and they have built trusted relationships in the infrastructure provider community. Nascent communities of researchers in academia and security services providers in the private sector are emerging to focus on critical infrastructure protection.

Where should we go next?

First, the federal government should create a single point of focus for critical infrastructure protection in government. Over the years, a number of efforts throughout the government and private industry have been created to focus on protection of critical infrastructure. The shifting responsibilities for various aspects of critical infrastructure protection have led to a fractured approach, often changing from year to year, based more on budget allocation across agencies than on an overall national strategy. The locus of responsibility has not only moved throughout the government, but it has also shifted back and forth between the government and the infrastructure providers. The assembly of DHS (a massive merger of 22 agencies) created funding discontinuities and more uncertainty as to roles and responsibilities for critical infrastructure protection, which were divided across a variety of departments at DHS by such categories as attack type, defense type, and sector, and have continued to shift from year to year. Now is the time to create a single point of focus for all of the disparate efforts throughout the government, the critical infrastructure provider community, academia, and private industry.

The government should also create a coordinated and focused national program for critical infrastructure protection. Over the past decade, there have been significant pockets of good individual work in the arena of critical infrastructure protection. What has been lacking is an enduring program with the vision to assimilate the various challenges of critical infrastructure protection into a coherent national strategy that balances threats, vulnerabilities, and consequences across the sectors and against similar national-level issues such as CBRNE vectors. Now is the time to consolidate the variety of efforts and expertise into a comprehensive program to protect the nation's critical infrastructure.

This national program should provide a single point of overall focus and accountability for U.S. critical infrastructure protection, including sector leaders who are fully accountable for their sectors. These sector leaders should provide a visible and consistent point of contact for the infrastructure providers, government agencies, academia, and the private sector.

The national program should develop and maintain a national strategy for critical infrastructure protection across all sectors.

The national program should develop a rational analytical basis for critical infrastructure protection work and decision making. The foundation for this would begin with the compilation of a single national list of key assets (based on objective criteria) and the development of a uniform methodology for threat, vulnerability, and consequence assessment. The methodology should be not only credible within and across sectors, but it also should locate critical infrastructure in the greater context of threats, vulnerabilities, and consequences under consideration by DHS. This methodology should encourage keen awareness of the many ways critical infrastructure can be leveraged – as a target, weapon, consequence transmitter/multiplier, and a detection/response element. In addition, the methodology should employ an efficient and defendable cutdown scheme to focus the effort.

The national program should devise and execute a regular program of assessments that are strategically designed to make the most effective use of government and infrastructure provider resources. The assessments should address the full spectrum of threats, vulnerabilities, and consequences and provide an overall risk characterization. Additionally, the assessments should establish an initial sector-by-sector baseline, provide lessons learned to peer providers, and include periodic follow-up assessments.

Another aspect of the national program should be to focus effort on identifying cross-sector leverage points (such as SCADA, modeling and simulation, and cyber and physical security) and work them as national critical infrastructure protection issues versus sector issues. The program should direct a national research agenda that addresses systemic issues, develops novel solutions, and decodes the complexity of regional and national meta-systems of critical infrastructure. It should lead in commercializing research and making the private sector aware of critical infrastructure protection issues of the greatest concern and opportunity. Finally, the program should lead an effort to eliminate barriers and disincentives (legal, regulatory, financial) for infrastructure providers to fully participate in critical infrastructure protection efforts.

For such a program to succeed, it would need to be led and staffed by people with a depth and breadth of real-world experience with, and passion for, critical infrastructure protection. To have significant bureaucratic leverage, the program must control (or significantly influence) critical infrastructure protection funding across agencies. The mindset needs to become much more strategic – shifting from funding individual year-to-year projects to instead making multi-year investments in the development and ongoing support of serious national capabilities in various core specialties (e.g., sector specific, analytic, cyber, physical, SCADA, methodology, intelligence) that can then be used to support specific work for the enduring program.

Second, the nation needs to understand the meta-system and shift that system from interdependency to inter-support. We missed the boat the first time around as the complexity and interdependence of the nation's critical infrastructure moved rapidly beyond our ability to understand and secure it. Now, we are likely down to our last inflection point where we can realistically try to get our arms around the bigger issue and design in workable solutions up front (versus trying to retrofit sector-specific security on the backend at a prohibitive cost). If we want to try to do that, we need to move aggressively now.

This work would have multiple benefits, making our critical infrastructure more resilient to natural disasters and accidents, in addition to terrorist attack. The meta-system understanding developed by this effort would likely lead to the identification of new opportunities for efficiency and other improvements to individual infrastructure as well as the operation of the meta-system.

This effort at the meta-system level would require a much more fundamental and deep understanding of the complexity of our infrastructure and its interdependency. If the nation wishes to leverage the trends of increasing interconnection and interdependence (currently a major security nemesis), we must begin now to invest heavily in gaining an understanding of how critical infrastructure operates as a meta-system and develop ways to secure that meta-system. We must begin to design security and reliability not just at a technology level, or at just at an individual company, region, or sector level, but at a cross-sector, meta-system, national and international level.

NOTES

1. Supervisory Control and Data Acquisition (SCADA) systems are used in a wide variety of critical infrastructure sectors to remotely monitor and control the infrastructure (which is typically distributed across a large geographical area such as a city, state, or multiple states).
2. To truly simulate an outsider, the assessor needs to start with what the outsider starts with: nothing. If an assessor can get in starting with nothing, it does not take much imagination to understand how much faster and more effectively an outsider can be with each successive piece of information gleaned due to poor security practices.
3. The OPSEC assessor may gain knowledge in a variety of ways, including everything from dumpster diving to social engineering (posing as a maintenance technician asking for "help diagnosing a problem" or a third-grade teacher requesting a "big colorful diagram for the class") to obtaining uniforms, badges, entry codes, passwords, and other materials. This task often entails weeks of unglamorous surveillance work.
4. Lopez 2000a.
5. Lopez 2000b.
6. Lopez 2003.
7. Lopez 2004.

PART III

Managing Organizations

6

MANAGING FOR THE UNEXPECTED

Reliability and Organizational Resilience

Todd M. La Porte

The way issues are framed determines much about how they are managed and decided. We noted in the introduction to this volume that the domain of critical infrastructure protection is no exception. Since the issue surfaced in the early 1990s, public and business leaders have directed the public's attention toward *critical infrastructures*, rather than, say, *essential services*; toward *protection* of those infrastructures, rather than *assurance* of the services these infrastructures deliver. The widespread adoption of the terminology of critical infrastructure protection focused scarce attention on basic protective measures, such as erecting better perimeter controls around sensitive areas, checking for redundancy in cable routing, and avoiding collocation of several sensitive systems and potential single points of failure. Taking such protective measures was an obvious first step after the abrupt realization, forced by the attacks of September 11, 2001, that our society was remarkably vulnerable to predatory action.

Disaster and emergency management communities, however, describe their core concerns differently. They would emphasize mitigation of potential disasters by building away from hazardous areas; prevention of emergencies through prudent management or maintenance; response to disasters by mobilizing emergency fire, medical, police, and rescue crews to help people in dire need; and recovery of disaster zones through clean up of damaged areas, restoration of services, relocation, and rebuilding.

Despite the valuable contributions of both these approaches, they obscure an important dimension of essential service assurance: reliable and continuous operations of large technical systems at times of extreme stress during natural disasters such as hurricanes Katrina or Rita, technological disasters, such as the U.S. and Canada blackout of August 2003, or terrorist attack, such as those of September 11, 2001. Maintaining operation of these systems – "keeping the lights on" – is of the utmost importance for operators and for society.

But the more commonly assumed critical infrastructure protection perspective focuses primarily on asset protection. The disaster management perspective focuses on anticipating or dealing with the effects of a disaster. It typically does not include a view of how organizations themselves, either in the public or private sectors, keep essential systems functioning.

This gap in understanding is dangerous and costly. Lives can be lost without adequate communications, power, transportation, and access to healthcare. Interruptions to critical infrastructure services can result in widespread uncertainty about restoration of services, lack of viable economic and social networks, serious loss of public confidence, and even social collapse. The shocking disorder accompanying Hurricane Katrina and the painful recovery of the Gulf Coast show the importance of operating essential services without interruption.

This section fills a gap in the disaster studies and emergency management bodies of literature, among others, by shedding light on the following questions:

What does it take for essential service organizations and critical infrastructure service providers, most of which are in the private sector, to maintain operations in the face of extreme events? Most organizations operate with some degree of slack, where production or distribution breakdowns can occur without incurring draconian penalties, or where the tempo of operations can vary without causing much harm. Most of what is known about operations, management, and administration is based on such "normal" organizations.

But many critical infrastructure service providers function quite differently. They operate large, complex, technical, and highly integrated systems, structured in networks that span regions and some that even encompass the whole country. The services they provide are expected to be available in real time, without fail, nearly all the time, regardless of the weather, time of year, state of the economy, or any other contingency. And extreme events are no exception: emergencies are, in fact, times when essential services are most needed by vulnerable populations and those whose job it is to assist them. "Normal" management theory and practices do not help much in such circumstances. The new realities of complex, large-scale, technological organizations and systems demand new vocabularies to describe operating realities, and new tools for managing systems, than we have inherited from the past.

How does the mounting pressure for efficiency affect efforts to adopt the management requirements of extraordinarily high reliability? As formerly closely regulated firms become exposes to market pressures for profitability, efficiency values increase in importance. The push for greater efficiency implies close attention to minimizing costs. But cost cutting may conflict with management practices that contribute to high degrees of operating reliability, including redundancy, intensive and repeated training, frequent equipment testing and replacement, and the like. The requirements for operating complex technical systems reliably are demanding, and they are not easily fulfilled by firms that must pay primary attention to a financial bottom line.

As their systems become increasingly interdependent with one another, what analytic and management challenges for reliability improvements do critical infrastructure service providers face? It is one thing for a single organization to figure out how to operate reliably on its own, and then to carry out the required structural and management reforms successfully. It is another for a *web of interdependent organizations* to do the same thing. In tightly coupled systems, simply identifying vulnerabilities, let alone managing them, is a daunting task. In a sense, risk migrates to the weakest part of the system, but due to overall complexity, the migration occurs without anyone's knowledge, and without a clear understanding of where the weakest links are located. Yet not identifying such vulnerabilities and risks leave systems unprepared to function during extreme events. Resolving this analytic problem will require much greater transparency and knowledge of operations across organizations than has ever existed in the past.

How might highly reliable operations be fostered in organizations that currently do not exhibit them? The chapters in this section point the way to understanding some of what is involved in making organizations work in ways that are highly reliable. But understanding what makes them work so well is not the same thing as knowing how to make other organizations become more highly reliable. A wholesale adoption of the elements of highly reliable organizations, if that were even possible, would not guarantee success. Much work still needs to be done to know how to develop highly reliable operations within organizations that are not now so reliable.

This volume underscores the profound problem that society faces in reconciling efficiency pressures with security imperatives. Society may need to compromise one or the other of these objectives. But even if the efficiency–vulnerability tradeoff cannot be solved, society still needs organizations to function robustly and reliably when they face extraordinary challenges or attack. The chapters in this section outline strategies and organizational attributes that could help critical infrastructures function better during extreme events.

Robert Frosch provides an analysis of accidents, system failures, and terrorism from the perspective of an experienced senior official responsible for operations at NASA and at General Motors. He invokes complexity theory and the statistical mechanics of phase change to show the commonalities in physics and organization studies that bear on an understanding of organizational failures and dynamics of attack and protection. Engineered systems and organizations, for reasons of efficiency and economy, are both designed to operate close to their catastrophe frontiers, which can be characterized statistically. The compelling similarity to organization theories of highly reliable organizations suggests its fundamental value for analysts of critical infrastructure protection, emergency management, and counter-terrorism policy. When the researchers arrive at the same insights by different routes, then we can be confident that their findings are to be taken most seriously.

From the organization studies literature, Todd M. La Porte argues that critical infrastructures are so large and exposed that they cannot be fully protected. They all were developed in benign environments, when threats from terrorism were nonexistent, and when natural events such as weather and non-predatory human error were the main contingencies facing system operators. Natural and technological disasters will never be completely preventable. Terrorists will adapt tactics to defeat countermeasures that emphasize hardening or protection, and the Bush administration's "War on Terrorism" will not eliminate them permanently. Therefore, strategies that emphasize organizations' capacity to function during extreme events are needed. Research on organizational resilience, on highly reliable organizations, and on complex adaptive systems can help develop such strategies.

The chapter by Paul Schulman and Emery Roe focuses on the critical role of management in keeping essential services functioning. In their view, the key to increased organizational reliability, particularly in relation to resilience, lies not in the design of large technical systems but in their management. A preoccupation with design, which they argue is widespread in among critical infrastructure policymakers, may even undermine the managerial skills and strategies that help assure operational reliability.

Schulman and Roe single out what they call "reliability professionals" as unsung heroes of critical infrastructures. They are the middle managers from the technical ranks most responsible for keeping systems functioning, but whose contributions are almost never acknowledged. Schulman and Roe remind us that resilience is essentially an organizational phenomenon that depends on the commitment and skills of human beings. Their experience and ability to discern patterns helps them compensate for the inevitable shortcomings in system designs, especially when chaotic situations arise.

Todd R. La Porte's chapter on suicide terrorism and critical infrastructures assesses the requirements for operating large, complex organizations that deliver essential services, and for the political requirements for protecting them.

La Porte, a longtime student of highly reliable organizations, argues that special conditions such as corporate cultures that achieve extraordinary technical competence and performance, are necessary for successful highly reliable operations. However, these conditions must also permit great flexibility in structure, redundancy, and exercise of authority. He also observes that external authorities must continuously monitor but also support these internal arrangements, and they must do so over many generations of political leadership.

These conditions of high reliability are as demanding as they are rare, occurring in only a handful of organizations, such as nuclear power plant and air traffic control operations. Dealing with threats from terrorism – threats likely to continue for the foreseeable future – only adds to the challenge. Leaders will have a hard time assuring the public that they will honor far into the future their commitments to highly reliable operations. But honor them they must if they are to secure the public's trust and confidence in an increasingly uncertain and vulnerable age.

Together, the chapters in this section provide hints to organization strategies that assure robust and reliable operations of essential services. Only a few organizations needed such strategies in the past, and only a few have them now. The authors here attest to the fact that strategies do exist and are effective for robust and resilient operations under extremely demanding technical and operating conditions. In the future, many more organizations and networks of organizations, in both the public and private sectors, will need these strategies as well.

However, it is not clear to researchers how such capabilities can be developed where they do not now exist. In some cases, economic or policy changes, such as deregulation or introduction of market competition, may threaten their development, for example, by increasing competitive pressure on firms and leading them to cut back on redundancy or training. Tempering or reversing corrosive forces that threaten the resilience of critical infrastructure operations is essential, as is disseminating their characteristics in organizations responsible for essential service provision and protection.

Thus, the demands, and the stakes, are extraordinarily high for operating highly reliable systems in the face of overwhelming disasters such as Hurricane Katrina or adaptive predation such as terrorism. We cannot radically reconfigure critical infrastructures to be inviolate, even in the long term, because of their embedded nature in our economy and society. We cannot defeat terrorists who might threaten critical infrastructures, because terrorism as low-intensity warfare in a globalized world is now a fact of life. We cannot accept the failure, even for short periods, of these systems, because any down time would create social chaos, sow widespread uncertainty, and impose great costs on an increasingly interdependent economy. We will always need organizations to keep the lights on, the water running, the planes flying, and the phones and computer networks functioning, regardless of the economic or political or social circumstances. In the past, when there were few if any requirements for just-in-time operations, and when organizations had more slack and society had more tolerance for temporary system failure, we had only modest needs for such a degree of system reliability. But highly reliable organizations are now an indispensable attribute of advanced industrial societies if they are to survive in a more turbulent, uncertain, and dangerous future.

7

NOTES TOWARD A THEORY OF THE MANAGEMENT OF VULNERABILITY

Robert A. Frosch

> *"For want of a nail the shoe is lost,*
> *for want of a shoe the horse is lost,*
> *for want of a horse the rider is lost,*
> *for want of a rider the battle is lost,*
> *for want of a battle the kingdom is lost,*
> *all for the loss of a horseshoe nail."*
>
> — Benjamin Franklin, *Poor Richard's Almanack*, 1733–1758

> *"So, naturalists observe, a flea*
> *Hath smaller fleas that on him prey;*
> *And these have smaller still to bite 'em;*
> *And so proceed* ad infinitum.*"*
>
> — Jonathan Swift, *On Poetry.* "A Rhapsody," line 337 (1733)

> *"If a sufficient number of management layers are superimposed on top of each other, it can be assured that disaster is not left to chance."*
>
> — Norman Augustine, *Augustine's Laws*, 1997

INTRODUCTION

In these notes I outline a set of observations about accidents and system failures drawn partly from different parts of the literature than are apparently commonly used in the subject.[1] While they do not form a complete and connected theory of vulnerability, my intent is to point in some directions from which

Some of the material in this chapter (particularly most of the section headed "A More Formal Theory") was previously published in "Appendix A, Letters to the Committee" in "Accident Precursor Analysis and Management," NAE, NAP, Washington, DC, 2004.

one may be developed. I put the possible theory in the context of complexity and the statistical mechanics of physical phase change. In addition, I give some anecdotal examples of the concepts, drawn from my experience, and intended to enhance the reality of the concepts.[2,3] I draw a parallel between accidents and terror events, intended to show that the theory of accidents and system failures may be useful in creating a theory of vulnerability, and thus in protecting against terror.

I begin with a discussion of the nature of accidents and risks, and some of the key concepts used in dealing with them. I then turn to a theory of accidents that is applicable to vulnerability in general. Some of this material may be elementary, especially to those oriented toward mathematical and physical theory, but may be new to those not so oriented.

RISK

Everyday life is a series of events, each event chosen from a variety of possibilities. Thus, the train of events may be seen as a branching sequence, a multifurcation tree. (I use multifurcation by analogy with bifurcation to mean multi-branched, as bifurcation means two-branched.) I choose one of a number of places to cross the street, I walk rapidly or slowly, I look carefully, or not, there is traffic, or not, a car is coming, or not, rapidly, or not, I have to dodge, or not. . . . Most times there is no danger; sometimes there is a near accident; some time I may be hit, injured, or killed. I plan for this chain of events by considering various risk comparisons and countervailing risks.[4] An assassination, or a terrorist event, is only an adjustment to the normal risks, and fits within the theory: the terrorist arranges to cause an accident. This model will appear later in this chapter as percolation theory on a Bethe tree (also known as a Cayley tree).

A terrorist must also navigate through a multifurcating (multi-branching) chain of events: selecting and obtaining materials and means, getting to the target, approaching the target closely enough, etc.

COMPARATIVE RISK

In planning my day I continually, mostly automatically, make use of the concept of 'comparative risk.' I choose where to cross the street in terms of traffic patterns, lighting at night, etc., but I make this choice by comparing risks. If the street is icy, I may choose to cross in a place that is less icy, even if there is likely to be more traffic there. This is a constant problem in risk analysis and risk avoidance: there is no such thing as one single risk, all alone; it is only possible to choose among risks. Exercising produces a risk of accident, strain, or a fall. Not exercising produces a risk of heart problem and obesity. To the extent that we make rational decisions about what we do, we always balance risks.

In the same way, a terrorist must also balance risks: more explosive is more destructive and surer, but easier to detect. Closer to the target is better, but more likely to be defended.

The defender, with finite resources, must choose among a vast set of possible things and places that could be attacked, and among a vast array of ways to defend them. This is choosing among risks. Deciding what must be protected, and where, for one reason or another, one chooses not to protect, or not to protect as heavily, is a key decision in both accident and terror protection.

Terrorists, on the other hand, can use their scarce resources strategically, as they have much less to defend than the defenders generally do. Their resources can therefore be used more judiciously, and they are required to weigh many fewer risks.

Further, as defensive measures increase, the ability of infrastructure and systems to perform is likely to be compromised. In the automobile industry, there is a constant battle for vehicle security against theft. As security measures increase, it becomes clear that the vehicle becomes harder and harder for the owner to use and continue to use. (Special keys may be lost and be difficult to replace because security measures rightly make them difficult to replace. Pass codes may be forgotten, and tedious to replace or refresh.) Eventually one must choose between vehicle security and vehicle use. Given enough security, the owner cannot use the car conveniently. Absolute security of a vehicle is impossible. When some valuable vehicles left on the street proved impossible for thieves to open or start, they were lifted up and trucked away, to be worked on at leisure.

This trade-off between security and ease of use is common to many systems: computers, credit cards, alarm systems, bank accounts, and many others. There is always a problem of balance between 'doing business' and 'protecting the business.'

I observe also that many difficulties with classified material systems over the years, in the Pentagon and elsewhere, have not been because the security systems did not work, but because the people who had to use the classified materials could not do their work properly, or reasonably efficiently, unless they defeated the system. These 'defeats' sometimes led to security breaches, but most breaches probably went undetected.

A classical 'comparative risk' problem is posed by the choice between 'errors of the first and second kinds' in detection systems. Errors of the first kind are 'false alarms,' supposed detections, when, in fact, there is no target there to detect. Errors of the second kind are failures to detect when there is a target there to detect. Detection is part of protection, while false alarms are problems for customers and those doing business.

The probabilities of the two kinds of errors are connected by the detection capability of the system, and must always be 'traded off'; they pose a comparative risk problem. In the presence of noise (and there is always noise present), the only way to ensure zero false alarms is to accept zero detections: turn the system off. One must choose an operating point: how probable (and disruptive) false alarms are allowed to be must be traded off with how probable (and dangerous) it is to miss detections. To ensure 100% detection, one must accept the possibility that they will all be false alarms.

Let us consider inspecting passengers' baggage at an airport, or employees' and visitors' briefcases, lunchboxes, and clothing at the entrance to a plant. By noise is meant that some things that might be dangerous might not look dangerous, and some things that are not dangerous might look dangerous. With a given amount of effort and time for inspection, it is possible to think that innocent things are dangerous (false alarms), and that dangerous things are innocent (missed detections). If we want to be very sure to stop entry of anyone with something dangerous, we will also stop innocent people (carrying something that looks dangerous); if we want to be sure to let in many innocent people, we will also let in dangerous ones (carrying something that looks innocent, but really is not).

Of course, we can increase the effort and time (e.g., have a second inspection for anything that looks dangerous, separating the dangerous from the 'only looks dangerous' with more care). However, we might still miss something dangerous that we thought was innocent, and we could increase our effort further. However, as long as it is possible to confuse innocent objects with guilty objects (which is always), we have to keep increasing the effort to get more perfect results. Eventually, no one gets in at all.

(It is worth noting, that from the overall terrorists' strategic point of view, it may be worth devoting some effort to carrying, or somehow have others carry, innocent things that look guilty, but are not. This could be a way to make the operation of the detection system so troubling to the innocent that the system eventually decreases its detection effort, so that the system which is being protected (e.g., air travel) can continue to operate. This can be described as raising the noise level to decrease the signal to noise ratio; making detection more difficult, as opposed to decreasing the detectable signal in order to decrease the signal to noise ratio to make detection more difficult.)

I recall hearing that when the U.S. Navy SOSUS (SOund SUrveillance System) system of passive detection of Soviet submarines off the U.S. coast was operating, one Chief of Naval Operations (CNO) inadvertently turned off the system by not understanding the connection between errors of the first and second kinds. After a sequence of occasions on which he was awakened at 3 A.M. to be warned of a Soviet missile submarine off the U.S. coast, only to be told at his office in the morning that it was a false alarm, he said, seriously, or in jest: 'I don't want to be awakened by any more false alarms in the middle of the night.' The comment was taken as an order, and, after a while, it was noticed that there were now no verified reports of Soviet submarines too close to our coast. There were no reports at all. In their effort to not have any false alarms, the system operators had been so cautious as not to have any true alarms either. The system was, effectively, turned off.

When an outside advisory committee looked at the problem of no detections, they tracked down the difficulty, and the system was turned on again, by allowing some false alarms. When the problem was explained to the CNO, he agreed that keeping the system working, and keeping him informed, meant he had to accept some 3 A.M. phone calls, or wait until morning to know! (This may be a case of bureaucratic 'amplification downwards,' in which a comment by the CNO, which he may have intended not to be taken too seriously, was taken very seriously by lower echelons, with bad results.)

COUNTERVAILING RISK

A particularly interesting version of comparative risk is 'countervailing risk': the attempt to counter a risk introduces a new risk, which may be greater or lesser than the original risk. In therapeutic pharmaceutical applications, countervailing risks are known as 'side effects.' Highly toxic chemotherapy agents are appropriate for treating deadly cancers, but would not be appropriate against the common cold. (Life has serious side effects, including death!)

In the late 1980s or early 1990s, while Vice President of General Motors in charge of Research Laboratories, I was suddenly called to an emergency meeting, and asked to bring a metallurgist with me to the meeting. The corporation had learned of 15 cases in which a rear half-axle (on a rear drive car, of which there were at least a million on the road) had separated from the differential, and the half-axle and wheel had 'walked off the car.' Fortunately there had been no serious accidents, and no injuries or deaths.

The question was to determine the cause of the problem and decide on what actions to take. The key question was whether these 15 were isolated incidents, or whether there would be more, and, indeed, whether all the rear wheel drive cars were at risk. The metallurgist, looking at one of the half-axles, thought there was something not right about the appearance of the metal at the separation point, but it would take some days for an analysis.

The meeting turned, in the face of the continuing uncertainty, to the possibility of prompt action, in case there was further danger. A proposal was made for recall of the cars and inspection or replacement of all the half-axles. This would require the disassembly of very many differentials (at least hundreds of thousands, depending upon how many owners responded to the recall). At this point the question was asked: How much experience have mechanics in car dealers' service shops (or in other car repair shops) had with disassembly and reassembly of differentials? It turned out that this was very rare; most shops would never have done it at all. Thus, the question became: What would the error rate be in reassembly, and how many accidents might those errors cause? Given the number of vehicles potentially involved, any reasonable estimate of the error rate suggested that, even with a very active training program (which would take time), the accidents caused by the errors might be much greater in number than those caused by faulty half-axles, unless the fault was ubiquitous.

A further question was raised: The probability that a particular driver/vehicle is involved in an accident is generally proportional to the number of miles driven. Thus, if a recall leads to drivers driving more miles, because of the recall, than they would otherwise have driven, the recall might cause more accidents, some serious, than might be prevented by the recall. On the other hand, if the recall did not lead to more miles being driven (e.g., the driver left the car at the dealers while doing other errands in the neighborhood), then this countervailing risk would be unimportant. In reality, the effect of a recall would probably be mixed; some drivers doing one thing, some another. Since no one knew of any relevant statistics on such behavior, this possibility was noted, but did not really contribute much to the decision.

The decision was made to await either analysis, or reports of more cases, and meanwhile to begin development of a suitable training system for a possible recall. Upon analysis and investigation, which did take several days, it turned out that there had been a heat treating control failure, which had been corrected in a short time, so the 15 bad half-axles were probably all there were. We did not subsequently hear of any more cases and there was no recall.

An additional interesting automotive case is posed by air bags. Air bags clearly save lives, but they also can kill, and that was particularly true of the first generation of inflatable restraints that were fielded. When small people, whether belted or not, are behind the steering wheel, they are likely to be close and low. ('Small people' are defined as 5% females; females in the smallest 5% of the female population, and men of about the same size.) If the air bag of a small driver inflates, even in a 'supermarket parking lot fender bender' it may wrap around the neck, and break it. This is generally fatal, and there have been a small number of such accidents. This is a particularly troublesome 'side effect': it puts a particular population at risk, even in the case of minor accidents that otherwise would not pose much risk of injury or death. While later generations of air bags are 'gentler,' some of this risk probably still exists. Most people seem to be unaware of this risk, and the automotive safety regulators have been unwilling to do much about it.

While building the space shuttle, NASA had a design rule that all flight critical sensor and control elements had to be at least 'doubly redundant.' (This term is not in itself a redundancy; we also used the term 'triply redundant.') While Administrator of NASA, the design engineers came to me with a request for an exception to the redundancy rule. They could not find any way to make the actuator set for the main rudder (which also opens out like a clam shell to be an air brake) to be redundant; there was simply no space, or way, to make the system independently double. After many attempts to find a way (and being sent back to try again), the proposition was advanced to replace redundancy with a 'battleship actuator,' one so straightforwardly strong that it 'would not fail'; that is, failure was expected to be extremely improbable. We accepted the countervailing risk of failure, and this solution was allowed, with special provision for inter-flight test and inspection. As far as I know, the solution was successful, and this mechanism has not failed.

It must be noted that the very act of choosing what to protect, and how to protect it, will raise countervailing risks, created by the means chosen. For example, hiring more guards is likely to place a greater strain on the means used for selecting them, and the greater number also means there are more insiders (possibly less carefully chosen) for terrorists to recruit. Protecting Target A to a higher level than before may make Target B, previously not as interesting to the terrorists, more interesting to them, thus requiring more effort to protect Target B. (I understand that economists refer to this as the "substitution effect.") As noted above, the sheer bureaucratic load of increased protection may be such that both the operators and the 'customers' start 'cutting corners.'

If tight security controls on visas for immigrant professionals lead to a shortage of skilled software people needed for security systems, or a shortage of skilled translators and interpreters, the countervailing risk is that the tight controls become 'self-defeating': the act of tightening the controls makes it difficult or impossible to tighten the controls. There is a forced trade-off between two risks.

From the terrorists' point of view, there is also a series of branching events. Terrorists choose targets, plan operations, obtain materials and means, such as explosives, vehicles, learn to fly, hijack airplanes, etc. At each branch point there are several possibilities, each with some different probability of an accident to the plot, a failure, being discovered, suffering an accident, and the possibility that the choice made creates new risks for the plan. The underlying phenomena, and the rules that govern them, apply always and to everyone.

A MORE FORMAL THEORY OF ACCIDENTS (AND OF ACCIDENTS CAUSED BY TERRORISTS)

I now turn to some theoretical background models for risk analysis, in which some of the previous ideas will be seen to fit.

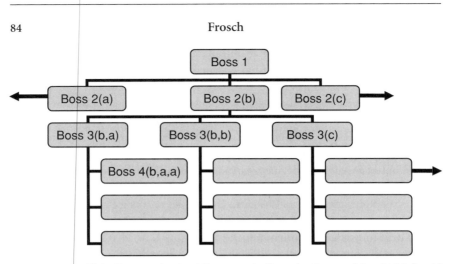

Figure 7.1. A self-similar organization. The arrows indicate that Bosses 2(a) and 2(c) should have organizations similar to that under Boss 2(b) under them, and a similar continuation of that under Bosses 4 (baa), ad infinitum if required.

THE FRACTAL NATURE OF MACHINES AND ORGANIZATIONS

Machines and organizations are designed to be fractal, that is, self-similar at all scales: the subparts look the same as the whole, the sub-subparts look the same as the subparts, etc. Machines are made of parts (little machines) assembled into components (bigger and more complex machines), which are assembled into subassemblies (even bigger machines), which are assembled into subsystems (still bigger machines), etc. until finally assembled into a complete machine. A shrinking engineer in the machine will be surrounded by machinery at any scale. Hierarchical organizations are specifically designed to be fractal; all levels of local organization are similar, as any organization diagram will show. (Organizations consist of collections of sub-organizations, each of which, in turn, consists of sub-sub-organizations, and so on, down to the individual worker. While all of the sub and sub-sub, etc. organizations do not look precisely alike, the whole system looks about the same at any level of the organization. The workers may be doing different tasks, but there is generally a group of co-workers reporting to a 'boss'; the 'boss' has a group of co-bosses, and they, in turn, report to a boss. Each boss has n assistant bosses, each of whom has n assistant-assistant bosses, and so on to $[(\text{assistant})^m]$ bosses.) (Figure 7.1: A Self-Similar Organization)

Neither machine nor organization is, of course, a regular, mathematically precise fractal; they may be described as 'heterogeneous fractals.' While not homogeneously fractal (the same at every level), we expect the distribution of the (number of parts of a machine) vs. (the masses) of the parts (or their volumes) to follow an inverse power law, where the power describes the dimension

Table 7.1. This table illustrates the values for several inverse power functions of the form $10/X^a$ where a takes values from 1 to 3.

X	10/X	$10/X^2$	$10/X^3$
1	10	10	10
2	5	2.5	1.25
3	3.33...	1.111...	0.37037...
4	2.5	0.625	0.15625
5	2.0	0.4	0.08
6	1.66...	0.2777...	0.04629...
7	1.4285...	0.20408...	0.02915...
8	1.25	0.15625	0.01953...
9	1.111...	0.12345...	0.01371...

of the fractal (Mandelbrot 1982).[5] For machines I would expect the dimension to be between two and three. For organizations I would expect the dimension to be between one and two.

Being fractal, both machines and organizations are approximately (heterogeneously) 'scale free'; they look the same at any scale. [Scale free is used in the sense that: $f(kx)/f(x)$ is not a function of x. Most functions are not scale free. Power laws are scale free functions since: $(kx)^a/x^a = k^a$.]

ORGANIZED CRITICALITY

Many natural (and human) systems appear to develop to a 'Self Organized Critical' (SOC) state where they have a scale free fractal structure, and are on the edge of catastrophe (Bak 1996; Buchanan 2001).[6] Such systems appear to undergo disasters of all scales, from the miniscule to the completely destructive.[7] The distribution of the structure of these systems is fractal, and the distribution of the (size vs. number of occurrences of a given size) of catastrophe follows an inverse power law in the vicinity of catastrophe. Examples include: sandpile (more correctly, rice pile) collapses, earthquakes, pulsar glitches, turbidite layers (fossil undersea avalanches), solar flares, sounds from the volcano Stromboli, fossil genera life spans, traffic jams, variation in cotton futures, people killed in deadly conflicts, and research paper citations. This is also the case for the ranking of the frequency of words in the English language, and the ranking of cities by size (Zipf, as cited by Bak[6]) (Table 7.1: Several Inverse Power Functions). This Zipf's Law inverse power behavior is closely related to Pareto's Law, the latter being the integral (area under the curve of), or cumulative, statistic of Zipf's Law inverse power statistics.[8]

For reasons of economy and efficiency, engineered systems (which I will loosely refer to as machines) and organizations (including those in which the design and operations of the machines are embedded) are designed to be as close to catastrophe as the designer dares. In the case of machines, the 'distance' from envisioned catastrophes is called the 'factor of safety,' and varies depending upon the stresses predicted to be placed on the machine during its operating life. Organizations (as operating machines) are designed to be as lean (and mean and cheap) as seems consistent with performing their functions in the face of their operating environment. In this sense, these fractal systems may be described as being 'Design Organized Critical' (DOC). I argue that the physics which applies to phase changes in natural SOC systems may be applied to DOC systems.

PERCOLATION THEORY

I now introduce percolation theory, which has been used as a theoretical framework for natural phase change (Stauffer & Aharony 1994; Grimmett 1999).[9] Percolation is a formal theory of the way in which, for example, water moves, or does not move, through tightly packed coffee grounds. Think of a barrier in a plane consisting of a square grid of blocks (or links, or pipes) separating water from a dry area (Figure 7.2a: Percolation – 0.5, and Figure 7.2b: Percolation – 0.7). If all the blocks are intact, water cannot flow through the barrier. If, however, enough of the right blocks are open (broken), there may be a path for the water to flow from one side of the barrier to the other. In percolation theory one assigns a probability p, that any link may be broken. The percolation problem is then, for a given p: What is the probability that there is at least one path for the water to flow from one side of the barrier to the other?

I assert that percolation theory provides a suitable 'spherical cow' or 'toy model' of vulnerability in machines and organizations. There are a number of possible percolation models, such as lattices of any dimension. I will use percolation on a Bethe lattice[9] (Cayley tree), although percolation on other lattices gives similar results. A Bethe lattice is a multifurcation (multi-branched) diagram which starts from a single nodal point, then descends through n branches, at the end of each of which there is a split into n branches, and so on, into a hierarchical, many-branched tree. (The simplest nontrivial case, in which multi = 2, consists of a tree of repeated bifurcations, or splits into two new branches, at the end of each branch.) (Figure 7.1 is a hierarchical organization in the form of a Bethe, or Cayley, tree). The asymptotically infinitely large case can be solved exactly. It has been shown (both by approximation and computation) that in less than infinite cases the phenomena approximate those proven for the infinite case, particularly around the critical value (see below).

In our model, a link between two nodes may be conducting or non-conducting. If conducting, we regard it as a failure of that link. Strings of connected link failures are interpreted as accidents of various sizes, and a string

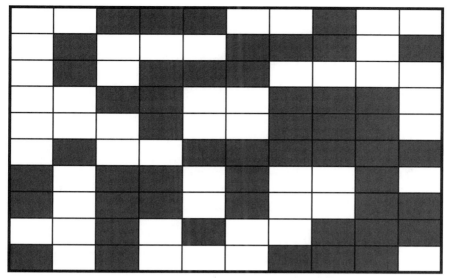

Figure 7.2a. An example of a 10×10 percolation diagram. The vertical sides are taken to be closed, while the top and bottom are taken to be open, with water above and nothing below. A white block is considered closed, and a dark-colored block is open to being filled. This diagram illustrates a case in which the probability of a block being open is 0.5. The rule is that blocks with a bottom, top, or side in common are connected, and liquid can flow between them, but touching corners are impervious (not like Tic Tac Toe, where diagonals are allowed). In the random sequence of open and closed blocks in this diagram, there is no path from top to bottom. Other random sequences would lead to other versions of the diagram, the statistical behavior being obtained from a large number of such examples.

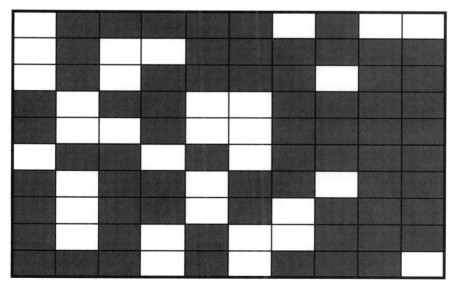

Figure 7.2b. As Figure 2a, but the probability of a block being open is 0.7, and here a clear path exists.

of link failures to the central (or origin) node is interpreted as a complete catastrophe. We examine the probability of catastrophe, and the distribution of lesser failures as p, the probability of failure of any link, increases from zero.

We first would like to know the percolation threshold: the value of $p = p_c$ for which there is at least one infinite path through the infinite lattice. This may be shown to be $p_c = 1/(z - 1)$ where z is 'multi,' the number of links at each node.

We next would like to know P, the probability that the origin (or any other arbitrarily selected site) belongs to the infinite (or catastrophic) cluster. Stauffer and Aharony[9] prove the example for $z = 3$:

$$p_c = 1/2 \qquad P = 0, \text{ for } p < p_c \qquad P/p = 1 - [(1 - p)/p]^3, \text{ for } p > p_c.$$

(In general, it may be shown that $p_c = 1/(z - 1)$ for a Cayley tree having z branches.[10])

Further, it may be shown that $n_s(p)$, the average number of clusters (per site) containing s sites goes asymptotically to: $n_s(p_c) \sim s^{-\tau}$. More generally, the mean cluster size (S) near the critical threshold $(p = p_c)$ goes as $S \sim |p - p_c|^{-\gamma}$, where γ is a constant. This distribution of cluster sizes describes cluster distributions near phase change in many physical systems, including the Ising model of magnetization, and clusters of water molecules near the phase change from steam to liquid water.

Catastrophic system failures are what they seem to be: phase changes, for example, from organized shuttle to rubble (a 'liquid'). (In the case of the shuttle failure, the simple percolation model [the spherical cow] is too simple; one ought to use an 'elliptical cow': a cascade model, in which a percolation link failure increases the probability of failure of other links.) I note also that the percolation model leads to the suggestion that the 'Heinrich diagram,' or 'Occurrence Pyramid,' is likely to be correct. This diagram, based upon anecdotal evidence,[14] suggests that in accident statistics, the ratio of "consequentials" (real accidents) to "near misses," to "compromises" (of system integrity), to "infractions" (of system rules), is likely to be $\sim$1:10:100:1000. This is a discrete version of a power law distribution (10^{-x}).

It is also interesting to note that Reason's[11] 'Swiss cheese model' of accidents is a percolation model, although he does not call it that, or formally develop the statistical implications. Any occurrence may be an accident precursor. The 'Swiss cheese model' is clearly closely related to (really the same as) the percolation model.

Terrorist plots have the same properties as other systems with DOC properties: they are designed to be economical, and, because of the hazards of discovery, are generally designed to be especially small and lean, so they can be easy to conceal. They are generally based upon a series of events that must happen in sequence, and be undetected. The sequence generally involves penetration of detection or other barriers to reach an objective for the actual final attack. These properties define a percolation problem through a set of detection or other barriers. (This cow is not spherical: the probabilities of link failure do not all have the same distribution. The spherical cow model can only be a crude simple approximation, but it demonstrates some key features of the phenomena. More complex models are possible, for example, with probabilities of link failure that vary across the links [an ellipsoidal cow, perhaps], or with probabilities of link failure in which later link failures become more probable following earlier link failures [as mentioned above, a cascade model, possibly applying to earthquakes and other phenomena,[12] but perhaps not clearly to terrorist penetrations.].)

It is likely to be useful to divide the vulnerability problem into two modeling problems: a percolation ('Swiss cheese') model of events leading to an incident (accident or attack) and a percolation model (possible a cascade model) of the consequences of the event.

An attempt to examine actual terrorist incidents (e.g., the World Trade Center catastrophe of September 11, 2001) finds a complex communication network whose organization is apparently like the normal fractal structure of other self-organized networks, like the Internet.[13]

COUNTERMEASURES TO VULNERABILITY

What can one do? Clearly, as suggested elsewhere (e.g.,[14]), we may redesign the system to be simpler, and to function without subsystems or components likely to fail in a way that leads to accidents. If this is not feasible, the system will need to be strengthened; moved farther away from its breaking point. For machines, this can be done by strengthening elements that appear most likely to fail, and whose failure is likely to lead to disaster, by introducing redundancy, more (or larger, which is equal to more) mechanical strength elements, redundant sensors, controls and actuators, etc. The trick is to find the elements most likely to fail, singly or in combination, so that only they are strengthened, and 'unnecessary' redundancy is not introduced. These critical elements are found by engineering intuition, engineering analysis, and/or by probabilistic risk assessment analysis of some variety.

In organizations one can add redundant organizational elements intended to increase strength against 'mistakes' of various kinds. These may include people to watch for safety or security problems or breaches, safety organizations, inspectorates, or auditors. Adding people, or organizational structure, however, invokes a countervailing risk: it increases the 'coordination tax,' the management load necessary to keep the system coordinated and operating, and may in itself lead to failure due to communication problems. There is thus a competition between the efficiency of operation of the organization and its management (which in extreme cases can lead to the weakness of organizational anorexia), and the necessity to have enough redundancy (fat) to protect against failures leading to accidents, or security breaches leading to vulnerability.

Over-redundancy can lead to an unmanageable organization, or one which is too 'brittle' bureaucratically, and fails by the necessity of operating by 'work to rule.' The organization 'seizes up,' and ceases to function for its purpose, or the organization itself, and its rules, must be circumvented so that it can continues to perform its rewal functions at all.

However, other organizational means may also function to provide the necessary redundancy. In an organization with a reasonable atmosphere of trust among its members and echelons, juniors formally or informally bring their problems and troubles to peers, and to their seniors, who may have other and/or broader means for attacking them. Seniors are attuned and attentive to rumors and concerns of both peers and juniors. These are strengthening elements, that 'bridge over' portions of the organizational 'tree,' and bring additional strength to the organization. They may be likened to 'bringing in reinforcements.' Within this theoretical framework, these horizontal and vertical communication means are strengthening elements that move the organizational structure away from p_c without adding new sub-organizations or people.

Organizational redundancy by terrorists for a particular terror plot seems unlikely: it can greatly increase the probability of detection. Redundancy for terrorists seems likely to continue to reside in multiple plots, either serially (as in most of the history of suicide bombings) or in parallel (as on 9/11/2001).

In the scientific and engineering communities, peer review plays this communication role. The prime purpose of peer review is not to provide confirmation of excellence, but to find errors and omissions that might be damaging or catastrophic.

It is interesting that in their work on high reliability organizations, LaPorte, Roberts, and Rochlin[15] (cited in Reason, p. 213, op. cit.) describe the field reorganization of hierarchies into small teams whose members communicate directly with each other, particularly in warning of danger. For example, the usually highly hierarchical Navy crews, when working together as flight deck teams on an aircraft carrier during flight operations, become a flat, highly communicating group, in which authority comes from knowledge and perception of problems, rather than from organizational position.

A sports team (e.g., basketball, football, soccer) when it is 'hot' seems to operate like a high reliability organization: flat organization on the field, direct communication, authority to initiate lies with everyone, etc. It also appears that a member of the team taking a 'prima donna' approach can destroy this hot teamwork.

Another case touching on the high reliability organization is that of the shuttle Columbia accident. In the report of the Commission on the Columbia Accident (NASA, 2003), there is a discussion of NASA safety organization and procedures, high reliability organizations, and a comparison with two Navy safety systems: the nuclear propulsion safety system and SUBSAFE, the safety system put in place after the loss of the submarine USS Thresher. The Navy systems are characterized as independent of the operating systems for which they are the safety controllers.

As Assistant Secretary of the Navy, I was very familiar with the two Navy systems in the period from 1966 through 1972, and as NASA Administrator, with the NASA systems from 1977 through 1980. The characterization of 'independent' is generally correct for SUBSAFE in the years in which I knew it, but certainly not correct for the nuclear propulsion system. While there was an 'independent' safety organization at the Atomic Energy Commission (AEC) (and its successor agencies, and the Department of Energy), for the entire period from the beginning of naval nuclear power, until his retirement from the Navy in 1983, Captain, then Admiral Rickover served as Director of the Naval Reactors Branch in the Bureau of Ships in the Navy, and as chief of the Naval Reactors Branch in the Division of Reactor Development at the AEC.[16]

The independence of the safety office was an illusion; Admiral Rickover at the Navy might send a letter to himself at the AEC requesting a waiver, and might then send a letter from Mr. Rickover at the AEC to Admiral Rickover refusing the waiver. (I recall him saying to me something like: 'That sounds like a good idea, but I'm not sure I can get the AEC to approve it.') The remarkable safety record of Naval nuclear reactors systems was not due to a really independent safety organization, but rather to Rickover's single-minded and obsessional insistence on rigid and demanding selection, education and training of officers and men, careful engineering with great attention to detail, and carefully worked out and religiously followed operating procedures.

Each nuclear trained officer in command of a nuclear powered Navy ship, and each chief engineer of a nuclear powered ship wrote a monthly letter report to 'The Admiral' (also known in later years to many as the 'k.o.g.,' or 'kindly old gentleman,' because he was not). The letter report was expected to be detailed, and to report any anomalies, variances from normal operation, etc. They were read, and frequently replied to, sometimes with considerable asperity.

During my time as NASA Administrator, I depended on the Office of the Chief Engineer, and upon internal communication upwards for safety and other engineering oversight, rather than depending completely on the internal safety organizations, and our explicitly independent external safety committees. (We were not engaged in manned flight at the time; we were building the Space Transportation System, and Apollo had been over for some time.) The style of the agency at that time included a great deal of internal open discussion and critique. Walt Williams, the Chief Engineer at the time, was a long-term, highly respected, senior NASA engineer who had come to NASA from its predecessor organization, the National Advisory Committee on Aeronautics (NACA), and had been a key player in Mercury, Gemini, and Apollo. Walt and his staff (because he introduced them) were welcome in any NASA meeting. (I augmented Walt's staff with others, including Harry Sonnemann, an engineer with great practical experience in building large systems, and with whom I had worked for many years, including while he was a member of my personal staff in the Navy Department, where he played a similar role.) Walt and his staff roamed the agency, finding and solving problems, and occasionally involving the Administrator's office, or the Administrator if it seemed necessary.

As we came close to the first flight of the shuttle (which happened after I was Administrator), we convened independent advisory engineering groups, both from within the agency (using senior people not directly involved in the shuttle program) and from the aerospace community outside of the agency and not directly involved in the shuttle program.

There is an obvious case to be made for the standing independent safety group, but there are also some countervailing risks. If an independent group is insufficiently knowledgable of, or involved in, the details of the operations, and the day-to-day work, it is unlikely to understand what is really happening, and how the system really works, well enough to be of valuable critical help. If it is too involved, it can understand difficulties too well, become too sympathetic, and be 'captured,' or even become indistinguishable from, the group for which it has oversight. Thus, there is a tendency for standing independent groups to teeter between ignorance and capture.

Maintaining independence while achieving, and maintaining, sufficient knowledge of the operations requires continuing management of the relationships; the organizational arrangement does not appear to be stable on its own. (Recent difficulties with financial auditing seem to be evidence of this point; distancing auditors from the organizations they audit sometimes results in insufficient knowledge to make a satisfactory audit possible.) In my experience, establishing and maintaining satisfactory open communication is key to keeping such organizational oversight relationships healthy.

A means of coping with the instability can sometimes be found in the use of part-time groups (internal or external), with slowly changing member-ship. If properly managed, such a group can establish and maintain sufficient intermittent contact with the operating organization to come to understand what it does and how it does it, while remaining independent enough not to be captured, and to remain a useful critic.

In my experience, few organizations operate according to their organization diagrams, and would probably collapse if they were forced to do so. This is another version of 'work to rule,' always a devastating bureaucratic device for hampering the functioning of any institution.[17] For this reason, while there are organizational arrangements which can be destructive of function, many somewhat different reasonably appropriate organizational arrangements are likely to work well for a given task, if well led and managed. No organizational arrangement can save an institution from inadequate leadership and management.

SUMMARY REMARKS

What do I make of all these somewhat disparate, and not all obviously connected, ideas?

It seems clear that there are a number of useful principles and theoretical structures that can be used for the analysis of terror (and accident) possibilities. It remains to exercise the ideas and theory usefully.

Safety and security are problems difficult to address and be alert to in a world in which, most of the time, one is not in an accident or being attacked. Safety and security are, most of the time, dynamic non-events: when nothing happens, safety and security have been achieved. However, one can never be certain that something is not about to happen. In high reliability organizations it appears that everyone expects a bad day *every day*, and this attitude is in itself a protection against accidents or attacks.[18]

The statistical properties of designed machines and organizations are similar to those of natural 'self-organized' systems (SOC systems). We should expect the same theoretical framework that applies to them, and to statistically similar physical phase changes, to apply to machines and organizations. Therefore, we can expect to predict the general statistical properties of accident precursors and catastrophic system failure in human-made systems from well-known theoretical structures. The results also suggest why commonly used means to strengthen systems work to move the system state away from the critical p_c.

It seems clear that the dynamics of vulnerability and protection against accidents has many characteristics very like those of protecting against terrorist attack. Protectors and attackers face similar problems as they each attempt to pursue their complementary goals. In both cases, there is a multifurcating chain of events percolating to a conclusion: an accident or being attacked, or attacking to create an accident. In both cases there is a comparative risk analysis to be undertaken, and each measure or countermeasure may create countervailing risks, which may be 'better' or 'worse' than the previous risks.

In that sense, it may be said that the problem of coping with terror attacks has been reduced to a previously unsolved problem (but one about which a good deal is known): preventing accidents. Further development and application of this theoretical material will require its development and application specifically to machine and organizational system accidents, and the testing of this framework against real system data.

The situation may be seen as a warfare game on a percolation board or tree. Both sides face the trio of 'knowns' (what we know about the system), 'unknowns' (what we know we don't know about the system), and 'unknown unknowns' (what we don't know about the system that we don't even know we don't know). Tic Tac Toe is a very simple version of a percolation board game, with one player placing pieces to create percolation paths on a grid; the other placing pieces to block possible paths. In Tic Tac Toe the object is to percolate along a row, column or diagonal, or to gain a draw by blocking the percolation. Tic Tac Toe has been generalized beyond 3 × 3.[19] Chess and Go are also versions of percolation games: penetrate to the King, or capture (and prevent capture of) territory.

Chess and Go, and, I assume, Tic Tac Toe played in a larger than 3 × 3 matrix, while deterministic, have proven to be so large in their possibilities that we have not really exhausted them, and they are still popular. One might go further, and introduce chance into the effectiveness of each play (e.g., with dice, a spinner, or cards), and even go beyond the featureless (checkerboard-like) grid of blocks to a board with varying places and events, and so on to "Terror Monopoly," to be played on a grid of blocks (see Figures 7.2a and 7.2b: Percolation). Such games, and even more elaborate versions, with their theoretically manageable mathematics, might be analyzable enough to provide some theoretical guidance. In any case, they might be turned into useful, simple ways to explore strategies and, possibly, train players in a simple way.

Mathematical and statistical modeling of possible chains of events and of the game, and actual game playing which tests the theories will certainly continue to be useful. However, some of the problems met in the past need to be kept in mind.

Useful models may clearly be overcome by the combinatorics of examining 'all possible' (or even very many) chains of events for both sides. Computer chess playing software must operate by heuristics and general rules, since the combinatorial problems make exhaustive search and analysis even a few moves ahead impractical. Models therefore need to be simplified, and this can be a problem giving rise to misleading results, unless the simplifications and assumptions are carefully examined and tested.

I recall that after the 'six-day war,' which the Israelis won in less than a week, Harold Brown, then Director of Defense Research and Engineering (DDR&E), asked that the applicable Pentagon warfare model be run on the case. The model had the Arab side winning handily in three days! People take actions in warfare that reasonable models do not always predict. The model failed because it left out the effect of strategic and tactical behavior: it assumed that the war (or each battle) was a series of small force encounters in which the (even slightly) stronger force always had a higher probability of winning: for example, in the model, if three tanks met two tanks, the three always beat the two, regardless of tactical skill, and if tanks met infantry, infantry always lost. However, in real life the Egyptians did not use infantry to protect their tanks against infantry, and, since tank operators cannot see well out of tanks (or could not in those days), it was possible for Israeli infantry to ambush and disable tanks, then kill the crews.

In terms of the percolation model, I interpret this as suggesting that the model had much the wrong probability of failure of a link. It could also be said that the simple tree model, in which the tree is completely homogeneous and the probabilities are static, and all the same, is much too spherical a cow to be trustworthy for detail. The model is only the beginning of a way to think about the modeling of such event chains.

In the attempt to create a high reliability organization, the greatest problem seems to be achieving the balance between organizational discipline (necessary for its existence and stability) and the open, informal structure needed for a functioning team. The countervailing risk to the high reliability team is that bureaucratic niceties will become a kind of self-defeating solution to problems. Formal discipline can destroy exactly those properties of the team that make it function.

However, note that Admiral Rickover managed to keep many high reliability teams functioning in an apparently hyper-disciplined atmosphere. Also, however, note his use of non-bureaucratized communication systems, albeit to and from himself. An interesting conundrum: an unlikely personality produced a desirable result in an unlikely way. Nevertheless, improving discipline, organization, and process to excess may be the easiest way to destroy a high reliability team.

There is a clear trade-off between protection and functionality. A completely unprotected subway system is easy prey, but the only absolutely complete protection is to let no one in. Somewhere between these two limiting cases, one crosses the line between reasonable protection and reasonable functionality. A reasonable point might be found by game playing or simulation, or experiment. The ability for continual adaptation seems important.

In the search for useful redundancy (increasing the factor of safety), a balance must be struck between redundancy and organizational efficiency, leanness, and cost. Organization anorexia can be an invitation to accidents and attacks. Therefore, there appears to be a connection between the search for organizational efficiency and private (and public vulnerability).

THE CEO'S QUESTIONS

What questions should a CEO ask of himself/herself and the organization?

"How easily can someone percolate themselves or a weapon to a place in my organization, plants, facilities where they can attack? (Are they already there?) How can I decrease the probability without destroying the organization or its functions?

Are we furnishing the weapons for our own destruction? (Are some of our materials explosive, toxic, or hazardous if released or triggered?) Will the effect go beyond ourselves to the public? What can we do about it: Can we protect the materials and the processes they are used in, can we have less such material around at any one time, or can we substitute less hazardous materials?

What are the cost and organizational trade-offs among the various possibilities, and with the business liabilities of various protective measures, including insurance, against these risks? (I understand that many large firms do not buy insurance [other than that required by law, such as workers' compensation insurance], but are self-insured. While at General Motors, I inquired, and was told the Corporation was self-insured. It assumed that it was solvent enough to cover any liabilities that were not so widespread as to be universal, and therefore shared public responsibilities, and that, in any case, premiums would be prohibitive.)

Are we too lean to deal with these problems? Given the liabilities, what is the optimum level of internal protection and redundancy to cope with emergencies? (I note that one of the considerations in setting manning levels for marine safety, especially on Navy ships, is the necessity to cope with damage control emergencies, whether caused by the sea, equipment failure or accident, or enemy action. This is a conscious setting of a redundancy level for a foreseeable, but generally rare, threat of unknown probability. While combat damage and loss can be expected, many Navy ships go through a war, even World War II, without serious damage, or with none.)

Do we have contingency plans to deal with the obvious possibilities (whether terror induced or not): fire, flood, earthquake, explosion, even absurd weather?

Is there outside expertise I should seek? Where?"

THE GOVERNMENT'S QUESTIONS:

With regard to industry, the government might ask:

"How can we engage companies in looking at their vulnerabilities, particularly those that might become public vulnerabilities?

How can we provide technical help so they may devise ways that are most effective and efficient in protecting against, and coping with the results of terrorist attacks?

Where is the appropriate interface between industrial and commercial self-protection, and public protection; who should take responsibility for doing what?"

FINAL COMMENT

This chapter seems continually to return to questions of balance: between risks and comparative risks, risks and countervailing risks, high reliability teams (with internal and external freedom of action) and organizational discipline, organizational redundancy and organizational efficiency, percolation attempts and percolation blocking. As always, the search for 'the middle way' seems best.

There is considerable work still to be done to understand how to analyze and protect ourselves against the chains of events that lead to accidents and to successful terror attacks, but some of the possible directions that such quantitative thinking may take are beginning to be clear.

NOTES

1. The editors have pointed out that there are literatures on security, and on organizational theory, to which I do not refer. I am not familiar with those literatures, but have come at the problem from a different direction.
2. Personal memories are notoriously unreliable when undocumented. The tales I tell are clear and vivid memories for me, and I tell them as I remember them, but the reader may choose to regard them as illustrative parables.
3. Or as "Merely corroborative detail, intended to give artistic verisimilitude to an otherwise bald and unconvincing narrative." Pooh Bah in "The Mikado," by W. S. Gilbert.
4. Graham and Weiner 1995.
5. Mandelbrot 1982.
6. Bak 1996; Zipf 1929, 1935, 1965; Buchanan 2001. While 'popular,' the Bak and Buchanan books have excellent scholarly citations and bibliographies, and figures drawn from many sources. See also Barabosi 2003 for an account of self-organizing processes in networks.

7. "Catastrophe" and "disaster" are used here in their technical sense, meaning 'a collapse of part or all of the system,' as in a sand pile partial or total collapse, an earthquake of some size, or a traffic jam from mild to complete. From a terrorist's point of view, causing such an event is, presumably, a success on some scale.

8. See, for example: http://www.hpl.hp.com/research/idl/papers/ranking/ranking.html.

9. Stauffer Aharony 1994; Grimmett 1999; see also Braga et al. 2005.

10. See, e.g., http://mathworld.wolfram.com/CayleyTree.html.

11. Reason 1997.

12. See, e.g., Gabrielov et al. 2000; Barabasi et al. 1996; Nickel and Wilkinson 1983.

13. Fellman and Wright undated.

14. Hendershot 2004.

15. LaPorte et al. 1989; LaPorte et al. 1991.

16. http://www.hidtory.navy.mil/bios/rickover.htm, and http://www.bartleby.com/65/ri/Rickover.html; also see Schratz 1983 for an interesting commentary on Rickover's influence.

17. This comment is not meant as an attack on systems of rules, which are necessary for an institution to function, but only to note that rule systems must be interpreted in a sensible way that leads to function, not in such a way that the rules overpower and destroy function.

18. Coincident with the final writing of this chapter, there appeared: A Reporter at Large, The Terrorism Beat, *Inside the city's defense command centers* (Finnegan 2005), which illustrates many of the points about high reliability organizations: continuous concern; flat organization with broad internal, informal communication across functions; easy, non-bureaucratic access to senior management, etc.

19. See, for example: http://boulter.com/ttt/.

8

CHALLENGES OF ASSURING HIGH RELIABILITY WHEN FACING SUICIDAL TERRORISM

Todd R. La Porte

America's critical infrastructure, if it is to adapt to today's threat environment, needs to demonstrate qualities of high reliability and extended continuity. Critical infrastructure must be prepared for the uncertain conditions arising from a newly recognized source of aggression – the prospects of sustained social predation, sometimes delivered with a very destructive sacrificial twist. What some mislabel as "suicide terrorism," others more properly term "martyr operations."

How might these unexpected developments be viewed through the lenses of organization/institutional perspectives and the challenges of operating America's critical infrastructure? At least five characteristics of current U.S. infrastructure are relevant: (1) The infrastructure is widely dispersed geographically. (2) It is tightly coupled physically with interdependent organizational elements. (3) It is, in part, highly hazardous to operators, users, neighbors, and citizens. (4) The infrastructure is increasingly spare, with reduced component redundancy and organizational robustness and fewer alternatives if failures occur (telecommunications are the exception). (5) Finally, the infrastructure is critical to citizen well-being. Even limited incapacity of systems is perceived to have unacceptable consequences.

We also live in a time of reasonably high economic uncertainty, amid abiding skepticism of large institutions – sometimes crystallizing as overt public distrust. These conditions have shaped the evolution of U.S. infrastructure communities, an evolution that has resulted in the provision of services we

This chapter is based on La Porte 2004. Portions of this chapter draw strongly from La Porte 2003. Because these sections have been used in discussions with quite different, nearly mutually exclusive audiences, the conference sponsors have allowed it to be published in this volume.

experience today. The evolution is marked by increased opportunities to operate with less regulation and constraint, in an economic environment that propels senior management to search for efficiency-enhancing tactics. In this context, how well do our current ways of thinking about operational dynamics and public policy serve us as we face the novel and perplexing developments of martyr operations?

The depth of the challenge to protect critical infrastructure is signaled by several characteristics of what may be an age of perpetual aggression. Many U.S. citizens fear a kind of "fluid terrorism," rooted in clashing world-views in which our adversaries have taken the very long view, one cloaked in a mantle of righteousness and a cultural nostalgia of past empire.

Unlike any other time in U.S. history, we now face an increasing likelihood of confronting unpredictable social predation that may involve martyr operations. That is, some adversaries have motivations that no longer include a deep attachment to physical survival as a defining element in their notions of self-interest. Notably, all of our contemporary management and/or organizational perspectives, as well as most public policy notions, have been developed with the opposite assumption. We have also never before faced adversaries whose organizational bases are not firmly grounded within national systems of legal and police activities. The legal practices of nation-states are therefore less effective as means of control.

Partly as a consequence of this change in the type of adversary, the public feels a sense of apprehension and fear – a kind of free-floating dread, fed by a range of threats amplified by terror attacks.[1] In response, the public is calling for better preparation across a much wider range of "first responders," and at a far higher level of operating reliability than has ever been demanded of public institutions or private enterprises. The emphasis is predominantly on prevention of an attack. Less attention is being devoted to resilient recovery after an attack.[2] Perhaps the closest examples are the demands on the operations of our air traffic control system, nuclear power plants, and water systems – now in an environment where these critical infrastructures could be the objects of deliberate attack not merely equipment, procedural, or financial malfunction.

The increased intensity of demands confront institutional leaders and analysts who now must understand new behaviors of adversaries, new needs for cooperation, and domains of operations that were not key premises in the development of the institutional/management strategies or organizational understanding. Thus, doubt is cast on the efficacy of a good deal of our current analytical bases for strategic institutional and organizational thinking, and with it public policy formulation and enactment.

In the face of these new uncertainties, I offer some observations about dynamics to consider and improvements to seek. The perspective I outline in this chapter is mainly from the vantage of infrastructure operators. It is informed by the study of institutions whose core technologies prompt the public and its managers to seek extraordinarily high levels of operating reliability – and the harder part – that should be expected to continue for a number of management generations.

RUSH TO RESPOND: REQUISITES THAT UNSETTLE, VECTORS WITHOUT MARKERS

As threats of terrorism on U.S. soil have become vivid, agencies, legislatures, and think tanks have rushed to offer policies and measures to reassure the public with visible evidence of "effective response." Much of the U.S. agencies' responses have been based on existing institutions and received ways of dealing with surprises, but few of these responses were fashioned in the context of the conditions I have just noted. Will continuing to do the things we have known based on the past harbor the "seeds of distressing surprise" and major disappointment?

In the face of demands for nearly failure-free, pre-emptive detection of social predators, society presses institutions to demonstrate extraordinary reliability, enhanced capacity, extensive coverage, and faithfulness. These demands are happening in the midst of current policy regimes that expect "economizing" – that is, rigorous application of cost-reduction measures promoted by the rhetoric of institutional competition that anticipates the failure of operations that do not meet the "expectations of the market." Notably, the players in this market themselves have little experience with sustained social predation.

Demands for highly reliable operations imply stringent measures, not only for the immediate generation but perhaps for several political and management generations of 10 to 15 years each. These demands add to the institutional challenges facing U.S. institutions.

PURSUING HIGHLY RELIABLE OPERATIONS

Organizations that have successfully achieved extraordinary levels of reliable performance share certain common qualities.[3] Those qualities listed in Box 8.1 have been associated with organizations that have evolved with the aim of avoiding certain failures altogether and have largely succeeded. They have, so to say, nullified "Murphy's Law" year after year. This is a remarkable feat, and it is associated with both internal processes and external relations. Their work exhibits the qualities that seem to be necessary if the managers and overseers of U.S. critical infrastructure earnestly seek to enhance super-reliability.[4]

BOX 8.1 CHARACTERISTICS OF HIGHLY RELIABLE ORGANIZATIONS

(Bold items are given special emphasis in the text.)

Internal processes

1. Strong sense of mission and operational goals, commitment to highly reliable operations, both in production and safety
2. Reliability enhancing operations

   - Extraordinary technical competence
   - Sustained, high technical performance
   - Structural flexibility and redundancy
   - **Collegial, de-centralized authority patterns in the face of intense, high tempo operational demands**
   - **Flexible decision-making processes involving operating teams**
   - Processes enabling continual search for improvement
   - **Processes that reward the discovery and reporting of error, even one's own**

3. Organizational culture of reliability, including norms that stress the equal value of reliable production and operational safety

External relationships

1. External "watching" elements

   - **Strong super-ordinate institutional visibility in parent organization**
   - **Strong presence of stakeholding groups**
   - Mechanisms for "boundary spanning" between the units and the "watchers"
   - **Venues for credible operational information on a timely basis**

INTERNAL PROCESSES[5]

Organizationally Defined Intention

Highly reliable organizations exhibit a strong agreed-upon sense of mission and operational goals that stress providing ready capacity for production and service. These operations are equally committed to reliability, and they are backed by a readiness to invest in reliability-enhancing technologies, processes, and personnel resources. When applied to critical infrastructure operations, these goals are strongly reinforced by a clear understanding that the technologies upon which the organizations depend are intrinsically hazardous and potentially dangerous to human and other organisms.

Notably, organizations within the United States often do not have the extraordinary levels of agreement internally about the objectives of operations that are found in the organizations from which this summary was drawn. In highly reliable organizations, there remains high agreement within the operating organizations and in the society at large about the seriousness of operating failures and their potential costliness, as well as the value of their primary missions. This consensus is a crucial element underlying the achievement of high operational reliability. If consensus is absent or attenuated, so is the assurance of the resources needed to carry out failure-preventing, quality-enhancing activities. Agreement of objectives also serves to stiffen corporate or agency resolve to provide the organizational status and financial and personnel resources such activities require.

Reliability-Enhancing Operations

Reliability-enhancing operations include the working dynamics that arise when extraordinary performance must be the rule of the day, and the norms that reinforce an organizational culture of reliability.[6] A dominant quality associated with highly reliable operations is an intensive technical and social interdependence. Highly reliable organizations characteristically contain numerous specialized functions and coordination hierarchies, which prompts patterns of complexly related, tightly coupled technical and work processes that shape the organization's social, structural, and decision-making character.[7]

The social character of highly reliable organizations is typified by high technical and professional competence, technical knowledge of the system, and a demonstration of high performance and awareness of the system's operating state.

Extraordinary technical competence in the case of those who operate critical infrastructures almost goes without saying. But continuously attaining very high quality in these institutions requires close attention to recruiting, training, staff incentives, and ultimately the authority relationships and decision processes among operating personnel who are, or should be, consummately skilled at what they do. This vigilance requires a premium placed on recruiting members with extraordinary skills and an organizational capacity that allows employees to burnish their skills in situ via continuous training. The organization must also emphasize reliable knowledge of the fundamentals of the operating systems. Maintaining high levels of competence and professional commitment also means assuring elevated organizational status and placing high-reliability professionals in positions with ready access to senior management.[8] In aircraft carrier operations, for example, high-ranking officers are assigned to positions of safety officers reporting directly to the ship's captains.

Highly reliable organizations achieve high levels of operational performance by accompanying their operations with stringent quality assurance maintenance measures, buttressed by procedural acuity.[9] Extensive performance databases track and calibrate technical operations and provide unambiguous descriptions of the systems' operating states. The level of attention to such self-scrutiny varies significantly from one critical infrastructure domain to another. Some of the most vigilant, such as the nuclear industry, have devoted extraordinary effort to the investment of collecting system performance data. These data inform reliability statistics, quality control processes, accident modeling, and interpretations of system readiness from a variety of perspectives. In some organizational settings, the effectiveness of these analyses is enhanced by vigorous competition between groups formally responsible for safety.[10]

The operations of highly reliable organizations are further enabled by structural features that exhibit operational flexibility and redundancy in simultaneous pursuit of safety and performance. They also feature overlapping or nested layers of authority relationships.

Working with complex technologies is often hazardous, and operations are often carried out within quite contingent environments. Critical infrastructure operations vary considerably in this regard, but all face publics that insist on uninterrupted provision of services. Effective, continuous performance calls for flexibility and reserve capacity to ensure safety and protect performance resilience.

Structural flexibility and redundancy are evident in three ways: key work processes are designed so that parallel or overlapping activities can provide backup in the case of overload or unit breakdown, and operational flexibility in the face of surprise; operators and first-line supervisors are trained for multiple jobs via systematic rotation; and jobs and work groups are related in ways that limits the interdependence of incompatible functions.[11] The three characteristics command the attention of systems engineering and operational managers in most infrastructure operations and other large-scale technical programs. But there is usually less explicit attention to understanding the organizational relationships that enhance their effectiveness. Notably, many of these activities become the objects of close scrutiny when economizing efforts are mounted.

Formal authority in large organizations is likely to be predominately hierarchical although these dynamics may have as much to do with adjudication as command. In highly reliable organizations, top down, command-like authority is most clearly seen during times of relatively routine operations. But importantly, two other authority patterns are also nested within or overlaid upon these formal relations: one is collegial and functionally based relationships; another is emergency responses. Participants who during routine times act out hierarchical roles, switch to these other patterns in extraordinary times when the tempo of operations increases. Members who are the most skilled in meeting the increased demands step forward without bidding to take charge of the response, while others who may "outrank" them slip informally into subordinate helping positions. During acute emergencies, another well-practiced, almost scripted set of relationships take over, again carried out by the same operating members. Thus, as routine operations become high tempo, and perhaps giving way to emergencies, an observer would see communication patterns and role relationships changing to integrate the skills and experience called for by each situation.

Within highly reliable organizations' structural relationships, decision-making dynamics are flexible, dispersed among operational teams, and include rewards for the discovery of incipient error. Decision making within the shifting authority patterns, especially operating decisions, tends to be decentralized to the level where actions must be taken. Tactical decisions often develop on the basis of intense bargaining and/or collegial interaction among those whose contributions are needed to operate effectively or problem solve. Once determined, decisions often are executed very quickly with little chance for review or alteration.[12]

Due in part to the perceived irreversibility of decisions, highly reliable organizations place a premium on increasing the likelihood that decisions will be based on the best information available. They also try to ensure that their internal technical and procedural processes, once enacted, will not become the sources of failure. This leads to quite formalized efforts continually in search of improvement via systematically gleaned feedback and periodic program and operation reviews.

These feedback and review systems are frequently conducted by internal groups formally charged with searching out sources of potential failure as well as improvements or changes in procedures to minimize the likelihood of failure. On occasion, several groups are structured and rewarded in ways that puts them into direct competition with each other to discover potential errors. They are also likely to be formally attached to different reporting levels of the management hierarchy, thus encouraging the quick forwarding of information – even negative information – about potential flaws to higher authority.[13]

Notably, in many organizations not considered highly reliable, the identification of potential flaws is seen intrinsically as blame putting. While negative reporting may be sought by upper management in a wide variety of other types of organizations, they are rarely conducted with much enthusiasm. In contrast, highly reliable organizations exhibit a quite unusual willingness to reward the discovery and reporting of error, without peremptorily assigning blame for its commission. This pertains even for the reporting of one's own error in operational and procedural adherence. The premise of such rewards is that it is better and more commendable for one to report an error immediately than to ignore or to cover it up. These dynamics rarely exist within organizations that operate primarily on punishment-centered incentives, that is, most public and many private organizations including those that operate critical infrastructure.

Organizational Culture of Reliability

Sustaining the organizational supports for reliability and the processes that increase it put additional demands on the already intense lives of those who operate and manage large-scale advanced technical systems. Operating effectively calls for a level of personal engagement and attentive behavior that is unlikely to be manifest merely on the basis of formal rules and economic incentives. Fully engaged "reliability professionals" respond as much to norms of individual and group relations that grow out of the particular demands and rewards of the hazardous systems involved as they do to financial rewards.[14] The slippery concept of "organizational culture" roughly describes this phenomena: a culture of organizational reliability refers to the norms, shared perceptions, work ways, and informal traditions that arise within the operating and overseeing of groups closely involved with hazardous systems.[15]

While highly reliable organizations strive equally for high levels of production and safety, they face the challenge of being reliable both as producers (many under all manner of demanding conditions) and as safety providers (under conditions of high production demands). Although most other types of organizations combine varying degrees of production plus service/safety emphases, highly reliable organizations must continuously strike a balance regardless of operating circumstances. In times of routine, safety wins out (although watchfulness is harder to sustain); in times of high tempo or emergency, this becomes reordered (although watchfulness is much more acute). This shift suggests an organization flexibly integrating the familiar norms of mission accomplishment and production with those of the so-called safety culture.[16]

Elements of the results are operator/member élan, operator autonomy, and intrinsic tension between skilled operators and technical experts. Operating personnel hold strong expectations for themselves about the value of skilled performance. In the face of hazard, they exhibit a kind of prideful wariness. There are often intense peer group pressures to excel as a highly competitive team and to cooperate with and assist each other in the face of high operating demands. Operators are expected to fulfill responsibilities that often go well beyond formal role specifications. For example, there is a view that "whoever spots a problem owns it" until it is mitigated or solved. This sometimes results in operators realizing that, in the face of unexpected contingencies, they may have to "go illegal," that is, to go against established formal standard operating procedures if these procedures appear to increase the difficulty of safely meeting the service demands placed on the organization. Operator élan is reinforced by clearly recognized peer group incentives that signal high status and respect, pride in one's team, emphasis on peer "retention," and social discipline, and rewards for contributing to quality-enhancing, failure-preventing activities.

Hazardous operations are often critical, and effectiveness depends on keen situational awareness. When it becomes clear that speedy decisive action must be taken, there is little opportunity for assistance or approval from others.[17] Partly as a result, "reliability professionals" come to develop and insist upon a high degree of discretion, autonomy, and responsibility for activities on their watch.[18] Often typified as being "king of my turf," this attitude is seen as appropriate by both other operators and supervisors.

But operator autonomy often comes with significant tensions. The highly reliable organizations we studied all operated complex technical systems that put a premium on technical engineering knowledge as well as highly skilled operating knowledge and experience. These two types of skills are usually formally distinct in the occupational role designations within highly reliable organizations. Each has a measure of status and each depends on the other for critical information in the face of potential system breakdown and recovery, if problems cannot be contained. But the operators view themselves as having the ultimate responsibility for safe effective operation. They also have an almost tactile sense of how the technical systems actually function in the organization's operating environments – environments that are likely to be more situationally refined and more credibly understood than can be derived from the more abstract, cognitively based knowledge possessed by engineers. The result is a tension between operators and technical experts, especially when operators judge an activity to require extensive on-the-ground operating and tacit knowledge about system operations that is based on long experience.[19]

These dominant work ways and attitudes about behavior at the operating levels of highly reliable organizations stem from carrying out hazardous activities and suggest the important affective nature of highly reliable operations. These patterns provide the basis for the expressive authority and "identitive compliance"[20] norms that sustain the close cooperation necessary for people facing unexpected high tempo/high surge situations while minimizing internal harm to people and capital.

EXTERNAL RELATIONSHIPS

Highly reliable operations depend on extraordinarily dense patterns of cooperative behavior within the organization. These are extensive and often quite intense – unusual both in terms of achieving continuous reliability and in incurring higher costs. As such, they are difficult to sustain in the absence of external reinforcement. Continuous attention both to achieving organizational missions and to avoiding serious failures also requires repeated interactions with elements in the external environment, not only to ensure resources, but, as importantly, to buttress management resolve to maintain the internal relations outlined above and to nurture highly reliable organizations' culture of reliability.

External "watchers" can enter at any point, but they are especially common when major failures are seized upon as a chance to ventilate concerns about operational reliability. Watchers include externally situated independent public bodies and stakeholding interest groups, and the institutional processes that assure their presence, efficacy, and use of tools for external monitoring in the interest of hazard evaluations. Aggressive knowledgeable watchers increase the likelihood that reliability-enhancing operations and investments will be seen as legitimate by corporate and regulatory actors. Watchers also promote the view that such costs *should* be incurred and that regulations and internal social demands should be allowed in the interest of safety. Achieving an effective watcher community may mean, on one hand, investing in development and training of external review groups and investing in behavioral surveillance instruments (e.g., random drug tests), and, on the other hand, assuring the watchers that organization leaders will quickly be held accountable for changes that could reduce reliability in service or safety.

Clear institutional interests are crucial to highly reliable performance. These interests should be evident in strong, super-ordinate institutional leadership in the parent organization, such as corporate- or command-level officers (e.g., utility corporate headquarters, higher military command, Washington, D.C., agency headquarters) and industrial association watchdogs (e.g., the nuclear industry's Institute for Nuclear Power Operators).[21]

At the same time, the persistent presence of external stakeholding groups assures attentiveness. These groups range from formal public watchers, such as regulatory overseers (e.g., the Nuclear Regulatory Commission, Environmental Protection Agency, Federal Emergency Management Agency, Occupational Safety and Health Administration, and public utility commissions), user and client groups (e.g., commercial pilots and members of Congress), and a wide sweep of "public interveners" (e.g., state and local governments, land use advocates, and citizen interest groups). Finally, the important function of watcher is also played by professional peer bodies and by organization alumni who are seen as operationally knowledgeable observers. They are likely to be accorded respect both by other outsiders and by the operators themselves.

An abundance of external watchers is crucial in attaining continuous high reliably operations and a culture of reliability. Likewise, boundary-spanning processes are also important. Through these processes, encouragements and constraints are exercised in the interest of product safety and reliability. Two types are evident: First, there are formally designated positions and/or groups who have oversight responsibilities. One example of a formalized channel within critical infrastructure operations is the Nuclear Regulatory Commission, which assigns two or three residents to each nuclear power plant. Residents have nearly complete access to power plant information, meetings, and other operations. Another example is the military's liaison officers assigned to air traffic control centers. Sometimes boundary-spanning activities take place in aircraft carrier operations via dual reporting requirements for nuclear engineering officers – the officers must report problems immediately to both the ship's captain and a central nuclear affairs office at Naval Headquarters in Washington, D.C.

The second type of boundary spanning occurs in the form of periodic formal visits from review groups who can exercise powerful sanctions if their reviews do not measure up. Some examples of these reviews include phased inspections and training checks in aircraft carrier combat preparations, Inspector General inspections of performance, and rigorous reviews by the Independent Nuclear Powers Operators, and the Nuclear Regulatory Commission, which mandates biannual activation of power plant emergency scenarios (these scenarios engage the relevant local and state decisionmakers in a day-long simulation leading to possible regional evacuation under the watchful eye of agency inspectors).[22]

External watchers, however well provided with avenues of access, must have available full, credible, and current information about system performance. These data, often in the form of annual evaluations, hazard indices, statistical summaries, and indicators of incipient harm and the early onset of danger, become a crucial bases for insightful reviews and public credibility.

Together, the activities noted previously signal the demanding nature of highly reliable performance requirements. Perhaps the most arresting is the need to reward the discovery and reporting of error, even one's own. This is a formidable array of conditions for any organization to seek or to sustain, even for short periods of time. But achieving very high reliability across a widely dispersed domain for a short time, while quite important, is not the only institutional challenge, and it is perhaps not even the most central one in the case of critical infrastructure.

In providing adequate responses to martyr operations, potentially to be launched by radical Islamic networks, the period of watchfulness is likely to extend well into the middle of the 21st century. Nearly failure-free performance, then, should be sought over the lifetime of the threat – perhaps at least the next 60 years.[23] The long time frame signals the need for institutional stability for at least 15 presidential terms and at least 6 significant changes in worker and management generations (assuming 10-year generations).

Resolving to attain highly reliable performance for all relevant critical infrastructure operations – even without the possibility of predatory attack – is a remarkable reach. It implies that in a democracy reliable service can be provided in such a manner that it will also nourish the public's confidence in the infrastructure's long-term consistency. To shoulder the burdens of retaining consistency in the face of social predation adds greatly to the institutional challenges of infrastructure management.

ASSURING INSTITUTIONAL CONSTANCY AND FAITHFULNESS IN THE FUTURE

Many organizations operate systems for which the full range of positive and negative outcomes can be perceived more or less immediately. If there is full disclosure of failures and successes, organizational leaders can be held accountable and rewarded. Indeed, some highly reliable organizations such as aircraft carrier operations and air traffic control systems can be judged in this fashion. So can many of the infrastructures critical to everyday life. But three conditions now combine to dramatically alter the relationship between present action, measured results, and subsequent reward.

First, a growing number of large-scale systems – infrastructure operations among them – address missions for which success depends on persisting well beyond the life span of their initiating management generation and on assuming relative institutional stability across several decades. Second, many of these large-scale systems are capable of severe, often widely distributed harm (even if they are not intentionally damaged), some of which may not occur or be detected for several operational generations. Third, since entering the post-9/11 world, the emerging threats from radical Islamic groups means that infrastructure operators must plan for infrequent, unpredictable attack and disruption for perhaps the next 100 years.

Critical infrastructure operations in the United States vary in the degree to which they exhibit different combinations of these conditions. As these vary, so do the institutional challenges that arise from them. For the discussion in this chapter, the U.S. public will be assumed to insist on high quality service

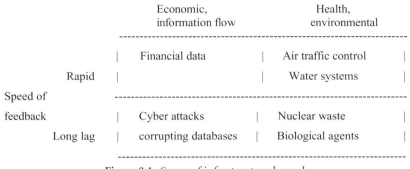

	Economic, information flow		Health, environmental	
Rapid	Financial data		Air traffic control	
			Water systems	
Long lag	Cyber attacks corrupting databases		Nuclear waste Biological agents	

Figure 8.1. Scope of infrastructure hazard.

uninterrupted across the foreseeable future from all the infrastructures considered critical. Holding these two conditions constant, these critical systems will differ in the degree to which failures can results in economic, health, and environmental damage, and in the speed with which such damage is detected (Figure 8.1).

The array in Figure 8.1 assumes that these conditions take place in times of more or less benign normal operations. Notably, when feedback is rapid, the familiar processes of accountability work as expected. As the time lengthens before failures and damage are detected, these processes of accountability falter. How can the decisionmakers be held accountable if the results of their decisions cannot be judged until perhaps years after they have retired or died?

As the sensitivity of infrastructure failure to time lag is recognized, infrastructure overseers and the public are likely to be concerned that some critical infrastructure operations, such as nuclear power and biological engineering, need to be worthy of the trust placed in them across many management generations. In more extreme cases (e.g., the management of nuclear weapon materials), obligations can be expected to continue for perhaps as long as a century. These and other cases suggest an obligation to demonstrate faithful adherence to a mission and its operational imperatives for a remarkably long time – and in the face of a variety of social and institutional environmental changes.

A requirement to take into account the inter-generational nature of infrastructure operations, such as nuclear power and other hazardous systems, presents particularly troublesome challenges for managers and for students of organization.[24] It is these aspects of highly reliable operations about which the social and management sciences have the least to say. This is the case even when these institutions operated in a more or less peaceful and stable environment. If one adds to Figure 8.1 the variable of "likelihood of aggressive attack at irregular, unpredictable intervals via shadowy, unexpected means," the institutional challenges mount quickly. In the face of this kind of social predation, social science, management studies, and systems engineering have even less to say.

As a step toward addressing the analytical deficits facing inter-generational operations, the concept of "institutional constancy" applies.[25] More formally, institutional constancy refers to "faithful, unchanging commitment to, and repeated attainment of performance, effects, or outcomes in accord with agreements by agents of an institution made at one time as expressed or experienced in a future time."[26] It includes assuring continued or improved performance in the spirit of the original public's policy bargain as new information, technology, or changed conditions develop. An organization exhibits institutional constancy when, year after year, it achieves outcomes it agreed to in the past (even in the face of virulent attacks from social predators).[27]

CONDITIONS ENCOURAGING INSTITUTIONAL CONSTANCY

Although scant attention has been paid to the systematic examination of the remarkable intentions embodied in institutional constancy, it seems to require demonstrating to the public and major opinion leaders that the agency, public contractors, or firms in question can both be trusted to keep its word for long into the future and to show the capacity to enact programs that are faithful to the original spirit of its commitments.[28] What conditions signal continued political and institutional will, steadfastness in "keeping the faith"?

Constancy is about future behavior, and the organization must signal its collective resolve to persist in its agreements, especially with strong commitments to trusteeship in the interests of future generations, even in the face of attack. Measures that reinforce this perception are listed in Box 8.2.

Assurance of an organization's steadfast will involves the formal, usually written goal of unswerving adherence to the spirit of the initial agreement or commitment. This formal goal may take the form of documents that can be used in the future to hold each generation's organizational leaders accountable for their actions. Steadfastness also involves strong public articulation of commitments to constancy by high-status figures within an agency or firm, calling especially on professional staff and perhaps key labor representatives to emphasize the importance of constancy. Coupled with formal declarations, consistent emphasis upon steadfastness within an organization reinforces the otherwise difficult commitments of resources, energy, and public witness that are needed by key members of the technical staff and work force.

Along with commitment from leadership, organizations need to exhibit strong evidence of institutional norms and processes that reinforce the resolve to persist across many work generations, including (in the public sector) elements in labor contracts that extend over several political generations.[29] When

BOX 8.2 CHARACTERISTICS ASSOCIATED WITH INSTITUTIONAL CONSTANCY

(Bold items are given special emphasis in the text.)

1. Assurance of steadfast political will

   - Formal goal of unswerving adherence to the spirit of the initial agreement
   - Strong articulation of commitments by high-status agency leaders calling on staff in achieving constancy
   - **Clear evidence of institutional norms that nurture the persistence of commitments across many generations**
   - **Vigorous external reinforcement from regulatory agencies and public watching groups**

2. Organizational infrastructure of constancy

   - Administrative and technical capacity to carry out constancy assurance activities re-enforced by agency rewards
   - **Adequate resources to assure the "transfer" of requisite technical and institutional knowledge across worker and management generations**
   - **Analytical and resource support of "future impact analyses"**
   - **Capacity to detect and remedy the early onset of likely failure that threatens the future, with the assurance of remediation if failures occur**

these contracts exist, they bind workers and their leaders to the goals of the agency that transcend management generations. The content of these norms and the processes that reinforce them are not well calibrated, though examples can be found in public activities that evoke the deep loyalty of technical staff and former members. This seems to be the case for elite military units (e.g., the U.S. Marine Corp and Navy SEALs), groups within the Center for Disease Control, and elements within U.S. Air Traffic Control circles. A close examination of the internal processes of socialization that produce such loyalty is warranted.

Constancy involves commitments to courses of action, particularly those for which benefits may be delayed until a succeeding management or political generation. Such commitments are difficult to sustain in the face of U.S. political metabolism. Therefore, vigorous external reinforcement from both regulatory agencies and public watcher groups must be present to assure that the relevant agencies and their contractors will not flag in the performance promised by one generation to the next. In turn, the vigor of outside groups must be reinforced by regularly assuring their formal involvement, providing sufficient resources to sustain their expectations, and prompting their demands for consultation, lest the next generations of leaders waiver in their resolve. The optimum would be when these measures lead to laws, formal agreements, funding, and infrastructure for continual encouragement and sanctions in support of "keeping the faith." The threat of unpredictable social predation introduces a particularly excruciating twist. Acts of social predation can result in great physical and psychic damage, but if they do not occur with some frequency temptations to reduce commitments to the future almost inevitably arise unless concentrated efforts to affirm them are made.

THE INFRASTRUCTURE OF CONSTANCY

While strong motivations and earnestness are necessary, they alone do not carry the day. Other institutional conditions should be present to assure that interested outsiders will perceive that committed actions will, in fact, be carried out across multiple generations.

Technical capabilities and administrative infrastructure are needed to assure performance, along with agency or contractor rewards and incentives for articulating and pursuing measures that enhance constancy and inter-generational fairness. A culture of constancy is nurtured by executive socialization and training processes to reinforce commitments and long-term perspectives. Such processes and resources, however, are rarely provided in today's institutional environments. Rather, perspectives and rewards are typically short term and strongly reinforced by contemporary business and legislative cycles.

The resources and activities needed to transfer the organization's critical operating, technical, and institutional knowledge from one work and management generation to the next include systematic capture of critical skills and operating histories, as well as continuous training and evaluation of each generation's capabilities. A portion of each future generation's presence in the current one helps with the transfer of such institutional knowledge.

Analytical supports should be evident for analysis and decision making that takes into account the interests of the future. For example, "future impact analysis" identifies the effects of present institutional actions on future capabilities. Something like this goes on during budgetary planning efforts but, in the U.S. system, the time frames are invariably short term and tied to the legislative or corporate profit-reporting cycles. Scanning further into an institution's future – at least beyond the present generation – is also called for. Analytical capabilities to assess the future impacts are likely to require at least a small cadre of highly skilled professionals, incentives for rewarding their efforts, and organizational and agency venues where their reflections will have a respected voice. The advent of predatory threats to infrastructure operations, as with other aspects of reliability- and constancy-enhancing activities, greatly adds to the analytical burdens for most infrastructure operators.

Finally, and perhaps most obviously, effective capacity needs to be in place to detect the early onset of likely failures related to the activities that could threaten the future. This analytical capacity should then be joined with institutional capabilities to initiate remedies, along with the assurance of remediation resources in the event failures should occur.[30] Without quite visible, publicly evident, and well-exercised capacity for early warning and pre-emptive remediation, the public is likely to remain skeptical, potentially suspicious, and ripe for mobilization into recalcitrant opposition.[31] Again, a perception that failures could now be perpetrated not only due to the intrinsic demands of infrastructure technologies, operations and natural environments, but the willful action of social predators sharply amplifies the need to demonstrate visibly an institution's capacities to respond to severe damage.

The conditions intended to reinforce the public's sense of assured institutional constancy, however, are demanding and costly. Institutional leaders are not likely to seriously consider developing them without strong external demand. Assurances of constancy are demanded when programs (1) are perceived to have large-scale efforts that may occur across broad spatial and temporal spans and that pose potentially irreversible effects; (2) are also seen as hazardous if failure occurs even if it is unlikely and there are substantial gains for the program's prime beneficiaries; and (3) pose significant risks for which the costs are likely to be borne by future generations that will receive few benefit. While these conditions are evident during benign periods, the threat of social predation is likely to greatly increase the sense of vulnerability.

This third program characteristic – temporal asymmetry of costs and benefits – raises a particularly difficult dilemma: Should current populations endure costs today so that future populations will not have to?[32] Leaders of U.S. critical infrastructure operators and overseers may be reluctant to make present investments to avoid future risks, rather than accruing present benefits. Uncertainty about the knowledge and technological capacity of future generations exacerbates the problem. An optimistic view assumes that difficult problems of today will be more easily solved by future generations.[33] Skepticism about this, however, can hamper proceeding with multi-generational programs. An important part of assuring constancy would be an agreed-upon ethic of how costs and benefits should be distributed across generations. This is especially true when negative operational effects extend far into the future, because it demands that each succeeding generation have the means and capabilities to acquire new information about long-terms effects and consider how to respond, perhaps in the face of changing values about coping with them.

Implementing this array of constancy-enhancing characteristics raises serious operational, political, and ethical questions. Indeed, assurances of institutional constancy for critical infrastructure, such as the management of water and public heath systems, are likely to be demanded as a substitute for accountability.[34]

An apprehensive public seeks assurances that critical infrastructure providers will be uncompromising in their pursuit of highest quality operations through the relevant life times of the systems in question. This means that the quality of both external relations and internal operations should ensure that stakeholders' views will be taken seriously and that organizational processes will result in immediate adjustment to potential errors. If harmful effects are visited upon future generations, assurances of continuity or institutional constancy take on increasing importance. Leaders of such institutions are likely to be pressed to assure the public that, as a condition of winning approval and resources to initiate or continue programs, their agencies and corporate contractors can be expected to keep agreements and commitments far into the future.

EARNEST RESPONSES FROM OBSOLETE INSTITUTIONS?

The array of organizational conditions implied by institutional commitments to achieve extraordinary levels of operational reliability present formidable challenges to political and enterprise leaders. They are very demanding conditions for organizational leaders to consider, much less actively insist upon, encourage, and nurture. It would not be surprising if these conditions were so challenging that infrastructure leaders argue that they are not so "critical" after all.

Many unanswered questions illustrate the shortfalls in the present institutional capacities and the gravity of these gaps. For example, how many of the characteristics of high reliability and institutional constancy presently exist within the private enterprises managing our infrastructure and the public agencies swept up in the homeland security and defense communities? Despite the importance of these high reliability characteristics, very few organizations possess them, and currently they have only modest ideas of how to realize them. The challenge is compounded by the fact that organizations now exist in a public atmosphere of disenchantment with large institutions and distrust in most public agencies, legislative bodies, and major economic institutions.

We must find ways to provide protection against shadowy, sometimes self-sacrificial adversaries bent on delivering economic destruction and culturally disabling fear across our society. This will be doubly difficult for our existing infrastructure institutions and ways of doing things, which have evolved in a social climate where we could assume that our adversaries valued their own survival, we could be comfortable to learn from trial and error (less need for high reliability), and we could imagine global admiration for our culture.

In the past, these conditions have evolved within institutions and society in a good deal of openness, in relatively limited public skepticism, and in only modest acquaintance with social hostility and the need to recover from humanly rooted disaster. But now, persistent threats of social predation on U.S. soil (even with only rare demonstrations of martyr operations) is surely increasing strain within existing public and corporate institutions and throughout the rest of U.S. society. And it is social strain experienced now in the face of strenuous efforts to economizing and continued capital accumulating policies on the parts of major infrastructure institutions.

What are the implications of assuring reliability over many operating generations, and what are the resulting dynamics and cultures of infrastructure institutions across the United States? What changes would we as a society need to make in order to take long-term preparedness seriously and in the face of economizing strategies currently in vogue?

Posing these questions rigorously results in a deepening sense of analytical pessimism. This pessimism is especially acute when considering the analytical means we currently use in operating institutions in contemporary American society. Enterprises and public agencies charged with preparing and responding to terrorist attacks confront a tactical situation that presents novel conditions: conditions that have been rarely taken into account in the development of management concepts and advice. There are many questions, and few answers are possible without considerable systematic reflection.

Agencies and some infrastructure operators are gathering themselves to respond if attacked. These responses, however, are likely to depend heavily on institutional experiences that rarely include the new conditions of a future threat. Errors and unexpected outcomes are likely – this is a relatively familiar lesson of institutional history. Institutions must become especially alert for surprises and errors arising from radical Islamic hostility as firms continue to adopt economizing strategies. While economizing efforts may reduce operating and social vulnerabilities, they more likely (and perhaps inadvertently) intensify them.

We already find ourselves engaged in heated exchanges about the need for early detection of error and self-correction in the interest of homeland security. It is hard to imagine that current economic strategies and public policies will have *only* functional effects on infrastructure robustness (reliability and resilience) in the face of social predation with a sacrificial twist.

We need to prepare our institutions and the public for the likelihood of substantial surprises and shortfalls in operational effects (not an easy thing in our current political culture.) And as we prepare to respond in the face of likely surprises, we should develop ways of doing things that reduce the likelihood of economic, political, and social–psychological damages if attacks do occur. In particular, we should avoid reactions that risk sacrificing social conditions and values that would be unlikely to be recovered when these attacks subside. We need to avoid the erosion or substantial loss of trust in U.S. institutional capacities to ward off or contain threats and occasional severe damage. Likewise, we should be work against the degradation of the nation's capacity to engage in public discourse and judicious behavior with citizens, overseers, and civic leaders about the meaning of casualties, the erosion of civic society, and changes in everyday life and culture.

The picture I have outlined is daunting for institutional leaders, the hard-working operators and reliability professionals, and for policy analysts and researchers more generally. Both our analytical and management communities are behind the curve of confident understanding. Thus, analyses should be done to review the economic, operational, and legal measures proposed to undergird ourselves for an unpredictable future by addressing the following issues: given a variety of plausible institutional responses, which ones would have significant distorting effects, and if these occurred, how much effort and cost would be involved in reversing them? Without such analyses, selecting policy responses are likely to return even greater surprise.

NOTES

1. Glassner 1999.
2. Resilience refers to recovery after a major collapse of service, that is, disaster recovery. Resilience is certainly important and should have a central place in policy and operating considerations, but it needs to be combined with developments that maintain service in the face of extraordinary threat as well.
3. For an overview, see La Porte 1996 and Rochlin 1996.
4. Highly reliable operations have become keenly sought goals for situations that are not so dramatically hazardous in the physical sense (for example, highly reliable organization operations in financial transactions, or in the performance of sophisticated computer chips or large software programs). See Roberts Libuser 1993. In these situations, motivation stems from fear of serious losses that are seen as amounting to institutional (not physical) death. Caution should be taken in drawing generalized inferences from this discussion. These findings are based mainly on three types of organizations, each with a limited number of cases, with bits from others (e.g., Roberts 1993 "Some aspects of organizational cultures and strategies to manage them in reliability enhancing organizations"). Although these organizations operate in different institutional milieu, we cannot say they represent a systematic sample. No one now knows what the population of highly reliable organizations might be.
5. This section draws strongly from La Porte and Consolini 1991; Rochlin et al. 1987; La Porte 1996; Rochlin 1993; Roberts 1990b; and Schulman 1993c.

6. Weick 1987; Roberts 1993.
7. La Porte and Consolini 1991; Rochlin 1993; Perrow 1984; Roberts and Gargano 1989.
8. Schulman et al. 2004.
9. Schulman et al 2004; Bourrier 1996.
10. La Porte and Thomas 1994.
11. See especially Landau 1969; Lerner 1986; Chisholm 1989; and Heimann 1993, on functional redundancy.
12. Roberts 1992; Schulman et al. 2004.
13. La Porte and Thomas 1994.
14. Weick 1987; Roberts 1993; Schulman et al. 2004.
15. The concept of organizational culture captures the sense that there are norms, values, and "taken for granted" modes of behavior and perceptions that shape interpersonal and group relations. At the same time, the concept retains a high degree of operational ambiguity, its use subject to stiff criticism (Ott 1989; Roberts 1993; Rochlin 2001); Trans. of Highly Reliable Organizations: Past Research and Future Explorations. Presented to the workshop on "Approaches to Organizational Reliability", Department Technologies et Sciences de l'Homme, Universite de Technologies de Compiegne, Compiegne, France, Oct. 7–8, 1999. See also Roberts 1990b; Rochlin and von Meier 1994.
16. See Rochlin 1999; cf. Weick 1987.
17. See Weick et al. 1999.
18. Roberts et al. 1994.
19. Rochlin and von Meier 1994; Rochlin 1999.
20. Etzioni 1965 discusses the case of "identitive compliance" as following instructions due to respect for the professional status of those issuing them.
21. Rees 1994.
22. La Porte and Thomas 1994.
23. This timeframe is based on an estimation that radical Islamic leadership will be sustained for this generation, and replicating itself at least twice more. It is possible that the threat of violence on U.S. soil could extend even further than 60 years if the West's response to this conflict is unable to erode the ideological jihadist opposition to "the White Nations and their friends."
24. Two conditions increase the public demands for constancy by undermining the typical means of assuring accountability (and they are sometimes characteristic of hazardous technical systems): (1) when the information needed to provide unequivocal evidence of effects is so extensive and costly that the public comes to expect that it will not be forthcoming, and (2) if harmful effects occur, they are unlikely to be unequivocally detected for some time into the future, due to the intrinsic properties of the production processes and their operating environments. While public sector organizations may come to mind first, the conditions apply with nearly equal force to the private sector in the United States.
25. This section draws from portions of La Porte and Keller 1996. It is also strongly informed by my work at Los Alamos National Laboratory exploring the organizational challenges posed for the laboratory by its missions of "science based stockpile stewardship (of nuclear weapons), "nuclear materials stewardship," and sometimes "environmental stewardship." While the operations of the first two contrasted to the latter are very different, the challenges provoked by the longevity of the materials involved prompts very similar organizational puzzles. For a similar rendering, see La Porte 2001.
26. La Porte and Kelle 1996.

27. For example, the Federal Aviation Administration's air traffic control operations and private air carriers. They have consistently achieved a high level of flight safety and traffic coordination in commercial aviation and flight operations. Other examples include the nuclear navy, which has consistently achieved high levels of safety aboard nuclear submarines and flight operations at sea, and electric utilities, which have achieved remarkably high levels of availability of electrical power. Many universities exhibit constancy in commitments to intellectual excellence by producing highly skilled academics and professionals as well as path-breaking research.

28. There are strong analytical and practical limitations to attaining institutional constancy over many generations, especially (1) weak analytical bases for confidently predicting the outcomes of institutional activities over long periods of time, (2) limited means of reinforcing or rewarding generations of consistent behavior, and (3) scanty knowledge about designing institutional relationships that improve rather than degrade the quality of action taken in the future that is faithful to the spirit of present commitments and agreements. Incentives to improve conditions that would assure institutional constancy are scant, as is interest in analysis that would improve the understanding of institutional and administrative design. Indeed, almost nothing insightful appears in the literature about increasing institutional inertia or constancy. Furthermore, while the two qualities of steadfastness and capable faithfulness to the original spirit of its commitment are closely related, a firm can succeed at one without achieving the other. A highly reliable organization might be able to persuade the public of its firm commitment to certain objectives but actually turn out to be in no position to realize them. Conversely, a highly reliable organization could very well be situated, motivated, and structured to carry out its commitments for years to come but be unable to convince the public of its steadfastness.

29. This point is akin to the arguments made classically by Selznick 1957, about the importance of institutional leadership and the character of the organization's sense of mission.

30. See, for example, La Porte and Thomas 1994. Cf. Shrader-Frechette 1993 and Clarke 1993, for discussions of the conditions that result in operator misperception of risk; conditions that would require strong antidotes if constancy is to be assured.

31. This seems clearly the case in the political and legal travail experienced by the Department of Energy for a number of years. See U.S. DOE 1993.

32. See, for example, Green 1980; Howarth 1991; Norton 1982; and Wenz 1983.

33. For comment of how responsibility should be divided between generations that accounts for changes in knowledge, see Halfele 1990 and Perrings 1991.

34. For those highly reliable organizations whose technical operations and consequences of failure can be seen as having constancy-evoking characteristics (especially in the face of uneven distribution of costs and benefits among generations and the potential for a long lag in discovering information about possibly grievous damages), ignoring constancy imperatives is an institutionally risky business. Setting these matters aside allows suspicion to fester and multiple and, if coupled with conditions that also evoke "reliability and regulatory magnets," they are likely grounds for political opposition and rigorous regulation as a condition for initial approval for new projects.

9

MANAGING FOR RELIABILITY
IN AN AGE OF TERRORISM

Paul R. Schulman and Emery Roe

Imagine a coordinated attack by terrorists striking major electric power transmission lines and facilities in strategic places throughout the American Midwest and Northeast. They are able to knock out more than 250,000 megawatts of peak load electrical capacity and throw more than 50 million people into darkness over a 240,000-km area in the United States and Canada. Without electric power, a variety of other critical services also fail, including water supplies, hospital facilities, and major financial markets all over the globe. Ultimately, security systems are themselves disabled, leaving key infrastructures vulnerable to additional terrorist attacks.

Sound improbable? Many of these conditions actually occurred during the U.S. and Canada blackout of August 14, 2003, caused not by terrorists but by the failure of electric transmission systems themselves.[1] While power was restored quickly in some areas, other portions of major metropolitan centers were without power for more than 24 hours, and some lost service for several days. A report issued in 2002 by a task force headed by former senators Gary Hart and Warren Rudman concluded that as a consequence of a coordinated terrorist attack, because of the lack of replacement parts for aged or customized equipment, "acute [power] shortages could mandate rolling blackouts for as long as several years."[2]

Unprecedented electric power grid failures, information networks under assault by computer viruses and hackers, large-scale transportation systems and water supplies open to terrorist attack, even the prospect of electronic voting exposed to all manner of fraud and undetected error: everywhere our critical infrastructures are vulnerable, "brittle," and less robust than we had thought. Contrary to previous assumptions, it is not enlarging their power or capacity but rather safeguarding the reliability of these complex systems that has become a great preoccupation of the twenty-first century.

"Reliability" has become the watchword of citizens, clients, leaders, and executives. In some cases it means the constancy of service, in others the safety of key activities and processes. Increasingly in an era of terror, reliability means the resilience of operations – their ability to absorb or recover from a shock or attack.

Across sectors and in a number of cases, the approach taken to promote reliability is remarkably similar. Most people assume that the answer to improved reliability lies in better design of complex systems. If we make them more fail-safe or less tightly coupled or more physically dispersed, we will improve their reliability.[3] A variety of re-designs in data processing and electronic communications, and airport and other security systems have already taken place to increase reliability in the face of terrorist threats. More design changes are planned for electricity grids and air traffic control systems.[4] Recent public discussions of business continuity have focused almost exclusively on design solutions to problems of business protection or recovery from external threat.[5]

We question this approach and offer an alternative perspective. The key to increased reliability, particularly in relation to resilience, lies not primarily in the design of large technical systems but in their management. Moreover, the preoccupation with design diverts attention from managerial skills and strategies that could improve reliability. In addition, some design changes already undertaken in these infrastructures actually undermine managerial resources that are needed to better protect the nation. From our research into nuclear power plants, electricity grid control rooms, water system control rooms, and air traffic control centers, we sketch the specifics of the skills set and managerial approaches that promote reliability in settings where high reliability has long been the essential condition, not only of operational success but of organizational survival.[6] We believe that managers and executives, as well as system designers in varied settings, can learn useful lessons from these examples. Further, we believe that in the absence of this understanding, many critical infrastructures are increasingly precarious with respect to reliability, entirely within their own designs, operating on their own terms, and wholly apart from the external threat of terrorist assault.

FOUR PROPOSITIONS FOR RELIABILITY MANAGEMENT

We cast our argument around four propositions about organizations and complex technology:

1. There is an important divergence between dominant approaches to designing systems and the process of managing them. The difference between design and management is above all a difference in cognitive

orientation – ways of seeing, knowing and responding – between different classes of professionals.

2. A distinct set of "reliability professionals" exists, often among middle managers in organizations, who operate complex technical systems. These individuals are specially motivated to make things "turn out right," and they have largely unheralded skills for understanding the world that lies between the general principles and deductive orientations of designers and the case-by-case, experience-based preoccupation of many technicians and front-line operators.

3. Successful reliability management focuses less on safeguarding single-factor performance than on maintaining a set of key organizational processes within acceptable "bandwidths." The boundaries of these bandwidths can be adjusted but only in proportion to improvements in the knowledge base (both formal and experiential) of the organization.

4. Despite the vulnerabilities they generate, centralization and interdependence among the component parts of a complex technical system can be significant resources for managers to draw on to promote high reliability. Despite the efforts of designers to design away these properties to protect against terrorism, they provide options and a frame of reference within which reliability professionals can maximize the resilience of an organization.

THE MANAGERIAL CHALLENGE OF MODERN DESIGN

The world of design – including policy and technical design – is becoming more and more hostile to good practices of organizational management. Several factors are at work. Legal and regulatory policies constrain managers and their decisions. Shifting standards for health, safety, or protecting the environment add confusion to the life of executives and managers. Regulatory demands for transparency of records and decision processes increase the risk of public exposure and/or liability for many management personnel. Yet perhaps the most significant challenge policy poses for managers is that policy is increasingly formal – in standards, analyses, and language – as opposed to the many informal, even ambiguous, processes by which good managers work.

Many policies, be they public or private (a safety regulation or a marketing strategy), rest upon formal models or protocols such as an epidemiological analysis, marketing survey, economic model, or econometric forecast. Their findings are expressed in formally specified terms, far different from the ambiguity of meaning in the ordinary language of everyday use. The standards and conditions specified in the policies are frequently legally defined – in concepts such as "due diligence" or "reasonable risk" or in quantitative terms such as "parts-per-million" or "market-clearing price." Often policy design is founded on a careful legal or technical worst-case standard. Rules are directed to protect against the worst, not the most likely outcome; safeguards against legal liability are imposed, and contracts are written to bind the least trustworthy parties.

The foremost pressure in policy is to be consistent and clear. The maxim of policy design is: "Spell it out, nail it down and, above all, put it in writing." This can be said also of technical designs that follow deductively from formal principles and models of how a complex technology or production process should be expected to work.

Managerial requirements can be quite different. In the world of management, ambiguity can be a strength. Much is accomplished by good judgment, rather than explicit instruction. Ambiguity allows discretion and protects against error in formal commands. Whereas designers value clarity, precision, and consistency, managers value judgment, discretion, and trust. Indeed, in the world of management, judging each case on its own merits may well be the very best analysis possible.

Both sets of values among designers and managers are important. Neither is "incorrect" from the standpoint of its own domain. That said, it is important to understand the differences. First, the two domains are populated by different sets of individual with different outlooks, values, and skills. Design is a province dominated by lawyers, economists, engineers, model-builders, and technical consultants – what organization theorist Henry Mintzberg has called the "technostructure" of an organization.[7] The managerial and operations levels, on the other hand, require a different set of cognitive orientations and skills from those dominant in the design professions.

Their approach to error exemplifies the differences between the two groups of professionals. Designers frequently underestimate the prospects of human error or are committed to its elimination through anticipation and proscription. As one engineer once remarked, "I try to design systems that are not only fool proof but damned-fool proof!" But managers approach error complex systems as inevitable.[8] In fact, good management is in many respects the management of error. Effective training often rests upon trial and error in learning. In some organizations, managers even argue that people are not trying hard enough if they do not make mistakes.[9]

Despite the most careful efforts, design errors or lapses are inevitable. In California electricity deregulation, despite the stated and restated conviction of policy architects – economists, regulators, and legislators – that electricity markets would quickly evolve and attract new players in electricity generation as well as keep wholesale prices down by market forces, managers of the grid confronted quite different conditions. At the height of California's 2001 electricity crisis, controllers encountered many mornings when the few bids to the power pool could not cover anticipated demand for the day. At other times, generators were unavailable to offer power to the state until the last minute during times of peak demand. Large generators came to dominate the market and exercised market power to drive up electricity wholesale prices far beyond what policy architects had anticipated. Skyrocketing energy prices caused the bankruptcy of one of the two major electricity utilities in the state as well as the Power Exchange (an organization established to coordinate and pool market transactions). Finally, the state of California used billions of its budget surplus to support power demands by buying power in spot markets to prevent continued blackouts. The state's electricity crisis created political turmoil that led ultimately to the recall of the governor and a financial catastrophe from which the state has yet to recover. This was hardly a scenario the deregulated system was designed to accommodate. In fact, design errors led to an unstable cycle of underperformance leading to ever more frantic efforts at re-design.[10] As a result, grid managers had to cope with considerable turbulence, unpredictable and substantially unrelenting, and still had to balance load with generation hour after hour.

THE WORLD OF RELIABILITY PROFESSIONALS

What has become evident in our research into how high reliability is achieved by organizations that have to manage critical infrastructures is the importance of the efforts of special individuals. These individuals are likely to have had careers that expose them to many facets of the systems being managed. They are likely to be positioned as shift supervisors, department heads, or technical specialists, to span both the higher-level arenas of design and strategy and the lower-level posts of operations and maintenance. This bridging function is connected with their special cognitive orientation to the work of the organization (Figure 9.1).

From a cognitive standpoint, the quest for reliability in an organization involves at least two dimensions: (1) the types or base of knowledge brought to bear on efforts to make an operation or system reliable, and (2) the focus of attention or scope of these reliability efforts. The knowledge base from which reliability is pursued can range from formal or representational knowledge, in which key activities are understood through abstract principles and deductive models based upon these principles, to experiential knowledge, in which activities are understood based on informal or tacit understanding, generally derived from trial and error. At the same time, the scope of attention can range from an orientation that conceives reliability as a stream of system outputs

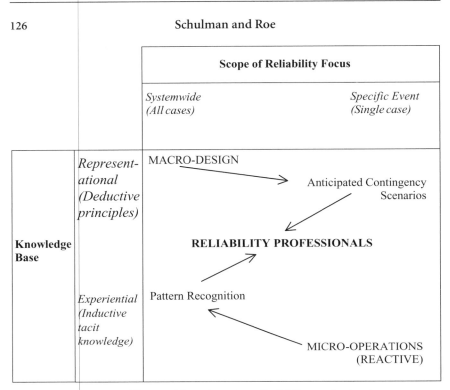

Figure 9.1. The cognitive orientation of reliability professionals.

(the inevitable consequence of having under control many variables associated with producing reliable results), to a case-by-case focus in which each case is viewed as a particular event with distinct properties or characteristics.

Toward one extreme of both scope and principles is the formal design approach to reliability. Here formal deductive principles are applied to understanding a wide variety of critical processes. In a formal approach, it is considered inappropriate to operate beyond the design analysis, and that analysis (and procedures in support of it) is meant to cover an entire critical system, including every last case of possible performance. The design in this sense is more than analysis; it is a major control instrument for the behavior of the system. This is the approach that dominates in a nuclear power plant, where operating "outside of analysis" constitutes a major regulatory violation.

Toward the other extreme is the activity of constant reactive behavior in the face of case-by-case challenges. Here reliability resides in the appraisal and reaction time of operators, rather than in the anticipation of system designers. In air traffic control, for example, it is assumed that the major element in reliability is the skill and judgment of the individual controller applied to specific problems in maintaining aircraft separation in sectors.[11]

The extremes of design versus reactive operation are each insufficient as an approach to providing reliability. Designers cannot foresee everything, and some design errors are inevitable. On the other hand, case-by-case reactions by their very nature are likely to give the operator too specific and individualized a picture, obscuring the proverbial forest for the trees. Experience can become a "trained incapacity," leading to actions that undermine reliability, because operators may not be aware of the wider ramifications of what they are doing.

Given the limitations of the extremes in the orientation to reliability, it is important to operate closer to a shared center by (1) moving from reactions to recognizing patterns beyond individual cases and (2) by moving from designs to contingency planning through the formulation of alternate scenarios. This middle ground is difficult to find for a complex system. But in this middle ground doctrine is tempered by experience, discretion is added to design, and individualized perspectives are reconciled with shared views.

The middle ground is the realm in which reliability professionals function, and their cognitive perspectives are reflected in their managerial strategies. As managers, reliability professionals are likely to relax their commitment to drawing up procedures that fully determine the operations within their organizations. They are likely to embrace contingency analysis, thinking of strategy as a probabilistic, rather than deterministic, undertaking. An example is the "what if" game frequently played by managers pushing their employees to use their imaginations to anticipate responses to a wide variety of potential cases. These professionals are also likely to think of decisions as the beginning, not the end, of options by encouraging consideration of alternative scenarios for decision outcomes.

At the same time, reliability professionals encourage a shift away from crisis management toward recognizing and evaluating patterns over a number of cases. This is really a form of adaptive management – recognizing common patterns and evolving norms, strategies, and even routines to cover similar categories of events or cases. These norms, strategies, and routines are likely to be different from formal procedures and protocols closely linked with design principles. The managerial perspective of a reliability professional is also likely to take into account a larger portion of the system, even larger than the area officially controlled by the manager.

Precisely this approach is well suited for responding to a turbulent environment, whether created by market failure, the failure of equipment, or the failure of available generation to match load. It is also well suited for responding to turbulence introduced by terrorist assault. In practice, however, reliability professionals' perspectives and skills are typically neglected by lawyers, economists, regulators, stakeholders, and the public. Their value is not captured in market pricing or in the internal accounting of organizational assets. Yet it is with this group and their professionalism that we believe the greatest gains in protecting critical infrastructures are to be found.

BANDWIDTH MANAGEMENT FOR ORGANIZATIONAL RELIABILITY

A great deal of research and argument in management theory centers around the question of whether an organization should attempt to design and manage away error through fiat, formal rules, and a mixture of rewards and punishments oriented toward compliance with those rules, or whether managers should embrace error as a necessary requirement for training and an inevitable characteristic of human performance.[12]

Managers who attempt to eliminate error or punish its every instance run the risk of discouraging the reporting of error and propagating an illusion of infallibility that not only precludes learning but leaves the organization unprepared to cope with error when it does occur. On the other hand, tolerating error is also risky in an era of strict legal liability and demands for regulatory transparency.

What we have discovered among high reliability organizations is that the error-avoiding or error-embracing approaches are really not either/or scenarios. The real requirement for high reliability is the management of key organizational activities (including errors) and their outcomes within an acceptable "bandwidth" – or envelope of fluctuations – in important performance factors. The key to reliability in complex operations lies not in attempting to achieve invariance in performance but in trying to put boundaries on deviations and their consequences. Managers try to reduce errors where possible, but they do so as a process of refining the bandwidth, and the reductions cannot be taken for granted but must be continually and actively managed.

In one nuclear power plant, for example, valve technicians in the maintenance department experienced a given rate of "wrong-unit" errors – entering the wrong one of two identical reactor units to do a job. To reduce the rate, a department head introduced a form to be signed by each technician and countersigned by a coworker before starting a job. The form identified the unit to be serviced and the unit the technician was currently in. This added paperwork requirement significantly reduced the number of wrong-unit errors. After a time, however, signing the form itself became part of a routine, and the error rate began to rise again. The department head saw this as an expected part of the continual process of managing error. As he put it, "we'll have to come up with something else to rekindle the fervor."[13] Similar tactics are necessary when work settings call for high levels of mindfulness, close communication and coordination, or even mutual understanding and trust. These properties are all subject to erosion over time. They are not locked-in by rules; they must be actively managed.

A critical issue in managing the reliability bandwidth of an organization is whether the operational area within the bandwidth consists largely of controllable and knowable variables or whether unknowns permeate the operational core of the organization. All else being equal, the more the managers know about what they are managing, the closer in they can draw the boundaries of the bandwidth. Conversely, when significant variables are unknown or uncontrolled, the bandwidth must be wider. It is important that the leaders and managers of an organization, as well as its clients and regulators, understand this, because an attempt to narrow the performance bandwidth on a foundation of uncertainty invites disaster.

A nuclear power plant, for example, can be operated within a narrow regulatory bandwidth because the basic knowledge of the physics and mechanics of the reactors is well understood. In fact, it is legally prohibited to operate outside this narrow performance bandwidth and the system conditions defined within it, either in error or through experimentation.

But in its large-scale electric power grid management, the California Independent System Operator confronts a wide variety of variables that it can neither fully anticipate nor control. Loads may peak at levels that elude forecasts. Transmission lines may be struck by lightning; large generators may go off-line unexpectedly. Here the resilience aspect of reliability becomes the requirement. The operational bandwidth must be wider and the boundaries of acceptable performance more ambiguous, albeit still present and agreed upon. Successful performance may rely more upon improvisation, experimentation, and risk-taking. Operating outside of prior analysis may well be unavoidable.

Understanding the difference between these two types of circumstances and adapting a managerial strategy for each is a reliability requirement. Shrinking the bandwidth is an important reliability commitment when operations rest upon settled knowledge. Indeed, high reliability organizations we studied were constantly attempting to extend careful analysis and control over operational variables. Attempts included automating and continually increasing mindfulness and care among employees. These organizations acted as if reliability improvement were essential in order not to lose the reliability already attained.

For organizations operating within unsettled domains, negotiating boundaries and reliability standards with forces in their environment is an important process. For the California Independent System Operator, negotiations might include the possibility of relaxing regulatory standards regarding transmission line temperature limits and modifying environmental standards for generators during power emergencies.

In brief, it is not management, but hubris, to attempt to shrink bandwidths by political fiat, legal rules, or regulatory punishments that do not rest upon a firm foundation in settled knowledge based on the mix and interaction of formal and informal understandings of the system. Such an attempt would be building control frameworks upon foundations of illusion – hardly a recipe for enhancing the performance reliability of any organization, let alone our critical infrastructures. Yet many system designs and redesigns are currently conducted within this realm of illusion, and they have left our critical infrastructures less reliable, wholly apart from the potential onset of a terrorist assault.

PRICING AND VALUATION ERRORS IN INFRASTRUCTURE DESIGN

As has been observed in the introduction of this volume, security against a terrorist attack has the characteristic of a public good, the costs of which are difficult to internalize in private transactions. For critical infrastructures in particular, the services delivered closely depend upon network capacity to handle many services simultaneously. This means that each transaction has an effect, as an externality, on the reliability of the others. Yet the service price does not reflect this reliability externality. In electricity generation, for example, when load changes unpredictably, or when it increases in the face of uncertain generation or difficult line conditions, the reliability of the entire grid can be affected. Each consumer (and competitive supplier) can have a marginal or even a threshold effect on the managerial challenges facing reliability professionals. But notwithstanding the promises of market designs, it is difficult to isolate and individually price for these effects.

Furthermore, the reliability we seek from these infrastructures is not a property that can be marginalized. Widespread grid blackouts or the destruction of major grid elements are events we must preclude from happening, particularly in light of terrorism. Consumers individually, and the public collectively, do not wish to trade off security against cost savings at the margin. Consumers can scarcely make intelligent trades between the marginal risks associated with these events because neither consumers nor market analysts can appraise the probabilities for such low-frequency occurrences.

Finally, reliability research indicates that the designers, analysts, managers, and top executives of critical infrastructures do not have a clear picture of the "value added" to their services by their own reliability professionals. High reliability is organizationally a holistic property, the value of which is difficult to isolate and assess at the margin. Nor is it easy to identify the point of diminishing returns for reliability investments. As one engineer at a large electrical utility commented, "we may have overbuilt for reliability, but who the hell wants to scale back to find out?"

Reliability professionals themselves make it difficult for their organizations to understand their reliability costs at the margins because they do not signal the approach to edges of reliable performance. With their frequently intense "can do" attitude toward the provision of reliable services, they accept growing challenges to their tasks as part of their responsibility. While they can readily perceive unsafe system conditions, they do not as readily perceive the limits to their capacities under increased load or stress, nor are they likely to complain about these increases. As a consequence, pressure on reliability professionals is all too often treated as a "free good" by system designers and top executives who are trying to maximize efficiency or service loads for critical infrastructures. The moral hazards of such situations only add to the problem.

As we see it, designers, top executives, and consumers all operate with illusory perspectives regarding the reliability and security of critical infrastructures. We all focus on service – its cost, capacity, and quality – but we tend to ignore the actual institutional infrastructure and the organizational tasks, roles, and skills that undergird the service.

DESIGNING FOR RESILIENCE

A monumental debate is taking place among policymakers, executives, and technical experts over how best to protect our critical infrastructures against terrorist attack. These infrastructures include our electricity grids, water supplies, telecommunications, health care system, transportation, and banking and financial services. In the business world, "business continuity" has become the focus for this reliability challenge.[14]

What are the key vulnerabilities? To what extent must the operation of critical services be centralized and "hardened" or decentralized and dispersed to best protect them against assault? Confronting these questions, a panel of the National Research Council of the National Academies released its major findings on counter-terrorism and critical infrastructures in 2002. Its report, *Making the Nation Safer*, asserts that for a variety of infrastructures "interconnectedness within and across systems . . . means that [the] infrastructures are vulnerable to local disruptions, which could lead to widespread or catastrophic failures."[15]

At issue is the notion that critical infrastructures have discrete choke points of vulnerability. If they are attacked or fail, the performance of the entire infrastructure is threatened, according to the current view. Indeed, the existence of choke points, it has been argued, signals the vulnerability of these systems, both inviting and guiding terrorist attack.

From the designers' viewpoint, the only remedy to the vulnerability of complex, tightly interconnected systems is to redesign them to simplify and/or decouple the parts and render them less interdependent. Such a strategy would decentralize power grids and generators, making smaller, more self-contained transmission and distribution systems.[16] In business continuity programs of large companies, the decentralization strategy has involved diversifying the hardware systems and geographically dispersing the databases and data processing.

Our research into the resilience dimension of reliability and especially the world of reliability professionals suggests that this decoupling strategy may be misguided as a means to mitigate vulnerability to terrorism. In fact, redesigns undertaken to decrease interdependence can undermine some of the very features that ensure the operational reliability of these systems in the first place.

As we have indicated, a great deal of the reliability of systems such as the California electricity system is a result of middle-management processes rather than formal design. Grid and service reliability would be impossible without the shift supervisors, dispatchers, technical department heads, and plant managers. These people have established their own informal communication networks, adjust and adapt to the constantly changing circumstances and conditions of the grid, and bring to bear their long experience with all facets of electricity generation, transmission, and distribution for on-the-spot problem solving. Significantly, the absence of such rich communication networks has been cited as factors in blackouts in the northeastern United States and Europe, and has hampered recovery operations in the U.S. Gulf Coast following Hurricane Katrina.

Over the past several years, there has been tremendous turmoil in the restructured California electricity system, including the break-up of three major utilities and the bankruptcy of one of them, the demise of the California Power Exchange, the depletion of the entire state budget surplus through power purchases in the "spot" market in order to keep the lights on, the unprecedented merging of northern and southern California grids into one integrated grid, and the creation of the novel California Independent System Operator to manage that grid. Add to this turmoil the continuing high turbulence in the energy markets, most notably rising energy prices along with the bankruptcy of Enron and the increasing financial difficulties experienced by the remaining large energy suppliers for the state. Surrounding these developments have been pitched battles between the subsequently recalled governor of California and the Federal Energy Regulatory Commission as well as battles between the California Public Utilities Commission, the former governor, and major power generators. Now federal Energy Policy Act of 2005 promises to make major changes in current practices by imposing national reliability standards on both electric grid operators and their power suppliers. Yet through it all, the middle-level managers and control room operators have kept the electrical system operating. Even rolling blackouts – when electricity reserves fell below safe levels relative to peak power demand – were relatively few and short-lived. The real story of California's restructuring is that the lights stayed on, and they stayed on through many close calls because of the dedication, cooperation, and virtuosity among controllers, supervisors, and operators in the middle (in the middle of the "perfect storm in electricity," as many termed it).

The skills, experience, and knowledge of reliability professionals, however, is being lost in the design- and technology-focused efforts of homeland security. Ironically, from an operational standpoint, the prevailing view about terrorism can be stood on its head. Complex, interdependent systems convey reliability advantages to those trained professionals who seek to protect or restore them against terrorist assault. Their complexity allows for multiple strategies of resilience and recovery. Their tightly coupled choke points allow these professionals to see the same portion of the system as do the terrorists, and it positions them to see it whole against a backdrop of alternatives, options, improvisations, and counter-strategy. In contrast, decentralized systems present a great many independent targets to terrorists – they can strike anywhere and, while they may not bring down major portions of the grid, they can still score psychological points. The local managers would probably not have a clear picture of what is happening overall, nor would they have as wide a range of alternatives and recovery options available to them.

The scenario of highly interrelated complex technologies cascading out of control under precisely targeted destruction by saboteurs is not one that anyone should lightly dismiss. But before society starts redesigning critical infrastructures under the assumption that dispersion or decentralization is better than integration or centralization, the undertaking merits a pause and serious thought about what research has already uncovered.

The nation's first lines of defense are its reliability professionals. They are the first ones who should be asked about proposed "improvements." They should be asked how these changes might increase their options to respond to threats and/or enhance their ability to match options to vulnerabilities. Some answers will doubtlessly be both surprising and enlightening to many designers and leaders of organizations – and they may save lives and critical assets in the future.

NOTES

1. U.S.–Canada Power System Outage Task Force 2004.
2. Regalado and Fields 2003.
3. National Research Council 2002b; Farrell et al. 2002; Perrow 1999.
4. For example, see Apt et al. 2004.
5. For example, see *Financial Times* 2005.

6. Research has been conducted over many years as part of understanding the challenges and competencies of "high reliability organizations" (see LaPorte 1996; Rochlin 1993a; Schulman 1993b, 1993c, 2002). The analysis of electrical grid reliability has been undertaken over a five-year period and has involved more than 85 interviews with managers, dispatchers, engineers, and regulators within private utilities and power generators, the California Independent System Operator, the California Public Utilities Commission, and the California Energy Commission. Our research is also informed by more than 100 person-hours of direct control room observation. Findings regarding the effect of the California electricity crisis on grid and service reliability can be found in Roe et al. 2002, 2005; Schulman et al. 2004; De Bruijne et al. in press; and Van Eeten et al. in press.
7. Mintzberg 1979.
8. See Apt et al. 2004.
9. Bosk 2003.
10. For a parallel example in regulation, see Mendeloff 1988.
11. Schulman 1993b.
12. Researchers argue that an organization's capacity to persist and grow depends on its ability to embrace error and learn from failure. Michael (1973) puts it this way: "future-responsive societal learning makes it necessary for individuals and organizations to embrace error." Korten (1980) maintains that the best organizations are ones "with a well developed capacity for responsive and anticipatory adaptation – organizations that: (a) embrace error; (b) plan with the people; and (c) link knowledge building with action." Bennis and Nanus (1987) conclude from studies on leaders that they must embrace error and not be afraid to make mistakes, and admitting them when they do. Schein (1994) sums up: "We come to embrace errors rather than avoid them because they enable us to learn." More recently a *Harvard Business Review* article, "The Failure-Tolerant Leader," reports that such leaders "don't just accept failure; they encourage it" (Farson and Keyes 2002, p. 66). Whereas an error-intolerant perspective would view the organization only as reliable as its first failure, an error-tolerant perspective would view the learning organization as failing every time until the last one.
13. Schulman 1993a.
14. Shrader and Woolsey 2002.
15. National Research Council 2002.
16. Farrell et al. 2002.

10

ORGANIZATIONAL STRATEGIES FOR COMPLEX SYSTEM RESILIENCE, RELIABILITY, AND ADAPTATION

Todd M. La Porte

With thousands of miles of unprotected borders, tens of thousands of critical power generating plants, chemical processing units and other hazardous manufacturing facilities, and hundreds of thousands of miles unprotected roads and rail, electric, gas, and telecommunications lines, the United States is impossible to protect completely against terrorist attack. In addition to military action against terrorists abroad and use of intelligence to intercept attacks before they are launched, what organizational strategies are best suited for providing homeland security and protecting critical infrastructure? In this chapter, I address the problem of critical infrastructure protection from an organization studies perspective. I begin by discussing the nature of critical infrastructures as large technical systems with distinct organizational properties. I then turn to organizational strategies to deal with what is identified as a "wicked" problem. While no specific organizational solution will solve critical infrastructure protection, a number of strategies may help solve it, notably the encouragement and protection of high reliability organizations and professionals who work in them. Finally, I argue that political leadership will be necessary to effect the changes proposed.

THE NATURE OF CRITICAL INFRASTRUCTURES

Critical infrastructures exhibit characteristics of large technical systems.[1] Their technology and organization are highly complex. Key elements are geographically dispersed, but they are linked together in networks and nodes, with varying degrees of connectivity. Some systems, such as telecommunications and electric power, operate in real-time (meaning that there is no possibility of stockpiling or scheduling demand – the whole system, from end to end, is "on" all the time). Other systems are less subject to the requirements of real-time operations, but even short or unexpected interruptions, for example in local road or container cargo traffic, can cause major economic and social disruption. The disruptions caused by Hurricanes Katrina and Rita on oil wells and refineries in the Gulf Coast region are cases in point.

As examined in more detail in Part IV of this book, most critical infrastructures are highly interdependent: telecommunications and electric power systems require each other to function, and both support the operations of almost every other element of infrastructure, including the Internet. Water distribution depends to a great extent on electric power for pumping and water treatment. Road traffic would quickly snarl if control systems were without electricity and telecommunications. Electric power generation would be compromised by disruptions in pipeline, rail, or truck transportation.

Large technical system organization is tightly coupled as well, which for normal operations improves efficiency. However, it is increasingly recognized that tight coupling can also lead to increased vulnerability to disruption, prompting many organization managers to adopt defensive management practices, stockpiling, and extensive relationship-building with outside organizations, which can reduce the very efficiency tight coupling is intended to increase.

Sociologist Charles Perrow argues that failure is inherent in complex tightly coupled systems: the centralization of decision-making authority required to manage tight coupling conflicts with the decentralization of authority required to deal with unanticipated problems by those closest to them throughout the organization.[2] Operators of complex tightly coupled systems need, but generally cannot have, both centralization and decentralization to make sure that such systems do not fail across a wide variety of operating conditions.

These management requirements are different from those of loosely coupled systems, such as most manufacturing, mining, office work, and lab research, where authority can be either centralized or decentralized, as the task dictates. The management requirements of tightly coupled but linear systems, such as continuous process industries, most transportation, and regulated electric power, are also different: authority by operators can be centralized because the information needed is easily provided and acted upon.

Technological change in and of itself may be a source of disruption to large complex systems, or at least it may establish conditions that make disruptions easier to achieve. New technologies require new organizational structures and processes and often demand that employees acquire new skills and ways of working.[3] When change is very rapid, the gap between the new technological capabilities and the capacity to regulate, monitor, or mediate the effects of these technologies may be wide enough that economic or social problems arise.

The history of most important technologies demonstrates this. It took some years, and many accidents, after automobiles were introduced for traffic regulation systems to be instituted. The electricity crisis in California in 2000 and the August 14, 2003, blackout in the United States and Canada both show how technological change, in these cases arising from deregulation, make system stability more problematic. The lag between a technical system's new operating conditions and the economic, regulatory, and social frameworks that shape and moderate the effects of the newly "liberated" technologies, means that unintended negative consequences may accompany the intended positive ones.

THREATS TO CRITICAL INFRASTRUCTURE PROTECTION

Different types of potential disruptions demand different types of organizational responses, some of which contradict others. Relatively well-understood and regular sources of disruption, such as hurricanes or other severe weather, permit routinized responses. These responses often include well-structured organizations, relatively predictable budget requirements, building codes to reduce vulnerability, and standardized emergency preparedness procedures.

On the other hand, terrorism exhibits high variability and dynamic uncertainty.[4] The unpredictability of the threat demands that organizations become more internally complex, engage in more interaction with outsiders, become more flexible in their organizational structures, and become more adaptive to a wide range of possible contingencies. In terrorism, purposive actors or predators may seek vulnerabilities in complex systems and try to exploit them for maximum disruptive effect. Terrorists understand that disrupting infrastructures multiplies damage throughout society, signals that public authorities are powerless to stop attackers from pursing their political objectives, and limits the ability of the government to provide for its own citizens.

Attacks involving chemical, biological, or nuclear weapons pose the possibility of far greater damage to life and property than is likely to be achieved by conventional weapons. Preliminary data suggest that chemical, biological, and nuclear attacks may be increasing in frequency, but they are still rare and difficult to carry out.[5] Creating a highly effective weapon of mass destruction from toxic chemicals, infectious diseases, or fissionable nuclear material – a process called "weaponization" – is more difficult than many believe. Nevertheless, security authorities are concerned that the technologies of weaponization will spread as familiarity with the technologies increases, particularly with the availability of freelance unemployed former Soviet and South African weapons scientists, and as costs of biotech equipment and supplies continue to decline.[6]

Terrorist attacks are serious challenges for many organizations that have previously faced stable environments and no predators, as well as for organizations that face regular or predictable extreme events, such as hurricanes. Both types of organizations may be called on to deal with both routine and non-routine types of events, but for them to do so will entail the ability to operate in both modes interchangeably. More importantly, multiple-mode readiness will require that organizations maintain multiple operational capabilities, and that they protect those capabilities in often difficult budgetary and political circumstances. Emergency management and preparedness organizations find it difficult to sustain public and policy attention to their needs once a disaster has passed.

As early as 1976, sociologist Barry Turner studied disasters to find out why many organizations fail to heed what in retrospect were signs of impending disaster.[7] He found that the conditions under which large-scale intelligence failures result include: rigid institutional beliefs, disregard of outside complaints, difficulty handling multiple sources of information, and the tendency to minimize danger. These elements incubate until they become part of the organizational culture, setting the stage for a serious problem to be triggered by an event that in other circumstances might be easily dealt with.

Turner argues that organizations perform poorly when faced with ill-structured problems, which they generally attempt to address by simplifying reality, falling back on habit or ritual, or resorting to rules of thumb. Some organizations attempt to deal with uncertainty by identifying goals and developing plans to achieve them, but in contingent and complex situations they have a hard time knowing whether they have done enough. Thus, organizations that fail to take steps to develop flexible, complexity-embracing and problem-seeking capabilities – and fail to develop organizational cultures that learn from their environments – are likely to experience a disaster in one form or another.[8]

Such observations have important implications for public safety and homeland security organizations. Emergency management and fire and police forces each have a clear mission and have operated in stable task environments, and they have largely been ability to manage most contingencies successfully. Changes have come, to be sure: over the last several decades, the "all hazards" approach to dealing with disasters has supplanted the segmented approach to emergency management and public safety, resulting in increased attention to cross-training and coordination among different emergency response units.

Terrorism, however, poses fundamental challenges to first responders and public safety practices. One wonders how effective any U.S. public safety organization can be in the face of suicide bombers or biological attacks, for example, neither of which have been used widely, if at all, in the United States. Even countries such as Israel, where suicide bomb attacks occur regularly, have great difficulty in combating the problem and reorganizing both organization struc-tures and practices to attempt to keep on top of it.

Given the difficulties facing public safety organizations, it should be no surprise that serious challenges are also facing the operators of large tech-nical systems. In the United States, these systems are mostly held in private ownership, and their public regulators are mostly unfamiliar with day-to-day operations. Firms and their regulators each have a history of operating in a safe domestic environment, often as regulated monopolies, with linear and less tightly coupled systems and, until more recently, have operated with relatively low levels of system interdependency.[9]

Today, however, with greater interdependency, more exposure to market forces, greater geographic dispersion, and, in some cases, more components that are unique and difficult to replace (as is the case with aging transformers in electric power distribution), large technical systems are more difficult than ever to manage successfully.[10] In addition, many of these infrastructures have themselves become more complex, through new developments in technology and/or as they face newly deregulated markets. Even without the added threat of terrorism, these systems are facing unprecedented stress, increased operating volatility, and occasionally costly system failures.[11]

RESPONSE STRATEGIES

Despite advances in risk assessment methods and improvements in the gov-ernment's ability to manage disaster response successfully, extreme events – particularly technological or industrial disasters – appear to be increasing in frequency and severity. Terrorist attacks, while historically insignificant sources of harm to the United States, are increasingly worrisome because of their unpre-dictability in type, scale, and timing. Industrial accidents and terrorist attacks may be characterized by indeterminate but potentially catastrophic damage over large areas, poor and/or rapidly changing situational information, lack of precedent on which to base problem assessment and response, unfolding of events in real time, and active mass media coverage worldwide.[12] This combi-nation could be termed a "wicked problem" of crisis management and critical infrastructure protection. [13]

Rittel and Weber coined this term to describe a class of problems for which there is no definitive problem formulation, for which it is difficult to tell when the problem is solved, – that is, there is no "stopping rule" – and for which there are no unambiguous solution criteria, or in fact any well-described set of possible solutions, because such problems are essentially unique. Wicked problems are often symptoms of other wicked problems, because they often interlock, change over time and depend highly on specific contexts. In fact, different stakeholders will describe the same wicked problem in quite different ways. What is more, in working on these problems, analysts do not have the luxury of failing, or of learning by trial and error. Examples of wicked problems include thorny value-laden issues such as siting of toxic waste facilities, dealing with environmental problems, reforming social security systems, and establishing fair taxation schemes. Ordinary problem-solving techniques cannot yield unambiguous or widely accepted solutions.

The implications of wicked problems for critical infrastructure protection are serious. Their wickedness implies that solutions that aim to maintain current ways of life without any change may not be possible, or if possible, may not be beneficial. The inherent openness of the United States, both culturally and geographically, limits the ability of any strategy of "hardening" to be completely effective. As government officials often assert, the nation's defenders have to be successful *all* the time, whereas terrorists only have to be successful once. While the homeland security initiatives undertaken by the government are mostly prudent, worthwhile, and uncontroversial, they will not completely protect the nation from another serious terrorist attack. Therefore, it is worth exploring additional strategies to anticipate, adapt to, or respond to attacks or extreme events. These may be divided in three major groups:

- *Macro strategies* – strategies implemented by the government to address external threats: border control, asset hardening, protection, and coordination of emergency response
- *Micro strategies* – strategies implemented by specific organizations to limit vulnerability to disruption or to prevent predators from using organization as launching pads for attacks: vulnerability assessments, contingency and continuity of operations planning
- *Structural strategies* – strategies implemented by government together with key private or non-governmental organizations to deal with industry operations on a sector-wide or intersystem basis

Macro strategies are the essence of what the federal government has undertaken in the months following September 11, 2001. Asset identification and protection is at the heart of critical infrastructure protection as defined by the Office of Homeland Security and later the Department of Homeland Security. Strengthening emergency response capabilities by improving first responder coordination across various governmental and territorial jurisdictions is another type of macro strategy.

Micro strategies are essentially what public and private businesses and organizations do in conducting infrastructure vulnerability assessments. Contingency planning, business continuity planning, and incident management are all terms to describe the analysis of business processes with a specific focus on minimizing obvious weaknesses that predators could use to disrupt operations or launch further attacks. Perimeter and facilities access control, employee background checks, co-location of utilities, siting of key facilities and the like make up the core elements of these micro strategies of critical infrastructure protection. These measures are less often the subject of governmental policy and more often the result of prudent operations management and planning.

Macro and micro strategies are reasonably well understood as matters of policy, as the recent series of homeland security presidential directives indicate. Implementation may be difficult, as long-standing federal–state relationships are challenged, and as standard operating procedures, budgets, oversight, and accounting are pressured to reorganize. Nevertheless, these strategies are likely to improve the capacity of the nation to deal more effectively with extreme events or terrorist attacks.

Structural strategies are less well developed in critical infrastructure and homeland security policies. Such strategies focus largely on organizations and their relationships with one another, where organizations are considered as purposive actors in their own right. This perspective is also concerned in part with the interaction of public policy with private business: whether or not 85 percent of all infrastructure is owned and operated by the private sector, as is often claimed,[14] it *is* true that infrastructure operators have more extensive relationships with federal, state, and local public and regulatory authorities than do other types of private enterprises. Thus, an important component of an overall critical infrastructure protection policy requires attention to structural and organizational strategies.

ORGANIZATION STUDIES AND CRITICAL INFRASTRUCTURE PROTECTION

From an organization studies point of view, what strategies might be appropriate for organizing long-term critical infrastructure protection? Several approaches can help answer this question: anticipation and resilience, organizing for high reliability operations, and reframing the question to permit consideration of more fundamental alternatives.

ANTICIPATION AND RESILIENCE

Because societies depend on a wide range of infrastructures and services, preventing their disruption and restoring their functioning become important policy concerns. But prevention and restoration are two end points in a continuum that also includes middle-range concerns: assuring organizational or system robustness (the ability to fail gracefully rather than catastrophically) and organizational or system resilience (the ability to recover quickly once a disruption has occurred).

Political scientist Aaron Wildavsky proposes that strategies of anticipation work best against known problems, whereas strategies of resilience work best against unknown ones.[15] Anticipatory strategies can immobilize much wasteful investment against threats that may never materialize, whereas resilience strategies involve the potential for small or short-term sacrifice in the interest of long-term survival. Furthermore, an over-reliance on anticipation can lead to loss of capacity of an organization to adapt to changing conditions or threats, which can lead to even more vulnerability in the future. As Wildavsky writes, "grass bends before wind but usually does not break; it is temporarily unstable. Trees maintain strong stability under high winds but when they break, they have no resilience. The damage is irreversible, even after the wind has died down."[16]

Wildavsky argues that each strategy is appropriate to specific conditions. When uncertainties are large, resilience is probably the most appropriate. When conditions are stable, and when projections about the future are generally correct, anticipation works best, although it should be used judiciously, as hazards come in many shapes and sizes, and the future is inherently difficult to predict. Strategies of anticipation require exclusively dedicating resources in specific or concrete ways, so there is always the risk that an anticipatory strategy will end up being costly in the long run. As Wildavsky says, "real human situations usually involve a mixture of the known and unknown; hence, there is a tradeoff – the most likely large dangers, if they are known and can be countered without making things worse, can, and should be, prevented."[17]

Resilient systems and organizations are those that rapidly acquire information about their environments, quickly adapt their behaviors and structures to changing circumstances, communicate easily and thoroughly with others, and broadly mobilize networks of expertise and material support.

An approach that emphasizes resilience is compelling for many types of hazards, though adopting it may be more feasible in the long rather than short-term. Accepting mass casualties from a terrorist attack would be unacceptable for most societies, and most would choose a strategy of anticipation to prevent one from occurring. Yet anticipation against the dynamic uncertainty of terrorism has its drawbacks as well. Organizations facing low probability but high cost consequences and dynamic uncertainty confront contradictory imperatives that can produce a schizophrenic response, or worse, organizational paralysis.

HIGH RELIABILITY ORGANIZATIONS

Most large organizations exhibit such characteristics as highly formalized structure, long-standing operating procedures, lack of adaptability in the face of new problems or changes to their environments, and the like. Small organizations are less rigidly structured, engage in more ad hoc business processes, and are generally more adaptable to change, but they are also generally less complex and cannot sustain stressful operations for long without collapsing.

Resilience as a strategy for typical organizations is appropriate when trial-and-error learning is acceptable and when the cost of errors is low. But when the potential or expected cost of error is high, successful organizations tend to assume behaviors of high reliability or mindful organizations.[18]

This unusual class of organizations addresses the apparent contradiction between anticipation and resilience. Organizations such as nuclear power plants, air traffic control centers, and certain types of military operations have come to perform nearly flawlessly even under the most stressful of conditions. Yet these operations are also extraordinarily complex, operate hazardous processes, function within very tight time constraints, and are technically or organizationally tightly coupled, either among subsystems or with outside systems.

In addition, these organizations are able to shift seamlessly from routine operating modes, where formal organizational attributes such as hierarchical authority and standard operating procedures dominate organizational activities, to "high tempo" activities, where more informal organization norms dominate. During high tempo periods, operating experts are given great latitude to control operations, communication flows where needed (unhindered by the chain of command), and the problem is the focus of everyone's activities, regardless of their formal position in the organization.[19] These organizations' ability to function well in times of normalcy and chaos defies conventional understandings of how large complex organizations operate.

The ability to switch between two modes of operations – one emphasizing planning and routines, and the other focusing on contingency and rapid response and adaptation – appears to reconcile the competing requirements of both anticipation and resilience in highly reliable organizations. These properties also characterize much of the most demanding activities involved in critical infrastructure operations, particularly if they are attacked or must operate under unusually stressful conditions. These overall properties of highly reliable organizations should make them extremely attractive to critical infrastructure operations, and in fact a number of them independently possess these characteristics.

In addition to being able to switch easily between normal and crisis modes, highly reliable organizations essentially perform with high levels of technical competence over long periods. One way they do this is to reward error discovery and correction. They are occupied with failure, something regular organizations often do focus on. In addition, they avoid simplifying information about environment or tasks, also an unusual characteristic (as noted earlier by Turner in the previous passage). Authority systems inside the organization are unique as well, in that they often have redundant operational and supervisory systems that are relatively collegial and decentralized. People with technical expertise, regardless of status or rank, are given great deference in making decisions, and they receive intensive and regular training. No matter the economic fortunes of the organization, training is simply not negotiable. Finally, highly reliable organizations share information openly with external overseers, regulators, and the public, but they also protect their sensitive operations from external interference at nearly any cost.[20]

It is important to note that an organization cannot calibrate its degree of reliability by choosing some features and leaving others aside, perhaps as too costly or inconvenient. These attributes evolve in organizations tasked with extraordinarily demanding functions where funding is generous and the mission supported by key external overseers. They are difficult to maintain without constant attention and overall institutional stability. They cannot be transferred into organizations from outside, as they are tightly knit into the fabric of organizational culture and the specificities of the work process. If the conditions that have given rise to these organizations change, their continued ability to perform so reliably cannot be assured.

RELIABILITY PROFESSIONALS

A common thread in resilient and reliable organizations is active and engaged management by highly trained professionals. Compared with automated systems, human professionals in sensitive decision-making positions have far greater ability to adapt quickly in these complex systems. Automated systems cannot acquire information outside the parameters the system designers envisaged, and they cannot develop novel problem-solving routines on the fly.[21] An often-noted characteristic of key operators in such systems as air traffic control and electric grid operations is that they "have the bubble." This state of hyper-awareness is critical to successful high-tempo operations.[22] Therefore, processes that depend on automated decision support have difficulty coping either with extreme complexity arising from system behavior or with dynamic uncertainty created by adversaries who learn.

Schulman and Roe, in this book (Chapter 9) and in previous work, emphasize even more strongly the importance of what they term *reliability professionals* in sustaining the effective functioning of critical functions in large technical systems.[23] They argue that essential but largely unrecognized staff members of critical infrastructure system organizations are vital to the task of "keeping the lights on" in the face of extraordinary system volatility or stress. These professionals cycle between their on-the-job knowledge of how large-scale systems typically function and their ability to understand the systems' overall macro-design. In this sense, they embody characteristics analogous to those of high reliability organizations.

Schulman and Roe (Chapter 9) and their colleagues argue that reliability professionals both look at the detailed day-to-day problems they face and develop sophisticated pattern recognition capabilities, where they use trial and error learning to develop their deep and often tacit knowledge of the system they are operating. They know the formal attributes of the designed system in which they work, but they are required as a condition of keeping the system running to depart from these design principles and develop contingency scenarios or workarounds to compensate for shortcomings in the original design. This dual cognitive/operational activity enables these staff members to keep systems from failing, even in the face of a wide variety of contingencies. They are thus essential elements of an overall strategy for maintaining system reliability.

In addition, the existence of organizational slack – in terms of resources, control, and conceptual understanding of the system and its environment – permits organization managers to hedge against surprise and to exercise the authority they need to manage the unexpected.[24] While slack has negative connotations for many, depletion of slack in many critical systems limits the ability of managers to run them successfully. This is all the more alarming because many of these systems control powerful and hazardous technologies vital to society.

SYSTEMS OF SYSTEMS

As society increases its reliance on critical systems, maintaining conditions for high reliability operation of larger systems of systems will be essential. It is already demanding enough for single organizations to carry out these requirements. Sustaining reliability across large systems of organizations will require extraordinary effort, both by operators of technical systems and the regulatory and political authorities that oversee them. Yet economic pressure to improve efficiency by utilizing complex and interdependent systems is difficult to resist, despite evidence that such a strategy also entails increasing vulnerability to disruption and makes these systems more attractive targets for terrorism or any sort of sabotage.

Competitive pressures in market environments also require organizations to deploy all resources, both physical and human, at or close to the margin. This increases pressure on line managers to reduce organizational slack to a minimum. Where challenges can be predicted, where warnings are timely, or where the threats are not fatal, organizations can afford to operate close to the margin, because they can react before disaster strikes.

But under conditions of competition associated with deregulation, many large-scale technical systems do not exhibit the same degree of inherent robustness that normal competitive organizations have. For large technical systems, competition leads to eliminating redundancies, cutting excessive staff, paring down non-essential programs such as training, and operating close to margins to achieve short-term economic objectives. Pains have been taken to construct market rules for formerly regulated services (e.g., electricity and telecommunications), but these have had mixed results, as demonstrated by the August 14 blackout of 2003 and the California energy crisis of 2000.[25] For other technical systems such as NASA's space shuttle program, time and economic pressures led to similar corner-cutting, with the well-known disastrous results.

For large technical network systems, increasing interdependence among many organizations intensifies the problem of assuring failure-free operations. For example, the tension between organizational autonomy and independence of the constituent units of the large-scale system makes communication among elements critical. As discussed in more details in Part IV of the book, managers face great difficulty knowing what remote units are doing, which makes decision making problematic because an action in one unit may have unintended consequences elsewhere in the system. Systems of interdependent organizations or complexes are only as reliable as their least reliable part. Risk migrates to these weak links, unknown to other system operators.[26]

Providing sufficient slack, encouraging constant and clear communications, and creating a consistent belief structure and safety-embracing culture help reduce the problem but cannot eliminate it entirely. Risk migration may be limited by ensuring that large-scale systems have a variety of organizational structures, but these structures need to be flexible in adapting to rapidly changing situations if crises or breakdowns are to be avoided.[27]

In addition, there is considerable concern about "cascading failures" among tightly interdependent infrastructure systems.[28] This concern has provoked a number of efforts to understand the technical and operational dimensions of interdependence through modeling and simulation.[29] Although the technical community strives to understand the causes of cascading failures and to design and build systems that will resist them, it is unclear whether technical solutions can ever permanently prevent large-scale outages.[30]

MULTI-ORGANIZATIONAL COORDINATION

How can one improve resilience in a context of large system interdependence? Critical infrastructure protection will not be secured by a single organization. Rather, it will be the outcome of many organizations working together in concerted fashion. However, it is a common problem in public administration that the coordination and cooperation needed for effective performance is nearly always lacking. As Pressman and Wildavsky put it in their classic text on implementation, "no phrase expresses as frequent a complaint about the federal bureaucracy as does 'lack of coordination.' No suggestion for reform is more common than 'what we need is more coordination.'"[31]

Guy Peters, a respected scholar of public administration, adds that "the fundamental problems of coordination have been exacerbated by the growth and structural elaboration of modern governments, but the coordination problem appears endemic to all large organizations, or collections of organizations, whether public or private."[32]

These conclusions are reinforced by recent experience in critical infrastructure protection and homeland security. The decision by Congress to create the Department of Homeland Security from 22 separate agencies in a number of federal departments was a response to the coordination issue: supporters of the decision believed that by putting all the relevant parts under one institutional umbrella, better coordination and control of the issue could be achieved. Observations by many close to the department indicate otherwise, however, and some worry that if the department does not clarifying its goals and rethink its structure and priorities, the United States will continue to remain vulnerable to attack.[33]

Although these claims of continued vulnerability may be exaggerated, it certainly will take some time for the new department to forge the cooperative ties among constituent bureaus, and among outside organizations with a stake in its work.[34] This is all the more pressing a concern given the multi-dimensional and dynamic nature of the problem, the requirements for extremely high standards of performance, and the complex and politically charged environment in which the relevant agencies operate.

Peters argues that lack of coordination arises from different operational responsibilities and legal requirements that place significant barriers between organizations, and that this is as much a policy issue as it is one of implementation or execution. Government reform efforts that include privatization and competition make the problem of coordination even more difficult. Three classic organizational responses are possible – hierarchies, markets, and networks. Hierarchies can solve coordination problems by fiat, and they may reduce transaction costs among organization subunits. But hierarchies generally require such a large degree of centralization of information that they restrict the degree of autonomy of "lowerarchs" to act as circumstances dictate. Markets require means of exchange and lots of participants to be effective in coordinating a large number of individuals and organizations. These conditions, however, may violate the spirit or even the letter of the law in cases involving coordination in multi-organizational systems, particularly those dealing with specific actions for public safety. Networks can effectively coordinate policy and operations (and professional networks can be especially useful in multi-organizational systems), but they work by bargaining among network participants and lack accountability or the ability to direct certain action. Furthermore, people and organizations can be part of multiple networks, so it may be difficult to discern conflicts of interest.[35]

Peters concludes that reform of governmental structures is not enough to improve coordination. Active and sustained intervention by political leaders will be necessary to achieve lasting results.

COMPLEX ADAPTIVE SYSTEMS

A final organizational strategy potentially useful for critical infrastructure protection comes from scholars of complex adaptive systems. Kauffman observed that some biological systems appear to organize themselves at the "edge of chaos," that is, there is enough order for information to be exchanged and stored, but there is sufficient flexibility of structure or procedure to adapt quickly to rapidly changing external situations.[36] Comfort examines a number of disasters to which she applies the "edge of chaos" idea and derives four conditions for effective, adaptive response: (1) articulation of commonly understood meanings or understanding of the threat between a system and its members; (2) sufficient trust among leaders, organizations, and citizens to overcome uncertainty and enable members to accept direction; (3) sufficient resonance or support of the community between the emerging system and its environment to gain support for action; and (4) sufficient resources to sustain collective action under varying conditions.[37]

These conditions can be measured technically, organizationally, and culturally. Technical measures include the state of the infrastructures used by the system to respond to disasters, such as communications or transportation. Organizational measures pertain to the degree of organizational adaptability to new and changing situations, style of communications among system participants, and character of leadership. Cultural measures include willingness to accept new ideas or new types of action. Comfort argues that variations in each of these characterize different degrees of system adaptability, as shown in Table 10.1.

Comfort argues that the overall homeland security system response to the attacks on September 11, 2001, was that of an "operative-adaptive" system. Moving to an "auto-adaptive" system (the most desirable state) will take concerted effort. She suggests three broad policy directions to improve governmental response to such attacks and to reduce future threats. First, organization leaders should improve complex inter-organizational system performance by

Table 10.1. Stages toward adaptive responses

System type	Technical	Organizational	Cultural	Characteristics
Non-adaptive	Low	Low	Low	System operates only with outside assistance during crisis, returns quickly to non-adaptive state
Emergent adaptive	Low	Medium	Medium	System develops way of responding during crisis, but cannot sustain collective response once threat has passed
Operative adaptive	Medium	Medium	Medium	System functions well during crisis, but cannot sustain new responses and threat reduction
Auto-adaptive	High	High	High	System functions effectively in response to varying threats, continues to develop new means of learning and acting

Source: Developed from Comfort 2002.

studying past failures, with particular attention to communication and coordination problems in multi-jurisdictional settings. Second, leaders need to recognize that emergency operations are inherently non-linear and dynamic, and they are not manageable by traditional rational and linear methods. Willingness to permit dynamic rescaling of response will result in more creative and effective operations against unpredictable threats. And third, leaders should facilitate the transition to continuous organizational learning by making substantial investments in information technology and organizational reforms to take advantage of new information technology-enabled capabilities.

POLICY APPROACHES FOR CRITICAL INFRASTRUCTURE PROTECTION

Critical infrastructure protection in the context of anti-terrorism is fraught with difficulties arising from the dynamic uncertainty of the threat, the organizational demands for reliability of infrastructure systems, the problems associated with multi-organizational coordination, and the challenge of achieving continuous organizational learning in these conditions. What is more, the infrastructures must respond to these difficulties while also remaining competitive in the long run.

Individually, each one of these is an extraordinarily difficult problem. In the context of critical infrastructure protection, the difficulty of addressing them together justifies our earlier characterization of them as "wicked." The problem of terrorist attacks, like other extreme events or disasters, is not one that can be definitively solved, despite presidential campaign rhetoric to the contrary. But progress can be made.

In addition to the obvious macro and micro strategies of infrastructure protection, infrastructure vulnerability assessments, and continuity of operations planning, there is a set of related structural and organizational strategies that should be considered to improve the capacity of the nation's critical infrastructure service providers and public authorities to perform their functions. I conclude this chapter by highlighting six of them.

First, organization leaders should seek to strike a balance between strategies that emphasize anticipation with those that emphasize resilience. The critical infrastructure protection debate has quickly moved toward anticipation and the accompanying efforts to prevent entry of hostile actors, to identify and harden assets, to simulate and then eliminate or protect system vulnerabilities, and so on. This may be the right solution, but given the nature of the large technical systems with which we live, an externally oriented approach that emphasizes hardening is likely to be economically and politically costly. Should it fail once, consequences could be catastrophic.

Therefore, strategies that emphasize resilience – by keeping critical infrastructure protection activities constantly engaged in improvement and learning – should be explored, both because they are likely to be less costly and because they are likely to increase success against actors trying to use dynamic uncertainty to their advantage. Resilience cannot be the only strategy; a catastrophic attack on a major city such as New York, Tokyo, or London might be so costly that protection would be worth the economic and political expense.

Second, strategies that recognize the importance of high-reliability organizations and auto-adaptive systems are essential. These organizations and systems may help point the way to addressing the operational problem of low frequency, high consequence events. Sustaining attention or watchfulness over long periods of time and getting the proper response at the right time will require an extraordinary organizational effort. High-reliability organizations appear to be better equipped than most to do so. Buttressing them with overall systems that promote continuous organizational learning, even in the face of long periods of threat quiescence, are necessary to deal with the twin problems of low frequency and terrorist attackers.

However, the literature on highly reliable organizations does not cover the way in which organizations come to possess their special characteristics, or what managers have done, not to mention what they should do, to steer their organizations in this direction. Researchers in this field assert that identification of the characteristics of highly reliable organizations is not the same thing as knowing how to make them so. More research is needed to learn how such organizations evolve and what can be done to stimulate their development to suit new homeland and national security purposes.

Third, strategies that promote and protect the professionalization of reliability are needed. It should be recognized that people make organizations work, particularly in the demanding domain of critical infrastructure. Minimizing the conditions that disrupt or impede the work of reliability professionals is essential to their ability to maintain the edge they need to keep the lights on and vital systems running. This means taking a close look at the policies that affect major systems, such as deregulation, and asking, "how will these changes affect reliability?" rather than only "how will they affect efficiency?" There appears to be an imperfect market for reliability, and this imperfection demands attention by public authorities to ensure it is provided at the highest possible level.

Fourth, risk will migrate over time to the weakest element in systems of organizations without operators knowing it or being able to manage it. These systems characterize increasing portions of our economy and society, making the migration of risk especially troubling. Policies will need to focus attention on the problem, reward sharing of information about technical and organization changes, encourage strong safety cultures, and protect against the consumption of slack.

Fifth, the classic approaches to taming wicked problems should be pursued: extensive dialogue should take place, by various means, among citizens and stakeholders about the meaning of critical infrastructure protection and homeland security, and the consequences of proposed security solutions. Rittel and Webber argue for "an argumentative process in the course of which an image of the problem and of the solution emerges gradually among the participants, as a product of incessant judgment, subjected to critical argument."[38] It is only through such processes of deliberation, critique and interpretation that problem re-formulation or re-framing can occur, which can ultimately lead to acceptance of problems as less wicked, more amenable to conventional problem solving, and more legitimate.

Finally, political leadership is essential for sustaining the appropriate degree of attentiveness to the problem of coordination across many organizations. Reform fixes may help improve the ability of many agencies to work closely with one another, but in and of themselves will not do the trick. Classically, reform efforts typically occur in the immediate aftermath of a disaster when public attention and political will is high. As time passes, attention and concern wane, unless reinforced by additional catastrophes. As the record shows, sustaining watchfulness and the ability to anticipate and deal with low-probability high-impact events is the single most difficult policy issue facing emergency management and homeland security.

No single answer will solve critical infrastructure protection. This multifaceted problem requires a variety of responses. A perspective that recognizes the large-scale technological system dimension of critical infrastructures, their wicked nature, and crucially, their organizational attributes and dynamics is vital to identifying both the structural and policy issues that can lead to better, if not definitive, solutions. Critical infrastructure protection needs to be understood not only as deploying a tougher "exoskeleton" of infrastructure hardening and counter-terrorist anticipation, but also organizational "antibodies" of reliability that enable society to be more resilient and robust in the face of new, dynamic, and uncertain threats and contingencies.

ACKNOWLEDGMENT

This research was supported by a grant from the Critical Infrastructure Protection Project, George Mason School of Law.

NOTES

1. For a discussion of large technical systems, see, e.g., Mayntz et al. 1988.
2. Perrow 1984 (2nd edition 1999).
3. Zuboff 1988.
4. Michel-Kerjan 2003.
5. See Tucker 1999; Tucker and Sands 1999.
6. See National Center for Infectious Diseases 1999.
7. Turner 1976. Turner expanded on this in a book-length study. See Turner 1976, 1978.
8. On organizations not learning from their environments, see also Crozier 1964.
9. For example, traditional telephone systems provide their own electric power to run the public telephone network and have back-up batteries capable of keeping the systems functioning for about six hours. Electric power system operators have their own telecommunications networks to coordinate geographically dispersed operations, and the reliability operatives in the system have their *own* telecommunications system because they are concerned that the regular corporate network is not adequately managed for their needs.
10. For a discussion of the challenge of transformer replacement, see Chapter 13 of this volume.
11. Roe et al. 2002; U.S.–Canada Power System Outage Task Force 2004.

12. For a discussion of these characteristics within the case study of the 2001 anthrax attacks, see Chapter 25 of this volume.
13. Ritte and Webber 1973; Roberts 2001.
14. The first reference to private sector ownership of 85 percent of infrastructure appears to be in remarks by Sen. Robert F. Bennett on September 25, 2001, following his introduction of S. 1456, *Critical Infrastructure Information Security Act of 2001*, introduced in the U.S. Senate on September 24, 2001. See Bennett's remarks at http://bennett.senate.gov/press/record.cfm?id=226479, accessed October 7, 2005. See also President's Council of Advisors on Science and Technology 2002; Office of Homeland Security in the Office of the President 2002.
15. Wildavsky 1988.
16. Wildavsky 1988, 79–80.
17. Wildavsky 1988, 80.
18. The "high reliability organization" literature is identified mainly with researchers at the University of California at Berkeley and Mills College in Oakland, California. For other perspectives on the composition of high reliability organizations, see Chapters 8 and 9 in this volume. See also Rochlin et al. 1987; La Porte and Consolini 1991; Roberts 1990a; Schulman 1993a; Schulman 1993b; Rochlin 1996; La Porte 1996. For "mindful organization" literature, see Weick and Sutcliffe 2001.
19. Rochlin et al. 1987.
20. See La Porte, Todd R., 1996, for more detailed discussion of these points.
21. Rochlin 1993b.
22. The personal dynamics of trying to maintain the ability to "have the bubble" are well illustrated in the film, *Pushing Tin,* 1999, directed by Mike Newell, based on Frey 1996.
23. See Chapter 9 of this volume and Schulman et al. 2004; Schulman and Roe 2004.
24. Schulman 1993b.
25. Roe et al. 2002; U.S.–Canada Power System Outage Task Force 2004.
26. Grabowski and Roberts 1997.
27. Grabowski and Roberts 1997.
28. Little 2002; Heller 2001.
29. The literature on network modeling and simulation is growing rapidly. For examples, see Gorman 2004; National Infrastructure Simulation and Analysis Center 2003.
30. Fairley 2004.
31. Pressman and Wildavsky 1984.
32. Peters 1998.
33. Kettl 2004.
34. Kettl 2004, pp. 97–117.
35. Peters 1998.
36. Kauffman 1993.
37. Comfort 2002a. See also Comfort 2002b.
38. Rittel and Webber 1973, p. 162.

PART IV

Securing Networks

11

COMPLEXITY AND INTERDEPENDENCE

The Unmanaged Challenge

Philip E. Auerswald

Managing a particular firm or organization, with all its complexity, to ensure reliable service and resilient response to disaster is a significant challenge in and of itself. However, the magnitude of the challenge has dramatically intensified in recent years due to deep and growing interconnections among organizations that provide critical services. Some connections occur among firms comprising a single infrastructure industry; these compel direct competitors in the marketplace to cooperate in security matters. In other cases, where the physical infrastructures are owned by the government (for example, harbors, airports, and highways) and services using these facilities are provided by commercial firms (for example, ships, planes, and trucks), interdependence crosses public and private institutional boundaries.

Considerable concern exists about cascading failures among tightly interdependent infrastructure systems.[1] This concern has provoked efforts to understand the technical and operational dimensions of interdependence through various forms of modeling and simulation.[2] Large-scale systems have a variety of organizational structures. These structures need to be flexible in adapting to rapidly changing situations.[3] Most pervasive and difficult to manage are the interdependencies that exist among firms in different infrastructures – water authorities that depend on electric power for their pumps, or hospitals that depend on transportation providers for the delivery of needed supplies. In all of these cases, accountability for assured continuity of service is limited. Managers of firms providing infrastructure services must consider the implications of these interdependences and devise ways to address them.

The chapters in Part IV consider the limits of design and engineering approaches to the challenge of securing complex and interdependent networks. One key component on which we focus is the interdependent aspect of their operation today. Network interdependencies wreak havoc on business-as-usual approaches for both technical and organizational reasons. The technical reason is that the systems involved are highly complex. While particular interrelationships are more obvious – for example, traffic signals powered from the grid will not function during a power failure – predicting the manner in which "systems of systems" will behave in a disaster is extremely difficult. The institutional reason is that no one is really in charge of managing network interdependencies. Not only are the interdependencies, almost by definition, beyond the scope of single firms, but they also frequently cut across the domains of regulatory agencies and other "stovepipes" in which national government agencies operate. The cross-industry institutions that do exist have not, to date, proven effective.

Authors of the chapters in Part IV look at the issue of interdependencies from the standpoint of three specific industries. In Chapters 12, by Jacob Feinstein, and 13, by Michael Kormos and Thomas Bowe, experienced industry professionals offer their perspectives on the means for assuring high reliability and resilience in the recently deregulated electric power distribution industry. In Chapter 14, a Carnegie Mellon University team composed of Jay Apt, M. Granger Morgan, and Lester Lave focus on the important topic of interdependencies between different infrastructures providing critical services, also using electric power as a focal point. Chapter 15, by Sean Gorman, considers another core infrastructure, the Internet along with other cyber systems, whose failure can affect the reliability of multiple critical services. Finally, Chapter 16 by Geoffrey Heal, Michael Kearns, Paul Kleindorfer, and Howard Kunreuther discusses supply chains in modern manufacturing. Because these supply chains are typically transnational, their global security is particularly difficult to assure.

Through considering complexity and interdependence from difference vantage points, the chapters share some common themes.

THE FAILURE TO COMMUNICATE

For many large technical network systems, increasing interdependence among many organizations intensifies the problem of assuring failure-free operations. For example, the tension between organizational autonomy and interdependence of the constituent units of a large-scale system makes communication among elements critical. When managers are not fully informed (or worse, are misinformed) regarding the actions and status of remote units, effective decision making is not possible. Actions in one unit can have unintended, and perhaps serious, consequences elsewhere.

Systems of interdependent organizations or complexes are only as reliable as their least reliable part. However it may be very difficult for system operators to identify that part. Chapter 16 offers as an illustration the crash of Pan

America's flight 103 over Lockerbie, Scotland, in December 1988. In this case, poor security systems at one node in a large network provided an opportunity to attackers, which they exploited. The same logic applies to the incentive of a single division within a large organization to invest in protecting against a catastrophic accident that could bankrupt the entire firm. The actions of Nick Leeson at the Barings Futures' Singapore office were primarily responsible for bringing down Barings Bank. Arthur Andersen was sent into bankruptcy not due to bad results of all branches of the firm worldwide, but mainly due to actions of one element of the whole organization, its Houston branch.[4] Providing sufficient slack, encouraging constant and clear communications, and creating a consistent belief structure and safety-embracing culture throughout the company can help reduce the problem of local under-investment in actions enhancing global security.

THE BOUNDARIES OF PRIVATE ACTION

As indicated by the chapters in Part III, the permanent race for economies of scale and just-in-time processes in a highly competitive world does not preclude a firm from improving the security of its operations and safety of its own employees. In fact, it should be in the firm's direct interest to better secure its operations to assure business continuity in case of disaster. Nor does competition preclude establishing ex ante effective catastrophe risk financing mechanisms (which can result in much more efficient outputs than if the firm relies for its security and resilience on government intervention ex post; see Part V). What are often not of direct interest, even for such safe firms, are the external effects their failure might have on others – the security externalities. If market forces do not sufficiently motivate firms to integrate such externalities in their decisions, society faces an important challenge: how will governments assure a certain level of public security and the continuity of critical services?

Of course, businesses do not make decisions solely on the basis of maximizing short-term efficiency of specific projects; they must maximize their global competitiveness and long-term survival. To do so, executives make many decisions that contribute to their costs, but which are intended to avoid technical or operational failures, to improve the attractiveness of their products in the eyes of consumers, to lower the risks of public criticism, to avoid expensive litigation, and to comply with government regulations. Most manufacturing firms place great emphasis on reducing injuries to their workers to the minimum, not only because of the cost of workers' compensation and federal workplace regulations, but also because a good safety record is a sign to the public of both good management and an appropriate set of corporate values.

The parallel with environmental risks is interesting. Before the 1970s, most firms expected their public relations offices to deal with complaints by environmentalists. Neither expenses to reduce the likelihood of polluting events nor the benefits of having a good record of environmental stewardship were built into business resource allocation systems of the firms. Over time, however, as the regulatory environment became more stable, and technologies and procedures for mitigation of environmental damage became better understood, firms built the business value of a good environmental record into their investment plans. Today many, if not the majority of, firms see environmental regulatory compliance as both a legal necessity and evidence of responsible public-interest stewardship.

In certain cases, such as nuclear power generation, compliance with the highest safety and security standards is a first-order public priority; realistically government officials would not have the option of shutting down the entire U.S. nuclear industry if an accident occurred on the scale of the Chernobyl meltdonwn.

WHERE MODELS FEAR TO TREAD: THE LIMITS OF DESIGN

In some respects, environmental externalities may provide elements of a model for security externalities. Major business-related environmental disasters, such as large oil spills, burst tank cars of chlorine, or unexpected releases of toxic gases from chemical plants, have been quite infrequent. Predicting how often they might happen, despite efforts to prevent them, is difficult. To that degree, there is a similarity between environmental stewardship and investments to reduce infrastructure vulnerability to disasters.

However, while the spatial and temporal scales of impacts make accounting difficult, whatever impacts occur can generally be measured directly in terms of the firm's output – for example, the amount of sulfur dioxide emitted as air pollution. Effluents can be monitored on a minute-to-minute basis. The same does not hold for security externalities, where the consequences of lapses in security may not materialize for months or years. Even more important, environmental compliance, like worker safety, is principally under the control of the firm. Natural disasters are under no one's control, and attacks by terrorists are under the control of the attackers. Furthermore, the interdependence of elements of infrastructure makes firms in one sector subject to errors or accidents occurring in another. Thus, firms can focus on recovery from such externally caused disasters, but alone they can do little about their incidence. The ongoing debate over who should pay for economic consequences of terrorism illustrates this fact. In some areas of natural disasters, such as earthquake and hurricane risks, firms have access to technology to reduce the risk, and specialized insurance companies can price their products to reflect the investments and business management processes their customers make to reduce exposure to natural disasters and their consequences. There is debate today about the extent to which the same conditions can be applied to terrorism risks. These issues are discussed in detail in Part V.

ACCOUNTING FOR COSTS, CONSEQUENCES, AND ASSIGNMENTS OF RESPONSIBILITY

Private-sector actors can reduce system vulnerability by decreasing dependence on vulnerable external services, decentralizing critical assets, and decentralizing core operational functions.[5] However, organizations may face strong sanctions from markets for taking such actions if they reduce efficiency, raise costs, or reduce profits in the short term. Similarly, markets rarely reward investments that reduce vulnerability to events perceived as so rare that there is no statistical basis for quantitative risk assessment.[6]

As we discussed in more detail in Chapter 1, the terrorist attacks against the United States on September 11, 2001, made clear that the nature of the international terrorism threat had changed over the past two decades – from more political and local attacks to extremist religious-based terrorist groups, many of whom advocate massive casualties and directly target U.S. economic interests.[7] Despite the terrible shock of 9/11, few private firms internalize the risk of terrorism in their operation costs today. The estimates of private-sector expenditures on vulnerability reduction vary widely and often fail to specify what domain of expenditures their estimates cover.[8] A survey undertaken by the Washington-based Council on Competitiveness only one year after 9/11 indicated that 92 percent of the 230 senior executives surveyed did not believe their companies would be targeted. Seventy percent of the survey respondents said that they saw no way to implement needed security measures in a way to bolster future productivity.

The investment in protection of critical infrastructures suffers from the so-called "tragedy of the commons."[9] This is the problem of financing investment to reduce negative security externalities, as discussed by the editors in Chapter 1. Chapter 16, by Heal and colleagues, describes how the presence of security externalities causes investment dilemmas for private firms. Consider, for instance, a poultry farm considering a pre-emptive investment in measures that would mitigate against the spread of the H5N1 (avian flu) virus. If poultry farm A substantially increases its expenses to make its farm less likely to host or spread the virus, it places itself at a competitive disadvantage. If firms B, C, and D, with which A competes do not support similar investment, they can still benefit from the actions by A. In the short term, their negligence provides a cost advantage, at the same time that they "free-ride" on the investments of the forward-looking firm; in the same manner, farm A is doubly penalized. If farms B and C decide to make investments similar to those made by A, then D's continued irresponsibility jeopardizes the entire industry: In large, interdependent systems, the risk is often the one associated with the weakest link. Unlike the Arthur Andersen case, the different farms are not part of the same organization; rather each operates independently. Without coordination, peer pressure, or even coercion, global underinvestment in security is likely.[10] In that context, it is unlikely that any private firm will try to endogenize such externalities if that decision will result in a weakened business position.

One solution is to compel all firms to abide by the same security requirements; ideally by the establishment by government or trade associations of enforceable global standards at the national and international levels. Developing market-sector incentives (e.g., subsidies, tax reductions, and the possibility of selling the safer product/service at a higher price) could also contribute to motivating private-sector enterprises to invest in infrastructure protection. It is likely to require more systematic collaboration between the private sector and the government than exists today.

Steering between market approaches that tend to remove system slack (and thus impeding efficient recovery from a catastrophic system failure), and the redesign of private infrastructures to ensure more reliable functioning (though at higher cost to consumers), the federal government has generally opted for policies of "partnering" and information sharing among private-sector operators, government regulators, law enforcement agencies, and intelligence services. Consensus around the goal of public–private partnerships to protect critical infrastructure has not yet translated into clarity as to how such policies should be implemented and improved over time. For example, information sharing on terrorism-related issues is far from optimal, as is discussed by Daniel Prieto in Chapter 23. Chapter 24, by John Donahue and Richard Zeckhauser, proposes that the manner of engagement required goes beyond public–private partnerships to "collaborative governance."

The tensions resulting from the separation of accountability among business executives and the collective institutions of government (federal, state, and local courts; legislative and executive bodies) are particularly strong and difficult to accommodate in market economies like that of the United States. Firms may be aware of the hazards of national disasters, war, or terrorism, but feel that these events are unpredictable, likely to be experienced by a large segment of the economy, and ultimately prone to have consequences of such magnitude that only government can address their risks and consequences. For all of these reasons, securing complex and interdependent networks that provide critical services constitutes an unmanaged dimension of the infrastructure challenge.

NOTES

1. Little 2002.
2. Gorman 2004; National Infrastructure Simulation and Analysis Center (2003).
3. Grabowski and Roberts 1997.
4. Kunreuther and Heal 2003.
5. See Kunreuther and Heal 2003 and Howard Kunreuther et al. 2002.
6. See Kunreuther 2002.
7. Hoffman 1998; Enders and Sandler 2006.
8. See, for example, Hobijn 2002, pp. 21–33; Congressional Budget Office 2004.
9. Harding 1968.
10. Kunreuther and Heal 2003.

12

MANAGING RELIABILITY IN ELECTRIC POWER COMPANIES

Jack Feinstein

When asked to name the largest machine ever built, people invariably respond with "the Boeing 747" or perhaps "a nuclear-powered aircraft carrier." The correct response, however, is the electric power system.[1] The electric power system consists of three components: power production, transmission, and distribution (see Figure 12.1). Power plants use either fossil fuels (oil, coal, or natural gas), nuclear energy, or hydropower to produce electricity; some alternative electricity sources include solar, wind, and biomass. The transmission system consists of high-voltage overhead or underground feeders that are used to deliver large quantities of bulk power to substations. The high voltage is transformed to lower voltages at these substations and then delivered to end-use consumers via distribution feeders.

The critical infrastructure components of the power system are those that are part of generation and transmission (including substations), because a coincidental loss of several of these components can cause large-scale blackouts. Although the distribution system would seem critical as well, because it affects every individual consumer, a deliberate widespread failure is virtually impossible to achieve. On the other hand, natural disasters such as hurricanes or ice storms, which can impact thousands of square miles, have destroyed many distribution systems over the past century and will continue to do so into the future.

The electric power system in the United States has more than 16,770 individual power-generating units installed in some 2,800 plants, with a combined capacity exceeding 1,000 million kilowatts.[2] They are all interconnected by high-voltage transmission lines approaching 160,000 miles in length.[3] When a generating unit is connected to the power grid, it works in conjunction with all other units on the power system. This creates a continuous balance between

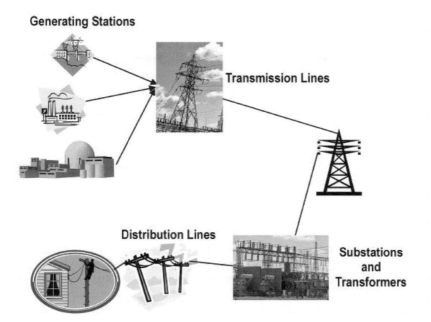

Figure 12.1. Basic electric power system.

customer demand and generation output and thus the reason for claiming that the power system is the largest machine ever built.

Despite the size and complexity of the power system, it historically has demonstrated exceptional reliability. A typical residential customer may experience on average one or two hours of power outages per year (which equates to about 99.98 percent availability), with most of those outages attributed to local distribution outages (e.g., weather-related causes or vehicles hitting utility poles). Large-area blackouts usually result in outage times that exceed the annual average with some extending to several hours, days, or (very rarely) weeks. According to the Department of Energy, a large-scale blackout is defined as one in which at least 100 megawatts of load has been intentionally interrupted, a power outage that affects 50,000 or more customers, or mechanical equipment failure that results in 200 or 300 megawatts (depending on the size of the power system) of load interruption. Without question, because of our interdependence on electricity, the longer the blackout the more significant the economic losses sustained by both the consumer and the utility.

The devastation that resulted in September 2005, as Hurricane Katrina passed over New Orleans was an unprecedented example of such losses. Nearly three months after the storm, nearly 40 percent of New Orleans was still without power. The storm flooded more than half of the city's 42 substations and 2 of its generating stations. On November 19, 2005, the *New York Times* reported that the agreed-upon goal was to restore power to at least 80 percent of the electric customers by year end 2005.[4] The local utility, Entergy New Orleans, was in a financial quandary. Not only did it experience damage in the range of $260 million to $325 million, but it also lost most of its customer base and the associated revenue they generated. Entergy New Orleans declared bankruptcy and borrowed approximately $200 million from its parent company to pay for repairs to its power system. Moreover, the overall recovery of New Orleans has been significantly delayed by the slow restoration of the electric system.

It is realistic to estimate that a high-magnitude earthquake in a highly populated area would also inflict the same devastation on an electric utility. In fact, it could be worse. The materials used to support and electrically isolate the high-voltage cable, wire, and buses that comprise the power system's equipment and feeders are usually fabricated from compounds of either porcelain or glass. They are both extremely brittle and subject to failure from shocks such as those experienced during an earthquake. This brittleness was experienced in California during the Northridge earthquake in January 1994 and the Kobe (Japan) earthquake in January 1995. The Los Angeles power system was blacked-out when the 1994 earthquake struck, although service to the entire city was restored within 24 hours. The California earthquake (magnitude 6.7) caused hundreds of millions of dollars in damage to substation equipment. The Kobe earthquake (magnitude 6.9) resulted in power system damage amounting to several billion dollars and a three-day blackout. A higher-magnitude earthquake would cause considerably more damage, with longer restoration times, perhaps similar to the damage experienced in New Orleans.

Several organizations have developed estimates of the cost of the 25-hour blackout on August 14, 2003, which affected approximately 50 million people and thousands of businesses in the Midwest, New York, and Ontario. The consensus is that the cost was in the range of $4 billion to $10 billion, with most studies indicating that $6.0 billion was the most likely cost.[5] The costs included in the estimate were (1) lost income to workers and investors, (2) emergency service and overtime costs to governmental agencies, (3) expenditures for material and labor by utilities to restore the system, and (4) losses due to food and commodity spoilage.

An extrapolation of these costs for a blackout of the entire continental United States and Canada would be in the range of $36 billion to $40 billion per day, and this does not include the impact it would have on the world economy.

In this chapter, I review some power system blackouts to identify performance characteristics of utilities. I also focus on power companies that have used a structured managerial approach to their system design, maintenance, and operation to both minimize and limit the duration of these events.

ANATOMY OF FAILURE

Because of the self-healing characteristics of the power system, large-scale blackouts rarely happen. Self-healing occurs whenever either a generator or transmission line trips out of service. The other generators and transmission lines that remain in service then pick up a proportionate share of the load carried by the lost resource. This is all done automatically without human intervention.

For the power system to continue to operate in a reliable manner and survive these events, the system depends on dispatchers to monitor and operate the system within established procedures and criteria.[6] As contingencies occur, the operators must adjust the power system to withstand any additional outages of generation or transmission.

Over the past 40 years, the utility industry through experience and knowledge has developed detailed criteria, design standards, and procedures such that almost all blackouts are prevented. Yet they continue to occur, and most of them have resulted due to utility managers (at all levels, including senior executives) failing to appropriately focus on reliability, including not closely monitoring their company's operational performance.

For example, a lesson learned from the "Great Northeast Blackout" of 1965 is that a power system must be operated in a manner that if any single element (e.g., generator, transmission, circuit) trips out of service, the system needs to remain stable. The experience of the 1965 blackout resulted in the development of criteria to establish transfer limits, that is, the amount of power that can safely be transferred between two areas. To comply with the criteria, utility operation control centers should have reliable computer systems to monitor these power transfers. As described later in this chapter, a failure of a computer system contributed to the 2003 blackout.

Notwithstanding the publication of criteria and procedures, there are many examples of blackouts occurring as a result of similar initiating event. A major contributor to the 2003 blackout was the failure of the First Energy Corporation's Ohio utility to properly maintain vegetation (particularly trees) clearances for high-voltage transmission lines along the lines' right-of-ways. This is the very same cause cited for blackouts that occurred in a portion of northeastern Wisconsin and the Upper Peninsula of Michigan in November 2001, when a transmission line sagged into trees. Likewise on July 17, 1998, a Public Service of Colorado transmission line sagged into trees and resulted in the interruption of about 300 megawatts of load (a rule of thumb for approximating a blackout's impact on a community is that 1 megawatt of load equals about 1,000 homes). The Pacific Northwest and California in both July and August 1996 experienced widespread blackouts, all attributed to transmission lines sagging into trees.[7] All of these outages encompassed widespread areas, and although not very long in duration, they resulted in inconvenience and economic impact to those affected.

When managers fail to adequately budget for necessary facility maintenance or fail to monitor procedural compliance of personnel, blackouts will eventually occur. Likewise, managers increase the risk of blackouts when they fail to keep abreast of incident reports, lessons learned, and other aids prepared annually by the North American Reliability Council (NERC).

For example, the United States–Canada Power System Outage Task Force's "Final Report on the August 14, 2003 Blackout in the United States and Canada," indicates that First Energy Corporation failed to follow NERC reliability criteria, manage tree growth along its transmission rights-of-way, to have adequate system monitoring at its operation control center, and to adequately train operators in emergency response.[8] Many of these issues have been experienced by other utilities over the past 40 years and are widely known in the industry. However, First Energy's management did not learn from them (see Box 12.1).

The task force report describes a sequence of events that day that illustrates a typical anatomy of failure: First, a First Energy generating unit in Eastlake, Ohio, shut down in the early afternoon, followed about an hour later by the failure of a transmission line south of Cleveland. A few minutes after that, the voltage dropped on the Ohio portion of the electric grid, which increased the current on all remaining transmission lines to compensate. The power shift and increased transmission line loading caused a different line to sag into a tree and fail about a half-hour after the first line had failed. At that point, system operators were trying to understand the problem, but they failed to inform system controllers in nearby states of their emergency. To compound the lack of information sharing, during the course of these incidents critical computer control systems at First Energy failed and thus did not automatically alert the system operators to the transmission line overloads. About five minutes later, another line tripped out of service, and two minutes after that, one more line sagged into a tree and shut down, but operators took no action (such as load shedding) to relieve the severely overloaded transmission lines. Still more transmission lines failed one minute late, followed by more and more lines within another half-hour. Finally, a little more than two hours after the initial failure of the Eastlake generating

BOX 12.1 LESSONS LEARNED FROM EXPERIENCES – A MANAGEMENT
TOOL

Con Edison experienced a total system blackout on July 13, 1977, with restoration
of electricity to all customers taking more than 24 hours to complete. After the
blackout, Con Edison executive management realized that a thorough review of the
incident needed to be undertaken to assure that it would never happen again. This
resulted in a multi-phase report examining every contributing factor to the blackout.
The areas investigated included planning, engineering, maintenance, operations,
training, personnel selection and recruitment, and others.

The blackout report then included recommendations addressing all of the items
that contributed to the blackout. The company followed up by implementing many
of the recommendations – for example, additional operators (including a senior
operator with an engineering degree) were added to the control center, additional
relay protection was added to transmission lines, testing of transmission tower
grounding was upgraded, and severe weather operating procedures were implemented. All of these changes were tracked until they were fully implemented, and
for the past 28 years Con Edison has not experienced another system-wide blackout
that was within their control to prevent.

Con Edison went even further. Because a common cause of blackouts is the
failure of managers to learn from their own and other utilities' experiences, Con
Edison institutionalized the passage of information within the company and to
others outside it. To ensure that the lessons would not be forgotten, a seminar was
developed in 1985, entitled "Lesson Learned from the 1977 Blackout." The seminar
was video taped and shown to personnel throughout the company, as well as new
engineering recruits. In addition, the seminar was discussed at various industry
meetings, such as the Pennsylvania Electric Association (now the Energy Association
of Pennsylvania), which attracted participants from the many utilities that operated
in the states bordering Pennsylvania. The seminar was so well received that copies
of the tape were sent to several utilities that requested it.

In 2000, the Internet-based "Blackout History Project" was initiated to produce a
history of the causes and effects of the 1965 and 1977 blackouts. The Web site contains
an interview with two former Con Edison's executives who were the assistant and
chief system operators in 1977. They also discuss their insights about the 1965
blackout. The Web site also provides a written description of the sequence of events
and a summary of the lessons learned from the 1977 blackout. Thus, lessons learned
from these watershed events have been recorded for future generations of utility
engineers, planners, and operators.

unit, a cascade of power surges and transmission line failures in Michigan
and Ohio blocked the eastward flow of power, shutting down generators and
creating a huge power deficiency. In seconds, power surged out of the East Coast,
tripping East Coast generators to protect them, and the blackout was on.

PREVENTING BLACKOUTS

It should be pointed out that it would be virtually impossible to build a power system that could be made blackout-proof. Managers can invest massive sums of money to harden their transmission and distribution systems to withstand destruction, but at some point a decision has to be made to stop spending when it becomes uneconomical to further reinforce the system. For example, utilities that are subjected to hurricanes can build there transmission towers to withstand hurricane winds of up to 200 miles per hour, such as might be experienced during a "Category Five" hurricane. However, they cannot account for wind-blown debris moving at high speeds or whether the debris will then hit their transmission lines causing short circuits. A response might be to build more underground transmission lines, costing at least a tenfold increase in the investment for a transmission system that most likely will never experience a Category Five hurricane in 100 years. Is it worth the money to avoid damage from such a low-probability event?

A good example of a utility's management making all the right decisions and still experiencing a devastating blackout is Hydro-Québec, the province-owned utility in Quebec, Canada. During the 1970s and 1980s, Hydro-Québec built some of the world's largest hydroelectric generating stations in the northern reaches of Quebec at James Bay and Churchill Falls in Labrador. Some of these facilities are 1,000 miles from Montreal and required innovative engineering, especially in using extra high voltage transmission circuits to deliver the electric power to the load in southern Quebec. Although the citizens of Quebec were able to purchase some of the cheapest electricity available, the great distance of the generators from the load centers resulted in a series of province-wide blackouts during the 1970s and 1980s. In particular, their power system was unable to remain stable during certain types of transmission outages, subsequently resulting in blackouts. Hydro-Québec managers decided that even though their customers were receiving very low cost energy, they still deserved to have more reliable service. At a cost in excess of US$1 billion, Hydro-Québec initiated projects during the 1990s to correct the stability problems they were facing. Upon completion of the projects, the Hydro-Québec system met the design criteria of the Northeast Power Coordinating Council (a NERC regional reliability council).

Then came what has been described as a "once in a hundred years" ice storm in January 1998, which affected areas of northern New York state and southern Quebec. The ice that enveloped the transmission towers in Quebec was in some cases three or more inches thick and was so heavy that it caused the transmission towers to collapse into piles of steel. The thickness of the ice exceeded any in recorded modern history and was well beyond Hydro-Québec's engineering factor of safety for tower design. The towers collapsed along four of the five transmission lines serving Montreal and resulted in a blackout affecting millions of people. This blackout occurred during a harsh Canadian winter and lasted for many days.

Thus, Hydro-Québec management had successfully taken action to prevent repetitive blackouts but was unable to prevent one caused by an unprecedented natural disaster.

The Hydro-Québec experience could give one the impression that notwithstanding a significant investment, it is not possible to prevent devastating extended blackouts. On the contrary, the investment paid off in the sense that Hydro-Québec no longer experienced the periodic shutdowns of the 1970s and 1980s. Yet, still dissatisfied with their exposure to the devastation and destruction of ice storms, the utility has been reported to have contracted for a US$32 million de-icing system to be installed by the fall of 2006.[9] The system will use high voltage direct current – or HVDC – technology to melt ice on some 323 miles of transmission lines in southern Quebec. When not in use, the de-icing equipment will be configured to provide added stability to the Hydro-Québec power system.

An argument can be made that Hydro-Québec had been too economical in its transmission design, and if the company had installed additional transmission lines it could have avoided the ice storm blackouts. However, redundant lines would have been subjected to the same ice storm and most likely would have also collapsed. Underground cables may have been reliable against ice storm damage, but Hydro-Québec, a government-owned utility, could not justify the added expenditure for such a rare occurrence.

Consolidated Edison Inc. (Con Edison)[10] experienced a major mid-town Manhattan substation shutdown in the early 1960s. After a transformer failed, the shutdown was initiated by the company to avoid damaging the remaining two in-service transformers. At that time, Manhattan distribution substations had been designed to sustain the load if one transformer was out of service for repair during peak periods. But because of the need to assure reliable service to Manhattan customers, both the company and the New York Public Service Commission (NYPSC) came to the conclusion that every Manhattan substation required an additional spare transformer to allow the substation to sustain two contingencies without the need to disconnect customer load. The NYPSC concurred that the new design criteria was prudent and allowed Con Edison to recover the additional costs by raising electricity rates.

These two examples and the others in this chapter counter the argument that private efficiency leads to high public vulnerability. The nature of the electric demand is that peak load only occurs for several hours per day during the hottest weather. The peak may last a total of 100 or so hours per year or about 1 percent of the time. As a minimum, all systems are designed for the next-worse or "N-1" loss of transmission facilities during peak load, so some resilience is built into the system for peak load (for a discussion of N-1 criteria, see Chapter 13). At all other times, the power system is even more resilient and can sustain additional contingencies beyond the design criteria.

POWER SYSTEM ATTRIBUTES CAN REDUCE TERRORIST TARGETING

Two overarching attributes of a blackout may reduce an attraction to the power system as a terrorism target. First, the 2003 blackout did not cause an economic system collapse, because restoration of the system was achieved in a little more than a day. This is similar to other short unscheduled outages, such as regional blizzards, that have an economic impact but do not result in a economic system collapse. A report by the Financial and Banking Information Infrastructure Committee found that the 2003 blackout had "no discernable effects on consumer confidence in the U.S. financial system." The report characterized consumers as patient and coping, even with the temporary loss of their banking access; overall, no extremes ensued, such as runs on the banks or massive stock market activity. The committee attributed the public's level-headedness to the quick action by the government to find the cause of the outage and assure the public that it was not caused by terrorism.[11] The second attribute is that the blackout did not cause significant civil unrest, injury, or death. In fact, the orderly evacuation of millions of New Yorkers from the business districts of Manhattan demonstrated the resilience of Americans.

Similarly, while the 9/11 World Trade Center attack damaged the infrastructure and shut down some financial markets for almost a week, those same financial markets did not collapse upon reopening. It was the office building destruction and displacement that had the major impact on the New York City economy, especially in the downtown financial district.

The economic and societal (such as injuries and loss of life) consequences of a long-term blackout depends on the area affected and the duration of the outage. For example, an outage encompassing the financial industry in New York City for an extended period would have worldwide economic consequences. The attacks of September 11, 2001, on the World Trade Center, which resulted in 3,000 deaths and shut down the financial capital of the world for almost a week, also destroyed two Con Edison substations (see Box 12.2).

BOX 12.2 SEPTEMBER 11, 2001, RESTORING POWER TO LOWER
MANHATTAN

The office building known as Seven World Trade Center was built in 1985 atop two
existing Con Edison substations, identified as Trade Center substations numbers 1
and 2. The electrical load in Manhattan is the most concentrated in the world. To meet
the demands for reliable electricity in this environment of tall buildings, Con Edison
developed electric distribution networks throughout Manhattan. A distribution
network is a geographical area supplied by multiple high-voltage feeders. Attached
to those feeders are transformers that reduce the voltage to the 120V distribution
service level and then tie into a grid of cables that run along every street within the
network geographical area. The supply to this network is an area substation with
multiple transformers that are supplied from the high-voltage transmission system
feeders. Thus, the network with multiple sources and redundant feeders experience
exceptional reliability. Con Edison network connected customers experience service
interruptions at an annual rate of about 15 per 1,000 customers served versus about
1,150 interruptions per 1,000 on a national average rate for customers that are
more likely to be served by the traditional radial distribution configuration. The
substation serving a network area has from three to five transformers to meet the
load requirement and by design can experience the loss of two transformers without
impacting any customers. This second contingency design criteria for substation
design in Manhattan is unique in the electric power industry. On the hand, because
the supply to the network is in one substation, a loss of the substation would result
in the loss of all customers served by the facility. This occurred on 9/11 when the
collapse of Seven World Trade Center destroyed the two-Trade Center substations.
Since the five-138 kV transmission feeders also supplied power to another substation
that also served the downtown load area, Con Edison had to take a multifaceted
approach to restoring the impacted networks. They had to disconnect the five-138kV
feeders into the Trade Center substations so that the other substation could be re-
energized. This is a very complex operation that normally takes weeks to perform,
yet the skilled Con Edison workforce, working around-the-clock, performed this
feat in a matter of days. The disconnection of the 13kV distribution feeders from the
Trade Center substations and reconnection to other substations and feeders in lower
Manhattan involved very innovative planning and installation. These feeders are
normally installed in underground ducts, which is a very time-consuming process.
To expedite the restoration, Con Edison elected to run the feeders along the gutters of
the street and build temporary plywood boxes to protect the feeders and pedestrians.
At intersections trenches were dug, the feeders placed in the open trench and then
a steel plate was used to cover the trench so that motor vehicle traffic could safely
pass over them. This work was performed under adverse environmental conditions
that resulted from the Trade Center Towers collapse, yet was completed in time to
assure that the financial markets could reopen by Monday, Sept. 17.

(continued)

BOX 12.2 *(continued)*

One other factor in Con Edison's restoration effort has largely gone unnoticed. That is, due to its superior credit rating, Con Edison had access to lines of credit to help pay for the material, labor, and services required to expedite the 9/11 electric service restoration. Just think of the delays that would have occurred if their suppliers and vendors required payment before or upon delivery. This is an excellent example of how the NY Public Service Commission can be proactive and understand the need to keep utility rates at an appropriate level so that the financial community views the NY regulated utilities as credit-worthy organizations.

Another attribute that reduces the power system as a terrorist target, although to a lesser extent than those described previously, is that many commercial and industrial companies and hospitals have emergency power backup systems to assure safety during power failures. Virtually every hospital has an emergency backup generator with fuel storage for continuous operation for 24 or more hours. Similarly, most if not all commercial and financial institutions have emergency power to assure continuous operation of their computer and data processing infrastructure. Some industrial companies have emergency backup power to assure that critical production facilities can be safely shut down. In New York City, many office buildings have emergency generators to power elevators (to free trapped passengers). The New York Stock Exchange, American Stock Exchange, and the Federal Reserve Bank have arrangements with Con Edison for support to provide emergency power to their complexes in lower Manhattan. None of these organizations have physical room to install emergency generators in their facilities. Instead, they have purchased mobile emergency generators and contracted with Con Edison to store, maintain, transport, connect, and operate them until regular power is restored.

Following the 1965 blackout, Con Edison installed gas turbine generators at several generating stations to supply emergency power to the New York City subway system. The generators were intended to allow trains to move to nearby subway stations to facilitate the evacuation of passengers (today, however, an update to the power supply used by the subway system from an antiquated 25 Hertz to a modern 60 Hertz system has eliminated this back-up power source).

REDUNDANCY AS A DETERRENT

To date, the electric power system in the United States has not experienced an overt large-scale terrorist attack, although there have been many small individual acts of sabotage and vandalism over the years.[12] These acts did not affect many facilities at the same time, and the self-healing attributes of the power system helped reduce the inconvenience in these occurrences. A coordinated terrorist attack would be expected to cause far greater and more widespread problems, similar to a major blackout.

The one major exception to the physical separation and redundancy of power system facilities is the power system control centers. The complexity of the operation and control of the power system is such that only through the use of computer monitoring and control systems can the power system operate in a reliable manner. The manufacturers of these systems build redundancy into their design with the expectation they will achieve 99.99 percent availability. This equates to about a one hour total of computer system downtime per year, consisting of a minute or so outage per occurrence. The weak link is that most utilities house their control systems in one facility – a fire or terrorist attack could shut down the control center and make control of the power system very difficult, if not impossible, to accomplish. The historical reason why the control center's computers are housed in the same facilities was that the data used by the computers to monitor the status of the power system was traditionally transmitted from generating plants and substations via direct-leased or utility-owned communications circuits. In many cases, many hundreds of individual communication lines would be routed into the control centers. Because of the quantity of circuits needed, the cost of providing redundant communication lines and facilities into an alternate control center was economically prohibitive.

A technological alternative has been developed to allow for the installation of computers and telecommunication facilities into back-up control centers. Through the use of the Internet (with appropriate security safeguards), primary and backup computers no longer need to be installed in the same location. System operational data from generating plants and substations are transmitted via the Internet to both the primary and back-up control center sites, so that if one is destroyed the other can continue to operate the power system.

An important lesson from the 9/11 attack is that financial institutions needed to have redundant facilities to back up their systems against loss of power or telecommunications. Destruction of certain critical facilities on the electric power system can result in extended outages. News accounts have indicated the most financial institutions have applied the lessons from 9/11 by installing backup systems and acquiring backup facilities away from lower Manhattan so that recovery can be accomplished in a relatively short time frame.[13]

RAPID RESTORATION AS A DETERRENT

Given that there was no social chaos, no economic collapse, and a very low or nonexistent fatality rate during the 2003 blackout, which affected some 50 million people and lasted one to two days, it would seem that the type of societal impact that a terrorist would want to achieve would not be through initiating blackouts. On the other hand, if these blackouts were to be instigated very frequently, the societal impact would be significant. However, if the power system could be restored in minutes or a few hours, then the impact on the public would continue to be minimized, and the rapid restoration of power would deter the terrorists.

An analogous example of how terrorism can be deterred through rapid response can be examined in the way the New York Metropolitan Transportation Authority eventually reacted to the prolific graffiti that plagued the subway system in the 1970s. The graffiti adversely affected New Yorkers' quality of life and feelings about themselves as well as the way the city was perceived by others, especially tourists. In other words, it had a societal impact for all those who lived, worked, or visited New York City. Politicians, pundits, psychologists, and citizens complained, deplored, and gave advice on how to stop the onslaught of graffiti that was engulfing the city, especially the subway system. An extensive rehabilitation of the subway system was initiated in 1984, including an effort to rid the subways of the graffiti. During that time, in became apparent that graffiti art required extensive time, effort, and danger to complete, and that the artists were motivated by the gratification they received from seeing their artwork on the passing subway cars day after day after day. As a counterattack, the transit authority immediately cleaned or painted the subway cars as soon as they were painted with graffiti. The "restoration" of the subway cars to a non-graffiti state was so traumatic to the artists they just stopped doing it. Concurrently, the transit authority also deterred artists by initiating better security in the subway car storage facilities.

This analogy can also hold true for the electric power system. That is, the electric power industry can minimize the consequences of a blackout by reducing the restoration time so that it is perceived as an inconvenience rather than a catastrophe, and therefore deter power system terrorism. If terrorism against the electric power system does not result in loss of life, and if restoration could be accomplished in a few hours, then the power system would no longer be a logical target.

To accomplish the sort of rapid restoration needed to reduce the attraction of the electricity grid to terrorists, innovative design changes to power plant equipment is required, transmission system elements will need modification, and revisions will need to be made to operational procedures and practices. Because the ownership of the majority of the electric power systems is private, regulatory changes and financial incentives may be necessary to provide incentives to the companies to implement rapid system restoration.

Notwithstanding the need to deter terrorism, it would be good public policy to reduce power system restoration times, due to the significant cost a widespread blackout imposes on those who are affected. To implement rapid restoration, utilities will need to work with their regulators to assure that changes are understood to be prudent and to assure that their costs are recovered via rate adjustments.

INTERRELATIONSHIP BETWEEN UTILITY EXECUTIVES AND REGULATORS

Operational reliability is largely a question of management priorities. Managers vary in how they view their regulatory, operating, and financial environments, and these variations affect their willingness and capacity to improve the reliability of their systems.

Many executives of investor-owned utilities can be categorized, based on historic actions, as (1) overly concerned about how the regulatory institutions will react to their managerial decisions, (2) primarily focused on rate of return on investments and dividend coverage, and (3) tending to short-change reliability whenever financial issues reach crises.

Executives' concerns about the regulatory institutions often stem from cases in which regulators have more sway over a utility's management than its own board of directors. Executives worry about such things as rate increase approval and after-the-fact prudence investigations. An investment-centered focus also has grounds in historical actions. Utilities have been viewed as an investment vehicle by financial institutions, because they provide reliable returns on investment. The tendency of executives to short change reliability during a crisis has contributed to several notable system failures. For example, whenever a nuclear plant is forced to come out of service due to mechanical failure or regulatory intervention, the owner can expect to spend hundreds of million dollars to fix the problems. A 1997 blackout involving a Commonwealth Edison substation in Chicago, and First Energy's performance on August 14, 2003, can be correlated to their companies' nuclear power plant(s) performance. To pay for the repairs or upgrades to the nuclear plants and not affect earnings per share, dividends, or credit ratings, senior managers reduced budgets to their transmission and distribution organizations. They then compounded this bad decision by allowing their focus and attention to be diverted away from these two important parts of the power system to concentrate on fixing the nuclear problem. Thus two bad decisions affected the company's performance: The first was reducing funding to critical infrastructure organizations and the second was not monitoring the situation to assure that these budget cuts did not impact reliability.

On the other hand, executives' behavior is also driven by the regulators' actions, which tend to be reactive to events, rather than proactive (especially when the utilities need additional capital improvements and ask for a rate increase). Regulatory agencies are political by nature, as their members are either elected or appointed by governmental leaders. Their staffs, although not political appointees, do reflect the commission members' mindsets by waiting to react to events to prove to the general public that they are looking out for their welfare. Regulators do not engage in open non-adversarial discussions of utilities' long-range planning and operation needs – discussions which, if encouraged, could result in better planning and operation.

Regulators also tend to hold prudence hearings after the fact to extract revenues from the utilities. If the regulatory staff were more attuned to the utilities day-to-day operations, the hearings could be avoided. An example of regulators being out of touch is the handling of a utility that conducted a detailed engineering analysis and inspection before determining that a project at its nuclear plant costing $300–400 million could be safely deferred until additional deterioration was detected. This action saved the consumers significant money in reduced energy charges. When an unexpected premature failure occurred, however, and the project had to be expedited, the regulatory commission then opened a prudence hearing to determine why the repair had not been made sooner. Had the commission been more attuned to the utility's operations, it might have reviewed the utilities' annual report and financial statements, which identified the deferment strategy, and evaluated the strategy ahead of time.

These characteristics of utility executives and regulators often result in bad decisions. However, there have been some bright spots over the past 40 years. For example, the Federal Power Commission supported the formation of NERC after the 1965 blackout. In addition, following a July 13, 1977, Consolidated Edison of New York blackout, the NYPSC hired Power Technologies Inc. to develop a criteria for the design and operation of the New York Bulk Power System.[14] The collaborative effort, with input from the New York utilities, incorporated many of the lessons learned during the Con Edison investigation of the blackout. This was an important step in that there were managers in charge of operations of upstate New York utilities who were still questioning why reliability was being emphasized more than the economic dispatch of generation at the New York Power Pool.[15]

Another example of positive collaboration between executives and regulators occurred subsequent to the 9/11 blackout in lower Manhattan, when regulators backed Con Edison's efforts to rebuild the destroyed substations. Regulators understood and supported the need for Con Edison to increase its capital construction program to build new substations that would meet increasing load throughout its service area.

The NYPSC also proactively fostered reliability is its June 20, 2005, order to improved vegetation management along the New York electric utility rights-of-way. This order, developed with input and comments from the utilities, directs the electric utilities to have personnel knowledgeable in right-of-way vegetation management.[16] The NYPSC also directs specific details regarding vegetation management and annual reporting requirements for the New York utilities.

CHARACTERISTICS OF RESILIENT AND LEARNING ORGANIZATIONS IN THE ELECTRIC POWER INDUSTRY

As previously noted, most blackouts have resulted from managerial failure, including improper funding for system maintenance, inadequate control center facilities, inadequate training, failure to enforce adherence to procedures, and lack of managerial oversight. However, some utilities have taken steps to minimize their exposure to blackouts – Hydro Quebec and Con Edison, among others. Specific organizational attributes that promote reliability work to prevent and minimize interruptions to their customers. An organization that is focused on reliability will pay attention to details; prepare procedures to cover normal and emergency operations and audit to assure compliance; prepare procedures that empower, not direct employees; examine every incident (whether significant or not) to measure the performance of system(s) and people; learn from experience by memorializing and sharing findings for those presently within the organization and those who will succeed them; install new systems and/or procedures to correct any identified deficiencies; implement routine and emergency procedures that are complementary; and periodically train and drill personnel in emergency procedures.

ATTENTION TO DETAILS

Many people have the misconception that when managers are promoted into positions of greater responsibility, they no longer have to worry about the mundane details of the business. In the electric power industry, which invests billions of dollars in generation, transmission, and distribution assets, small details such as vegetation management may not be high on the list of issues many utility executives worry about, but it is these small details that cause significant events, as demonstrated by the 2003 blackout (see Box 12.3). Yet some executives do worry about the details. For example, Charles Luce, the chief executive officer of Con Edison from 1967 to 1982, started his career as an attorney and thus did not have the depth of technical knowledge that engineers have of the operation of generating plants and substations. However, he knew that if these facilities were well maintained, he could then be confident that they would perform reliably. He decided that the way to foster in his managers the need to pay attention to details was to insist that critical facilities be maintained in a "hospital clean" condition. If he saw oil or water spills during plant visits, it was a sign to him that plant managers were not paying attention to details. It took only a few plant manager firings to change the culture within the company. He retired more than 23 years ago, yet Con Edison still has a culture that pays attention to details.

BOX 12.3 VEGETATION MANAGEMENT – A TUTORIAL

Vegetation management is perhaps the most cost-effective, simplest, and easiest maintenance action a utility can undertake to reduce the risk of blackouts. Yet time and again, it contributes to the causes of blackouts. Because tree growth is constant and predictable, any transmission maintenance organization has a good idea of when trees and vegetation need to be trimmed to maintain proper clearances to the transmission lines.

The problem begins when budget reductions are issued. Cutting budgets in transmission and distribution organizations is difficult to achieve because a major cost factor is the fixed labor payroll of the operation and maintenance employees. Some savings can be accomplished by reducing additional maintenance work, which also reduces spare parts purchases, but then the mechanics have nothing to do. Most utilities would rather not lay off their skilled labor force, because it would be difficult to replace them after budget cuts are restored. The first to be cut is overtime, which generally affects equipment maintenance backlogs. The next easiest way to reduce expenditures is to reduce contractor labor costs. Because almost all vegetation management for utilities is done by contractors, this becomes an easy target for spending reductions. Generally, the transmission departments may get away with deferring vegetation management for one growing season, but it does catch up with them – sometimes very quickly. Accompanied by other conducive system conditions, blackouts follow.

PRAGMATIC OPERATIONAL PROCEDURES AND COMPLIANCE AUDITS

Malfunctions and loss of life are often caused by the failure of people to follow procedures. Upon investigation after accidents, it is commonly determined that procedures had not been followed for a long period and that employees and managers took no initiative to understand why they were not being followed or to revise them to improve performance. The October 17, 2003, New York City Staten Island Ferry accident that resulted in death and injuries to passengers is a prime example of procedures not being followed. The ferry pilots had not been following the safety procedures for years. After the accident, both ferry boat operations personnel and their management faced criminal proceedings as a result of their inaction.

Con Edison audits procedural compliance at several levels. For example, department managers periodically listen to audio tapes of control center operators giving orders to field personnel. They verify that the orders are being given and received in a manner consistent with communication procedures. All operating organizations prepare a list of all items that require periodic inspection per procedures, and executives conduct monthly or quarterly audits of their organization's compliance with the inspections. On a corporate level, the staff of the general auditor of the company conducts annual audits of compliance within specific organizations.

PROCEDURES THAT EMPOWER EMPLOYEES

Many managers mistakenly believe that the only purpose of procedures is to direct personnel to respond in a given precise manner to specific events. On the contrary, procedures work best when they are written so that employees feel enabled and authorized to direct specific actions during both routine and emergency situations. For example, under normal conditions, an operator does not have the authority to interrupt electric power to the utility's customers, yet under emergency conditions the operator must be empowered to shed load without consulting with management. In the early 1980s, the New York Power Pool (now NYISO) replaced its emergency response procedure with a blanket procedure that covers all operating states of the power system. The five states – normal, warning, alert, major emergency, and restoration – are each defined by specific parameters so that the operators know when power system conditions are deteriorating to a less stable condition. At each defined state, specific corrective actions and authority is given to the NYISO operator as well as to each utility's control center operator. Thus, this procedure empowers the operators at the NYISO and utilities to initiate corrective strategies for all system conditions (see Box 12.4.).

EXAMINATION OF INCIDENTS TO MEASURE SYSTEM AND PERSONNEL PERFORMANCE

All past major system emergencies or failures have been the result of a series of minor errors that individually would not have led to catastrophic failure. However, as with the straw that broke the camel's back, tolerance of each additional error eventually has led to a sequence of events that culminated in a disastrous incidence. The only logical way to cut the chain of events leading toward disaster is to review every incident, critique both people and system performances, determine the cause, and make necessary changes to reduce the likelihood of recurrence.

BOX 12.4 POWER SYSTEM OPERATING STATES

In the early 1980s, the utility companies that operated as the New York Power Pool (NYPP) were given a report prepared by Power Technologies, Inc. for the New York Public Service Commission. The report was initiated by the commission to address issues related to the Con Edison 1977 blackout. In addition to other recommendations, the report also contained criteria for utility companies to follow in the operation of the New York Bulk Power System.

A unique item in the report was the notion that the condition of the power system under various operating scenarios could be identified as different operational states of "health." A good analogy would be a person who would be considered "normal" when specific physiological observations are met (e.g., body temperature, reflexes, pupil response). Other states of being for a person are sometimes defined as not feeling well, seriously ill, or critically ill. The condition of the power system can be described in a similar manner. As power operating conditions change, so does the system's operational state. Just as doctors respond differently to each state of health for a person, system operators must also take different corrective actions depending on the system conditions to return the power system to the normal state.

The NYPP operating committee established a task force to develop an operating procedure incorporating the operational state system to be used by both the NYPP control center operators and the utility control center operators in their control of the New York Bulk Power System. The procedure's purpose was to help the operators identify a change in the state of the power system as conditions degraded and then to provide guidance and assign responsibility and authority to the operators to implement corrective strategies to return the power system to the normal state.

The success of this application is demonstrated by the fact that notwithstanding several incidents with severe contingencies occurring on the NYS power system, no major blackouts due to operator error or inaction has occurred since 1977. The operating personnel in New York have successfully responded to emergencies using this procedure.

Operational States

The operational state of a power system can be determined by monitoring system conditions such as line loading, area control error, frequency, and voltage against assigned criteria for acceptable limits of these monitored items. The system is considered to be in the normal state if all system conditions do not deviate from the limits set for the power system (e.g., no transmission line overloaded). The system is considered be outside of the normal state if any condition exceeds predefined limits. The operational states are defined as normal, warning, alert, major emergency, and restoration.

Each power system designates the monitored elements and criteria that will be used to determine the state of the system. For example, New York developed its criteria based on NERC and Northeast Power Coordinating Council procedures and criteria as well as the historical operating experiences with the New York power system. Utility managers can customize the criteria based on operational needs of their systems or those of the regions in which they operate.

Operational Procedures

The success of implementing operational states as an operating tool also depends on the preparation of procedures that clearly define the actions that the operators are expected and authorized to follow (without the need to consult with supervisors) to restore the system to the normal state. The monitored system conditions (that is, voltage, current, power flow, and frequency) are analyzed using a comprehensive software application that is continuously running in the control center computer system. This computer application is a very potent operating tool because it immediately makes the operators aware of any change in the power system state and then displays on their computer terminals the authorized corrective strategies to be used to return the system to the normal state. Typical corrective strategies for each operational state might appear as follows:

Normal

   Adjust generation
   Adjust interchange schedules
   Adjust transformer tap positions
   Activate reserves
   Recall facilities out of service

Warning

   All of the above
   Implement manual voltage reduction

Alert

   All of the above
   Remove facilities from service
   Curtail interruptible load
   Request voluntary customer curtailment
   Request assistance from adjacent control areas

Major Emergency

   All of the above
   Implement quick response voltage reduction
   Order generation to maximum or emergency ratings
   Shed firm load

Restoration

   Initiate system restoration plans to restore load

For example, on December 29, 1989, a 30-inch diameter high-pressure gas main ruptured in the Hell Gate section of New York City's borough of the Bronx, resulting in loss of life and significant fire damage. An investigation determined that the cause was a gas main damaged by a backhoe in combination with an unrelated subsequent short circuit of a distribution feeder in a nearby manhole, which provided the ignition source for the gas explosion. The backhoe operator was killed by the explosion, however, and no one could confirm that he had indeed hit the gas main while excavating. Because Con Edison engineers were not satisfied until they could clearly establish the root cause of the incident, the final report was not issued, and the engineers continued to look for other possible causes. Approximately two years after the explosion, the actual root cause was found: Several years prior to the explosion, Transco, the gas transmission pipeline company that supplied gas to Con Edison, increased the transmission system supply pressure to enable higher quantities of gas to be delivered Con Edison and other customers. Because the Con Edison system pressure needed to remain at the same level as before the increase, Transco compensated by reducing the pressure of the gas delivered elsewhere in the system. A consequence of Transco's action was that the gas became colder than it had been prior to the pressure change. The colder gas made the steel couplings used to assemble the sections of the mains more brittle and thus not strong enough to withstand the stress put on them. In all likelihood, the nearby backhoe had not struck the gas main, but rather the combination of the gas pressure and brittle steel couplings eventually failed and caused the explosion. With this discovery, Con Edison initiated a program to inspect and repair all gas main couplings affected by the colder gas temperatures. This very thorough root cause analysis prevented another similar reoccurrence.

MEMORIALIZED EXPERIENCE AND SHARED FINDINGS

Every organization probably has examples of past errors that are repeated whenever new personnel replace retiring experienced workers and managers. The large utility boiler manufacturer Babcock and Wilcox endeavored to avoid this problem in the early 1970s. The company had determined that with each new generation of engineers and managers, it was repeating the same mistakes that had been made and corrected in the past. The company developed a computer database of its manufacturing and design errors.

On the other hand, a chief operating officer of a large Northeast utility had a plaque in his office that read "Use imagination, not memory." The intent of the plaque was to instill a new approach to how things were done, that is, to stop people from answering his questions with "we have always done it that way." His intent was correct in that fresh ideas are always desired, but he also sent a message that he did not place value on any previous lessons learned and even discouraged discussion of past events. Some high-profile incidents occurred on his watch as chief operating officer that were very similar to past events.

SYSTEMS AND PROCEDURES TO CORRECT DEFICIENCIES

Preparing written critiques, revising procedures, and installing new systems will have significant payback in the prevention of system failures. New technologies are always being developed so that problems previously addressed with new procedures may now be corrected with system changes or enhancements, thus reducing human error.

For example, the report prepared after the 1977 Con Edison blackout recommended adding an experienced engineer with power system experience to the control center staffing. After implementing this change, it became apparent to Con Edison that although the additional operator was helpful, management was not satisfied with the timely decision making during the period immediately following an abnormal operation or condition on the power system. Con Edison control center managers then initiated a requirement that the on-duty senior system operator prepare a critique of every abnormal event that occurred on the operator's watch. The critiques included the sequence of events, the cause of the incident, the operator actions taken to restore the system to a normal (secure) state, and the time frame to complete these actions. The critique then compared the responses of all personnel and equipment to those required by engineering and operational procedures. The senior system operator also included in the critique recommendations for changes in equipment and procedures to improve the overall performance of response to incidents on the power system. A draft of the critique was given to the chief system operator within one day of the incident. All operators had to read the critiques so that they would also learn from other operators' experiences. The critiques were kept on file in the control room for operators to use as references. Recommendations to change procedures were implemented, in many cases, on the same day as the initial draft of the critique was issued. Since 1978, thousands of critiques have been prepared, and they have become an invaluable tool for teaching lessons learned from experiences.

COMPLEMENTARY ROUTINE AND EMERGENCY PROCEDURES

The duties of an operator can sometimes be described as 99 percent boredom and 1 percent terror. During normal system conditions, operation of the power system is routine. Emergencies are infrequent but require the operator's immediate and correct response; failure to do so results in further deterioration of the system. To facilitate the operator's response during an emergency, the actions outlined in the emergency should build upon those conducted during normal procedures. This reduces stress during emergencies.

TRAINING AND DRILLING OF PERSONNEL
ON EMERGENCY PROCEDURES

It is not enough for procedures to cover all aspects of operations; personnel must understand why the procedures exist (or have been revised) and be thoroughly trained in applying them.

Following the 1977 Consolidated Edison of New York blackout, Con Edison's management team determined it to be unacceptable to have another blackout that could be attributed to its failure to properly plan, design, maintain, and operate the power system. It implemented a number of managerial initiatives to both improve procedures and train its personnel. In the early 1990s, Con Edison took another step in assuring that lessons learned would be memorialized. The company built a learning center (see Box 12.5) to centralize all training programs within the company. The learning center assured a consistent approach to training, and it fostered the initiation of a cultural change as the utility business became more competitive. In addition, Con Edison established a business academy to train managers for future leadership roles within the company. The unique business academy centered around course material developed and presented by senior managers and officers of the company.

BOX 12.5 THE CON EDISON LEARNING CENTER

Eugene McGrath, the visionary chief executive officer of Con Edison from 1990 to mid-2005, is an engineer and former power plant manager. Such a background is quite unusual in the electric utility industry, where most leaders have either finance, accounting, or legal training. His background in power plant operations made him very sensitive not only to the types of people to best recruit for Con Edison, but also to the level of training necessary for them to do their jobs. Well-trained employees are more likely to be productive, happy, safe, and less likely to make errors. As the electric utility industry deregulated, he was aware of the need for a cultural change at Con Edison. He oversaw a demographic review of the union and management workforce, which also identified that a significant part of the workforce would be reaching retirement by the end of the decade. This had both good and bad implications for the company. It would allow the company to continue to downsize and reduce layers of management without the need for layoffs, but it also meant the loss of a workforce with 30–40 years of experience in operating and maintaining the power system.

The company faced another issue as a result of the 1970s-era decentralization of its distribution operations into six divisions. There was considerable duplication in training of personnel, with no overarching organization to assure consistency in the training, especially because much of it was done on the job.

In 1991, Mr. McGrath made a decision to build a central training facility for Con Edison employees that would encompass both skills and safety training for the non-supervisory workers who performed construction, maintenance, and operating functions for the company, and management training and development for the technical, professional, and supervisory staff. All organizations would transfer their training responsibilities to the new training facility.

The Con Edison Learning Center was completed in an unprecedented nine months in 1993 and cost $60 million. The 168,000-square-foot center includes a large entry space filled with special displays and information kiosks. The training facility uses state-of-the-art technology, and where needed, duplicates the field conditions the workers will experience. Thus workers splice high-voltage cables in simulated manholes that mimic the close quarters of manholes buried in the streets of New York City. The training staff is recruited from within the company and serve for three years, after which they are expected to return to their previous or another department. This assures a flow of fresh ideas from people with field experience. In many cases, trainers join the learning center staff knowing they will be retiring in a few years. After a long and successful career, they transfer their knowledge just before they retire to the new employees joining Con Edison. In its first 10 years of operation, 59,000 classes and 18,000 meetings were held, involving approximately 475,000 students and visitors.

A major initiative for the learning center was the development of the Business Academy. Middle- and higher-level managers are sent to the academy for a two-week course that encompasses a range of topics, including utility accounting, planning, regulatory issues, and learning from experiences. The courses were developed by Con Edison's executives and outside experts. The success of the academy can be measured in the number of graduates who are now executives of Con Edison.

As a result of the 2003 blackout, more utilities are beginning to understand the need for becoming a learning organization. NERC has been a driver in implementing the lessons gained by experience from this blackout – it conducts onsite audits of both utility and regional operating organizations to monitor implementation of the recommendations from its blackout report.[17]

DESTABILIZING THE ELECTRIC POWER GRID – A WORST-CASE SCENARIO

The electric power grid of continental North America consists of three separate areas – the Eastern Interconnection, comprising the United States and

Canada generally east of the Rocky Mountains; Texas; and the Western Systems Interconnection, encompassing everything else. Because each of these areas operates independently, it is thought that a scenario in which an event shut down the North American grid would not be possible. However, in light of the 9/11 terrorist attacks, possible scenarios have been suggested.

Within each of the three areas, the electric power grid is highly interconnected between electricity providers. The interconnection of utility companies and the exchange of power between them were made possible by the growth of the telecommunications industry. To safely and effectively interchange power between power companies, there has to be a means of continuously monitoring the flow of energy. Whereas today that information flows between interconnected companies and regional control centers via the telecommunications infrastructure using either direct communications lines and/or the Internet, the first groups of power system operators manually controlled the power flow. As the interconnections between utilities became more complex, analog computers were developed to assist in the control. In the 1960s, digital computers were introduced, and they now control all aspects of power interchange. The computers use the real-time data on power flows at the interconnection points with other utilities to calculate the internal generation requirements needed to meet the utility's service area load. They simultaneously take into account any power being imported or exported. All of the interchange power and generation data are transmitted to the utility control centers from substations and generating stations via the telecommunications network. In addition, other critical information such as transmission line power flow, equipment status, and any abnormal conditions is also sent the control centers. The control center computers analyze the data in real time and present to the system operators a comprehensive account of the state of the power system. As conditions change on the power system, the operators are alerted, and they can initiate loading level changes to generators and/or adjustments to transmission line power flow to assure the system operates within established criteria and procedures. Without this continuous flow of data to the control centers, the operators would not be able to control the power system. Thus, the stability of the power system is a function of the quantity and accuracy of the information sent to the operation center computers.

The worst-case scenario for destabilizing the power grid would start with the complete shutdown of the North American telecommunications network. A sequence of events would follow:

1. Following the telecommunications network failure, nothing would immediately change within the power system, because the generators would continue to operate and produce power at the same level as they were just prior

to the communications failure. This would occur because the balance of customer demand and generation output would be maintained by each generator's governor (internal output controller), which would independently adjust generation levels to maintain the system frequency at 60 Hertz (cycles per second).

2. After the shutdown of the telecommunications network, commerce would almost immediately stop, and the United States and Canadian workforces would depart for home, causing a significant reduction in the demand for electric power. The generator governors would sense this and respond by reducing generation levels. The generator governors would act independently and reduce their generation levels at different rates, resulting in some geographic areas being deficient in generation and others having too much. This would happen because with the interruption of telecommunications, control centers would not be able to monitor and coordinate the operation of the power system. As the changes in generation levels occur, unintended (and unmonitored) power flows between areas would cause some power lines to overload. Without data being sent to the control centers, no adjustments would be made to correct the overloads, and the power lines would fail. Other lines would pick up the loading of the failed lines, but they would overload and eventually fail, resulting in more cascading failures and eventually instability and regional shutdown, as was experienced on August 14, 2003. The regional blackouts would then spread across the United States and Canada.

3. In response to the blackouts, emergency generators would start up and supply power to the telecommunications network facilities, where technicians would have been attempting to re-establish the network. Because the network would be down, they would be unable to communicate with technicians at other locations to troubleshoot the cause of the failure. Eventually, the emergency generators would shut down after running out of fuel (the telecommunications facility staffs would not be able to order more fuel, and even if they could contact the fuel depots, there would not be any power to pump fuel into delivery trucks).

4. All efforts to re-establish the telecommunications network would cease until restoration of electric power.

5. In addition, the natural gas transmission and distribution system would be shut down – either manually or automatically – to prevent explosions because it too relies on the telecommunications network for dispatch and pressure control.

6. Although many of the out-of-service generating stations have emergency shutdown and black-start capability, they would be unable to communicate to the system control centers their stand-by status. They would risk extensive

damage if they attempted to send power into the grid without knowing the status of the system. System dispatchers would be attempting to communicate with the generating stations and substation personnel using back-up radio systems, but the back up would be cumbersome, and not all substations would have personnel available to report circuit breaker and other equipment status.

7. All efforts to re-establish the electric power system would cease until restoration of the telecommunications network.

The end result of this worst-case scenario would be reminiscent of the eighteenth century, where lighting was by candles and communications was by courier. But things are far different now. For example at that time, the infrastructure to feed the approximately 5 million people living in the United States depended on sailboats and horses. Now, however, the U.S. population is more than 280 million, and the food distribution network could not possibly operate without electricity and telecommunications.

While this worst-case scenario builds on a premise that feels like science fiction (*can* the telecommunication network across the North American continent be shut down?), the intent of this scenario is to show the complete interdependence between the electric power grid and the telecommunications industry. Both are effectively privately owned (public power companies are managed no differently than investor-owned ones) but rely on the public sector for protection from terrorism. A terrorist attack on several telecommunications facilities or utility operation centers could result in isolated blackouts, but recovery could be facilitated if the telecommunications network remains available (for example, a fire in a New York Telephone Company switching center in lower Manhattan in the mid-1970s affected Con Edison substation monitoring and relay protection facilities, but engineers from both companies were able to work around the problem while the switching center was repaired). The challenge to the public sector, therefore, is to prevent a coordinated attack on the telecommunications network that might cripple it and take down the electric power systems as well.

IMPROVING POWER SYSTEM INFRASTRUCTURE PROTECTION

The electric power industry was awakened by the findings of the 1997 Presidential Commission on Protection of Critical Infrastructures, especially the potential vulnerability of their operation centers' computer systems to outside attacks. Some utilities had already recognized that as they expanded their control systems to include use of the Internet, they had to take proactive steps to assure protection from attacks. Other utilities had done nothing to protect themselves. After the commission reported its findings, the vendors that build the power system control computer system took a much more proactive role in making certain that their products were protected from attacks. One protection is a specialized communications protocol used by these systems.

After 9/11, the utilities started to be concerned with the prospect of a physical attack. Although utilities use private protection services to guard their facilities, local police departments must be attentive that these critical facilities exist and need to be periodically patrolled and safeguarded. Some municipalities have closed local streets to traffic near these facilities, utility companies have removed identification from their facilities, and some have installed barriers to prevent vehicle access.

No one can predict whether the electric power system will become the target of a coordinated terrorist attack. As noted elsewhere in this chapter, attacking only one power company facility may result in local interruptions, but not a massive regional power failure. It would take the efforts of a well-coordinated paramilitary organization to simultaneously cause a large-scale blackout. The formation of regional joint task forces made up of both state and federal law enforcement agencies as well as representatives from local utilities would be helpful in identifying areas of vulnerability within the power system infrastructure and then developing strategies to mitigate the impact of a terrorist attack on them. The advantage is that the experts in each field (law enforcement and utility operations) can contribute their expertise to protecting the power system.

Other steps are also necessary, because there is no assurance that management of utilities will continue to heed the lessons learned from the August 2003 blackout. Although NERC's new role in conducting reliability audits is a step in the right direction, additional initiatives should be considered. A good example is the actions that were taken by the nuclear power industry after the Three Mile Island nuclear accident in March 1979 – the Nuclear Regulatory Commission stepped up its enforcement and auditing function. This is similar to what NERC is now doing. The next step would be for the formation of a power industry self-examination organization, comparable to the Institute for Nuclear Power Operations, which was founded by the nuclear power industry after Three Mile Island. The institute is a good example of industry response to poor management within a critical infrastructure.[18] A new self examination organization for the electricity industry would complement the reliability issues that NERC attempts to address, while at the same time maintaining NERC as the appropriate organization to develop and enforce reliability criteria. A new organization modeled after the Institute for Nuclear Power Operations would work with the utility industry to examine itself and help develop organizations that achieve high performance in issues impacting reliability.

NOTES

1. The electric power system is actually an interconnected network of power companies that are either investor owned or owned by government-sponsored entities. The original developers of these companies were private entrepreneurs who developed power systems in densely populated areas and cities. Government-sponsored companies later evolved to fill the void in areas where the private developers did not expect to profit, due to the low population density of potential customers. When a reference is made in this chapter to a utility company, it refers to either investor-owned or governmental (public) entities. In reality, there is no difference in the management of either organization type. Both produce and deliver the same product. They purchase generating, transmission, and distribution equipment from the same manufacturers. Both types of utilities must raise capital in the financial markets and earn a return to pay for it. The significant difference between private and public entities is that the investor-owned companies raise capital in both the equity (common and/or preferred shares) and debt (corporate bonds) markets, whereas the public companies have access to the lower interest rate municipal bond market. There have been many efforts to convert investor-owned utilities into public companies, because the public companies traditionally have lower electric rates per kilowatt-hour (kW-hr). This chapter, however, does not discuss the pro and cons of investor-owned versus public power companies.
2. Energy Information Agency 2004.
3. Energy Information Agency 2003.
4. Gary Rivlin 2005.
5. Electricity Consumers Resource Council (ELCON) 2004.
6. Criteria and procedures complement each other. Following the "Great Northeast Black-out" of 1965 (affecting northeastern United States and eastern Canada), public and private electric power companies of the United States and Canada founded the North American Electric Reliability Council (NERC) to coordinate the planning, design, and operation of the North American electric grid. The NERC criteria can be viewed as overarching criteria for the overall grid. NERC now consists of eight Regional Councils that represent geographical segments of North America, with each region also preparing planning, design, and operation criteria based on specific needs of the region, all within the framework of the NERC criteria. Within the NERC regions, individual power companies and/or regional transmission operators develop procedures for the generating plants and transmission facilities under their control. These procedures are developed within the framework of the NERC and regional council criteria, and they include the experiences within the electric power industry from past incidents that form the basis for best industry practices. Each utility then prepares design and operation procedures using the above framework.
7. North American Electric Reliability Council (NERC) 1996, 1998, 2001.
8. U.S.-Canada Power System Outage Task Force 2004.
9. Transmission & Distribution World 2005.
10. Consolidated Edison, one of the nation's largest investor-owned energy companies, encompasses a number of subsidiaries, including Consolidated Edison Company of New York, Inc. (serving New York City and Westchester County, New York) and Orange and Rockland Utilities (serving a portion of southeastern New York state, northern New Jersey, and northeastern Pennsylvania), according to Con Edison Reports 2005.

11. Financial and Banking Information Infrastructure Committee (FBIIC) 2003 (FBIIC is sponsored by the President's Working Group on Financial Markets and is chaired by the Department of the Treasury).

12. For example, during an extended strike by Con Edison's workforce in 1983, a small unattended substation was broken into, and a valve was opened to drain the insulating oil from the power transformer, which would have caused it to fail and blackout the local distribution customers (a scheduled visit by a non-striking supervisor prevented the transformer from failing). The vandal was assumed to be a Con Edison employee, who would have known the consequences of the vandalism. This internal vandalism case also points to a particularly troubling possibility that is very difficult to solve: internal sabotage or terrorism by an employee who is a covert member of a terrorist organization. The 1993 World Trade Center bombing serves as an example of this type of plot. The convicted terrorists who designed the bomb included a young chemical engineer from Egypt. He had attended Rutgers University to earn his chemical engineering degree and had been hired by a New Jersey chemical company upon graduation. He had used his workplace personal computer to design the bomb.

13. U.S. Federal Reserve System, U.S. Department of the Treasury, Office of the Comptroller of the Currency, and U.S. Securities and Exchange Commission, Interagency Paper on Sound Practices to Strengthen the Resilience of the U.S. Financial System (Federal Reserve System Docket No. R-1128, Department of the Treasury, Office of the Comptroller of the Currency Docket No. 03-05, Securities And Exchange Commission Release No. 34-47638, File No. SS7-32-02).

14. The New York Bulk Power System is composed of all transmission facilities that operate at or above 115kV and all generators that are interconnected to the bulk power transmission facilities. Transmission lines that operate below 115kV are not considered part of the bulk power system and are the operating and planning responsibility of electric utility that owns these facilities.

15. The New York Power Pool (NYPP) was created after the 1965 Northeast blackout. The NYPP was a consortium of the eight electric utility companies that operated within New York State. Seven of the utilities were investor owned and the eighth was the New York Power Authority, a publicly owned entity. As a result of the lessons learned from the 1965 blackout, it became apparent that an organization had to be created that could coordinate the long-range planning and day-to-day operation of the eight companies that produced and distributed power to New York customers. A control center was constructed in the early 1970s by the NYPP, and computer directed dispatch of the New York-based generation was implemented in 1977. When the New York Independent System Operator (NYISO) was created in the late 1990s, the facilities and personnel of the NYPP were transferred to the NYISO.

16. CASE 04-E-0822 – In the Matter of Staff's Investigation into New York State's Electric Utility Transmission Right-of-Way Management Practices, filed in Case 27605. http://www3.dps.state.ny.us/pscweb/webfileroom.nsf/ArticlesByCategory/BDB52B0CC15BBE74852570260063242B/$File/301.04e0822.pdf?OpenElement, accessed February 9, 2006.

17. United States-Canada Power System Outage Task Force 2004.

18. For further information, see Rees 1996.

13

COORDINATED AND UNCOORDINATED CRISIS RESPONSES BY THE ELECTRIC INDUSTRY

Michael Kormos and Thomas Bowe

Electricity. Like air and water, most Americans take it for granted. And that is just fine with the electric industry, a 125-year-old business that takes pride in its ability to deliver affordable electric power reliably, without interruption, and always on demand.

But unlike virtually every other business or commodity, the electric industry provides a product that operates at the speed of light. The ultimate in instant gratification, electricity is consumed the instant it is generated. It is the unique on-demand, light-speed characteristics of electric power that makes securing the national electric grid a truly exceptional challenge, compared with other commodities.

The nation's electric power grid is too large and complex to completely secure its many components. In the 12-state U.S. region served by PJM Interconnection, a regional transmission organization based in Valley Forge, Pennsylvania, there are some 50,000 metered components – transmission lines, transformers, and circuit breakers – which would require policing. Add in the rest of the United States, and the number of metered components reaches the hundreds of thousands. Now include components such as transmission lines and towers, and the number of physical parts that would need securing reaches into the millions.

That said, a strong level of security is built into the power grid's physical design, as well as the operational processes system operators use to maintain the grid's day-to-day reliability.

Yet even with a high level of operational security built into the grid's design and operation, it is not fail-safe, as the Northeast blackout of August 14, 2003, demonstrated. To address the weaknesses leading to the blackout, key members of the electric industry have been pursuing a number of economically and politically sustainable initiatives to enhance the resilience of the national electric infrastructure by strengthening its interdependent infrastructures. Many

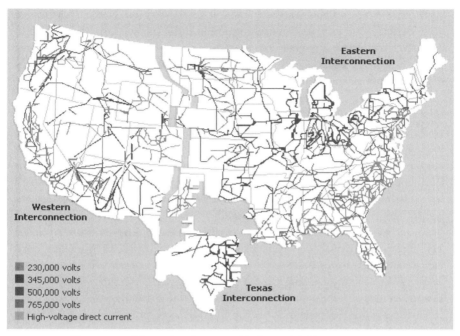

Figure 13.1. The national power grid. *Source:* MSN Encarta 2006.

of these initiatives are being led by the regional transmission organizations approved by the Federal Energy Regulatory Commission (FERC). The operators, with a combination of effective market designs, clear operational authorities, and centralized planning, are improving the grid's reliability to meet the security challenges of the twenty-first century. In addition to enhancing security, these regional operators are working to provide greater efficiency to the grid's operations.

Using the September 11, 2001, terrorist attacks and the August 14, 2003, blackout as real-world examples of potential threats and unanticipated events, we consider how PJM Interconnection, with responsibility for ensuring the reliability of the largest centrally dispatched control area in North America, is bolstering grid security and resilience through recent initiatives.

HOW THE NATIONAL ELECTRIC POWER GRID WORKS

Every second of every day, hundreds of millions of Americans rely on the transparent, continuous operation of the nation's electric power system. The system is divided into three grids: the Eastern, Western, and Texas Interconnections (Figure 13.1).

Balance must be achieved within each of these grids by the coordinated activities of 3,700 entities – including public utilities, metropolitan cooperatives, municipalities, independent generator owners, large and small customers, federal agencies, and more – all with shared responsibility for the operation and reliability of the system. When all is in balance throughout the national interconnection, electricity is available the instant a customer flips the 'on' switch.

As a result of the nation's utilities and system operators proven ability to sustain this state of balance, the United States has absolute confidence in its electric infrastructure. As a result, Americans have far less tolerance for disruptions than they might if they did not find it so reliable. Indeed, expectations for electric service performance have reached the point where most Americans take the high levels of service for granted.

To achieve and sustain such high performance levels, along with the resulting expectations of availability, system operators must continually and economically balance the output of energy-producing resources (coal, oil, gas, nuclear, and renewable energy generators) to every customer's demands ("load") every minute of every day. That done, operators must then balance the energy flows from the generation resources to the load, along a complex array of transmission lines and facilities. To do this, system operators must monitor and control a system composed of tens of thousands of transformers, breakers, and other capital-intensive assets with strict operational limits within which each component must remain. These interdependent assets are located across geographically dispersed substations and connected to generators and loads by transmission lines and towers that criss-cross the United States.

STRENGTH IN INTERDEPENDENCE

The electric grid's interdependencies contribute to its resilience. The large, integrated electrical system allows for more flexible response to minute-by-minute changes, such as demand spikes and sags, generator or major transmission failures, or overloads throughout the system. As such, the effects of changes to the system are dynamically distributed throughout the grid, according to the laws of physics, which determine how electricity will naturally flow, and the impedances of the grid itself. This "dynamic distribution" and the mere size of the electric grid allow the grid to more readily absorb changes to the grid's operations, whether these changes be the result of a planned outage, tornado, or human-caused attack.

Additionally, the three large grids that make up the national system have been planned and are operated to serve the nation's varying energy demands, despite daily challenges such as generators going off-line for maintenance, transmission lines sagging into untrimmed trees, lines falling down as a result of a storm, or other act of nature. In fact, the grid has enough resilience to withstand emergency demands that arise from heat waves, cold snaps, ice storms, tornados, and hurricanes that can disrupt hundreds of miles of transmission and distribution lines.

From a security perspective, the sheer number of the grid's interconnections and the scale of its dispersed parts on the one hand make total physical protection of the grid impossible. On the other hand, much of the security – or what might better be termed "survivability" – of the electric grid is inherent to its design and operations. The grid's survivability is its ability to automatically adapt, or heal itself, in response to the failure of a component or to inadequate balance (e.g., transformer taps changing, generation control systems adjusting to dips in frequency, special protection schemes being activated). Survivability is only achieved, however, through effective design and planning. Because system planners cannot predict most planned or unplanned changes to the grid, they design the system to withstand the loss of multiple elements.

Additionally, the majority of grid system operators manage the system to remain within "acceptable operating limits" even after the loss of any large generator, transmission line, or transformer. Acceptable operating limits are based on ratings determined by the equipment's manufacturer and owner/operator to ensure the equipment can operate at a particular point for a defined time, without suffering any damage. This operating paradigm is known in the industry as the "N-1 criteria," which allows system operators to maintain a level of operational resilience within the system. Operating within N-1 protocols allows the operator sufficient time to return the system to a state ready for the next contingency (N-2), without any equipment violating acceptable operating limits.

In addition, when the nation or electric industry upgrades its security postures, many operators conduct additional analysis of the maximum credible disturbances, which are events that are highly probable and, more importantly, would have high impact. Such analysis can assist operators in understanding how to pre-position the system to survive such an event or, at a minimum, to create an incident response plan for quick implementation tailored to that day's operational dynamics.

GRID VULNERABILITIES

While the dynamics of the interconnected grid makes it resilient, its interdependence also presents risks. The collapse of one system can bring down neighboring systems. Failures can cascade throughout the entire grid if it is not rapidly contained.

The sheer size of the interconnection and its geographically dispersed components makes physical protection of the entire grid impossible. It is simply not feasible to deploy guards to watch over every large transmission tower and sub-station. For example, as of January 2005 the PJM Interconnection system alone contained 1,001 generating stations and 49,970 miles of transmission lines, distributed over 138,510 square miles among 12 U.S. states – and that is just one section of one part of the overall national grid. Complicating the physical security equation is the fact that many of component sites are located in remote areas that are often difficult and time-consuming to reach.

Due to the many interconnections of the electrical grid systems, each operating entity/utility is co-dependent on the planning, operations, data feeds, and contingency responses of many partners. Balancing the grid's needs requires that each system operator be a good neighbor to its other interdependent, interconnected neighbors. Because of this interdependence, system operators have, at a minimum, an informal understanding of their commitment to one another. This informal understanding is best summarized by Alexandre Dumas' *The Three Musketeers*, who lived by the motto, "All for one, one for all!"

Being a good neighbor requires that every operating entity manage the system's ever-changing demands with uniform, well-coordinated standards of good utility best practices. This is the key to ensuring sufficient operational resilience within the system to withstand the unexpected. When operating entities cannot maintain shared expectations or meet required standards of the grid's interconnected whole, events such as the blackout of August 14, 2003, become possible.

The interdependence of the system also highlights the trade-off between economies of scale and system resilience that a large interconnection provides, compared with smaller more isolated interconnections, which are far less susceptible to another party's failures. However, with many smaller, more isolated grids, the ability of one grid to assist another during a crisis or high demand would be significantly limited.

GRID INTERDEPENDENCE WITH OTHER CRITICAL INFRASTRUCTURES

The scope of the challenge of the electric grid's vulnerability is increased further because the grid's interdependence extends to other critical national infrastructures as well (Figure 13.2). These include, but are not limited to, the national telecommunications network, information system networks (private and public Internet), and other facets of the energy infrastructure (such as gas pipelines, barges, coal deliveries, oil deliveries). The telecommunications and information

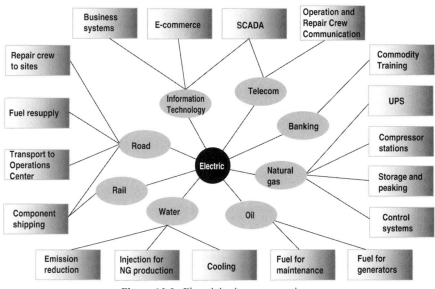

Figure 13.2. Electricity interconnections.

services networks are perhaps the most crucial interdependences in terms of vulnerability of the electric grid.

TELECOMMUNICATION INTERDEPENDENCE

Telecommunication is a crucial interdependent infrastructure for the electric industry. The computer and control systems that keep the electric grid balanced send and receive vast amounts of data – about 25 terabytes every two to four seconds – transmitted over private and public communication networks.

The interdependence of these two national infrastructures was illustrated during the "Millennium," or "Y2K," debate that raged throughout the late 1990s. Many believed that the electric grid would crash when the date changed from 1999 to 2000, because not all the computers tied to running the two infrastructures would be able to handle a date that did not begin with "19." The electric grid operators asserted that the grid would remain operational as long as the telecommunications industry stayed "up." The telecommunications operators countered that the telecommunication system would remain operational as long as the electric grid stayed "up."

In an effort to address this cross-industry interdependence, grid operators build redundancy into their communication systems. Most grid operators work to maintain telecommunication redundancy by using different carriers as their primary and alternate service providers. Recent merger-mania within the telecommunications business, however, has increased the difficulty in sustaining redundancy. Indeed, these ongoing mergers create a new challenge: how to overcome vulnerabilities of the "last mile," introduced when formerly independent telecommunication providers merge their networks. This problem occurs when formerly redundant lines suddenly terminate at single points of failure within the last mile of the telecommunications network. As a result, instead of lines being fully redundant from one point to the other, the redundancy ends too frequently in the "last mile," and a failure in that last mile would strip an operator of both its primary and alternate service.

Business pressure has also changed the vulnerability of the grid by encouraging the migration from private communication networks to public networks. While private networks are used for the most critical reliability data, these networks are very expensive. To cut costs, the industry has been turning to public communications for connecting business facilities and utility control centers.[1]

INFORMATION SERVICE INTERDEPENDENCE

Information systems are another set of crucial, interdependent infrastructures. Virtually all of the command-and-control systems used by operators to manage the grid depend on computers. These computers, in turn, depend on myriad software programs developed by in-house developers or consultants, or they are provided by independent software vendors.

The computers that once dominated grid operations were highly customized, extremely expensive standalone systems. But business pressures, coupled with the emergence of ever more complex systems, shifted grid operators from a reliance on propriety mainframe control systems to "open" systems and industry-standard protocols. These "commodity" computer hardware and off-the-shelf applications satisfy the same operational requirements as their mainframe counterparts of the past, but because they are no longer proprietary, they are more vulnerable to attack. Likewise, the increasing reliance on public communications networks (such as the Internet) for normal business transactions heightens the electric system's risk.

The growing dependence on commercial software, open source programming, and public networks introduces a host of other potential risks that must be managed, such as denial of service attacks, viruses and worms, computer exploits, hackers, and even basic hardware failures and software bugs. Indeed, one of the greatest challenges facing grid operators today is keeping large-scale information technology systems in sync with the steady march of security patches issued by mainstream hardware and software vendors. When information technology vendors release a patch to repair a vulnerability, they in effect notify the world of the grid's deficiency, and grid operators must install and test that fix as quickly as possible, before anyone else has a chance to compromise the systems via the publicized vulnerability. In the regional operator PJM's case, for example, each new patch must be distributed and tested on hundreds of servers in a race against the possibility of exploitation of the vulnerability.

A COORDINATED RESPONSE: PJM INTERCONNECTION, SEPTEMBER 11, 2001

PJM Interconnection, as a regional transmission organization, plays a vital role in the Eastern Interconnection. Started in 1927 as a way to pool the associated power resources of a few members located in Pennsylvania, New Jersey, and Maryland (hence the initials "PJM"), PJM has grown as a result of its demonstrated ability to enhance reliability and lower costs through coordinated operations and development of transparent markets for electricity. Current operations encompass most of the Mid-Atlantic region. In its new, expanded footprint, PJM serves more than 50 million people and is responsible for ensuring the reliability of the largest centrally dispatched electric grid in the world. The transmission organization coordinates the movement of electricity in all or parts of Delaware, Maryland, New Jersey, Ohio, Pennsylvania, Virginia, West Virginia, Illinois, Kentucky, Michigan, North Carolina, and the District of Columbia. It also operates the largest wholesale electricity market in the world. Additionally, PJM manages a sophisticated regional planning process for generation and transmission expansion to assure future electric reliability, and it facilitates a collaborative stakeholder process, in which stakeholders are participants that produce, buy, sell, move, and regulate electricity. PJM oversees nearly 10 percent of the Eastern Interconnection in its role of regional transmission organization.

As an interconnected operation and high reliability organization, PJM illustrated many of its strengths in its coordinated response with other system operators on 9/11. As with many other system operators that morning, PJM's managers found themselves facing multiple terrorist attacks on their borders: the World Trade Center's Twin Towers in New York City, the Pentagon in Arlington, Virginia, and another aircraft that ultimately crashed near Shanksville, Pennsylvania, all within or immediately bordering the PJM region of operation.

The day started when a PJM employee walked into the control room and announced, "An airplane just hit the World Trade Center!" At first, system operators thought the incident might be a tragic accident. Eyes throughout the control room turned to the television news monitor. Then PJM system operators watched in horror as the second hijacked aircraft stuck the World Trade Center. At that moment, they began executing well-rehearsed plans to position the electric system to withstand additional attacks.

While the system operators had not specifically rehearsed for a terror-ist attack, they had been trained extensively to respond to daily operational demands and events and also had drilled extensively in preparation for Y2K. Possible "millennium bug" emergencies had required the electric industry to be capable of responding to simultaneous failures within the electric industry and between interdependent infrastructures. Although PJM's Y2K contingency plans had not been needed on January 1, 2000, they proved their worth less than two years later, when they were used by system operators to shore up the grid during the 9/11 terrorist attacks.

Using their Y2K plans as a road map, PJM's system operators assessed the state of the system and then began modifying the Y2K operational guidelines to fit the demands of this new crisis. First they leveraged PJM's state-of-the-art decision support systems to assess additional contingencies (N-1 events) and conduct a "worst case" analysis of the electric system's response to potential N-2 and N-3 events. By combining multiple contingencies, the system operators were able to assess whether the grid could withstand the simultaneous loss of these critical assets. This analysis highlighted that, had one of these worst case scenarios occurred, other equipment components would have exceeded their operating limits.

Not knowing if the attack on the World Trade Center was an isolated attack or a wider terrorist assault, PJM operators and engineers adopted an ultra-conservative perspective and began operating as if under these worst-case mul-tiple contingency scenarios. As a result, the system operators directed many of the company's fleet of 540 generators to different operating points. This, in turn, reduced energy flows across the system by nearly a third of the system's capability. The decision to reduce demand on the overall grid made the system capable of withstanding any number of contingencies, such as multiple lines tripping out or nuclear generators going off-line, and the probability of a cas-cading failure was therefore minimized. By reducing the overall energy flows on all the lines, PJM's system operators gave the grid more room to absorb redistributed electric flow should the need arise. (For a discussion of power surges due to redistribution, see Chapter 12.)

PJM was then able to direct the running of this more geographically diverse set of generation by using market signals that incented generators to rapidly move their generator outputs in the desired direction. This is an advantage unique to PJM and other regional transmission organizations. As a regional transmission organization, PJM has the ability to direct generators owned by multiple owners out of normal economic operation, and financially compen-sate them for that. Generators that do not operate within a market such as PJM have little incentive to operate outside of their "economic" envelope. In con-trast, PJM's market ensures that generator operators either raise or lower their generation based upon the market signal sent to them. The resulting control of generation allows PJM to rapidly reduce flows across the transmission system making the grid far more stable as load is served by generation closer to the demand.

PJM also pre-positioned a greater portion of this generation to act as a large reserve above already significant daily reserve requirements (Operational standards require system operators to maintain sufficient reserves to cover their "greatest contingency" in 15 minutes or less.).

After switching to an ultra-conservative mode to increase resilience in the system, PJM communicated with its transmission and generation owners through a rapidly assembled series of conference calls and announcements, in an effort to provide all interdependent operating entities with synchronized directions, a clear explanation of actions taken, and discussion of proposed actions. These calls also guided PJM's asset owners in dispatching technicians to critical sites, which would allow them be ready to communicate vital readings back to control centers in the event that other communications channels failed. They also served as a first line of passive defense for targeted sites. These technicians were positioned at locations precisely as had been planned for possible Y2K emergencies. PJM also asked members to independently work with local law enforcement authorities to coordinate the physical protection of critically important stations in the grid.

Just as important as communicating with entities that report to PJM was communicating with all interconnected neighbors. These calls provided status updates and the latest analyses, and it also served to reinforce neighbors' restatement of their long-standing commitments to bilateral support, if needed. Most of these actions were taken within minutes of the second terrorist attack, without need for management approval. The actions exemplify the interdependent relationships of the interconnected neighbors – not one operating entity questioned the appropriateness of these emergency actions. Everyone responded supportively because they understood the gravity of the situation and because PJM carried FERC-approved authority for its actions, as well as having won the trust with its members through years of close collaboration in developing effective procedures, training, communication, and sound and flexible solutions to operating challenges. That said, while PJM's steps were significant, they were also simply logical extensions of typical grid operations, designed to respond to the ever-changing demands of electrical operations. Although the electric grid did not turn out to be the target on September 11, these actions would have remained appropriate.

Whether an operator loses a generator because a bomb explodes, a cooling pipe cracks, an earthquake, or some other event, operations must be ready to respond in a rapid, flexible, and ultimately effective manner. Because of the interdependent coordination between PJM and its member utilities, the grid operators were able to rapidly and effectively communicate on September 11 and successfully responded to the terrorist attacks.

LESSONS LEARNED FROM 9/11

The actions set into motion in response to the terrorist attacks on September 11 emphasize the importance of grid operation organizations to develop plans, such as PJM's Y2K contingency, that consider the potential for multiple failures. Current business continuity plans should include the probabilistic analysis of system vulnerabilities and interdependencies, and mitigating strategies for the potential simultaneous losses of telecommunications, data, and control and monitoring systems. System operators must have the pieces in place to conduct real-time, worst-case analysis on thousands of contingency combinations. This makes certain the grid can be put into a more conservative state to respond to multiple credible disturbances.

In addition, organizations must ensure that system operators have internal and external authority to respond to crises immediately, without seeking additional management approval. Reinforcing this authority in training and evaluations will ensure that (1) system operators act with total flexibility and alacrity, even if it means dropping a city's services to save the network and remaining customers; (2) member (interdependent) companies understand each other's emergency protocols and therefore do not need additional time to respond; and (3) parties understand they will be held accountable if they fail to act in accordance with the directives of the regional authority (such as PJM).

PJM's ability to send market incentives (the correct price signals to generators) as part of its role as a regional transmission organization guaranteed that PJM's members responded to these signals without PJM having to assert formal authority. Proper market signals reinforce grid reliability in day-to-day operations as well as during a crisis. Without a market to fairly compensate for actions that support reliability, generators would be exposed to potential losses when asked to operate at a potential loss. In its capacity as a regional operator, PJM can direct all generators within the region to take a specific action – such as those demanded by the 9/11 crisis – and ensure all parties are properly compensated. Regional operators are responsible for maintaining reliability over large regions, which in turn promotes unity of command over a vast array of resources. PJM has this authority through the FERC, which has vested PJM with making emergency management decisions and cost allocations. The operator's Operating Agreement and Tariff documents, developed mainly through an independent stakeholder process, define PJM's responsibilities, authorities, business rules, and settlement methodologies. The stakeholder process also enhances participant response to PJM's directives, because they are based on completely independent rules that favor no single party. This centralized, independent command ensures that the best course of action is selected and rapidly deployed. As such, FERC initiatives and policies to promote regional transmission organizations' market operations and, through that, greater reliability of the electric grid can be economically and politically feasible in the long run.

Even with market signals, market/system operators must have the ability to direct emergency action. Likewise, the market rules must ensure that participants who respond are paid for lost opportunity costs, and that these costs are distributed across the market. This ensures all members take the right actions during a crisis.

Finally, effective crisis response requires regular, intensive training that uses simulations that mimic the uncertainty, pace, and potential data saturation of theoretical events. With the benefit of effective tools, training, authority, communications, and flexible solutions, the operators of the electric power grid in the region affected and potentially affected during the 9/11 crisis acted in a coordinated fashion. Since then, the electric industry has made security of the grid a top priority.

AN UNCOORDINATED RESPONSE: THE NORTHEAST BLACKOUT, AUGUST 14, 2003

In contrast to the events of September 11, 2001, during which large portions of the Eastern Interconnection responded as a coordinated whole, the events of August 14, 2003 – and the ensuing blackout of nearly 50 million people in the northeastern United States and Canada – reflected a lack of coordination. When northeastern North America went dark on August 14, the cause was not terrorism: The blackout was the result of fundamental violations of effective operations. These violations included ineffective monitoring systems, inadequate training (particularly crisis response), lack of clear authorities within the responsible entities, and unclear industry standards.[2]

August 14, 2003, was a summer day that started like any other in grid operations. But problems surfaced in Ohio (outside of PJM's operating area) in the afternoon, when a critical generator near Cleveland went off-line. As Chapter 12 details, additional flows in the Cleveland area caused the transmission lines to heat up, expand, sag into untrimmed trees and other obstacles. The lines began failing as they came into contact with the obstacles or energy jumped across the remaining gap.

When a transmission line fails, it behaves like a blown fuse in a home, shutting down to protect equipment and people. As the Ohio system began failing, the alarm functions within its energy management system failed too, making it difficult for the operators to know they had lost a major line. Without that line, the transmission system had to absorb the additional flows needed to serve the Cleveland load. This additional loading created more heat, more line sagging, and eventually the loss of a second major line (N-2), then a third (N-3). It was not until the responsible grid operators reached the N-3 contingency that they recognized the emergency – despite earlier warnings from neighboring operators (including PJM's operators) who saw peculiar activity at their borders. Confusion mounted, and more lines were opened to protect the system. Without proper training and regular emergency drills with agreed-upon coordination plans, however, the Ohio operators failed to act or otherwise notify their neighbors of the emergency.

Approximately 20 minutes after the N-3 event, a fourth major line, and some 20 smaller transmission lines in the Ohio area, tripped. The Eastern Interconnection tried to achieve balance, but due to the rapid loss of load, equipment started automatically going off-line to protect the system from damage. It was by then beyond any operator's ability to save the system.

In contrast to operations on 9/11, the responsible operators involved in the Northeast blackout lacked many of the authorities, capabilities, and market signals that a regional transmission organization has at its disposal to rapidly move generation. The result, as the major crisis unfolded, was difficulty for the operators to react as a coordinated whole over a large area. If PJM's operators had failed in alarming the rest of the system of a problem, one of the members would have called PJM to report a violation when the first line tripped out. PJM is guided by a standing order to operate to the "most conservative" reading seen between its operations and another member's, until the difference in readings has been resolved. Therefore, even if PJM had not seen the loss of the first line, it would have operated as if it had lost the line once its owners had reported its loss. This standing order (an operational guideline) requires operators to mutually ensure that resilience stays within the system. The value of a regional transmission organization operating as a coordinated whole over a large area is the key point. Regional organizations with the right authorities and capabilities allow the grid to rapidly respond to crisis because there is no question of responsibility, and the large operators can more rapidly position the grid to withstand the challenges of the crisis.

OPERATIONAL COORDINATION INITIATIVES

While the two events demonstrated very different outcomes, September 11, 2001, and August 14, 2003, were catalysts for initiatives to provide greater resilience to operating the electric grid. The events demonstrated that for interdependent entities to coexist, there must be detailed coordination at their increasingly larger shared borders.

PJM and the Midwest Independent System Operator (MISO) embody the electric industry's progress toward greater coordination. These two regional transmission organizations have approached the industry and the FERC for permission to expand (in PJM's case) and establish markets (in MISO's case). These market expansion and creation efforts are the result of the FERC's and the regional transmission organizations' members recognition of the value of increased competition and enhanced reliability through larger, more robust markets.

In essence, these market-growth initiatives are designed to deliver greater market efficiencies. In addition, with the FERC-appointed authorities of a regional operator, these efficiencies can enhance security to the public rather than promote vulnerability.

A key component to enhancing resilience and reliability of the grid is minimizing the inefficiencies of poor coordination at the operational "seams." These seams, which may be physical borders or operating protocols, are where the questions of responsibility for problem identification and response often arise. PJM and MISO codified their commitment to resolving these seams in a historic joint operating agreement in December 2003. This agreement, filed with FERC, committed both organizations to implementing a detailed coordination plan at every point of grid operations. The agreement addressed everything from operating during emergencies to communications, data exchange protocols, planning, market coordination, and resolving congestion at points where the system is stressed. By codifying the means to extract greater efficiencies between the two regional transmission organizations, they are better able to quickly react and implement the most reliable solution during crises.

As a result of PJM's and MISO's strong leadership, the electric industry now sees the value of developing other joint operating agreements. In fact, agreements modeled on PJM's and MISO's joint operating agreement are rapidly becoming the standard for operating entities to include other regional transmission organizations.

WIDE-AREA PLANNING INITIATIVES

Although it may at first appear counter-intuitive, the Northeast blackout actually demonstrated the robustness of the power grid. Even after the third major transmission line failed, the system contained enough resilience that it still continued to operate for an additional 24 minutes before it collapsed. In essence, the grid's response demonstrated its designed resilience, in that the grid's eventual failure happened only after escalating to an N-4 scenario.

A cascading failure such as that seen on August 14, calls for holistic planning over a broader geographical and system expanse so that studies reflect the true nature of how the whole system will react to grid enhancements. This type of integrated planning would also benefit from the regional transmission organization model. A regional operator is responsible for the coordinated regional planning and direction of necessary transmission expansions, additions, and upgrades that enable it to provide efficient, reliable, and non-discriminatory transmission service – and it must do so by coordinating efforts with appropriate state authorities and other regional operators.

In PJM's case, its regional authority has resulted in more than $1 billion in transmission enhancements throughout PJM's region since 1998. Most of these enhancements have been paid for by generator developers interested in building units within PJM's market area. These generators are only interested in such large capital investments because of the demonstrated success of PJM's market. As a result of this success, generators are being built where the market signals are the highest, which also correlates directly with locations in the system containing the least resilience.

Considering that the electric grid is a synchronized system, the larger the footprint considered during expansion planning, the more likely that such changes will enhance the coordinated whole. The larger footprint provides for a more realistic assessment of how the whole grid will actually react to changes throughout the system. When the planning and the resulting construction are carried out without a regional perspective, the resulting changes could be detrimental to neighboring grid entities. On the other hand, coordinated planning ensures that future grid enhancements are improvements for the interconnected whole, and not just one entity. Coordinated planning will create a more efficient grid that can withstand an array of contingencies, as well as one that is more likely to survive unpredictable demands, because each grid change has rigorously been tested throughout a wider range of possibilities.

An example of highly coordinated system planning to enhance the grid's resilience is PJM's Probabilistic Risk Assessment Transformer Replacement Initiative. This initiative was started by the PJM planning staff to assess actual transformer failure rate against the predicted rate. The transformers, as with other highly critical components to the grid, present special problems, because they are often designed as individual unique instruments and not mutually replaceable. They are vulnerable to physical attack and are expensive to replace (roughly $6 million each). Transformers also can take a year or more to replace, due to the limited overseas manufacturing base. These problems, combined with the observed transformer failure rate, highlight the need to replace most large transformers over the next decade. PJM staff analyzed market data that quantify the cost of transformer failures, along with a reactive response to returning the system to a state of resilience. The staff found that the cost of waiting for failure can exceed the cost of proactively investing in a stored replacement by an order of magnitude. Through the community of PJM members, the PJM staff is taking its analysis to committees of stakeholder groups to illustrate the value of investing today, rather than down the road.

This standard design will overcome the problem that the unique transformer designs of most transmission owners will not function from one portion of the transmission grid to the next. Standardization will reduce the needed investment in spares, because fewer types of spares would need to be maintained (as this standardized spare could be used in many locations). Having such flexibility of response with a standard transformer will enable PJM to respond to either multiple transformer failures (due to simple aging), or to a multi-pronged attack of some sort on PJM transformers.

Based on the success of the transformer replacement initiative, PJM will examine its application of probabilistic risk assessment and member investments to other transformers and other critical portions of the infrastructure. PJM will continue to assess the needs of the system and evaluate (either through planning or market structures) available resolutions.

INDUSTRY SECURITY COORDINATION INITIATIVE

The leadership of regional transmission organizations in engaging the industry to resolve operating seams and enhance overall coordination has been significant. Other industry-wide initiatives are also protecting the electric infrastructure. For example, significant initiatives that directly address the security of the electric infrastructure have been undertaken by the leadership of the North American Electric Reliability Council (NERC). NERC monitors and analyzes the broad physical and cyber-based risks facing the electric industry. The council draws on the practical experience of industry experts, other critical infrastructure industries, and government agencies to understand where these threats might emerge, how they are changing, and to help the industry anticipate and respond to them.

NERC is, in essence, the electricity sector coordinator for critical infrastructure protection. NERC works closely with the Department of Homeland Security, the Department of Energy, Public Safety and Emergency Preparedness Canada, and Natural Resources Canada to make certain that crucial infrastructure protection functions are fully integrated and coordinated with government. NERC also maintains its Information Sharing and Analysis Center for the electric industry. NERC members use the center to report security incidents and threats. NERC shares this information, when appropriate, with industry participants, other critical industry sectors, and U.S. and Canadian governments.

Through its Critical Infrastructure Protection Committee, NERC facilitated development of physical- and cyber-security standards, guidelines, and industry workshops to ensure the reliable operation of the North American bulk power system. In addition, the council's American National Standards Institute-accredited standards development process includes an open, inclusive public review and consultation process, which works to ensure NERC's security standards are vetted by industry experts.

The end result of these NERC initiatives, and particularly the Department of Homeland Security outreach and industry standards, is that the electric industry is better able to address internal interdependencies and engage the federal government in helping address interdependencies between infrastructures.

CONCLUSIONS

When power system operators manage the electrical grid within established standards and policies, there is a great deal of inherent resilience. However, threats to the electrical infrastructure – whether from aging equipment, heat wave, tornado, terrorist attack, or other unimaginable event – requires that operating entities continue to integrate best business practices to be certain that each is abiding by the tenants of good utility practice.

With the advent of independent regional transmission organizations, the electric grid and its stakeholders have been able to experience immediate benefits through market design and market signals, unity of command and efficiencies in operations, joint operating agreements, and regional planning. These regional transmission organizations have greatly enhanced the efficiency of operations and markets without increasing public vulnerability. Indeed, the operators have strengthened the grid. As a result of the operators' initiatives, the industry will be far more flexible and responsive to the demands of the next unforeseen crisis, and the system efficiencies will continue to enhance security.

NOTES

1. Jones and Skelton 1999, pp. 46–48.
2. See also U.S.–Canada Power System Outage Task Force 2004.

14

ELECTRICITY: PROTECTING ESSENTIAL SERVICES

Jay Apt, M. Granger Morgan, and Lester B. Lave

The record of the past 40 years shows that in the nation's system for generating, transmitting, and distributing electricity, some blackouts are inevitable. Natural hazards produce many local and regional blackouts (Table 14.1), and society has learned to cope with them. Power outages occur more frequently than theory predicts, however, and despite years of promises and technology development, the frequency of large blackouts has not decreased over time (Figure 14.1). Making cost-effective improvements in control and operation of the grid[1] is important; however, data suggest that reducing the frequency of these low-probability, high-consequence events will become increasingly expensive.[2]

The U.S. and Canada blackout on August 14, 2003, revealed that many private institutions are far ahead of the public sector in defining their critical missions and taking steps to protect them when the lights go out. During the one-day blackout, some hospitals and television stations in New York City, Toronto, Cleveland, and Detroit were able to stay open because they had backup generators. Services in other sectors, however, could not be delivered. Elevators in office buildings were stuck between floors, trains stopped between stations, traffic signals went dark, cell phones lost reception, and, in Cleveland, water ceased to flow and sewers overflowed when the electric-powered pumps stopped functioning. If the blackout had persisted for longer than a day, the

Portions of this work have appeared in the following publications: S. Talukdar, J. Apt, M. Ilic, L. Lave, and M. G. Morgan (2003). "Cascading Failures: Survival vs. Prevention." *The Electricity Journal* 16(9): 25–31. J. Apt, L. B. Lave, S. Talukdar, M. G. Morgan, and M. Ilic (2004). "Electrical Blackouts: A Systemic Problem." *Issues in Science & Technology* 20(4): 55–61. J. Apt and M. G. Morgan (2005). "Critical Electric Power Issues in Pennsylvania: Transmission, Distributed Generation, and Continuing Services when the Grid Fails," Pennsylvania Department of Environmental Protection.

Table 14.1. Blackouts affecting many customers, 1965–2004

Date	Location	Number of customers affected (millions)
November 9, 1965	Northeastern United States	30
June 5, 1967	Eastern United States	4
May 17, 1977	Miami	1
July 13, 1977	New York City	9
January 1, 1981	Idaho, Utah, Wyoming	1.5
March 27, 1982	Western United States	1
December 14, 1994	Western United States	2
August 24, 1992	Florida (Hurricane Andrew)	1
July 2, 1996	Western United States	2
August 10, 1996	Western United States	7.5
January 1998	Québec (ice storm)	2.3
February to April 1998	Auckland	1.3
December 8, 1998	San Francisco	0.5
December 26–28, 1999	France (wind storms)	3.5
August 14, 2003	Great Lakes region, New York	50
August 30, 2003	London	0.5
September 2003	Atlantic region of United States (Hurricane Isabel)	4
September 23, 2003	Denmark, Sweden	4
September 28, 2003	Italy	57
November 7, 2003	Chile	15
July 12, 2004	Athens	3
September 5, 2004	Florida (Hurricane Frances)	2.8
August 31, 2005	Gulf coast of United States (Hurricane Katrina)	2.3
September 12, 2005	Los Angeles	1
October 25, 2005	Florida (Hurricane Wilma)	3.3

Source: Data on the U.S. and Canadian outages between 1984 and 2000 are from the North American Electric Reliability Council (NERC); data on other outages are from press reports.

region's public health and welfare would have begun to suffer from the failures of more and more socially critical missions (see Appendix 14.A for the effects of blackouts on an array of critical services).

Before the next blackout strikes, whether caused by natural elements or human sabotage, private and public institutions need to decide which of their missions (of those requiring electricity) are critical, and then protect them. In this chapter, we review the vulnerabilities of many critical systems and discuss cost-effective ways to reduce their vulnerability. Throughout our discussion, we approach the challenge of reducing vulnerability from the perspective of not simply protection of the electrical grid, but protection of the social services that rely on the grid.

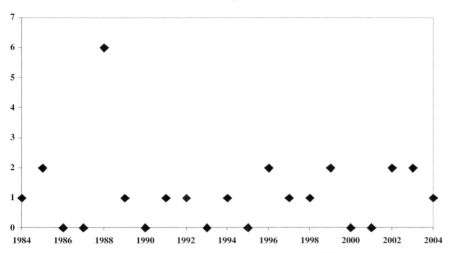

Figure 14.1. Number of blackouts in North America affecting 1 million or more customers, 1984–2004. No statistically significant trend showing improvement or worsening with time is evident in the data. Analysis is based on North American Electric Reliability Council Disturbances Analysis Working Group database and public reports.

Private institutions delivering critical services face additional challenges in that while the social benefits of keeping services running during an outage are large, these benefits are dispersed among society as a whole. The capital costs, however, are concentrated in the hands of the service providers. Therefore, there is little incentive for the private service providers to change. We discuss public policy measures that could alleviate this benefit–cost dilemma.

CRITICAL SERVICES: A CASE STUDY

To develop specific data on the fate of critical social services when the electric grid fails, the Carnegie Mellon Electricity Industry Center assigned students in a 2004 engineering project course the task of assessing the vulnerability of such services in the Pittsburgh area. Students also developed options and benefit–cost ratios for sustaining those critical services during grid power unavailability.

The case study found that while some important services in Pittsburgh, such as hospitals and the 911 emergency response system, have taken measures to ensure continued service during a blackout, several other vital services would lose power. These vulnerable services include both privately and publicly owned assets. For example, important private services such as grocery stores, gas stations, and cellular phone service are vulnerable. Traffic networks are also vulnerable, because Pittsburgh's traffic signals would fail during a blackout, and many tunnel ventilation fans would become inoperable. The study also found that three of the five Pittsburgh police zone stations do not have on-site backup generation. In addition, liquid fuel storage tanks, which rely on electricity to pump fuel, generally have no electric backup. Some fuel can be released from storage tanks via gravity flow, but the switchover from pump to gravity flow can be time-consuming.

The study found that Pittsburgh's natural gas system is highly reliable; possibly more so than the diesel supply chain. Although natural gas backup generators are typically more expensive than those powered by diesel, natural gas powered backup is a viable option for high value services, especially if the generators are used to produce electricity and heat during normal operating conditions. However, local law specifies in some cases that backup systems be fueled by diesel. Furthermore, critical service providers such as financial institutions prefer diesel – they can control their own fuel storage supply, independent of the natural gas supply. However, only a few days of diesel is usually on hand even in the best facilities. Propane can be used for backup fuel in certain locations.

As proven in the Paris heatwave of 2003 and the Quebec ice storm in 1999, an outage during extreme hot or cold weather could significantly damage health and the economy. If an outage were to occur during hot weather, air conditioners would fail. In very cold weather, forced-air heaters and electronic ignition boilers would not operate. In addition, an extended outage during the winter could cause pipes in homes to freeze and burst, putting more stress on emergency management personnel. In either hot or cold weather, some people would be at risk for health problems, and emergency shelters would need to be available. An effective information campaign (which takes into account that television sets would not be working) would need to disseminate information about the availability of emergency services. While plans do exist for handling weather-related emergencies in some cities, it is important that such plans be regularly reviewed and updated to ensure that regions are well prepared for an extended power outage.

RE-FRAMING THE PROBLEM: WHAT SERVICES MUST BE CONTINUED?

While much of the government and the research community, including many of those concerned with the electric power industry, have focused on the protection of networked infrastructure, what really matters is the social services that those networks provide. Three strategies can be pursued to assure that critical social services are maintained: (1) harden the network to make it less vulnerable to disruption; (2) make the network more robust so it can survive disruptions and continue to operate (perhaps at a reduced level of service); and (3) pursue alternative strategies to keep services operating when power from the network is no longer available.

Because networked infrastructures are physically dispersed, there is no way to harden every piece against accidental or intentional disruptions, although increased protection for some system components would make sense.[3] Researchers in cyber security understood the limits to system hardening many years ago. Indeed, it was the desire to produce a computer communication system that could continue to operate when parts of it were disrupted that led to the architecture of ARPAnet, the forerunner of today's Internet. Computer security theorists have therefore largely abandoned the model of a computer system as an impenetrable fortress. Rather, they seek to design a "survivable" system – that is, one that can fulfill its mission in a timely manner, even in the presence of attacks, failures, or accidents.[4] Making the electric infrastructure similarly more robust is feasible, and many improvements are possible in operations and standards.

A focus on survival of missions stands in contrast to survival of the generation and transmission grid through approaches such as "islanding" (separating the survivable parts of a grid from those that are critically wounded), which have long been used. These are good tools, but their implementation over the past two decades has failed to eliminate low-probability, high-consequence outages, nor are they likely to do so in the future.

Ensuring the fulfillment of critical missions is also different from either a traditional vulnerability assessment approach or the approach of making the electricity delivery system 100 percent reliable.[5] Invulnerability is not only very expensive, but it is also impossible to test and probably impossible to achieve for a complicated system like the electric grid. Rather, a fresh approach is needed to prevent society from incurring large costs during the inevitable next blackout or from attempting to entirely prevent such a blackout.

SEVEN STEPS TO ASSESSING READINESS

The goal of a socially oriented approach is to lower the social costs of grid failures, rather than preventing all of them. More specifically, the goal is to reduce the costs of the inevitable grid failures by assuring the continued availability of critical services and subsystems, such as traffic signals in urban cores, pumps for water and sewer systems, urban mass transit, emergency service systems, subway and elevator egress, and crucial economic functions.[6] Verification could be accomplished in a number of ways, including actual tests conducted on the services and subsystems (something that cannot be done on the full grid).

The first step in defining and verifying solutions to the survivability of critical missions would be to determine a set of design reference events that

Table 14.2. Three representative blackout events

	Temporal duration	Spatial extent	Reference frequency	Likely causes
Reference event 1	4 hours	1 circuit (about 1,000 people)	1 in 22 months	Load shedding, weather
Reference event 2	2.5 days	400,000 people	1 in 6 years	Weather, disruption of transmission or generation
Reference event 3	2 weeks	All of a region	1 in 50–100 years	Weather, terrorism

would mimic outages of varying lengths and geographical locations. The system would be evaluated on the basis of whether it fulfills critical missions during these design events. An example of a set of design reference events is given in Table 14.2.

The second step would be to define the missions that must be fulfilled. This step would results in enumeration of life-critical and economically impor- tant missions that are provided by electric power, together with a list of mis- sions which, if unfulfilled, would have important socio-economic consequences (such as reducing gross domestic product or inducing terror).

The third step would be to prioritize the missions. The priority list would be different for different design reference events. For example, a 12-hour out- age from a cascading grid failure would have different priorities than would a month-long blackout from a severe ice storm or human attack on system components. Similarly, some services, such as delivering potable water, could carry on uninterrupted for a day or more because of water stored in the system. Thereafter, however, water delivery would be far more problematic. Others ser- vices, such as sewage treatment and disposal, might be an immediate problem.

The fourth step would be to determine which missions are already protected (e.g., hospitals and navigation aids for air traffic). Weak links in the chain would be identified at this step. For example, while the New York City area's Newark and Kennedy airports quickly restored power for passenger screening and other boarding functions the day after the 2003 blackout, LaGuardia could not because it had insufficient backup power, and its grid power was slow to be restored. As a consequence, East Coast air traffic was snarled by the closing of a busy hub.

The fifth step would be to determine which missions require procedural changes or new hardware.

The sixth step would focus on the missions in step five that require new hardware. This step would seek cost-effective technologies that could fulfill critical missions during the design reference events. For example, light-emitting diodes (LEDs) could produce traffic signals with only a small fraction of the energy required to light the incandescent bulbs currently housed in traffic lights. Inexpensive batteries and trickle chargers of LED traffic signals could ensure that lights could continue to operate without additional electricity for days during a power outage. Other cost-effective devices might include those that make elevators return to the ground floor or allow subways and elevated trains to creep to the next station. Some devices would be attractive for private investment (for example, tenants may be willing to pay higher rent for a building that has its own micro-grid with backup power). For public goods at this stage, the costs of fulfilling the missions would be compared with the value of the missions, and alternative methods of fulfilling the missions could be evaluated. Effects of the candidate solutions on the nominal and recovering grid would be assessed and verified during this step by building and testing prototypes where necessary. For example, loads would be tested for their smooth transfers from distributed power systems to and from the grid to ensure that the transfer would not affect grid stability – this could require hardware and operations changes and would certainly require tariff changes.[7]

The seventh step would be to build a system for allocating competing resources required for these missions during an extended blackout. This is often the first step considered by managers trained in emergency response, but it would be much more effective if preceded by steps one through six.

Performing the tasks outlined in these steps can yield an up-to-date assessment of the readiness of the system to respond to challenges. Knowing the available hardware and procedures, governing authorities can estimate which missions could be accomplished and where the greatest trouble spots are likely to be.

PRIVATE AND PUBLIC INVESTMENTS IN SOCIALLY CRITICAL MISSIONS

During a large power outage such as one caused by a hurricane or ice storm, the best that government agencies can do by way of social services is to provide a limited number of shelters and very limited distribution of water. Most of the organizations in a position to assure that important social services continue during a power outage are private companies. While it might be to the collective benefit of society for these organizations to make investments that will make services more robust, it is often not in their private interest to do so. In other cases, the investments may be in the interest of private entities but not properly identified as an opportunity. Or it might be possible to provide incentives or information to make these investments more attractive to private entities.

Private entities such as supermarkets and gas stations have no responsibility to secure their operations to make them more robust to blackouts – they are responsible only for their owners. If it is possible to avoid loss or increase profits during a blackout, a profit-maximizing firm will do so. For example, the decision for a private company to install a backup system involves the calculation of the cost of a backup system, how often it would be needed, and whether it would generate net benefits.

Most backup systems required to provide services independent of grid power have associated capital and maintenance costs. When a purchase of a given capital expense is contemplated, the decision maker estimates the frequency of power outages at the location being considered, and the cost of the power outage. If a 100-kilowatt generator (appropriate for a heat treating furnace, for example) costs $76,000 and is financed over its 12-year lifetime, the annual cost of capital to purchase the generator at an interest rate of 7 percent is $9,400. Operations and maintenance costs for this size a generator, if properly maintained and operated at full load once a month, are approximately $1,900 annually, for a total yearly backup cost of $11,300. If the generator is used during a power outage to back up a service that incurs losses of $25,000 (perhaps in lost product during a furnace heat-treating cycle), then the generator would be a sensible purchase if the company expects the power to fail long enough to ruin production more frequently than once every two years. Figure 14.2 illustrates the decision process.

As another example, a multi-story apartment building owner with a typical small traction elevator faces a product differentiation backup decision. The elevator would be backed up by a 12-kilowatt generator, with capital cost of $13,200 and annual maintenance cost of $240. Using a discount rate of 7 percent and a 12-year equipment lifetime, the amortized monthly cost of the backup would be $160. For a five-floor apartment building with six apartments per floor, a monthly rent increase of less than $5 would pay for the backup. While some tenants might not value this service, others might seek out such a building and willingly pay the increase.

SUGGESTED POLICY CHANGES TO ASSIST INVESTMENT

Policies to encourage survivable services can be win–win situations. At present, however, institutional or informational barriers inhibit more widespread installation of backup systems, even when they generate net benefits. State and local governments could encourage or require private parties to improve the reliability of important social services in a number of ways. For example, governments could modify electricity tariffs to permit load serving entities to recover costs associated with designing, installing, testing, and maintaining backup on-site power systems for individual customers who sign up for this service.

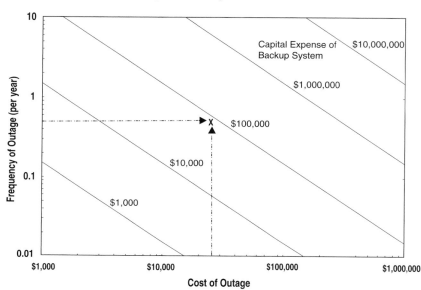

Figure 14.2. Decision support tool for backup systems. Example analysis for backup systems with 12-year depreciation at 7 percent discount rate and annual operations and maintenance costs equal to 2.5 percent of capital cost. If the capital cost of the backup system is lower than the point at the intersection of the assumed cost and frequency of a power outage, the purchase of a backup provides greater benefit than cost.

State and local governments could also provide information and suggestions to private parties to help them see how they might benefit from strategies that would make their services more robust in the face of power outages. A prime candidate might be a multi-story retirement home that installs backup power for its elevator and then finds that advertising this fact provides it with a competitive advantage.

Governments could encourage firms to offer "preferred customer" services that would assure continued availability of services, such as access to gasoline and ATM machines, to customers who have paid a fee that allows the companies to make the necessary additional investments. Preferred customers would be offered special service during an emergency. Alternatively, government might approve a special surcharge for businesses during blackouts, analogous to the surcharge collected by taxicabs during a snow emergency. The surcharge would enable a service provider to recover the cost of an already installed backup system. In addition, states should study whether barriers exist to fostering backup power installations funded through surcharges.

States or localities could require businesses to post publicly accessible information on the presence or absence of back-up devices. In much the same way that the publication of the U.S. Environmental Protection Agency's toxic release inventory has induced many companies to cut emissions, such postings might induce companies to take steps to make their critical services more robust.

Changes to building codes and other legal requirements could also change business practices. For example, a decade ago some U.S. cities adopted a building code that requires elevators in newly constructed buildings of more than seven stories to have backup power. Similarly, a community could require, as a condition of doing business, that firms operating gasoline pumps, ATM machines, or similar devices must work together to arrange for a percentage of these services to remain operational in the event of a power outage.

Governments could also provide tax incentives, subsidies, or grant programs to support the development of needed facilities. Given limited resources, this option should be used sparingly. Some circumstances, however, such as certain upgrades to emergency rooms of private hospitals, may warrant modest assistance.

Finally, communities could facilitate the construction, interconnection, and operation of distributed generation systems, and the operation of competitive micro-grid systems. In much of the United States today, rules granting utilities exclusive service territories make such micro-grids illegal; these rules could be changed.[8]

State and local governments could also encourage or require public and non-profit parties to improve the reliability of important social services. For example, information and suggestions to local governments and non-profit organizations could help them see how they might benefit from strategies that would make their services more robust in the face of power outages.

However, because most power outages arise from failures in the local distribution system, some jurisdictions have adopted regulatory requirements to foster retail competition based on reliability. This is most prevalent in New Zealand and Australia, where up-to-date reliability indices are posted on utility and government websites.[9] Transparency of this sort aids consumers, but it is uncommon in the United States.

TEMPTING TARGETS

Electric infrastructures have been targeted for destruction by, for example, the North Atlantic Treaty Organization (NATO) in the southern Yugoslav province of Kosovo, the Farabundo Marti National Liberation (FMLN) in El Salvador, radical environmentalists in the United States and the Czech Republic, and labor movements and disgruntled landowners in several countries. They have also proven to be tempting targets to hunters practicing their sharp shooting. Iraqi insurgents have attacked European and U.S.-manufactured hardware in

Iraq, and presumably some information on vulnerable features has been shared with groups outside Iraq.

Several general areas of vulnerabilities may be tempting targets for sabotage. For example, often many of the main transmission lines feeding cities travel over a single corridor, providing a target for both natural hazards and human disruption. A 2002 study by the National Research Council identified large transformers as a critical area of vulnerability, because they are often unique and take many months to construct.[10] Spare relays and transformers are sometimes stored at substations.[11] Indeed, substations have been the subject of domestic attacks with some frequency. On the generation side, however, vulnerability due to a fuel shortage is now lower, because past labor actions in the coal mining industry were frequent enough that generators now have many weeks of coal on hand.

Several companies maintain large portable generators that can be brought in to provide power in emergencies. Analysis should be undertaken to examine whether the country has enough such capacity, and whether other portable equipment (such as transformers on rail flat cars) are needed. Navy and other ships are also a potential source of power during disruptions in coastal cites, and diesel locomotives can be used in inland locations, but all of these options require advanced preparation and planning.

Although a potential target of attack, the electric grid is not particularly effective for causing psychological disruptions. Because the average U.S. customer loses electricity for 2–8 hours one or two times per year,[12] it is difficult to incite terror by turning out the lights. There are conditions, however, under which a blackout can cause terror. For example, riots occurred during the 1977 New York City blackout (3,500 arrests were made amid widespread looting) but not during the 1965 or 2003 blackouts.[13]

On the other hand, the psychological value of attacking nuclear generation stations and their associated fuel storage facilities is substantial, and these installations have received additional physical security attention in recent years. An attack would not need to cause a core meltdown or the release of radioactivity to generate a public outcry. Public concern that leads to plant closures could quickly reduce generation margins in countries such as France, where nuclear power provides 85 percent of electricity, and the United States, where roughly one-third of all power in the eastern United States is generated by nuclear stations. The public's concerns may be especially important in nations that have experienced a nuclear power plant or fuel cycle mishap (the United States and Japan, for example). Continued attention to the physical and cyber security of these facilities, including personal reliability programs to reduce personnel vulnerabilities, is warranted.

A recent review by Farrell and colleagues identifies additional areas of vulnerability, such as tank farms associated with the U.S. Strategic Petroleum

Reserve.[14] While petroleum distillates fuel only 2 percent of U.S. generation, diesel (a petroleum distillate) provides much of the nation's emergency backup capability. The study points out that liquefied natural gas (LNG) storage facilities could be a target. LNG is stored at roughly 150 peaking generation facilities worldwide, and more than 100 LNG tankers ply the seas. An attack on an LNG terminal could leave the public much less likely to accept an increase in the number of LNG terminals, which are projected as trade in LNG becomes more global. One response to the risk of disruption of gas supply would be dual-fired generation units, which can burn whichever of two fuels costs less or is available if supply of the other is interrupted.

Computer-based failures or attacks on infrastructure have also become a concern. Farrell and colleagues describe the U.S.-led 1982 cyber attack on the Soviet Union's natural gas pipeline infrastructure as evidence of similar current vulnerabilities. More recently, consolidation in the power industry has increased the number of devices running the same computer software (making more systems vulnerable to a single attack), and pressures from competition leave little money for large expenditures for cyber security. The U.S.–Canadian commission investigating the 2003 blackout established a special task force to look into whether the blackout was caused by cyber attack. The task force concluded that it was not, but nonetheless significant architecture and operation vulnerabilities existed in the control software and hardware. Organizations such as the Computer Emergency Response Team Coordination Center may be able to work with vendors and operators to reduce such vulnerabilities, but the threat of insider action is significant.

A 2003 study by Watts describes instructive South American experiences in reinforcing their grids.[15] For example, Chile, which first deregulated electricity in 1982 and faced domestic attacks throughout that decade, constructed mobile substations, accompanied by transportation plans to move these large-wheeled units and coordinated in advance with urban law enforcement units. Some standardization of transformers at subtransmission voltages was made, with spare units stocked at low power levels. Substations were protected with double fences 4–5 meters high and solid steel doors with sensors to detect intruders. Transmission tower bases were protected with fences. However, Watts notes that "after more than two decades of deregulation in Chile and in absence of terrorist attacks, some secure physical policies have been forgotten in order to reduce 'unnecessary' costs." Watts notes that Brazil has established a monitoring and control network based on power line communication, which can isolate some locations to reduce the extent of cascading outages. This system uses an automated protection scheme based on both central and distributed agents to control generation and load, and is said to achieve stable operation within seconds of loss of a major substation.

RECOMMENDATIONS FOR GRID IMPROVEMENTS

While completely eliminating blackouts is an unrealistic (and expensive) goal, it is quite possible to improve upon the current record of blackouts while at the same time decreasing the extent of cascades caused by deliberate human actions.

Investigations of blackouts such as those listed in Table 14.1 reveal a number of common problems that need to be addressed.[16] Significant improvements can be made within the next few years. We recommend a near-term plan based on our analysis of what has worked in other interconnected systems. These proposed improvements recognize that real people make mistakes, and that the system should be designed to reduce both the number and effect of those mistakes. Some of these recommendations are hardware-related, but all are designed to reduce both accidental and deliberate large blackouts.

MONITORING AND DATA COLLECTION

Ineffective monitoring, or lack of monitoring, comes up regularly as a problem leading to blackouts. While there is great variability in the quality of system monitoring across the country, monitoring of the power system overall is more sparse than it should be, both within regions and between them. Market pressures are not likely to improve matters.

Systems to display these data to operators vary as well, and most control centers ignore decades-old recommendations to display the information in a format that enables operators to identify the extent of a disturbance. The present representations of system state, particularly indicators of danger, are too complex. They stress accuracy over clarity. And even the limited and poorly displayed monitoring data that are collected are not shared among power companies.

National standards for telemetry data on power flows and transmission system components must be established and enforced. Operators can no longer be expected to make the right decisions without good data. Control centers must have displays and tools that allow operators to make good decisions and to communicate easily with operators in different control areas. There must be backups for power and data, and clear indications to all operators that data are fresh and accurate. The emphasis should be on data and presentations that support decisions.

Grid operators also need much clearer metrics of danger and suggestions for action (similar to collision avoidance alarms in aircraft and in air traffic control centers). A better warning system does not have to be expensive, however. For example, if the existing 157,000 miles of transmission lines in the United States were fitted with $25,000 sensors every 10 miles, and if each sensor were replaced every five years, the annual cost would be $100 million, or roughly one-tenth the lower bound of the estimated annual cost of blackouts. From a consumer's standpoint, the cost would increase the average residential electricity bill (now approximately 10 cents per kilowatt-hour) to 10.004 cents per kWh.

As described in more detail in Chapter 13, the data systems that monitor and control the grid in most large utilities formerly were proprietary systems with limited or no connections to the rest of the world. However, partly in response to cost pressures, some system functions in some utilities are no longer isolated. This leaves these systems vulnerable to cyber attack. Because the arcane nature of proprietary systems no longer protects utilities that adopt a common system, they must pay much more attention to the threats posed by hackers who can develop one exploit and use it on many power systems.

TRAINING

Another issue to address is operator training. Training, as with monitoring, varies widely between power companies. Most operators are not trained routinely with realistic simulations that would enable them to practice dealing with the precursors to cascading failures and the management of large-scale emergencies.

All grid operators must be trained periodically in contingency recognition and response using realistic simulations. These simulations must include all operations personnel in a way that exposes structural deficiencies such as poor lines of authority and insufficient staffing. The goal should be to recognize and act upon signs of extreme system stress that may be well outside daily operations experience. The description of piloting an aircraft as "years of boredom interrupted by moments of stark terror" applies also to grid operations, and training should be as rigorous as that undergone by pilots. Grid operators must have the systems and training that only realistic simulation, using their specific control center configuration, can provide. Federal standards for training, licensing, and certification of grid operators and control centers are warranted to ensure against a single weak control center bringing down a large area. No federal entity mandates such realistic training for grid operators, but the owners of nuclear generation plants proved (after Three Mile Island) that it can be done.

EQUIPMENT

Power companies widely vary in their system abilities and equipment sophistication. Some companies can interrupt power to customers quickly during an emergency, whereas others are nearly helpless. This patchwork ability to shed load is not appropriate to the current interdependent transmission grid.

Some systems can interrupt power automatically, but some cannot even do it manually from the control center. Operation control centers must be able to actually control.

Shedding of load in the near term would probably take the form of preemptively blacking out large areas. Some power companies have customers who have agreed to be blacked out in emergencies, but this practice is not uniform. In a future decade, it may be possible on a large scale to provide signals to consumers to shed parts of their load in exchange for lower tariffs, but this partial load reduction solution has not been economically feasible with current systems in the United States.

Sensors, load-shedding devices, and other system components must be checked on a more systematic basis than they are at present. The August 30, 2003, London blackout resulted from an undersized component that had not been checked. Five hundred thousand people were stranded during rush hour. In today's highly competitive environment, chief financial officers may frown upon periodic checking and testing – it should therefore be mandated by national standards.

INDUSTRY STANDARDS

Industry standards are lax across the grid, and this also can lead to outages. For example, in many systems vegetation under transmission lines is trimmed only every five years, instead of more frequently. As was recorded in the 2003 U.S.–Canada blackout, lines sagging into untrimmed trees contribute to blackouts. Industry standards for tree-trimming under transmission lines must be set with the costs of failures in mind, not just by the competitive constraints of the immediate marketplace. Companies that do not comply should be penalized. These standards could vary by region and should be set by regional bodies such as the regional transmission operators.

NATIONAL COORDINATION

A national grid coordination center should be established and run as a national asset by a private body. It would stimulate research and development to support the data needed for grid monitoring. A national center would also monitor the grid at regional and larger levels, provide national flow control, and perhaps act as a backup for computer failures in individual control regions. As with air traffic control, the roles and responsibilities of the local and national centers would be neither perfect nor without infighting, but they would complement each other to avoid the complete lack of "big picture" awareness seen in so many blackouts.

In addition to the national coordination center, a permanent government investigation body should be appointed, including professional accident investigators who are trained to look for systemic as well as discipline-related causes. This body should be an entity separate from the operators or regulators of the grid.

INNOVATIVE THINKING

In the longer term, more serious consideration should be given to changing the basic geometry and operation of the transmission system. For example, advanced power electronics could be use to control exactly where power flows through the lines.[17] Advanced systems could also be used to better compensate when industrial customers add or drop very large loads. In addition, direct current transmission lines could reduce the loss of energy that occurs in transmitting alternating current power long distances. Other technologies, such as robust automatic control systems to reduce dependence on human operators, might be feasible in a decade.

If properly implemented with intelligent controls, generating electricity in relatively small plants located close to consumers, rather than in large central generation plants, could reduce blackouts.[18] Such distributed generation could also lead to dramatic increases in overall system efficiency because excess heat need not be thrown away, as it is in large central plants, but could be used for space conditioning or process heat. Such distributed generation now accounts for 7 percent of the United States' capacity, and the Energy Information Administration calculates that a three-fold expansion is possible. This distribution could dramatically increase reliability, if local fuel storage is used (to avoid reliance on the natural gas network). However, while distributed generation holds promise, for the foreseeable future the U.S. power system will primarily rely on centrally generated power sent over the existing transmission grid.

The need for innovative thinking suggests that an expert commission should be created to advise the body setting mandatory standards. The commission should have experts from operating companies, systems operators, the Federal Energy Regulatory Commission (FERC), and academia to take a fresh look at how to design both engineering and operation standards to satisfy the goals of the system.

INFORMATION SHARING

Information is required to convince decision makers to invest in survivability. However, organizations that hold important information about survivability and the power network are highly protective of their information.

The sort of information needed to assist governments in the decision-making process can be summarized in three groups: (1) models of the storage, transportation, and consumption of fuel and other goods during a blackout; (2) catalogs of the electrical needs and generating abilities of facilities, agencies, businesses, and communities; and (3) quantification of the criticality of different services during design reference power interruptions.

Obtaining the information necessary to assess the vulnerability of important services in the face of power outages and proposing solutions may be at odds with the desire of many organizations, especially those involved with homeland security, to keep information about vulnerabilities out of the public domain so that pernicious persons or groups cannot exploit those vulnerabilities. The problem is that if groups performing system-level analysis for state or local governments cannot access important information, it is extremely difficult for policymakers to develop rational policies to reduce future vulnerabilities. We encountered such difficulties when we performed a preliminary analysis for one agency of the state of Pennsylvania and found that even with the state's assistance it was impossible to obtain important data from other state agencies.

Public utilities are particularly protective of information about their emergency preparedness. For example, community water systems have prepared vulnerability assessments and emergency response plans. When questioned about any aspect of emergency operations at water system facilities (including the number and size of generators, the amount of fuel stored at pumping stations, or the parts of the water system that will first lose service in a crisis), facility managers will most likely answer by saying that the information is contained in the emergency response plans. These documents are reviewed but not retained by the states before being sent to the federal level. They are not available to the public.

This lack of information sharing is a problem even for responsible government agencies: one county emergency management coordinator described hitting an information "roadblock" when requesting information from local utility companies in an attempt to develop a critical infrastructure plan. A 2003 survey of public utility commissioners found that 54 percent "believe that utilities are either somewhat or very reluctant to share their security information with the commission."[19] The purpose of protecting information about emergency preparedness is to assure the public that emergency plans will not be compromised. This must be balanced by releasing enough information to assure the public that emergency plans are effective.

At the moment, the pendulum appears to have swung too far in the direction of compartmentalized information. For example, certain actions by the Department of Homeland Security to centralize and then compartmentalize information about vulnerabilities are not conducive to developing corrective action. For example, a 2004 Associated Press report describes the process by which landline phone networks must alert federal regulators of service outages and report how the problems will be avoided in the future, a process that Federal Communications Commission (FCC) asserts has improved the landline phone networks; however, attempts to apply the same process to the wireless and cable phone networks have met with opposition.[20] Neither the companies themselves nor the Department of Homeland Security want the information made available to the public for fear the information will provide "blueprints for terrorists bent on wrecking U.S. communications systems." Rather than filing with the FCC and allowing public access, the reports would be filed with the Department of Homeland Security.

The problem, of course, is that the Department of Homeland Security and other similar organizations have neither the resources nor the authority to develop and implement most of the changes that would be needed to make important social services less vulnerable. Those resources and responsibilities are widely distributed among state and local governments and in the private sector. It would help if the Department of Homeland Security and other similar organizations at sub-national levels could develop a greater ability to engage in system-level analysis that considers and balances a range of legitimate but perhaps conflicting social objectives. They would also need a greater ability to think about problems in terms of preserving social services as opposed to a unitary focus on protecting "critical network services." Furthermore, the department would benefit from having a greater ability to develop and promote a range of alternative polices that states and private entities might adopt to promote viable solutions to reduce vulnerabilities. Finally, the department would need to provide arrangements that allow informed independent analysis by academic and other groups following the lead of other agencies that deal with sensitive information, such as the Bureau of the Census (i.e., academics and others can become sworn Census Officers) and the Department of Defense (e.g., the JASONs, a rotating group of the nation's top scientists, have been providing classified analysis to the department since 1959).

In the meantime, the states would be well advised to develop an interagency arrangement, perhaps in the form of a standing interagency committee, which is charged with better balancing the conflict between the short-term need to protect information about vulnerabilities and the long-term need to encourage responsible parties to use such information to develop and implement solutions. Such an interagency committee should also have responsibility for exercising oversight to assure that solutions and systems developed by others would actually provide the protection they promise. Too often, entities provide assurances that everything is under control, only to find that back-up systems fail to operate when an actual outage occurs.[21]

Every organization faces a dilemma over releasing potentially harmful information. The more people who see the information, the more likely it will get into the hands of people who seek to harm the organization. But the more people with access to the information, the more likely that it will be thoroughly critiqued and that better plans will be developed.

The dilemma is particularly acute in a democratic nation under threat of terrorist attack. Not only is a great deal at stake in ensuring that proposed actions are efficient and cost effective, but the public has a stake in knowing what is to be done to protect them. A nation must strike a balance between open information (no one wants to tell terrorists how to do the most damage) and cost-effective actions. We know from published information on military programs that classified programs generally are not cost-effective and often are ineffective. Indeed, organizations often try to limit the release of data to shield themselves from scrutiny that might show that they are doing their job badly. In the United States at the moment, only a few individuals in the Department of Homeland Security have access to data, and there is little effective outside review of how their $41 billion is being spent.

Regardless of attempts to obscure it, however, much of the desired information can be obtained through other sources, from current employees to past computer postings. While publishing the information might make it easier for terrorists to disrupt society, it also is very likely to lead to improving the systems and possibly preventing or at least lessening the potential impact.

HOW MUCH PROTECTION?

The cost of failure of the grid can be substantial: the outage that affected 50 million people in August 2003 cost $4–6 billion. Given the high potential cost of a widespread outage due to a terrorist attack, government and private entities will face substantial pressure to encourage or require protection of a wide range of assets. However, no nation has unlimited resources to dedicate to countering the many threats that could be directed at symbolic targets and critical infrastructures.

How should a balance be struck between protecting assets and continuing robust economic activity? We can use the figure of cited above to estimate that attacks that black out 10 million people may take place every year in the absence of increased protection, costing $1 billion annually; if the system were up-graded at a cost of $100 million per year, the number of blackouts might be reduced to once every 10 years. With this assumption, we calculate that upgrading the system is worth $900 million in expected savings. In fact, this savings might justify an upgrade that cost $9 billion. Of course, different assumptions of attack frequency will change these estimates greatly. If attacks on the grid succeeded in causing blackouts every three years (with no additional protection), then the justifiable expenditure for additional protection would be $300 million annually.

Whatever level of expenditure on new protection is agreed upon, mechanisms must be in place to decide on whether a particular expenditure should be made, and to allocate its costs. O'Hanlon and colleagues argue that the most efficient mechanism to allocate costs is "a combination of regulatory standards and antiterrorism insurance" whose premiums would be shared between the government and the users.[22] We note that the insurance industry is very slow to insure newly identified risks, so such insurance may be unavailable. We have also argued earlier in the chapter that national standards for grid operation and data can dramatically improve reliability. These will be viewed by industry as "unfunded mandates," but their cost may be viewed by society as justified.

In the energy sector, the FERC has indicated that it will approve applications to recover prudent costs for protection of electric power assets.[23] Burns and colleagues have discussed principles that state public utility commissions might use to determine whether protection-related expenses should be passed on to customers.[24] These authors conducted a survey of public utility commissioners in 2003, finding that 83 percent have no special guidelines for determining the acceptability of protection measures. They suggest that commissioners might use rules developed during the expenditures of funds to upgrade software to avoid the Y2K problem as a starting point. In any case, there should be enough flexibility to allocate some costs to protection for systems that have both public and private benefits. For example, the Department of Homeland Security could provide financial incentives to distributed generation systems that decrease the probability of grid failure.

We now consider the question of how to judge which expenditures to make, because the nation cannot afford to protect everything. If one target is hardened, an attacker will switch to a softer target. One way to study such interactions is through game theory. Another is through large-scale war gaming. Used together, both approaches have the potential to identify cost-effective areas for protection expenditures.

Keith Florig examined whether the U.S. Postal Service should extend its existing program to irradiate mail bound for certain destinations in the wake of the anthrax attacks.[25] He estimates that irradiation of all mail would raise postage costs by 1–2 percent, delay delivery by several hours, and cause harm to some materials shipped by mail. He finds that mail sanitization "would have to avert at least a hundred casualties per year to be as cost-effective as most other societal investments in public and occupational health." But Florig then goes on to note the enormous disruptiveness of the anthrax scare, and that "society's willingness to pay for preventing future incidents of terrorism through the mail should be based on the combined economic, institutional, psychological, and public health damage that such mischief can inflict. . . . Before committing billions of dollars to technologies for the long-term enhancement of mail safety, federal authorities would be wise to ask the public how they weigh these costs and benefits."

This formulation addresses a key point: protection expenditures can be large enough that the public, not just experts or lawmakers, should be involved in judging which systems should be protected. Risk communication is often thought of as a way to lessen the impact of a disaster on society but, as noted by Morgan and colleagues, it is a two-way street whereby the public and experts can jointly shape policy.[26]

In the United States, substantial roadblocks exist to both analysis and policy for protecting the electricity infrastructure. It is perfectly possible for any group isolated behind walls of secrecy to make enormous expenditures that are ineffective, directed at unimportant targets, and impose substantial penalties on individual liberties and the economy. Decisions must be made only after thorough examination of alternatives by a diverse range of analysts, and after wide-ranging and open discussion. Such a conversation is overdue.

In summary, the terrorist threat has prompted a more general examination of the reliability of the electricity system. The examination is welcome in that considerable costs inflicted on individuals and the economy could be lowered by focusing on ways to fulfill critical missions during a blackout. Because the costs of defending against both natural hazards and terrorists could be considerable, the public needs to be brought into the discussion to find out what interruptions they find most bothersome and what they are willing to pay – through higher taxes, higher product prices, or annual fees – for increased reliability.

ACKNOWLEDGMENTS

The authors thank the students of the Carnegie Mellon Electricity Industry Center 2004 engineering project course, who developed and assessed the data in the vulnerability study of the Pittsburgh area. The student members of the team were Benjamin Anderson, Erik Andreassen, Michell Birchak, Barbara Blackmore, Laura Cerully, Helen Davis, Jonathan Fasson, Dominic Fattore, Sandra Gani, Wenyao Ho, David Lagattuta, Emily Lauffer, Rachel Lin, Landon Lochrie, Nick McCullar, Ben Mosier, Jonathan Ng, Laura Sperduto, Marena Tiano, and Jennifer Wong. The Ph.D. candidate project managers were Kyle Meisterling and Paul Hines. Course faculty were Dmitri Perekhodtsev, Marija Ilic, Jay Apt, and M. Granger Morgan.

Appendix 14.A. Taxonomy of critical services

Service category	Specific service	Time, duration, and scope of outage during which service is critical	Typical existing backup	Health and safety risks	Economic risks
Emergency Services	911 and related dispatch centers	All outages	Most systems have comprehensive backup power systems	Risk of injury and fatality; inability to report and prioritize emergencies, potentially leading chaos	Indirect costs associated with increased chaos after an outage; businesses and stores may delay re-opening
	Police headquarters and station houses	All outages	Varies; some stations have backups; AC power is often required for recharging hand-held radios	Risk of injury and fatality; inability to report and prioritize emergencies, potentially leading to chaos	Indirect costs associated with increased chaos after an outage; businesses and stores may delay re-opening
	Fire protection services	All outages	Varies by location	High risk of injury and fatality	High risk to businesses and residences
Medical Services	Ambulance and other medical transport services	All outages	Limited; many require AC power to charge batteries for radios and cell phones, and to pump fuel at commercial gas stations	Risk of injury and fatality	Injury and fatality, loss of workforce
	Life-critical in-hospital care (e.g., life support systems, operating rooms)	All outages	Full, but some failed during the August 14, 2003 blackout; some systems have inadequate testing procedures	High risk of fatality	Fatality, loss of workforce
	Less-critical in-hospital services (e.g., refrigeration, heating and cooling, sanitation)	Medium and extended duration	Varies	Increased risk of infection	Indirect risk

Non-electric public utilities	Water treatment	Extended duration	Typically very limited	Risk of illness if system pumps untreated water	Incapacitation and workforce productivity
	Drinking water	Extended duration; immediately in areas with wells	Limited gravity-fed areas; some pumps have backup power	Risk of dehydration and/or disease, especially during hot weather	Incapacitation and workforce productivity
	Sewer treatment	Medium and extended duration	None in most areas	Risk of disease from untreated sewage in water supply	Incapacitation and workforce productivity
	Sewer pumping	Short duration, high use periods (morning, evening); long duration	Very limited	Risk of disease from sewage buildup in low elevation areas	Incapacitation and workforce productivity; damage to buildings in low-lying areas
	Natural gas	All outages (including some critical backup generation fueled with natural gas)	Most pipelines use the materials being transported as the pumps; in-home furnaces require power for pilot lights and fans	Significant health risk for customers using gas heat during cold weather	Pipes may burst in cold weather if homes/buildings are left without heat
Communications	Radio broadcast media	Medium and extended duration	Most stations have backup systems with several days of stored fuel	Radio is important for distributing emergency information; risk of chaos if stations fail to disseminate information	Increased chaos costs from decreased communications
	Television broadcast media	Medium and extended duration	Many stations have backup power systems with several days of stored fuel	Less vital than radio communications as most TV sets require electricity	Most risk is borne by broadcasters and advertisers
	Cable television and broadband services	Medium and extended duration	Minimal	Less vital than radio communications as most TV sets require electricity	Risk for businesses that rely on cable broadband services

(continued)

Appendix 14.A (*continued*)

Service category	Specific service	Time, duration, and scope of outage during which service is critical	Typical existing backup	Health and safety risks	Economic risks
	Wired telephone systems	All outages	Most systems have good backup power systems; some fiber optic systems depend on grid power, as do many new phones	High risk as many vital services rely on the wired telephone system	Very high economic costs; communications are vital to every sector in an emergency
	Wired data service	All outages	Varies	Minimal risk, unless used by medical or emergency services	Significant risk, as many business functions require broadband connectivity
	Wireless (cellular) telephone and data systems	All outages	Minimal; battery backup provides only 2–8 hours of service at most base stations	Possible risk to those unable to make emergency calls	Significant risk to customers who rely on cellular phones
	Computer services (on- and off-premise)	All outages	Data centers typically have good backups with several days of stored fuel and priority fuel contracts; on-site uninterruptible power supplies are typically limited to several minutes of computer backup power	Loss of data	Minimal risk, if computers use commercially available automatic shutdown software sensitive to power supply; significant for unprotected businesses
Non-emergency government services	Information service offices	Medium and extended duration	Varies with location and type of building	Important for distributing emergency information; risk of chaos if information is not available	Increased chaos costs from decreased accurate information

	Prisons and other detention facilities	All outages	Varies	Potential risk to prisoners, guards, and public if security systems fail	Indirect risk from increased chaos
Transport and mobility	Building elevators	All outages	Varies with local building codes, height, and age of building	Decreased mobility for elderly and disabled	Indirect risk from lost time
	Traffic signals	All outages, particularly in urban areas	Traffic police; a very few locations have battery backup	Risk of injury and fatality due to emergency vehicle delays; could be especially serious in conjunction with a terrorist attack	Large social costs associated with traffic delays
	Tunnels	All outages	Generally none for ventilation; lighting has limited backup	Accident risk if lighting fails; possible congestion disruption of emergency vehicles	High social cost resulting from traffic delays and closure if air quality becomes too bad
	Light rail systems and subways	All outages, evacuation immediately after event	None aside from emergency lighting	Some risk to elderly or disabled if adequate evacuation plans are not in place; high health risk if ventilation is inadequate	High social costs from workforce delays in urban areas
	Conventional rail systems including railroad crossings	Extended duration	Crossings have backup batteries	Some additional accident risk at busy intersections	Fatalities at rail crossings
	Air traffic control, navigation, and landing aids	All outages, immediately after event	Federal Aviation Administration requires backup power systems to be in place	Some risk of airplane accidents that would result in a large number of fatalities	High social costs resulting from air traffic delays and in-airport delays

(continued)

Appendix 14.A (*continued*)

Service category	Specific service	Time, duration, and scope of outage during which service is critical	Typical existing backup	Health and safety risks	Economic risks
	Airport operations including security and on-airport ramps, luggage systems, transportation, and food	All outages, immediately after event	Partial backup power is typical	Some health risk during extreme weather conditions	High social costs resulting from air traffic delays and local and system-level airport delays
	River lock and dam operations	Extended duration	Varies	Minimal risk, unless there is a diesel shortage and river transport is required	Significant costs if there is a diesel shortage; lost trade
	Buses	Medium and extended duration	Varies, but generally minimal; problems with fuel pumping and traffic congestion	Minimal risk	Significant social costs due to loss of access to gasoline for personal vehicles
	Drawbridge operations	Varies	Varies	Minimal risk, unless there is a diesel shortage and river transport is required	Significant costs if there is a diesel shortage; lost trade
Lighting	Building evacuation and stairwell lighting	All outages	Trickle charge battery lighting required by building codes	High risk of injury and fatality without emergency lighting, especially in densely populated locations	Injury and workforce incapacitation
	Residential lighting	All outages	Flashlights, candles, and lanterns	Some risk of injury in stairwells; risks due to makeshift lighting	Injury and fatality from fires due to candles and makeshift lighting
	Indoor commercial and industrial lighting	All outages	Varies	Varies	Varies

	Security lighting	All outages	Varies	Varies by location	Potential for high economic losses
	Street lighting	All outages	None typically	Increased accident risk when roads are unlit	Indirect costs
Retail grocery	Cash registers, lighting, refrigeration, security	Medium and extended duration	Varies with location and firm preferences	Risk of food and emergency supply shortage during an extended outage	Large social costs resulting from insufficient access to food and supplies
	Wholesale grocery distribution networks	Medium and extended duration	Generally minimal	Risk of food and emergency supply shortage during an extended outage	Large social costs resulting from insufficient access to food and supplies
Financial	Cash machines	Medium and extended duration	None typically	Minimal	Significant social costs resulting from inadequate access to cash
	Bank branches	Medium and extended duration	Only for security systems	Minimal	Minimal risk, if some other access to cash exists
Financial	Credit card systems	Extended duration	Some backup power typically	Minimal	High risk during an extended outage (if also a shortage of cash)
Fuel infrastructure	Pipeline and pumping systems	Medium and extended duration	Full for natural gas (because the system uses its own gas), typically none for other products	Indirect risk for vital services if fuel pumps fail to supply required fuel	High risk to services that rely on diesel to backup important systems
	Local storage infrastructure	All outages	Varies; many locations must switch from pump to gravity feed systems	Indirect risk for vital services if fuel cannot be distributed	High risk to services that rely on diesel to backup important systems
	Non-pipeline transport and distribution systems	All outages	Backup not required as long as truck fuel is available	Indirect risk for vital services if fuel cannot be distributed	High risk to services that rely on diesel to backup important systems or propane for heating and cooking
	Retail gasoline sales	Medium and extended duration	None (a few exceptions exist)	Significant risk if emergency services cannot obtain gasoline for vehicles	High social costs associated with lack of mobility if gasoline is unavailable

NOTES

1. Apt et al. 2004.
2. Talukdar et al. 2003.
3. High-voltage transformers are especially vulnerable – they are easy to incapacitate (e.g., some could be disabled with a single shot from a high-powered rifle) and very difficult to replace. Other elements of the power system, while not a risk to system reliability, could be used by terrorists as a vehicle for damage. For example, some cooling towers could be used to disperse chemical or biological warfare agents, and nuclear spent fuel storage facilities could be attacked in a way that dispersed waste. For more information, see Farrell et al. 2002.
4. Lipson and Fisher 1999.
5. Our proposal that in addition to addressing the security of the transmission system we should focus on sustaining critical social services when the transmission system fails has stimulated some allergic reactions among traditional power engineers. For a discussion, see Fairly 2004.
6. Farrell et al. 2002.
7. Morgan and Zerriffi 2002.
8. King and Morgan 2003.
9. New Zealand's reliability information is posted on the website of the Ministry of Economic Development; see "Electricity Information Disclosure Statistics," http://www.med.govt.nz/ers/inf_disc/disclosure-statistics/2003/2003-08.html, accessed July 14, 2004. Australian companies similarly posts information on the Internet; see http://www.qca.org.au/files/EnergexServiceQualityReportSeptQtr2004.pdf, accessed February 2, 2006.
10. National Research Council 2002b.
11. Farrell and Zerriffi 2004.
12. Short 2002.
13. For more information on the riots during the 1977 blackout, see *Time Magazine* 1977.
14. Farrell et al. 2005.
15. Watts 2003.
16. See also U.S.–Canada Power System Outage Task Force 2004; Western Systems Coordinating Council 1996; Energy Advisory Board Task Force on Electric System Reliability 1998.
17. At the moment, the United States and Canada are divided into just three synchronously interconnected regions in the east, west, and Texas. In principle the large eastern and western regions could be sub-divided to reduce system-wide vulnerability.
18. Zerriffi 2004.
19. NARUC/NRRI 2003.
20. *Wired* 2004.
21. Two notable recent examples are a large hospital in Cleveland that lost power during the U.S.–Canada blackout of August 14, 2003, and the air traffic control tower at Los Angeles International airport that experienced a power outage on April 12, 2004, and disrupted nearly 100 flights.
22. O'Hanlon et al. 2002.
23. 96 FERC ¶61,299, Docket PL01-6-000 (September 14, 2001).
24. Burns et al. 2003.
25. Florig 2002.
26. Morgan et al. 2001.

15

A CYBER THREAT TO NATIONAL SECURITY?

Sean P. Gorman

Since the attacks on the World Trade Center and the Pentagon on September 11, 2001, the nation has increased its attention on cyber security as an important facet of national security and critical infrastructure vital to the functioning of the U.S. economy. The White House's National Strategy to Secure Cyberspace states that "by 2002, our economy and national security are fully dependent upon information technology and the information infrastructure. A network of networks directly supports the operation of all sectors of our economy."[1]

Cyber security is also highlighted as an area critical to national security by the National Research Council's Critical Infrastructure Protection Board and National Security Telecommunications Advisory Committee.[2] This point, though, has not been without contention, especially with regards to the threat posed by cyber terrorism. *Washington Monthly* editor Joshua Green maintains that a myth of cyber terrorism has been imagined or created by the current administration: "There is no such thing as cyber terrorism – no instance of anyone ever having been killed by a terrorist (or anyone else) using a computer. Nor is there compelling evidence that Al Qaeda or any other terrorist organization has resorted to computers for any sort of serious destructive activity."[3]

The recurring theme in this book is the question of private efficiencies resulting in public vulnerabilities. In no other critical infrastructure sector are vulnerabilities more publicly seen than in cyber systems, which include the logical and physical network of computers, servers, fiber optic cables, and other components that constitute the nation's information infrastructure. Worms, viruses, and denial of service attacks happen daily, and the largest and most devastating are regularly covered in the media. The costs are not trivial, and they impact the private and public sector at a national level. For example, analysis by Lawyer indicates that computer virus attacks in recent years amounted to approximately $10–17 billion annually in terms of lost productivity and clean-up costs; the Love Bug, a particularly virulent attack, alone cost approximately $8.7 billion.[4]

Each of these attacks exploits vulnerabilities, most often known, in computing software and operating systems. Most computer users are familiar with the process of downloading patches or updates to safeguard their computer from the latest known vulnerability. This makes cyber systems unique among critical infrastructures because hackers are persistently finding and publicly exploiting vulnerabilities, and thus there is not the information-sharing problem seen in other infrastructures regarding vulnerability information. Vulnerability information is regularly supplied to the consumer in an ongoing race to keep computers patched and secure from exploitation.

There is little question that these vulnerabilities result from a drive for efficiency. In cyber systems, vulnerabilities are most often the result of exploits found in the code of a piece of software or operating system (in software terminology, an "exploit" is a vulnerability in programming code that allows a malicious actor to take control or advantage of a computer system). The exploits are what are not found in the quality assurance testing of the product before it is released. The number of known vulnerabilities in database of the National Institute of Standards and Technology totaled 14,400 at the end of 2005.[5] It would be impractical and most likely impossible to test to the point of zero exploits, but the number of exploits and cyber attacks is testament to the private efficiency public vulnerability trade-off. The question with cyber security is not whether there are vulnerabilities, but whether there is a threat that warrants federal involvement, or whether it is simply a business issue that should be left to the market. To provide perspective on this issue, this chapter examines whether a credible threat to cyber security exists from terrorism, organized crime, or other nation-states. The paper does not address the government's ability to deal with cyber security or policy steps that could be taken to improve cyber security.

To analyze whether cyber security poses a threat to national security, I analyze two sides of the issue and discuss a range of potential threats. I also analyze the incidence and effect of the failure of critical infrastructure. I base my analysis on a wide variety of public documents and media outlets, because there is little written in the academic literature on the specific topic. The sources of material vary in their credibility and should be taken on face value. Often the most intriguing information comes from sources that are difficult to verify but provide a valuable insight not available in academic or mainstream literature. Weight has been appropriately distributed to sources depending on their credibility, but all sources are presented and discussed to cast the widest possible net of knowledge.

THE MYTH OF CYBER TERRORISM?

Green's myth of cyber terrorism opened a policy debate on the issue of cyber security in the context of national security, specifically with regard to the possible threat of terrorists implementing a cyber attack on the United States. *CIO* senior writer Scott Berinato extended Green's argument, stating that terrorist organizations like Al Qaeda will follow the path of least resistance and suggesting that physical attacks and bombs offer a cheaper and easier alternative than the sophistication of a cyber attack.[6] Even the use of a cyber attack to control physical infrastructure electronic systems has only been considered as a worst-case scenario causing minor inconvenience. The majority of cyber security reports have been from investigative reporters relying on interviews with experts in the field like Georgetown University Professor Dorothy Denning, who Green cites as stating that "not only does [cyber terrorism] not rank alongside chemical, biological, or nuclear weapons, but it is not anywhere near as serious as other potential threats like car bombs or suicide bombers."[7]

A more analytical approach was taken by the U.S. Naval War College in conjunction with Gartner Research to simulate a "digital Pearl Harbor" attack against the nation's critical infrastructures. The study found that "a group of hackers couldn't single-handedly bring down the United States' national data infrastructure, but a terrorist team would be able to do significant localized damage to U.S. systems."[8] The researchers of this study mention a further caveat that such an attack would require $200 million in funding, country-level intelligence, and five years of preparation.

Whether there is an enemy that could undertake such an offensive is an open question. Is national security realistically threatened by critical infrastructure and cyber security, or is it an oversold myth? To date most available evidence of cyber threats in the public domain is anecdotal. It is useful, though, to examine the anecdotal evidence of critical infrastructure threats. To provide some structure to the wide range of attack examples considered, I divide them into physical failures (unintentional and intentional), malicious cyber attacks, and developing cyber warfare capabilities.

ATTACK OF THE BACKHOES AND MASSIVE PHYSICAL TELECOMMUNICATION FAILURES

While cyber attacks tend to attract the majority of media coverage, it is also important to note damage of critical infrastructure from physical failures to illustrate the interconnection of the two. Hacking is not the only way to cause disruption of the nation's cyber command-and-control structure. Cyber assets are affected by physical infrastructures just as physical infrastructures can be affected by cyber assets in their complex interdependency.

Physical failures in the telecommunications grid are probably the most frequent type of infrastructure failure. These failures result largely from accidental fiber optic cable cuts from backhoes and shovels. The prevalence of accidental fiber cuts can be seen in the number of local "call before you dig" and "Miss Utility" programs. While most fiber cuts result in minor inconveniences such as the loss of localized service, several cuts have resulted in major outages. Fiber cuts have often plagued airport air traffic control. In 1990, a fiber cut shut down Chicago's O'Hare International Airport, and the following year a cable cut in New Jersey shut down all three New York airports and caused air traffic control problems from Washington, D.C., to Boston.[9] Fiber cuts often reveal the interdependency of several critical infrastructures – the same fiber cut that shut down New York City's airports also shut down the New York Mercantile Exchange and hampered long-distance calling for nine hours.[10] Furthermore, fiber cuts can often be time-consuming to repair. In 2000, a San Jose cut left customers out of service for more than a week; repairs to the fiber optic wires had to be hand-spliced one by one and each splice tested.[11] More recently, a train derailment and chemical spill in Baltimore's Howard Street tunnel slowed Internet traffic coast-to-coast. While the robust SONET[12] ring technology employed by several providers who lost circuits did reroute traffic in short order, the flood of rerouted traffic along poorly capacitated alternative routes slowed traffic as far away as Seattle and Los Angeles.[13]

TELECOMMUNICATION FAILURE DURING 9/11

The single largest physical loss of telecommunication infrastructure happened with the fall of New York City's World Trade Center towers on September 11, 2001. Federal Communications Commission records report that the telecommunications provider Verizon alone had to replace 1.5 million voice circuits, 4.4 million data circuits, and 19 SONET rings. In addition, 112,000 private branch exchange trunks and 11,000 fiber optic lines dedicated to Internet service providers were destroyed.[14] Furthermore, Verizon lost its primary central office at 140 West Street, resulting in the loss of telecommunication service to 34,000 businesses, including the New York financial district.[15] The loss of the Bank of New York's primary data center caused nearly $80 billion in securities trades to fail.[16] Following the destruction on 9/11, the federal government called for firms to locate backup facilities 120 miles from Manhattan, but this was rejected by the financial community, and most vulnerabilities are considered to still be unfixed.[17] Some of the vulnerabilities of the fiber optic system that were realized in the 9/11 attacks had been predicted as early as 1995 – a government document reported that use of fiber optics reduces transmission routes, concentrating traffic within the fewer routes; it also decreases use of alternative transmission technologies, which restricts spatial diversity.[18]

While only a few cases of fiber optic sabotage have been documented, their effects have been dramatic. Over the past two years, the Seattle area has been plagued by a fiber optic saboteur who has taken out 911 emergency services four times with strategic fiber cuts; the most recent cut on September 3, 2003, disabled 911 services for nearly nine hours.[19] A somewhat mistaken but common belief is that fiber optic networks are fully redundant rings that would prevent these types of cuts from disrupting critical resources. In an August 5, 2003, court case involving the Maine Public Utility Commission, an expert witness from Verizon stated that only 10 percent of the fiber rings in Maine are fully redundant, and 90 percent are at least partially collapsed (meaning both sides of the ring are located in the same right of way) and vulnerable to single cut failures.[20] Further, the standard operating procedure for restoring a failed line is to locate the lead engineer for the region, consult paper maps, manually identify an alternate route, and send technicians to wire a jumper around the outage. This very manual, people-dependent process is far different from the perception of self-healing, instantly rerouted networks seen in marketing literature.[21] While the difficulties imposed by dependence on telecommunications fiber and anecdotes of fiber failures are well documented, there has been little organized effort to quantify the impact of the vulnerability at a national level. Without such analysis, it is difficult to understand the magnitude or consequence of the nation's vulnerability, and whether market forces alone are sufficient to provide an adequate level of security.

EFFICIENCY AND VULNERABILITY IN THE TELECOMMUNICATIONS SECTOR

These trend of efficiency at the sake of diversity has only increased as aspects of the telecommunications industry have consolidated in an effort to cut costs, many times resulting in increasing public vulnerabilities. Since the telecom boom of the late 1990s, a belief pervades that there is a glut of telecommunications fiber – as much as 40 million miles laid and 80 percent of it unused. This belief has led to the perception that the United States has an overabundance of telecommunications infrastructure. Many assume that the United States is so densely wired with fiber, physical attacks on it are unlikely to cause significant outages.[22] Scant empirical research means that this conclusion cannot be supported.

While it is true that the United States has an overabundance of fiber optic cable, the nation does not have an equal amount of diversity for routing the cables (commonly called rights-of-way). The cost of securing unique rights-of-way has resulted in many providers co-locating their fiber optic conduit with other types of providers along the same rights-of-way. A fiber optic cable right-of-way typically shares space with roads, rail lines, gas pipelines, electric transmission lines, and even sewers. The laws governing where rights-of-way can be granted for installation of fiber optic cable also vary greatly across jurisdictions. Cities, counties, state, and even the federal government can set their own right-of-way rules across geographies for which they have jurisdiction. The result is a patchwork of fiber optic cable routes across the United States, greatly varying in resilience.

Compounding the variance of right-of-way regulations is the financial position of the telecommunications sector and the fiber aggregation trends. The heavy build-outs of the telecommunications boom came at a heavy price when the market fell in 2000/2001. Most firms were left with staggering debt and falling prices for their services. These issues have been further compounded by the fraudulent activities of several large players including MCI/WorldCom, Tyco, Adelphia, and Enron. As a result, the industry has little disposable capital for investments in laying fiber cable. In fact, many current engineering approaches in the sector are predicated on having no additional physical diversity (i.e., not laying additional fiber paths or rights-of-way) because it is cost-prohibitive. A Sprint technical report details the company's aversion to installing new cable because of costs and geographic barriers, as well as the slowness of installation as compared with increasing transmission capacity over existing cables.[23] Most providers' solution to network survivability and resilience, therefore, has become over-provisioning – that is, using 50 percent spare capacity as a design rule of thumb.

A second complication to increasing diversity and resilience in the telecommunications sector is market consolidation, specifically for fiber routing. The number of large players in the telecommunications sector is rapidly shrinking. SBC, a carrier composed of the former companies Ameritech, Southwestern Bell, Pacific Bell, Nevada Bell, and SNET, recently also bought AT&T and Verizon, and has agreed to purchase MCI/WorldCom. In each of these acquisitions, cost savings must be realized for the strategic move to be profitable for the acquirer. For fiber optic systems, this means aggregation and consolidation of rights-of-way. As more telecommunication routes are groomed to single fiber rights-of-way with each acquisition, they reinforce a sector-wide trend of sacrificing diversity for cost savings.[24]

As a result of these divergent and interdependent market and policy forces, it is imperative to have a more fundamental understanding of the resilience of the nation's fiber optic grid.

LIGHTS OUT

Cyber assets do not operate in a vacuum – they are interdependent with other critical infrastructures such as electric power. Examination of these interdependencies and the result of failures are therefore useful for understanding the extent of resilience in the cyber system. While physical telecommunication failures may be the most common types of failure affecting cyber systems, by far the most obvious to the public are electrical power grid failures. The huge U.S. and Canada blackout on August 14, 2003, was one of the largest and most recent, but it is far from singular. (For detailed description and analysis of the 2003 blackout, see Chapters 12 and 13.) Another major outage on August 10, 1996, blacked out the western United States after sagging power lines came in contact with untrimmed trees and shorted out. The conditions during the 1996 and 2003 blackouts were quite similar. Both occurred during August, when power consumption peaks along with the summer heat. As with the 1996 outage, over-capacitated lines resulted in a cascading failure that spread throughout the region. The effect of the blackout can be seen in satellite images of the Northeast before and during the blackout (Figure 15.1).

The 2003 blackout also poignantly illustrated the interdependencies between the United States' electric power network and Internet infrastructures. As power failed, many regional and enterprise networks experienced outages, although most national backbone networks had adequate backup power supplies to survive the outage.[25] Figure 15.2 illustrates the scope of Internet routing outages during the blackout.

Each dot on the map represents the location of a network that failed as a result of the 2003 blackout. As seen by the failure in Florida, the interdependencies between the Internet and electric power are not always geographically correlated.

CYBER ATTACKS COME OF AGE

Critical information infrastructure has two fundamental components: the physical aspects (e.g., fiber optic cables and support devices) and the data and systems that run over them. Physical infrastructure is the less studied of the two components, but accidental and planned failures have damaged areas as diverse as financial systems and air traffic control. While there is a consensus that physical failures can be very damaging, little is understood about which parts of the infrastructure are most vulnerable or how to quantify (or justify the cost of) the areas in need of protection.

Cyber vulnerabilities are better documented and have many more cases of actual exploitation but also lack thorough analysis of protection strategies and

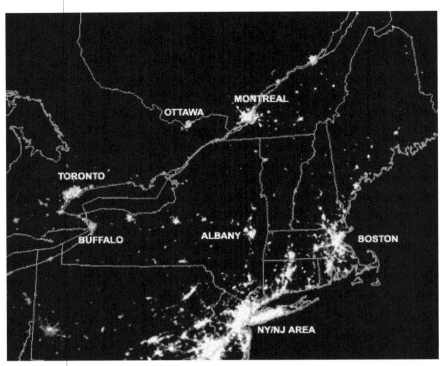

August 13, 2003, Satellite image of Northeast US and Canada. *Source:* Platts Inc.

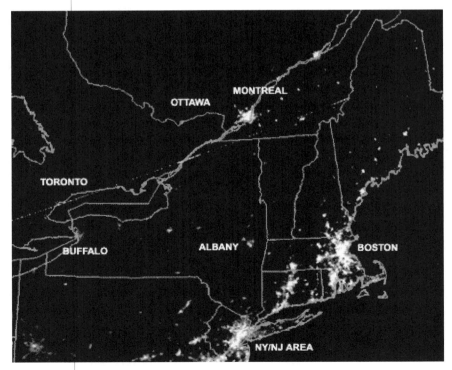

Figure 15.1. Satellite images prior to and during August 13, 2003, blackout. *Source:* Platts Inc.

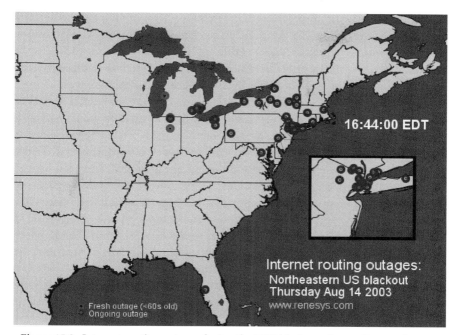

16:44:00 EDT

Internet routing outages:
Northeastern US blackout
Thursday Aug 14 2003
www.renesys.com

Fresh outage (<60s old)
Ongoing outage

Figure 15.2. Internet routing outages during the 2003 blackout. *Source:* Renesys Inc.

costs and benefits, especially in the realm of policy. Cyber attacks have become increasingly sophisticated, and the motivations behind them has moved beyond simple Web defacements and teenagers hacking for fun. Mounting evidence shows cyber attacks being orchestrated by crime syndicates with connections to terrorist organizations. Furthermore, more and more evidence indicates a heavy involvement of nation states in developing cyber attack capabilities. The nature of both sources of threat points to a fundamental understanding of information infrastructure as an area of critical national security. While cases of major catastrophes from cyber attacks have not yet been documented, the tools, motivations, abilities, and potentials have been documented.

Tracking cyber attacks and discovering the culprits is incredibly difficult and rare, but the few successes and best guesses expose some disturbing trends. The following brief scenario is intended to illustrate the sophistication of attacks, their economic motivations, and possible implications for national security.

Millions of packets flood through a data pipe into a major Manhattan bank, crashing upon the firewall acting as the bank's first line of defense. The tidal wave of packets overwhelms the firewall's ability to sort the traffic, shutting it down and denying any traffic entry to the bank network. The attack causes a temporary network outage, but on the surface it has not violated the security of the network. Hidden in the flood of packets that saturates the firewall is a "packet sniffer," which acts as a traffic spy gathering data unbeknownst to the network administrator. When the network administrator reinitializes the downed firewall, the packet sniffer grabs the administrator's user name and password and passes it along to the bank's anonymous assailants. Money is then withdrawn from the compromised bank, sent to a second bank, and then sent to a third or fourth bank. By the time the breach has been discovered (typically a two-hour operation), the money has been withdrawn from the final bank and transferred from the intervening bank as a valid transaction. Only the intervening bank and originating bank created and authorized the fraudulent transfer, and the terminating bank is not held liable. The monetary loss is covered by insurance, and the system continues to operate. According to a veteran security executive who requested anonymity, "successful and unsuccessful attacks like one just described happen on a daily basis throughout the financial community."[26] The attack described in this case was traced back to a nation-state actor. The majority of cyber-based bank attacks are tightly covered from public attention by strict non-disclosure agreements in the name maintaining public confidence.

THE RUSSIAN CONNECTION

While the above incident comes from an undisclosed source and cannot be verified, a growing number of public accounts of cyber attacks are increasingly linked with Russian organized crime. The growing problem of Russian cyber crime and the resulting financial loss led the Federal Bureau of Investigation (FBI) to issue a public warning about "organized hacker groups from Eastern Europe, specifically Russia and the Ukraine" exploiting Microsoft vulnerabilities for financial gain.[27] Russian organized crime has been documented by various media outlets to be responsible for a stream of high-profile cyber attacks, including "stealing secret Microsoft source codes, ransacking the Pentagon's computers, hacking into NATO's military websites, posting thousands of credit card numbers on the Internet, and stealing millions of dollars from Western banks."[28]

Specifics that outline targets and actors in cyber attacks are often difficult to come by. The few cases that have been prosecuted do offer insight into the nature of these operations. In 2001, the FBI arrested two Russian hackers by tricking them into coming to the United States for job interviews with security firms and hacking into the Russians' computers for evidence. Although the Russian government protested the FBI's tactics, the two hackers were tried and convicted in U.S. court. The court cases revealed that the Russian pair first hacked into

CTS Network Services to launch attacks on two credit card processing centers (Sterling Microsystems and Transmark), while also stealing financial data from Los Angeles-based NaraBank and FSI Inc. The second part of their strategy was breaking into Glen Rock Financial Service and then threatening the exposure of credit card information if the company did not pay a ransom.[29] Hacking and extortion techniques have been frequent tactics employed by Russian organized crime, the most prominent being the theft of 300,000 credit cards from CD Universe, which were then held for ransom.[30] One report maintained that Moscow houses the Civil Hacker School, which is funded by Russian intelligence agencies and Russian crime syndicates to ensure a steady supply of cyber crime talent.[31]

A WEEK IN THE LIFE OF INTERNET PREDATORS

Possibly the best recent example of the growing weight and sophistication of cyber attacks on the Internet was the attack by multiple predators across the Internet in August 2003. The first instance was the Lovesan worm, which attacked Windows XP and Windows 2000 operating systems starting August 11 with an executable file that randomly turned off the affected computer. Three different mutations of the worm infected hundreds of thousands of computers. Lovesan was followed by the Nachi worm, which used the same exploit but also affected Microsoft IIS 5.0 servers. In a twist, the Nachi worm killed the Lovesan worm and patched the vulnerability that allowed the Lovesan worm to propagate. The negative externality of this was a tremendous amount of Internet traffic, which overwhelmed and shut down many networks, including the world's largest intranet belonging to the U.S. Navy and Marine Corp.[32] The third of the deadly trio was the Sobig.F virus that propagated through Microsoft Windows electronic mail. The address from which the e-mail arrived was spoofed with domain names associated with the end-user. If the attachment was downloaded, it executed a program that told the affected computer to download a program from 20 different servers located across the United States, Europe, and Korea. The virus also opened proxies on affected machines, allowing them to be used as unsolicited bulk commercial e-mail (spam) gateways to the Internet. One source attributes the Sobig worm to a Russian spammer.[33] Finally, the big three predators spawned scavenger predators such as the Dumaru virus, which sent a spoofed e-mail from "support@microsoft.com" alleging to have a patch for the Lovesan worm. The e-mail's attachment left a backdoor into the affected computer, allowing it to be remotely controlled.

These cyber attacks not only illustrate a higher level of sophistication than just hacking incidents; it also illustrates an increasing level of impact. Detailed analysis of the attacks has uncovered some disturbing implications: Peter Simpson, manager of ThreatLab at Clearswift (a security software company), maintains that the Sobig virus was developed by organized crime syndicates to facilitate spam scams.[34] Viruses like Sobig leave backdoors or Trojan horses on computers that allow them to be remotely controlled at a later date. Most often, these backdoors are used to send spam "undercover," to keep it from being filtered out as coming from known spammer addresses. While spam is annoying, in the past it hardly seemed to constitute a high level threat. This conception is beginning to change, however. One of the latest discoveries reveals the utilization of these backdoors in a sophisticated credit card fraud scheme again linked to the Russian underworld. In such as scheme, computers that have been remotely controlled by virus-enabled backdoors are linked in a ring, and each computer hosts a pornography site for a few seconds before it is passed off to another site. The ring also rotates compromised computers to send spam, directing surfers to disreputable Web sites.[35] The sites then swipe unsuspecting customers' credit card numbers. A similar plot by a group of Polish hackers uses worm-enabled backdoors to route traffic through compromised computers so that cyber crime activities cannot be traced. The group's corporate front – Bulkertraffic.com – offers service to spammers, purveyors of Internet fraud, and other nefarious groups as a form of invisible hosting.[36] The same Polish group also offers for sale the use of 450,000 hijacked computers with high-speed connections for a variety of illicit activities. There is a growing black market for hijacked computers that can be used for everything from spam dispersal to distributed denial of service attacks. This black market provides a growing resource that significantly changes the scale at which cyber attacks can be waged.

Are cyber attacks from organized crime syndicates a national security issue, and do they constitute cyber terrorism? The cyber terrorism question is a matter of definition, but a reasonable case can be made that organized crime does play a role in funding and equipping terrorist groups. The academic literature and news reports indicate a strong link between organized crime, cyber crime, and the funding and growth of terrorist groups.[37] Many of the cyber attack techniques outlined above have been directly linked to funding terrorist groups through such "businesses" as spam/porn, credit card theft, identity fraud, and money laundering.[38] Reports also have connected Russian organized crime with Al Qaeda in the appropriation of weapons of mass destruction and the utilization of Al Qaeda operatives in Russian apartment bombings.[39] While the majority of evidence comes from often-unverified news reports, the existence of growing cyber attack capacity in Russian and other organized crime syndicates is without doubt. Furthermore, the connection between these crime syndicates and terrorist organizations is well documented. At a minimum, a growing number of cyber attacks and related financial crimes are funding terrorist groups, and it would not be a far leap to believe that terrorist groups may evolve cyber attack tactics to aid their own missions. Both aspects point to cyber security as an area of increasing importance to national security.

AL QAEDA AS A CYBER THREAT

The vulnerability of critical infrastructure is well documented from actual failures, and the sophistication of growing malicious cyber attacks has been laid out. But are these areas that terrorist organizations are looking to exploit? Al Qaeda may be capable. The group's connection to the technical skills to implement infrastructure attacks appears to be in place, but Al Qaeda and other terrorist groups have always used physical attacks focused on inflicting the loss of human life to force world attention to their causes (and as stated at the beginning of this chapter, no terrorist has ever used a computer to kill a person). Without precedent to point to, is their compelling evidence to call for precautions against a cyber threat that has yet to occur?

A good place to start answering this question is by examining Al Qaeda's own rhetoric on the matter. On December 27, 2001, Osama Bin Laden put out a statement that "it is very important to concentrate on hitting the U.S. economy through all possible means."[40] This statement has become a mantra within Al Qaeda to focus on striking the "key pillars" of the U.S. economy. Quoting this communiqué by Bin Laden, Arabic newspaper *Al-Hayat* reported that Al Qaeda's Abu Hafs Brigade claimed responsibility for the August 2003 U.S.–Canada blackout.[41] He also stated that the blackout attack was "a message to all the investors that the United States is no longer a safe country for their money, knowing that the U.S. economy greatly relies on the trust of the investor." While post-blackout analysis and statements by the Bush administration ruled out any terrorist involvement in the blackout, the statement does make clear the attention Al Qaeda has focused on critical infrastructures and the U.S. economy's dependence on them.

While the statement was most likely opportunist propaganda, it does point to an evolution in the strategies and tactics of Al Qaeda. Apparently Al Qaeda has come to believe that targeting the U.S. economy can have a large damaging effect, and that the U.S. economy's reliance on vulnerable critical infrastructures makes them easy targets. Last, that guerilla attacks and tactics on these infrastructures will erode public confidence, thus affecting long-term devastation on the U.S. economy. In a 2002 interview with author Dan Verton, Sheikh Omar Bakri Muhammad (the leader of Al-Muhajirun, an Islamist group supporting Al Qaeda) stated that "in a matter of time, you will see attacks on the stock market."[42] Bakri expands this statement by outlining how such an attack might go forward and how resources are being developed to do so: "I would not be surprised if tomorrow I hear of a big economic collapse because of somebody attacking the main technical systems in big companies. There are millions of Muslims around the world involved in hacking the Pentagon and Israeli government sites." The Sheikh concluded with a caution that Al Qaeda was seriously interested in "cyber weapons" and advocated using them "to destroy the economy of capitalist states."

While the statements of Sheikh Bakri are definitive, it is suspect as to how much of the statement is inflammatory rhetoric to promote Al Qaeda's cause and how much is actual threat. According to a special report on Internet security featured in the *Economist* in 2003, American intelligence uncovered an Al Qaeda hide-out in Pakistan that had been used to train hackers to attack the computer systems of power grids, dams, and nuclear plants.[43] While none of this is a smoking gun, it does point to a growing threat that U.S. policy would be wise to prepare for.

CYBER WARFARE AND NATION-STATES

Perhaps an even stronger argument for including both cyber security and critical infrastructure as integral aspects of national security is the growing cyber warfare threat posed by nation-states. Conservative reports indicate that 20 to 30 countries are developing or already possess cyber warfare capabilities.[44] The growing dependence of nation states on information technology for economic viability and military capabilities have led to grandiose statements like:

> ... cyberspace has become a new international battlefield. Whereas military victories used to be won through physical confrontation of weapons and soldiers, the information warfare being waged today involves computer sabotage by hackers acting on the behalf of private interests of governments.[45]

Cyber warfare itself dates back to the Cold War, when Sandia laboratories traced virus attacks on U.S. computers to their origins in Bulgaria and East Germany.[46] Malicious attacks against U.S. Department of Defense computers have risen from 225 in 1994 to 40,000 in 2001.[47] Perhaps the most widespread and damaging attacks occurred in March 1998 and code-named "Moonlight Maze," which resulted in the theft of "thousands of files containing technical research, contracts, encryption techniques, and unclassified but essential data relating to the Pentagon's war-planning systems."[48] Red-teaming exercises (in which a group simulates the activities of malicious actors by trying to break into or compromise a system or target) that tested the strength U.S. computer defenses like "Eligible Receiver" and "Zenith Star" illuminated several vulnerabilities – including the ability to shut off the power grids of nine cities, control 911 emergency systems, and "paralyze" military command and control systems.[49] Although the point has been made that there is no hard evidence of foreign government involvement in any cyber attack,[50] the ability to mask the origination of an attack makes the possibility of producing hard evidence dubious, but other avenues to investigate the role of nation states in cyber attacks are highlighted in the next section.

CHINA'S CYBER SOLDIERS

The most well-documented cyber warfare initiative belongs to China, which has been conducting cyber warfare exercises since 1997 and has been operating an information warfare military unit since 2000.[51] The ability to wage cyber warfare with information technologies is considered a critical component of China's national strength.[52] The growth and reach of China's information warfare capabilities are impressive, including the establishment of a cyber warfare complex in Bejucal, Cuba, to monitor data traffic and intercept U.S. communications.[53] Security experts state that Chinese hackers are probing and mapping critical U.S. systems, especially financial networks, on a daily basis.[54] The gravity of these capabilities becomes more disturbing when placed in the context of Chinese military strategy documents. The release of the book *Unrestricted Warfare* provides a perspective on the development of China's cyber warfare capabilities; specifically, the book "proposes tactics for developing countries, in particular China, to compensate for their military inferiority vis-à-vis the United States during a high-tech war."[55] The document praises computer hacking as more influential than a nuclear bomb, and it reveals a strategy of asymmetric warfare that uses non-traditional tactics to defeat a military superior foe (explicitly the United States):

> As we see it, a single man-made stock-market crash, a single computer virus invasion, or a single rumor or scandal that results in a fluctuation in the enemy country's exchange rates or exposes the leaders of an enemy country on the Internet, all can be included in the ranks of new-concept weapons.[56]

> While few may argue in current times that a hacker with even the most sophisticated cyber warfare capabilities matches the threat of a nuclear weapon, elements of the Chinese military see it as the future and are investing heavily in that future.

Investment in cyber capabilities may not be confined to China's military expenditures. Since the telecommunications collapse of 2001, Chinese buyers have purchased the telecommunications companies PSINet, Level 3, Asia Global Crossing, and Global Crossing Inc. – a total original U.S. investment of $20 billion, purchased for 3 cents on the dollar by various Chinese interests.[57] Robert Fonow of the National Defense University asserts that these Chinese acquisitions could provide a platform for espionage and network warfare, citing that 95 percent of Department of Defense traffic uses the international telecommunications system.[58] With these recent Chinese telecommunications acquisitions, he calculates that most military and diplomatic traffic passes over Chinese-owned networks, with some traffic passing through facilities in the Chinese mainland. His over-riding belief is that China plans to use its cyber warfare capabilities to prevent the projection of U.S. force by preventing command-and-control apparatuses that guarantee supply lines and troop coordination. In fact, many of these same tactics were successfully employed by the U.S. military in the invasion of Iraq to render the enemy immobile. A combination of such tactics in conjunction with disruptions of the domestic financial system paints a bleak if hypothetical picture.

THE MAGNITUDE OF THE CYBER SECURITY THREAT

Green, in his *Washington Monthly* article, correctly concludes that terrorists cannot kill people with computers, and moreover, that no one has been killed by hacking or even cyber warfare incidents. Just because lapses in cyber security have not resulted in bloodshed, however, should not prevent U.S. cyber systems from being an issue of importance to national security. Terrorists have not used nuclear weapons to kill anyone either, but that does prevent the possibility from being a topic of grave concern. Green and other do make a valid point that the hype and hyperbole of threat and reality do need to be investigated analytically.

JURISDICTION OVER CRITICAL INFORMATION INFRASTRUCTURE

In the aftermath of 9/11, critical infrastructure protection came to the fore in the U.S. government, and telecommunication and cyber security became one of the most immediately identifiable areas of focus. Currently the security of the nation's telecommunication system, which is in vast part controlled by private interests, falls under several federal jursidictions. Unlike in the financial sector, no firm regulatory body or framework exists when it comes to security aspects of telecommunications. In general, telecommunications fall under the Federal Communications Commission, but when it comes to security the federal mandate becomes less clear. The White House's National Communications System was created for coordinating and planning the telecommunication sector to assist during crises and disasters. This role has grown since the agency's inception in 1962 to include the security of telecommunication infrastructure, as well as the Internet. The Clinton administration formed the White

House's Critical Infrastructure Protection Board to look after the security of the nation's core infrastructure including telecommunications, and its former head Richard Clarke was the federal government's cyber security czar. Agencies such as the Federal Reserve Bank and Departments of the Treasury and Justice have also become involved in telecommunication security when it has been an integral part of their domains, as in the case of financial services and their related networks.

The creation of the Department of Homeland Security has again changed this landscape. On March 1, 2003, the National Communications System moved into the new Department of Homeland Security under the Information Analysis and Infrastructure Protection Directorate. According to the President's fiscal budget, \$4.2 billion will be spent on cyber security in 2003, and \$4.5 billion has been requested for protection of critical infrastructure.[59]

POLICY SOLUTIONS

Even with the considerable institutional investments and money spent addressing the issues surrounding cyber security, significant obstacles remain. What are the policy mechanisms that are best suited to addressing issues? Is it an area that can be solved by purely market mechanisms, or has there been market failure that need to be remedied by government intervention? If government intervention is warranted, what form should it take – incentives, standards, or regulations? Many questions arise, but currently few have answers. One answer that has been put forward from many perspectives is the use of insurance as a mechanism for promoting investment and establishing standards for cyber security. While insurance theoretically offers a well understood and effective mechanism for addressing cyber security, one variable is missing from the equation. For insurance to effectively remedy the problem, metrics need to be developed by which to base actuarial science. If risk cannot be quantified and mitigation/prophylactics cannot be measured, then actuarial tables cannot be created and the fundamental mechanisms required for insurance companies to issue coverage are lacking.

The insurance sector is an area in which the public could contribute by helping to establish standards and metrics in conjunction with the private sector to determine best practices and bases for insurance discounts. This exercise would be the cyber version of a Good Housekeeping Seal to create incentives for private-sector businesses to invest in security while also contributing to their bottom line and creating shareholder value. The only solution outside of regulation to solve the trade-off between efficiency vulnerability is to provide the private sector with an alternative that either provides them a competitive advantage in the marketplace or adds to their bottom line, both of which create shareholder value to firms. To do otherwise is at best a Sisyphean task. Insurance combined with a Good Housekeeping Seal approach is one possible way to address the problem and create value for the private sector. Another possible approach is to set up anonymous data pools where telecommunication infrastructure providers submit routing data to a secure and trusted third party. This set up would allow potential clients to obtain a market signal of how diverse each provider is for the unique set of buildings (for example) that need to be networked. A diversity index for each query could provide a market signal that would help optimize the resilience and diversity of currently available fiber. Currently little to no information is provided to the market on the diversity of the cyber infrastructure they depend on.

Insurance and anonymous data pools are just two ideas for market mechanisms to help remedy the multitude of infrastructure security problems. The one certainty is that the government, explicitly the Department of Homeland Security, must make a business case to the private sector if there is going to be progress securing national infrastructure, and specifically cyber infrastructure. A discontinuity exists between the level of security required by the public sector and that which for which the private sector is currently willing to pay. Further, the growing threat to and vulnerability of the nation's critical cyber infrastructure demand a solid strategy for meaningfully integrating the public and private sectors to achieve a satisfactory level of security for the nation's at-risk nervous system.

NOTES

1. White House 2003b, p. 3.
2. White House 2003b; National Research Council 2002a; NSTAC 2002.
3. Green 2002, p. 1.
4. Lawyer 2003.
5. NVE 2005.
6. Berinato 2002.
7. Green 2002, p. 2.
8. Kane 2002, p. 1.
9. Neuman 1991.
10. Neuman 1991.
11. Neuman 2000.
12. SONET stands for "synchronous optical network," which can be built as self-healing rings that use two or more transmission paths between nodes; if one path fails, traffic can be rerouted along another path.
13. Lindstrom 2001.
14. FCC 2001; Government Accountability Office 2003b.
15. Government Accountability Office 2003b.

16. Newman 2002.
17. Government Accountability Office 2002; Newman 2002.
18. NIST 1995, p. 23.
19. Halsne 2003.
20. Maine PUC 2003.
21. Maine PUC 2003.
22. NRC 2002; NSTAC 2002.
23. Iannaccone et al. 2003.
24. Coluccio 2005.
25. Renesys 2003.
26. Anonymous 2003.
27. FBI 2001.
28. Lunev 2002, p. 1.
29. DOJ 2001.
30. Lunev 2001.
31. Lunev 2001.
32. Messmer 2003.
33. Seltzer 2004.
34. Sturgeon 2003.
35. GRID Today 2003.
36. McWilliams 2003.
37. Bequai 2002; Philippsohn 2001; Furnell and Warren 1999; Lunev 2001.
38. Bequai 2002.
39. Lunev 2002; Gertz 2001.
40. Verton 2003, p. xv.
41. Mohamad 2003.
42. Verton 2003.
43. *Economist* 2003.
44. Vegh 2002.
45. Adams 2001, p. 98.
46. Guttman and Elburg 2002.
47. Vegh 2002.
48. Adams 2001, p. 99.
49. Adams 2001.
50. Vegh 2002.
51. McDonald 2003.
52. Yoshihara 2001.
53. McDonald 2003.
54. Anonymous 2003.
55. Liang and Xiangsui 1999.
56. Liang and Xiangsui 1999, p. 44.
57. Fonow 2003.
58. Fonow 2003.
59. Dean 2002; Green 2002.

16

INTERDEPENDENT SECURITY IN INTERCONNECTED NETWORKS

Geoffrey Heal, Michael Kearns, Paul Kleindorfer,
and Howard Kunreuther

In an interdependent world, the risks faced by any individual, firm, region, or country depend not only on its own choices but also on those of others. In the context of terrorism, the risks faced by any airline, for example, are tied to the security standards of other carriers and airports.

To illustrate this point, consider the destruction of Pan Am flight 103 in 1988. In Malta, terrorists checked a bag containing a bomb on Malta Airlines, which had minimal security procedures. The bag was transferred in Frankfurt to a Pan Am feeder line and then loaded onto Pan Am 103 in London's Heathrow Airport. The transferred piece of luggage was not inspected at either Frankfurt or London – the assumption in each subsequent airport being that baggage had been inspected at the point of origin. The bomb had been designed to explode above 28,000 feet, a height normally attained only on the transatlantic route. The bomb exploded over Lockerbie, Scotland, killing 259 passengers and crew, and another 11 people on the ground. Failures in a peripheral part of the airline network, Malta, compromised the security of a flight leaving from a core hub, London.

A great deal of work on the vulnerability of critical infrastructures to terrorist attacks is described elsewhere in this book. These other chapters focus on individual firms or systems, such as the electric grid, telecommunications services, and the cyber network, and ask how much their security depends on the actions of others due to the transmission of harmful effects from one agent to another (which from now on we refer to as contamination). The analytical framework related to interdependency of the participants in a risk-exposed

Support from NSF grant number CMS-0527598 and the Wharton Risk Management and Decision Processes Center is gratefully acknowledged.

network has important implications for public policies intended to motivate private investment in reducing vulnerability of the system as a whole.

Interdependence does not require proximity. Hence the antecedents to catastrophes can be quite distinct and distant from the actual disaster, as in the case of the September 11, 2001, attacks on the World Trade Center and the Pentagon, when security failures at Boston's Logan airport led to crashes in New York City, Arlington, Virginia, and rural Pennsylvania. The same was true in the case of the August 2003 power failures in the northeastern United States and Canada, where the initiating event occurred in Ohio, but the worst consequences were felt hundreds of miles away. Similarly, a disease in one region can readily spread to other areas, as was the case with the rapid spread of SARS from China to its trading partners.

Two studies by Kunreuther and Heal introduced the concept of "interdependent security" using game-theory models to investigate how the optimal decision of one unit in a system regarding how much to invest in security depends on what others in the system do.[1] More specifically, the interdependent security paradigm raises the following question: To what extent will one agent (e.g., an individual, an organization, a division in a firm) invest in protection, when it is connected to and dependent on others whose failures may compromise its own operations, as the failure at Malta airport compromised security at London airport and led to the crash of PanAm flight 103?

Two characteristics of these interdependent security problems underlie the incentives that organizations face in their efforts to reduce their risk exposure. One is that the risky event occurs only once, and the second that the risk facing one agent is determined in part by the behavior of others. In the equilibria that arise in these problems, it is possible that a change in the behavior of one agent could tip the system from one equilibrium to another.[2] A related phenomenon is "cascading" – in which a change by one agent leads to a change by a second, which provokes a change by a third, and so on.[3]

IMPACT OF CONTAMINATION FOR INTERDEPENDENT NETWORKS

The challenges of managing risks within interdependent networks are faced by firms throughout those networks – for example, firms in a computer network, a power grid, or a supply chain. The firms must develop appropriate strategies for reducing risks in a cost-effective manner. If each firm wants to maximize the expected returns from its resources, each needs to determine whether to invest in a risk-mitigation measure such as reducing the likelihood of losses from a terrorist attack. When the firms are interdependent, each has less incentive to invest in protective measures if the others have not taken similar action.

To illustrate this point, consider two firms, DataCollate and InfoAware. Each firm faces a certain probability of a terrorist attack that damages itself, and another probability that such an attack on itself disrupts the activities of the other firm due to interdependencies through a network. Suppose DataCollate invests in security measures, and by so doing avoids incurring an attack on its own firm. If, however, InfoAware does not invest in its own security, DataCollate faces an additional risk that it will be harmed by an attack at InfoAware. More specifically, even if DataCollate invests in security measures, there is still a probability that InfoAware will be attacked, in which case DataCollate also incurs a loss (and this loss comes at a cost in addition to the amount it has already paid for its own security measures). This possibility reduces the incentive for DataCollate to invest in protection. Why? Because investing in security buys less protection when there is the possibility of contamination from others due to interdependencies. (Appendix 16.A presents a more formal analysis of this interdependent security problem for the case of two firms.)

The results for the two-firm interdependent security case carry over to more general settings with some increase in complexity. The incentive for any firm to invest in protection depends on how many other firms there are and on whether these other firms are investing. Other firms that do not invest in security reduce the expected benefits from one's own protective actions and hence reduce a firm's incentive to invest.

If there are many identical firms, and all firms invest in security, then the probability that any firm will experience a loss will be low. If, however, no firm invests in security (and assuming that these firms can contaminate the others), then the likelihood of a loss to any firm in the network increases. Therefore, the greater the number of unprotected firms, the lower the incentive for any firm to invest in protecting itself against a catastrophe.

Intuitively, this result is due to interactions of weak links on others in the system. One unprotected firm endangers all of the other firms, even if they have invested in security. As more firms decide not to invest in security, the probability of a failure in the system increases and the economic incentive for any specific firm to undertake protection decreases. As the number of firms gets large, this probability approaches 1, and a firm will not be willing to incur any costs to invest in security because it knows it will be contaminated by one or more of the many unprotected firms.

TIPPING AND CASCADING BEHAVIOR

The fact that significant negative externalities are imposed by some firms on others in an interdependent security context is both a curse and a blessing.

The curse derives from the scenario noted above; the blessing may come about through leveraging reduced externalities to induce phenomena known as tipping and cascading, in which one firm after the next finds it in its interest to invest in protective behavior because others are taking such actions. There may be ways of inducing tipping and cascading so that everyone's welfare is improved. If firms are heterogeneous (so that they have different risks and costs associated with their activities), some firms in the previous example may have much higher risks than others of a large-scale accident that has system-wide implications.

Heal and Kunreuther show that one firm may occupy such a strategic position that if it changes from not investing to investing in protection, then all others will find it in their interests to follow suit.[4] Even if no single firm can exert such leverage, a small group may be able to do so. More specifically, the firm that would create the largest negative externalities for others in the system should be encouraged to invest in protective behavior, not only to reduce its own losses but also to induce other firms to follow suit.

This type of tipping behavior is in the spirit of the many interesting examples described by Schelling, where one equilibrium suddenly changes to another due to the movement of a few agents (e.g., the sudden change in the racial composition of a neighborhood).[5] Tipping and cascading behavior implies that one needs to focus on only certain key parts of a system to convince others to follow suit. This behavior suggests the particular importance of persuading some key players to manage risks more carefully. Working with them may be a substitute for working with all firms.

APPLICATIONS TO SUPPLY CHAIN MANAGEMENT

Interdependencies exist across supply chains in every industry, and the complexity of these interdependencies has been growing by leaps and bounds as industry has become more globalized through outsourcing and off-shoring activities. The result is that global supply chains that source from one country for manufacturing or retailing operations in another now dominate many of the major economic sectors, from the automotive industry to semiconductors to the huge retail industry represented by giants like Wal-Mart and Home Depot.

The increased complexity of such global supply chains has added levels of risk and interdependence that are sometimes not evident until disaster strikes, exposing hidden vulnerabilities and leading to large economic losses. The Taiwan earthquake of September 1999, which sent shock waves through the global semiconductor market,[6] the 9/11 terrorist attack on the World Trade Center, and the August 2003 blackout in the northeastern United States and

Canada are but a few recent reminders of the potential for significant disruptions to supply chains. More recently, hurricanes Katrina and Rita in 2005 have led to huge disruptions in economic and business activity in the affected states, which are likely to far outstrip the significant property losses of these events. Interestingly, the Taiwan earthquake was largely seen as a business disruption, with responsibility for recovery falling on the business community, while hurricanes Katrina and Rita were seen for their effects on human suffering, with the government responsible for response and recovery. Whatever the perceptions of these events, the fact is that firms that are better prepared for such supply chain disruptions are increasingly being favored in the market place as better economic risks. We consider first the evidence for this claim, and then note the challenges presented in managing interdependent security problems across such supply chains.

The effects of supply chain disruptions (whether from natural disasters, terrorists, or other unexpected events) on the profitability of supply chain participants are now recognized as being potentially very large. Hendricks and Singhal analyze announced shipping delays and other supply chain disruptions reported in the *Wall Street Journal* during the 1990s and show that companies experiencing such disruptions under-perform their peers significantly in stock market performance as well as in operating performance, as reflected in costs, sales, and profits.[7] Coping with the management challenges of such disruptions is, however, a very difficult matter, as the interdependencies involved require cooperative activity and monitoring across the supply chain in ways that are not captured in the traditional intra-supply-chain metrics of price, cycle time, and product quality. To comprehend the problem, it is necessary to understand the background underlying supply chain management as it has evolved in the recent period of increasing globalization.

Supply chain management has grown steadily in importance over the past two decades.[8] First came the "just-in-time revolution" in the 1980s, which led to increased efficiency, both internal to companies and between companies and their suppliers and customers. The just-in-time revolution led directly to the recognition of a host of hidden costs associated with supplier and customer relationships, and it resulted in further initiatives in the early 1990s for companies around the world to re-engineer and rationalize procurement functions and interfaces with customers. With the continuing liberalization of international trade, and the associated emergence of China and India as important manufacturing sources, companies around the world looked increasingly to outsourcing and off-shoring activities for sourcing labor-intensive manufactured goods.

The effect of all of these trends has been the globalization of supply chains and head-to-head competition among manufacturing and raw material sources across the planet. The resulting supply chains are considerably more complicated than their earlier cousins of a few decades back because of their length and their multi-national character. Moreover, these same supply chains are under constant pressure to become leaner, with less inventory and less redundancy. These trends, visible from commodity metals to semiconductors to textiles, imply both increasing efficiency of supply chains and increasing vulnerability of such supply chains to disruptions. Longer paths and shorter clock speeds imply more opportunities for disruption and a smaller margin for error if a disruption takes place.

There are many sources of potential disruption to global supply chains, some of them just from pure congestion in ports and other (de-)consolidation centers. Today security and concerns with global terrorism have become central drivers of senior management concerns for disruption management of global supply chains, partly because of the sinister and unpredictable character of terrorism that makes traditional financial and operational response strategies less effective against it. These underlying reasons, together with the increasing evidence of the profit impact of good disruption risk management noted above, have made security of global supply chains and multi-modal logistics systems an important focus of supply chain disruption management.

Effective management strategies for security in global supply chains cannot be specific to one company. Rather, these strategies need to encompass the entire supply chain of all the organizations participating in the supply chain. But one cannot stop there either, because much of the infrastructure, such as ports and (de-)consolidation centers, serves multiple organizations, including end users and shippers, some in private hands and some under government control. To deal with the security problem, a broad private and public partnership is required. One public–private partnership, launched between the container traffic industry and the retail industry, is effectively dealing with the interdependent security problems in global retail supply chains.

THE CUSTOMS–TRADE PARTNERSHIP AGAINST TERRORISM APPROACH

Spurred by the new U.S. Department of Homeland Security's (DHS's) assessment of needs for protection of critical infrastructure, major retailers and the transportation and logistic specialists that provided shipping services to them were brought together in 2002 to discuss the requirements and responsibilities that the private and public sectors should respectively bear in meeting the new challenges of interdependent security in global supply chains. The key objective of both the private and public sectors in these early discussions was to determine the partnership principles to guide the development of standards and certification procedures for improved security for these companies. Major retailers involved in container-based trade (such as Wal-Mart and Home Depot) recognized the primacy of developing a joint solution that assured continued facilitation of international trade with a high level of security. Major disruptions to any major trans-shipment point, such as a port or (de-)consolidation center, would have significant negative externalities for many retailers, and not just the retailer whose shipment had been the target of a terrorist attack.

These early discussions were eventually synthesized in the United States into a voluntary public–private partnership approach to cargo security that was named Customs–Trade Partnership Against Terrorism (C-TPAT). The principles of C-TPAT were then further elaborated in the National Defense Transportation Agency's Security Best Practices Committee, operating in cooperation with DHS and the Transportation Security Administration. The idea of C-TPAT was to develop basic principles, and associated best practices, for all participants in a global supply chain in four areas: site security, personnel (including background checks), material movements, and process control.[9] Right from the start, these discussions elicited the idea that large retailers would use their buying power to insist that all elements of their supply chains, beginning with manufacturers, comply with the emerging best practices in these areas. Retailers would also submit to having their compliance audited by the appropriate DHS systems, as well as those of relevant international customs agencies. This tipping strategy has been quite effective in promoting enrollments within the United States; the Customs and Border Patrol noted that, as of November 2004, C-TPAT had more than 7,400 enrolled partners, including 86 of the top 100 U.S. importers by containerized cargo volume. The 7,400 partners cover more than 40 percent of all the imports by dollar value into the United States and more than 96 percent of all the U.S. inbound maritime container carrier traffic.[10]

The C-TPAT approach foresees integrating the activities of three types of key actors: (1) private companies that manage supply chains (including manufacturers at the front end and retailers and shippers downstream); (2) port authorities and (de-)consolidators (in the United States and elsewhere) that have the responsibility for clearing cargo and for its loading/unloading; and (3) local, regional, and national agencies (including DHS and the Transportation Security Administration) that have the responsibility for assuring homeland security, including responding to threats and abnormal conditions.

At the company level, the C-TPAT approach to supply chain security management encompasses concerns from the originating manufacturer to the final wholesale and retail outlets. Large companies have developed security metrics (including the scope of integrity of seals, continuous movement of the container, length of time in exposed areas such as foreign ports, and a number of cost metrics) to evaluate approaches to improving global supply chain security. The available methods and technologies for mitigation include certification of

Establish voluntary security standard ⇨	Assess risk across supply chain ⇨	Evaluate, study costs and benefits, and prioritize ⇨	Build strategic improvements and public–private partnerships ⇨
1. Design voluntary standard for supply chain security management that will allow private firms to achieve reasonable "internal levels" of security 2. Set standards to be compatible with current best industry practices and available technology 3. Coordinate with key private players to achieve "critical mass" to achieve tipping	1. For each sector (e.g., shippers, consolidators, retailers) determine main assets/processes 2. Assess vulnerabilities of each asset and process 3. Categorize according to level of vulnerability under various scenarios 4. Determine synergies with reduction in theft losses and other key matrics	1. Develop and validate models for assessing costs and benefits of security-related interventions 2. Value potential damage of a security breach for each asset class: • direct/indirect • externalities 3. Prioritize mitigation initiatives for various processes and asset classes	1. Analyze alternative strategies to reduce risks of security breaches/attacks 2. Evaluate direct and indirect costs of best available actions 3. Analyze alternatives to re-align public and private interests: • tax incentives • legal reform • required insurance 4. Design audit system to monitor effectiveness and compliance

Figure 16.1. Security Management in Global Supply Chains.

personnel, audit procedures, and approaches to assuring the integrity (tamper-proofness) of containers. The key to the success of this approach is leveraging those organizations in the global supply chain that have the resources and the information to undertake necessary precautions locally, while assuring that larger problems arising from interdependencies are addressed at the level of the entire supply chain.

Figure 16.1 illustrates the general approach being pursued in the United States for security management in global supply chains. The approach begins with the adoption of a voluntary standard (e.g., in retailing, the principles embodied in C-TPAT and associated relevant metrics for the retail sector). It is envisaged that the adoption of this standard by the major players in global supply chains will lead, via the tipping effect, to widespread adoption of the standard. For those having adopted the standard, best practices are identified along the supply chain, including tracking, monitoring, new technologies, and security metrics. These best practices are further refined in specific companies and sectors and shared among all supply chain participants, which leads to improved private-sector solutions. These solutions are then integrated into evolving public-sector initiatives to yield the desired public–private partnership that will define security management systems and their interfaces with public responders and law enforcement officials, including those at DHS and its subsidiary organizations (such as the Transportation Security Agency and Customs and Border Control).

In terms of the interdependent security framework described earlier in this chapter, interdependencies are evident in two fundamental areas: (1) in the adoption and implementation of the voluntary standard for security management by each private company in a supply chain, and (2) in the adoption of global standards and technologies across the supply chain. Both of these activities have essential elements of the interdependent security problem embedded in them.

The adoption and implementation of a voluntary standard such as C-TPAT requires more than just lip service to be effective. Personnel screening, vulnerability assessment, and monitoring of material movements throughout the supply chain are required to cope with interdependent security issues. One weak link is enough to allow penetration of a purposeful agent and to undermine the risk mitigation actions of all others in the supply chain.

Improvements to monitoring could contribute to the security of the supply chain. For example, companies could adopt uniform global technology standards, such as radio frequency identification (RFID) technology. RFID technology allows for micro-chips to be installed in each product shipped as well as in pallets and containers. While such technology has considerable potential for enhancing inventory control as well as for contingent responses to terrorist events, it is potentially costly, and the costs may fall unevenly on different supply chain participants. For global retail supply chains, RFID technology requires both significant costs at the originating manufacturer as well as at the final wholesale or retail outlets where such RFID technology would replace barcoding equipment at checkout counters. How such costs would be shared through direct pricing or other funding mechanisms (possibly subsidized by the government) is a thorny problem. It requires that all participants in a supply chain or in a sector agree on a timetable to implement it. The resulting bargaining problem bears a strong resemblance to the interdependent security problem analyzed in Appendix 16.A.[11]

In addition to adopting specific technologies, other options include implementing information and monitoring programs that would require each participant in a sector or a supply chain to gather, verify, and share certain information on a routine basis. The information could be on security breaches, on facility or company-wide audit results according to specific standards, or on supply chain metrics such as speed of movement through various facilities or other indicators of vulnerability to security breaches. Such information systems would be critical to the risk assessment process for the entire supply chain, and they would help identify weak links where risk mitigation would have the highest payoff.

This sketch of the interdependent security challenges in global supply chains only scratches the surface of the interdependency problems inherent in security management. As predicted by the interdependent security framework, one encounters the expected problems of obtaining compliance across large and small organizations in the same supply chain or sector, given the externalities associated with contamination. Free-rider problems also arise, along with the challenges of inducing tipping and cascading when risks are shared across different units in the system. Added to the complexity is the multi-jurisdictional nature of the problem, which mixes the involvement of private companies, publicly owned ports, and multiple national governments in defining and enforcing the standards that would lead to credible public–private partnerships. Given the importance of international trade (currently estimated by the World Bank to be roughly $8 trillion and growing), the problem of global supply chain security is likely to remain a major concern for the foreseeable future.

APPLICATIONS TO COMPUTER SECURITY

Another important domain in which interdependent security models seem both appropriate and promising is that of computer network security. The very term "computer virus" highlights the fact that many modern computer security exploits spread in the same manner as do diseases such as SARS: through contacts in a complex (virtual) network of communication. While this epidemiological metaphor has been present in computer security circles for some time now, the game theory aspects of such problems have received less attention, yet they are good targets for interdependent security modeling. The notion of a (relatively) catastrophic event is certainly present, as the most malicious modern computer exploits can effectively destroy important machines, documents, and other resources. However, if an individual's electronic mail contacts are sufficiently "immunized" against transmitting viruses and worms (for instance, through the diligent application and maintenance of commercial or other anti-virus software), that person may have relatively little incentive to maintain best security practices. If the same contacts are routinely forwarding viruses, the individual has great incentive to immunize. Such an incentive structure can be mapped into the interdependent security framework.

There are also computer security settings in which catastrophic risk has a more collective nature, as an example adapted from Kearns[12] demonstrates. Imagine the user population of a large organization in which each individual has a desktop computer with its own local software and memory, but in which users also maintain important data files or documents on a shared disk drive accessible to the entire organization. From the perspective of the organization, the primary security concern – the "catastrophic event" in interdependent security parlance – is that an intrusion (whether by a piece of malicious software or a human hacker) might erase the contents of the shared hard drive.

Each user's desktop computer and its contents – including e-mail, downloaded programs or files, and other components – is a potential point of entry for such intrusion.

Users must at least implicitly decide about many aspects of their individual security practices: how often they change their passwords (and how secure those passwords are against dictionary attacks and other common attacks), whether they enable encryption in their Web and e-mail communications, how careful they are in not downloading suspicious files and programs, whether they maintain their anti-virus software, and many other features. The vulnerability of the shared hard drive is determined by the collective behavior along these dimensions.

If individual users feel quite confident that the overall population is adhering to fairly diligent security practices, their incentive to also be diligent is high, because their negligence would constitute a first-order contribution to the shared disk's vulnerability. Conversely, if individuals are convinced that their colleagues are lax on security, and if there are many colleagues, this diligence incentive may be sharply reduced – the disk is already so vulnerable from the collective behavior of others in the system that one user's rigor will have only a marginal impact.

This scenario is just one of many good matches between the original interdependent security model and problems in computer security. Moreover, such matches can drive new research in interdependent security in both theoretical and experimental directions.

SHARED RESOURCES AND PARTIAL CATASTROPHES

One generalization of the basic interdependent security model that arises naturally in many computer security problems involves the complexity and heterogeneity of shared resources. In many interdependent security problems, catastrophes are "private" – for instance, in the airline security problem, individual airline carriers suffer explosions. In the shared disk example above, however, the catastrophe is "public" – the disk's erasure damages the entire organization. This damage is similar to the problem of supplying power in an integrated network or the global supply chain problem discussed earlier, where there is a weak link in the system.

Computer security overall exhibits many potential problems falling in between the wholly public and wholly private extremes. For example, on many shared computing and file servers, resources may be accessible by only subsets of the population. Thus, a file that is accessible only to one set of users may be erased by certain breaches of the accounts of those users, but not by breaches of the accounts of other users. Such partially shared resources might arise from organizational structure (e.g., only managers are permitted to read and write to personnel files), informal working groups (e.g., a research team sharing data files), and many other sources. The pattern of subsets of shared resources can be complex indeed on systems of even moderate population size.

In an interdependent security setting, such partially shared resources lead to the notion of a "partial catastrophe." If the account of user A is breached and all resources accessible to A are destroyed, this is a "full catastrophe" for user A, but it might be one of varying severity for other users, depending on the number and value of resources they share with A.

FUTURE EXPERIMENTS IN COMPUTER NETWORK SECURITY

Another appealing feature of the computer security applications of interdependent security outlined above is the potential for numerical experiments, due to the availability of relevant data. To date, discussion of interdependent security models in the context of specific problems has been largely conceptual and theoretical. The lone exception to this is a numerical model and study in airline security.[13] This study was handicapped by the unavailability of data pertinent to the estimation of certain parameters in the interdependent security model, which had to be set to default values. In contrast, we believe that much more complete, realistic, and informative experimental interdependent security case studies could be performed in computer security.

In the networks of many organizations, detailed information is routinely logged that could be directly or indirectly used in the derivation of interdependent security models for some of the security scenarios we provide. For example (and setting aside non-trivial privacy issues), to estimate the direct risk parameter associated with a particular user of a system, one could examine the historical record of security flaws or breaches associated with that user's resources, measure the frequency of his password changes, monitor the rate of virus and worm arrivals in his e-mail, and check the freshness of his anti-virus signatures. Many other measurements are also possible. Similarly, in the "partial catastrophe" scenario described in the previous section, one could directly examine (for instance) file permissions to determine who has a shared stake in each resource. One could even use the time the user takes to edit a document as a measure of the "value" of that document to the user, and incorporate such valuations in to the numerical interdependent security model.

Many interesting and important security questions could be addressed by such detailed numerical interdependent security models. For example, what is the "distribution of vulnerability" across users in a typical or specific organization's computer network(s)? Building on that, are there a small number of users whose practices and exposures render them much more vulnerable than the average, or is the vulnerability more evenly spread? Another question might be, given limited resources or budget, what are the best policies for improving the overall level of security of a network? This is related to the first question, as it could dictate (for example) the dramatic improvement of security for a few individuals or incremental increases in security across the entire population.

Such sociological and strategic studies are particularly timely, because the technical computer security community is largely concerned with technological "solutions" or approaches to such problems, and thus less likely to undertake such a line of work.

STRATEGIES FOR REDUCING INTERDEPENDENT SECURITY RISKS

If firms are reluctant to adopt protective measures to reduce the chances of catastrophic losses due to the possibility of contamination from weak links in the system, the private and public sectors may have a role to play in addressing this problem. Strategies will require both structural and communications relationships within the private sector and with government at all levels.

TRADE ASSOCIATIONS AND KEY FIRMS

Leadership from industry, either through trade associations and/or through influential firms that take the lead, can convince others of the need to adopt security measures. A trade association can play a coordinating role by stipulating that any member must follow certain rules and regulations and has the right of refusal if they are asked to do business with an agent that is not a member of the association and/or has not subscribed to the ruling. In the example of baggage security, an airline trade association could require all bags to be reviewed carefully, and each airline could indicate its unwillingness to accept in-transit bags from airlines that do not adhere to this regulation.

Even without a formal mechanism, if a few airlines were to voluntarily undertake these measures they could convince others to follow suit. Kearns and Ortiz use computational algorithms to analyze behavior of airlines with respect to investing in security measures.[14] They analyzed data from 49 major international airlines using airline passenger reservations covering all bookings – including transfers between airlines – in a commercial air reservation system on a single day. Their model suggests that three carriers form a tipping set. These carriers' decision to invest creates an economic incentive for a large population of otherwise skeptical carriers to follow suit. Kearns and Ortiz' simulations suggest that a small group of firms may be able to tip the entire industry from a starting equilibrium in which no one invests in security, to a new equilibrium that improves security and increases expected profits of all firms in the network.

THIRD-PARTY INSPECTIONS, INSURANCE, AND REGULATIONS

There may be a role for governmental standards and regulations coupled with third-party inspections and insurance for enforcement purposes. For example, third-party inspections coupled with insurance protection could encourage decentralized firms in the supply chain to reduce their risks from accidents and disasters. Such a management-based regulatory strategy would shift the locus of decision making from the regulator to individual firms. The firms would then be required to do their own planning as to how they would meet a set of standards or regulations.[15]

If these firms take preventive action, they can encourage the remaining ones to comply with the regulations to avoid being caught and fined. This is another form of tipping behavior. Without some type of inspection, low-risk divisions that have adopted risk-reducing measures cannot credibly distinguish themselves from the high-risk ones that have not. By delegating part of the inspection process to the private sector through insurance companies and certified third-party inspectors, regulatory agencies such as DHS can provide a channel though which the low-risk firms can speak for themselves. If a firm chooses not to be inspected by certified third parties, it is more likely to be a high-risk rather than a low-risk one. If a firm does agree to inspection and receives a seal of approval that it is protecting itself against catastrophe, the firm will pay a lower insurance premium than one that does not undertake actions to lower its risk. In this way, regulatory agencies can reduce the number of audits they need to undertake, because they know who has received seals of approval from private third-party inspectors.[16]

Third-party inspections complement existing regulatory oversight. DHS, which has limited personnel and funds, has restricted capability to audit for itself all the firms in the supply chain. Without a relatively plausible expectation of inspection, however, firms could not be expected to adopt new behaviors. For example, chemical firms, particularly smaller ones, demonstrate little financial incentive to adopt certain requirements if they perceive that they are unlikely to be inspected and/or they know that the fine is small if they are caught. In such cases, they may be willing to take their chances and risk the financial penalties. The combination of third-party inspections in conjunction with insurance, however, is a powerful duo of private-market mechanisms that can convince many firms of the advantages of implementing security measures to make their operations safer.

OPEN ISSUES

A number of open issues need to be considered when addressing interdependent security issues and the management of risk, including multi-period and dynamic models, behavioral considerations, and endogenous probabilities.

In multi-period and dynamic models, deciding whether to invest in security normally involves multi-period considerations, because the upfront investment cost needs to be compared with the benefits over the life of the protective measure. From the point of view of dynamics, the decision to invest depends on how many others have taken similar actions. How does one start the process of investing in security? Should one subsidize or provide extra benefits to those willing to be innovators in this regard to encourage others to take similar actions?

Regarding behavioral considerations, the interdependent security models to date all assume that individuals make their decisions by comparing their expected benefits (with and without protection) to the costs of investing in security. This is a rational model of behavior. A growing literature in behavioral economics suggests, however, that individuals make choices in ways that differ from the rational model.[17]

With respect to protective measures, evidence from controlled field studies and laboratory experiments suggest that many individuals are not willing to invest in protection for a number of reasons that include myopia, high discount rates, and budget constraints.[18] In the models considered in this chapter, no internal positive effects were associated with protective measures. However, many individuals invest in security to gain peace of mind and to relieve anxiety about their perceptions of what might happen to themselves or to others in the event of a security-related incident.

The interdependent security model described previously implicitly assumes that the risks faced by the firms in the network are independent of their own behavior, rather than being endogenous. In reality, if some firms are known to be more security-conscious than others, they are presumably less likely to be terrorist targets. In this sense, investing in security has similarities to theft protection: if a house announces that it has installed an alarm, then burglars are likely to turn to other houses as targets instead.[19] Similarly, in the case of the chemical supply chain, terrorists are more likely to focus on targets that are less well protected.[20]

For interdependent security problems, a firm is more likely to invest in security when probabilities are endogenous than when these probabilities are exogenous, because of the increased likelihood of being a target when others invest in protection.[21] Future research should examine how changes in endogenous probabilities affect interdependent security solutions, and the appropriate strategies for improving the performance of individual firms as well as the security of multiple companies whose security is interdependent with others.

CONCLUSIONS

Our objective in this chapter has been to lay out the logic of interdependent security through a set of examples, notably airline security, global supply chain management, and computer security. The interdependent security model characterizes the nature of the problem facing individual agents as well as the need for public–private partnerships for coping with the negative externalities generated by the linkages between units in the system. Other chapters in this volume point to similar interdependent security effects in areas of critical infrastructure. Indeed, the very character of infrastructure is that of a supporting mechanism for economic agents. Thus, whether in electric power, ports, chemical manufacturing, or the Internet, the value of these major pieces of critical infrastructure systems is their use by multiple organizations and individuals for other economic or social purposes.

The key externalities identified by the interdependent security framework are determined by the nature of the protective actions taken or not taken by others using or having access to the system. This particular characteristic implies that individual decisions regarding risk-reducing measures based on the usual cost–benefit analysis will be influenced in fundamental ways by the behavior of others. In particular, the reliance on pure market solutions that depend solely on individual initiatives may fail in interdependent security environments. Thus coordinative mechanisms are needed through trade associations and sharing best practices across individuals and companies to promote actions that enhance individual and social welfare. Alternatively, private-sector initiatives such as third-party inspections, and insurance can be combined with public sector actions such as well-enforced regulations and standards. The many applications in this book illustrate how such coordinating mechanisms are developing across multiple areas of critical infrastructure.

As the other chapters in this book note, interdependencies and coordination are further exacerbated by the complexity of purposeful agents acting out of complex motivations to do harm. Thus, while the interdependent security framework provides some insights as to the nature of needed strategies and policies to combat this, we still have much to learn about the behavior of agents facing interdependency problems and the impact of firms' actions on developing private–public partnerships for protecting our critical infrastructures.

APPENDIX 16.A. FORMAL GAME THEORETIC ANALYSIS OF THE INTERDEPENDENT SECURITY PROBLEM

The Two-Firm Case

Let Y be the assets of each firm before it invests in security or incurs any losses during the year from a terrorist attack. If the firm incurs a cost of c for security, it will be totally protected against a terrorist attack of its own firm but still may be contaminated by the other firm if that firm does not invest in security. Each firm has two choices: invest in security, S, or do not invest, N. A simple 2×2 matrix of the four possible paired outcomes illustrates what happens to the expected returns of each firm as a function of the choices each makes (Table 16.A).

To illustrate the nature of the expected returns, consider the upper left hand box where both firms invest in security (S,S). Then each firm incurs a cost of c and faces no possible catastrophic accidents so that each of their net returns are Y-c.

If A_1 invests and A_2 does not, then this outcome is captured in the upper right hand box (S,N). Here A_1 incurs an investment cost of c, but there is still a chance, q_2, that A_2 will suffer a terrorist attack that will impact $A1$ causing a loss of L. This type of contamination imposed by A_2 on A_1 is referred to in economics as a negative externality. A_2 incurs no cost of protecting itself and faces no risk of a loss from A_1, but it does face the risk of a terrorist attack to its own firm with an expected loss of $p_1 L$. The lower left box (N, S) has payoffs which are just the mirror image of these.

Suppose that neither firm invests in protection (N, N) – the lower right hand box of Table 16.A. Then each firm i has an expected return of Y- $p_i L$ -$(1$-$p_i)q_j L$, where j refers to the other firm. The expected losses can be characterized in the following manner. The term $p_i L$ reflects the expected loss originating from an accident in one's own firm i. The second term reflects the expected loss from an attack originating at firm j that contaminates firm i ($q_j L$) and is multiplied by $(1$-$p_i)$ to reflect the assumption that a terrorist attack during a given time period can only occur once. In other words, the risk of contamination only matters to a firm when that firm does not have a terrorist attack itself.

Because each firm i wants to maximize its expected returns, the conditions for it to invest in protection against a catastrophic accident are $c < p_i L$ and $c < p_i (1$-$q_j)L$. The first constraint is what one would expect if firm i was totally independent of firm j: that is, the cost of investing in protection must be less than the expected cost of a terrorist attack. If firms A_1 and A_2 are independent, this tightens the constraint by reflecting the possibility of contamination from the other firm.

Table 16.A Expected returns associated with investing in security measures (S) and not investing in security (N)

		Firm A_2	
		S	N
Firm A_1	S	Y-c, Y-c	Y-c-$q_2 L$, Y-$p_1 L$
	N	Y-$p_1 L$, Y-c-$q_1 L$	$Y - [p_1 L + (1$-$p_1) q_2 L]$, $Y - [p_2 L + (1$-$p_2)q_1 L]$

The Multi-Firm Case

Consider the case in which there are n identical firms. As shown by Kunreuther and Heal,[22] if none of the other firms are protected, then the condition for any firm to invest in protection is given by the following condition:

$c < p[L-X(n,0)$, where $X(n,0)$ represents the negative externalities to the firm if none of the other firms in the system invests in security]. Let c^* be the value of c where the firm is indifferent between investing and not investing in protection when j of the other firms have invested in security: $c^* = p[L-X(n,j)]$. If there are no negative externalities because all the other firms have invested in security, then $c^* = pL$, which is the same as if the firm were operating in isolation. As more firms do not invest in protection, c^* decreases, so that the firm is less likely to take security measures if it is maximizing its expected returns.

NOTES

1. See Kunreuther and Heal 2003 and Heal and Kunreuther 2005a.
2. See Schelling 1978.
3. See Dixit 2002 and Farrell and Saloner 1985.
4. Heal and Kunreuther 2006.
5. Schelling 1978.
6. Papadakis and Ziemba 2001.
7. Hendricks and Singhal 2005.
8. Kleindorfer and Van Wassenhove 2004.
9. See Kleindorfer and Saad 2005 for a discussion of how C-TPAT integrates with other supply chain security and risk management practices.
10. See USCBP 2004.
11. See Heinrich 2005 for a detailed discussion of the costs and benefits of RFID technology for security and other purposes.
12. Kearns 2005.
13. Kearns and Ortiz 2004.
14. Kearns and Ortiz 2004.
15. Coglianese and Lazer 2003.
16. For more details on this approach, see Kunreuther et al. 2002a.
17. See Kahneman and Tversky 2000.
18. For more details, see Kunreuther 2001.
19. Kunreuther and Heal 2003.
20. Keohane and Zeckhauser 2003.
21. Heal and Kunreuther 2005b.
22. Kunreuther and Heal 2003.

PART V

Creating Markets

17

INSURANCE, THE 14TH CRITICAL SECTOR

Erwann O. Michel-Kerjan

Insurance is a kind of game in which one needs to be extremely cautious.
Chance must be analyzed, and players be skilled in the science of calculating
*   probabilities;*
they need to foresee hazards at sea, and hazards wrought by bad faith;
they must not fail to keep watch for exceptional and bizarre events;
they must combine all together, compare with premium rates,
and assess the final result.

Such speculation is the work of genius.
However, if theory, guided by experience, is only too often fault,
what of the fate of tradesmen who, lured by the prospect of gain,
sign policies presented to them without due consideration
for the dangers into which blind fortune
and their own recklessness may lead them?
*   – B. M. Emerigon, Treatise on Insurances, 1783*

Part III of this book examined the protection of critical infrastructure and services by the development of more resilient technological and organizational systems. In Part IV, we highlighted the growing interdependent nature of economic and social activities, which leads to more global and interdependent risks: the failure of one organization is more likely to have an effect on others. This new reality needs to be better understood and worked out quite specifically, something we addressed in the previous part and for which we suggested some strategies and policies to better respond to these challenges.

A more detailed analysis of questions addressed in this chapter is provided in Michel-Kerjan 2006.

Whereas the suggested actions should limit the occurrence and/or the impacts of major catastrophes, the possibility that such extreme events will occur anyway cannot be disregarded. If that were to happen, the question of the economic consequences of the catastrophe is likely to take center stage. Who should pay? The victims themselves (self-protection)? Their insurers (if they had purchased coverage against the event)? The shareholders (e.g., firms publicly traded)? The government – present and future generations of taxpayers – in the interest of national solidarity? What proportion should each of these stakeholders pay?

Because the last few years have seen large-scale catastrophes that severely hit the insurance business, insurers and their reinsurers may want to strongly limit their coverage for certain types of risks or in specific high-risk areas, or even stop covering them at all. This possibility raises the question of the roles and responsibilities of both the public and private sectors in providing adequate financial protection to victims of disaster, both people and firms. More broadly, it also requires that every country develop global strategies to recover from such large-scale destabilizations. Strategies are needed for the three sources of disaster this book analyzes: terrorist and malevolent acts, natural disasters, and technogenic risks. Of these risks, terrorism poses certainly the most challenging question as to who should be responsible for the economic consequences.

In fact, the U.S. President's National Strategy for Homeland Security in July 2002 defines "homeland security" as "the concerted effort to prevent attacks, reduce America's vulnerability to terrorism, and minimize the damage and *recover* from attacks that do occur."[1] This White House definition is of prime importance. Clearly here, homeland security is said to be a two-part strategy: the ex ante approach, to deter new attacks on U.S. soil (prevent and reduce), and the ex post approach, the reaction capacity to an attack (minimize and recover). Part of the ex post "recovery" consists of emergency measures and crisis management, which are known to have the potential to seriously reduce (if effective) or seriously increase (if not) the ultimate level of losses. The other aspect lies in the financing of the damage/indemnification of victims of such attacks.

To succeed, catastrophe risk financing must be a comprehensive national effort. While most decisionmakers recognize that the nation's preparedness for additional mega terrorist attacks is an important tile within the mosaic of homeland security, it seems that almost all of the time, energy, and funding allocated to homeland security has been devoted to the ex ante phase. This emphasis is somewhat surprising because while the physical impact of a smaller terrorist strike may be local, the economic and social impacts could be national, or even international. As we discussed in Chapter 1, the national impact of the threat of terrorism is all the more evident as terrorists shift their focus toward inflicting massive casualties and damaging the U.S. economy. The potential for mega-terrorism reveals a risk that seriously challenges a critical market of our economy: the insurance and reinsurance industry.

As we analyze throughout the next four chapters, terrorism might very well be the most difficult risk to consider from an insurability perspective, the most extreme in a sense. Because of that difficulty, the contributions in this part of the book focus mainly on it. Our discussion, however, is also relevant for other sources of extreme events. Another important element that impacted on our choice is the fact that before the September 11, 2001, attacks, terrorism was included in most commercial insurance coverage without being singled out; in other words, there was nothing resembling a market for terrorism risk coverage in the United States. The same was true in several other industrialized countries. This market exists today, and nearly 50 percent of commercial enterprises have bought terrorism coverage in the United States. How such a new market has come to emerge, with specific interaction between the private and public sectors, with specific demand and supply drivers, with specific prices, provides an interesting perspective on the creation of new markets.

In this fifth part of the book we concentrate our analysis on the role that market mechanisms, specifically insurance/reinsurance, can play in the whole dynamic of sustaining critical services, namely by (1) facilitating economic and social recovery in the aftermath of a disaster by rapidly providing insured victims with compensation, and (2) improving the bridge between higher investment in security and mitigation before the fact, to limit the damage afterward.

A close examination reveals that insurance may not have received the attention it deserves. This is somewhat surprising, because insurance ought to constitute an important nexus linking risk assessment, risk mitigation, and risk financing. Moreover, insurance has historically played a fundamental role of social cohesion and continuity in the face of adversity. Confronted with the unprecedented extreme events that have occurred recently, the resilience of the insurance infrastructure is thus of prime importance. We argue that there is a need to rethink the appropriate role of the public and private sectors, not only in providing financial protection to those at risk, but also in encouraging risk reduction measures that would reduce future losses and hence the need for government disaster assistance after another 9/11-type disaster.

One way to facilitate such a market-based process would be to officially recognize the critical nature of the insurance sector and consider it the nation's 14th critical sector. Indeed, an unnoticed paradox exists. On the one hand, insurance has not yet been officially considered a critical sector on its own. On the other hand, the recognition of the criticality of the insurance infrastructure is implicit for anyone who observes the collection of partnerships within insurance, developed over the years between the government and the private sector to provide coverage against extreme events.

INSURANCE AND RISK PRICING

Insurance, in its two main types – risk pooling and individually based coverage – is now everywhere in most industrialized countries and is growing extremely rapidly in developing countries. For car owners, some minimum insurance coverage is required by law in most developed countries. If a commercial aircraft takes off, the airline is covered for third-party liability. The CEO of a large company might want to purchase Director and Officers insurance. Insurance can also cover special events, such as an international painting exposition or the final game of a world sports championship.[2] Most individuals and firms, consciously or unconsciously, live and operate in an insured world. As a result of that evolution, the insurance sector is today the world's largest industry.[3]

How can we describe insurance? In simple terms, insurance is a contractual transaction that guarantees financial protection, through the advance payment of a relatively small sum (premium), against substantial loss. By the transfer of all or part of one's exposure to more broadly based financial structures with greater capacity for diversification (therefore less vulnerable to an individual risk), the individual or commercial enterprise is relieved of a risk that would be difficult to cope with unaided if it ever materialized.

From a market mechanism perspective, the price of insurance can therefore be viewed as a good indicator of the level of risk of certain activities. For instance, a young inexperienced driver should pay a higher insurance premium (other things being equal) than someone who has been driving a car regularly for 20 years without ever having had an accident. In that case, the principle of risk-sharing in exchange for the advance payment of a pre-determined premium is based on sound knowledge of the risk associated with such activities (car insurance), for which there is a great deal of historical data regarding claims and for which accidents are typically independent.

THE CHALLENGES OF LINKING INSURANCE TO MITIGATION

Insurance can also play a key role in improving the bridge between higher investment in security and mitigation in exchange for lower insurance price or better coverage, which should limit the damage after a catastrophe has occurred.

In an ideal theoretical world, the risk is perfectly known. It is possible to determine the distribution of probabilities, based on a huge collection of historical data that also facilitate determining with great certainty the average loss per year, per risk, or per region. As a result, the insurer diversifying risks among a large number of identical and independent agents will charge its insured the actuarial premium plus administrative costs. If the insured decides to invest in mitigation/security measures that are known to reduce to some extent the probability and the associated magnitude of the loss, then the insured would expect to pay a reduced insurance premium (or to obtain other rewards such as a higher limit of coverage or a lower deductible).

This perfect theoretical world, however, does not exist. Reality severely limits this scenario in several important ways. We discuss five of them now.

First, there is often asymmetry of information between the insured and the insurer as to the level of risk or the effort undertaken to mitigate the risk. The way in which information distribution about the risk affects risk sharing is certainly an important question in which economists and practitioners have developed a prime interest over time.

Second, as discussed earlier, for the large-scale risks we focus on in this book, there are far less data, and thus much more uncertainty associated with the occurrence of these events and the potential losses associated with them. This lack of data is even more the case for terrorism than it is for natural hazards, which is very problematic. Indeed, if one cannot know with enough confidence the likelihood of a specific risk, how can one estimate the effectiveness of specific security/mitigation measures and the quality of security investment? What should the price of insurance be based on? And without a good price scheme based on risk, how can one reward such investment? Actually, results of a recent Wharton Risk Center survey of leading insurers in the United States indicate that none of them had linked the price of terrorism insurance they provide to their policyholders with their efforts in security whatsoever; the situation is similar in Europe.[4]

Third, in most industrialized countries insurance is a highly regulated market, so it is not always possible for insurers to set up premiums at the level they would like, which might limit their willingness to offer incentives for security efforts as well. At the end of 2002, the Insurance Services Office used the estimates provided by AIR Worldwide (one of its subsidiaries) to file advisory loss costs with the insurance commissioner for each state. The Insurance Services Office defined three tiers for the country, placing certain areas within Chicago, New York City, San Francisco and Washington, D.C., in the highest tier, with assigned loss costs of approximately $0.10 per $100 of property value.[5] In pre-filing discussions with regulators, the Insurance Services Office's advisory loss costs were challenged by some regulators who felt that such premiums would lead businesses to relocate to other areas. Negotiations ensued, compromises were made, and eventually nowhere did the filed loss costs for the first tier exceed $0.03 per $100 of property value; that is, three times less than originally determined.[6] Thus, while the new levels no longer adequately reflected the risk in the eyes of the modelers, they became more palatable to other stakeholders.

Fourth, on the demand side, with time potential purchasers tend to underestimate the real level of risks ("it will not happen to me") and dismiss insurance premiums as being too expensive, thus limiting the level of coverage.

In that regard, decisions by local, state, and federal governments also play an important role both in terms of risk financing and in the attempt to encourage (or discourage) people and firms to invest in mitigation ahead of time. Indeed, government traditionally is instrumental in the aftermath of a disaster in providing financial relief to those who went without (or extremely limited) insurance coverage. Under public pressure in the aftermath of a catastrophe, the government will likely assist the citizens and firms that were victims of the catastrophe through emergency measures, crisis management, and disaster relief to uninsured citizens in the form of low-interest loans and grants. While such action is legitimate in some sense, over time it also develops the expectation of public assistance, which presents drawbacks. This expectation might reduce incentives to purchase adequate insurance (or even to be covered at all) and implement adequate but costly mitigation measures. While the effect of individuals' expectations is difficult to measure, it certainly plays a role. When a disaster occurs, the rules of the game are often instantaneously modified – there was "before" and there is "now." In the immediate aftermath of a catastrophe, instant political pressure often overpowers long-term economic efficiency.

Fifth, one must consider equity issues. For instance, should poor families living in flood-prone areas (where real estate prices are typically lower) be asked to pay the actuarial price for flood insurance? As it is likely that they cannot afford to pay that amount, they will go without coverage if not required by law or other institutions (e.g., banks for mortgage), which would increase the need for the government to step in afterwards anyway.

THE LIMIT OF INSURABILITY

In the field of insurance and risk management, catastrophes present very specific characteristics, as they can have long-term impacts on the social and economic continuity of the firm, region, or country they affect.

One of the central issues at stake in the financing of catastrophe risks is to determine appropriate insurance mechanisms with specific premiums for events with relatively low frequency and with the potential to inflict massive disruption and/or destruction.[7] Those two factors pose great difficulty for insurers.

IMPACT OF UNCERTAINTY

Two conditions must be verified for a risk to be considered insurable. First is the ability to identify and quantify (or at least to evaluate partially) the probability of an event occurring, and the amount of associated loss incurred if it does occur. Second is the capacity to establish a premium that reflects the level of risk. If both these conditions are verified, the risk may be considered insurable. This does not, however, signify that it is a profitable activity for an insurance company. The insurer, if not obliged by regulation, may well decide that it will not cover this risk if it estimates that covering it is not sufficiently profitable.

The case of terrorism risk is a comprehensive illustration of the traditional limit of insurability. The changing nature of the risk, combined with the lack of data and the possibility of terrorists adapting their attack strategies depending on our own security effort, make this risk extremely difficult to quantify. It is thus impossible to establish an actuarial price for terrorism, and terrorism insurance pricing is thus very likely to be subjective. For example, who could say for sure that New York City faces a higher risk (or a lower risk) of terrorist attack than Miami or Houston in the next five years? How should terrorism insurance premiums differ between these three cities? In the same vein, should firms in the financial sector pay double or half of the price paid by hospitals in one of these locations? Moreover, government plays a key role in influencing the level of risk either ex ante (positively or negatively, for example through specific security measures, counter-terrorism, and foreign policy) or ex post, depending on how the crisis is managed by government authorities. This variability makes the estimation of the likelihood of an attack on a specific location and the potential losses extremely difficult to quantify with certainty.

HIGHLY CORRELATED RISK: A NEW LOSS DIMENSION

To understand challenges faced by the insurance sector vis-à-vis terrorism risks, one needs to consider the evolution of the threat toward attacks that inflict massive casualties and major economic disruption (see Chapter 1).[8] The nearly $35 billion of insured losses from 9/11 illustrate the high degree of risk correlation between different lines of insurance coverage. Indeed, these attacks not only affected commercial property (the World Trade Center towers and adjacent buildings) and caused major business interruption and aircraft hull damage, but also led to billions of dollars in claims from other lines of coverage: workers' compensation, life, health, disability, and general liability insurance. The high correlation among different lines of insurers' portfolios is likely to be seen again after future large-scale attacks.

As discussed in Chapter 1, the evolution of economic and insured losses due to disasters is even more significant if we consider natural catastrophes in addition to the new threat of terrorism. Table 17.1 provides a list of the 20 most costly natural and human-caused catastrophes for the insurance sector over the past 35 years. Among these 20 record holders, 18 occurred in the past 15 years, and 10 between 2001 and 2005 (in constant price indexed to 2005).[9]

Table 17.1. The 20 most costly insured losses in the world, 1970–2005

Rank	U.S.$ billion (indexed to 2005)[a]	Event	Victims (dead or missing)	Year	Area primarily affected
1	45	Hurricane Katrina	1,326	2005	United States, Gulf of Mexico
2	35	9/11 Attacks	3,025	2001	United States
3	22.3	Hurricane Andrew	43	1992	United States, Bahamas
4	18.5	Northridge Quake	61	1994	United States
5	11.7	Hurricane Ivan	124	2004	United States, Caribbean
6	10.0	Hurricane Rita	34	2005	United States, Gulf of Mexico
7	10.0	Hurricane Wilma	35	2005	United States, Gulf of Mexico
8	8.3	Hurricane Charley	24	2004	United States, Caribbean
9	8.1	Typhoon Mireille	51	1991	Japan
10	6.9	Winterstorm Daria	95	1990	France, United Kingdom
11	6.8	Winterstorm Lothar	110	1999	France, Switzerland
12	6.6	Hurricane Hugo	71	1989	Puerto Rico, United States
13	5.2	Hurricane Frances	38	2004	United States, Bahamas
14	5.2	Storms and floods	22	1987	France, United Kingdom
15	4.8	Winterstorm Vivian	64	1990	Western/Central Europe
16	4.7	Typhoon Bart	26	1999	Japan
17	4.2	Hurricane Georges	600	1998	United States, Caribbean
18	4.1	Hurricane Jeanne	3,034	2004	United States, Caribbean
19	3.7	Typhoon Songda	45	2004	Japan, South Korea
20	3.5	Tropical Storm Alison	41	2001	United States

[a] Figures on economic and insured losses due to a specific disaster can vary throughout the book, depending on whether the figure is indexed to a specific year price. Data on natural disasters in Table 17.1 are provided in Swiss Re (2006), "Natural catastrophes and man-made disasters in 2005," Sigma, #2, February 2006, Zurich; and Wharton Risk Center (2005), "TRIA and Beyond. The future of terrorism risk financing in the U.S." The Wharton School, Philadelphia.

In the United States alone, catastrophes in 2005 inflicted twice as much insured losses than in 2004, the previous record holder. This is the new loss dimension the insurance infrastructure faces today.

How long insurers and reinsurers will continue to cover such events on their own and under what conditions is a central question in the debate on how to better protect firms in critical sectors. Indeed, with recent disasters and their resulting effects on the liquidity or even solvency of insurance companies, insurers may be reluctant to cover these untoward events alone. Traditionally, the insurance industry has avoided these problems by transferring such risks to the reinsurance market. However, the current reinsurance capacity for coverage against terrorism has been seriously reduced after 9/11, and prices of catastrophe reinsurance tend to increase significantly in the aftermath of major catastrophes.

These recent disasters have encouraged systematically the development of cooperation between the private sector and federal or state governments, acting as insurer or reinsurer of last resort. In fact, today in the United States insurance of extreme events is often addressed through some forms of collaboration between the private and public sectors (for many years floods, hurricanes, and earthquakes, and more recently terrorism). Of course, such involvement by the government in insurance programs aims at providing potential victims with sufficient availability of risk coverage. But it also constitutes an implicit recognition of the government's role and responsibility in sustaining the operation of insurance infrastructure.[10] In Chapter 18, Rand Corporation's Lloyd Dixon and Robert Reville argue that the federal responsibility vis-à-vis national security calls for the development of long-term partnerships between government and the insurance sector to provide financial coverage to victims of devastating attacks. They also discuss how a strong insurance infrastructure can reduce the will of terrorist groups to attack the country, as economic disruption would be reduced.

THE TERRORISM RISK INSURANCE ACT OF 2002 AND ITS EXTENSION

Quite surprisingly, no state or federal insurance legislation was enacted during the year following 9/11 in the United States. As a result, many firms remained largely without coverage at the time of the first anniversary of the 9/11 attacks. The lack of available terrorism coverage at an affordable price delayed or prevented certain projects from going forward due to concerns by lenders or investors in providing financing for these efforts. These concerns led to the passage of the Terrorism Risk Insurance Act of 2002 (TRIA), signed into law by President Bush on November 26, 2002. TRIA established a three-year national program, based on a public–private risk-sharing arrangement that provides up to $100 billion of commercial coverage against terrorism losses perpetrated by foreign interests on U.S. soil.

Although TRIA and its two-year extension – passed in the 11th hour before congressional recess at the end of December 2005 – have temporarily solved the problems faced by commercial firms in obtaining adequate terrorism coverage after 9/11, I do not believe it is the appropriate long-term program the country needs. Chapter 19 by James Macdonald and Chapter 20 by Wharton's Howard Kunreuther and Erwann Michel-Kerjan provide important points of view on the ongoing terrorism risk financing debate, with a special focus on

TRIA operation, terrorism insurance market regulation, and potential terrorism loss-sharing among different stakeholders. These chapters offer exclusive and complementary perspectives on the broader question of insurance and protection of critical infrastructure to deal with extreme events, a central theme addressed by Franklin Nutter's chapter that analyzes the re-insurance aspect of it.

INSURANCE, THE 14TH CRITICAL SECTOR

So far, existing programs for a public–private role in financing catastrophe recovery have not addressed critical infrastructure as such. Except for airline transportation and nuclear plants (one of the so-called key assets of the nation), no program has been designed to cover risks associated with a specific critical sector.[11] As Franklin Nutter concludes in Chapter 21, "financing the recovery of critical infrastructure has not received the attention it deserves." On the other hand, firms in each of these sectors use insurance mechanisms to cover some of the risks they are exposed to on a daily basis. Insurance and, more broadly, risk financing market mechanisms are common to all 13 other critical sectors.

Hence, how policymakers and executives in the private sector can best utilize the insurance infrastructure to develop a cost-effective strategy for preparation, prevention, and recovery from catastrophic risks is of prime importance. For example, the Department of Homeland Security has recently started considering insurance (and more generally private risk financing solutions) in its strategy for protecting the nation.

INSURANCE AS A CRITICAL SECTOR

Has insurance ever been viewed as a critical sector for the nation, and one which should require specific attention on its own? To our knowledge, such a question has not been raised explicitly. If society agrees that insurance and reinsurance play such a key role in protecting the nation against economic and social discontinuity, then thinking of insurance as comprising "identifiable industries, institutions, and distribution capabilities that provide a reliable flow of products and services essential to the economic security of the Unites States" makes sense. That is, precisely, the definition of a critical sector.

Some steps in the direction of identifying insurance as a critical sector have been taken by recognizing the banking and finance sector as a critical infrastructure, and within that, insurance is included as a financial service.[12] In its *Agenda for 2005*, the Financial Service Sector Coordinating Council

(FSSCC)[13] recognizes that "coordination between the insurance industry and governmental authorities also can facilitate disaster preparedness and disaster response efforts, and mitigate financial losses." However, insurance has not yet been considered on its own as a critical infrastructure to be protected. As stated by this FSSCC report, "the insurance industry will seek to form strong working relationships with governmental authorities to establish a foundation for future cooperative efforts."[14] But 10 years after the Presidential Commission for Protection of Critical Infrastructure (the Marsh Commission), these strong working relationships have not been solidified yet.

Officially recognizing the insurance infrastructure as one of the top critical sectors of the nation would certainly contribute to accelerating these needed collaborative actions. It would also better structure the debate on the roles and responsibilities of the public and private sectors in providing adequate protection to victims of catastrophes and in more systematically linking risk financing and risk mitigation.

As discussed in Chapter 1, the notion of critical services has been a fluid concept over the past decades, and 13 critical sectors have been identified today. The list is likely to evolve further. The number of infrastructures recognized as "critical" will continue increasing as some sub-sectors become singled out to better tailor protection to their specific vulnerabilities and modes of operation. In that same process, insurance should be the next one to be singled out – the 14th critical sector.

With growing global international interdependencies, that recognition should apply beyond the United States and be integrated in all industrialized and emerging economies' strategies to protect their critical services. For instance, on the other side of the Atlantic Ocean, the European Commission is now moving to develop the "European Program for the Protection of Critical Infrastructures" (see Chapter 26). Financial coverage should be an integral part of that program. It is not today.

Beyond the imperative recognition of insurance as the United States' 14th critical sector, it is worth noting how the general approach within the U.S. government to analyzing the protection of critical services remains largely "physical" or "cyber" (as detailed in Chapter 15). That duality is well illustrated by two recent important documents released as part of the overall effort to protect the country – the *National Strategy for the Physical Protection of Critical Infrastructures and Key Assets* and the *National Strategy to Secure Cyberspace*, both developed by the White House and published in February 2003. However, the financial protection perspective is missing. A "National Strategy for Financial Protection" has not yet been developed. The White House, working with key interested parties and experts, could take the leadership on this vital issue. With growing threats on the international scene, the American public and business enterprises deserve nothing less.

NOTES

1. Emphasis added.
2. The first catastrophe bond, which transfered the risk to financial markets rather than being covered by an insurance policy, was issued in Europe in August 2003. The world governing organization of association football (soccer), the FIFA, which organized the 2006 World Cup in Germany, developed a $262-million bond to protect its investment. Under very specific conditions, the catastrophe bond covers against *both* natural and terrorist extreme events that would result in the cancellation of the World Cup game without the possibility of it being re-scheduled to 2007.
3. The word "insurance" is viewed here in its general meaning of risk coverage in exchange of the advance payment of a premium. This infrastructure is combination of insurers, reinsurers, incident management, asset management, and other forms, in the United States and abroad. With about $3.24 trillion in revenues in 2004, it would be the third largest economy in terms of GDP.
4. Wharton Risk Center 2005. See also Michel-Kerjan and Pedell 2005.
5. A second tier consisted of Boston, Houston, Los Angeles, Philadelphia, and Seattle, as well as other portions of the highest rated cities; the rest of the country fell into the third tier.
6. The second and third tiers settled at $0.018 and $0.001 (respectively) per $100 of property value.
7. There is an important literature on the economics of insurance and extreme events; among the earliest works, see Dacy and Kunreuther 1969 and Kunreuther et al. 1978. For a collection of journal publications in this field, see Kunreuther and Rose 2004.
8. For insightful analyses of the evolution of terrorism risks, see Enders and Sandler 2006; see also Enders and Sandler 2000; Hoffman 1998; Pillar 2001.
9. The Indian Ocean tsunami that devastated southeast Asia on December 26, 2004, killed 220,000 people, but because of a low insurance market penetration inflicted "only" $2.07 billion of insured losses – making it only the 34th most costly event for insurance over the past 35 years (Swiss Re 2006).
10. For example, the Federal Victim Compensation Fund was established by Congress in the aftermath of 9/11 and provided nearly $7 billion in payments to 9/11 civilian and first responder victims' families. The fund actually requires the beneficiaries to relinquish their rights to sue, thus limiting liability losses that might otherwise have ended up in court and possibly paid by the insurance industry. All but a few 9/11 victims' families went through this compensation fund for benefits.
11. Since the terrorist attacks of September 11, 2001, the U.S. commercial aviation industry can purchase insurance for third-party liability arising out of aviation terrorism. The current mechanism operates as a pure government program, with premiums paid by airlines into the Aviation Insurance Revolving Fund managed by the Federal Aviation Administration (FAA). The Price-Anderson Act established to provide private–public coverage for nuclear plants has been another exception.
12. The White House 2002.

13. The FSSCC is a U.S. network of financial trade associations and private firms representing thousands of financial services organizations. The network works closely with the U.S. Department of the Treasury, financial regulators, and other government agencies to coordinate private sector preparation for events that could disrupt the normal business of financial services.
14. Financial Services Sector Coordinating Council 2005.

18

NATIONAL SECURITY AND PRIVATE-SECTOR RISK MANAGEMENT FOR TERRORISM

Lloyd Dixon and Robert Reville

Government policies and programs have been developed over many decades in the United States to address risks to private businesses and individuals associated with a wide range of disasters and adverse events. Programs such as riot insurance, unemployment insurance, and workers' compensation have been created to cushion the effects of urban riots, job loss, and workplace injuries. Programs have been developed at the federal and state levels to share risks and provide compensation for losses due to large natural disasters such as earthquakes, floods, and hurricanes. Another risk to citizens and businesses in the United States became more evident on September 11, 2001: the risk of terrorism. Stakeholders and the policy community have been proposing and discussing government programs and policies for addressing this new risk, although the need for a public role is still being debated. This chapter explores the public role in addressing terrorism risk, and specifically the role of terrorism insurance and compensation in national security.

Much of the recent debate on terrorism risk management has focused on insurance and the Terrorism Risk Insurance Act of 2002 (TRIA). Insurance is just one tool for addressing risk, however, and we begin this chapter with a brief description of the broader set of mechanisms that have been used in the United States to provide risk management and compensation for adverse events. The next section discusses unique public policy issues that arise in the context of terrorism risk, and in particular how national security considerations set this risk apart from other risks. How the compensation system can contribute to national security is then illustrated with the experience after 9/11. We then describe trends in terrorism since 9/11 and the increasingly complex public–private interdependence of terrorism risk. Finally, we explore some of the policy challenges at the intersection of public policy and private risks for terrorism. We identify several policy issues that should be researched and ultimately addressed in crafting the public role.

THE RISK SHARING AND COMPENSATION SYSTEM

The institutions, programs, and policies that provide benefits to businesses and individuals affected by an accident, natural disaster, terrorist attack, or other type of loss can be thought of as a system composed of four primary compensation mechanisms: insurance, the tort system, government programs, and charity. Together these mechanisms determine the fraction of losses borne by injured parties, the parties responsible for paying for the losses, the time to payment, and the transaction costs associated with the transfers. Together they also create incentives for physical and financial risk management for both businesses and individuals.[1] Ultimately, their combined operation contributes to the resilience of a local economy or a country to a catastrophe. Very little research has explored the appropriate roles and interrelationships of these institutions for terrorism.

The role that each compensation mechanism plays in the United States varies by the type of injury or loss. For example, the tort system and life insurance play the lead role in providing benefits to individuals who are killed or injured in commercial aviation accidents. In contrast, the tort system does not play a major role in compensating losses caused by floods. Instead, flood insurance, Federal Emergency Management Agency disaster assistance programs, and charities provide benefits to flood victims. It may be stating the obvious, but in the absence of benefits from insurance, the tort system, the government, or charity, the business or individual harmed bears the loss.

Failure to consider the larger system when evaluating proposals for any one mechanism can lead to unsatisfactory conclusions for two basic reasons. First, focusing on only one mechanism can result in neglect of approaches that may be more effective. In particular, the recent debate on terrorism compensation policy in the United States has focused almost exclusively on TRIA (see Chapters 19 and 20). Broader questions about whether insurance is the best mechanism for addressing terrorism risk have rarely been addressed. Second, the interactions themselves between the different mechanisms can be important, and focusing on only one aspect of the compensation system can result in overlooking significant indirect impacts caused by those interactions. The interaction between the extent of tort liability for terrorism and the cost and availability of terrorism insurance is an important example.

THE LINK BETWEEN COMPENSATION AND INSURANCE
FOR TERRORISM LOSSES AND NATIONAL SECURITY

Insurance and compensation for terrorism losses have implications for national security. This link with national security is typically absent from insurance and compensation policy for other disasters, such as earthquakes and hurricanes. As a general rule, the provision of national security is an accepted role for government. Thus the connection of terrorism compensation and insurance policy with national security provide another rationale for public involvement in markets for terrorism insurance. This involvement goes beyond the different types of market failures in terrorism insurance markets discussed in other parts of this book and elsewhere.[2] Three aspects of national security are related to the compensation system: reducing physical vulnerability, promoting solidarity, and enhancing economic resilience.[3]

REDUCING PHYSICAL VULNERABILITY

The compensation system can alter incentives to reduce physical vulnerability to terrorism. This connection between terrorism and national security is the most direct and obvious, but the extent to which compensation and insurance affect terrorism risk mitigation decisions is not well understood. Several issues need to be further explored. An important one is the extent to which subsidies for insurance or extensive government assistance after an attack reduce the incentives for a firm to avoid risky situations or invest in security measures. Recent work by the Congressional Budget Office has raised the prominence of this issue.[4] However, some analysts have argued that left to themselves, private markets may create excessive incentives to take security measures. Lakdawalla and Zanjani point out that because terrorists can adapt their strategies in response to security measures, securing one target may just cause terrorists to switch their attention to another target.[5] The outcome may be a security arms race that results in over-protection. Possible policy responses to such interdependencies include government subsidies of terrorism insurance, which would reduce the likelihood that firms would take excessive protection measures.

PROMOTING SOLIDARITY

RAND Corporation counterterrorism expert Bruce Hoffman has described terrorism as the use of violence by non-state actors with the goal of changing the policies of governments by dividing them from their citizens through the use of fear.[6] Countering terrorism fundamentally involves countering this fear, which undermines the terrorists' goal of dividing the government from its citizens. While providing security is the most direct way to reduce fear, the government may be able to reduce fear by demonstrating solidarity with victims through government assistance and compensation. Such compensation policies that encourage cohesion and solidarity may frustrate the terrorists' aims. For example, in the aftermath of 9/11, federal, state, and city governments all scrambled to offer assistance to businesses and individuals, which was no doubt intended in part to offer reassurance to citizens to counter the fear stoked by the terrorists. Policies that spread the cost of providing compensation broadly across the nation may further the perception in the United States that terrorism is an attack on the nation as a whole.[7] Whereas promoting solidarity does not immediately deter future attacks, it could deter them in the long run by causing terrorism to be less effective in achieving the ultimate goals of terrorists.

ENHANCING ECONOMIC RESILIENCE

Economic resilience refers to the speed with which the economy bounces back after an adverse event. By enhancing the resilience of the economy to attack, the compensation system can reduce economic vulnerability to terrorism. Insurance payments (and other types of compensation for losses) allow disrupted businesses to continue operation, allow owners of buildings to rebuild, and provide income support and medical care for the families of the deceased and injured. Without insurance or some other means of managing the risk, terrorist attacks targeting businesses will lead to greater disruption, dislocation, and joblessness, which will increase the fear of future attacks. Putting productive assets and people back to work reduces the economic ripples that can result from major terrorist attacks. Reducing the economic impact of attacks can help control the hardship and fear caused by attacks, thus thwarting the aims of terrorists, and it is not inconceivable that thwarting the aims of terrorists could ultimately reduce the likelihood of attacks.

Further investigation is needed to understand the complex role that resilience and solidarity play in security against terrorism. In addition, it is unclear which specific approaches to insurance or compensation are more or less effective in improving resilience or solidarity. For instance, Ken Feinberg, the Special Master of the federal September 11th Victim Compensation Fund (VCF; discussed in the next section), has noted that paying different amounts to victims, as was done through the VCF, may increase divisiveness. Further investigation is needed to relate particular policies with solidarity and resilience, and to relate improved solidarity and resilience to the inability of terrorists to achieve political goals, and ultimately to deterrence of future attacks.

THE RESPONSE OF THE COMPENSATION SYSTEM
TO THE 9/11 ATTACKS

The response of the public and private sectors to the 9/11 terrorist attacks illustrates how the compensation system can further national security goals.

The 9/11 attacks caused tremendous loss of life, health, property, and income to individuals, businesses, and public assets. The attack also resulted in a massive multi-pronged compensation response. Insurance payouts to businesses, homeowners, and individuals injured or killed in the attacks (including loss adjustment expenses) are expected to total $32 billion – the largest amount for any single event in U.S. history up to that time.[8] Congress limited the role of the tort system in compensating losses after the attacks and set up the VCF to provide compensation to those who suffered serious physical injury or to the families of those who were killed in the attacks. Overall, the fund distributed more than $7 billion to 2,680 individuals who were injured and to the survivors of 2,880 people killed in the attacks or in the rescue efforts conducted thereafter.[9] The federal government also provided billions to compensate businesses and workers, and to rebuild New York City. The charitable response was unprecedented. Approximately two-thirds of U.S. households made contributions to charities for victims of the 9/11 attacks, and charitable donations exceeded $2.9 billion.[10]

The economic effects of the 9/11 attacks were far-reaching, but the compensation response after the attacks arguably reduced economic impacts and sped economic recovery, compared to what would have occurred in the absence of such programs. Insurance payments for property damage and business interruption allowed businesses to repair damages and pay their workers for at least part of the time that operations were interrupted. Government grant and incentive programs encouraged small businesses to return to Lower Manhattan at a time when the prospects for Lower Manhattan were extremely uncertain.[11] The response of government, insurers, charity, and plaintiff lawyers who donated their time to help victims apply to the VCF, was a demonstration of national solidarity against the aims of terrorism. Special Master Ken Feinberg has described the VCF as "vengeful philanthropy" – showing the terrorists that they cannot hurt or divide the country because the United States will support the families of the dead and seriously injured.[12] Arguably, the response limited the effectiveness of the attacks in causing economic damage, and therefore to some extent, frustrated the ultimate aims of the terrorists.

The insurance system provided more than half of the total payout of the compensation system after 9/11.[13] Insurance payments were so large because terrorism was not yet recognized as a distinct peril by insurers (despite the previous attempt to destroy the World Trade Center in 1993), and therefore was neither excluded nor priced as a stand-alone policy. In addition, insurers did not attempt to invoke war damage exclusions. As a result, a large number of insured businesses and individuals received payouts on their policies.[14] This, too, contributed to the national response and likely improved resilience from the attacks.

The benefits paid out after the 9/11 attacks were the result of a unique combination of resources from insurance, government programs, and charity. There is, however, no guarantee that a similar mix of resources will be available for victims of future attacks: The VCF was event specific, the take up of terrorism insurance has been spotty even with TRIA, and the charitable response for future attacks is unpredictable.

FUTURE ATTACKS AND THE EVOLVING RISK

Terrorism is an evolving risk. New groups engage in terrorism, and existing groups cease to exist or discontinue terrorist activity. Technology evolves, and the capabilities of terrorist groups evolve accordingly. In addition, existing groups react to government counterterrorism strategies by adapting their methods of operation. This constant change complicates the design of institutions to address the risk. In this section, we describe some research on the evolving threat of terrorism in the United States and its implications for terrorism insurance policy.[15]

Three trends in the threat of terrorism in the United States have emerged since 9/11 that together portend a significant shift of the risk of terrorism from the public sector to the private sector. The three trends are the degradation of Al Qaeda's capabilities, the shift of risk toward softer targets due to the hardening of government facilities, and the increased targeting by Al Qaeda and its affiliated groups on attacks that lead to cascading economic effects.[16]

Since 9/11, Al Qaeda has seen significant damage inflicted on its Afghanistan safe haven, its top leadership, and its ability to operate unnoticed or unimpeded. As a result, Al Qaeda has shifted from a centralized and hierarchical organization to a "movement of movements," with affiliated local cells in multiple countries. These local cells are technologically and organizationally less capable of complex attacks on high-profile targets, but they are able to attack in many places around the world, leading to an increased tempo of attacks focused on more accessible, less protected, civilian-centric targets.

Simultaneously, there has been a dramatic increase in security at many of the traditional targets, such as embassies and other government properties. Strengthening security is referred to as "hardening," and many terrorism experts have noted that the hardening of one kind of target displaces risk toward other "softer" targets. In combination with the transformation of Al Qaeda, this displacement of risk phenomena has been used to explain Al Qaeda's post-9/11 attention on targets such as hotels, nightclubs, places of worship, transportation systems, office complexes, passenger aircraft, commercial shipping, and foreign workers and contractors.[17]

This displacement of risk toward softer targets also shifts the targets from predominantly government facilities to those that are typically privately owned.[18] This implies that there has been a displacement of risk toward targets that are more likely to result in private sector losses – and if insured, insurance losses. Ultimately, the displacement of risk to the private sector is one part of a broader set of policy questions that are only now being explored by researchers and policymakers alike: what is the appropriate allocation of security resources across targets, and what are the vehicles for encouraging this allocation? Among the unexplored questions is whether government support of terrorism insurance encourages a more appropriate allocation of security resources in circumstances where government security measures tend to shift risk onto the private sector.

A third recently observed trend in terrorism is the increased interest by Al Qaeda in wreaking economic damage. Osama bin Laden's rhetoric has glorified the economic damage that the 9/11 attacks generated. He has claimed that this damage exposes the fatal weakness of the United States – that it is a "paper tiger," and that attacks focused on undermining the country's economic pillars will topple it, like the Soviet Union during its ill-fated occupation of Afghanistan. As a result, he has exhorted his followers to plan future attacks on targets that lead to damage to the economy. Realizations of such a shift in targeting strategy include the alleged plots against financial institutions in New York and New Jersey, as well as the terrorists' interest in attacking targets that would lead to economic disruptions that would exceed the losses to the particular target, such as airlines, oil shipping, and tourist destinations.

As with the first two trends, the third trend shifts risk to the private sector and highlights the role of insurance. In this case, however, because causing economic damage is an explicit goal of the terrorists, institutions that prevent or buffer the cascading economic effects are directly countering the terrorists' aims. To the extent that targeting economic damage is the terrorists' strategy for achieving their ultimate goals, encouraging insurance and other financial terrorism risk management is explicitly a counterterrorism policy.

As with the displacement of risk through hardening of government targets, the increased focus on causing economic damage has also shifted risk to the private sector. Not only does this change in focus increase risk to insured property and assets, but it also increases risk in areas where losses are only partially insured. In particular, much of the follow-on economic losses from a terrorist attack, such as increased hotel vacancies as a result of decreased travel, are uninsured. This suggests that new government policies to mitigate indirect effects of terrorist attacks should be considered.

These three trends in the threat of terrorism underscore the complex public–private relationship that is intrinsic to terrorism risk. Government and private sector actions combine to shape the character of the risk at any given time. Physical and financial security are equally interwoven. Ultimately, research and policy must consider both financial and physical protection in the design of robust and effective institutions to address this risk. As these interdependencies are often not recognized, and certainly poorly understood, considerable work remains.

NATIONAL SECURITY CHALLENGES IN PUBLIC–PRIVATE RISK SHARING FOR TERRORISM

Terrorism experts expect terrorism to be increasingly targeted at private sector assets that have the potential to lead to substantial economic disruption. In this section, we explore several issues related to national security that should be addressed in developing risk-sharing mechanisms for terrorism. We focus here on insurance, but additional work is needed to understand how policies focusing on government compensation, liability, and charitable organizations should be integrated with government policies on insurance.[19]

COVERAGE REQUIREMENTS

Even with the federal TRIA, insurance coverage for losses caused by foreign acts of terrorism is currently only carried by about one-half of firms that buy property and casualty insurance.[20] What is more, many of the firms that do buy insurance do not buy it up to the same coverage limits they purchase for other perils. One approach for ensuring that resources are available to cover property losses and rebuilding after an attack is to require the purchase of insurance. Other countries (such as Spain and France) require terrorism insurance, and the United States requires insurance for some other risks in certain settings – such as flood insurance for properties with federally regulated mortgages in flood-prone areas.

Mandatory coverage would likely increase the resilience of the economy to terrorist attacks, and priority could be placed on requiring firms in economic sectors that are critical to the continued operation of the economy (such as transportation and communication) to hold appropriate amounts of insurance coverage. Requiring insurance would also solve any under-estimation of risk by firms that would cause them to decline terrorism insurance. A downside of mandatory coverage is that there are many different ways for a firm to spread risk, and purchasing insurance may not be the most efficient approach for all firms (for example, a firm could spread its risk by diversifying its holdings geographically and across different sectors of the economy). Another drawback of mandatory insurance is that government interventions in insurance markets would likely be necessary to ensure that adequate insurance capacity were available at reasonable rates. Such an intervention may involve the federal government acting as the insurer of last resort. Insurance can in principle also deter investments in measures that enhance security or resilience (moral hazard) although, as discussed later, insurance also has the potential to encourage such investments by linking premiums to risk-mitigation practices.

THE CHALLENGES OF INFORMATION SHARING

One challenge that has received scant attention in the literature on terrorism insurance is information sharing, and specifically the implications of government control of information about the risk. Intelligence agencies have greater knowledge of the risk of terrorism than do the private sector targets increasingly at risk. Considerable recent controversy has accompanied the attempts to share information among intelligence agencies; sharing information with the private sector is arguably the next frontier in intelligence policy.

Intelligence agencies must limit the information they provide to insurers and policyholders about terrorism risk to avoid compromising sources or causing terrorists to simply alter their targets or attack modalities. However, withholding information from the private sector may hinder efforts by businesses to take appropriate risk mitigation measures and may hinder insurer ability to set insurance rates accordingly. Complex issues also arise in deciding just who intelligence agencies should share information with in the private sector. The first inclination may be to share information only with the firms subject to increased risk and not with their insurers. But such a policy could lead to asymmetric information about terrorism risks between the insurer and the policyholder. This asymmetry is a classic cause of market failure, because businesses that have private information that they are at greater risk will be more likely to buy insurance, and low risk firms will increasingly be priced out of the market.

PRE- VERSUS POST-FUNDING

Insurance premiums are typically collected up front to pay for later losses, but it is very difficult to set premiums for terrorism coverage with any level of confidence because of the difficulties in predicting the type and frequency of attacks. If losses were post-funded, surcharges could be placed on a wide range of property–casualty policies (for example all commercial property–casualty policies in the United States) to cover the losses.[21] An advantage of broad-based post-funding is that it avoids setting rates and collecting premiums before an attack. Also, spreading losses broadly with ex post surcharges would be consistent with the belief that terrorism is directed at the country as a whole and that the country should come together to reimburse losses. A potential disadvantage (discussed later) is that insurance premiums could not be used to signal firms about what types of risk mitigation and security measures are prudent. Broad-based post-funding might also be perceived as unfair by some who argue that low-risk areas of the country should not subsidize high-risk areas. Finally, it is worth noting that in practice, mechanisms for post-funding may not in fact be applied if policymakers determine that they are better uses of post-attack resources.

LINKING INSURANCE PREMIUMS TO RISK MITIGATION PRACTICES

No broadly accepted standards for protecting against terrorism attacks currently exist in the private sector, and interdependencies between firms and national security ramifications make it very difficult to determine the appropriate risk mitigation and security measures.[22] Some progress might be made on identifying the appropriate types of security measures by developing national security standards through a public process that weighs the broad social and national security implications of different standards. At one extreme, firms could be required to adopt such standards as a condition of buying terrorism coverage.[23] Alternatively, the standards could be voluntary, and insurers could be allowed (or perhaps required) to provide premium discounts to firms that adopt such practices.

Developing national terrorism risk standards would combine the expertise and experience of the public and private sectors. A disadvantage of heading in such a direction is the potentially massive complexity of the resulting regulations. For example, variation in magnitude and type of risk across industries and geographic regions may necessitate a complex set of standards. In addition, given the difficulty insurers have in pricing terrorism risk, they would presumably find it very difficult to set premium reductions that would reflect differences in expected losses in any defensible way.

CONCLUSIONS

Terrorism creates challenges for many of the public and private approaches that have been used to address risks facing individuals and businesses in the United

States. A fundamental difference between terrorism and many of these other risks is that terrorists are purposeful actors. The capabilities and strategies of terrorists change in response to actions by their targets. The shifting nature of the threat makes it extremely difficult for insurers to price insurance with any degree of confidence. In addition, risk management and compensation policies may dampen terrorist activity by helping reduce the economic impacts of and social divisiveness caused by terrorist attacks. Indeed, even if compensation and insurance policies do not influence terrorist activity, they can reduce the impact of terrorism on the economy by reducing the effectiveness of terrorist acts.

Risk management and compensation policies for terrorism have national security implications, and these implications should be considered in designing such policies. Even absent failures in the market for terrorism insurance, however, decisions that are efficient from the firms' point of view will not necessarily produce outcomes that optimally limit vulnerability to terrorism from a societal point of view.

Our review of the changing capabilities and aims of terrorists suggests that terrorists will increasingly focus attacks on the private sector, and their goal will increasingly be economic disruption. These trends underline the importance of public–private sector coordination in addressing terrorist threats. The focus on economic disruption also suggests increased attention should be paid to policies that address the vulnerability and resilience of the economy to attack. Policies that reduce the vulnerability and resilience of infrastructure that is critical to economic activity, such as transportation and communication systems, merit particular attention.

We also emphasize that many tools are available to manage risks and provide compensation for terrorism. Insurance policies are often the focus of discussions on risk sharing, but the liability system, government assistance programs, and even charity all interact to determine the effectiveness of the risk management and compensation system. The advantages and disadvantages of each mechanism should be evaluated in crafting an integrated system tailored to the attributes of the terrorism threat.

NOTES

1. Dixon and Stern 2004, 5, 145–149.
2. For an extensive discussion of the challenges of insuring terrorism, see Kunreuther and Michel-Kerjan 2004, 2005a.
3. See Dixon and Reville 2005 for an additional discussion of the links between national security and terrorism insurance and compensation.

4. The Congressional Budget Office argued that by subsidizing insurance rates, the Terrorism Risk Insurance Act weakens the incentives of property owners to adopt measures that would reduce losses from terrorist attacks (Congressional Budget Office 2005, p. viii).

5. Lakdawalla and Zanjani 2005.

6. Hoffman 1998.

7. Spreading losses broadly could also encourage resentment in areas where the terrorist threat is low.

8. The Insurance Information Institute currently projects that insured losses due to the 9/11 attacks will total $32.5 billion (Hartwig 2004). The $20 billion in insured losses due to Hurricane Andrew in 1992 is the second largest amount in U.S. history through 2001 (Tillinghast-Towers Perrin 2001). Estimates of private insurer losses due to Hurricane Katrina in 2005 are on the order of $40 billion to $60 billion (Marsh 2005a), with an additional $20 billion to $25 billion in losses for the federal National Flood Insurance Program. Litigation continues over whether the 9/11 crashes of the two planes into the World Trade Center constitute one event or two from the point of view of insurance coverage. For the discussion here, however, the 9/11 attacks are considered to be one event.

9. Feinberg et al. 2004.

10. Renz et al. 2003. For a detailed evaluation of the performance of the compensation system after 9/11, see Dixon and Stern 2004.

11. For example, the World Trade Center Small Firm Attraction and Retention Grant program provided grants of up to $5,000 per employee to firms with 200 employees or fewer that signed leases for five years or more in Lower Manhattan. Federal Liberty Zone tax benefits provided tax credits for firms that moved into the area south of Canal Street in Lower Manhattan, an additional 30-percent depreciation on property rehabilitated or replaced after the attacks, and a five-year recovery period for depreciation of leasehold improvements. Government benefits to business are expected to exceed $6 billion (Dixon and Stern 2004, 109–125).

12. Feinberg 2005.

13. Dixon and Stern 2004, p. xviii, found that insurers, government, and charities paid 51, 42, and 7 percent (respectively) of the benefits provided to those killed in the attacks at the World Trade Center, the Pentagon, and the Pennsylvania crash site and to businesses and individuals in the New York City affected by the attacks on the World Trade Center.

14. Dixon and Stern 2004.

15. This section is based upon Chalk et al. 2005.

16. Chalk et al. 2005 also describes a fourth trend, the rise of anti-globalization among homegrown extremists. This trend has implications similar to the ones described here in terms of terrorist targeting strategies.

17. Chalk et al. 2005, 17–18.

18. The RAND database of global terrorism events (which includes Islamic terrorism as well as other types of terrorism) shows that attacks on government, diplomatic, military, and police facilities accounted for 41 percent of all attacks between 1980 and 1989, versus 32 percent of attacks between October 2001 and December 2004. Businesses, private citizens, and private property were the target of 23 percent of the attacks between 1980 and 1989, versus 38 percent of attacks between October 2001 and December 2004.

19. For a discussion of other issues and options that should be considered in discussion of government interventions in the market for terrorism insurance, see Dixon et al. 2004 and Kunreuther and Michel-Kerjan 2004.

20. U.S. Department of the Treasury 2005.
21. Under TRIA, a substantial portion of payouts would be post-funded in the event of a large loss.
22. See Kunreuther and Heal 2003 for a discussion of the interdependencies among firms inherent in efforts to improve security against terrorist attacks.
23. Such requirements to would be analogous to the floodplain management requirements for communities participating in the National Flood Insurance Program.

19

TERRORISM, INSURANCE, AND PREPAREDNESS

Connecting the Dots

James W. Macdonald

"We cannot enter data about the future into the computer because such data are inaccessible to us. So we pour in data from the past to fuel the decisionmaking mechanisms created by our models, be they linear or non-linear. But therein lies the logician's trap: past data from real life constitute a sequence of events rather than a set of independent observations, which is what the laws of probability demand.... Even though many variables fall into distributions that approximate a bell curve, the picture is never perfect... resemblance to truth is not the same as truth. It is in those outliers and observations that the wildness lies."[1]

— Peter Bernstein, *Against the Gods*, 1996

The shocking terrorist assault on September 11, 2001, was one of those "outliers" where, as Peter Bernstein might say, "the wildness lies." In the immediate aftermath, the coordinated attacks on the Pentagon, on the World Trade Center, and in the air over Pennsylvania appeared to defy all logical explanation and rational analysis. The previous comparable attack by foreigners on continental United States soil occurred almost two centuries ago, when British soldiers burned District of Columbia government buildings during the War of 1812. Prior to the 1990s, the most serious act of domestic terrorism had arguably occurred more than a century earlier with John Brown's 1859 attack on a federal arsenal at Harper's Ferry.

Throughout the 1990s, America witnessed a growing frequency of large and small domestic and foreign terrorist incidents. But the picture was never perfect. Domestically, the perpetrators represented an eclectic mixture of apparently unrelated "dots" such as the Unabomber's luddite attacks on the growth of industry and technology, increasingly violent clashes between the federal government and radical right-wing militias (consummated in the 1995 attack on the Oklahoma City Murrah Building), pro-life attacks on abortion doctors and clinics, environmentalist attacks on pollution emitters and SUVs, animal rights group protests against furriers, and importantly, the isolated attacks by radical Islamic terrorists – including the 1990 assassination of Jewish activist Rabbi Meir Kahane, the 1993 bombing of the World Trade Center, and the interdicted December 1999 attack planned for Los Angeles International Airport. Hindsight quickly showed that we had not "connected" the domestic radical Islamic "dots" to the related events occurring internationally (including the 1996 bombing of the Khobar Towers in Saudi Arabia, 1998 bombings of American embassies in east Africa, and the October 2000 attack on the USS Cole). In most cases, we believed that domestic events were isolated criminal acts.[2] Once the "bad guys" were in jail, "normalcy" returned to our daily personal and business lives, or so we hoped.

The size of the insured loss was as stunning as the event itself: The estimated $32 billion pre-tax insured loss from 9/11 was 30 times more financially damaging than the previous record terrorist insured loss of $907 million (from the 1993 bombing of the NatWest Tower in London). The insured 9/11 losses were more than 50 percent worse than the largest natural catastrophe at that time (i.e., the approximately $20 billion in insured losses sustained in 1992 from Hurricane Andrew).[3] The total additional economic loss (including uninsured losses from reduced travel and tourism) was estimated by New York City alone to be at least $83 billion. In early 2002, a Milken Institute report estimated the total national economic loss from the 9/11 attacks at $175 billion.[4]

Insurers are in the business assuming risk. We are well aware that the past does not necessarily predict the future. But no insurance underwriter anticipated an assault on such a devastating scale as 9/11. Like most Americans, insurers would agree with President Bush's comments in an April 2004 press conference: "nobody in our government, at least, and I don't think the prior government, could envision flying airplanes into buildings on such a massive scale."[5] Prior to 9/11, most underwriters considered a major terrorist attack inside the United States to be one of the many unlikely exposures that are tolerable for no additional premium (being only slightly more probable than an asteroid hitting the earth). Although "war risk" exclusions were common on commercial insurance policies, terrorism was rarely specifically excluded. On 9/11, however, insurers' collective understanding of terrorism risk, insurance, and risk management was thrust into unchartered waters.

At an insurer's level, a host of new underwriting questions urgently needed to be answered: How should a prudent company prepare for the next possible attack? Can we underwrite terrorism on the scale of 9/11 or worse? What are the new questions we need to ask? Will risk managers be willing to give us the possibly confidential and highly sensitive information we need? How will the answers to these questions alter our risk selection and pricing decisions?

And perhaps most importantly: Is America willing to "think the unthinkable" strategically, as we did the early years of the Cold War? Can we develop a holistic risk management solution for what appears to be a new age of "non-state sponsored, asymmetrical warfare"?[6]

In this chapter, I provide one underwriter's response to some of these important questions. In the first section, I review and provide commentary on the original Terrorism Risk Insurance Act of 2002 (TRIA) and the Terrorism Risk Insurance Extension Act of 2005. I then review four important developments that explain the decision to extend the act for another two years. At least three of these developments should continue to influence American public policy thinking for the foreseeable future. In the third section, I define what appears to be an emerging consensus on some of the critical issues driving the national debate on the federally backed terrorism insurance program. I also consider three important "dots" that remain "unconnected": preparedness, perception of risk, and pricing. In closing, I offer specific recommendations that could help develop a long-term solution to the insurability of terrorism risk.

THE TERRORISM RISK INSURANCE ACT OF 2002 AND THE TERRORISM RISK INSURANCE EXTENSION ACT OF 2005

On November 26, 2002, with the nation's economy weak and thousands of construction jobs reportedly at risk because of terrorism insurance cost and availability problems, President Bush signed into law the Terrorism Risk Insurance Act of 2002. The expressed purposes of the law were for the federal government to provide "temporary financial compensation to insured parties, contributing to the United States economy in a time of national crisis in order to: (1) protect consumers by addressing market disruptions and ensure the continued widespread availability and affordability of property and casualty insurance for terrorism risk; and (2) allow for a transitional period for the private markets to stabilize, resume pricing of such insurance, and build capacity to absorb any future losses, while preserving state insurance regulation and consumer protections."[7] The federal program was originally scheduled to expire at the end of 2005.

TRIA seeks to achieve its goals through a "transparent" private and public sector insurance program (called the Terrorism Risk Insurance Program). To qualify for the program, a loss must be "certified" by the Secretary of the Treasury in consultation with the Secretary of State and the Attorney General. The act of terrorism must occur on U.S. soil (with a few exceptions for American foreign missions, aircraft, and watercraft). With the exception of workers' compensation insurance, all losses from formally declared "war" are excluded. These are the most important provisions of the law that have *not* become the subjects of debate.

There are at least six important provisions in the law that immediately became the subjects of considerable disagreement. First, TRIA mandates *supply* by requiring insurers to "make available" terrorism insurance, but *demand* is voluntary. The voluntary nature of most purchase decisions results in closely watched "take up" rates. In addition, to qualify for certification, a terrorist attack must produce a total insured loss of $5 million or more (or only about 15 percent of the insured loss sustained on 9/11). Second, the law also limits coverage to acts of terror conducted "on behalf of a foreign person or foreign interest." Domestic acts of terrorism are not covered. American citizens independently acting but in sympathy with a foreign cause would also most likely not be covered.

Third, with only a few exemptions, the TRIA law does not preempt state insurance regulations.[8] It also does not supersede most of the insurance provisions that would otherwise apply. Insurers must "make available" the terrorism insurance on a basis that "does not differ materially" from the terms and conditions that would otherwise apply. It is therefore possible that one or more of the standard policy limitations could result in a "certified" loss being excluded, even if the policyholder has paid an additional premium for that coverage.

Fourth, TRIA is criticized because it limits the risk of loss to the federal government and American taxpayers by including only certain commercial lines of insurance. By omitting personal lines, medical malpractice, life insurance, health insurance, assumed reinsurance, and several other lines, the industry-wide base premium subject to the law was reduced from approximately $1 trillion (if every form of insurance had been included) to only slightly more than $210 billion in 2004.[9] In 2005, this limitation reduced the hypothetical total industry deductible (assuming every insurer's deductible was exhausted) from about $150 billion to only slightly more than $30 billion.

Fifth, insurers are allowed to charge a premium for the TRIA coverage, subject to state controls. If no loss occurs in a given year, the premium is subject to federal taxation and increases insurers' capital base. However, the federal backstop requires no up-front premium charge to be paid by insurers. The leads many critics to refer to the federal backstop as a questionable form of "free reinsurance." The larger question related to this issue is that of the relative role that up-front and after-the-fact charges should serve in any new, long-term approach.

Sixth, TRIA includes two significant features intended to motivate the private sector to create new financial solutions or reinsurance capacity to insure terrorism risks: insurer deductibles and coinsurance, and policyholder surcharges.

Regarding insurer deductibles and coinsurance, insurers are required to retain all losses up to an annual deductible that increases during each year of the program. They also must retain 10 percent of all certified losses above their deductible. The deductibles are defined as a percentage of the prior year's "direct earned premium" (DEP). The federal government is responsible for 90 percent of insurers' certified losses in excess of their deductible. Total annual payments by insurers and the government are capped at $100 billion. In 2003, the insurer deductible was set at 7 percent of the prior year's DEP, rising to 10 percent in 2004, and then jumping to 15 percent in 2005.

The Department of the Treasury is empowered to charge an annual policyholder surcharge as a post-loss "recoupment" surcharge. In the event that the sum of annual certified losses payable by insurers (equaling the total of all insurer payments within their deductibles and coinsurance obligations) does not exceed a stipulated annual "insurance marketplace aggregate retention," the federal share of the losses is subject to mandatory recoupment. The maximum annual surcharge is 3 percent of the total commercial policy premium, applicable to all policyholders of lines subject to the law (including policyholders electing not to purchase the terrorism insurance). In 2003, the "aggregate retention" was $10 billion, rising to $12.5 billion in 2004 and then to $15 billion in 2005. If the unreimbursed insured certified loss amounts payable exceed these "marketplace aggregate retentions," the Department of the Treasury has the right, but not the obligation, to recoup the federal share of losses through the same maximum annual 3 percent policyholder surcharge.[10] There is no time limit to the possible duration of these required or discretionary annual surcharges.

In the next chapter, Michel-Kerjan and Kunreuther explore in detail the financial issues summarized in the latter points above. Based on the many lessons learned during its first three years, a summary review of TRIA's key provisions is incomplete without some consideration of what is *not* mentioned in the law. In hindsight, the federal architects of the U.S. terrorism insurance program made two important omissions:

First, unlike the European terrorism insurance programs (most of which were created or modified after 9/11), the law does not allow insurers to set aside pre-tax loss reserves. Under statutory accounting rules, loss reserves for natural or human-caused catastrophes may only be posted *after* a catastrophe occurs. In years with no losses, American premiums received for terrorism are taxed at a 35 percent federal corporate tax rate and the remaining 65 percent becomes an addition to the insurer's "retained earnings" (a component of net worth, also called the capital base, or "policyholder's surplus" in U.S. statutory accounting). If pre-tax loss reserving were allowed, as much as 100 percent of the terrorism premium could be posted in the liability section of insurer

balance sheets. Taking the latter approach exponentially increases the investment income growth available to develop these reserves over time, and thereby
increasing the ability of the private sector to absorb terrorism losses. The failure to make this accounting change means that a major terrorism attack would
likely result in a significant drain on individual insurers' capital and surplus
bases. In many cases, this sudden loss of capital could quite possibly present
the risk of financial impairment or insolvency.[11]

Second, TRIA is silent on the issue of preparedness. Virtually all forms
of insurance provide some financial incentives or requirements for preparedness incentives by policyholders. For example, the National Flood Insurance
Program requires communities to agree to loss-mitigation plans prior to any
resident in the community to qualify for the federal insurance. TRIA is unusual
in that it appears to conceive the challenge of insuring terrorism risk entirely
as a financial issue.

This does not imply that the Bush administration was less than focused
on reducing America's vulnerability to another major attack. Quite the contrary, the administration and Congress were highly focused on this issue. The
final legislation creating the Department of Homeland Security (DHS) was
signed into law only one day before TRIA became law. DHS was given principal responsibility for improving terrorism risk preparedness and information
sharing (discussed in the prior chapter). However, the "dots" between the preparedness mandate in DHS and the financial focus of the Department of the
Treasury were not formally connected. As I detail in the following sections of
this chapter, the reported lack of investment in preparedness became a central
focus of several influential assessments of the law's effectiveness.

On June 30, 2005, the Department of the Treasury issued a report showing
that between 2002 and 2005, despite the increased shifting of risk to the private sector, terrorism insurance pricing was becoming more competitive, three
modeling companies had developed new underwriting and portfolio management tools for terrorism risk, the "take-up" rates for property insurance were
steadily increasing, and insurers had more than replenished their capital bases
with the combined Property and Casualty capital base expected to achieve
a record high by the end of 2005.[12] The conclusions in the Treasury report
were confirmed by independent 2005 surveys completed by the two largest
insurance brokers, Marsh & McLennan and AON.[13] In addition, a competitive
specialty market for "stand-alone" terrorism property insurance had developed
with total "per risk" capacity estimated at $1.3 billion through 20 insurers.[14]
New possible capacity from hedge funds was reported to be developing in the
event that TRIA expired.[15] New terrorism capacity had also developed from
the alternative insurance market. In 2005, the Treasury report estimated that
"captive insurers" had underwritten 8 percent of the property terrorism insurance policies, more than twice the 3 percent reported in 2003.[16] The Treasury

report expressed basic agreement with an influential Congressional Budget Office (CBO) report published in January 2005. The CBO's central premise was that "by providing zero-premium coverage and not requiring policyholders to take actions to reduce their exposure to losses, TRIA effectively lessened incentives for property owners to make costly adjustments to a short-term threat."[17]

The third important report influencing policymaking was the Wharton School's influential study, *TRIA and Beyond*, published in August 2005. The Wharton report added a much-needed empirical assessment of terrorism risk, in combination with a progressive theoretical discussion of all the options available to policymakers. The authors conclude that TRIA should be replaced with "a more economically effective, socially equitable, and politically sustainable program."[18]

By all accounts, in late 2005 TRIA seemed to have achieved its "temporary" goals, and the likelihood that it would be extended was questionable. The House and Senate had passed very different extension bills, and the act's expiration deadline was fast approaching. Unlike November 2002, when the initial bill had been enacted, the American economy had improved significantly, and there were no immediate construction or job-related issues mandating an extension. On December 22, 2005, President Bush surprised many stakeholders, by signing into law the House and Senate's compromise legislation labeled the Terrorism Risk Extension Act of 2005.

The TRIA extension prolongs the federal program to the end of 2007. Based entirely on the bill previously passed the Senate (S.467), the major focus of the law is to accelerate the shifting of terrorism risk to the private sector. It undertakes to achieve this goal through five changes: (1) progressive 2.5 point-of-percentage increases in the insurer deductible to 17.5 percent in 2006 and 20 percent in 2007, (2) a reduction in the federal share of losses from 90 percent to 85 percent by 2007, (3) an increase in the "aggregate retention" from $15 billion in 2005 to $25 billion in 2006 and $27.5 billion in 2007 (greatly increasing possible size and duration of post-loss policyholder recoupment surcharges), (4) a slimming down of the types of commercial insurance that are subject to the law, and (5) the introduction of new minimum insurance industry insured loss "Coverage Triggers" of $50 million in 2006 (effective only after March 31, 2006) and $100 million in 2007. (For a summary of the important features of the TRIA and the extension act, see the side-by-side comparison in Appendix 19.A).

The TRIA extension also includes a requirement for the Presidential Working Group on Financial Markets to submit a report to Congress by September 26, 2006. The report is to address the "long-term availability and affordability of terrorism insurance," with specific focus on the issues of insuring nuclear, biological, chemical, and radiological attacks and group life insurance.

IMPORTANT DEVELOPMENTS REFINING THE TRIA DEBATE

Four developments most likely explain why TRIA was extended, despite the recommendations of the CBO and Treasury reports. The first has been cited by many observers: The changing nature of the global terrorist threat. The July 7, 2005, bombings in London by British subjects sympathetic to Al Qaeda were a "wake-up" call to the U.S. government. The London attack showed that the earlier bombing in Madrid had not been an anomaly – rather, the bombing supplied clear evidence of a new global trend toward regionally conceived, directed terrorism attacks.[19] Terrorists also benefited from communications and technical training stemming from the Internet. The suicide bombings of Western hotels in Amman Jordan on November 9, 2005, though thousands of miles from U.S. soil, were more brutal reminders of the continuing global threat.

Another development that contributed to extending TRIA was the increasing risk of an attack by a weapon of mass destruction (WMD). Public concern over the risk of a WMD attack began well before the 9/11 attacks. In fact, concerns over the threat of nuclear proliferation spans many decades, focused mainly on "rogue states" acquiring this capability. The 9/11 attacks shifted this focus to non-state sponsored organizations such as Al Qaeda, Hamas, and Hezbollah. In the many months prior to the March 2003 invasion of Iraq, non-stop warnings about "the next smoking gun" and "mushroom clouds" dominated the media. When no WMDs were discovered in Iraq, these concerns abated, but only temporarily.

In August 2004, the 9/11 Commission Report warned Americans that the next attack could exceed the magnitude of 9/11. The report stated: "The greatest danger of another catastrophic attack in the United States will materialize if the world's most dangerous terrorists acquire the world's most dangerous weapons."[20] Following this sentiment, Central Intelligence Agency Director Porter Goss told senators and the nation in his February 16, 2005, testimony that "it may be only a matter of time before Al Qaeda or another group attempts to use chemical, biological, radiological, and nuclear weapons."[21] Concerns over WMD attacks intensified throughout 2005. As the year ended, news that Iran was planning to recommence its nuclear planning compounded the seriousness of the increasing threat.

The third stage-setting development for the TRIA extension was its support from (then) Chair of the Federal Reserve Board, Alan Greenspan. In an appearance before the House Financial Services Committee in 2005, responding to a question about the looming expiration of TRIA, Greenspan replied: "There are regrettable instances in which markets do not work, cannot work"; and he added that he was not convinced that the terrorism insurance market could be made to work.[22] Five months later, less than three weeks after the London bombings, Greenspan reiterated his position: "I think that what Congress has got to do is to recognize it's a trade-off – that is, so long as we have terrorism that has the capability of a very substantial scope of damage, there is no way you can expect [the] private insurance system to handle that."[23]

Finally, the forces of nature influenced TRIA's fate. On August 29, Hurricane Katrina and the ensuing flood in New Orleans produced what Munich Re estimates will be a total of $45 billion of insured losses, more than twice the previous record hurricane loss from Hurricane Andrew. Quickly following Hurricane Katrina, Hurricanes Rita and Wilma increase the season's hurricane insured losses to more than $60 billion. The seven major hurricanes in 2004 and 2005 set new records, now representing seven of the ten worst natural catastrophes in the United States. By the end of 2005, the catastrophic losses, previously believed to present probabilities of only one occurrence in every 500 or 1,000 years, seemed to be becoming annual events.

In the final weeks of 2005, questions linking these four developments with TRIA's renewal were unavoidable: How much worse would the loss of life and property in New Orleans have been if terrorists had methodically bombed all of the levees and canal walls? If the nation were this unprepared for a risk as common as a major hurricane, what would be the consequences of a chemical, biological, or nuclear terrorist attack? Can insurers continue to risk capital by relying on the accuracy of natural-catastrophe or terrorism predictive modeling? And finally, why would anyone buy terrorism insurance voluntarily when Congress seems to be willing to dole out many billions of taxpayer dollars to compensate the victims (as manifested in the government's response to Hurricane Katrina and to the victims of 9/11)?

At a minimum, answers to such questions underscored the need for federal government leadership. There may be appropriate times for government to stand back and take a hands-off approach, but December 2005 was not one of those times.

AMERICA'S EMERGING TERRORISM INSURANCE SOLUTION

The 9/11 terrorist attacks began an intense and urgent search for understanding by senior Property and Casualty underwriters, starting in most cases from zero knowledge. Fourteen months after the attacks, the enactment of TRIA launched a national debate that has intensified over the years. The collective discourse took many forms: countless thought-provoking research reports, private sector and government funded surveys, feasibility studies, congressional hearings, and even a few old-fashioned, real-time debates. The often-passionate repartee ranged from significant disagreement over the macro-economic cost or benefit of a federal backstop, to the details of how the program should be designed, to whether the program was necessary at all.

The passage of the TRIA Extension Act in late 2005 led one of the major financial rating analysts, Moody's, to conclude that "the federal government is signaling its eventual exit from the terrorism risk reinsurance business at the end of 2007."[24] The fact that the act completely ignores the many innovations included in the version passed by the House appears to give substance to this position. There are many reasons to believe the opposite is true, however. For example, the Senate and House bills were passed by large majorities.[25] This arguably shows congressional support for a permanent government role. In addition, the act's inclusion of a Presidential Working Group report to Congress addressing the "long-term" availability and affordability of terrorism insurance supports the belief that the nation may be moving fairly quickly to the creation of a permanent solution.

WMD THREAT MANDATES A LONG-TERM PROGRAM

A close review of the positions of almost all stakeholders reveals a consensus on the need for a federal backstop as long as the United States is faced with the risk of a WMD attack. As the (then) CBO Director Douglas Holtz-Eakin succinctly stated, "the central issue is what is the correct economic response to a long-lasting terrorism threat and its economic consequences."[26] In its January 2005 report, the CBO showed considerable prescience in stating that "the gains in economic efficiency from allowing TRIA to expire could require a significant trade-off: without the TRIA program, an especially large loss from a terrorist attack would be likely to produce another episode of scarce coverage, rising prices, and uninsured assets."[27]

The Treasury report agreed with the basic conclusions of the CBO but did not opine of the risk of a major terrorist attack. It is important to emphasize, however, that this report was a response to a specific requirement in TRIA for an assessment of the effectiveness of the law. It was *not* a holistic assessment of the threat of terrorism and the best risk management solution that the nation needs to consider. In his July 13, 2005, testimony to Congress, Treasury Secretary Snow clarified the department's position regarding the insurability of a major terrorist attack: "in the case of terrorist risks ... there were risks of such a scale that aren't modelable, and of such size, that it is very difficult, at the present time, for the private insurance industry to properly assess the risks in order to be able to provide coverage."[28]

The above positions, although subject to caveats, suggest that an emerging consensus seems to exist that a federal financial backstop of the private sector is required, but only as long as the nation faces the foreseeable threat of a terrorist attack involving a weapon of mass destruction (with particular focus on nuclear, biological, chemical, or radiological agents or devices). If society accepts the important conclusion of the 9/11 Commission that America's ideological and military progress in the global war on terrorism will most likely be measured in decades and not in years,[29] the need for a "permanent" solution seems clear. As Peter Bernstein might say, the "outliers" where the "wildness lies" simply are not insurable by the private sector without government assistance.

Initially, underwriters asked the basic question of whether terrorism is insurable. The latest insurance textbook used for professional certification articulates six requirements for a loss exposure to be insurable: (1) the risk is "pure" and not "speculative" (a "pure" risk involves only the chance of loss, whereas a "speculative" risk offers either gain or loss), (2) the loss is accidental from the standpoint of the insured, (3) the loss exposure is "subject to losses that are definite in time and that are measurable," (4) the loss exposure is "one of a large number of similar but independent losses," (5) the loss should not be catastrophic, and (6) the loss exposure "must be economically feasible to insure."[30] When examined against these conditions, the insurability of terrorism fits well into the first three criteria. Without question, a terrorism loss is both "pure" and accidental from the standpoint of the insured. With the exception of some possible biological or chemical attacks, most foreseeable terrorism attack scenarios would produce losses that are definite in time and measurable.

Although terrorism losses may be accidental from the standpoint of the insured, however, there is certainly nothing accidental about a terrorist attack. Terrorism is distinguished from the natural catastrophic risks insurers normally underwrite because of three characteristics discussed in an important 2003 research paper by Kunreuther and colleagues: (1) the dynamic nature of the threat (in that terrorists can adjust their attack mode to counter any visible self-protection efforts, like concrete set off blocks in front of many government buildings); (2) the interdependence of our vulnerability to an attack, making our collective preparedness only as strong as the weakest link in the self-protection chain; and (3) the constraints on information sharing (discussed in the prior chapter).[31] Without even considering the crucial issue of a possible catastrophic loss, most underwriters would agree that these three characteristics alone make terrorism uninsurable on a traditional basis.

WORKERS' COMPENSATION PRESENTS UNIQUE CHALLENGES

Workers' compensation insurance is the single largest commercial line in the United States, with 2004 direct written premium of $52 billion.[32] Introduced in the early 1900s by individual states, workers' compensation is essentially a form of "no-fault" insurance. The state workers' compensation plans give workers

Table 19.1. Average estimated fatality and "permanent total" workers'
compensation benefits (US$) – selected states with major urban centers

State	Average expected fatality benefit (per employee)	Average expected benefit for a permanent total injury (per employee)
California	$408,000	$1,813,000
District of Columbia	$653,000	$2,192,000
Illinois	$347,000	$1,712,000
Massachusetts	$338,000	$2,100,000
New York	$508,000	$1,672,000
Texas	$555,000	$2,142,000
Washington	$493,000	$1,835,000

Source: Risk Management Solutions Inc. (RMS) 2006. Printed with permission of RMS.

the certainty of specified medical and lost income benefits in return for a strict
limitation on their rights to sue their employers for workplace injuries. In most
states, the purchase of this insurance by an employer is compulsory.

From a terrorism perspective, this insurance line presents three unique
underwriting and capital management challenges: (1) no state allows insurers to exclude terrorism, (2) workers' compensation policies have no policy
limit on the maximum amount of medical benefits that are payable for a given
occurrence, and (3) the average benefits for death, permanent disability, temporary and medical expenses vary widely from state to state. Unlike property
and liability insurance lines, insurers having no ability to limit the scope of the
terrorism insurance they provide.

Depending on the location of an attack and the nature of the injuries
sustained, the potential loss to insurers can vary by more than 300 percent
(Table 19.1). For example, an attack in Chicago similar to the airplane assaults
on 9/11 would on average have produced a fatality loss of about 40 percent lower
than the loss sustained in New York ($347,000 in Chicago versus $508,000 in
New York). However, if the attack had resulted in major burns or other possible forms of what workers' compensation coverage calls "permanent total"
disability, the average loss payment per employee in Chicago would have
been slightly more than the loss in New York ($1.7 million versus $1.6 million). The average fatality benefit is, in most cases, four to seven times lower
than the average permanent total injury, underlining the extreme difference to
insurers in the possible size of a loss depending on the nature of the injuries
sustained.

In addition, the specific attack mode used by terrorists presents insurers
with an unusually wide range of potential insured losses. For example, it is
not unusual for more than 2,000 employees of the same company to work

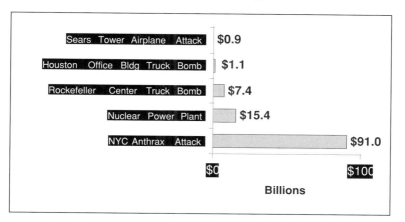

Figure 19.1. Probable costs of potential terrorist attacks. *Source:* Towers Perrin, "*Workers Compensation Terrorism Reinsurance Pool Feasibility Study*" (March 2004):42. The $91 billion figure for the anthrax attack would be a worst-case scenario (according to the report, a plausible major truck bomb attack might cause losses of as much as $16 billion and a large-scale anthrax attack $32 billion).

in the same large office building. This could expose an individual insurer to the significant risk of a large, uncorrelated loss. The insured loss estimates for workers' compensation alone could reach $90 billion, amounting to almost 25 percent of the entire 2004 capital base of the American Property and Casualty industry (Figure 19.1).

On a positive note, as the national terrorism insurance debate hit its zenith in mid-2005, it was becoming clear that important public policymakers were embracing the unique issues presented by workers' compensation. During one TRIA debate, for example, the influential former CBO director Douglas Holtz-Eakin indicated that he endorsed the need for a federally backed solution for workers' compensation, even if TRIA expired: "One possibility is let TRIA expire and rely entirely on markets. . . . We still have an issue with the nuclear, chemical, biological radiological attacks, which would not be covered, and a substantial policy dilemma with workmen's compensation if we go that route. And there may still remain a need for some sort of TRIA-like mechanism for workers' compensation if that was the route that the Congress chose."[33]

WORKERS' COMPENSATION AND PROPERTY LOSSES COULD EXHAUST THE CAPITAL BASE

If we combine the best estimates of possible property losses with the related workers' compensation losses, some scenarios exceed the total estimated capital

Table 19.2. Examples of potential losses to property and workers' compensation from selected attacks in Manhattan

Attack mode	Combined property and workers' compensation loss ($bn)	Property loss ($bn)	Workers' compensation loss ($bn)	Number of fatalities
Sarin gas (1,000 kg ground dispersal)	28	21	7	7,000
Dirty Bomb (15,000 curies of Cesium-137)	62	62	.2	Few
Anthrax (1 kg anthrax slurry)	61	35	26	40,000
Anthrax (10 kg anthrax slurry)	171	112	59	90,000
Anthrax (75 kg anthrax slurry)	340	266	74	120,000
Sabotage on nuclear power plant	217	202	15	1,000
Nuclear bomb (battlefield 1 kt)	240	140	100	130,000
Nuclear bomb (tactical 5 kt)	450	250	200	300,000

Source: Risk Management Solutions Inc., *A Risk Based Rationale for Extending the Terrorism Risk Insurance Act*, September 2005, p. 11. Reprinted with permission of RMS.

base of the Property and Casualty insurance industry. As I will discuss in the next section, this capital (policyholders' surplus) was estimated to be $414 billion at the end of 2005. The modeling firm Risk Management Solutions (RMS) projects a range of possible property and workers' compensation insured losses from WMD attacks in Manhattan (Table 19.2). For example, a 5-kiloton nuclear explosion is estimated at $450 billion in insured losses.

It is important to note that these insured loss estimates are simply best estimates. The inherent imitations in these estimates relate directly to the information-sharing challenge. As the Treasury report accurately states, modeling firms need to use subjective considerations in making their loss estimates given the lack of historical data. This produces "strikingly different predictions" of the potential scenario-based losses (called "deterministic" estimates).[34] However, a review of estimates by the two other modeling companies (AIR and Equecat) shows similar worst-case WMD loss estimates, ranging to a high of $700 billion in insured losses.[35] These high loss estimates show that terrorism is uninsurable on a traditional basis by the private sector.

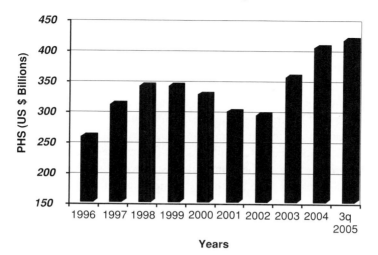

Figure 19.2. Property and casualty policyholders' surplus (1996 to third quarter 2005, in US$ billions). *Note:* Amounts include state insurance funds. *Sources:* Best's Aggregates and Averages, 2005 Edition (1996–2004) 3 Q 2005 Estimate; ISO/PCI cited in 1/9/06 National Underwriter article (see footnote).

POLICYHOLDERS' SURPLUS DOES NOT MEASURE INSURER ABILITY TO INSURE TERRORISM

Some observers have questioned why the Property and Casualty insurance industry is not collectively capable of insuring losses, even in excess of $100 billion. As the Consumer Federation of America stated in the introduction of its April 2004 report, "the primary question before Congress in considering any extension of TRIA beyond 2005, is what is the best estimate of the risk of terrorism available in the marketplace and can the private sector handle such risk absent taxpayer back-up."[36] In 2005, the Consumer Federation of America, Treasury report, and others accurately noted that the Property and Casualty insurance industry did rebound from the loss sustained in 2001, an explicit goal of the TRIA law. The total policyholders' surplus (capital) grew to a historic high, estimated by the Insurance Services Office to reach $414 billion as of the end of the third quarter in 2005 (Figure 19.2).[37]

The conclusion of these observers is that most large losses could be insured by the Property and Casualty industry. As cogent as this argument may seem, its limitation was articulated by the General Accountability Office (GAO) in a February 2005 report. The GAO questions the question itself: Is the total capital of the P&C industry an appropriate measure of the industry's ability to insure terrorism risk? Two limitations cited by the GAO suggest that the answer to this question is no. The first reason is that, in response to any given natural or terrorist attack, "only a portion of the industry's capital is available to pay disaster claims because the industry as a whole does not pay disaster claims." The second reason cited is the important insurance regulatory point that the main purpose for insurer capital is to provide assurance that the financial obligations of insurers on all of the business they have underwritten can be fully met, even if loss reserves prove to be inadequate.[38]

The Insurance Information Institute expands on these points, emphasizing that the U.S. Property and Casualty market is highly segmented. Personal lines (mainly homeowners and personal auto insurance) absorbed 42 percent of the total 2003 surplus (or $146 billion). After deducting the estimated $30 billion in reserve deficiencies (heavily weighted with asbestos losses), the institute estimates that at the end of 2003 only $114 billion in net surplus was available to pay for terrorism losses (equaling about one-third of the total Property and Casualty surplus that year).[39] If about 10 percent (at most) of this net capital (surplus) had been theoretically "available" to pay for a major 2003 terrorist attack, the total terrorism capacity of the Property and Casualty business would have only been $11.4 billion, or about one-third of the insured loss sustained on 9/11.

In addition, we need to consider the highly cyclical nature of the U.S. Property and Casualty market. As Figure 19.2 shows, the market is embedded with historical peaks and valleys. Until very recently, the industry had not produced total returns exceeding its cost of capital – a key measure of the success of any business. Economists with the Insurance Information Institute calculate that, between 1991 and 2003, the Property and Casualty Return-on-Equity failed to equal insurer cost of capital by an annual average of 6.4 percent.[40] Any solution we craft for a problem as apparently long term as terrorism needs to be grounded in an equally long-term understanding of the Property and Casualty insurance business, not just the horizon of the last four or five years.

In summary, key stakeholders appear to have resolved the initial major issues that absorbed the national debate. The WMD threat subordinates other arguments and demands a government-backed program as long as this threat persists. The next two areas of emerging consensus go behind the question of whether we need a public–private partnership to how that partnership should be molded. As always, the devil is in the details.

AMERICA NEEDS A NEW LONG-TERM APPROACH

Most of TRIA's opponents and most underwriters appear to agree that, if America has a terrorism insurance program after the TRIA Extension Act expires at the end of 2007, it should be a new program, not another extension of the existing law. The far-reaching changes included in the House extension bill (H.R. 4314) demonstrate support for a significantly new approach. The need for a beginning with a "blank page" in designing the next program becomes evident as we consider the main technical issues that have become important parts of the national debate.

COVERAGE CLARITY

The TRIA law requires insurers to "make available" insurance for terrorism on a basis that is "not materially different" from the coverage otherwise provided in a given commercial policy. The result is that even a policyholder who has paid a premium for the TRIA terrorism coverage could have this coverage denied if one or more of the terms and conditions of the policy excludes the given loss. Critics argue that TRIA coverage regarding (at the very least) an attack involving a nuclear, biological, chemical, or radiological agent or device should supercede other terms and conditions. The June 2005 Department of the Treasury TRIA Assessment documents the extent of the marketplace uncertainty: Less than 3 percent of surveyed policyholders believe they have purchased nuclear, biological, chemical, and radiological protection in property and liability lines, but the same survey showed that insurers believe that they sold some amount of such coverage to 30 percent of their policyholders.[41] The issue has led one critic to conclude that the current approach presents a "delusion of terrorism insurance" and needs to be entirely reconsidered.[42]

From a conceptual perspective, the questionable design aspect of TRIA was in the decision to essentially retrofit terrorism insurance into policies designed almost entirely for accidental losses. Most likely, in late 2002 with the New Year and a large percentage of commercial policy renewals on January 1, 2003, looming, this seemed to be the expedient way to inject a healthy dose of terrorism protection into what, at the time, was a weak economy and a fragile insurance market. This retrofit approach, however, made the coverage clarity problem unavoidable. The best way to resolve this problem is to develop a new generation of model endorsements and policies designed to insure terrorism. The stand-alone property terrorism insurance market is a logical beginning place.

DEFINITION OF "TERRORISM"

As discussed in the prior chapter, the global terrorist threat itself has changed significantly since 9/11. To be responsive to this new reality, many critics agree that the definition of "terrorism" in TRIA needs to be broadened to include acts conducted on behalf of a foreign person or foreign interest. At minimum, critics argue that this important definition should include coverage for domestic terrorism or independent actions by U.S. citizens sympathetic to the goals of foreign terrorists. The House extension bill expanded the definition by eliminating the TRIA limitation to foreign sponsored acts. Ideally, to limit the risk of gaps between the federal and private-sector insurance, the "terrorism" definition in the law should be as close as possible to the most common standard wording developed in the private sector. There are many variations globally, but the definition adopted by the stand-alone property terrorism market deserves the most serious consideration: "An act of terrorism means an act, including the use of force or violence, of any person or group(s) of persons, whether acting alone or on behalf of or in connection with any organization(s), committed for political, religious, or ideological purposes including the intention to influence any government and/or to put the public in fear for such purposes."[43] The argument against this change is not clear. The Senate extension bill and the TRIA Extension Act seem to reflect a reluctance to recognize domestic acts as political rather than criminal.

INSURANCE LINES SUBJECT TO TRIA

To limit taxpayer exposure, the initial TRIA legislation excluded the federal backstop from specified lines of commercial insurance. Group life insurance is the most notable line not originally included in the TRIA law. The argument for including this line in the federal backstop program is fairly compelling. Along with individually purchased life insurance, commercially purchased group life insurance sustained a $1 billion loss on 9/11. This equals 3 percent of the total insured losses. The Department of the Treasury estimates (based on a report by Swiss Re) that group life was less than half of the total insured life loss on 9/11.[44]

Instead of specifically excluding group life insurance, the TRIA legislators required a study by the Department of the Treasury, empowering the department to decide whether this line should be included. Using the aftermath of 9/11 as its sole data point, the June 2005 Treasury concluded that, "while there was a general lack of catastrophic reinsurance for insurance companies that offer group life coverage, there had been no appreciable reduction in the availability of group life insurance coverage for consumers." Implicitly relying on "market failure" thinking, the Department of the Treasury concluded that this line of insurance did not need the benefit of a federal backstop.

From an underwriting perspective, the Department of the Treasury's logic appears to penalize prudent risk management. Presumably, if these insurers had managed their capacity poorly, with a market failure resulting in the months after 9/11, the department would have concluded that this line needed to be included in the federal program. This kind of logic appears to ensure what insurers call "adverse selection." In theory, for any insurance program to be sound, a spread-of-risk is needed, including unrelated risks that have higher and lower probabilities of a loss in a given year.[45] In addition to the significant loss sustained on 9/11, the underwriting argument in favor of including group life is almost identical to the argument industry leaders have accepted for including workers' compensation. With the exception of the limits on their policies (typically some percentage at or above the employees annual base salary), group life underwriters are challenged with the same aggregation risks that confront workers' compensation underwriters.

Opponents of the current approach of limiting the lines of insurance included in the program argue that no one knows what may happen next or who may be impacted, so almost all lines of insurance should be included. The House extension bill included group life insurance (but not individually purchased life insurance). Advocates of the current approach counter that expanding coverage to all lines would present an unacceptable exposure to U.S. taxpayers. Group life insurers have argued (to no avail) that they should be included in the TRIA program. There is no consensus among Property and Casualty insurers on this issue, nor is one likely.

STATE INSURANCE REGULATION

Because TRIA leaves the state regulatory system mostly unchanged, insurers argue that a "free market solution" is not possible to achieve. Some large states have refused to allow terrorism exclusions. As mentioned earlier, no state allows workers' compensation insurers to exclude terrorism. Many states have "fire following" regulations that do not allow property insurers to exclude payments for fire losses even if the proximate cause of the loss is explicitly excluded (such as terrorism). Federal preemption of state form and rate controls is therefore frequently argued by senior Property and Casualty insurance executives to be a necessary part of any new legislation attempting to optimize traditional insurance, reinsurance, and capital market solutions.[46] Interestingly, one of TRIA's most outspoken critics, Wharton's Kent Smetters, offers support for regulatory changes. After emphatically rejecting the "market failure" economic argument, Smetters concludes that: " ... if there is any 'failure,' it rests with government policies. Government tax, accounting, and regulatory policies have made it costly for insurers to hold surplus capital. They have also hindered the implementation of instruments that could securitize the underlying risks. In other words, the 'market failures' that appear to justify government intervention into the terrorism insurance market could be best viewed as 'government failures.' "[47]

Most underwriters would likely agree that consumers and small businesses need the protections afforded by state insurance departments. The House extension bill contains an innovative compromise solution, enabling "exempt commercial purchasers" freedom from state form and rate qualifications if they meet numerous, detailed requirements.[48] Many states already give this right to larger commercial insurance buyers. A consensus is unlikely on this issue, but the precedents are abundant for some limited preemption of state form and cost controls.[49]

PRE-LOSS TERRORISM CATASTROPHE LOSS RESERVING

Unlike the European terrorism insurance programs created after 9/11, TRIA does not give insurers the right to post pre-tax loss reserves for terrorism or natural catastrophes. As explained earlier, under the rules of statutory insurance accounting, loss reserves for catastrophes may not be posted until after the catastrophe has occurred. As a result, terrorism insurance premiums are taxable as income in a loss-free year. Support for the introduction of an allowance for catastrophe reserves includes both insurers and some of TRIA's harshest critics. The Consumer Federation of America supports this concept in the event the federal backstop is discontinued.[50] The House extension bill contained an innovative provision to allow insurers the *voluntary* option to post catastrophe reserves, called a Capital Reserve Fund. The legislation also included a thought-provoking option allowing the Department of the Treasury to use these reserves in the event of a major loss (subject to long-term replenishment). Essentially, the House approach appears to create a virtual pool. This is one of the most novel ideas in the House bill, and it is worthy of further consideration. One possible argument against this specific approach would be the probability that only those insurers with material exposures to terrorism attacks in major urban centers would likely select this approach, creating a probable "adverse selection" and limiting the scope of the reserves created in the entire industry.

CONNECTING THE DOTS – PREPAREDNESS, PERCEPTION OF RISK, AND PRICING

Three related issues that require immediate attention are preparedness, perception of risk, and pricing. Let us begin with the crucial preparedness and loss mitigation point and then consider the next two integrally related items.

As I describe in previous sections of this chapter, many critics of a federal role conclude that the artificially low cost to commercial insurance buyers created through the "free" reinsurance "subsidy" to policyholders has created a disincentive for the private sector to make even minimal investments in terrorism loss mitigation. This is a fundamental line of thinking in both the CBO's January 2005 report and in the Treasury report. As an underwriter engaged in many meetings to discuss post-9/11 loss mitigation initiatives with Fortune 1000 customers, I found the conclusion surprising and even counter-intuitive. In this circumstance, it is important to look closely at the specific survey questions asked by the Department of the Treasury that form the basis for its conclusions. A close review of the survey questions shows that one or two of the most important loss-mitigation areas related to terrorism are entirely missing.

In framing their loss-mitigation survey questions, the authors of the Treasury report limited themselves to the logical parameters of the economic theory called the "Good Samaritan's Dilemma." Basically, this argument holds that carelessness and lack of attention to loss preparedness can become a serious problem when individuals know that they will be fully compensated after a loss occurs. In this case, the inexpensive terrorism insurance made possible though the "free reinsurance" from the federal government is postulated as a disincentive for minimum loss prevention efforts by commercial insurance buyers.

Using this conceptual starting point, the survey queried five points reflecting the degree to which the policyholder organization has undertaken "efforts to reduce potential loss associated with a foreign or domestic terrorist attacks," specifically from increased expenditures on security, decentralized operations, new egress and fire prevention plans, employee incentive schemes to reward safe practices, or restrictions in their products or services. The survey results suggest that policyholders were not investing meaningfully in these limited mitigation efforts. For example, the authors report that "small changes in egress and fire prevention plans were reported by 16 to 22 percent of respondents, and large changes in egress and fire prevention plans were reported by an additional 6 to 7 percent."[51] The conclusion reached by the authors, which I believe is entirely correct, states that: "Without knowing more about the baseline of activities and vulnerabilities, it is difficult to draw a conclusion about whether these results should be viewed as encouraging or discouraging." Not surprisingly, the impact of the TRIA "subsidy" on loss mitigation and preparedness is not mentioned in the executive summary."[52] However, the study results speak for themselves. The response of most observers was that the Treasury report supports the key argument in the January 2005 CBO report that artificially low terrorism insurance market premiums were discouraging investments in preparedness.

From an underwriting perspective, this is a classic example of "right answers" never being the product of "wrong questions."

The theoretical risk management tradeoff of cost of insurance versus investments in preparedness is arguably irrelevant in terrorism risk management because there are no consensus measures for exactly what constitutes "prudent" mitigation efforts post-9/11. If the designers of the survey had started with a "blank page" approach (as opposed to the narrow parameters of the Good Samaritan's Dilemma), they almost certainly would have added a question about the single most important form of terrorism loss mitigation: business continuity planning (BCP). The Business Continuity Forum in England estimates that diligent continuity planning can reduce the economic impact of a terrorist attack by a remarkable 50 percent to 90 percent.[53] Not surprisingly, the DHS Web site for guiding businesses in their preparedness measures focuses almost entirely on post-loss continuity planning and emergency action planning.[54] The commercial line of insurance responding to losses from this source is called "business interruption" or "business income" insurance. It is normally included as a coverage part within property insurance policies as a supplement to protection for direct physical damage. At 34 percent of the total $32 billion loss on 9/11, business interruption insurance sustained the largest loss on 9/11. The importance of this line to the resiliency of the American economy has resulted in RAND researchers labeling business interruption insurance a "counter-terrorist tool."

Business continuity planning is one of the "material risk" controls required by the Sarbanes-Oxley Act of 2002. Although it was mainly passed to address the many corporate scandals of the time (including Enron and WorldCom), the Sarbanes-Oxley law created new governance controls in some cases overlapping with terrorism preparedness. Unlike TRIA, the Sarbanes-Oxley legislation is not scheduled to expire. If the Treasury survey had asked broader risk-management questions, including continuity planning (and the even more comprehensive emerging discipline called "enterprise risk management"), the survey's conclusion most likely would have been that America has made important strides in terrorism and extreme event preparedness, but the reason was mainly Sarbanes-Oxley, not TRIA.

A basic rule of risk management theory (and what most people would consider common sense) is that in order to consider either loss mitigation or buying insurance, the prerequisite is that there must be a perception of risk.[55] The Treasury report itself shows that the vast majority of policyholders not buying terrorism insurance based their decision on the perception that they are not at risk. The authors note "a substantial increase, from 49 percent in 2003 to 89 percent in 2004, in the percentage of policyholders without terrorism coverage who selected 'we feel our company is not at risk' as one reason they declined the offer of insurance for acts of terrorism covered under TRIA."[56] The mid-2005 Marsh survey confirms that the "perception of risk" issue in driving terrorism insurance buying decisions, with the cost of insurance a distant secondary reason for non-purchase decisions.[57]

A related problem to the "perception" issue is the fact that the United States has no minimum standards for preparedness. Even if a policyholder believes there is a risk, there is no clear guidance from the Federal Emergency Management Agency or other agencies regarding exactly what minimum mitigation efforts or building standards should be applied.

The lack of any minimum preparedness standards also impedes the ability of insurance underwriters to provide and financial incentives to encourage preparedness. Because no research to date has defined causal relationships linking specific mitigation measures with quantifiable reductions in terrorism loss, there is no technical basis for an insurance pricing credit. For an underwriter or a state insurance regulator to approve a "schedule" credit for a given loss prevention measure, there must be some credible support to justify a reduction. For example, there is no consensus on whether office buildings should have concrete set-off blocks limiting the possible damage from a truck bomb. Analysts with the Rand Corporation have argued that this just shifts terrorism risk to an unprotected target, with no net improvement or social benefit.

Second, even if there were agreed-upon minimum preparedness standards, and if further research showed that a pricing reduction were justified, the credit would be applied not to the total policy premium, but only to that part of the premium related to terrorism risk. In a hypothetical example, assume that a 10 percent credit could be justified for a new anthrax filtration system in an HVAC system or for concrete set-off blocks around a large office building. Assume as well that the office building benefiting from these improvements is paying a $1 million premium for property insurance. If that the terrorism premium loading is the same as the national 2004 average of 1.8 percent, the total pricing credit for either of these improvements would only be $1,800 ($1 million × 1.8% × 10% = $1,800). Thus, the financial benefits from any possible pricing reductions are marginal at best, even for a large office building. If future research can establish credible financial benefits from specific mitigation measures, financial incentives or altered program structures (such as lower deductibles) should be possible.

On a positive note, progress has reportedly been achieved in meetings held among private-sector companies, DHS, and the National Fire Protection Authority. The goal of these meetings has been to refine the voluntary preparedness guidelines outlined in the National Fire Protection Association's NFPA 1600 to better reflect the new scale of terrorism risk created by the attacks on 9/11.[58] DHS has also funded a New York University initiative called *Intercep*.[59]

One of the goals of this group has been to reach out to insurance underwriters and policyholders to better understand the interaction between insurance and self-protection. At one roundtable I attended, a consensus developed that that the key to making progress is the development of government-endorsed minimum preparedness and construction standards.

DHS representatives and Secretary Chertoff have rejected any role in explicitly endorsing any minimum preparedness standards. At one Intercep roundtable discussion I attended in early 2005, in which Secretary Chertoff fielded questions, a large New York City commercial real estate developer raised this issue immediately. The developer explained that he was about to construct a large building close to Times Square, and he urgently needed to know what standards the government recommends for mitigation. He cited specific issues very much related to the World Trade Center and the 9/11 attacks such as the width of egress staircases and the minimum recommended heat tolerance levels for wall insulation. Secretary Chertoff's reply was that defining or endorsing new minimum construction and safety standards were not within the role of DHS. Instead, he stated that he expected the private sector to meet this need. However, this expectation is not realistic for at least two reasons: (1) defining informed and effective new construction standards would require access to classified information, available to DHS but not to the private sector, and (2) it is extremely unlikely that the 6 million businesses in America (or their trade associations) could voluntarily form a consensus on what minimum terrorism mitigation costs they should incur.

Breaking this logjam should be a top priority of public policymakers. The benefits of formal government-endorsed minimum mitigation standards transcend the two obvious improvements of reducing the vulnerability to people and property to terrorist attacks, and avoiding costly investments in loss mitigation with little real value. A third less-than-obvious benefit would likely be improved affordability and availability of liability insurance. This is particularly true of perceived high-risk exposures such as port authorities, hotels, and all office buildings in the vicinity of "trophy" sites. As demonstrated in the October 2005 jury verdict holding the New York Port Authority 68 percent liable for the 1993 World Trade Center terrorist attack (and the terrorists therefore only 32 percent liable!), absent some clear standards for what constitutes "prudent" mitigation behavior, no one knows how future American judges and juries will define what constitutes "negligence" after the next major terrorist attack in the United States.[60]

In summary, although much progress has been made, a long-term solution is not possible until America connects the dots of preparedness, perception of risk, and pricing. That connection simply is not possible without the active involvement of the federal government.

RECOMMENDATIONS FOR A LONG-TERM SOLUTION

Despite the moments of occasional hyperbole and vituperation (or perhaps even because of these ice-breaking moments), the 2005 U.S. terrorism insurance debate defined important areas of emerging agreement. Furthermore, Hurricane Katrina has shown that extreme events demand hands-on leadership from the federal government, both before and after a loss occurs. Based on the considerations in this chapter, I offer specific recommendations for the development of a possible long-term solution. First, as suggested earlier in this book, public policymakers should consider whether commercial insurance itself should be formally classified as "critical infrastructure" within the DHS charter. In fact, the Terrorism Risk Insurance Program should be entirely moved from the Department of the Treasury to DHS. Moving the program to DHS would integrate all of the critical needs for a holistic risk management solution based on preparedness, information sharing, and risk financing.

With its charter formally expanded, DHS should then be required to develop reasonable, economically feasible minimum preparedness and construction standards in collaboration with the private sector. As suggested by the Consumer Federation of America and others, policymakers should consider requiring compliance with new, minimum loss mitigation standards as a prerequisite for the availability of any insurance policy backed by the federal program.

A long-term terrorism insurance program should entirely discard the current approach of attempting to retrofit terrorism insurance into policies designed mainly for accidents. Risk managers, state insurance regulators, and insurers should replace this approach with a new set of policies designed specifically for terrorism risk. Alternatives to traditional insurance should be explored to mitigate the current areas now considered uninsurable in the traditional market (such as the alternatives discussed by the GAO in their September 2003 report to Congress, titled *Catastrophe Insurance Risks: Status of Efforts to Securitize Natural Catastrophes and Terrorism Risk*).[61]

Although there is at least some theoretical justification for "free" reinsurance, there are practical benefits to making an up-front charge. Consideration should be given to setting the charges at some level above the best actuarial estimate to encourage private-sector alternatives. Properly conceived in a new program, up-front charges could be invaluable in building a "bank" to limit taxpayer risk.

Policymakers need to consider the possibility that the issue of an up-front federal premium charge is integrally related to the question of which lines of insurance should be included in the program. If no premium is charged for the federal backstop, public policymakers may logically want the included lines limited to minimize taxpayer risk. However, if an up-front premium becomes part of policy, the program could expand to include additional lines. This would accelerate the development of a federal "bank" to pay losses before the taxpayer is exposed to loss. A risk-adjusted formula for the federal premiums, properly designed, could encourage less-exposed lines of business into the program, improving the diversification and financial stability of the program. The major segment offering mostly uncorrelated loss (and improved spread-of-risk) to the newly designed program is personal lines (at more than 40 percent of the total Property and Casualty premium).

Policymakers should use the House extension bill (H.R. 4314) as a model for further changes, with special attention to (1) the limited regulatory exemption for certain qualified commercial insurance buyers, (2) the concept of creating a "virtual" pool by enabling terrorism pre-tax terrorism loss reserves, and (3) the risk-adjusted approach of adjusting the insurer deductible percentages (and even the federal coinsurance share) based on the size of the loss and the relative terrorism risk exposure presented by each line of insurance.

TRIA requires that the amount of terrorism insurance written by the insurance industry be reported annually to the Department of the Treasury. Because this money would be available to pay for losses in any given year prior to a depletion of surplus, no assessment of the reasonableness of the current or future cost-sharing structures is complete without this information. At best, the various reports that have been produced provide only rough estimates of the probable TRIA premium. Most reports contain no premium information at all. This information should be publicly available for the Terrorism Risk Insurance Program to achieve its explicit goal of "transparency." This information also needs to be made available for future research.

Perhaps most importantly, as many observers have commented, American risk managers, insurers, and policymakers need to understand that, although the risk of terrorist WMD attack must be addressed, terrorism is only one of the risks we need to face. Extreme events come in many forms. However, our resources are finite. Not every possible target for a terrorism attack can be defended. From a global underwriting perspective, 40 other nations are at greater terrorist risk than the United States in 2006.[62] Terrorism is one of the many risks we now need to confront on a daily basis. The wisest investments in loss mitigation are mostly those offering fungible benefits regardless of the cause of loss, such as improved first responder capabilities, improved emergency action training, and continuously refined business continuity planning.

Some policymakers will undoubtedly continue to believe that a federal role is not justified because of the lack of a "market failure" after 9/11. One of the philosophical forefathers of this thinking appears to be Thomas Paine, who penned the late eighteenth-century credo: "The government that governs best is the government that governs least." It is important to remember that this staunch libertarian is also the person perhaps most responsible for rallying colonists to join the Revolutionary War. Thomas Paine understood that, when we are confronted with historically unique situations challenging our collective security, Americans need to put aside traditional thinking and ideological differences, and be both "open and resolute." He knew that when national security is at risk, a hands-off approach is impossible. If Paine had witnessed the tragedies of 9/11 and Hurricane Katrina, his opinion on the need for improved federal leadership and commitment would, almost certainly be "yes" because, in our new world of risk, it is a matter of "common sense."[63]

APPENDIX 19.A

Side-by-side comparison of TRIA, extension Act, house extension bill

Issue	TRIA (H.R. 3210)	Extension Act (S. 467)
Duration	11/26/02–12/31/05	1/1/06–12/31/07
Definition of "Terrorism"	To qualify for reimbursement, an "act of terrorism" must be "certified" by the Secretary of the Treasury. Must be a "violent act."	No change.
"Make available" requirement	Insurers subject to the program must "make available" terrorism insurance subject to the law in all covered lines that "does not differ materially" from the terms and conditions that would otherwise apply under the given policy (other than price). Only provides federal backstop for certified losses that are otherwise covered by the terms and conditions of each policy.	No change.
Insurers included in the program	Includes: All state licensed insurers NAIC listed surplus lines insurers State workers' compensation insurance funds Federal insurance programs for marine, aviation, and transport Secretary of the Treasury is authorized to issue guidelines (pre-event) applicable to captive insurers and other non-licensed insurers or self-insurance.	No change.
State insurance regulation	States maintain the right to approve policy forms and premium rates.	No change.
Insurer right to post pre-tax terrorism loss reserves	Not included.	Not included.
Covered Lines of Insurance	Limited to commercial lines, other than: Medical Malpractice Surety Crop Private Mortgage	Excludes all of the lines previously eliminated plus: Commercial Auto Surety Professional Liability

	Assumed reinsurance Financial Guarantee NFIP Flood Insurance	Farm owners Multi-Peril Burglary & Theft Includes Directors and Officers Liability. No change. No change.
Loss from declared war Territory	Does not include Personal Lines, Life (whether individual or group), or Health. Excludes all other losses other than workers' compensation Limited to the United States, the premises of a U.S. mission, or a U.S. flag vessel or air carrier.	
Minimum required industry insured loss "triggers"	$5 million Applicable to any one qualifying act of terrorism, specified through definition of a qualifying act of terrorism	2006: $50 million 2007: $100 million Applicable to the sum of all annual acts of terrorism (specified as new "Coverage Triggers") No change.
Nuclear, biological, chemical, or radiological (NBCR) attacks	Covered only if the underlying insurance policy provides coverage.	
Insurer financial obligations – insurer deductibles	a) 100% of all certified losses within Individual insurer deductibles applicable on a group basis set as a percentage of the prior year's direct earned premium: 2003: 7% 2004: 10% 2005: 15%	Insurer deductibles set as percent of prior year DEP: 2006: 17.5% 2007: 20%
Insurer and federal coinsurance obligations	In excess of the deductibles, insurers pay 10% of additional losses, and government pays 90%, subject to the annual program cap.	Insurer share: 2006: 10% (no change) 2007: 15% Federal share: 90% in 2006 and 85% in 2007. Subject to the annual program cap.
Annual program cap	$100 billion	No change.

(continued)

333

APPENDIX 19.A *(continued)*

Issue	TRIA (H.R. 3210)	Extension Act (S. 467)
Post-loss policyholder recoupment surcharge	Requires the Department of the Treasury to make a maximum 3% annual charge payable by commercial insurance buyers to reimburse the federal share of any certified annual losses which are less than specified "marketplace aggregate retentions": 2003: $10 billion 2004: $12.5 billion 2005: $15 billion If the annual certified losses exceed these amounts, the Secretary of the Treasury has discretion to apply a surcharge on the same basis. There is no limit to the possible duration of these charges. Policies covering rural and "smaller commercial centers" may be subject to lower surcharges.	Continues the progressive increases in the "aggregate retentions": 2006: $25 billion 2007: $27.5 billion
Litigation management	Mandates a federal cause of action for property damage, personal injury, and death from a certified loss. Pre-empts state causes of action. Eliminates punitive damage awards from federal reimbursement.	Continues the initial TRIA approach but codifies regulations issued by TRIP into the new law requiring advance approval of certain planned settlements by the TRIP.
Availability and affordability of terrorism insurance	Required the Department of the Treasury to produce a report to the Congress assessing the impact of TRIA not later than June 30, 2005.	Requires the President's Working Group on Financial Markets to produce a report to Congress not later than September 26, 2006, addressing the "long-term" availability and affordability of terrorism insurance with specific discussion on group line insurance and NBCR.

NOTES

1. Bernstein 1996.
2. For a comprehensive discussion of the domestic and international radical Islamic attacks preceding September 11, 2001, see Posner 2003.
3. For a detailed review of the financial implications to insurers of major terrorism attacks, see Hartwig 2004.
4. William C. Thompson Jr., the comptroller of New York City, issued a September 4, 2002, report estimating the total economic impact of the 9/11 attacks ranged from $82.8 billion to $94.8 billion. See *One Year Later: The Fiscal Impact of 9/11 on New York City.* http://comptroller.nyc.gov/bureaus/bud/reports/impact-9-11-year-later.pdf, accessed February 25, 2006. The Milken Institute estimates the total impact of 9/11 on the nation's gross domestic product at $175 billion in a January 2002 report, *The Impact of September 11 on U.S. Metropolitan Economies.* http://www.milkeninstitute.org/pdf/National_Metro_Impact_Report.pdf, accessed February 25, 2006.
5. Bush 2004.
6. Peters 1999.
7. "Terrorism Risk Insurance Act of 2002," Public Law 107-297, Section 101(b).
8. The two exceptions are a provision in TRIA that superseded any explicit "terrorism" provisions in a commercial policy subject to the law, and the specific terrorism insurance premium (still subject to state approval).
9. These estimates are based on direct premium from Best's Aggregates & Averages, 2005 and from the Insurance Information Institute 2006.
10. TRIA, ibid: Section 103 (e) (6), page 9.
11. The General Accountability Office provides an excellent review of many of the key issues composing the TRIA debate and a review of the European government-backed natural catastrophe and terrorism insurance programs in its February 2005 report. See Government Accountability Office 2005b.
12. In the executive summary, the Treasury report states that "...the cost of terrorism coverage for paying policyholders in high-risk cities declined substantially from 6.1 percent of premium in 2002, to 5.1 percent in 2003, and further to 2.6 percent in 2004." Page 4.
13. The Marsh study provides detailed information based on a customer survey through the end of 2004; the study considers all lines of commercial insurance included in the TRIA law (Marsh 2005b).
14. This AON survey focuses on property insurance and provides customer survey information through the first half of 2005 (AON 2005). The stand-alone property market is discussed on pages 20–25. Notably, $850 million of this capacity is from just four companies: Berkshire Hathaway ($500 million), AXIS ($150 million), AIG ($100 million), and Hiscox ($100 million).
15. Benfield Group Limited 2005.
16. These estimates are cited in the Treasury Report, ibid: p. 88. The report defines a "captive insurer" as "an entity formed primarily to insure or reinsure the risks of one policyholder. It may be owned by a corporation or an association, domiciled onshore or offshore, and has the option of writing the business of unrelated parties" (p. 88).
17. Congressional Budget Office 2005.
18. Wharton Risk Management and Decision Processes Center 2005.

19. For a detailed discussion of the increasingly decentralized nature of the jihadist threat, see Simon and Benjamin 2005.
20. National Commission on Terrorist Attacks upon the United States 2004, p. 380.
21. Goss 2005.
22. Coalition to Insure Against Terrorism (CIAT) 2005.
23. Insurance Journal 2005.
24. Brady 2006.
25. The Senate passed S. 467 unanimously; the House passed it by 371 to 49.
26. American Enterprise Institute (AEI) 2005. This debate was televised by C-Span.
27. Congressional Budget Office 2005.
28. Snow 2005 testimony. Comments during the subsequent questioning are quoted from AON Risk Services 2005.
29. National Commission on Terrorist Attacks upon the United States 2004.
30. The American Institute for Chartered Property Casualty Underwriters / Insurance Institute of America (AICPCU/IIA) is a not-for-profit educational organization offering degrees and certifications in insurance. Wiening 2002.
31. Kunreuther et al. 2003.
32. For an excellent detailed discussion of the implications of an expiration of the federal backstop to workers' compensation, see Carney 2005.
33. American Enterprise Institute (AEI) 2005, p. 6.
34. U.S. Treasury Report, ibid: p. 124.
35. American Academy of Actuaries 2005.
36. Hunter 2004.
37. Scalfane 2006.
38. Government Accountability Office 2005c.
39. Hartwig 2004, Slide 26.
40. Hartwig 2004, Slide 30.
41. Department of the Treasury, Assessment: ibid, p. 105.
42. Boardman 2004.
43. AON 2005, p. 25.
44. U.S. Treasury Report, ibid: p. 26.
45. For a detailed discussion on this issue and the other basic insurance issues discussed in this chapter, see Wiening 200.
46. For a detailed discussion of this issue, see Degnan 2003.
47. Smetters, 2004, p. 2.
48. H.R 4314, ibid: p. 8.
49. For a more detailed discussion of the U.S. state insurance regulatory system and the role served by other stakeholders such as financial rating agencies, see Chapter 1 of Wharton Risk Management and Decision Processes Center 2005. The June 30, 2005, Treasury report also provides a good summery review of the U.S. Property and Casualty operating environment in Section 2 "Overview of the Insurance Industry," pp. 10–17.
50. CFA 2005; p. 9.
51. U.S. Treasury Report: ibid, p. 107.
52. U.S. Treasury Report: ibid, p. 7.
53. AP Online 2005b.
54. See http://www.ready.gov/business/, accessed March 3, 2006.
55. Wiening 2002, Section 1, p. 3.
56. U.S. Treasury Report: ibid, p. 109.

57. The Marsh survey reports that 90 percent of the 232 companies not buying property terrorism insurance in 2004 reported that the major reason was the perception that they are not at risk. Marsh 2005b, p. 14.

58. The National Fire Protection Association's "codes and standards influence every building, process, service, design, and installation in the United States, as well as many of those used in other countries." For further information on the 1600 guidelines, see http://www.nfpa.org/assets/files/PDF/NFPA1600.pdf, accessed February 25, 2006.

59. For detailed information on the DHS-funded initiative to improve private-sector enterprise preparedness, see http://www.nyu.edu/intercep/, accessed February 25, 2006.

60. Hartocollis 2005.

61. Government Accountability Office (GAO) 2003a.

62. This is based on the 2006 Global Terrorism Ranking issues by a leading broker in terrorism and political risk insurance, Jardine Lloyd Thompson. The ten countries considered at greatest risk are Iraq, India, Russia, Israel, Nepal, Pakistan, Colombia, Indonesia, Philippines, and Turkey. The complete listing and an introduction from JLT Emerging Markets is at http://www.jltgroup.com/files/PR/051222JLTTop50RiskiestCountries.pdf, accessed February 25, 2006.

63. Paine 1776. In closing his argument, Thomas Paine states: " ... instead of gazing at each other with suspicious or doubtful curiosity, let each of us, hold out to his neighbor the hearty hand of friendship, and unite in drawing a line, which, like an act of oblivion shall bury in forgetfulness every former dissention. Let the names of Whig and Tory be extinct; and let none other be heard among us, than those of a good citizen, an open and resolute friend, and a virtuous supporter of the rights of mankind ... " (p. 35).

20

LOOKING BEYOND TRIA

A Clinical Examination of Potential Terrorism Loss Sharing

Howard Kunreuther and Erwann O. Michel-Kerjan

The evolution of international terrorism is now well accepted. Still mainly organized as local political actions twenty years ago, it has continuously expanded to include a large portion of extremist religious and other groups seeking to inflict fear, mass-casualties, and maximum disruption to Western nations' social and economic continuity. Most of these groups operate internationally.[1] Indeed, the world's 15 worst terrorist attacks (based on the number of casualties) all occurred after 1982, more than three-quarters of which took place between 1993 and 2005. A large portion of all terrorist attacks in the world during this period have been directed against U.S.-related interests and personnel. The Madrid train bombings on March 11, 2004, the coordinated London bus and underground bombings of July 7, 2005, and the bombings in Amman, Jordan, in November 2005 – attacks against three countries that were allies of the United States in the war in Iraq – suggest that the United States remains a principal target for several international terrorist groups adhering to al-Qaeda's ideology.

Although the United States has been successful since 9/11 in preventing terrorist attacks on its own soil, the impact to the economy of another mega-attack or series of coordinated attacks pose serious concerns to the government, the private sector, and citizenry (Kunreuther and Michel-Kerjan 2004, 2005).[2] With security reinforced around federal buildings, the commercial sector constitutes a softer target for terrorist groups to inflict mass-casualties and stress on the nation. These threats require that the country as a whole develop strategies to prepare for and recover from a (mega-)terrorist attack. Insurance is an important policy tool for consideration in this regard.

Quite surprisingly, even after the terrorist attack on the World Trade Center in 1993 and the Oklahoma City bombing in 1995, insurers in the United States did not view either international or domestic terrorism as a risk that

338

should be explicitly considered when pricing their commercial insurance policy, principally because losses from terrorism had historically been small and, to a large degree, uncorrelated. Thus, prior to September 11, 2001, terrorism coverage in the United States was an unnamed peril included in most standard all-risk commercial and homeowners' policies covering damage to property and contents.

The 9/11 terrorist attacks killed more than 3,000 people from more than 90 countries and inflicted insured losses currently estimated at $32.5 billion that were shared by nearly 150 insurers and reinsurers worldwide. Reinsurers (most of them European) were financially responsible for the bulk of these losses. These reinsurance payments came in the wake of outlays triggered by a series of catastrophic natural disasters over the past decade and portfolio losses due to stock market declines. Having their capital base severely hit, most reinsurers decided to reduce their terrorism coverage drastically or even to stop covering this risk.

Hence, in the immediate aftermath of 9/11 U.S. insurers found themselves with significant amounts of terrorism exposure from their existing portfolio with limited possibilities of obtaining reinsurance to reduce the losses from a future attack. The lack of availability of terrorism insurance soon after the 9/11 attacks led to a call from some private sector groups for federal intervention. For example, the U.S. Government Accountability Office (GAO, formally General Accounting Office) reported in 2002 that the construction and real estate industries claimed that the lack of available terrorism coverage delayed or prevented several projects from going forward because of concerns by lenders or investors (U.S. GAO 2002).[3]

In response to such concerns, the Terrorism Risk Insurance Act of 2002 (TRIA) was passed by Congress and signed into law by President Bush on November 26, 2002.[4] It constitutes a temporary measure to increase the availability of risk coverage for terrorist acts. TRIA is based on risk sharing between the insurance industry and the federal government. While today it is unclear what type of long-term terrorism insurance program, if any, will emerge for dealing with the economic and social consequences of terrorist attacks,[5] it is of prime importance to understand how different types of attack would translate into different loss.

This chapter provides an extensive series of empirical analyses of loss sharing under the TRIA program for 2005 that was undertaken as part of a nine-person team research initiative we co-directed at the Wharton School last year, in collaboration with numerous firms in the insurance industry and other critical sectors, and federal and international organizations, that resulted in the Wharton Risk Center *TRIA and Beyond* report.[6] President Bush signed into law a two-year extension of TRIA on December 22, 2005, the Terrorism

Risk Insurance Extension Act (TRIEA) that expanded the private sector role and reduced the federal share of compensation for terrorism insured losses. We also present some analyses for the years 2006 and 2007 based on the new loss-sharing design (see Appendix 19.A for a side by side comparison of TRIA 2005 versus TRIEA).

The chapter is organized as follows: The next section focuses on the loss-sharing process between insurers, policyholders, and taxpayers for 2005 and 2006. Using data collected on the top 451 insurers operating in the United States, Section 3 examines the impact of the deductible on insurers' losses from terrorist attacks and provides also a simulated analysis for the 30 largest insurers (70 percent of the market) for 2006 and 2007. Section 4 presents the financial impacts of terrorist attack simulations on the different stakeholders based on the explosion of a five-ton truck bomb or the crash of a commercial aircraft against one of the top 477 tallest high-rises of the country. Section 5 presents the results of a loss-share analysis for three major cities: Los Angeles (California), Houston (Texas), and New York City (New York) by combining the simulations with market share data for different lines of insurance coverage in these cities. Section 6 provides a discussion as to how loss sharing between the relevant stakeholders is likely to evolve in 2006 and 2007.

In Section 7 we present a conceptual analysis as to what would happen if TRIA were made permanent. Using data on insurance markets, we show that it would be possible for some very large insurers to game the system. They would collect large amounts of premiums for terrorism insurance but be financially responsible for only a small portion of the risk. Commercial policyholders from all insurers and the federal government will absorb the residual insured losses. Such strategizing raises important equity issues as to who should pay for terrorism losses.[7] We conclude the chapter by reviewing a set of possible alternatives or complementary options to the current design of TRIA that could become important features of a permanent program.

LOSS-SHARING DESIGN

ELIGIBILITY FOR COVERAGE

Under both TRIA and TRIEA, insurers are obligated to offer terrorism coverage to all their commercially insured clients. Firms are not required to purchase this insurance unless mandated by state law, as is the case for workers' compensation lines in most states.[8] The stated coverage limits and deductibles must be the same as for losses from other events covered by the firm's current policy.[9] This implies that if there are restrictions on a standard commercial insurance policy, then terrorism coverage will also exclude losses from these events. Thus, the risks related to a terrorist attack using chemical, biological, radiological, and nuclear weapons (so-called CBRN) are covered under TRIA, only if the primary policy includes such coverage.[10]

Commercially insured losses are eligible for coverage under TRIA and TRIEA only if the event is certified by the Secretary of Treasury (in concurrence with the Attorney General and Secretary of State) as an "act of terrorism." As stated under TRIA, an "act of terrorism" has to be "committed by an individual or individuals acting on behalf of any foreign person or foreign interest, as part of an effort to coerce the civilian population of the United States or to influence the policy or to affect the conduct of the U.S. Government by coercion" (TRIA, 2002). This distinction has been maintained under TRIEA. Therefore, an attack like the Oklahoma City bombing of 1995, which killed 168 people and had been the most damaging attack on domestic soil prior to 9/11, would not be covered under TRIA and TRIEA because it would be considered "domestic terrorism." Under TRIA a condition for certification was that total losses from the attack must be greater than $5 million. TRIEA establishes a "per event trigger" for federal participation: aggregate insured losses must be at least $50 million from March 31, 2006, to January 1, 2007, and $100 million for losses occurring in the 2007 Program Year.

While this chapter focuses on commercial terrorism coverage, one should note that individuals at risk are also covered against terrorist attacks. Life insurance policies typically cover loss of life from terrorism attacks. TRIA and TRIEA do not provide insurers with special protection against any of these individual risks (i.e., life, homeowners, automobile).[11]

STRUCTURE OF THE PARTNERSHIP

Under TRIA's three-year term that ended on December 31, 2005, there was a specific risk-sharing arrangement between the federal government and insurers for a certified event. The same logic applies under TRIEA. Figure 20.1 depicts the public–private loss sharing for an insurer when total insured losses are less than $100 billion. If the loss suffered by an insurance company i is less than its deductible (ID_i), the insurer does not receive any reimbursement from the federal government. This situation is illustrated by an insured loss of L_1 in Figure 20.1 where the insurer's payment is represented by the oblique lines. If the insured loss due to a certified terrorist attack is greater than its deductible, as depicted by L_2 in Figure 20.1, the federal government will initially reimburse

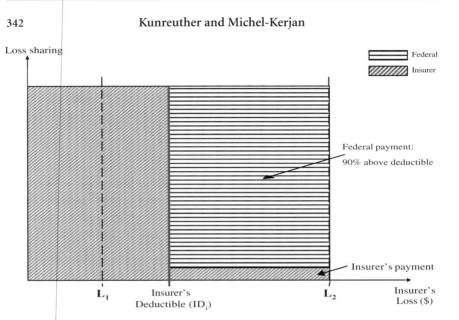

Figure 20.1. Loss sharing under TRIA and TRIEA between an insurer and the federal government. *Note:* If the insurance company *(i)* loss is less than its deductible (ID_i), the insurer is not reimbursed by the government (e.g., for an insured loss of L_1). If the loss is greater than the deductible (L_2), the government reimburses the insurer for 90 percent of the losses above its deductible, and the insurer pays 10 percent.

the insurer for 90 percent of the losses above its deductible, and the insurer will end up paying only 10 percent of it up front. The federal payment is represented by horizontal lines in the figure. This federal backstop provision is equivalent to free up front reinsurance above the deductible. As will be discussed later, the federal government will recoup part or all of this payment from all commercial policyholders.

The insurer's deductible is determined as a percentage of its total direct commercial property and casualty earned premiums of the preceding year for TRIA/TRIEA lines (that is, lines covered by the act), and not just the premiums of clients that purchase terrorism coverage. In 2005 the premium was set at 15 percent – if an attack had occurred in 2005, insurers would have been responsible for losses equal to 15 percent of the direct commercial property and casualty revenues that had been earned as premiums in 2004.[12] If an attack occurs in 2006, insurers will be responsible for losses equal to 17.5 percent of the direct commercial property and casualty earned premiums in 2005 (20 percent in 2007). This deductible plays a very important role in determining loss sharing between insurers and the federal government and can be very large for many insurers. Using data provided by A.M. Best on their estimates of TRIA retentions for major publicly held insurance companies for 2005, we determined this deductible to be $3.6 billion for American International Group (AIG) and $2.5 billion for St. Paul Travelers. Four other companies on the list of top ten insurers, based on TRIA-line direct earned premiums, had TRIA deductibles between $800 million and $2.1 billion in 2005. These are Zurich, Liberty, Chubb, and ACE. In the next section of the chapter we provide an extensive analysis of this issue both for the top 30 and top 451 insurers in the United States.

If the insurance industry suffers terrorism losses that require the government to cover a portion of companies' claims, then these outlays will be fully or partially recouped *ex post*. More specifically, the federal government will recoup the portion of its payment between the total insurers' outlays and a market aggregate retention amount, which is defined by the law ($15 billion in 2005; $25 billion in 2006; $27.5 billion in 2007); that is called the "mandatory recoupment." This mandatory recoupment[13] is obtained by levying a surcharge on all commercially insured policyholders, whether they had purchased terrorism insurance or not. If the insured losses exceed $100 billion during the year, then the U.S. Treasury will determine how the losses above this amount will be covered.[14]

This federal recoupment surcharge "may not exceed, on an annual basis, the amount equal to 3 percent of the premium charged for property and casualty insurance coverage under the policy."[15] Insurers play the role of intermediaries by levying this surcharge against all their property and casualty policyholders,[16] whether or not they had purchased terrorism insurance, and transfer the collected funds to the Department of Treasury. In other words, taxpayers would have paid insured losses between $15 billion and $100 billion in 2005. In 2006, they will pay insured losses between 25 billion and 100 billion dollars. The law indicates that the federal government could also recoup part of that payment (so-called "discretionary recoupment") but is not clear on that process; in this chapter we assume that this is not the case.

Figure 20.2 depicts the repayment schedule in 2006 between the insurers (the area comprising oblique lines), all commercial policyholders (solid gray area), and the taxpayers (area comprising horizontal lines) after the federal government has reimbursed all insurers for 90 percent of their claims payments above their deductible level (for those suffering loss above their TRIEA deductible). In the example we consider here, since the total insured losses L are greater than $25 billion but total payments by insurers are below the market aggregate retention of $25 billion, we assume the government recoups a portion of its payments from commercial policyholders with the remaining amount paid by U.S. taxpayers.

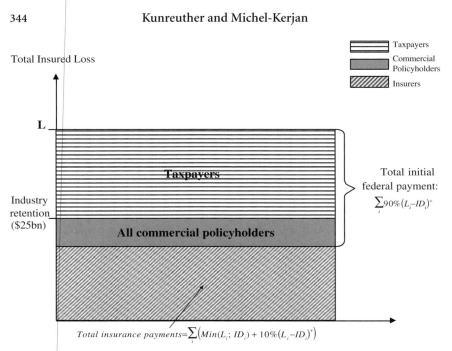

Figure 20.2. Loss sharing under TRIEA between insurance industry, all policyholders, and taxpayers in 2006. *Note:* In this example, because the total insured loss *L* exceeds $25 billion, but total payments by insurers are below the market aggregate retention of $25 billion, we assume the government recoups a portion of its payments from commercial policyholders with the remaining amount paid by U.S. taxpayers.

EMPIRICAL ANALYSIS OF INSURER DEDUCTIBLE/ SURPLUS RATIOS

We conducted a series of empirical analyses on the impact of TRIA and TRIEA on loss sharing between those directly targeted by a terrorist attack, their insurers, and other interested parties such as commercial policyholders and U.S. taxpayers.[17] In this section and the next two others, we concentrate our analyses on the following two aspects: the effect of the program's deductible feature, and the effect of different terrorist attacks on losses and loss sharing.

We first examined TRIA and TRIEA's deductible feature and its effect on the level of exposure to a terrorist attack insurers might have. We found that the larger an insurer's Deductible/Surplus (*D/S*) ratio, the more exposed the insurer is to losses from any given terrorist attack. We determined how the *D/S* ratio for the top 451 insurers operating in the country[18] has changed over the three years of TRIA's operation (2003–2005). Data necessary to do a similar analysis for 2006 (TRIEA line insurers' direct earned premiums) are not available yet. For that reason, we also computed the D/S ratios for 2006 and 2007 for the top 30 insurers under the deductible increases to 17.5 percent in 2006 and to 20 percent in 2007 but using extrapolated figures from the last three years. We then compared D/S over the five-year period 2003–2007 for each insurer (see Appendix 20.1).

We then analyzed in the next sections the impact of different simulated terrorist attacks on the losses experienced by the victims, insurers, policyholders, and taxpayers, and the likely differences in large urban areas. We differentiated workers' compensation from other TRIEA-covered lines. While we have the data to undertake such analyses for large cities throughout the country, in this chapter we provide the results only for one or two cities in three states: Texas (Houston and Dallas), California (Los Angeles and San Francisco), and New York (New York City).

THE NOTION OF POLICYHOLDERS' SURPLUS

We start with our analysis of the impact of the deductible feature of TRIEA. Insurer *capital* represents the net worth of the company (assets minus liabilities). Capital enables the insurer to pay any losses above those that were expected. It serves as a safety net to support the risk an insurer takes on by writing insurance, and it helps ensure that the insurer will be able to honor its contracts. As such, insurers' capital supports the personal safety nets of homeowners, business owners, workers, dependents of heads of households, and others who rely on insurance to provide financial compensation to rebuild their lives and businesses after covered losses occur.

Insurer capital is traditionally referred to as "*policyholders' surplus*" (also called "surplus" for short). Despite the connotation of the term "surplus," there is nothing superfluous about it – it is, in fact, an essential component supporting the insurance promise. The cost of that capital is an insurer expense that must be considered in pricing insurance, along with expected losses, sales, and administrative expenses for policies written. Consider, for example, insurance for property damage caused by hurricanes. An insurer's expected losses are relatively low, because in a typical year the policyholder will not suffer a hurricane loss. However, losses could also be quite high – far in excess of those expected at the time policies are priced – as illustrated by the 2005 hurricane season. In the event of a serious hurricane, a substantial portion of the loss must be paid from insurer capital. For terrorism coverage, maximum losses are extremely high relative to expected losses, which makes the capital issue critical.

THE EVOLUTION OF THE *D/S* RATIO UNDER THE THREE-YEAR TRIA TERMS: 2003–2005

Given the obligation of insurers to offer terrorism insurance to all their commercial policyholders under TRIA, the amount of loss that an insurer will eventually bear is based on its deductible. As described in the previous section of this chapter, the insurer's deductible under TRIA (and TRIEA) is determined as a percentage of its total direct earned premiums (DEP) during the preceding year for TRIA lines. For each of the top 451 insurers, A.M. Best provided us with the premiums written in TRIA commercial lines,[19] to allow us to determine what the deductible (*D*) of each of these insurers had been under TRIA. Although we do not know the insurers' exact terrorism exposure,[20] we will assume that they are providing this TRIA-based coverage to a large proportion of their policyholders in the urban areas we consider here. We can also distinguish P&C from workers' compensation market shares. Our interest is in determining how vulnerable insurers are to the possibility of suffering a large loss relative to their surplus. Those insurers with large deductibles (*D*) relative to their surplus (*S*) are the ones most at risk if they are providing terrorism coverage to most of their policyholders.

Figure 20.3 depicts the evolution of the *D/S* graphically for our sample of 451 insurers for these same three years (2003, 2004, and 2005). For each year, we plot the number of insurers whose *D/S* ratio lies between different percentage ranges in increments of 5 percent (e.g., [0% and 4.99%]; [5% and 9.99%], etc).

Of the total, 294 insurance companies providing terrorism insurance in the United States had a *D/S* ratio lower than 10 percent in 2003, compared with 139 insurers in 2005. If we consider higher *D/S* ratios, more than half of the firms had a *D/S* ratio greater than 15 percent in 2005 compared with less than one-sixth of the insurers in 2003. In 2003, only 36 insurers had a *D/S* ratio above 20 percent. There were 80 such insurers in 2004. In 2005, 162 insurers (more than 35 percent of the sample) had a *D/S* ratio greater than 20 percent.

FOCUS ON THE TOP 30 INSURERS – TRIA AND TRIEA, 2003–2007

Insurers writing policies in an urban area know that there is some chance that the loss from a terrorist attack could reach or exceed their deductible (*D*). We focus our second series of analyses of the impact of TRIA on insurers for

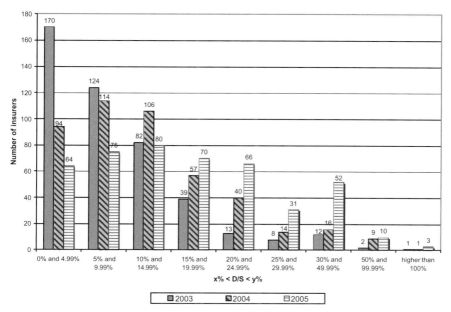

Figure 20.3. Change in *D/S* ratio for the top 451 insurers under TRIA (2003–2005).

the 30 largest companies based on direct earned premiums in TRIA lines the preceding year. These companies wrote premiums that comprised 70 percent of the total insurance market.[21]

This analysis is based on the TRIA deductibles of 7 percent (2003), 10 percent (2004), and 15 percent (2005) of the direct earned premiums (DEP) for TRIA line policies during the previous year. The data show clearly that there has been a major shift over the past 3 years as the TRIA deductible percentage has increased. For example, as shown in Figure 20.4, only 5 insurers had a *D/S* ratio exceeding 10 percent in 2003 while more than half were in this category in 2005. Of the top 30 insurers, 8 of them have a *D/S* ratio exceeding 20 percent in 2005, while only 1 was in this range in 2003.

It is interesting to see how the extension of TRIA affects the *D/S* ratio of these 30 insurers for 2006 and 2007. We thus also analyze an increased deductible up to 17.5 percent of TRIA-line direct earned premiums (DEP) in 2006, and to 20 percent in 2007. However, in order to determine "*D/S* (2006)" and "*D/S* (2007)" for each of the 30 companies under this scenario, we need to know what would be their TRIA-line DEP and their surplus in 2005 and 2006, respectively. As these data are not available yet, we do extrapolate from the past. We base our analysis on the annual percentage change in these two numbers over the three-year period (2002–2004) for each of the thirty companies.[22] We then extrapolate

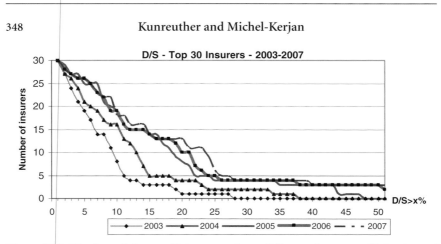

Figure 20.4. Number of the top 30 insurers whose *D/S* exceeds pre-specified values of *x* percent.

these figures for the next two years to estimate direct earned premiums (DEP) for TRIA lines and surplus (*S*) for 2005 and 2006.

Figure 20.4 depicts the number of insurers (y-axis) whose *D/S* exceeds pre-specified values of *x* percent (x-axis); years 2003, 2004, and 2005 are exact figures, and 2006 and 2007 result from our prospective analysis. Should this estimation be right, 18 of the top 30 insurers would have a TRIEA deductible higher than 10 percent of their surplus in 2007; for 13 of them that would be higher than 20 percent (vs. 8 in 2005 and 1 in 2003), including for 6 of the 10 largest insurers (Appendix 20.1 provides the complete set of results). Moreover, none of these 30 insurers had a *D/S* ratio higher than 50 percent in 2005. There will be 3 such insurers in 2006 (50 percent, 56 percent, and 66 percent, respectively) and 2007 (the *D/S* ratio increased dramatically up to 57 percent, 70 percent, and 100 percent).

CONSTRUCTING TERRORIST ATTACK AND LOSS-SHARING SCENARIOS

Due to the difficulty in estimating the likelihood of a terrorist attack, insurers utilize scenarios to determine their maximum exposure to a range of possible attacks that vary by location and mode of attack.[23] However, few insurers consider the likelihood of these scenarios occurring in determining their exposure.[24]

Given insurers' interest in determining their exposure using deterministic scenarios, and to more fully understand the nature of the economic and human losses from a terrorist attack on business property, we constructed a set of scenarios to analyze the impact of financial losses between the non-insured victims, the insurers, and the taxpayers under TRIA and TRIEA. We also utilized these scenarios to analyze the effect on the distribution of losses should TRIA not have been renewed so that the private market (e.g., insurers, property owners, and/or employers) would be responsible for all the losses.

As discussed earlier, there are no easy answers to these loss allocation questions – they will be determined by the nature and location of the terrorist attacks and the number of insurers providing coverage. For example, if the attack is a relatively small one on a single building, and if large insurers with high deductibles cover the target building, then there will be little, if any, federal government involvement in loss payments. However, if a few smaller companies with low TRIA deductibles cover the target building, then the federal government will pay a significant portion of their losses, and then will partially or fully recoup these payments later from all policyholders purchasing commercial insurance.

Evidence indicates that most insurers focus on damage from two-to-ten-ton truck bombs in determining the losses they could suffer from a terrorist attack.[25] As an element of comparison, the attack in the front of the Alfred P. Murrah Federal Building in Oklahoma City in 1995 was perpetrated with a two-and-a-half-ton truck bomb. One reason for this focus is that A.M. Best uses this type of scenario in analyzing the impact of a terrorist attack on insurers' balance sheets. Although other scenarios could be used to evaluate losses from a terrorist attack,[26] we analyze the effect on property damage and workers' compensation losses of a five-ton truck bomb exploding in each of the United States' 447 largest commercial high-rise buildings.[27]

SCENARIO METHODOLOGY

Figure 20.5 describes the methodology for allocating losses from a specific scenario to the potential victims as well as to the insurers and the federal government immediately after a terrorist attack.

The loss allocation process can be divided into several steps:

- *Step 1:* Identify the nature of the terrorist attack: What is the target (represented by the target picture in figure below)? What mode of attack? Is the attack considered a "certified" or "non-certified" event? What are the direct losses potentially by insurance?
- *Step 2:* Determine losses covered by insurance. What was the insurance take-up rate at the target location? What portion of the losses is actually covered by insurance (by line)?

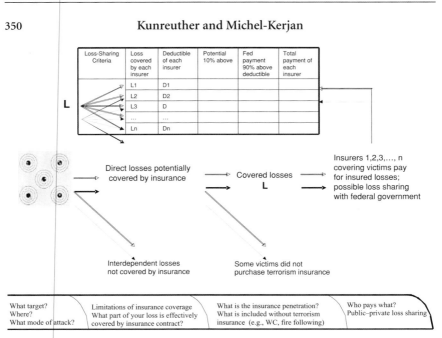

Loss-Sharing Criteria	Loss covered by each insurer	Deductible of each insurer	Potential 10% above	Fed payment 90% above deductible	Total payment of each insurer
L1	D1				
L2	D2				
L3	D				
...	...				
Ln	Dn				

Direct losses potentially covered by insurance → Covered losses → **L**

Insurers 1,2,3,..., n covering victims pay for insured losses; possible loss sharing with federal government

Interdependent losses not covered by insurance

Some victims did not purchase terrorism insurance

What target? Where? What mode of attack?	Limitations of insurance coverage What part of your loss is effectively covered by insurance contract?	What is the insurance penetration? What is included without terrorism insurance (e.g., WC, fire following)	Who pays what? Public–private loss sharing

Figure 20.5. Methodology for loss-allocation process.

- *Step 3:* Determine what proportion of losses is assumed by each of the affected parties. Who is paying what? What insurers are responsible for which part of the insured losses? How does the loss-sharing process under TRIA and TRIEA operate (see the table at the top of the figure below)?

Figure 20.6 provides the distribution of loss for each of 447 commercial high-rise buildings on two major insurance lines covered by TRIA (and TRIEA): property (including business interruption) and workers' compensation. The explosion of a five-ton truck bomb would inflict not only disastrous damage to the specific building that terrorists want to target, but also to other adjacent structures. The impact would mainly depend on the type of building and the number of employees who work there.[28] For example, the distribution of losses described in Figure 20.6 indicates that a five-ton truck bomb on Building A would inflict $4.7 billion in workers' compensation losses and $3.9 billion in property losses.[29] An attack on Building B, in a different city, would inflict $6.8 billion in workers' compensation losses and $8.7 billion in property losses. The maximum combination of property and workers' compensation losses is estimated to be between $15 billion and $16 billion for a single event (Buildings B and C).

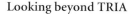

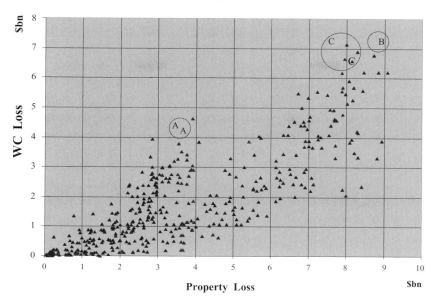

Figure 20.6. Projected property losses and workers' compensation losses from five-ton bomb attacks to 447 high-rise buildings in the United States (in $ billion). Each triangle represents one specific high-rise building used in the simulation; Triangles A, B, and C are three specific buildings we discussed in the core of the text.

Similar simulations can be run using a scenario of an aircraft crashing against each of the 447 high-rise buildings (Figure 20.7). Such a simulation reveals that the magnitude of loss for property and workers' compensation for each of the 447 simulations would be lower. Workers' compensation maximum losses are likely to be capped at $3 billion[30] and property at $8 billion for different buildings. As with the truck bomb scenario, if simultaneous attacks were to occur in different locations, the losses would be additive.

EFFECT OF LOCATION AND ATTACK SIZE ON LOSS SHARING UNDER TRIA

How would losses from foreign terrorist attacks on U.S. soil be distributed across the relevant affected parties? This question can be answered differently, depending on different risk-sharing scenarios that vary with respect to location, magnitude of damage, and terrorism risk insurance take-up rate.

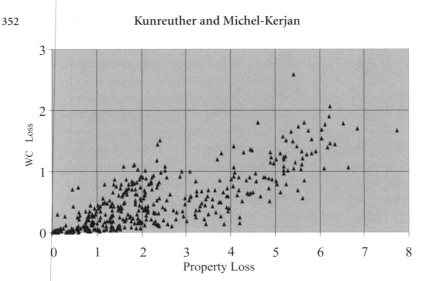

Figure 20.7. Projected property losses and workers' compensation (WC) losses from aircraft attacks to 447 high-rise buildings in the United States (in $ billion). Each triangle represents one specific high-rise building used in the simulation.

ASSUMPTIONS

We make a number of assumptions to examine these losses. Because data are not available on individual insurers' terrorism exposure, we utilize *market shares* of insurers to allocate losses from a terrorist attack between the 451 largest insurers that comprise 97 percent of the market with respect to 2004 TRIA-line direct earned premiums (DEP). Market shares appear to be the most reasonable proxy for analyzing loss sharing across the affected parties. In addition, we separate property insurance lines from workers' compensation lines. In the case of property coverage, we utilize premiums written for nationwide commercial coverage. With respect to workers' compensation (WC) coverage, we have access to insurers' market shares in the relevant states and therefore allocate losses using these data.[31]

We first undertake a comparative analysis of loss distribution between the affected parties as we vary location, level of loss, and take-up rate under a scenario in which the terrorist attacks take place in 2005 with TRIA in place. In this scenario, insurers will pay their entire loss up to their TRIA deductible (D: 15 percent of the TRIA-line DEP in 2004) and then an additional 10 percent above D, with the federal government paying the other 90 percent.[32] Under TRIA the federal government would levy a surcharge against all policyholders purchasing commercial insurance to recoup part of its payment within the total insurers' payments and the insurance industry retention ($15 billion in 2005) ("mandatory recoupment").

Table 20.1. City comparison of simulated scenario involving five-ton truck bombs ($25 billion in losses: 50 percent coverage for property; 100 percent coverage for workers' compensation [WC]); 2005 TRIA

City comparison	Not-insured[i]	Total insured	Loss sharing		
			Insurers' payments	All policyholders[ii]	Final government taxpayers
New York, NY	**$7.5bn**	**$17.5bn**	**$13.27bn**	**$1.73bn**	**$2.5bn**
	Insured loss sharing		*76%*	*10%*	*14%*
Los Angeles, CA	**$7.5bn**	**$17.5bn**	**$13.1bn**	**$1.9bn**	**$2.5bn**
	Insured loss sharing		*75%*	*11%*	*14%*
Houston, TX	**$7.5bn**	**$17.5bn**	**$14.5bn**	**$0.5bn**	**$2.5bn**
	Insured loss sharing		*83%*	*3%*	*14%*

[i] Retained by policyholders who suffered the losses but were not covered against terrorism.
[ii] The federal government recoups the 90% portion of the insured loss it initially paid above insurers' payments up to an industry aggregate of $15 billion in 2005 (see TRIA design above).

EFFECT OF ATTACK LOCATION

The effect on loss sharing of two 5-ton truck bomb attacks varies greatly depending on the location of the attack (Table 20.1). Under our simulation, we compare the total property loss ($15 billion) and workers' compensation loss ($10 billion) in three major cities (New York City for New York, Los Angeles for California, and Houston for Texas). We also assume that half of the property damage to commercial enterprises in the buildings is covered by either terrorism insurance or fire-following insurance, and that all the workers' compensation losses are covered by insurance. This scenario results in a $17.5 billion in insured loss out of the $25 billion total. A sensitivity analysis relative to the insurance take-up rate is undertaken later in this subsection.

Under this scenario, the insurers and policyholders will absorb $15 billion of the $17.5 billion insured loss in each of the three cities. However, the distribution of payments between insurers and all policyholders differs across metropolitan areas (due to different workers' compensation market shares). In both New York and California, two or three large insurers provide a very large portion of workers' compensation coverage for the entire state – they will have a much higher loss relative to their TRIA deductible than workers' compensation insurers in Texas, where there is less concentration of coverage in one company. Hence, the federal government will initially pay more in New York and California (the 90 percent portion above the deductible of the few key workers' compensation insurers), and then recoup part of that payment against all policyholders. In all three cities, the federal government covers $2.5 billion of the loss, which is shared by all U.S. taxpayers.[33]

EFFECT OF SIZE OF LOSS

Changing the size of the loss from $0.5 billion to $100 billion affects the distribution of payments (Table 20.2). We detail the effect in one specific metropolitan area (New York, NY), using the same assumptions as in the previous section: half of the property damage to commercial enterprises in the buildings is covered by either terrorism insurance or by fire-following insurance, and all the workers' compensation losses are covered by insurance.

The figures reveal that, if losses from terrorist attacks do not exceed $15 billion, the insurance companies and policyholders will bear all of the losses. We considered two cases for which the total loss is $40 billion. In Case 1, property loss is $28 billion and workers' compensation is $12 billion. In Case 2, the dollar figures are reversed: property loss is $12 billion and workers' compensation is $28 billion. Even if the total loss is the same, the loss sharing differs considerably between these two cases. While taxpayers would end up paying $5.4 billion in Case 1, they would pay $15.3 billion in Case 2. The difference is due to both the level of insured loss and the distribution of loss among insurers who have different deductibles under TRIA. In other words, a $1 billion loss due to property damage is shared differently than a $1 billion loss of workers' compensation, because the insurers are different. If the terrorist attacks lead to losses of $100 billion, under a scenario in which losses are half property, half workers' compensation, then the U.S. taxpayers will bear 54.5 percent of the total insured losses.

INCREASED BURDEN ON INSURERS AND COMMERCIAL ENTERPRISES (COVERED OR NOT AGAINST TERRORISM) IN 2006 AND 2007

How are these results likely to be modified this year and in 2007? There is no definitive answer to that question now. The design of the program requires one to specify direct earned premium under TRIEA lines collected the previous year (i.e., 2005), and these data will not be available before this book is published.

Some have used the "total industry DEP/deductible" as a proxy to measure how terrorism losses would be shared between insurers, all policyholders, and taxpayers. However, our data analyses have shown that the loss shares differed

Table 20.2. Impact of varying losses from 5-ton truck bomb attacks on New York City (50 percent insurance coverage for property; 100 percent coverage for workers' compensation [WC]); 2005 TRIA

Loss scenarios	Not-insured[i]	Loss sharing			
		Total insured	Insurers' payments	All policyholders[ii]	Final goverment taxpayers
Total: $0.5bn Property: $0.25bn WC: $0.25bn	$125mi	$375mi	$375mi	$0	$0
Insured loss sharing			*100%*	*0%*	*0%*
Total: $5bn Property: $2.5bn WC: $2.5bn	$1.25bn	$3.75bn	$2.97bn	$780mi	0$
Insured loss sharing			*79.2%*	*20.8%*	*0%*
Total: $15bn Property: $9bn WC: $6bn	$4.5bn	$10.5bn	$8.23bn	$2.27bn	$0
Insured loss sharing			*78.3%*	*21.7%*	*0%*
Total: $25bn Property: $15bn WC: $10bn	$7.5bn	$17.5bn	$13.27bn	$1.73bn	$2.5bn
Insured loss sharing			*75.9%*	*9.9%*	*14.2%*
Total: $40bn Property: $28bn WC: $12bn	$14bn	$26bn	$20.6bn	$0	$5.4bn
Insured loss sharing			*79.2%*	*0%*	*20.8%*
Total: $40bn Property: $12bn WC: $28bn	$6bn	$34bn	$18.7bn	$0	$15.3bn
Insured loss sharing			*55%*	*0%*	*45%*
Total: $100bn Property: $50bn WC: $50bn	$25bn	$75bn	$34.1bn	$0	$40.9bn[iii]
Insured loss sharing			*45.5%*	*0%*	*54.5%*

[i] Retained by policyholders who suffered the losses but were not covered against terrorism.

[ii] The federal government is assumed to recoup the portion of insured loss it initially paid above insurers' payments up to an industry aggregate of $15 billion in 2005.

[iii] Including $18.3 billion that would represent the 90% federal payment above the New York Insurance Fund's TRIA deductible.

very significantly depending on whether one considered such an – incorrect – aggregate approach or the more granular insurer-based one on which TRIEA is really based.[34] What can be done at this time is to understand in what directions loss sharing is likely to evolve under the revised design of the terrorism insurance program.

EFFECT OF THE INCREASED INDUSTRY MARKET RETENTION ON LOSS SHARING

While most of the debate has been focused on the increase in insurer deductible, the major change in TRIEA is the increase of insurance industry retention from $15 billion to $25 billion in 2006. In Table 20.3, we utilize the results of the analyses summarized in Table 20.2 but modify the retention level to reflect this change (results are indicated in [ ]).

For total insured losses under $15 billion, there is, of course, no difference. For the $25 billion loss scenario, however, the $2.5 billion that would have been paid by taxpayers in 2005 is now paid by policyholders. The difference is even more significant for the two $40 billion scenarios: commercial policyholders, whether they are covered against terrorism or not, pay $4.4 billion and $6.3 billion, respectively. For the same $100 billion scenario as the one used before, there is no difference because insurers already pay $34.1 billion in claims, which is above the $25 billion retention – in that case there is no mandatory recoupment by the federal government.

EFFECT OF THE INCREASED DEDUCTIBLE AND MARKET CONDITIONS

As discussed earlier, TRIEA increases the insurer deductible, as a percentage of the TRIA-line DEP in the previous year, from 15 percent in 2005 to 17.5 percent in 2006, and to 20 percent in 2007. While this represents a difference in 2.5 points of percentage each year, this translates into a 17 percent increase in 2006 and another 14 percent increase in 2007 (in absolute value). Between 2005 and 2007, for a given DEP level, there will be a 33 percent increase in the insurer's deductible under TRIEA.

The increased insurer deductible is affected by market conditions as well, if one expects TRIAE-lines premiums to evolve over time. For example, the total TRIA-line premiums for our 451-insurers sample evolved as follows: $170.9 billion in 2002, $197.2 billion in 2003 (a 17 percent increase from the previous year), and $210.6 billion in 2004 (a 7 percent increase from 2003). After the 2004 and 2005 hurricane seasons, it would not be surprising to see

Table 20.3. Impact of varying losses from 5-ton truck bomb attacks on New York City (50% insurance for property coverage; 100% insurance for workers' compensation; 2005; $15 billion industry market retention [$25 billion industry market retention])

Loss scenarios	Not-insured[i]	Total insured	Loss sharing		
			Insurers' payments	All policyholders[ii]	Final goverment taxpayers
Total: $0.5bn Property: $0.25bn WC: $0.25bn	$125mi	$375mi	$375mi [$375mi]	$0 [$0]	$0 [$0]
Insured loss sharing			*100%*	*0%*	*0%*
Total: $5bn Property: $2.5bn WC: $2.5bn	$1.25bn	$3.75bn	$2.97bn [$2.97bn]	$780mi [$780mi]	$0 [$0]
Insured loss sharing			*79.2%*	*20.8%*	*0%*
Total: $15bn Property: $9bn WC: $6bn	$4.5bn	$10.5bn	$8.23bn [$8.23bn]	$2.27bn [$2.27bn]	$0 [$0]
Insured loss sharing			*78.3%*	*21.7%*	*0%*
Total: $25bn Property: $15bn WC: $10bn	$7.5bn	$17.5bn	$13.27bn [$13.27bn]	$1.73bn [$4.23bn]	$2.5bn [$0]
Insured loss sharing			*75.9%*	*9.9%*	*14.2%*
			75.9%	*[24.1%]*	*[0%]*
Total: $40bn Property: $28bn WC: $12bn	$14bn	$26bn	$20.6bn [$20.6bn]	$0 [$4.4bn]	$5.4bn [$1.0bn]
Insured loss sharing			*79.2%*	*0%*	*20.8%*
			[79.2%]	*[16.9%]*	*[3.9%]*
Total: $40bn Property: $12bn WC: $28bn	$6bn	$34bn	$18.7bn [$18.7bn]	$0 [$6.3bn]	$15.3bn [$9bn]
Insured loss sharing			*55%*	*0%*	*45%*
			[55%]	*[18.5%]*	*[26.5%]*
Total: $100bn Property: $50bn WC: $50bn	$25bn	$75bn	$34.1bn [$34.1bn]	$0 [$0]	$40.9bn[iii] [$40.9bn]
Insured loss sharing			*[45.5%]*	*0%*	*[54.5%]*

[i] Retained by policyholders who suffered the losses but were not covered against terrorism.
[ii] The federal government is assumed to recoup the portion of insured loss it initially paid above insurers' payments up to an industry aggregate of $15 billion in 2005.
[iii] Including $18.3 billion that would represent the 90% federal payment above the New York Insurance Fund's TRIA deductible.

the market hardening so that a 10 to 15 percent annual increase in TRIEA-line premiums for 2005 and 2006 appears to be a reasonable assumption.

Suppose now that the portfolio of a representative insurer X follows the same evolution of the aggregate sample. If annual TRIA-line DEP in 2004 of insurer X were $100 million, then its terrorism coverage deductible under TRIA for 2005 would have been $15 million. Assuming a 13 percent increase in TRIA-line DEP in 2005, then insurer X's deductible under TRIEA for 2006 would be $19.775 million (i.e., .175 × $113 million). This represents a 31.8 percent increase in its terrorism deductible from the previous year in absolute value. If premium increases follow a similar pattern between 2005 and 2006, then insurer X's deductible under TRIEA for 2007 would be $25.54 million (i.e., .20 × $127.69 million).

This reflects a 70 percent increase over its deductible in 2005. The impact on the precise amount of terrorism loss sharing can be determined after data from 2005 become available. What is clear is that insurers and policyholders will pay a much greater loss share in 2006 and 2007 than under the 2005-attack scenario due to the higher deductible and higher market retention and hence the general taxpayer will incur a smaller portion of the loss.

PRIVATE EFFICIENCY, PUBLIC VULNERABILITY: WILL INSURERS STRATEGIZE IF THE CURRENT PROGRAM IS MADE PERMANENT?

We can use the scenario methodology to analyze the question as to how insurers will react if the program is made permanent in its current form. Will insurers' exposure to terrorism losses change from what it currently is under TRIEA and, if so, what would be the impact on loss sharing between the affected parties following a large-scale terrorist attack on U.S. soil?

To examine this question, we assume that TRIEA officially becomes a permanent program with the insurer's deductible at 17.5 percent of their TRIEA-line DEP from the previous year. All insurers know that they will have to pay for all losses they incur below this deductible (D) and 10 percent of the loss above it, with the remaining 90 percent eventually paid by other parties (taxpayers, policyholders). An insurer with a very low deductible/surplus ratio would have a rationale for this insurer to take advantage of the small percentage it will have to absorb if its loss exceeds the TRIA deductible. Any insurer with a low deductible/surplus (D/S) ratio would have an economic incentive to write a large number of policies in a concentrated area subject to a terrorist attack (e.g., Times Square, Wall Street area) due to the positive correlation in these losses. In other words, the insurer knows that if one of these buildings is damaged or destroyed, the surrounding ones are also likely to suffer severe damage.

DETERMINING TERRORISM COVERAGE USING AN "E^* GAMING STRATEGY"

To examine how the aggregate exposure/surplus ratio affects the amount of coverage an insurer will want to provide if the current program is extended indefinitely, we use the following notation:

E^* = maximum insured terrorism exposure (i.e., worst case scenario)
E = actual dollar claims incurred by an insurer from a worst case scenario
DEP = direct earned premiums written for TRIA lines of coverage
$D = aDEP = $ TRIA/TRIEA deductible determined by the percentage a
   (e.g., a = 17.5% in 2006)
S = current surplus
$X = E/S$ = aggregate exposure for terrorism/surplus ratio
$Y = D/S$ = deductible/surplus ratio

Given the difficulties in estimating the probability of a terrorist attack, rating agencies focus on deterministic scenarios in evaluating an insurer's credit rating. We focus our estimates on insured losses from a five-ton truck bomb scenario in determining the maximum exposure an insurer will be willing to accept. If an insurer experiences insured losses of E^*, it determines its dollar claims (E) with one of two equations:

$$E = E^* \quad \text{if} \quad E^* \leq D \tag{1}$$

$$E = D + .1(E^* - D) \quad \text{if} \quad E^* > D \tag{2}$$

A possible line of analysis would be to suppose that the maximum amount of terrorism exposure (E^*) that an insurer wants to write is determined by a desired aggregate exposure/surplus (E/S) ratio given by x (e.g., $x = 10\%$). To determine the value of E^*, the insurer first computes $D/S = y$ and compares the value of y with x.

- If $y \geq x$, the insurer knows that its claims are determined by the first equation (1) (i.e., $E = E^*$), because it is responsible for the entire loss on its own given that $D/S > x$. The insurer thus sets $E^* = xS$.
- On the other hand, if $y < x$, the insurer knows that its claims are determined by the second equation (2), and the government will cover 90 percent of the insured loss above its TRIA deductible, given the federal backstop provision of TRIA. In this case, the insurer computes $E/S = D/S + .1$ $(E^*/S - D/S)$, which can be written as

$$x = y + .1(E^*/S - y) \quad \text{or} \quad E^* = (10x - 9y)S. \tag{3}$$

To illustrate this strategy with a simple numerical example, we assign the values of $D = 10$, $S = 200$, $y = .05$, and $x = .10$. Since $y < x$, E^* is determined by (3) as follows:

$$E^* = (1 - 0.45)200 = 110$$

If an insurer were responsible for the entire loss, then $E = E^*$ for all values of E^* so that $E^* = xS$. For this example, $E^* = .10(200) = 20$, which is considerably lower than the scenario in which the insurer is responsible for only 10 percent of the loss, as it was under TRIA and still is under TRIEA in 2006.

To examine the impact of a permanent TRIA-like program on the amount of terrorism coverage written by insurers, we assume that each insurer is concerned with maintaining an aggregate exposure from deterministic scenarios at 10 percent of its surplus (S).[35] E, then, is the *ultimate exposure* of the insurer; that is, what it will pay after sharing part of the loss with other parties.

E^* represents the *aggregate exposure* that an insurer is willing to risk if it is responsible for 10 percent of the loss above $D = 15\%$ (e.g., the arrangement under TRIA in 2005) and it wants to set a value of $E/S = D + .1(E^* - D) = 10\%$.

We define an E^* *gaming strategy* as the decision by an insurer to increase significantly the amount of coverage it provides in order to take advantage of the 90 percent risk-sharing arrangement with the government, and at the same time to collect a significant amount of terrorism insurance premiums.

We focus on the locations where a large terrorism loss is more likely. To make the data analysis manageable, we have limited our sample of insurers to those who already provide the largest terrorism coverage in urban areas. We focused on the top 30 insurers based on TRIA-line direct earned premiums in 2004 and then eliminated the 7 companies who are small business and personal lines writers. This group of 23 large insurers actually accounts for about two-thirds of the TRIA-lines direct earned premiums of the market. For the sake of simplicity, we then make the assumption that these 23 insurers cover 100 percent of the insured losses in the city we consider. We then analyze how losses would be shared under TRIA and compare this with a design of a "permanent TRIA."

For each insurer, we can determine its aggregate terrorism coverage in urban areas. For insurers with a D/S ratio greater than 10 percent, insurers limit their exposure to 10 percent of their surplus ($E^* = E$). Those with D/S less than 10 percent could offer much more coverage than under TRIA, particularly those with very small D/S due to a large surplus ($E^* > E$). Figure 20.8 depicts the difference that fixing a threshold of $E/S = 10$ percent would have on insurers' decisions regarding how much terrorism coverage to offer, depending on whether the insurer had a D/S ration higher than 10 percent (Insurer (a); left part of the graph) and those with D/S less than 10 percent (Insurer (b);

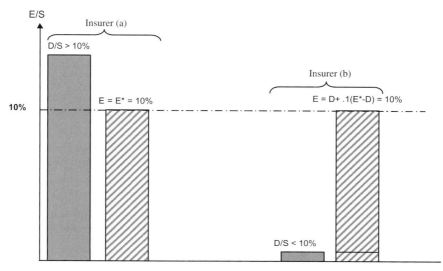

Figure 20.8. Insurer's exposure limited to 10% of its surplus.

right part of the graph). In both cases, there are two bars. The solid gray one on the left indicates the D/S ratio of the insurer in 2005; the one made up of oblique lines on the right indicates exposure based on the constraint that $E/S = 10$ percent.

The aggregate exposure for each of these two types of insurer is depicted in Figure 20.9. An insurer with considerable business in non-TRIA lines such that its surplus is high but its deductible is quite low will take advantage of the structure of TRIA's program (if it is made permanent) by increasing its aggregate exposure considerably from the current level, up to E^*. For example, Insurer (b) on Figure 20.9 will pay only 10 percent of any loss above its deductible (D; the portion represented by oblique lines) with the other 90 percent paid by taxpayers and possibly all policyholders under the federal government's recoupment arrangement under TRIA (the area represented by horizontal lines).

An important difference from the analyses undertaken in the previous section of the chapter is that market share is now based on each insurer's E^*. In this case, we assume that E^* is composed of both property and workers' compensation coverage. As a result, the market shares of insurers providing terrorism coverage would be quite different if a TRIA-like program were made permanent. In particular, the New York State Insurance Fund would likely not be the major provider of workers' compensation coverage anymore, as its surplus is much lower than other large insurers; the company is therefore constrained in how much terrorism insurance it will be willing to write.

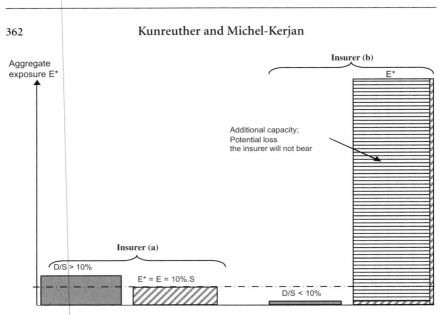

Figure 20.9. Aggregate exposure of insured losses; additional capacity provided by insurers with D/S < 10%.

Using E^*, one can then determine how the coverage from a terrorist attack would be spread across insurers. Because insurers with low D/S ratios are willing to write considerably more property coverage at relatively low prices in metropolitan areas if TRIA is made permanent, all commercial enterprises will expect to be insured against property losses (we assume a 100 percent take-up rate).[36]

ALLOCATION OF LOSSES ACROSS AFFECTED STAKEHOLDERS

As mentioned earlier, data for 2006 are not available yet, so we provide the analysis by making the design of TRIA-2005 permanent. We discuss in this section who pays for the losses under TRIA in 2005, and should TRIA be made permanent, for two scenarios in New York City: a $25 billion and $100 billion terrorist attack using five-ton truck bombs. Under TRIA in 2005, the allocation of losses is based on each insurer's market share of total property-casualty premiums for commercial coverage, and insurers are assumed not to be using an E^* *strategy*. The now 100 percent take-up rate when TRIA is made permanent results in a shift of non-insured losses ($7.5 billion and $25 billion, respectively) to either all the policyholders or the government/taxpayers (Table 20.4). On first glance it seems counterintuitive that insurers will pay less for terrorism losses when their take-up rate is 100 percent rather than 50 percent. The reason is that insurers with low D/S ratios will increase their exposure very significantly,

Table 20.4. Distribution of losses under TRIA-2005 and if TRIA is made permanent ($25 billion loss in New York City)

		Insured loss sharing			
	Non-insured	Total insured	Insurers' payments	All policyholders[i]	Final ged. gov. taxpayers
Scenarios					
TRIA-2005 – 50% take-up rate on Property Insurance – 23 insurers					
Total: $25bn Property: $15bn WC: $10bn	$7.5bn	$17.5bn	$13.3bn	$1.7bn	$2.5bn
Insured loss sharing			76%	9.8%	14.2%
TRIA Extended Indefinitely – 100% take-up rate – 23 insurers					
Total: $25bn Property: $15bn WC: $10bn	$0	$25bn	$8.4bn	$6.6bn	$10bn
Insured loss sharing			46%	14%	40%
Change in final payments			−37%	+288%	+300%
TRIA-2005 – 50% take-up rate (TRIA-line premium market) – 23 insurers					
Total: $100bn Property: $50bn WC: $50bn	$25bn	$75bn	$24bn	$0	$51bn
Insured loss sharing			32%	0%	68%
TRIA Extended Indefinitely – 100% take-up rate – 23 insurers					
Total: $100bn Property: $50bn WC: $50bn	$0	$100bn	$20.7bn	$0	$79.3bn
Insured loss sharing			20.7%	0%	79.3%
Change in final payments			−14%	0%	+55%

[i] The federal government is assumed to recoup the portion of insured loss it initially paid above insurers' payments up to an industry aggregate of $15 billion in 2005.

as shown in Figure 20.9. Following a terrorist attack, these few insurers will be initially responsible for the largest part of the losses.

Under TRIA in 2005, these losses would have been spread over a much larger number of insurers, who collectively would have absorbed more of the loss because it would fall below their values of D. In other words, under a permanent TRIA program these few insurers will end up paying a very limited portion of their exposure (they actually pay E not E^*), while the federal government will cover 90 percent of the loss above their D levels. As with the other analyses, we assume that the federal government will pay for any losses above the $15 billion industry market retention without recoupment of any of their expenditures under the TRIA federal backstop provision.

Consider the insurance scenario with a $25 billion loss. Because the total loss will increase from $17.5 billion (with a 50 percent take-up rate) to $25 billion (with a 100 percent take-up rate), the general taxpayers' share of the loss will increase from $2.5 billion to $10 billion – that is, a 300 percent increase from the current TRIA program. The difference between the $15 billion insurance industry retention and insurers' payments of $13.3 billion will be charged against all policyholders, who will experience a 288 percent increase in payments. The difference in market shares induced by a few insurers playing an E^* strategy would result in a 37 percent decrease in insurance industry payments, even if all losses caused by the attacks are now covered (Table 20.4).

In the more extreme case of a $100 billion loss, when some insurers decide to significantly increase their aggregate exposure after learning that TRIA is renewed indefinitely, the insurance industry would pay considerably less in claims even though the take-up rate on property coverage is assumed to be 100 percent. More specifically, due to their higher exposures when TRIA is extended indefinitely, the insurers will receive a larger subsidy from the federal government than they would under TRIA today. Furthermore, the insurance industry loss with either a 50 percent or 100 percent take-up rate is greater than the $15 billion market retention rate. We assume that taxpayers cover the loss above this amount so there will be no recoupment of the subsidy by the federal government and the commercial policyholders will not be taxed at all. Hence, the insurers actually pay less when total insured losses are $100 billion than when they are $75 billion (Table 20.4). Indeed, the larger total insured loss due to the increased coverage amount is passed on to the U.S. taxpayers, who now absorb $79.3 billion in loss payments compared with $51 billion under TRIA in 2005.

If one wants to design a program that encourages insurers to write coverage, then a permanent terrorism insurance program like TRIA or TRIEA will be successful due to the very large subsidy the government provides to any insurer whose losses exceed D. The very large insurers with low D/S ratios will provide most of the coverage and pay very little after a terrorist attack compared with their aggregate exposure. They would keep all their premiums and transfer the loss to all commercial policyholders and taxpayers. This points to an inequity in this system, because the policyholders of those insurers who do not suffer any loss are responsible for the same amount of repayment to the government in the form of a surcharge as are policyholders in companies that suffered large losses and were subsidized by the government.

RATIONALE FOR LIMITING AGGREGATE EXPOSURE

There are several reasons why insurers may not be willing to assume the large aggregate exposure implied by an E^* gaming strategy. First, a larger E^* increases the likelihood that an insurer will experience medium to large losses below its TRIA (or TRIEA) deductible with the more structures insurers cover in high-risk areas. In this sense insurers may decide to limit their aggregate exposure by estimating the likelihoods of different terrorist attack scenarios occurring. Insurers may then reduce their aggregate exposure by utilizing their survival constraint in a manner similar to the processes they follow for other catastrophic risks. Second, when an insurer provides coverage against terrorism, it also provides insurance against all other events that could cause damage or losses to their property and/or claims from their workers' compensation coverage. When an insurer decides whether to write more terrorism coverage, it needs to consider its aggregate exposure from a much broader set of risks (e.g., fire, theft, job injury).

Insurers may be concerned that Congress will amend a permanent TRIA-like program if legislators observe the type of strategizing described above. Suppose insurers who expanded their coverage by focusing on E^* were to be held responsible for 50 percent of their losses above their TRIA deductible. These insurers will very likely want to cancel some of their commercial policies for fear of incurring large claim costs after a terrorist attack. One reason why these insurers have not followed an E^* gaming strategy today is their concern that a TRIA-like program will not be renewed in its current form.

THE WAY FORWARD: A PERSPECTIVE ON LONG-TERM OPTIONS FOR TERRORISM RISK FINANCING

Although TRIA has provided an important and necessary temporary solution to the problem of providing terrorism insurance to commercial firms, we do not believe it or its successor TRIEA is an equitable and efficient program in the long run. We now turn to a set of alternative options that involve the private and public sectors for providing protection against terrorism losses on a more permanent basis. These alternatives are not mutually exclusive. Some combination of these and perhaps other options should be considered in the design of a program that provides protection against terrorism losses while at the same time encouraging risk-reducing measures by those who are potential targets for a future attack.

DEPLOY CAPITAL OF POTENTIAL TARGET FIRMS

Modern enterprise risk management has shown that it often makes sense for a firm to use its own capital to absorb risk, rather than insuring against a loss. In these circumstances, the firm can manage the risk through its own capital management strategy. For example, the firm may lower its debt financing in relation to equity to be able to tolerate more risk. Other more focused strategies include the use of structured debt (e.g., warrants, convertible and forgivable debt) and more recently the use of contingent capital (i.e., financing that is contingent on the occurrence of specified events). Thus, we would envision that a large part of terrorism risk is, and will continue to be, absorbed by the firm's own capital, so that it is, in fact, self-insured.[37]

Those institutions providing long-term debt financing to developers could possibly underwrite potential losses from terrorism and charge higher interest rates to reflect the additional risk. Equity capital investors could hold more diversified portfolios, so no single investor would suffer a large and disproportionate diminution in the total value of assets in the event of an attack.

DEPLOY CAPITAL OF REINSURERS

One potential private market solution that has been discussed is to increase the transfer of risk through reinsurance (Congressional Budget Office 2005).[38] Since reinsurance portfolios normally cover sizable losses in the tails of the distribution, reinsurers normally need to hold relatively large amounts of capital compared with primary insurers. During the past several years, most major reinsurers experienced reductions in capital, in part due to the 9/11 attacks, and several of them were downgraded by rating agencies. They decided not to allocate much of their scarce capital to terrorism risk, instead focusing their capital on other lines.

Results from the survey of reinsurers undertaken, as part of the Wharton Risk Center *TRIA and Beyond*, by the Reinsurance Association of America indicate that the reinsurance industry's capacity for providing terrorism coverage under the TRIA program in 2005 was in the range of $5–6 billion. According to those surveyed, if a TRIA-like program were not in place, reinsurers would either maintain the same amount of reinsurance coverage or reduce the amount they provide.

More detailed analysis needs to take place as to the role that private reinsurance could play in providing protection against catastrophic losses from terrorism. One possibility would be a TRIA-like program without individual insurer deductibles that would only provide payments once losses exceeded a large aggregate threshold.[39] This approach would stimulate the demand for reinsurance and would avoid some of the distortions associated with individual insurer deductibles and inclusion of captives in the program.[40]

Another complementary option would be to base any federal reimbursement of terrorism losses on net (i.e., after reinsurance) losses without requiring reinsurers to make terrorism coverage available. Such a change might significantly increase the scope of reinsurance and associated risk spreading. The terms of reinsurance would reflect the federal backstop (i.e., the reinsurer's ability to be reimbursed for losses), thus reducing reinsurance prices. Primary insurers would be free to either buy reinsurance if available at the right price or keep similar exposures as under the current system.

REDUCE TAX COSTS FOR INSURERS AND REINSURERS TO HOLD CAPITAL

U.S. federal tax policy increases the costs of private-sector arrangements for spreading catastrophe risk, thus reducing the supply of insurance and alternative risk-spreading vehicles. Insurers cannot establish tax deductible reserves for events that have not occurred. More importantly, providing insurance against rare but potentially enormous losses requires insurers to hold large amounts of equity capital, which is primarily invested in marketable securities. Investors can readily purchase the same types of securities directly or through investment funds, in which case the returns on the securities are subject to personal taxes only. When held by an insurer to back the sale of its policies, the returns are taxed twice – at the corporate level and at the personal level – because insurers cannot hold such capital in tax-deferred accounts. For the securities to be used to back policies, the premiums must therefore be high enough to compensate investors for the extra layer of taxes. The total cost can be very large for the amounts of capital that must be invested to back the sale of insurance for rare but potentially extreme events, such as large losses from terrorist attacks.

The private sector's capacity to offer coverage for losses from terrorism (and other extreme events) would therefore expand if insurers and reinsurers were allowed some form of tax-deferred reserves for terrorism coverage. Such a policy could reduce the costs to insurers and reinsurers of holding the large amounts of capital necessary to provide coverage. This should increase supply and reduce premium rates. A tax-deferred reserve approach should be weighed carefully in light of a number of potential benefits and possible drawbacks: a short-term reduction of tax revenues, the disadvantage of industry-specific tax rules, and the challenges of designing a system that meets the objectives of expanding capacity to insure losses from terrorism (and possibly other extreme events) without allowing significant unrelated tax deferral.

FACILITATE THE USE OF TERRORISM CATASTROPHE BONDS[41]

A catastrophe bond transfers the risk of a large loss from the insurance/reinsurance industry to the financial markets. A significant market for catastrophe bonds to cover losses from terrorist attacks has not emerged since 9/11. To date, only three terrorism-related catastrophe bonds have been issued and these were part of multi-event coverage for other risks such as natural disasters and pandemics. For example, the first bond was issued in Europe in August 2003. The Fédération Internationale de Football Association (the world governing organization of association football [soccer]), which is organizing the 2006 World Cup in Germany, developed a $262 million bond to protect its investment. Under very specific conditions, the catastrophe bond covers losses resulting from both natural and terrorist extreme events that would result in the cancellation of the World Cup game without the possibility of it being rescheduled to 2007.[42]

The lack of interest in new financial instruments for covering terrorism risk may be due to concern by investment managers that potentially a large loss from a catastrophe bond would hurt their reputations (and possibly their compensation). Another reason why there has been no market for terrorism catastrophe bonds might be evident in the reluctance of reinsurers to provide protection against this risk following the 9/11 terrorist attacks. Financial investors perceive reinsurers as experts in this market. Upon learning that the reinsurance industry required high premiums to provide protection against terrorism, investors were only willing to provide funds to cover losses from terrorism if they received a sufficiently high interest rate.[43]

Most investors and rating agencies consider terrorism models as too new and untested to be used in conjunction with a catastrophe bond covering terrorism risks. The models are viewed as providing useful information on the potential severity of the attacks but not on their frequency. Without the acceptance of these models by major rating agencies, the development of a large market for terrorism catastrophe bonds is unlikely.[44] In addition, institutional, tax, and regulatory constraints have discouraged the growth of terrorism-related and other catastrophe bonds.

A study should be undertaken to analyze behavioral, institutional, and regulatory obstacles to the development of a more robust market for terrorism catastrophe bonds, as well as the steps that would need to be taken to modify the current situation.

MUTUAL INSURANCE POOLS

Another alternative would be to allow insurers to form an insurance pool to deal with specific lines of coverage, perhaps with some federal backing for large losses. In effect, a group of companies would provide reinsurance to each other. For example, firms insuring high-risk assets in the United States and around the world could form their own mutual insurance pools. This solution has the advantage of spreading the risk over a large number of insurers who join these pools, but it is unclear whether this alternative would provide adequate coverage against mega-terrorism. Pool solutions developed in several other countries should be analyzed in more detail to determine their potential application to the U.S. market.[45] The pool does not have to provide coverage for the entire country, but can be focused on certain types of risks and/or industries.

PUBLICLY ADMINISTERED MUTUAL INSURANCE

The need for federal protection against terrorism risks and those of other extreme events comes from the combination of two defects. The loss probability is highly uncertain and the maximum possible loss is considered to be large relative to the amount of private reinsurance and catastrophe bonds available to insurers. One strategy for addressing these two problems is to construct a type of publicly administered mutual insurance arrangement.

Two key conditions must hold for this arrangement to be feasible. First, although losses on individual properties can be highly correlated and aggregate damages can be large, the losses cannot be perfectly correlated. For example, the arrangement could absorb a severe attack on Houston, New York, or San Francisco, but not necessarily if the three cities were attacked simultaneously. Second, buyers need not agree on what they think the loss probability is in each site, but they must be able to agree (in the simplest case) that it is the same, or (in a more complex case) on what the relative likelihoods are. For example, all buyers might agree that a large-scale assault is twice as likely in Houston and New York as in San Francisco.

The insurance would work as follows for the case of a mutual insurance program protecting insurers providing terrorism coverage in these three cities.

Each insurer would choose a level of protection through the mutual pool and pay an estimated premium. If no attack occurs on either site after a predefined period of time, any excess premiums above a certain threshold are returned to these insurers in proportion to their original purchase. Suppose a loss does occur in Houston, for example, and if its magnitude is less than resources accumulated by the pool to that point, all claims are paid. But if total insured losses exceed claims, insurance buyers are assessed an additional amount to cover claims. In this example, New York and San Francisco policyholders furnish the capital to cover excess claims in Houston. In effect, this arrangement uses as its source of excess capital the undamaged assets of pool participants who have not suffered a loss. Such an arrangement might be voluntary, but it might be made compulsory as well, with the *ex post* assessments proportional to the additional coverage that was made mandatory.

FEDERAL REINSURANCE WITH EXPLICIT PREMIUMS

Another possible response to the limited capacity of private insurers and reinsurers to furnish coverage against catastrophic losses is a federal reinsurance program with explicit premiums. The most obvious technique for pricing federal reinsurance would be for the government to calculate a premium. It would make its own estimate of the probability of a major attack and the extent of the damages, calculate the expected value of the loss, add a modest amount for administrative expenses, possibly tack on a "risk premium," and offer unlimited amounts of coverage for sale at this premium.

Under a federal reinsurance program, in years without any major terrorist attack, no benefits would be paid out. But if an attack occurred, these government's collected funds would be used to cover the catastrophic portion of the losses against which insurers had purchased federal reinsurance. If the losses protected by federal reinsurance exceeded the premiums collected, the government would have to finance these claims from other sources of taxpayer revenue. Over time, if the premiums accurately reflected the risks of terrorist attacks, the government reinsurance fund would be replenished.

CONSIDERING COVERING BOTH DOMESTIC
AND FOREIGN TERRORISM[46]

Another question that needs to be addressed is whether the arbitrary distinction that the current U.S. terrorism risk insurance program makes between so-called "foreign" and "domestic" terrorism reflects the current nature of the terrorism threat.[47] This poses at least two major problems.

First, the evolution of international terrorist activities from more locally organized and even national groups to global organization makes it difficult to distinguish between domestic and foreign terrorism, as illustrated by the July 2005 bombings in London.[48] Some of these terrorists had been trained to kill in Pakistan. Should one thus conclude that they were "acting on behalf of a foreign person or foreign interest"? On the other hand, they had been living in London for years, studying or working there. Should one conclude they acted on behalf of their own ideology? In that case, should we conclude that the nearly 800 casualties were victims of domestic terrorism? Had these events been more devastating and occurred in the United States, would they have qualified for TRIA coverage? Today this gray zone is likely to inflict legal costs to both victims and insurers, and considerably delay claims payments to victims of the attacks.

Second, the decision to exclude domestic terrorism from TRIA and its extension because it was not considered a serious threat needs to be reevaluated in the light of the current threats posed by extremist groups in the United States.[49] Data on domestic terrorism from the U.S. Federal Bureau of Investigation reveal that more than 350 acts of domestic terrorism have been perpetrated on the U.S. soil during the period 1980–2001. Although the annual number of such attacks decreased during the 1980s and mid-1990s, it started increasing again in the past ten years, averaging 15 attacks a year nationwide during the period 1996–2001.[50] It is likely that this increase has been galvanized by anti-globalization imperatives.

Consideration should therefore be given as to whether it is desirable to include domestic terrorism as part of the events covered in a national terrorism insurance program. The analysis should consider whether the economic rationale for government involvement in covering the risk of large losses from domestic terrorism is any different from foreign terrorism, as well as the problems associated with the arbitrary distinction made by TRIA between "foreign" and "domestic" acts.

DEVELOPING INCENTIVE PROGRAMS
FOR ENCOURAGING MITIGATION

Moreover, further analysis is needed to link mitigation and insurance coverage in a more systematic way. It would be important to develop incentive programs to adequately reward private sector investment in security, for example, by lowering the price of terrorism risk financing and/or by providing any other economic incentives (e.g., more favorable tax treatment). It is worth noting, however, that the absence of a link between insurance and investment in security is not specific to the United States – most industrialized countries have not yet implemented such incentive programs either.

CONCLUSIONS

Today, five years after 9/11, the question as to who should pay for the economic consequences of a terrorist attack on the United States has not yet received the attention it deserves. As stated by the White House in its 2002 National Strategy, homeland security is "the concerted effort to prevent attacks, reduce America's vulnerability to terrorism, and minimize the damage and recover from attacks that do occur."[51] To succeed, security must be a comprehensive national effort.

The new law extending TRIA for two additional years directs the President's Working Group on Financial Markets to study long-term availability and affordability of coverage for terrorism losses. This group must submit a report of its findings to the House Financial Services and Senate Banking Committees by September 30, 2006. As we have already advocated,[52] Congress or the White House should consider establishing a broader National Commission on terrorism risk coverage before permanent legislation is enacted. Indeed, the challenges associated with terrorism risk financing are fundamental, and they will not be solved overnight. In addition to the insurance industry, there is a need to include representation on such a National Commission from sectors of the economy who are affected by the terrorism risk such as energy, transportation, real estate, and health. U.S. Treasury representation should be supplemented by key individuals from federal agencies, such as the Department of Homeland Security and the Department of Defense, who are concerned with national security issues.

Such a National Commission could explore the objectives of a terrorism risk financing program and how to achieve them through alternative risk-sharing mechanisms. In addressing these issues, there is a need for collaboration with the homeland security/intelligence community to measure what potential threats are. A National Commission could also examine how other countries cope with the terrorism risk to determine whether these approaches merit consideration for the United States. The insurance infrastructure would undoubtedly play a key role in such a program, but it should be viewed as part of a broader strategy for dealing with terrorism. For example, the public and private sectors could provide economic incentives in the form of lower taxes, subsidies, or lower insurance premiums to encourage those at risk to adopt higher security and loss reduction measures. There will likely be a need for well-enforced regulations and standards to complement these incentive programs.

The design of a terrorism insurance program reflects society's view as to who should pay for the losses from the next attack.[53] Hurricane Katrina is likely to impact how citizens, firms, and policymakers envision the role and responsibility of the public and private sectors in providing adequate protection to victims of large-scale disasters, and the importance of understanding how actions taken before a disaster impact on the need for financial assistance after a catastrophic event occurs.[54] Similar questions need to be posed with respect to terrorism risk. A well-designed terrorism insurance program has the potential of encouraging mitigation measures while at the same time alleviating the need for large-scale public sector involvement following the next attack.

APPENDIX 20.1. DEDUCTIBLE OVER SURPLUS RATIOS: 2003 TO 2005 AND PROSPECTIVE ANALYSES 2006–2007

Using data provided by A.M. Best, we undertook an analysis of the top 463 companies[55] ranked by their 2004 TRIA lines direct earned premiums (larger than $10 million). For each insurer, we had the following data:

- Total direct earned premiums all lines;
- Total direct earned premiums (DEP) for TRIA lines;
- Surplus (S).

We determined the deductible over surplus (D/S) ratio for the three years of TRIA operation: 2003, 2004, and 2005. Table 20.A provides the data for determining the D/S ratio for 2005 when D = 15 percent and it also shows these ratios for 2004 and 2003 when D = 10 and 7 percent, respectively, for the top 30 insurers (ranked by total TRIA DEP in 2004). Note that in 2003 only three insurers in the top 30 had a ratio D/S ratios equal to or higher than 15 percent, while this number increased to 14 insurers in 2005.

Prospective Analysis: Impact of TRIA Extended to 2007 on D/S Ratios

Below we show how the extension of TRIA would impact the D/S ratio for the top 30 insurers in the United States for 2006 and 2007. The new deductible is increased to 17.5 percent of TRIA-line DEP in 2006, and 20 percent in 2007.

Methodology The study is undertaken for the top 30 insurers. In order to determine D/S (2006) and D/S (2007) for each company under these two scenarios, we need to know what would be their TRIA-lines DEP and their surpluses in 2005 and 2006, respectively. We base our analysis on the annual percentage change in these two numbers over the three-year period (2002–2004) for each of the thirty companies. We then extrapolate these figures to estimate DEP for TRIA lines and surpluses (S) for 2005 and 2006. Table 20.A presents the result of this analysis. With the deductible increased to 20 percent in 2007, 6 of the 10 largest insurers will have a D/S ratio that will be 20 percent or greater.

Appendix 20.A. Prospective analysis *D/S* ratios for the 30 largest insurers, 2003–2007; D=17.5% DEP in 2006 and 20% DEP in 2007 (all amounts in $ million)

Name	Projected 2006 TRIA line DEP	Projected 2006 surplus	Projected deductible 07	D/S 2007 (20%)	D/S 2006 (17.5%)	D/S 2005 (15%)	D/S 2004 (10%)	D/S 2003 (7%)
AIG	32,663	110,524*	6,533	6%	5%	4%	3%	2%
St. Paul Travelers	20,069	16,907	4,014	24%	21%	17%	12%	8%
Zurich/Farmers	18,170	13,647	3,634	27%	25%	23%	18%	13%
Liberty Mutual	13,101	13,307	2,620	20%	18%	16%	12%	9%
CA State Comp Ins Fund	9,024	3,156	1,805	57%	50%	43%	37%	27%
CNA Insurance	9,024	7,436	1,805	24%	21%	17%	13%	8%
Chubb	9,365	13,608	1,873	14%	14%	14%	11%	9%
Hartford Insurance	9,901	18,006	1,980	11%	10%	10%	7%	5%
ACE INA	7,766	3,963	1,553	39%	37%	33%	22%	18%
Nationwide	5,376	12,159	1,075	9%	8%	7%	4%	3%
TOP 10:								
– Total	134,459	212,713	26,892	Mean ratio	Mean ratio	**Mean ratio**	Mean ratio	**Mean ratio**
– Average	13,446	21,271	2,689	23%	21%	**18%**	14%	**7%**
State Farm	4,898	68,565	980	1%	1%	1%	1%	1%
Allianz of America	3,524	4,626	701	15%	15%	15%	10%	9%
W. R. Berkley	5,510	4,639	1,102	24%	22%	20%	14%	11%
Great American P&C	3,592	3,109	715	23%	21%	20%	13%	10%
FM Global	3,006	6,500	601	9%	10%	11%	10%	8%
XL America	3,560	2,824	712	25%	23%	20%	14%	10%
Cincinnati Insurance	2,600	7,622	520	7%	8%	8%	8%	6%
Berkshire Hathaway	2,941	84,182	588	1%	1%	1%	0%	0%
Auto-Owners	3,032	4,346	606	14%	11%	9%	6%	4%
Safeco	2,560	4,699	512	11%	10%	9%	7%	5%
Progressive Insurance	3,059	6,508	611	9%	8%	6%	3%	2%
Old Republic General	2,501	2,215	500	23%	19%	15%	10%	6%
HDI U.S. Group	1,957	561	391	70%	57%	46%	33%	19%
Allstate Insurance	1,942	20,531	388	2%	2%	1%	1%	1%
Fairfax Financial (USA)	1,299	4,832	260	5%	6%	7%	5%	6%
Markel Corporation	1,990	1,967	398	20%	19%	18%	13%	10%
Arch Capital Group U.S.	3,323	663	665	100%	66%	42%	23%	3%
GE Global	1,478	8,467	296	3%	3%	3%	2%	2%
White Mountains	996	3,181	199	6%	6%	7%	4%	4%
Erie Insurance Group	1,724	3,967	345	9%	7%	6%	4%	3%
TOP 30								
– Total	189,951	456,717	37,982	————	Mean (average) ratios	————		
– Average	6,332	15,224	1,266	20%	18%	15%	11%	6%

* This represents shareholders' equity rather than policyholders' surplus that seems more appropriate here.

NOTES

1. Enders and Sandler 2006.
2. Kunreuther and Michel-Kerjan 2004, 2005a.
3. Government Accounting Office 2002.
4. U.S. Congress 2002; H.R. 3210, The Terrorism Risk Insurance Act of 2002 became Pub. L. 107–297, 116 Stat. 2322.
5. Works related to terrorism insurance in the United States that were published in the last year (other than by the authors or cited elsewhere in the text) include Cummins 2005; Jaffee and Russell 2005; Jaffee 2005; U.S. Department of Treasury 2005; Chalk et al. 2005; Government Accountability Office 2005c; CBO 2005; Brown et al. 2004; and Smetters 2004.
6. This study, undertaken in collaboration with numerous firms and federal bodies, was designed to understand the importance of the insurance infrastructure in our national security agenda. For more details, see the Wharton Risk Management and Decision Processes Center report *TRIA and Beyond* .
7. Analyses in Sections 4, 5, and 7 focus on 2005, which is the most recent year data are available for. It will be possible for us to undertake similar analyses for 2006 later this year.
8. Workers' compensation coverage is mandatory for a large majority of employers in all states other than Texas, where it is optional. Employers must either purchase insurance or qualify to self-insure. Workers' compensation laws do not permit employers or insurers to exclude coverage for worker injuries caused by terrorism, including those caused by acts involving nuclear, biological, and chemical agents.
9. In most instances, this "make available" requirement means that insurers are required to offer a policy without a terrorism exclusion or limitation. Once an insurer has satisfied this offer requirement, the insurer is permitted to offer other terrorism coverage options, such as a policy with a sub-limit.
10. The extension of TRIA based on Senate bill S. 467 directs the President's Working Group on Financial Markets to study long-term availability and affordability of coverage for terrorism losses, including (1) group life and (2) nuclear, biological, chemical, and radiological events. The President's Working Group has to submit a report of its findings to the House Financial Services and Senate Banking Committees by September 30, 2006.
11. After initial discussions in 2002 about the possibility of having life insurance benefit from TRIA protection, Treasury decided not to extend TRIA to group life. It concluded that since insurers had continued to provide group life coverage after 9/11 even though the availability of reinsurance was reduced, there was no need to include this coverage as part of the TRIA program; see Government Accountability Office 2004e. Whether group life will be included in the future will mainly depends on the conclusion of the President's Working Group to be released by the end of September 2006. It is worth noting that the extension of TRIA reduces the spectrum of coverage; for example, TRIEA excludes commercial automobile insurance, burglary and theft insurance, surety insurance, professional liability insurance, and farm owners multiple peril insurance. [D&O insurance is still covered.]
12. In 2003 the deductible under TRIA was 7 percent of direct commercial property and casualty earned premiums the previous year and 10 percent in 2004.
13. The law is ambiguous as to what will happen if the total insurers' outlays are above this market aggregate retention.

14. The TRIA legislation states that "If the aggregate insured losses exceed $100,000,000,000, (i) the Secretary shall not make any payment under this title for any portion of the amount of such losses that exceeds $100,000,000,000; and (ii) no insurer that has met its insurer deductible shall be liable for the payment of any portion of that amount that exceeds $100,000,000,000. Congress shall determine the procedures for and the source of any payments for such excess insured losses." §103(e)(2)(A). TRIEA does not modify this.

15. TRIA, Section 103(e)(8)(C).

16. There is no statement in the legislation or its interpretation that specifically indicates that only the commercial policyholders are taxed. We have discussed this point with insurers and reinsurers. They have assumed that because TRIA applies only to commercial enterprises, the Department of Treasury will tax only commercial entities after a terrorist attack.

17. The analyses undertaken in this chapter are based on data provided by A.M. Best and Risk Management Solutions, discussions with key stakeholders concerned with terrorism insurance, and on responses to a questionnaire designed by the Wharton Risk Center and distributed to insurers by the American Insurance Association and the Property Casualty Insurers Association of America in 2005.

18. The top insurers were those ranked by 2004 TRIA-line direct earned premium (DEP); that is the measure used to calculate insurers' 2005 deductible under TRIA. These insurers all had a total TRIA-line DEP equal to or above $10 million in 2004.

19. The original sample was made of all insurers with a TRIA-line total earned premium higher than $10 million in 2002, 2003, and 2004. Because the number of these insurers varied from one year to the next (establishment of new companies, mergers, bankruptcies, etc.), we selected a consistent sample of 451 insurers over the three years 2002–2004 that we used to determine the evolution of the D/S ratio under TRIA 2003–2005.

20. This information would obviously be highly valuable but is not yet publicly available.

21. The top 30 insurers' TRIA line direct earned premiums in 2004 were about $147 billion out of the $210 billion provided by the top 451 insurers of our sample in that same year.

22. This can be done for the largest companies as changes are "relatively" stable over these three years and consistent with the market. However, extrapolating that for the other 431 smaller insurers does not work well because for most of them there is a huge difference between (2004/2003) and (2003/2002): taking the mean is not likely to reflect what the evolution has really been from 2004 to 2005.

23. When asked the question "Does your company consider scenarios in its catastrophe/exposure management process?" 92 percent of the insurers who responded to the Wharton questionnaire answered "Yes." One company responded to the above question by noting: "Our company uses deterministic terrorist attack scenarios, and the associated Probable Maximum Loss (PML) estimates of these scenarios, to establish and manage exposure concentrations within major metropolitan areas and/or surrounding landmark properties."; see Wharton Risk Center (2005).

24. As illustrated by the following responses to the question: "Do you take estimates of the likelihood of the various known scenarios into account when making underwriting decisions?":

> "Not really. There is little historical data to predict future events."
> "Likelihood is very unpredictable for terrorist acts."
> "Our company does not believe that estimates of the frequency of terrorist attacks are credible at a country, regional or specific property level."; see Wharton Risk Center 2005.

25. For example, 90 percent of the respondents of the Wharton questionnaire discussed above indicated that they were using that type of scenario in evaluating their exposure: 7 of the 10 insurers responding to the questionnaire indicated that they used 5-ton truck bomb scenario and 2 insurers indicated they used a two-ton truck bomb scenario. See Wharton Risk Center 2005.

26. For example, the RAND Corporation has undertaken a detailed study on the impact of aircraft attacks on high-rises in the United States.

27. We are grateful to Andrew Coburn from Risk Management Solutions, who provided us with these data.

28. For the simulation, we assume that the attack would occur at 10 A.M. on a Wednesday – a time when most employees would be in the building.

29. For obvious reasons, we do not reveal here the nature of any of these targets.

30. The insured workers' compensation losses due to the 9/11 attacks were $1.3 billion.

31. For each of the three states on which we focus our analysis, there are major competitive workers' compensation insurers: New York State Insurance Fund, State Compensation Insurance Fund of California and Texas Mutual Insurance Company. The State Compensation Insurance Fund of California covers half of workers' compensation lines in the state while the major insurers in New York and Texas cover 40 percent and 20 percent, respectively, of the total workers' compensation coverage in their states.

32. We assume that insurers have not purchased reinsurance. If they have, then the amount of their loss would be somewhat reduced. We assume a zero deductible for the policyholder on their terrorism insurance policy. This assumption simplifies the analysis but does not affect the qualitative results.

33. The U.S. Department of Treasury has the authority to collect the $2.5 billion through surcharges if it elects to do so, but here we only allow a recoupment for losses between the insurer's payments and the $15 billion market retention in 2005.

34. While still imperfect because we consider each insurer's market share in the location where we simulate the attack, not the real coverage provided by that insurer for the specific target.

35. This assumption represents a very prudent behavior. Indeed, 17 of the top 30 insurers already have a D/S ratio equal or higher than 10 percent in 2005.

36. It is unclear how terrorism insurance will be priced under this scenario. Insurers with low D/S ratios competing for business in urban areas will have an economic incentive to reduce their price as they expand their coverage, because they know they will be only responsible for 10 percent of any loss greater then D – something an insurer with more limited surplus cannot do. As a result, the major providers of coverage will be winnowed down to only a few insurers.

37. For more details on strategies that firms can use to self-insurance against risks, see Doherty 2000.

38. Congressional Budget Office 2005.

39. Notably, the leading reinsurance companies reentered several European markets for terrorism insurance after 9/11. Most of them did so because their exposure was limited and they were all part of a pooled reinsurance tranche of a national program. See Michel-Kerjan and Pedell 2005. This article also discusses programs in Spain (established in 1954) and the United Kingdom (established in 1993; modified in 2003).

40. End of 2004, nearly $35 billion in terrorism coverage capacity was provided by industry captives in the states of Vermont and Hawaii only (the two largest on-shore captive states in the United States – 700 and 150 licensed captives end of 2004, respectively).

For a detailed discussion on captives in the context of terrorism insurance in the United States, see Wharton Risk Center 2005, Chapter 9.

41. This section is based on Kunreuther and Michel-Kerjan 2005a.
42. Congressional Budget Office 2005; Kunreuther and Michel-Kerjan 2005a.
43. Kunreuther 2002.
44. Government Accounting Office 2003a.
45. See OECD 2005.
46. We appreciated discussions on this domestic terrorism issue with James O. Ellis III (Memorial Institute for the Prevention of Terrorism in Oklahoma City), Mark Potok (Southern Poverty Law Center), and with Henry Schuster (CNN).
47. TRIA stipulates that a terrorist attack would be certified as an act of terrorism only if it is perpetrated by "an individual or individuals acting on behalf of any foreign person or foreign interest, as part of an effort to coerce the civilian population of the United States or to influence the policy or affect the conduct of the United States government by coercion."
48. For an insightful analysis of the London bombing in that regard, see the series of articles, "In Europe's Midst" (*Economist* 2005b).
49. For discussions on the nature of these groups and their operation, see Ellis (no date); Hoffman 199; Stern 2003; Potok 2004; Frey 2004; Chalk et al. 2005.
50. Federal Bureau of Investigation 2002.
51. White House 2002.
52. See Kunreuther and Michel-Kerjan 2005b. See also *Economist* 2005a, b.
53. Indeed, other countries have implemented programs quite different from TRIA; see Michel-Kerjan and Pedell 2005. See also OECD 2005.
54. Daniels et al. 2006.
55. The original sample of insurers with a 2004 total TRIA-line direct earned premium above $10 million was made of 466 insurers; but partial data were missing for three of them. As discussed, among these 463 insurers, our 2004 selected sample is made of the 451 insurers that also appear in the 2002 and 2003 data sets.

21

FINANCING CATASTROPHE RISK WITH PUBLIC AND PRIVATE (RE)INSURANCE RESOURCES

Franklin W. Nutter

At both the state and federal levels, the financing of recovery from catastrophic events has received considerable public attention, engendered heated debate, and at times resulted in the legislated adoption of peril-specific approaches. Yet most such public programs and much of the debate have failed to address recovery for damage to critical infrastructures. The insurance and reinsurance sectors have played a vital part in financing recovery from catastrophic events, but much of that financial support has been directed to losses related to damages to property owned by individuals (e.g., homes, autos) and to small commercial businesses. Critical infrastructures, however, have been treated differently from other assets, resources, or businesses. Most critical infrastructure assets have not been insured or found sufficient coverage in the private insurance market. The potential cost of losses to these assets from catastrophic events is either self-insured by government or business, or it goes uninsured or underinsured.

If critical infrastructure is defined to be public facilities (e.g., roads, bridges, public buildings), transportation facilities, energy resources and facilities, and networks (e.g., computer, financial), a public–private partnership will be needed to address recovery needs. Existing state and federal catastrophe financing programs and the recent debates surrounding them shed considerable light on potential options for a public–private partnership and present major considerations applicable to the exposure of critical infrastructure to catastrophic damage. At the end of the day, at least part of the solution will be found in the reinsurance industry.

Often described as "insurance for insurance companies," reinsurance is a sophisticated transaction by which one insurer indemnifies another insurer against all or part of a loss. Reinsurers provide protection for insurers in the case of large, infrequent, and extremely severe catastrophe losses. The fundamental objective of insurance – to spread the risk of loss – is thereby enhanced by the insurers' abilities to spread that risk through reinsurance.

The key reasons a primary company purchases reinsurance are (1) to limit liability of specific risk, (2) to stabilize losses, (3) to protect against large losses, and (4) to increase capacity so they can write more policies. Each insurer determines the degree to which it will utilize reinsurance for one or all of these purposes after assessing its own exposure to losses and its own capital resources.

REINSURANCE AND CATASTROPHES

Primary insurers, which provide coverage directly to individuals and businesses, customarily retain most of the insured exposure for catastrophic risk. Without adequate reinsurance for catastrophic losses, an insurer would either retain on its own account the insured exposure consistent with its appetite for large losses, or refuse to underwrite coverage that it deemed too risky or that exceeds its risk capital profile.

In the aggregate, nearly one-half of premiums ceded to reinsurers on U.S. risks goes to reinsurers based entirely outside the United States. Another 25 percent of the U.S. market belongs to the U.S. subsidiaries of reinsurers headquartered outside the United States. The capital base of the 30 U.S.-based reinsurers approximates $68 billion, supporting an annual premium volume of $30 billion. The global reinsurance market has a premium volume of approximately $164 billion, underwriting risks throughout the global economy.

Reinsurance has played a significant financing role in virtually all major catastrophes in the United States over the past century. For example, current estimates for insured losses arising from 2005 hurricanes Katrina, Wilma, and Rita range from $60 billion to $80 billion. Approximately one-half of this total will ultimately be paid by reinsurers. Insurance Information Institute figures reflect that Hurricane Andrew, which had been the costliest natural disaster in U.S. history before Hurricane Katrina, caused $22.3 billion in insured damage.[1] The reinsurance industry paid 25 percent ($5.6 billion) of the total for that event. With respect to Hurricane Hugo in 1989, the total insured loss was $6.6 billion; reinsurers paid roughly one-third ($2.3 billion). The terrorist attacks of September 11, 2001, cost insurers $31.7 billion; the reinsurance industry paid approximately two-thirds ($20.7 billion) of this amount.[2] In the case of the four hurricanes that hit Florida in 2004, the industry paid approximately $22 billion. Approximately 20 percent of this total was funded by reinsurers; another 11 percent was paid through the state-sponsored catastrophe reinsurance fund (discussed later in this chapter).

Although reinsurers assume the risk of a significant portion of insurance companies' catastrophe losses, the determination of whether to reinsure a risk is made by each insurer. Several of the largest national personal line insurers, for example, purchase very little, if any, reinsurance, because their capital and surplus resources are large enough to retain risk and absorb shock losses. In addition, they have significant expertise in evaluating their catastrophe risk and spreading it among a large policyholder base. On the other hand, a smaller or regional insurer, or a self-insurer, may rely more heavily on reinsurance to spread its risk of loss. No insurer should (or would want to) expose its entire capital base to the threat of a single catastrophe or an accumulation of catastrophes. In addition, insurers have a responsibility to stockholders (or, in the case of mutual insurers, policyholders) to see that their capital provides an adequate return on equity and is not exposed to a risk of ruin from catastrophes.

An insurer's capital base together with its reinsurance program serves as a buffer against infrequent yet severe events. The capital base over time is a function of a company's retained earnings, profitability, investment performance, and investor support. A shift in any of these may affect a company's reinsurance purchase decision. However, catastrophic reinsurance needs are more commonly affected by satisfactory rate adequacy at the consumer level and concerns by the insurer about geographical concentration of catastrophic risk.[3]

EFFECTS OF A MEGA-CATASTROPHE

A fundamental problem facing insurers and their policyholders is the threat of a mega-catastrophe that exceeds the committed resources of the insurance and reinsurance markets. A catastrophe that causes losses that exceed 20 percent of the aggregate capital of the industry, for example, would likely have a significant negative effect on the solvency of some companies and their ability to provide coverage going forward.

According to the National Association of Insurance Commissioners, U.S. insurance and reinsurance industry capital at the end of 2005 was approximately $420 billion. Reinsurance Association of America data indicate that the capital for the U.S. reinsurance industry for 2005 was $68 billion. Both capital amounts reflect a robust industry relative to historical norms.

Based on the combined U.S. industry capital insurance and reinsurance, a loss from a catastrophic event or from a series of events of 20 percent of capital would cost $80 billion – exceeding by nearly 300 percent the insured losses from 9/11, but approximating the high end of the loss range for the

2005 hurricanes. Industry experts generally believe that repeated losses of this magnitude could cause a significant number of insurer insolvencies and restrict access to insurance for consumers within and outside the affected loss area. Catastrophic loss models for acts of terrorism in a major city or a natural disaster affecting a large metropolitan area in California, Florida, or the East Coast do project losses at or exceeding this number. Such a series of catastrophes would potentially disrupt the normal functioning of the insurance market, not only for property insurance but also for other types of coverage. Experience suggests, and financial and insurance regulators would likely require, that following such an event insurers restrict writing coverages consistent with the negative impact on their capital base.

At the federal level, a safety net providing protection for insurers above which they cannot absorb catastrophe losses has often been advocated. The Terrorism Risk Insurance Act of 2002 is a successful example of just such a program (for detailed discussions of the act and its 2005 extension, see Chapters 19 and 20).

PREPARING FOR A MEGA-CATASTROPHE

To improve insurance affordability and availability of coverage, and to be better positioned financially for the losses of a mega-catastrophe, insurers have often advocated solutions based on changes to insurance rates, deductibles, building codes, and the federal backstop. For example, insurers assert that consumers who live in catastrophe-prone areas should pay a premium for insurance in direct relationship to that risk, rather than a premium that blends catastrophe-prone risks with less-severe exposures or with less catastrophe-prone geographic areas. In conjunction with risk-based rates, insurers would offer premium incentives for mitigation measures taken by policyholders. Lacking the authority of government, insurers cannot require mitigation; yet insurance can be used to provide financial incentives for mitigation in conjunction with rates based on catastrophe exposure.

Experimentation with deductible programs is frequently cited as a key component to ensure availability of insurance for consumers in catastrophe-prone areas. For example, earthquake programs have long been written with deductibles of 2, 5, or 10 percent of policy limits. Wind policies have typically offered a flat or fixed deductible. Many insurers today believe that creation of new deductible programs will provide affordable coverage with an incentive for consumers to take steps to mitigate property loss. Many states have taken action to approve such deductible programs.

Insurers also advocate that states and communities working with the federal government should institute pre-disaster mitigation programs, including appropriate building codes and mandatory hazard reduction measures.[4]

Hurricane Andrew emphasized the importance of building code enforcement in 1992. Dade County, Florida, experience prior to the hurricane indicates that little or no enforcement or compliance with building codes existed. The result was billions of dollars in additional damage. Subsequent hurricane experience in Florida validates damage reduction due to enforced building code improvements.

THE ROLE OF STATE GOVERNMENTS

States generally view their role as one of assuring affordable access to insurance protection for consumers. Because of the exposure to hurricanes in the coastal United States, as well as flood, tornado, and well-known earthquake exposure in California and other states, nearly every state employs a combination of mitigation, insurance coverage mandates, and insurance market mechanisms to address insurance availability for individual consumers. Most state initiatives, however, do not address commercial entities or critical infrastructures – private or public – because they either are not insured in the private market or are deemed insurance markets for sophisticated buyers of insurance coverage. Insurance regulatory coverage and rate approvals generally remain in place for personal lines (automobile and homeowners coverages) as a means to require insurers to provide coverage and guarantee insurance at rates deemed affordable in the context of exposure analysis. In addition, hurricane-exposed states have mechanisms for homeowners who cannot find coverage in the voluntary insurance market. Licensed insurers are required to provide insurance coverage for those deemed high risk relative to regulatory-approved premiums. By regulating rates that insurers may charge consumers, in combination with the use of residual, high risk, or "involuntary" market mechanisms (e.g., state funds or pools), these states are financing catastrophe recovery by appropriating the resources of private insurance capital. This combination of regulatory action and private capital often raises tension over the adequacy of insurance rates in catastrophe-prone areas and the appropriation of private capital to address the public's exposure to catastrophe.

Following Hurricanes Andrew (Florida, 1992) and Iniki (Hawaii, 1992) and the Northridge earthquake (California, 1994), Florida, Hawaii, and California each enacted legislation to create a state fund to finance catastrophe risk for consumers. Each state created a mechanism reflecting its own unique market environment and the state's role in addressing catastrophe risk. For example, the Hawaii fund provided direct hurricane risk insurance to the public. After the initial concern over potential hurricane losses was more fully assessed and an adjustment in insurance rates implemented, the private market has since returned, and the Hawaii state fund no longer provides insurance.

The Florida fund is a state-created and administered facility providing rein-surance capacity to insurers. Insurers may voluntarily purchase reinsurance from the state fund or from the private reinsurance market. In the event of a loss exceeding its retained earnings and bonding authority, Florida's fund is authorized to assess on a statewide basis most policyholders for the losses in the property lines. The Florida fund was called on in 2004 to pay reinsurance claims of $3.75 billion for four hurricanes that caused $21.7 billion in total insured loss. In 2005, the fund sustained losses approximating $2.6 billion and exhausted its cash position.

As with the Hawaii fund, the California Earthquake Authority provides earthquake coverage directly to the public. It was originally capitalized by contributions from insurers and funded by premiums paid by consumers. The fund purchases private reinsurance and has taxing and bonding authority as a quasi-state agency. It has not yet been called upon to pay claims and therefore remains untested.

Although most other states have been reluctant to create similar catastro-phe funds, New York, South Carolina, Georgia, Louisiana, Texas, Maryland, Virginia, and New Jersey have discussed it. Efforts to establish state funds in these states have so far failed, largely because insurers in the states have sought to retain private markets rather than promote a competitive government agency, and the states have feared exposing state coffers to catastrophic losses. These states have instead preferred polices of hazard mitigation, building codes, and flexibility in insurance, rates, and coverage. Legislators have also expressed concerns about the exposure of state treasuries to catastrophe risk and poten-tial assessments or taxes for funding shortfalls. In these states, consumers rely on private insurance coverage, opting to retain the catastrophe risk without adequate coverage or by applying deductibles, and, to some degree, federal financial assistance. In none of the states has financing for the recovery of critical infrastructure been enacted.

PROTECTING THE INSURANCE INFRASTRUCTURE: EXAMPLES OF U.S. PUBLIC–PRIVATE PARTNERSHIPS

Exposure in the United States to natural and human-caused catastrophes has been widely documented. However, the events of 9/11 and the hurricane losses of 2004 and 2005 exposed the U.S. insurance industry to a previously unknown level of calamity. Although insurers have successfully absorbed catas-trophe losses in the past, today's catastrophe loss model projections greatly challenge the industry's resources to absorb some high end projected loss events. Despite this potential problem, the role of government and its relationship to the private sector in financing such potential catastrophes still lacks a clear long-term policy direction. Federal policy with regard to financing recovery for catastrophes has largely been limited to response and recovery efforts funded by taxpayers or, in the case of the families of the victims of the 9/11 terrorist attacks, direct taxpayer-funded compensation, similar to a life insurance payout. For example, over the past 15 years, the Federal Emergency Management Agency has provided victims of roughly 650 declared catastrophes with immediate assistance, housing, and low-interest grants and loans. Disaster assistance in these events totals approximately $45 billion.

The future of insurance for public or private infrastructure cannot lie wholly within the responsibility of the federal government or the private sector. Rather, resolution of the issue may need to rely on public–private partnerships modeled after existing programs for other risks.

INSURANCE AGAINST FLOOD DAMAGE

The National Flood Insurance Program was adopted in 1968 to provide government insurance coverage to residential and small commercial risks. The program operates much like an insurance company with some limited subsidization of risk premium, but the program also has a stated goal of reducing disaster assistance by requiring those at risk for flooding to bear the cost of insurance and by requiring participating communities to adopt building codes with flood hazard reduction features. The financial backing of the federal government does permit the program access to below-market federal funds in the event it cannot meet liquidity needs. As a result of the hurricane losses of 2005, the program has borrowed $18.5 billion to cover insured losses of $23 billion, a sum exceeding the total program losses from all prior years. The program currently insures 4.6 million homes and businesses and has 20,000 participating communities, all of which are required to adopt flood hazard mitigation building codes and land-use restrictions as a basis for participation in the program. No insurance coverage for critical infrastructure (defined as utilities, public infrastructures, large commercial operations, and transportation and energy resources and facilities) is authorized under the program.

INSURANCE FOR CATASTROPHIC NUCLEAR ACCIDENTS

The Price–Anderson Act of 1957 is a public–private approach for mitigating commercial nuclear risk. The act limits the total liability of individual nuclear reactor operators for any accident. First, operators must obtain the maximum amount of private insurance available, which is currently about $200 million per reactor per accident. In the event of an accident at any single reactor that results in losses exceeding $200 million, all operators of commercial nuclear power reactors would be required to provide additional protection by paying into a secondary insurance fund. All operators would be required to pay as much as $10 million annually for nine years to fully fund the secondary fund.

If an accident involves damages that exceed the amount in the secondary insurance fund, the government is not explicitly required to fund the balance. Rather, Price–Anderson commits Congress to investigate the accident and to take whatever action it deems necessary. This action could include appropriating funds or requiring the nuclear industry to provide additional funding to satisfy remaining claims. Price–Anderson is viewed favorably by both commercial nuclear facility operators and public officials. Energy legislation in 2005 contained a 20-year extension applicable to new reactor facilities.

INSURANCE AGAINST URBAN RIOTS AND CIVIL DISORDER

While not specifically targeted at catastrophes, the National Insurance Development Program was established in 1968 to ensure the availability and affordability of fire, crime, and other property insurance to residential and commercial owners located in high-risk urban areas. The program responded to the urban riots and civil disorders of the 1960s, when many of America's cities suffered major property losses. It was designed to preserve businesses in the riot-stricken areas.

The program encouraged state insurance regulators and the industry to develop and carry out programs to make property coverage more readily available in inner cities. Under this program, federal reinsurance was made available to property insurance companies operating in states that voluntarily adopted Fair Access to Insurance Requirements Plans, which made insurance coverage available to urban property owners. Insurers were required to retain a small portion of the liability. Insurers could transfer most of the remaining risk by making a premium payment to the federal government, which then assumed the remaining liability. The program also included a requirement that states share in program losses with the federal government – to keep states from setting property insurance premiums too low. No coverage for critical infrastructure was provided.

As with most other government insurance programs, the National Insurance Development Program targeted a specific risk deemed uninsurable in the context of contemporary insurance market conditions. Once the perceived risk of urban riots subsided and insurance markets provided coverage, the program was not extended by Congress.

RECENT INITIATIVES INVOLVING PUBLIC–PRIVATE RISK SHARING

Segments of the insurance industry over the past 10 years have repeatedly sought the involvement of the federal government in financing catastrophe risk. Even before Hurricane Andrew, and as recently as the events of 9/11 and the hurricane losses of 2005, segments of the industry have promoted various approaches to secure federal backing of private-sector insurance coverage. Because the initiatives have been driven by homeowners and small commercial property insurance market problems, and because critical infrastructure is generally self insured or consists of government facilities, critical infrastructure has not been specifically addressed in any proposal. The proposals reflect four approaches: government-sponsored enterprise, federally backed reinsurer of state catastrophe funds, federal auctions of catastrophe bonds, and catastrophe reserves and tax shelters.

Early initiatives focused on the creation of a government-sponsored enterprise that would be privately managed but would have the backing of the federal government. The proposal involved federal loans to a government-sponsored corporation in addition to favorable tax treatment. Although later efforts expanded the authority to include insurance to consumers as well, the corporation would have been authorized to provide reinsurance to insurers. The principal resistance to the concept was the concern that insurers would bear no direct risk to their own insurance portfolio and therefore would have little incentive to underwrite and price coverage appropriately. Even suggestions to require the corporation and insurers to share the losses were met with opposition from those viewing a government-sponsored enterprise as a subsidy to insurers that could not be justified by the uncertain promise of more affordable or available insurance for catastrophe exposure. This concept was also opposed by private market advocates opposed to government programs where private markets are already providing insurance coverage.

Another proposal for a public–private partnership was a proposal for a federally backed reinsurer of state catastrophe funds. Opponents of this approach noted that state funds had been rejected by many states and that such funds exposed the federal government to actions by the states regarding insurance rates and coverage with no federal regulatory authority over state action. A proposed limited federal regulatory role over insurance created conflicts among those favoring the current system of state regulation and those wishing to expand federal oversight.

A proposal for a federal auction of catastrophe bonds provided for the federal government to auction reinsurance catastrophe contracts to qualified bidders. The government could control and limit its exposure, the industry would have additional reinsurance protection, and taxpayers would not subsidize the risk. Such contracts could be divisible and resold on a secondary market. Advocates of the proposal thought that this action would stimulate capital market products that would provide additional catastrophe capacity. State funds, private investors, and insurers could bid on the contracts. The approach, however, fell victim to a lack of insurance industry consensus. Reinsurers argued that such a program was attractive if the federal contracts attached at a point above private-sector capacity. Other insurers argued that the attachment point should be low ($2 billion of insured loss) to more easily access government reinsurance capacity.[5] The proposal saw limited Congressional attention.

Some have promoted allowing insurers to establish catastrophe reserves that would accumulate funds tax-free or tax-deferred for future catastrophe events. Current accounting and tax policy do not permit such reserves. While proponents argue that offshore insurers benefit from such reserves, tax and accounting professionals express concern over the potential misuse of such tax advantages for events that are unknown and perhaps unknowable. Similar proposals have been made to allow state-sanctioned special purpose reinsurers to be tax exempt. These special-purpose reinsurance vehicles would effectively be corporate accounts, not operating entities. Proponents argue that offshore tax havens have used these vehicles to create additional catastrophe capacity. Congress has not addressed these proposals, largely over concerns relating to tax shelters for corporate insurers and buyers.

THE 9/11 TERRORIST ATTACKS

Lacking policy exclusions for terrorism, the insured losses from the 9/11 terrorist acts were covered by many traditional insurance lines (e.g., property, business interruption, workers' compensation). The losses also fell within the same catastrophe coverages in reinsurance contracts as natural catastrophes. At the time, no specific underwriting for acts of terrorism had occurred nor had reinsurance contract provisions for or exclusions of terrorism been considered.

The insurance industry sought no federal assistance or reimbursement for losses from the 9/11 terrorist attacks. However, as had been the case prior to the establishment of several other federal programs aimed at specific risks mentioned previously, insurers approached the federal government for assistance on future insured coverages for terrorism. The industry proposed the creation of a pool of insurers, assisted by the federal government in the role of reinsurer, possibly along with a liquidity mechanism such as a letter of credit. The concept was modeled after the United Kingdom's successful Pool Re, which was triggered as a result of the London Terrorist Act of July 2005 and which provides capacity limited to acts of terrorism to U.K. insurers. While the insurer pool concept received near unanimous support from the industry, the Bush administration expressed concern over the creation of a federally backed monopolistic fund that it perceived would deter the development of a private market for terrorism insurance. The Administration supported a different federal role, however, and proposed a program whereby insurers and the government would co-insure losses for acts of terrorism, with the government picking up the vast majority of the exposure. This proposal differed from the industry's pool concept in that individual insurers, rather than a pool of insurers, would provide coverage. The proposal was criticized by many in Congress, who believed that the insurance industry must first bear some significant loss before any federal role would apply and that insurers must pay a premium for the government share.

Eventually Congress enacted the Terrorism Risk Insurance Act of 2002, providing a public–private partnership to employ a level of private insurance coverage backed by a federal reinsurance program. The federal program is limited to commercial insurance coverages. Except for the insurance coverage issued by insurers for the commercial sector (e.g., banks, commercial real estate), the program does not directly target critical private or public infrastructure. It does cover critical infrastructure to the extent that infrastructure is insured by private insurers or insurance captives created by corporations or groups of corporations. The act does not cover self-insured programs related to critical infrastructure.

LESSONS LEARNED AND FINAL THOUGHTS

A number of conclusions can be drawn from the successful and unsuccessful initiatives and debates in the last few years over the role of state or federal government in financing catastrophe losses. First, state and federal solutions tailored to specific issues or events (e.g., terrorism, hurricanes, earthquakes) are better received than broad, untargeted financing proposals. A legislated program for addressing specific natural or human-caused catastrophes or terrorism losses has more political traction than proposals for financing future unspecified events, for example.

In addition, experience with efforts to enact catastrophe-related legislation suggests that tax exemptions or tax offsets for insurers to finance catastrophe exposure have limited appeal to legislators. Clearly, any proposal that gives insurers tax breaks has a higher threshold to achieve in light of the government's own fiscal issues. Because of their tax exempt status, public entities and subsequently the public infrastructure they represent do not benefit from tax-driven proposals. Tax-driven proposals therefore do not seem to be viable options for addressing financial recovery from a catastrophic event affecting public infrastructure.

Furthermore, legislative history suggests that with respect to catastrophe exposure for which insurers have previously been providing coverage (e.g., hurricanes), a risk-bearing role for insurers in any government sponsored, backed, or funded program will be politically essential. Governments (state and federal) have shown little interest in fully taking on a risk being provided to some degree in the private market. Terrorism risk, for example, must be retained by insurers under TRIA, although it was not expressly covered or underwritten prior to 9/11.

Moreover, the federal government has been willing to step in if a government nexus clearly exists (e.g., terrorism), but it prefers a role that entails a limited timeframe, for limited purposes, and with capped funding obligations. The government strongly prefers a program that stimulates or facilitates a private market in the foreseeable future rather than a long-term government program. The government also prefers to be a backstop to insurers rather than to have any role directly related to consumers. In the case of infrastructure, this preference may necessitate a layer of coverage provided by the public or private entities responsible for their management or owned by them outright. Although the Federal Terrorism Risk Insurance Act preempted state insurance regulation to some degree, the federal government has little appetite to regulate insurers for solvency, insurance coverage, or rates.

Another point to consider is that the relationship between any federal (re)insurance program and state regulation of insurers is a critical issue that requires balancing many interests. Any insurance program that addresses infrastructure must balance the competing perspectives of the private sector (potentially unlimited risk but limited capital) and the public sector (regulatory priorities for financial oversight and solvency regulation).

Insurers, for their part, generally oppose government loans and prefer an insurance or reinsurance program that maintains the financial integrity of their balance sheets.

Finally, insurance or financing of catastrophe risk for critical infrastructure has received scant attention during the debates about proposed state or federal government programs. This oversight may be because the risk is not fully understood or defined, Congress has chosen not to address it, the advocates have been overlooked, or, most likely, the legislative initiatives have been directed at specific consumer-related catastrophic exposures deemed underserved by the traditional insurance market. Although existing programs and recent proposals for a public–private role in financing catastrophe recovery have not addressed critical infrastructure, they may serve as prototypes for establishing such a program.

Only the Price–Anderson Act, which provides insurance for nuclear facilities, directly relates to critical infrastructure. As a federally backed pool above private insurance market capacity, it represents a viable prototype for insuring critical infrastructure. As such, it reflects one of the most important lessons from the insurance debates: any new program needs to be specific to a type of risk or peril.

It is unclear (and perhaps doubtful) whether Congress would enact a program broadly covering critical infrastructure. To limit its exposure, Congress would likely require that any such program be defined narrowly (e.g., financial networks or energy transportation systems). Another option may be to define the insured risk more broadly, but by name, and limit the definition of the peril (e.g., acts of terrorism). Once these issues are resolved, the next step would necessitate an evaluation of the private sector's appetite for risk bearing. In the current political environment, a private-sector risk-bearing role that would be required to expand over time would be deemed essential to securing the government's risk-bearing participation. The case for a public role in financing recovery for catastrophe loss to critical infrastructure must be based on an assumption that private insurance markets or self-insured private or public entities have a financial stake in protecting the infrastructure and in financing its recovery.

NOTES

1. All figures in this section are expressed in 2005 dollars; for all damage amounts in this section, see Insurance Information Institute (undated; figures inflated from 2004 to 2005 dollars using the Consumer Price Index Inflation Calculator, http://data.bls.gov/cgi-bin/cpicalc.pl).
2. In the case of the event of September 11, reinsurers paid losses based on the terms of catastrophe contracts which did not specify terrorism coverage; therefore losses clearly exceeded coverage expectation. These coverages have subsequently been rewritten to address terrorism exposure specifically and moderate exposure to terrorism losses.
3. "Satisfactory rate adequacy" means that the consumers are actually being charged a premium that reflects the catastrophe exposure that they have – as distinguished from a rate that is set in the political process that understates the true "risk-based" premium.
4. See Kunreuther and Michel-Kerjan 2005b.
5. In light of the $32 billion of insured loss from 9/11 and the hurricane losses in 2005, and with no federal program in place, the issue of the industry's ability to bear insured losses from catastrophes may have been resolved in favor of a high attachment point for any federal program. The Federal Terrorism Risk Insurance Program also requires insurance company retention of 15 percent of commercial premiums before federal reinsurance attaches.

PART VI

Building Trust

22

PUBLIC–PRIVATE COLLABORATION ON A NATIONAL AND INTERNATIONAL SCALE

Lewis M. Branscomb and Erwann O. Michel-Kerjan

> *"Trust dies but mistrust blossoms."*
>   – Sophocles (497–406/5 B.C.)

> *"Emergency management officials should not be exchanging business cards during a crisis."*
>   – Senator Susan Collins, March 15, 2006

The challenges of the protection of critical services cannot be accomplished by government alone, despite responsibility for public security and safety. Nor can industry, which owns or operates most of the critical infrastructure, be expected to protect it alone. Given the emergence of a larger threat spectrum, combined with the growing globalization of economic activities, nations cannot expect to be successful without effective cooperation among each other. The world grows smaller as its components become more interdependent. How societies learn to work collectively to achieve the goal of safety and security and to sustain it in the long term is thus of prime importance. This collective approach would require, at a minimum, several mutual understandings and the trust to make them work. There is sensitive information to be shared – proprietary information from firms, intelligence information from government – shared accountability and responsibility to be negotiated, costs to be allocated, and benefits to be divided up, to name a few.

Creating and developing collective actions among commercial and government institutions is not an easy task. The habits and cultures and the legal, political, and financial power among a complex mosaic of stakeholders differ in many ways. This leads us to an essential element of all enduring and successful partnerships: the necessity for building trust between the parties. Part VI addresses three complementary elements of this problem: (1) the necessity (and difficulty) of sharing sensitive information, addressed by Daniel B. Prieto; (2) the principles that govern the allocation of responsibilities between private sector and government for sharing of risks, discussed in the chapter by John D. Donahue and Richard J. Zeckhauser; and (3) a framework for senior executives on how strategic partnerships within a specific industry can be developed internationally, proposed by Patrick Lagadec and Erwann O. Michel-Kerjan.

THE PROBLEM OF TRUST

Overcoming differences among competing firms in a particular infrastructure service industry, between members of that industry and their customers, and especially between public and private organizations is difficult and time-consuming. It is easiest to find common ground with someone in the same field, with the same points of reference, the same language and culture. It is more difficult (and takes longer) for a decision maker to built trust between partners who may have opposing interests and with whom the decision maker has little experience. But it will take even more time and effort to establish that trust when the circumstance that tests whether trust was merited has not yet been experienced by either party. Finally, and especially because governments must be participants in the trust relationship, the fact that many firms providing infrastructure services are foreign-owned, and that many of those services are linked across national boundaries, makes the problem more difficult still.

To make matters worse, the need for trust is not limited to assuring all parties that each will live up to its obligations when the crisis comes, because the very chaos created in a disaster like Hurricane Katrina or the September 11, 2001, terrorist attacks requires innovating on the spot, making important decisions amidst a high degree of uncertainty, and readjusting roles of the parties when the details of catastrophe are better known and available resources can be redeployed.

Internal tension within an organization, national and international competition within an industry, highly turbulent political processes during election years, and the image of a nation abroad are just a few of the elements that will put pressure on decision makers, all of whom have different agendas. These aspects of decision making, however, should not be ignored, but rather recognized as possible limitations to the establishment of collective actions, and reconciled to some extent in order to foster actions resulting in mutual benefit.

Efforts to integrate the private sector into domestic preparedness programs after 9/11 is taking a long time and creates strong concerns on both sides because of historical precedents, cost concerns, and legal impediments. For example, there were significant conflicts among political authorities during and after Hurricane Katrina, and also major difficulties experienced by private firms, including inadequate security and obstacles in gaining access to facilities requiring repair in affected areas.[1]

Trust is fragile.[2] Crisis episodes (perhaps more than any other situation), which are likely to arise from large-scale catastrophes, can destroy trust very easily. And when trust built over long-term relationships is lost, it is extremely difficult to restore. The implementation of "rapid reflection forces" based on a limited number of key decision makers who have learned to work together, as introduced in Chapter 25, is an innovative solution for maintaining a minimal level of trust and succeeding collectively. As Senator Susan Collins said, "emergency management officials should not be exchanging business cards during a crisis."[3]

BUILDING TRUST THROUGH INFORMATION SHARING

When it comes to collective action, who has information on what, and who does not have that information, is critical.[4] Information sharing thus becomes a critically important prerequisite for trust. Two types of information must be shared: information on prevention, mitigation, and recovery operations (including all the important infrastructure providers); and information about the risks and potential consequences (including intelligence information when available).

We start with operational information. In the United States, the private sector, which operates most of the critical services, will likely have much more information than the different levels of government on the capabilities of their own infrastructure firms. These firms will also be most knowledgeable on the efforts to make them more robust and resilient, and they will have a better collection of information about customer firms' needs and characteristics. However, none of these commercial enterprises would have all the information it needs to be best prepared: *each stakeholder's information is incomplete.* Only collective action to share data can make the information available to all partnering firms more complete. But even this partial information is seen – often rightly so – as highly valuable. As a result, everyone tends to keep it to themselves and protect their access to it.

Recently, there has been increasing recognition of the necessity of sharing information within specific critical sectors. As Daniel Prieto discusses in Chapter 23, the 1999-initiated national effort by leading firms in several critical sectors to establish Information Sharing and Analysis Centers (ISACs) has played an important role in the development of collective action, shared cost, and better understanding of emerging threats and best practices. Still, we are far from a trusted institutional framework that would enable business partners to exchange complementary sensitive data with one another and with government.

There are several reasons why private companies are reluctant to share information. First, proprietary information is the essence of competitive advantage. Second, most firms have confidentiality agreements with their customers not to reveal information about who they are, what their buying behavior is, among other attributes. Releasing that information, even only in part and in limited context, could not only compromise a firm's image, but could also send them to court (see below). Indeed, firms are reluctant to disclose information about their vulnerabilities for fear of disturbing customers dependent on them, for fear of exposing themselves to civil damage suits for negligence in the future, and for fear of inviting unwanted government regulation. Finally, although government officials say the sharing of security information has not so far raised substantive anti-trust problems, it is hard to know to what extent that concern lingers in the minds of corporate lawyers so long as anti-trust exemptions are not formally provided.

One possible solution would be the creation and implementation of trusted information sharing platforms with government/industry compliance auditing (limiting anti-trust issues). A third party would collect a set of partial information from a number of different organizations, assemble the dataset for all partners (so-called data fusion), and provide access to the global result or pre-specified metrics, without revealing the origin of the information. If the number of partners is large enough, each of them will know its own original dataset and final metrics, but will not be able to reconcile the sources and nature of other data provided by other partners (limiting competition issues).

This form of sharing raises important questions: who will assure the protection of these data? Who will pay, in the event of a breach in the system? One possibility would be to create an insurance market to cover such information breaches. After all, insurers cover against business interruptions and product recalls. Insurers could cover against the economic consequences of data loss in a more systematic way than what they do today. The insurance policy would be defined with very specific characteristics (limit of reimbursement, conditions under which the trusted platform fails to protect the information, potential commercial or malevolent use of lost data). Development of such products is currently in the research phase.

The second source of information relates to the risk itself. As discussed earlier in this book, terrorism and natural hazards present an important difference regarding information sharing. When terrorism threats are known to government agencies, they are likely to keep some information secret for national security reasons. Some of that information could be made public several years after special services gathered it, as happened a few years ago when the government issued warning in New York City based on threat warning collected several years before. Sharing of classified information, which comprises most of the intelligence about terrorist activities and capabilities, requires that infrastructure service firms have people with security clearance to receive it. Some progress in this direction has been made, but it is slow and limited in its coverage.

Information sharing among government entities is not less challenging. Indeed, assuming that information circulates easily from one government agency to another – or even within one agency among different levels of decision makers – is simply naive. Permanent tension between different agencies, even those designed to work toward the same goal, has led to agencies withholding important information. This practice contributed to the failure to intercept terrorists who hijacked the planes on 9/11.[5]

THE PROTECTION OF PRIVACY

The emphasis given by the 2004 National Commission on Terrorist Attacks Upon the United States[6] to the importance of information sharing among agencies, and evident need for sharing between public and private sector, leads one to ask how far sharing should go. From the critical infrastructure firms' perspective, the answer is: "only as far as my proprietary information and ability to compete are preserved." From the government sector, the need for sharing is limited by the need to protect intelligence information from disclosure to terrorists. But intelligence services themselves are as eager to acquire information from telecommunicating and Internet service providers, Internet browser service providers, financial services, libraries, and others, as they are reluctant to share it with other agencies of the government. Thus, the collection and analysis of masses of commercial and government data is the subject of political debate over the balance between the prevention of terrorism and the protection of civil liberties.

The passage of the controversial U.S. Patriot Act just 45 days after the 9/11 attacks, later revised and renewed at the beginning of 2006, raises critical questions regarding the scope of government empowerment in accessing private information in the interest of security. On the other hand, 9/11 has revealed a brand-new world of threats that calls for changes at home and abroad. Work by Harvard colleagues Philip Heymann and Juliette Kayyem has attempted to address these issues in a systematic way and has tried to reconcile the argument for expanded domestic intelligence powers with the need to preserve the anonymity of citizen communications and other benign activities. Heyman and Kayyem show that it is possible to propose new rules and government practices that would simultaneously address national security, democratic liberties at home, legal and human rights abroad, and broader foreign policy in the interest of the United States today and in the longer run. As they argue, "it is not possible to have minimal risk from terrorism and absolutely maximally protected freedoms, but it is possible to preserve 90 percent of what concerns each camp."[7]

Finding the right balance will certainly be a challenging exercise. It is also likely to evolve over time, depending on whether new attacks are perpetrated, and where. The trust that citizens have in their elected government is critical to assuring the capacity of a country to deal with the emerging nature of disasters it faces. The trust that customers have in the company that provides them with critical services and assures that personal information is not revealed is also critical.

How firms can comply with new legislation allowing local, state, and federal organizations to access personal data, and at the same time respond to the desire of customers for their information not to be revealed in a systematic way is already challenging. This conflict is illustrated by a recent example of plaintiffs going to court against airlines because of their sharing data about passenger travel with the federal government.[8] The Internet browser Google's initial reluctance to share search data with government – a conflict subsequently resolved by Google's sharing a much smaller random sample of data than was initially requested – has raised these questions again.

These Google and airline passenger examples are very different, both in terms of the kinds of shared – or to be shared – private data and government's goal in asking for access to these two sets of data. But generally speaking, it is prudent to say that today there is no clear political consensus and recognized legislative status on how to manage these information-sharing policies, as illustrated by the number of incidents taken to the courts to settle. As courts are all over the map on this issue, case-by-case judgments going in multiple directions will make decision making even more challenging. Indeed, it increases uncertainty related to legal and financial risks associated with sharing data. Congress, in consultation with federal bodies, industry representatives, and privacy protection groups, should put in place a better-understood statutory framework of data collection and use.

WHO SHOULD DO WHAT? THE RATIONAL ASSIGNMENT OF ROLES TO GOVERNMENT AND THE PRIVATE SECTOR

In Chapter 24, John Donahue and Richard Zeckhauser explore the problem of defining the roles for public and private sectors, noting that the United States has been experimenting widely with many new roles for both. Services normally under public management live side by side with services "outsourced" to contractors. But in the case of risk management, neither party can easily acquire all the needed information, resources, and incentives. Donahue and Zeckhauser explore the concept of "collaborative governance," in which both parties share in the decisions that must be made, the information on which those decisions rest, and the resources to accomplish the mission, along with the benefits from it. Their analysis of security externalities, a concept we introduce in Chapter 1, reveals that in most cases there are multiple stakeholders, with the government representing the aggregate interests of the largest number of affected publics, each of which has a proportionately smaller interest. The lack of information renders the logical negotiation of roles and responsibilities very difficult. Notwithstanding the uncertainties, however, the authors suggest a series of six steps that need to be taken before designing a collaborative infrastructure security effort. They conclude with a description of the "absolutely imperative" role for government that is "subtle, complex, and fundamentally analytical." Unfortunately the Department of Homeland Security (DHS) is not, today, structured or equipped to meet this requirement. This is certainly the main challenge DHS will have to meet successfully in the coming years if it is to bring safety and security to the nation's critical infrastructure.

BUILDING TRUST THROUGH COLLECTIVE PREPAREDNESS AND GLOBAL REACTION CAPACITY

Adequate preparation to deal with large-scale disrupting events is not something to be improvised on the battle field. Numerous exercises are run on a daily basis, but most of them are local and do not respond adequately to the new scale of potential disruption we face as a country or a group of countries. Strategic and operational answers have to be developed to deal with such events and to improve collective preparation through creative partnerships. But how to construct such international partnerships at senior-executive level and reach success?

Fortunately, there have been a few significant breakthrough initiatives: one was initiated under the leadership of the U.S. government. The second was initiated in Europe under the leadership of industry and associated senior executives from nearly 30 countries, including the United States. The first, the U.S. Top Officials Three (TOPOFF) exercises, was essentially cross-sector oriented; the second, the Paris Initiative, was sector specific.

From April 4 to 8, 2005, DHS ran the congressionally mandated TOPOFF-3 (the third of this sort) to enhance the nation's capacity to prevent, prepare for, respond to, and recover from a substantial terrorist attack involving the use of weapons of mass destruction. Simulated terrorist incidents originated in New London, Connecticut (chemical incident), and Union and Middlesex Counties in New Jersey (biological incident). With nearly 10,000 participants from 27 federal agencies and more than 200 government and private-sector organizations, as well as 13 countries participating as observers, this large-scale rehearsal constitutes the largest exercise ever undertaken in dealing with counter-terrorism. This exercise is part of a whole dynamic of global public policies and private strategies that aim at protecting Americans and the U.S. economy against terrorism, a goal that certainly echoes the need for international cooperation and the development of global reaction capacity, not only national ones.

The second initiative, which was launched in Europe in 2002, is discussed in Chapter 25 by Patrick Lagadec and Erwann Michel-Kerjan. In the aftermath of the 2001 anthrax crisis, they suggested launching an ambitious debriefing process on that unconventional episode. They coordinated a large pilot study, with the strategic purpose of bringing some hallmarks to help postal operators at the highest executive level. This pilot study led to the "Paris Initiative," in which senior executives of postal sectors from 30 countries met in Paris one year after the international crisis to share their experiences gained and to suggest new avenues of international partnerships. An innovative international platform for immediate cross-organizational response capacity resulted from the initiative as well; a partnership enabling the necessary common learning process. To date, postal operators have been among the very few to launch such an advanced international process to understand and meet the collective challenge of an increasingly interdependent world. The authors argue that while associated theoretical idea and concepts are more and more recognized today, the challenge is to implement them in the real world. In their chapter, the authors explain the process and experiences of the Paris Initiative, and they suggest strategies for applying the developed operational framework to other critical sectors at the international level.

To conclude that addressing the problem of critical infrastructure protection requires more open and informed dialogue between the private and public sectors is not sufficient. This process must be architected, tested, and adapted as circumstances change. Information will always be inadequate to optimize the process, but that is all the more reason for sharing it. Where the threats and solutions are transnational, as in most cases they will be, the role of government in defining what success means will require diplomatic and political skills as well.

NOTES

1. Telecommunication firms seeking to restore telephone service in New Orleans were required to provide security for their workers but were denied police weapons permits, and they were denied access to their own facilities by forces that sometimes confiscated the fuel they required to operate emergency power generators. A system for designating power, communications, and water companies, among others, identification cards qualifying them as "first responders" with authority like that of police and fire personnel is perhaps required.
2. For a nice discussion of the question of trust, see Seligman 2000; Slovic 1993, 1999.
3. Collins 2006.
4. For a conceptual analysis of the impact of government being more informed about the nature of relevant risks than other partners within a public–private partnership, and the implications on optimal risk sharing, see Michel-Kerjan and de Marcellis-Warin 2006.
5. The executive summary of the 9/11 Commission Report states: "The U.S. government has access to a vast amount of information. But it has a weak system for processing and using what it has. The system of 'need to know' should be replaced by a system of 'need to share'" (National Commission on Terrorist Attacks Upon the United States 2004).
6. National Commission on Terrorist Attacks Upon the United States 2004.
7. Heymann and Kayyem 2005.
8. In the days after the 9/11 terrorist attacks, some of the U.S. largest airlines, including American, United, and Northwest, turned over millions of passenger records to the Federal Bureau of Investigation. After years of debate and denial, Northwest confirmed in 2004 that it had "cooperated fully with the FBI in its investigation, including the provision of passenger name records for a 12-month period leading up to September 2001, as requested by the FBI." Northwest, along with other airlines, have been seriously challenged by groups of passengers and privacy watch associations.

23

INFORMATION SHARING WITH THE PRIVATE SECTOR

History, Challenges, Innovation, and Prospects

Daniel B. Prieto III

The terrorist attacks of September 11, 2001, fundamentally challenged two key aspects of U.S. national security thinking. First, it altered the relationship between the private sector and the federal government by squarely thrusting the private sector into a new and unprecedented national security role. Second, it challenged long-standing priorities regarding the treatment of national security information, increasing the importance of sharing information and making it more widely available at the expense of traditional limitations on access to and dissemination of classified and other sensitive information.

This chapter addresses the confluence of these challenges – information sharing by the federal government with the private sector to enhance national and homeland security. It provides a brief history of public–private information sharing efforts before 9/11, describes reforms and initiatives since 9/11, and assesses problems and prospects for improved information sharing in the future.

THE NEW NATIONAL SECURITY ROLE OF THE PRIVATE SECTOR

The use of commercial aircraft as missiles against the World Trade Center and the Pentagon, and subsequent Al Qaeda statements declaring its intention to "fill [American] hearts with terror and target [America's] economic lifeline,"[1] made it clear that private sector facilities – including transportation, energy, water, chemicals, telecommunications, computers, and the food supply – are attractive terrorist targets. More than 85 percent of the hundreds of thousands of critical infrastructure facilities in the United States are owned by the private sector. The federal government has acknowledged the private sector as a critical partner in homeland security in strategy, policy, and in the homeland security reorganization efforts of the federal government since 9/11.

The critical homeland security role of the private sector was again made clear in late 2005. Hurricane Katrina devastated New Orleans and other coastal areas in Louisiana, Mississippi, and Alabama, becoming the most destructive and costly natural disaster in the history of the United States, and one of the deadliest. The official death toll neared 1,400, an additional 1,300 were missing and "feared dead," damages were estimated between $100 billion and $200 billion, and more than a million people were displaced. The private sector played a key role in providing an effective response to Hurricane Katrina. In some areas, Wal-Mart, Target, and Home Depot provided manpower, materials, and logistics to become key distribution points for food, water, clothing, generators, and other supplies. Mississippi Power, a subsidiary of Southern Company, restored electricity to hundreds of thousands of customers well ahead of schedule. Starwood Hotels provided vital services to its customers, employees, and first responders during and immediately after the storm.

Hurricane Katrina illustrated the need for better integration of the private sector into America's security equation. For this to happen, information sharing between the federal government and the private sector needs to improve and be supported by more clearly understood roles and responsibilities, well-developed trust relationships, and clear protocols and mechanisms for sharing. While progress has been made since 9/11, more needs to be done.[2]

The 9/11 attacks demonstrated the ability and willingness of terrorists to target U.S. economic infrastructure and use it as a weapon against civilians. Katrina illustrated that the private sector brings resources and logistical capabilities that are a necessary complement to federal, state, and local homeland security capabilities. The private sector is now a critical front-line national security player that will be essential to detect, prevent, and respond to future terrorist threats.

POLICY AND INITIATIVES BEFORE 9/11

Spurred by the rapid growth in the use of information technology in the mid-1990s, President Clinton created the President's Commission on Critical Infrastructure Protection. The commission addressed vulnerabilities in key sectors in the U.S. economy generated by an increased reliance on and interconnectivity resulting from the expanded use of information technology. In 1997, the commission called for a national effort to address the growing vulnerability of these critical infrastructures on which the nation's health, welfare, and security relied. The resulting Presidential Decision Directive 63 (PDD-63)[3] identified 12 areas critical to the functioning of the country – information and communications; banking and finance; water supply; transportation; emergency law enforcement; emergency fire service; emergency medicine; electric power, oil, and gas supply and distribution; law enforcement and internal security; intelligence; foreign affairs; and national defense – and established structures at the federal level and in the private sector to address vulnerabilities in these critical infrastructures.

PDD-63 raised a number of the key questions surrounding information sharing between the federal government and the private sector that remain today: What is the private sector's willingness and ability to cooperate with the federal government in sharing information? To what extent will the federal government get involved in the monitoring of privately operated infrastructures? What are the legal issues – including privacy and liability – associated with information sharing between the federal government and private sector firms?

PDD-63 established a number of organizations – including the National Infrastructure Protection Center within the Federal Bureau of Investigation (FBI) and the Critical Infrastructure Assurance Office within the U.S. Department of Commerce – to coordinate infrastructure protection efforts nationally. It also assigned a federal lead agency to each of the critical infrastructure sectors. Lead agencies were to collaborate with companies on a sector-by-sector basis to facilitate information sharing on threats, vulnerabilities, incidents, protective measures, and best practices. PDD-63 also called for the private sector to set up Information Sharing and Analysis Centers (ISACs) to "provide an information sharing and analysis capability to support [company] efforts to mitigate risk and effectively respond to adverse events, including cyber, physical, and natural events."[4]

Only a handful of ISACs were created prior to the terrorist attacks of 9/11. Those included ISACs for financial services, information technology, telecommunications, and electricity. After 9/11, the imperative for improved information sharing and greater private sector involvement to address terrorism spurred the creation of new ISACs. By March 2005, there were 15 ISACs, including for chemicals, food, energy, public transit, surface transport, water, and real estate.[5]

While ISACs were established as a result of PDD-63, neither PDD-63 nor the policy changes after 9/11 clearly delineate how the ISACs should operate or how the relationship between the ISACs and the federal government should work. With each industry group free to set up their ISAC as they wished, the ISACs differ widely in quality and structure and in how they are funded, managed, and operated. Some operate as private entities, while others are part of industry associations. Some rely on member fees for funding, while others are sponsored by associations, contracts, or grants.[6]

After 9/11, a number of federal lead-agency designations changed as a result of the government reorganization that created the Department of Homeland Security (DHS).[7] Notably, DHS became the lead agency for information technology and telecommunications, transportation, chemicals and hazardous materials, postal and shipping, and commercial nuclear facilities. Water remained with the Environmental Protection Agency, energy with the Department of Energy, banking and finance with the Department of Treasury, and food and agriculture with the Department of Agriculture.

Since 9/11, sector-specific agencies have provided funding to ISACs to improve their capabilities, expand membership, and support exercises. Sector-specific agencies have hosted outreach events, assisted sectors to organize sector-wide efforts, recommended best practices, and issued information and threat bulletins.[8]

POLICY AND INITIATIVES AFTER 9/11

THE DEPARTMENT OF HOMELAND SECURITY

The Homeland Security Act of 2002, which established DHS, recognized the increased importance of information sharing with the private sector and created new mechanisms and organizations within DHS with that goal in mind. Increased information sharing with the private sector was also highlighted in the National Homeland Security Strategy,[9] the National Strategy for the Physical Protection of Critical Infrastructures and Key Assets,[10] Homeland Security Presidential Directive 7 (HSPD-7) regarding critical infrastructure identification, prioritization, and protection,[11] Executive Order 13356 "Strengthening the Sharing of Terrorism Information to Protect Americans," and Executive Order 13388 "Further Strengthening the Sharing of Terrorism Information to Protect Americans."[12]

INFORMATION ANALYSIS AND INFRASTRUCTURE PROTECTION DIRECTORATE

The Homeland Security Act created an Information Analysis and Infrastructure Protection (IAIP) Directorate as one of the five directorates within DHS. IAIP's mission is to protect critical infrastructure and to serve as a focal point for synthesizing terrorism-related information. IAIP then disseminates information to state and local government and private sector entities. In 2005, Homeland Security Secretary Chertoff announced that he would seek to rearrange IAIP, splitting infrastructure protection into a preparedness directorate and an Intelligence and Analysis division that would report through a new Chief Intelligence Officer directly to the Secretary.[13]

PROTECTED CRITICAL INFRASTRUCTURE INFORMATION

The Critical Infrastructure Information Act of 2002[14] allowed DHS to issue regulations regarding the transmission and protection of critical infrastructure information from the private sector to the federal government. The regulations created the Protected Critical Infrastructure Information (PCII) Program and established uniform procedures for the receipt, care, and storage of private-sector information submitted under the program. In particular, qualifying information is exempt from public disclosure. The goal of the program is to encourage private entities to voluntarily submit to DHS confidential, proprietary, and business-sensitive critical infrastructure information. DHS plans to use the information to assess vulnerabilities, secure critical infrastructure, issue warnings and advisories, and assist in recovery. With non-disclosure protections, the program is meant to allow the private sector to better assist in homeland security without publicly exposing potentially sensitive and proprietary information.

DHS OPERATIONS CENTERS

In addition to the PCII office, DHS also has been seeking to improve information sharing with the private sector by selectively including private sector representation within DHS' round-the-clock operations centers.

The Homeland Security Operations Center (HSOC) serves as DHS' nerve center to (1) collect and fuse information from law enforcement and intelligence sources to help deter, detect, and prevent terrorist attacks; (2) maintain and share daily domestic situational awareness and homeland security monitoring; (3) act as a single point of integration – federal, state, local, and private – for homeland security operational communications and information sharing pertaining to domestic incident management and response; and (4) issue advisories and bulletins concerning threats to homeland security, as well as specific protective measures.

The HSOC disseminates two types of domestic terrorism-related products: threat advisories and information bulletins. Threat advisories contain information about incidents or threats involving critical infrastructure and may indicate changes in readiness, protective measures, or response. Information bulletins communicate more general information relevant to critical infrastructures and are less time-sensitive and specific.

The HSOC comprises more than 35 agencies ranging from state and local law enforcement to federal intelligence agencies.[15] On an ad-hoc basis, it includes on-site representatives from selected private-sector critical infrastructure sectors, including trucking, rail, chemicals and petrochemicals, telecommunications, and nuclear. For example, the HSOC includes relevant private-sector representatives on site during periods of elevated alert or specific crisis-related or national-security special events, such as the Super Bowl or the presidential inauguration.

In addition to the HSOC, DHS' Transportation Security Operations Center (TSOC) serves as a round-the-clock operations center for transportation security-related operations, incidents, or crises. The TSOC communicates directly with the HSOC and also houses private-sector representatives as needed. The TSOC notifies ISAC leadership and sector coordinators of critical infrastructure events, including notification of imminent threats, dissemination of sector-specific warning products, and changes in national threat level.

HOMELAND SECURITY INFORMATION NETWORK

DHS has launched the Homeland Security Information Network, an Internet-based communications tool that includes directories, email, instant messaging, and geospatial mapping capabilities. The network provides connectivity to all 50 states, Washington, D.C., and more than 50 major urban areas. In June 2004, DHS in cooperation with the FBI launched pilot programs in Dallas, Seattle, Indianapolis, and Atlanta to provide unclassified information to private sector owners of critical infrastructure assets.

DHS PRIVATE SECTOR OFFICE

The DHS Private Sector Office seeks to provide "the U.S. business community with a direct line of communication to the Department of Homeland Security." But the Private Sector Office is not intended nor does it act as a conduit for national security sensitive information, either from industry to government or vice versa. It serves primarily as a liaison office that facilitates interaction between DHS and the private sector and as an outreach office that provides information and education to the private sector regarding the activities of DHS. The DHS Private Sector Office works directly with individual businesses, trade associations, and other professional and non-governmental organizations to share information about department programs and opportunities.

FBI JOINT TERRORISM TASK FORCES

Since 9/11, the FBI has increased the presence of its counterterrorism field offices and operations though Joint Terrorism Task Forces (JTTFs). The JTTFs are jointly staffed by FBI agents and local law enforcement officials who are assigned to work full time with the FBI. The FBI has increased the number of JTTFs from 35 before 9/11 to 100 in 2005. In addition, as of mid-2005, 56 FBI field offices maintain field intelligence groups to analyze and disseminate information. While none of these efforts explicitly incorporates private sector involvement, the field offices serve as a federal resource to private sector entities on a regional and local basis as needed.

INFORMATION SHARING CHALLENGES

Given the policy changes following 9/11, the creation of the Department of Homeland Security, and the proliferation of information-sharing mechanisms that began in 1998 and accelerated after 9/11, what is the state of public–private information sharing today?

Certainly improvements have been made to information sharing between the government and the private sector since 9/11. DHS has created a number of new offices and programs focused on information sharing with the private sector. At the same time, significant challenges remain. These challenges fall into three broad categories.

First, an unsettled organizational landscape at the federal level and in the private sector sharing mechanisms has left roles and responsibilities for increased and improved sharing unclear at multiple levels of government and, certainly, in the minds of members of the private sector.

Second, issues of trust and risk act as a serious impediment to holders of information for fear that information misuse by other parties might expose them to liability, punishment, or other negative consequences.

Third, the value of improved sharing is often not immediately apparent, leaving private-sector owners of information often seeking a quid pro quo: why should a company give up sensitive information on its facilities if it is not receiving relevant and actionable intelligence information from the government in return?

UNSETTLED ORGANIZATIONAL LANDSCAPE

Far-reaching and rapid organizational change in the federal bureaucracy has posed one of the greatest challenges to improving information sharing with the private sector since 9/11. DHS was designated by the Homeland Security Act to play a lead role in facilitating information sharing with the private sector. While DHS inherited significant assets, including the National Infrastructure Protection Center and the Critical Infrastructure Assurance Office, personnel turnover and disruptions during the transition significantly limited DHS' effectiveness. According to a report by DHS' Inspector General, to the extent that the certain preexisting federal efforts had achieved "one stop shopping" from the government for critical infrastructure information sharing after 1998, the difficult transition into DHS and associated personnel shortages have hindered information sharing efforts.[16]

The creation of DHS also unsettled the federal landscape by splitting duties for information sharing between industry sectors' traditional regulatory agencies and DHS. This split happened most notably in chemicals and hazardous materials, commercial nuclear plants, and transportation. The fragmentation has contributed to a lack of clarity regarding divisions of responsibility.[17] For example, the Department of Transportation is responsible for regulating transport, but DHS is responsible for transportation security; the Environmental Protection Agency is responsible for regulating chemicals, but DHS is responsible for chemical security.

As a result, private sector officials have complained about confusion, contradictory direction, and duplicative information requests and poor coordination between DHS and other federal agencies. Making matters worse, while DHS has lead responsibility for some sectors, it frequently lacks sufficient or comparable technical expertise in those areas traditionally regulated by other federal agencies, most notably, the Department of Energy, the Department of Transportation, and the Environmental Protection Agency. Near-term staffing shortages have made matters worse, but even when addressed, DHS may never match the sector-specific technical capabilities of counterpart agencies. Lack of deep industry-specific expertise on DHS' part will likely impede robust information sharing between DHS and the private sector.

Paul Kurtz, the former senior director for critical infrastructure protection on the White House Homeland Security Council, said in mid-2004 that "the state of relations between the private sector and DHS when it comes to critical infrastructure is strained, clearly strained, and it's sad."[18] According to other experts interviewed by *Congressional Quarterly*, the causes of the problems include a lack of "a core strategy or a list of priorities. And the near-constant staff changes . . . have led to communication problems."[19]

ISACs were envisioned as the primary node for information sharing with federal authorities, but they have struggled to fill that role. ISACs have suffered from the fact that many have been fee-based membership organizations. Information sent to the ISACs by the HSOC too often has been distributed only to ISAC member companies and has failed to reach non-member companies. As a result, DHS has declined to endorse the ISACs as the primary interface with the private sector. In fact, DHS conspicuously distanced itself from the ISAC model when it promoted the creation of Sector Coordinating Councils. As mandated by executive order (HSPD-7),[20] the councils were set up to be more inclusive than ISACs and to allow any company or association operating within a sector to become a member for free.

Information Sharing and Analysis Centers and Sector Coordinating Councils remain works in progress. DHS continues to suffer growing pains and must continue to improve its coordination with other federal agencies that have technical expertise and regulatory oversight for particular infrastructure sectors. The landscape for sector-based efforts to share information within industries and between industry and government remains unsettled. A clear model for the organizations, mechanisms, processes, and rules that will best serve information sharing with the private sector is still lacking.

TRUST AND RISK

Even if organizational structures at both the federal level and within industry were more mature, it is not clear that information sharing between the federal and private sectors would be dramatically improved. Much of the reason for this stems from a lack of history and familiarity in exchanging information between the public and private sectors. Corporations have legitimate competitive and liability concerns over the potential disclosure of business-sensitive information, while federal authorities have legitimate concerns over the disclosure of sensitive national security information. According to the Government Accountability Office (GAO), "the benefits [to a company] of sharing information are often difficult to discern, while the risks and costs of sharing are direct and foreseeable."[21]

The primary risks that the private sector perceives around information sharing include the sensitivity of information (for example, information that companies would not want competitors to discover or information related to a break-in that is relevant to ongoing or future law enforcement activities), legal limits on disclosure (such as Privacy Act restrictions on the disclosure of personally identifiable information of companies' customers), and contractual or business limits on disclosure (including non-disclosure agreements with business partners, clients, and customers).[22]

The depth of private sector concerns is reflected in the limited effectiveness of DHS' Protected Critical Infrastructure Information initiative. While the program is one of the federal government's flagship initiatives, it has yet to serve as an effective catalyst for significantly improving information flows. By March 2005, after nearly a year in operation, the PCII office had received only 30 submissions.[23]

For the federal government, an overarching challenge to sharing with the private sector is the security of classified information and a lack of security clearances among private sector officials. To the extent that most sharing with the private sector takes place, the information shared is unclassified/for official use only, and typically provides only general homeland security information that is not specific enough to be actionable by companies. Providing more sensitive threat information would require appropriate security clearances for private sector recipients of the information. While no specific data are available on security clearances for the private sector, the problem of providing security clearances for first responders and state and local officials provides some insight to the hurdles that would confront comparable efforts to provide clearances for the private sector.

To improve information sharing with state and local officials, Washington has sought to provide expedited clearances to first responders who are members of the FBI's JTTFs. According to the GAO, the FBI has done a good job of processing "top secret" clearances for state and local law enforcement officials who are part of the JTTFs within their target timeframe of six to nine months.[24] It has done a much poorer job of completing lower-level "secret clearances" for first responders who are not part of the JTTFs within their target of fewer than 60 days. According to *Congressional Quarterly*, by early 2005, only two dozen fire chiefs nationwide had security clearances, and critics voiced concerns that the FBI was not moving swiftly enough to expedite applications for fire chiefs.[25] Notwithstanding clearances, a 2003 executive order allows the FBI and other federal agencies to share classified information with first responders who lack security clearances in the cases of emergency.

Part of the difficulty in providing clearances for state and local officials comes from the sheer number required. There are more law enforcement *agencies* in the United States than there are FBI *agents*.[26] The volume problem is similarly evident in completing security clearances for civilian contractors to the Department of Defense, the one area where private sector employees routinely receive clearances.[27] As of 2004, the backlog of clearances was about 180,000, and the average time for completion of a clearance increased by nearly 20 percent to 375 days from 2001 to 2004.[28]

Another challenge posed by security clearances is oversight. In April 2005, Portland, Oregon pulled its police officers out of the Portland JTTF, making it the first city in the country to pull out of the FBI's expanded network of JTTF offices. The decision came, in part, as a result of the FBI's refusal to grant Portland's mayor a top secret clearance. The mayor argued that, unable to see what the Portland policemen on the JTTF saw, he would be unable to exercise full oversight of the police to ensure that officers did not "overstep their authority under state law while acting as federal agents."[29]

The volume and oversight problems would need to be addressed if Washington were to pursue a program of clearances to private sector officials on a meaningful scale. There are hundreds of thousands of critical infrastructure sites across the United States, a large multiple of the number of state and local law enforcement agencies. The backlog faced by civilian contractors to the Department of Defense would be small compared with the number of critical infrastructure employees who might seek clearances. Furthermore, companies could face oversight problems, similar to those in Portland, unless senior executives and board members also were to obtain clearances that would allow them to exercise oversight over other employees in their organizations who have clearances.

Finally, even if clearances were granted to industry officials on a sufficient scale, information sharing might still be slow to improve. Even within the federal government, where officials have requisite security clearances, information sharing improvements are occurring only slowly. Again, the benefits of sharing are often difficult to discern, while the risks and costs of sharing are direct and foreseeable. For the intelligence community, wider sharing increases the risk of compromising valuable sources and methods.[30] For the FBI, greater sharing increases the risk of compromising a law enforcement investigation. Furthermore, the government culture, developed over decades during the Cold War, has prized secrecy, information control, and data ownership, and it has lived in fear of leaks of classified information.

The obstacles to sharing within the federal government are also relevant when it comes to sharing information externally with state, local, and private sector entities. Even if the problem of clearances could be overcome, it is likely that challenges to information sharing beyond the federal government would remain.

VALUE PROPOSITION: THE QUID PRO QUO PROBLEM

Even if the organizational landscape could become more certain, mutual trust could be strengthened, and sufficient classification and non-disclosure regimes could be established, the information sharing paradigm presumes that the private and public sectors have useful information to share.

A common presumption in the private sector is that the federal government possesses a significant amount of classified information that is specific and actionable. According to the GAO, "most ISACs reported that they believed that they were providing appropriate information to the government but, while noting improvements, they still had concerns with the information being provided to them by DHS and/or their sector-specific agencies. These concerns included the limited quantity of information and the need for more specific, timely, and actionable information."[31] In short, many in the private sector believe that the federal government is withholding valuable information from them.

In truth, this may not be the case. While post-9/11 information-sharing efforts stress the critical need to "connect the dots," the federal government may not be in a position to provide the dots. U.S. intelligence capabilities declined significantly after the end of the Cold War due to budget and personnel cuts.[32] Even though intelligence budgets have grown since 9/11, it may take at least a decade to rebuild U.S. intelligence capabilities to a sufficient level to, for example, penetrate Islamist terrorist groups and provide adequate intelligence on terrorist threats.[33] As former Central Intelligence Agency (CIA) Director James Woolsey explained, "In intelligence, not only are not all of the dots there, but there are no numbers on them."[34]

The perception that the federal government is withholding information only heightens the reluctance by the private sector to share information with the federal government: why should the private sector give up sensitive information when it is not getting valuable federal information in return?

INFORMATION SHARING BY SELECTED SECTORS

Many of the federal efforts to broadly catalyze information sharing from the top down have had limited success. At the same time, greater sharing of private-sector information with the federal government is occurring on a case-by-case basis, and outside of the PCII program, in certain industry sectors. This is particularly true in aviation, telecommunications, and cyber security, where models of information sharing that existed prior to 9/11 have provided the foundation for current efforts. In air freight and cargo shipping, companies are using the rich availability of supply-chain data to provide federal authorities greater access to information about the shippers that use and packages that travel within their systems.

AVIATION SECURITY[35]

Private airlines began using passenger data – last minute reservations, payment by cash, short or one-way trips – starting in 1996 to assess the risks posed by passengers and checked baggage. In addition, federal authorities have routinely augmented the screening efforts of private air carriers by providing them with government watch list information on persons considered to be threats to aviation security.

Between 1999 and 2001, public criticism and civil liberties concerns led to restrictions on the Computer Assisted Passenger Profiling System (CAPPS I) so that it could only be used to target baggage and not travelers for screening. After 9/11, the restrictions on CAPPS I were lifted to allow it to again be used for targeting both passengers and baggage. In addition, federal authorities have sought to expand passenger screening with additional intelligence and law enforcement information, and to use passenger record data (including name, address, date of birth, and telephone number) augmented with commercially available consumer data. CAPPS II, as this initiative was known, was scrapped in 2004 under public pressure and privacy concerns after it became known that several airlines had turned over traveler records to federal agencies and defense contractors.[36]

DHS's Transportation Security Administration (TSA) modified the pre-screening initiative and renamed it Secure Flight.[37] Under Secure Flight, the federal government would take over from air carriers the responsibility for pre-screening airline passengers. TSA would receive passenger data from the airlines, and compare passenger information against data from a new consolidated watch list database created after 9/11. Additionally, TSA announced that it would test the use of commercially available consumer data (i.e., information that either identifies an individual or is directly attributed to an individual, such as name, address, and phone number) to enhance the efficacy and security benefits of the system.

In spring 2005, a TSA contractor tested the use of personally identifiable commercial data to see if such data could better enable Secure Flight to identify false or stolen identities. The manner in which the contractor collected, used, and stored the commercial data, however, was inconsistent with how TSA had previously publicly described how the program would use commercial data.[38] As a result, "individuals were not fully informed that their personal information was being collected and used, nor did they have the opportunity to comment on this or become informed on how they might exercise their right of access to information."[39] DHS' own privacy office investigated whether the tests violated DHS' own privacy rules.[40] In summer 2005, TSA issued revised privacy notices to more fully disclose the nature of its use of commercial data.

DHS' Data Privacy and Integrity Advisory Committee determined that TSA's commercial data test did not provide a reasonable case for using commercial data as part of Secure Flight. Going further, Congress restricted TSA from using commercial data or databases "obtained from or that remain under the control of a non-federal entity,"[41] which effectively ended the use of commercial data in Secure Flight during, at least, fiscal year 2006.

Secure Flight is a work in progress, and, like its predecessors, it remains controversial.[42] Shifting screening responsibility from the private sector to the federal government and expanding the program to include more personal data has raised criticism from privacy groups and heightened scrutiny on Capitol Hill.[43]

TELECOMMUNICATIONS

Historically, telecommunications companies have cooperated with federal authorities, providing information and access to systems that allow federal authorities to conduct surveillance. In the 1970s, for example, the National Security Agency (NSA) relied on major telegraph companies to provide copies of messages into and out of the United States.[44] Under the 1994 Communications Assistance for Law Enforcement, U.S. telecommunications carriers are required to make their networks available for wiretaps for domestic law enforcement. While such a requirement does not exist regarding intelligence agencies, the NSA maintains very close relationships with telecommunications and computer industries, even though only a very small group of senior company executives might be aware of such relationships.[45]

In domestic investigations, communication companies typically require court orders before cooperating.[46] But in December 2005, the *New York Times* first reported on a program authorized by President Bush soon after 9/11 allowing wiretaps without warrants on U.S. persons or people geographically located in the United States who might have links to Al Qaeda or Al Qaeda affiliates.[47] News reports indicate that large telecommunications companies, including AT&T, MCI, and Sprint, without warrants, granted access to their systems and provided call-routing information to help physically locate callers.[48] The existence of the program touched off a national furor over the legality of domestic eavesdropping without court approvals as well as a debate over the relative constitutional powers of Congress and the executive branch to authorize intelligence collection in the United States.

In February 2006, the Electronic Frontier Foundation, a privacy-rights advocacy group, sued AT&T, calling the company's participation in the NSA program an unconstitutional invasion of privacy.[49] For companies, the incident raised the potential risk of liability and brand damage due to providing commercial data for intelligence purposes to federal authorities, when a company's customers have certain expectations or even legal claims to privacy protections.

CYBERSECURITY

DHS' National Cybersecurity Division in September 2003 created a U.S. Computer Emergency Readiness Team (U.S. CERT) to provide a national focal point for analyzing computer-based vulnerabilities, disseminating cyber warnings, and coordinating incident and response activities. U.S. CERT links public and private response capabilities to facilitate communication about cybersecurity.[50] It works with the private sector and academia to coordinate responses to major cyber events and to provide information on vulnerabilities, prevention, and remediation to private-sector companies, small businesses, and home users.

DHS created U.S. CERT by integrating several preexisting federal cyber centers and drawing on the capabilities of Carnegie Mellon's CERT Coordination

Center, the country's leading university cybersecurity center.[51] The U.S. CERT is largely modeled after Carnegie Mellon's center but seeks to provide a greater national effort in education and warning for smaller businesses and home users.

The U.S. CERT encourages private-sector companies to report cyber attacks or discovered vulnerabilities. Information specific to the facility and company making the report remains confidential unless explicit permission is granted to release that information. Composite sanitized information is provided publicly so that other companies and individuals can avoid similar attacks and fix similar vulnerabilities.

In January 2004, U.S. CERT started a National Cyber Alerts System to provide cyber security information to the public. The alert system is managed in partnership between the DHS and the private sector. By June 2004, more than 250,000 subscribers were receiving cyber alerts.

SEA FREIGHT: CARGO SHIPPING[52]

Starting in 2003, DHS' U.S. Customs and Border Protection implemented a "24-hour rule" requiring private ocean carriers to provide the U.S. government with extensive data about all containerized cargo shipments – manifests, bills-of-lading, and entry and exit data – at least 24 hours before those containers are loaded onto a U.S.-bound vessel in a foreign port. Data are provided electronically via the Automated Manifest System and are evaluated by DHS' Automated Targeting System (ATS).[53] Each shipment is analyzed and scored according to more than 300 weighted rules derived from targeting methods developed by experienced customs personnel.

The higher the risk score of a shipment, the more the shipment warrants specific attention. The ATS analysis and score is used to decide which containers should not be loaded aboard the vessel at the foreign port, which containers should be inspected at either the foreign port or the U.S. discharge port, and which containers are considered low risk and can be transported without further review. All shipping containers that ATS identifies as posing a potential terrorist threat are inspected, usually with large-scale imaging and radiation detection equipment prior to or upon on arrival at U.S. seaports.

Currently, U.S. importers and foreign exporters are not required to file data that could be used in the security screening process, notwithstanding the fact that the law requires the cargo security screening and evaluation system to be conducted prior to loading in a foreign port. Such data would be valuable as they would provide information beyond what is in carriers' manifest filings. While importers are required to file merchandise entry data with the government, they do not have to do so until after the cargo shipment has already entered the United States or until it reaches its inland destination, which is too late for security screening purposes.

Customs may eventually require importers to file relevant entry data into U.S. Customs' targeting system 24 hours before vessel loading. Importer data could provide a more detailed and complete picture of cargo shipments and could augment the risk screening currently conducted by ATS.[54] Other information that could improve the quality of cargo risk screening includes more specific and precise cargo description, selling party, purchasing party, point of origin, country of export, ultimate consignee (final recipient), exporter representative, name of broker, and origin of container shipment (name and address of business where container was loaded).

AIR FREIGHT: FEDEX

International freight shipper FedEx provides homeland security officials access to the international portion of its databases.[55] Information provided includes credit card details, shipper name and address, and the package's origin and final destination. Agents cross reference information provided by FedEx with information in government databases. The relationship is mutually beneficial to both parties. With federal assistance and checks against government data, FedEx is better able to flag suspicious packages. Working closely with the government also helps FedEx prevent disruptions to operations and damaging publicity that might ensue if terrorists successfully exploited its systems. For federal officials, cooperation with FedEx provides the ability to see if credit cards have been used in other suspicious transactions and map the activities of and links between persons or organizations of interest.

In addition to providing access to portions of its consumer information database, FedEx encourages its work force to be on the lookout for suspicious activity. It is also building a special computer system to report on suspicious behavior directly to DHS.

FEDERAL INNOVATION

To overcome the problem of few security clearances in the private sector, federal authorities such as DHS and the FBI have sought greater use of "tear line" information. Federal authorities make information shareable by creating "tear line" reports, which contain classified and non-shareable information above the tear line, and then, below the tear line, the unclassified information that can be shared. The problem with this solution to date is that the process of redacting and summarizing classified information to create a shareable unclassified version of it frequently ends up making the shared information so general as to be not meaningful or actionable to non-federal entities.

Two potential solutions exist to improve the quality of information shared by the federal government with non-government entities. The first solution would be to "write to share" information, which would reverse the typical tear line concept by having government analysts write reports that are shareable in their original form. The information below the tear line would provide additional details that are classified and only accessible with permissions or authentication. While this seems like a minor change, a "write to share" philosophy would require a significant cultural change.[56] Federal officials normally write reports in classified form, and then subsequently extract the information they are willing to share with others. "Writing to share" would force officials from the very start to define what can be shared. This approach can help increase the amount and quality of shareable information and help prevent important information and context from becoming lost in subsequent rounds of redaction and summarization.[57]

Another potential solution that the federal government has begun to implement is for the government to increase its supply of valuable, but non-classified, information. The presidential commission investigating the failure of U.S. intelligence on Iraq's weapons of mass destruction recommended in March 2005 that the CIA establish an office to gather intelligence from "open" or non-classified sources, including newspapers and periodicals.[58] In congressional testimony, witnesses argued that mining unclassified sources could respond to the unique needs of first responders and other non-federal entities, who often lack access to classified information.[59]

DHS is increasingly recognizing the value of open-source information and is now publishing daily open-source infrastructure reports.[60] Open-source intelligence, combined with tear sheet information, has the potential to both increase the quality as well as the volume of information shared by the federal government with the private sector. Success on this front can help mitigate the need for security clearances and may also help address the quid pro quo problem that has contributed to a reluctance by private sector entities to provide information to Washington.

REGIONAL INNOVATION

Recognizing the difficulty of information sharing between the federal and private sectors, efforts are underway to increase regional information sharing between state and local authorities and the private sector. Portland, Oregon, for example, has launched the Connect & Protect™ program to provide automated, real-time emergency alert notifications from Portland's emergency 9-1-1 system to more than 100 schools and more than 50 homeland security, public safety, and private sector organizations on a secure Internet-based information network.[61] Incident alerts are automatically filtered and targeted to relevant organizations. Users receive alerts of 9-1-1 events and are able to receive additional descriptive detail on incidents, including photographs and maps. The system also provides valuable content to help organizations decide how to respond to the incidents, including materials on precautionary procedures, hazardous materials, evacuation planning, loss prevention, workplace safety, and guidance on training and preparedness.

In the system's first six months of operation between August 2003 and March 2004, it processed 87,000 and delivered 3,500 targeted alerts to network subscribers. The core technology – RAINS-Net – was developed in partnership between the state of Oregon, six research universities, more than 60 technology companies, and a variety of local first responder organizations.[62]

Regional innovation like Connect & Protect is essential to the future of successfully building better information sharing with the private sector. Building systems regionally leverages local geographic relationships to build trusted relationships between the private sector and state and local governments. Over time, as organic regional networks grow, they may be leveraged by federal authorities to build a national "network of networks" for information sharing relationships.

CROSS-SECTOR INNOVATION IN THE PRIVATE SECTOR

Innovative information-sharing projects are also taking place between consortia of companies from multiple industries and the federal government. In one example, technology consulting company C-bridge Corporation is developing a project to improve security at a number of private energy and manufacturing facilities in a concentrated geographic region. The project is aimed at reducing the risk of "insider threats," where current employees or other personnel within a facility might provide aid to terrorists or saboteurs. National labor union and trade groups representing the personnel being screened are also participating in the project.

C-Bridge is using technology from defense contractor Lockheed Martin, personal data from large commercial data aggregators, and watch list data from the federal government to run background checks and perform risk assessments on staff and contract personnel who have access to sensitive manufacturing and energy facilities. C-Bridge's personnel risk assessment pilot is modeled after risk assessment programs the company has built for DHS. The project utilizes software jointly developed with Lockheed Martin for the Department of Defense to protect classified data and ensure privacy protection for personnel subject to risk screening and background checks.

C-Bridge's approach to data theft seeks to ensure privacy protection by pre-defining data sharing rules and policies, protecting classified information, and providing continuous auditing and monitoring to ensure compliance with the sharing policies agreed upon by the participants. Continually monitoring how data is being shared allows for constant assessment and mitigation of risk by assuring the companies, personnel, and labor unions that their data are being used only for the purposes for which they are aware and have agreed upon beforehand. If successful, the C-Bridge project can provide lessons for future cross-sector information-sharing initiatives between the private sector and the government.

CONCLUSIONS AND RECOMMENDATIONS

Four years after 9/11, information sharing between the federal government and the private sector remains a significant challenge. While some progress has been made, federal efforts to share homeland security intelligence information with the private sector remain limited and ad hoc. According to the GAO, "DHS has not yet developed a plan for how it will carry out its information-sharing responsibilities.... In addition, DHS has not developed internal policies and procedures to help ensure effective information sharing by the many entities within the department that collect and analyze information that may impact the security of our nation's critical infrastructure."[63] According to Zoe Baird, president of the Markle Foundation, there is still no systematic and compre-hensive way to integrate the private sector into information sharing.[64]

Private-sector officials have an expectation that that the federal role in protecting their facilities should include as a top priority the transmittal of threat intelligence information. Information provided by the federal govern-ment should be consistent, accurate, clear, timely, and as specific about the potential threat as possible.[65] Sharing would be aided by the greater presence of private-sector representatives at DHS operations centers and at regional and field DHS and FBI offices. Sharing would also be aided by a greater use of tear line and open source information, and the growth in distribution networks like the Homeland Security Information Network and Portland's Connect & Protect. Sharing is made more difficult by the problem of getting large num-bers of security clearances for private sector personnel, by fear of improper disclosure of classified information, and by the fact that federal authorities may not possess actionable or specific intelligence. Finally, it is imperative that the federal government be better coordinated and, to the greatest extent possible, speak with one voice. In several instances since 9/11, that has not been the case, with the FBI and DHS releasing uncoordinated and conflicting messages regarding threats to the financial sector, oil refineries, and mass transit.[66]

The sharing of sensitive corporate information in the other direction – from companies to the federal government – also suffers from growing pains. The primary broad mechanism established to catalyze private-sector submissions of information to the federal government (the PCII Program) has gained little traction due to risk aversion by the private sector. Companies fear improper or inadvertent disclosure by the government of information sensitive to individual companies. When private industry and government both have a sense that the other side is holding information back, it perpetuates a lack of trust and creates an unproductive quid pro quo mentality in which each side waits for the other to be more forthcoming as a condition for sharing more themselves.

An unsettled organizational landscape at the federal level and within the private sector has not helped matters. DHS remains understaffed, suffers high personnel turnover, often lacks sufficient technical expertise, and is frequently poorly coordinated with counterpart agencies that possess greater industry expertise. Within the private sector, the primary information sharing nodes – ISACs and Sector Coordinating Councils – vary widely in quality and operations, are not yet mature, and lack clearly defined roles, responsibilities, and sharing protocols.

Given continuing challenges in broad-based sharing efforts, the sharing and innovation that does take place will likely continue to develop independently on a sector-by-sector or regional basis. Furthermore, sharing programs are more likely to occur in sectors where several conditions are met: First, programs for providing corporate information to federal authorities are more likely when there exists an established history of information exchange, often via a regulatory relationship. Preexisting relationships have provided the framework for experimentation in the passenger aviation sector, telecommunications, and cybersecurity.

Second, companies will be more likely to share corporate information when doing so can help them better protect their own assets, prevent misuse of their systems, and detect and reduce costs associated with crime or fraud. With cybersecurity, making up-to-date vulnerability information available to other companies and the federal government provides awareness of common vulnerabilities, a public good that benefits all community members. In aviation, screening passengers prevents airplanes from being hijacked or destroyed. With sea and air freight carriers, sharing shipper and supply chain data with federal authorities improves companies' ability to detect and prevent crime and fraud as well as potential terrorist attacks.

Third, companies are more likely to share information with federal authorities where existing geographic and regional relationships between firms can be leveraged, as in the case of Portland's Connect & Protect and C-Bridge's pilot program with a consortium of manufacturing and energy firms. Over time, pilots and regional programs have the potential to provide a model for or contribute to the creation of national programs. Just as importantly, innovative pilots help to build and strengthen trust relationships across the public–private divide.

At the same time, information sharing from the private sector to the federal government has the potential to become problematic where a company's sharing is not required by regulation or where it does not meet a company's direct self-interest in protecting its own assets against criminal or terrorist attacks. Information sharing where the primary goal is to provide intelligence information to the government – as in the case of cooperation by telecommunications companies on eavesdropping without warrants – has exposed AT&T to legal liability and brand reputation issues relating to the privacy rights of its customers. Similarly, the use of commercial consumer data to augment the screening of airline passengers has led to censure and protests of the program over privacy rights. FedEx's information sharing with federal authorities also raises privacy and legal issues. According to a former CIA official, "the new cooperation between business and the government takes place in a legal 'gray zone' that has never been tested in court. [These] relationships could undermine existing privacy laws."[67]

Faced with legal risk and ambiguity, many companies – including FedEx rival United Parcel Service, General Motor's OnStar in-vehicle emergency communications system, Internet service provider Earthlink, and cable service provider Cox Communications – say that, as a matter of policy, they do not disclose customer information to federal authorities without a subpoena, warrant, or court order.[68]

Improving information sharing with the private sector is a work in progress. The challenges to information sharing between government and the private sector are widely recognized. The federal government and the private sector must make better progress on a number of recommendations that have been made by both government and private-sector groups over the past several years.[69] The government needs to develop a comprehensive and coordinated national plan to facilitate information sharing regarding critical infrastructure protection. That plan needs to clearly delineate roles and responsibilities, craft data exchange and handling mechanisms and processes, define interim objectives and milestones, set timeframes for achieving objectives, and establish means to measure progress. Industry should become better integrated into the full government intelligence cycle (requirements, tasking, analysis, reporting, and dissemination). At the same time, the government must aggressively increase its analysis, use, and dissemination of open-source information both within and outside of government. Federal authorities should increase their industry expertise and better harness private-sector analytical capabilities to better develop sector-specific information and intelligence requirements.

While policy and institutional reforms since 9/11 have placed top priority on improving sharing between the government and the private sector, policy reforms must translate into meaningful and durable changes in behavior. It is critical to identify the mechanisms, rules, procedures, and incentives/disincentives that will promote information sharing and foster the creation of organizations, programs, and systems that will support it. Sharing information must become part of the DNA of the national security, intelligence, and homeland security communities, federal state and local officials, and the private sector. Viewing the private sector as an equal partner in detecting, preventing, and responding to terrorist attacks must become second nature to intelligence, law enforcement, and other government agencies. Dramatically improving information sharing between the government and the private sector will take creativity and persistence from the executive branch, Congress, state and local officials, and business leaders.

NOTES

1. Bergen 2002.
2. The 9/11 Public Discourse Project, which comprises the continued efforts of the National Commission on Terrorist Attacks Upon the United States (known as the 9/11 Commission), issued a report card in December 2005, in which it gave the federal government a grade of "D" for its information sharing efforts (see 9/11 Public Discourse Project 2005). Similar concern over progress in information sharing with the private sector was expressed in congressional testimony by Zoe Baird, President of the Markle Foundation, before the House Permanent Select Committee on Intelligence (Baird 2005).
3. U.S. Department of Justice 1998.
4. Government Accountability Office (GAO) 2004b.
5. GAO 2004b, Table 2.
6. GAO 2004b, Table 2.
7. These changes were reinforced by the National Strategy for Homeland Security in July 2002 and Homeland Security Presidential Directive 7 in December 2003.
8. GAO 2004b.
9. Office of Homeland Security 2002, p. xi: The National Strategy for Homeland Security identifies five major initiatives in this area: integrate information sharing across the federal government; integrate information sharing across state and local governments, private industry, and citizens; adopt common "meta-data" standards for electronic information relevant to homeland security; improve public safety emergency communications; and ensure reliable public health information.

10. Office of the President 2003, p. xi: Information Sharing and Indications and Warnings. This strategy identifies six major initiatives in this area: (1) define protection-related information sharing requirements and establish effective, efficient information sharing processes; (2) implement the statutory authorities and powers of the Homeland Security Act of 2002 to protect security and proprietary information regarded as sensitive by the private sector; (3) promote the development and operation of critical sector Information Sharing Analysis Centers; (4) improve processes for domestic threat data collection, analysis, and dissemination to state and local government and private industry; (5) support the development of interoperable secure communications systems for state and local governments and designated private sector entities; and (6) complete implementation of the Homeland Security Advisory System.

11. White House 2003a. "Coordination with the Private Sector: (25) In accordance with applicable laws or regulations, the Department and the Sector-Specific Agencies will collaborate with appropriate private sector entities and continue to encourage the development of information sharing and analysis mechanisms. Additionally, the Department and Sector-Specific Agencies shall collaborate with the private sector and continue to support sector-coordinating mechanisms: (a) to identify, prioritize, and coordinate the protection of critical infrastructure and key resources; and (b) to facilitate sharing of information about physical and cyber threats, vulnerabilities, incidents, potential protective measures, and best practices."

12. White House 2005.

13. Chertoff 2005.

14. See sections 211–214 of the Homeland Security Act.

15. A full list of HSOC participants includes the Federal Bureau of Investigation, U.S. Coast Guard; U.S. Postal Inspection Service; Central Intelligence Agency; U.S. Secret Service; Washington, D.C., Metropolitan Police Department; Defense Intelligence Agency; Federal Protective Service; New York Police Department; National Security Agency; U.S. Customs and Border Protection; Los Angeles Police Department; U.S. Immigration Customs Enforcement (including Federal Air Marshal Service); U.S. Department of Energy; U.S. Environmental Protection Agency, Drug Enforcement Administration; U.S. Department of the Interior (U.S. Park Police); Bureau of Alcohol, Tobacco, Firearms, and Explosives; U.S. Department of Defense; U.S. Department of State; U.S. Department of Transportation; U.S. Department of Veterans Affairs, National Capitol Region; Transportation Security Administration; National Geospatial-Intelligence Agency; U.S. Department of Health and Human Services; Federal Emergency Management Agency; National Oceanic Atmospheric Administration; and the Department of Homeland Security's Public Affairs, Office of State and Local Coordination, Science and Technology Directorate, Geo-spatial Mapping Office, Information Analysis Office, and Infrastructure Protection Office.

16. According to the DHS Inspector General, significant personnel shortages inhibited the integration process of DHS' Information Analysis and Infrastructure Protection directorate in its first years of operation. See Department of Homeland Security 2004.

17. For example, GAO noted a lack of clear roles for DHS and Department of Transportation when it came to transportation security (see Government Accountability Office 2003c). To clarify roles, GAO recommended that the Department of Transportation and DHS enter a memorandum of understanding, a recommendation with which DOT and DHS disagreed.

18. Starks and Andersen 2004.

19. Starks and Andersen 2004.
20. See White House 2003.
21. GAO 2004b, p. 10.
22. ISAC Council 2004b. See also Government Accountability Office 2004b. For text of the Privacy Act of 1974, see http://www.cftc.gov/foia/foiprivacyact.htm, accessed November 2005.
23. From Knake 2005.
24. GAO 2004d. The FBI's goal is to complete the processing for secret security clearances within 45 to 60 days and top secret security clearances within 6 to 9 months, beginning with the FBI headquarters' receipt of the application from the FBI field office. Since September 11, about 92 percent of applications for top secret security clearances were processed within the FBI's timeframe goals. During this same period, about 26 percent of secret security clearance applications were processed within the FBI's timeframe goals. The FBI was more successful with processing top secret security clearances within its stated timeframe goals than secret security clearances, in part because the FBI often assigns greater priority to processing applications for state and local Joint Terrorism Task Force (JTTF) members.
25. Madigan 2005.
26. Hamilton 2005.
27. Government Accountability Office 2004c.
28. Government Accountability Office 2004c and Harris 2004.
29. McCall 2005.
30. Hoekstra 2005.
31. GAO 2004b, p. 9.
32. Commission on the Roles and Capabilities of the U.S. Intelligence Community 1996. See also Federation of American Scientists 2004.
33. See, for example, Flynn 2005b.
34. Marks 2004.
35. For a thorough history and overview, see Elias et al. 2005.
36. See, for example, Goo 2004.
37. GAO 2005a.
38. GAO 2005b.
39. Berrick 2006.
40. Singel 2005b.
41. The Department of Homeland Security Appropriations Act, as cited in Berrick 2006.
42. CBS News 2005. See also Singel 2005a.
43. GAO 2005a.
44. McCullagh and Broache 2006.
45. McCullagh and Broache 2006.
46. Cauley and Diamond 2006.
47. Risen and Lichtblau 2005.
48. Cauley and Diamond 2006.
49. Associated Press 2006.
50. Yoran 2004a. See also Yoran 2004b.
51. The Carnegie Mellon CERT Coordination Center serves as a major reporting center for Internet security problems, provides technical advice and coordinates responses to security compromises, identifies trends, works with other security experts to identify solutions to security problems, and disseminates information to the broad community.

The coordination center also analyzes product vulnerabilities, publishes technical documents, and presents training courses.

52. Ortolani and Block 2005.
53. Although ATS inputs go well beyond advance manifest information, the scope and reliability of the cargo information currently received under the "24-hour rule" is reinforced by the Trade Act Final Rule published on December 5, 2003. This rule mandates advance electronic cargo information inbound and outbound for all modes of transportation.
54. See Coalition for Secure Ports (undated).
55. Block 2005.
56. Sarkar 2004.
57. Dempsey 2004.
58. Commission on the Intelligence Capabilities of the United States Regarding Weapons of Mass Destruction 2005.
59. Harrington 2005.
60. See, for example, http://www.globalsecurity.org/security/library/news/2005/02/dhs_iaip_daily_2005-02-28.pdf, accessed November 2005.
61. See http://www.rainsnet.org/files/PDF/RAINS_Connect_and_Protect_Fact_Sheet.pdf, accessed November 2005.
62. See http://www.rainsnet.org/downloads/RAINS_Fact_Sheet.pdf, accessed November 2005.
63. Government Accountability Office 2004b, pp. 9–10.
64. See, for example, Baird 2005.
65. Government Accountability Office 2005d.
66. Frank 2004; Strohm 2005; Mintz and Schmidt 2004; Sherman 2005; and Leavitt 2005.
67. Block 2005.
68. Block 2005; McCullagh and Broache 2006.
69. Ralyea and Seifert 2004. Also see GAO 2004a,b; and ISAC Council 2004a,b.

24

SHARING THE WATCH

Public–Private Collaboration for Infrastructure Security

John D. Donahue and Richard J. Zeckhauser

Vital physical assets must be protected. But against what risks? And how? And by whom? And at whose expense? After the terrorist attacks of 2001, these questions were propelled from back offices into boardrooms and cabinet meetings. The way American society resolves such questions will reshape broad swaths of the economy for the foreseeable future.

Security can be provided by the public sector, the private sector, or some blend of the two. The separability of financing and delivery further multiplies the options. For example, protection can be provided publicly but funded privately (through special tax levies on affected industries) or be provided privately but funded publicly (through tax subsidies or direct grants), or with various mixtures of public and private provision and funding.

This profusion of alternative delivery models is not hypothetical. Property owners defend against fire risks in part through private responses – alarms, extinguishers, sprinkler systems, fireproof materials – and in part through reliance on publicly provided fire fighters. Public police forces and private security services co-exist – although in the United States, the private force, in the aggregate, is larger (around a million private security guards, as of 2003, compared with about 600,000 police[1]) – and dividing lines can blur, as when public police officers moonlight for private clients. Airline security arrangements have skittered between public and private realms in recent years – from for-profit contractors employed by airports and paid for by airlines (prior to 9/11) to a federal agency partly funded by special taxes, with some recent moves toward a mixed system involving both public and private players.[2] The problem of determining who should do what, and what criteria should guide assignment becomes more complex and more consequential as the repertoire of delivery models expands.

Joint action for infrastructure protection is all but inevitable: Neither sector on its own likely possesses the requisite mix of information, resources, and incentives. And there is small hope that the nation will slide into the right arrangements along the path of least resistance.[3] For example, private owners of vulnerable assets, reasoning that war (including "war on terror") is government's concern, expect the public sector to do the heavy lifting. Government, in turn, sees firms' concentrated stakes in valuable assets as ample private incentive to invest in protection against low-probability but high-loss events. Efficient collaboration is not the natural outcome of incentives in alignment against well-posed threats, but a construct of analysis, transactional architecture, and management.

This chapter examines the application to infrastructure protection of a particular form of public–private collaboration that we term "collaborative governance." Drawing on our broader work on collaborative governance, we introduce policy challenges and responses that have been employed in other settings and that offer lessons for infrastructure protection. The policy record, with respect to low-probability, high-cost threats, provides many pitfalls to avoid and suggests few templates to apply. The ability of intricate networks to find fresh ways to fail tends to outpace society's ability to develop regulatory and other bulwarks against failure, as witnessed by power blackouts such as afflicted the northeastern United States in 2003. The government's stance on natural disasters is rarely prevention (the focus of this chapter), but rather mitigation of consequences. Here too, however, experience has shown the limitations of state and local regulations and response services, federal support, and private insurance markets. And the policy response to the grim possibilities illustrated by the 9/11 terrorist attacks is not fully formulated, let alone tested. Both success and failure, though, offer insight into how to align public and private interests and energies. Our intent in this chapter is not to definitively pinpoint the ideal configuration of collaborative arrangements for infrastructure security. Rather, we seek to array and illustrate the principles that guide wise choices in crafting and managing collaboration.

Elsewhere we have defined collaborative governance as "the pursuit of authoritatively chosen public goals by means that include engaging the efforts of, and sharing discretion with, producers outside of government."[4] Collaborative governance is distinguished both from simple contracting and from private voluntarism by the allocation of operational discretion. In a pure goods or services contract, the government retains all discretion – for example, New York City's government might hire a private firm to put up barricades along a Midtown parade route. Pure voluntary provision would be illustrated by the Midtown Manhattan Association hiring private guards to patrol a particular stretch of the route. Volunteerism places all discretion with the donor. At these two extremes, strategic interaction is relatively sparse.

In collaborative governance, by contrast, each party helps to determine both the means by which a broadly defined goal is achieved and the specifics of the goal itself. A charter school, for example, receives public funds to educate the children in its charge. Within the broad parameters set by its charter, it has considerable flexibility with respect to curriculum, staffing, the length of the school day and year, and other key determinants of education. The shared discretion that is the hallmark of collaborative governance can augment the capacity available for public missions and increase the flexibility with which such missions are pursued. But a price is paid: Authority becomes ambiguous, strategic complexity grows, and agency problems proliferate.

Debates over physical security have long featured both a privileging of the state in principle, and a blend of public and private responsibilities in practice. Max Weber explicitly defined government as "the human community that successfully claims the monopoly of the legitimate use of physical force,"[5] and Hobbes reluctantly prescribed submission to Leviathan as the only remedy to the "war of all against all." Yet the U.S. Constitution – often considered the blueprint for the modern state – was written in the wake of a war fought in part by extra-governmental forces – Hessian mercenaries on the British side and the "Pennsylvania Associators" on the other.[6] More currently, the United States has relied on private forces in Iraq and elsewhere for functions that are only marginally distinguishable from classic combat operations.[7]

Although large-scale armed conflict tends to be the state's province today, private forces routinely engage in lower-level security functions. Most large universities, for example, have their own police forces to maintain order on campus and protect prominent or controversial guests who might excite violent protest. When public figures who are potential terrorism targets visit Harvard University, they are protected by a mix of public and private forces. A senior federal official might be guarded by the Secret Service and campus police while he gives his speech, with a phalanx of off-duty local police (paid by the university) monitoring entrances and exits and state police escorting him to and from the airport.

In short, long before terrorism became a major concern in the twenty-first century United States, collaborative approaches to protection – although not discussed in those terms – were both a subject of debate and a practical tool in the provision of security. To reap the benefits and curb the risks of collaborative arrangements for infrastructure security, one must understand the phenomenon more generally. For example, an appreciation of how we protect our food supply against contaminants or our hospital care against costly error will help explain how to protect our ports and power plants against terrorism. Moreover, unless one can understand the forces that shape collaborative governance across a society, it is difficult to discern how best to allocate discretion and divide responsibility in the specific area of infrastructure protection.

This chapter begins with a few general observations on the rising – or to be more precise, restored – importance of non-governmental actors in public undertakings, a category that includes but goes beyond collaborative governance. Next, it probes some of the dynamics of shared discretion in the pursuit of public goals. Finally, it characterizes the fundamental challenge of a collaborative approach to infrastructure protection and the special imperatives the public sector must meet to perform its indispensable analytical and managerial functions within such arrangements.

Private engagement in governmental undertakings – both within and beyond the security arena – is neither new nor rare. Indeed, virtually every plausible blend of state and market organization has been observed in practice at some time and place. Nearly every developed nation's repertoire of collective-action models blends state and market components, but the preferred mix varies substantially by place, by time, and by project. Prominent private roles are the historical norm. But such roles seem novel against the backdrop of the extraordinary consolidation of federal authority in the mid-20th century. U.S. government spending exploded with the New Deal and World War II, from less than 4 percent of gross domestic product in 1930 to more than 44 percent 15 years later. Even after this wartime surge ebbed, federal spending rarely fell below 15 percent of gross domestic product, and the average for the second half of the twentieth century was 19.8 percent.[8] Quantitative expansion forced qualitative evolution as the mid-century heyday of the central government etched enduring patterns into organizational structures, administrative procedures, and the mindsets of scholars and practitioners.[9] Thus, we are apt to view delegated or shared public responsibilities as something novel. But constructing and maintaining arrangements for efficient and accountable public–private interaction has been, and is becoming once again, very much a mainstream task for managing the public's business.

RATIONALES AND RISKS OF INDIRECT GOVERNMENT ACTION

Non-governmental actors are appropriately enlisted into public undertakings – whether running a school or guarding a port – to improve performance in the creation of public value. Private entities may offer advantages over governmental organizations in several (partly overlapping) dimensions.

RESOURCES

Perhaps the simplest rationale for collaboration with the private sector arises when government lacks the resources (or the ability to mobilize the resources) required to accomplish a mission. Today, as empty public coffers coincide with urgent homeland security imperatives, this rationale holds special salience. In principle, "governmental resources" is both an imprecise and an elastic category. The U.S. government commands resources only as the citizens' steward, rather than on its own account. Its spending ability is not determined by its earning ability or its collateral available to support debt, but primarily by citizens' tolerance for taxation, including the future taxation implicit in public debt. So a declaration that government's resources are inadequate to realize some public goal translates to one or more possible scenarios:

- Citizens are unwilling to provide, through taxation, revenues to fund this particular undertaking – a situation that, if it strictly applied, should raise questions about whether the mission is accurately labeled as a "public goal."
- Citizens are not asked to provide designated resources for this particular goal, so one cannot assess their willingness to pay for it, but their tolerance of taxation in the aggregate is exhausted, or nearly so.
- Procedural impediments (budget rules, debt limits) preclude incremental funding for this goal independent of its merits, and resources cannot be or are not diverted from other purposes.
- Citizens are willing to devote resources to the mission, but not enough to accomplish it with public funds alone. Only if costs borne by government can be lowered through an infusion of non-governmental resources, or by improving operational efficiency through private involvement, will it meet the net benefits test from the public perspective.
- Some aspects of a public project provide benefits are so narrowly directed to particular groups – such as the owners of a chemical factory, nuclear facility, or port – that the electorate believes the prime beneficiaries should pay at least a share and are unwilling to fund the endeavor except on these terms.

PRODUCTIVITY

A second generic rationale for indirect government production is that external agents possess productive capacity and capability that government lacks. By collaborating with firms or non-profit organizations, the government can tap the outside entity's efficiency edge to improve performance or lower costs or both, relative to acting alone. In one variant of this rationale, technical know-how, proprietary intellectual capital, or other potentially transferable capacity resides in the private sector instead of in the government. In a second variant, productivity advantages are not accidental but inherent in the private form of organization. Potential reasons for private advantages are familiar – the focused incentives of the profit motive (at for-profits) and procedural flexibility (at both for-profits and non-profits), the ability to harvest economies of scale and scope by operating beyond jurisdictional boundaries, and the motives inherent in the prospect that the quality of performance will affect the odds of extension, merger, or extinction. A third variant of the efficiency case for delegation has to do with standby capacity. If the need for a public undertaking arises only episodically – such as snow removal, disaster relief, or the Christmas-season surge in postal demand – it may be less costly to rely on the private sector for peak needs than for government to build up the surge capacity itself. (Or it may not; the choice turns on which sector, public or private, can better employ the standby resources when they are not needed to meet surge requirements.) The more important and embedded are private productivity advantages, the stronger the rationale for delegated, collaborative, or otherwise shared production.

INFORMATION

Even if the government's resources and productivity are identical to the private sector's, an initiative can be improved through private involvement when the government does not have pertinent information and would find it very difficult or prohibitively expensive to acquire it.[10] The types of data needed to carry out some publicly consequential task – such as information on the relative volatility and toxicity of different compounds in use at different locales within a chemical plant, or the docking schedule and processing time for various vessels and cargoes at a port – are often embodied in private organizations in ways that make it hard to share them with or sell them to government.

LEGITIMACY

Fans of old-time Westerns know that a group of citizens in hot pursuit of the bad guy was called a "posse" if the sheriff was involved and a "mob" if he was not. However, in some circumstances private involvement may enhance the perceived legitimacy of an undertaking. A particular task may be seen as inappropriate for the government to pursue on its own. Or if government is held in systematically low esteem by the citizenry, as in failed states or corrupt regimes, collaboration with the private sector can shore up legitimacy independent of any task-specific factors. In such circumstances, private-sector involvement may be necessary for effective public activity.

Legitimacy considerations may cut the other way, of course. Most people find it unremarkable for a private company to post night watchmen to guard against pilferage. But not many would endorse permitting the same company to send private interrogators to raid the homes of suspected pilferers; that is the government's job. When Ross Perot engaged private commandos to rescue two of his employees held hostage in an Iranian prison in 1979, some found it noble and some foolhardy, but few called for disbanding the U.S. State Department and the Special Forces in favor of Perot's self-service model. There may have been more of an outcry about private usurpation of a public responsibility if the employees had been imprisoned in Indiana rather than Iran.

GENERIC RATIONALES APPLIED
TO INFRASTRUCTURE SECURITY

In many policy arenas, we have examined elsewhere – including park management, student loans, and foreign assistance – collaboration between the public and private sectors is an option that may or may not turn out to be superior to direct provision, regulation, simple contracting, or autonomous voluntarism.[11] In contrast, infrastructure protection by its very nature usually involves some degree of inter-organizational, cross-sectoral collaboration. In the United States, all chemical factories and airlines, most power utilities and electricity transmission assets, and many port operations and nuclear facilities are privately owned. Even when an airport or power plant is in the government's hands, it is usually far removed from the public entities responsible for security. Collaboration is thus a necessity, rather than an option – although the terms of that collaboration can vary over a wide range.[12] (In this chapter, we focus on the sharing of responsibility for terrorism loss *prevention*. Different considerations can apply to public–private collaboration for recovery from a terrorist attack.)

While a substantial private role in infrastructure protection may be all but inevitable, its extent and contours are open issues, and the generic rationales for private involvement – resources, productivity, information, and legitimacy – do come into play in the infrastructure arena, though often in distinctive ways. The change in airport security screening in late 2001, for example, illustrates a tendency to perceive the government as having an advantage in the security arena that departs from the general presumption of greater private-sector efficiency in delivery of services (see Box 24.1). On productivity grounds alone, a case could probably be made for government to handle most functions associated with infrastructure protection.[13]

BOX 24.1 AIRPORT SECURITY DOES AN ABOUT-FACE

The relative efficacy of public and private service provision was at the core of the debate over airport security that erupted immediately after 9/11. The existing system of private passenger screening was suddenly, and with near-unanimity, denounced as inadequate. A public mission newly perceived to be of paramount importance – ensuring that nobody bent on destruction could board an airliner armed – had been entrusted to a cheap, rickety delivery system. The airlines, many of them chronically on the verge of insolvency, had been required to pay for passenger screening, and they had bid out the work to a highly competitive industry of private security firms. But to eke out any profit from their lean contracts with the airlines, these security firms had drawn their workers from the bottom of the labor pool. Screeners' wages had been paltry and benefits generally negligible; standards, naturally, had been low and turnover high (for example, screener turnover at Chicago's O'Hare International airport had been more than 200 percent per year).

What was to replace this unacceptable status quo? One option was to move passenger screening alongside other crucial security functions carried out directly by the government. The other option was to continue to delegate screening to specialized private providers, but with more funding, far higher standards, and direct government oversight.

The Bush administration and its allies in the House of Representatives proposed an upgraded security system that would still rely on private providers. Rival Senate legislation crafted by Democratic leaders with the help of Republican maverick John McCain, called for making passenger and baggage screening a governmental function carried out by public employees. Many commentators predicted that President Bush would get his way, as he had with so much else in the wake of the terrorist attacks. But as the dust settled after a House–Senate conference on the airport security bill, the proponents of direct governmental delivery had won nearly every point. The final legislation called for virtually all passenger and baggage screening to be performed by federal employees under a new Transportation Security Authority. Applicants lined up for positions in the authority, and a year after the law was passed there were more than 60,000 federal passenger and baggage screeners on the job in America's airports. Their training was rigorous, their compensation far better than that of their private-sector predecessors, and their job satisfaction demonstrably higher; once hired as a government screener, few workers quit.

Security is very likely better than it was prior to 9/11 – although the overall rarity of hijacking makes it hard to measure – but it is less clear that the increment of increased safety is worth the sharp increase in costs, or that the Transportation Security Authority performs better than would have an upgraded private system. The gross flaws in the previous contractual model did not preclude structuring a sturdier contractual arrangement. The work, however vital, is readily specified: Inspect every passenger and every piece of luggage to ensure that no weapon can be smuggled onto an airplane. Evaluation is more straightforward for airport screening than for many other functions that are delegated contractually. The performance of individual screeners can be gauged through actions and devices, for example by constantly testing security with dummy weapons or bombs and levying painful financial penalties for any lapse. Several large firms already operate in the industry, and entry is relatively easy, making airport screening far more competitive than many other outsourced functions. Such arrangements are not merely hypothetical; they were and are the norm in Israel and in many European countries that are sadly familiar with terrorism.

It is almost unimaginable, however, that the private sector would be entirely absent from infrastructure security arrangements. Although a wholly private arrangement might not comport well with citizens' views of the private sector's proper role, a purely governmental arrangement could raise questions both about expansion of state authority and, on quite different grounds, about the propriety of sparing private organizations the potentially substantial costs of security for private assets.

The most consistently valid argument for a collaborative approach to infrastructure security turns on information. The government itself almost certainly lacks the fine-grained understanding of particular infrastructure assets (and their forward and backward economic linkages), necessary to mount the most robust and least costly defenses, and also to determine an appropriate level of effort. The private organizations that own, operate, or depend on physical assets would generally possess far more complete information of the sort relevant to the protection of those assets than would the government. Yet the public sector likewise can have privileged or exclusive access to information and procedural options – intelligence data, negotiations with foreign governments, the right to detain a suspect or tap a phone line – that could, in principle, be extended to the private sector but generally are not. The difficulty of efficient information sharing even between government agencies hints at the likelihood of even greater coordination hurdles for cross-sectoral security efforts. Indeed, serious legal barriers can prohibit or constrain private firms' efforts to share information with government.

COSTS AND RISKS OF PRIVATE ROLES IN PUBLIC MISSIONS

Indirect government action can expand the resources devoted to a mission, enhance the efficiency with which they are deployed, provide richer and more detailed information to guide the undertaking, or boost its perceived legitimacy.

Against these generic advantages, however, society must weigh a range of potential costs, which are commonly called "agency losses." That is, the private agents may not faithfully fulfill the public's mission; for example, they may purport to act at government's behest but instead give excess weight to parochial concerns. Direct government action often entails agency costs as well. Elected officials and government workers can and do pursue their own agendas at the expense of citizens' interests. Relationships that reach across sectoral boundaries summon four distinctive threats to effectively fulfilling public missions: diluted control, higher spending, reputational vulnerability, and diminished capacity.

Diluted control occurs as a result of indirect action that explicitly diminishes government's monopoly of authority for defining the mission, directing the means, or both. Beyond this open and accepted dilution of autonomy, indirect action also involves the risk of unanticipated or unrecognized losses of control.

Higher spending is also a potential threat. Indirect production can sometimes prove more costly than anticipated, and it can even be more expensive than direct production for the same output. This increased cost can be because of an erroneous prediction of private productivity advantages, because of transactions costs, because the dilution of control leads to a different and more costly definition of the mission, or because private actors are able to exploit and extract resources from their governmental partner.

Most forms of indirect action expose the government to some risk that the actions of its agents will adversely affect its reputation. For example, if the government requires (or merely allows) a nuclear plant operator to deploy a private security force, and if members of that force needlessly hinder innocent hikers in the surrounding woods, the citizenry's ire will fall on both public and private parties.

Diminished capacity can result when indirect production discourages or even precludes the maintenance of capacity for direct governmental action. To the extent government depends on private capabilities, it puts itself at a disadvantage in future rounds of negotiation with its agents. Whether such factors present trivial or profound barriers to reverting to direct governmental delivery, and whether reliance on external capacity entails minor or major future costs, will depend on the details of each case. If a village delegates trash collection to a private waste-management firm, it can later reconstruct the status quo by purchasing a truck and hiring two men; if a state privatizes its prison system, it would be far more costly to reverse course.

In complex, large-scale missions, including most instances of infrastructure security, neither a pure public nor a pure private solution is likely to be the best choice. The challenge is to develop a blend of public and private roles that amplifies the benefits and controls the risks presented by each sector. In this light, it is useful to focus on the predominant feature that distinguishes collaborative governance from other forms of indirect governmental production – the explicit sharing of discretion.

SHARED DISCRETION AS THE HALLMARK OF COLLABORATIVE GOVERNANCE

Collaborative governance is defined by a mixed allocation of discretion. For an endeavor to be considered "governance" at all, a large share of discretion must rest with a player who is answerable to the public at large (where government is absent, weak, or undemocratic this condition is unlikely to hold). Collaboration begins when government yields the monopoly of control. Collaborative governance exists in the mid-range of the distribution of discretion; neither extreme can be considered collaboration. For example, corporate philanthropy is not collaboration. Companies enjoy wide discretion over their giving, and within very wide parameters their choices are presumptively defined as "the public good" for tax purposes. Although the public sector surrenders tax revenue it would have otherwise received, it is essentially a passive partner to the company's actions.

Similarly, a municipal government's contract with a private waste-management company is delegation but not collaboration. The company's mission to pick up the garbage and dump it at the landfill is explicit, complete, and controlled by the government, and its motive is to maximize the net revenue it receives in return. The private player is a highly constrained agent, nothing more, and discretion rests with the government. Understanding the ramifications of alternative allocations of discretion requires distinguishing among three forms of discretion: those involving production, payoffs, and preferences.

PRODUCTION DISCRETION

A fundamental motive for indirect governmental action is the realistic prospect of efficiency gains (relative to direct provision) through engaging private capacity. But this motive does not, on its own, call for collaborative governance. The government can often harness private efficiency advantages, while avoiding the complexities of shared discretion, through simple procurement contracts. If the government requires a truck, a bus route, or a software package, and recognizes that acquiring it from the private sector is likely to be more efficient than producing it internally, it can specify its requirements, invite competing bids, and choose the provider that promises to deliver on the best terms.[14] The contractor, once selected, is permitted a good deal of latitude over how to go about meeting the terms of the deal, but the definition of ends remains government's prerogative.

In addition, in contracting for security services, it is often impractical, unwise, or flatly impossible for the government to fully specify its goals. For example, because the Department of Homeland Security has little understanding about what combination of ambulance drivers, nurses, and emergency room technicians would be most valuable to blunting a smallpox outbreak in Muncie, Indiana, it lets administrators at Ball Memorial Hospital set priorities for vaccinating "first responders." The Occupational Safety and Health Administration may focus on trash compactors as the greatest danger to grocery store employees, but the manager of the local Safeway may know that reducing loading-dock workers' risk of slipping on spilled produce would deliver far greater safety gains at the same cost. No government agency will likely match an automaker's judgment over the relative promise of innumerable changes in fuel, engines, design, and materials to boost mileage and hold down the costs of new-generation vehicles. And those who manage a liquefied natural gas (LNG) facility may know far better how to reduce its vulnerability to a terrorist attack than would government inspectors, both because of managers' familiarity with the operation of the facility and with other risks such as common crime, accidents, or disgruntled employees, all of which are somewhat analogous to, if less dire than, terrorism. Public goals often can be advanced more efficiently if private players are given some discretion not just over the means, but also over the ends to be pursued. When government yields a share of such discretion, it has crossed the line from simple delegation to collaborative governance.

In all but the most straightforward undertakings, permitting private agents to participate in the specification of what is to be produced, and how, greatly enhances the potential for efficiency improvements. Yet at the same time, the government may find it far more challenging to ensure accountability due to the two other forms of discretion that tend to be unwelcome concomitants of production discretion.

PAYOFF DISCRETION

Granting production discretion to private collaborators can increase the efficiency of governance and create more value than either direct government production or contractual delegation with tightly defined goals. However, the collaborating partners must deal with the distribution of that augmented pool of value. Allocating the payoff from any one productive arrangement can be conceptually rich and operationally complex, but matters become far more complicated when collaborations feature a choice among alternative arrangements that lead to different distributions of value. For example, an automaker would favor a new-generation car campaign that relies heavily on reformulated fuel (imposing a fixed cost on the oil industry) rather than absorbing its own fixed cost of redesigned engines. If there must be new kinds of engines, however, the automaker would like to maximize the government's share of the research and development investment required. Similarly, a company that has already made progress on diesel-electric hybrids would like the campaign to anchor on that design rather than alternatives that play to the strengths of rivals. In short, once given discretion, private parties will attempt to shape the undertaking to increase their parochial payoffs.

When production alternatives entail different distributions of value, production discretion is inevitably entangled with payoff discretion. This makes the government vulnerable when it lacks full information about each alternative's efficiency and payoffs. When information is incomplete or private actors possess information that the government lacks, collaboration is apt to yield results that fall well short of what the potential could be if all information were fully shared. At worst, collaboration may lead to a choice of ends, and net gains in public value, that are inferior to what could be obtained through direct governmental production or through delegation by means of fully specified contracts. This risk is recognized, however, and explains why the government is normally chary about sharing discretion. On the other hand, conventional tactics for limiting the government's vulnerability to payoff discretion – such as tight performance goals, ceilings on agents' payoffs, or aggressive after-the-fact auditing – frequently sacrifice some of the efficiency gains of production discretion.

PREFERENCE DISCRETION

Payoff discretion has to do with the distribution value that can be expressed in monetary form. Preference discretion is a related but broader concept. Payoffs come in various forms that collaborators may value differentially. It is in the very nature of public missions that parties will differ in how they define the good. For example, a new private security arrangement in midtown Manhattan – say creating a protective cordon around a several-block area with random inspections of entering vehicles – may yield greater protection for buildings, but new inconveniences, reduced freedom of movement, and greater privacy invasion for the public. This arrangement may please the building owners who control the Midtown Manhattan Association, but displease pedestrians and hence the City Council.

As with payoff discretion, the challenge to efficient and accountable collaboration comes from the tendency for preference discretion to be entangled with production discretion. Government cannot be sure that a collaborator

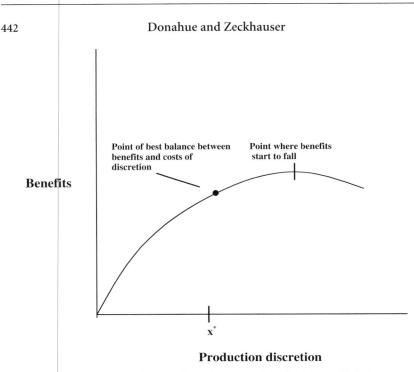

Figure 24.1. Production discretion boosts benefits (up to a Point).

is guided by his expertise or by his interests as he seeks to shape the mix of outputs the collaboration yields.

The central task for government officials attempting to create public value through collaborative arrangements is to maximize the efficiency gains of production discretion, after accounting for the losses associated with payoff and preference discretion. The optimal level of production discretion is found where the marginal benefit of production discretion equals the combined marginal costs of payoff discretion and preference discretion.[15]

The core task can be illustrated graphically, as well as stated in words and in equations. In Figure 24.1, the value gained through collaboration (relative to the polar cases of direct production or pure contracting) rises as private players are granted more production discretion. That discretion is exercised by choosing superior means for reaching a particular point, or by achieving production points unavailable to government acting on its own or through agents bound by tight contractual specifications. The gains of production discretion flatten as the potential of agents' productive and informational superiority is progressively exhausted. As discretion expands into areas where agents are less deft and worse informed than government – payoffs begin to diminish.

Alas, production discretion is generally accompanied by undesirable private discretion over payoffs and preferences. (To simplify the exposition, we

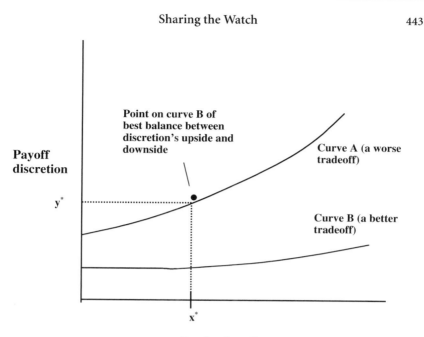

Figure 24.2. Payoff discretion as unwelcome fellow traveler of production discretion.

merely discuss payoff discretion here. The analysis for preference discretion would be much the same.) The ratio between production and payoff discretion is by no means a constant. Figure 24.2 shows two different trajectories of the relationship between these two types of discretion. Some payoff discretion is unavoidable, as shown by the vertical intercepts of the production possibility curves. Curve A illustrates a situation in which relatively little additional payoff discretion is incurred at the early stages of the range. The balance becomes somewhat worse as government continues to loosen constraints on private collaborators. Curve B illustrates a less-fortunate marginal relationship between production and payoff discretion.

Figure 24.2 might be thought of as illustrating two different arenas of collaborative governance, one with an inherently favorable relationship between good and bad discretion and the other with a more troublesome entanglement. Curve A might illustrate an "adopt a highway" program, in which local businesses take responsibility for clearing litter from a stretch of road in exchange for being allowed to post signs that publicize their civic-mindedness (as well as their donuts or health-care services through name recognition). Curve B might depict the hypothetical midtown-Manhattan security scenario addressed in the previous section, in which structures can be secured at a steep price in convenience and privacy. In the first case, the nature of the task itself presents private agents with limited opportunities to expropriate payoffs or insinuate

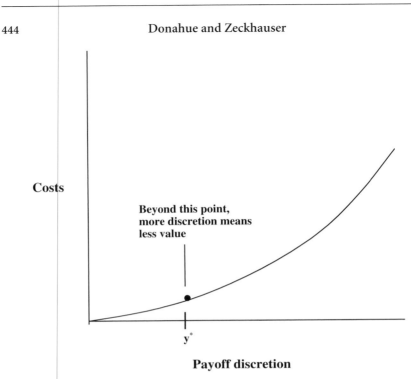

Costs

**Beyond this point,
more discretion means
less value**

y*

Payoff discretion

Figure 24.3. The degree of payoff discretion to accept.

preferences as they are given progressively more production discretion. In the second case, the temptation to push private interests, at the expense of the public interest, is pervasive.

Alternatively, and just as validly, Curves A and B can be thought of as referring to the same collaboration, but with more- and less-sophisticated governmental efforts to structure and manage the relationship. Curve B, in this version, would represent a feebly designed adopt-a-highway or city security program. Curve A would represent the same endeavor, but with more astute measures to harvest the gains while minimizing the losses that come with private discretion. In the highway case, for example, signs identifying benefactors might be smaller but more frequent to solidify the link between a company's image and the condition of a given stretch of roadway. In the security case, a Curve A scenario might involve the government requiring that arrangements be submitted to and approved by the City Council before being implemented, or it could institute a complaints process with stiff financial penalties levied against the private association in the event of unreasonable impositions on citizens.

While Figure 24.2 shows how payoff discretion rises with the level of production discretion, Figure 24.3 shows how much this costs. The value lost through payoff discretion grows as government loosens the reins, with the rate of loss accelerating as government exercises less control over its collaborators' ability to claim larger payoffs or to substitute their preferences for those of the public at large.

For simplicity, we assume there is no preference discretion, or that it is costless. The optimum allocation of discretion is derived from the three functions represented on Figures 24.1, 24.2, and 24.3. It is found at x^*, implying that payoff discretion will be at y^*, and that the program will operate at the points along the curves corresponding to y^* (note that the marginal benefit of greater production discretion, the slope at the point of the curve corresponding to x^* in Figure 24.1, just equals the marginal cost). The latter is the product of the slopes at points B and C in Figures 24.2 and 24.3. That product represents the increase in payoff discretion from a unit increase in production discretion times the marginal cost of that increase. Parallel figures to 24.2 and 24.3 could be presented for preference discretion. They would have the same general shape. In weighing how much production discretion to grant, the counterbalancing costs of the accompanying payoff and preference discretion would be added together.

The outcomes for the public of collaborative governance, as these illustrations hint, can range from spectacular to calamitous, depending on government officials' ability to determine when collaboration is a promising approach, to judge how much discretion to cede to private agents, and to fine-tune the terms of the collaboration so as to maximize the benefits less the costs associated with shared discretion.

RISKS OF COLLABORATIVE APPROACHES TO INFRASTRUCTURE SECURITY

The risks of a collaborative approach to infrastructure security involve both payoff and preference discretion. The most obvious vulnerability associated with payoff discretion involves the allocation of costs. The managers of private firms involved in collaborative security efforts – assuming that they are faithful stewards for their shareholders – would prefer to maximize the government's share of the protection bill, including costs incurred for security benefits that fall to the firm itself rather than to the public at large. This logic extends to firms' natural desire to minimize any cost-increasing or profit-decreasing constraints on their operations. For example, imagine that building a triple-fence security perimeter patrolled by National Guardsmen could reduce by 90 percent the public risks of an attack on a chemical plant, at a discounted lifetime cost of $100 million. And suppose that reformulating the plant's product line or performing strict security vetting of all employees could achieve the same reduction for a mere $50 million. If the government pays most of the cost for the first option and the firm pays all for the second, one would expect the private collaborator to use its discretion to tilt toward the perimeter patrol.

Similarly, firms will generally wield their discretion to favor anti-terrorism measures that offer ancillary private benefits. Installing floodlights throughout a port can deter petty theft and vandalism as well as terrorism, and a recent report from the Inspector General at the Department of Homeland Security suggests payoff discretion has been at work in the allocation of public port-security money. A port adjacent to a luxury entertainment complex (a target for security threats completely unrelated to terrorism) received a grant for surveillance equipment that the auditors found to "support the normal course of business" rather than respond to realistic terror threats.[16]

A systematic hazard involving payoff discretion is embodied (although experts differ as to what degree) in the Terrorism Risk Insurance Act of 2002 (TRIA), that introduced considerable public cost-sharing without curbing private discretion. This law was enacted in response to complaints that private terrorism coverage had become expensive and sometimes unavailable in the wake of the 9/11 attacks. There were respectable arguments for and against major government participation in the insurance market – arguments that continue today. TRIA ended up socializing the upper range of losses from terrorism damage to property (see Chapter 19 for a discussion of the components of TRIA). For risks covered by TRIA, private-property owners see little payoff in reducing their exposure to risks above the ceiling where government bears most of the cost, particularly because their insurance companies are unlikely to reward them for doing so. The distribution of losses from a terrorist act can be expected to dampen their incentive to invest in risk reduction, relative to alternative insurance arrangements, though the extent of the distortion is a matter of debate.[17]

Each firm in an industry would also like shared security regimes to be structured in ways that favor their business strategies over competitors'. A nuclear plant that has been operating for a long time, with 20 years' worth of spent fuel rods stored on the premises, will push for protection policies focused on nuclear waste; a newer plant will see more payoff in policies that concentrate on threats to the reactor itself. Requirements for a half-mile buffer zone around ports handling hazardous cargoes – accompanied by limited grants to buy adjacent land – would be devastating to a port in the middle of a dense, pricey city, but quite acceptable (and possibly even attractive for its competitive edge) for a port in an isolated community.[18]

Infrastructure security poses fewer obvious problems of conflicting preferences among collaborating parties than do some other arenas for public–private collaboration. Despite differing interests on the allocation of cost, and on the details of security arrangements, the basic goal of reducing expected terrorist losses is shared by government, private asset owners, and security owners. In social services, by contrast, some people consider it a very good thing if religious messages accompany substance-abuse counseling, and some people consider it a very bad thing. In matters of infrastructure protection, interests about salient choices are reasonably aligned. Everyone dislikes risk and would prefer to spend efficiently.

Yet even here there is room for divergent preferences at the margin, and private discretion can entail public costs. Private firms may also value the *perception* of security as well as its reality. Customers and possibly investors may find it hard to gauge levels of or changes in risk, and they may respond to visible risk-reduction measures as well as (or instead of) real but obscure reductions in the probability of a damaging attack. Private collaborators, moreover, will also prefer arrangements that give them privileged access to public security resources. To the extent that a major employer can shape the contingency plan for a regional alert, it would send more police and National Guardsmen to the local chemical plant than to the local hospital, school, or armory. Public and private players may also have different time preferences. A firm may doubt that investors will have much tolerance for short-term security spending in the name of long-term risk reduction. The government also has its own reasons for truncated time horizons, such as limited terms in office.

SECURITY EXTERNALITIES

In an alternative universe in which governments did not exist – but terrorism did – the private sector would assuredly take major steps to reduce the risk of attacks on infrastructure and to buffer the damage should an attack occur. Companies that own a particular asset would be motivated by the fact that terror attacks are bad for business. They destroy or damage capital assets, kill or injure employees with firm-specific skills, disrupt operations while facilities are repaired or rebuilt, suppress demand because customers are scared away, and raise the cost and reduce the availability of insurance against all these prospects. A rational company – with no motive other than maximizing the expected present value of net revenues – would spend on infrastructure protection up to the margin where its private value of incremental risk reduction reached its private cost of further security. Yet infrastructure protection is a governance challenge, not merely a business challenge, because threats to critical infrastructure have costs, and thus risk reduction has benefits, that extend far beyond private owners of infrastructure assets. Attacks on infrastructure can destroy neighboring assets. Collateral damage can be minor (the hot-dog stand adjacent to the oil pipeline pumping station) or major (the metropolis down-wind from the nuclear power plant). Beyond the direct cost of physical losses would be the loss of business for other companies that depended upon destroyed or damaged infrastructure. On the special ledger of human casualties, losses external to the private firm come in two forms. First, dead or injured employees are much more than bundles of firm-specific skills. Second, in many imaginable incidents involving infrastructure, employees themselves would account for a minority of human casualties. More generally, a private company would have only minor motives – proportional to its share of the economy – to worry about the prospect of diffuse economic damage as confidence drops in the wake of an attack.

The term "positive security externality" describes a situation in which protection spending by one party benefits another. Such externalities may stem from many sources. One party's security efforts may prevent damage that would spill beyond bounds of ownership; or the spending party may control one element in a vital chain of products; or information may be gained from the efforts of each party that purchases security. Private arrangements would recognize and respond appropriately to some of these external risks, even in a world without government. For example, a factory that depended on a rail link or pipeline would rationally pay some or most of the security costs for that asset, even if it did not own it. A sufficiently sophisticated insurance industry would lead firms to internalize many external liability costs. Even a rudimentary tort system would stimulate A to enhance safety for B beyond its own pure self-interested level. Quite apart from traditional incentive structures for exchange, insurance, and liability, one could expect to see cost sharing to protect assets. For example, citizens of a nearby city, recognizing their vulnerability, would likely chip in to protect a nuclear plant. But transactions costs are likely to be significant, and complex negotiations may degenerate into stalemate. Alas, there are apt to be impediments to highly efficient security arrangements when the owner of the asset to be protected collects only a small fraction of the benefits.

However inventive private arrangements might be, when externalities abound society should still expect an inadequate supply of security absent government participation. When there are multiple parties sharing in a public good, voluntary provision falls far short, and the tort system tends to get short circuited. Beyond this, security investments shift probabilities rather than creating certainties; this makes it harder to estimate production relationships or tell what level of security is being provided. The resulting information asymmetries create barriers to effective contracting, since participants cannot tell what they are getting for their contributions.

ALLOCATING THE COSTS OF SECURITY

In a world of underprovision, government may step in to help reach the appropriate social level of spending. The government has three main tools for altering

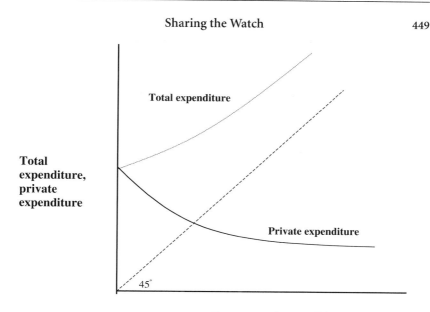

Government expenditure

Figure 24.4. As government spends more, private spending sags and total spending lags.

private decisions about security: direct provision, regulation, and collaboration. Private companies, with plenty of alternative claims on their own resources, would naturally prefer for government to provide and pay for any needed security investments. But government budgets are chronically strained. Moreover, if they faithfully represent taxpayers' interests, governments will spend to reduce the public, but not the private, damages that a terror attack would produce. If security is left entirely to the public sector, then, there would be less spending on protection, in the aggregate, than the combination of public and private stakes would warrant.

A second objection to declaring security to be primarily or solely the government's burden is the question of equity. If the government is supposed to spend significant dollars protecting infrastructure, those who create infrastructure are in effect imposing a tax on the body politic. Moreover, infrastructure owners will have insufficient incentive to make their assets easy to protect. The situation might be as shown in Figure 24.4. Here the level of private provision and total provision is a function of the level of government provision. For simplicity, assuming that only total expenditure mattered, if private provision were strongly responsive to the level of public provision (i.e., the bottom curve slopes steeply), government provision would primarily shift costs to itself rather than enhance security.

When the government wishes to economize on public spending, but still achieve adequate security, it often adopts regulation. For example, insurance companies must have adequate reserves, bicycle helmets must meet crash standards, and buildings must meet construction codes to protect against plumbing failures and fires. Some current regulations protect against terrorism. For example, nuclear power plants are required, as a condition of their licensing, to meet certain security standards. If the government knew precisely what should be done beyond these minimum standards, and if it had the power to impose desirable requirements, the regulatory approach would produce an ideal outcome for infrastructure security. But these are heroic "ifs." To some extent, these imposed expenditures offset other private expenditures. If the displacement is because those costs were inefficient, say because they tended merely to protect the spending party, then regulation can enhance efficiency. However, if the displaced costs would have created superior security, and the government regulation was chosen by mistake, say because of inadequate knowledge, or because certain expenditures are easier to monitor, then regulation will sacrifice efficiency.

In the collaborative governance approach, government extends certain benefits – such as cash or freedom from regulatory imposition, or the right to make claims on certain public resources – to private entities that agree to provide enhanced security. The advantages of collaboration are specific instances of the generic gains we discuss throughout this chapter. The deal the government strikes with the private players grants resources (which may include freedom from some governmental requirements) in exchange for the private sector taking on certain responsibilities. The private players may be protecting their own assets (e.g., the government could pay a third of the costs for a chemical company's security program); or they may be predominantly protecting other entities' private assets or even public assets (e.g., a port authority might hire a private firm to secure its facilities.) The nature, extent, and effect of private security efforts will be shaped by the government's stance, by the inherent interests of the private collaborators, and by the details of the collaboration's structure.

None of these three approaches to the problem of positive security externalities is likely to be fully successful, but some will be better than others at aligning resources with interests. When the externalities are small relative to the benefits going to the spending party, concerns should be minimal. When there is just one affected party, rather than many, efficient contracting on security levels will require only moderate transactional complexity. Time and money requirements for meetings, contracts, and lawyers will not be so burdensome as to deter rational security efforts. But when there are many parties with stakes in the same security arrangements; limited liability; and externalized losses that are large relative to internalized losses, security externalities are less tractable. Consider an LNG facility that is worth $20 million, owned by a company with a market value of $100 million. A potential terrorist attack could trigger an explosion that would produce a total of $3 billion in damages, with most of the losses suffered by neighboring populations, businesses, and interconnected systems.[19] For $10 million, the LNG facility can reduce the lifetime chance of such an explosion from 1.1 percent to 0.1 percent. Society at large would benefit from such an expenditure, because in probabilistic terms it saves 1 percent × $3 billion, or $30 million. Yet the owners of the LNG facility will not make the expenditure if their own risk is limited to the $20 million value of the plant itself. Even if tort claims by damaged neighbors meant large and inescapable liability costs in the event of an attack, the firm itself would never be willing to spend more than the $100 million it would lose if it were sued into bankruptcy. It would not be hard to imagine circumstances where the optimal level of security spending, for society as a whole, exceeded the market value of the asset owner.

When significant security externalities exist, the only way to achieve adequate investments in security is to have all affected parties contribute.[20] Economics provides a classic resolution to this problem, which is called the Lindahl solution.[21] Assuming that there is a public good (in this case security) that will be enhanced through expenditures by a particular party, the Lindahl solution finds the percentage shares of the costs that will lead all parties to demand the same quantity. We can illustrate this with another simplified hypothetical situation, this one involving a chemical plant that processes hazardous chemicals located next to a factory that is not a terrorist target, and near to a built-up commercial and residential zone. Suppose there is one spending party (e.g., the owners of the chemical plant), one external party with major stakes (e.g., the owners of the factory next door), and many other affected parties (e.g., nearby businesses and residents), each with relatively small stakes. The government represents the interests of the parties with individually small stakes. The Lindahl solution divides expenditures in proportion to benefits at the margin for the optimal total expenditure. If, for example, the spending burden were divided with 70 percent borne by the chemical plant, 10 percent by the neighboring factory, and 20 percent by the government, all three parties would favor a total security expenditure of $2 million. The chemical plant would spend $2 million on security, and collect contributions of $200,000 from the neighboring factory and $400,000 from the government.[22]

This sketch departs from reality in its assumption that the probabilities of an attack and, even more challenging, that the magnitude of risk reduction from the security measures, are known with some precision. Low-level probabilities are inherently hard to estimate because they offer little experience to rely upon. Normal statistical methods cannot be employed. Indeed, the vast majority of the time, nothing happens. Given that outcome, it is almost impossible to distinguish between situations where nothing would have happened absent the security measure and nothing happened because of the security measure. This estimation problem is redoubled because security measures affect the actions of the terrorists themselves. For example, if an intended target is protected, the terrorist can turn to a softer alternative target.[23] When an attack on a protected target is made, the security measure may prevent or ameliorate damage, and/or raise costs to the terrorists. Computing the benefits of security measures in such complex situations is extremely difficult.

Given that the public and private producers are sure to be tussling over costs, responsibilities, and credits, and that their interests diverge, each will have an incentive to provide its own estimates of the risks faced and the benefits (often probabilistic) that its own efforts provide. The challenges of probabilistic estimation – given the massive uncertainties here – exaggerate any natural tendencies to distort estimates to serve one's own purposes. These inherent uncertainties, and the likely disagreement on what expected benefits and costs would flow from potential actions, amplify the challenge of structuring a fair and feasible accommodation when security externalities are significant, as they usually are.

Moreover, while the balancing of burdens and benefits – and hence the management of payoff discretion – is challenging at any single point in time and in purely technical terms, it has important inter-temporal and political dynamics as well. Suppose government is able to structure an arrangement with a major port operator that features just the right blend of public and private expenditure and just the right pattern of risk-reduction investment at the start of the deal. The port operator is compensated just enough, and on just the right terms, to induce it to recognize the security externalities associated with its operations. Suppose, then, that many years pass without a major domestic terrorist attack. The port operator will be tempted – to the extent the terms of the deal and government's vigilance permit – to use its discretion to tilt security expenditures away from risk reduction and toward activities that boost profitability (e.g., installing attractive lighting in its tourist areas). To the extent this occurs, collaborative infrastructure protection is likely to be viewed as "corporate welfare," and to lose political legitimacy.

GOVERNMENT'S IMPERATIVES IN COLLABORATIVE INFRASTRUCTURE PROTECTION

Efforts to protect vital infrastructure in the coming decades will almost certainly involve extensive interaction between business and government, frequently featuring the shared discretion that is the hallmark of collaborative governance.

These arrangements could turn out to be flexible and effective, or rigid and lame. They may make a limited claim on resources and allocate costs in ways that are both fair and efficient, or they may entail bloated costs tilted toward the government in ways that undercuts private prudence and sap the public's willingness to pay for security. Which subsets of the many possible futures that turn out will depend on many factors, including revelations yet to come on the nature and extent of terrorism risks.

Thus, a pivotal determinant of whether infrastructure protection turns out to be efficient and robust, or expensive and flabby, will be government's ability to structure collaborative arrangements that give private players the proper incentives and focus public resources on broad public security. What does government need to get matters right in order to minimize the gap between the public and private benefits of investments in infrastructure security? The public-sector challenges in this arena are a particularly intense variant of the generic imperatives of collaborative governance. We array those imperatives as six distinguishable (though neither disjoint nor strictly sequential) steps:

1. *Appraisal.* Before designing a collaborative infrastructure security effort, government must first appraise the threat-reduction goal. It must map, as precisely as the data permit, both the public and the private risks embodied in the status quo – the nature and dimensions of the threat, the degree to which public and private vulnerabilities overlap or diverge, and the major uncertainties surrounding this appraisal. This first step, in short, involves figuring out what success looks like.

2. *Analysis.* Once the goal is tolerably well framed, the government needs to understand the capabilities and motivations of the players who may be engaged to help pursue it. The government must identify the array of private actors who are either inherently or potentially involved in security efforts; analyze the productive potential or resources they can bring to the enterprise; determine the preference and payoff motivations built into their economic structure and context; and identify the main points of congruence and conflict with broader public security goals. It must also predict how a particular configuration of security efforts is likely to influence external threats.

3. *Assignment.* Government officials, taking their cues from their appraisal of the mission and their analysis of private actors' abilities and intents, need to determine which security functions should be assigned to each party in the collaboration. These functions may be assigned across and within the public and private sectors, in accordance with the best fit between each function and the attributes of the various candidates to perform it. "Assignment" is only an approximate term for what is often a system of rules and incentives

meant to influence the probability that certain kinds of actors will take on certain kinds of tasks.

4. *Architecture.* Once the players are determined, their roles are specified through the development of accountability structures that are consistent with each actor's capabilities, incentives, and constraints, and that focus their energies on the common mission. This architecture can involve contractual relationships, financial incentives, regulation, tax preferences, public opinion, reputation, and other components in varying blends and degrees of complexity. The more that shared discretion – our hallmark of collaboration – figures in the relationship, the more subtle and more elaborate the architecture of accountability is likely to be.

5. *Assessment.* Even the most astute government official is unlikely to get the appraisal, analysis, assignment, and architecture exactly right, given the massive uncertainties involved. The government must assess the security collaboration as it matures – revising early appraisals of the threat to be confronted, revisiting first-round analyses of what private actors can do and what they want, rethinking the assignment of roles and the governance architecture that codifies responsibilities.

6. *Adjustment.* Because requirements change and analyses can be mistaken, the assessment stage may lead to significantly changed prescriptions. Thus, assignments and the architecture that coordinates them may have to be recalibrated. Adjustments will be undertaken as priorities change, new evidence comes to light, or experience reveals new problems or possibilities.

Each of these tasks is quite challenging on its own, and challenging along dimensions – differential treatment of outside parties, analytical and transactional precision, flexibility – that tend to be especially problematic for government. Taken together, they present a much more impressive set of requirements to master. This complexity is generally true of collaborative governance, and intensely so for collaboration on infrastructure protection. Appraising the array of risks in the status quo and analyzing the incentives of potential collaborative actors, for example, requires disentangling broadly shared vulnerabilities from firm-specific risks. It also demands a detailed appreciation of individual firms' competitive standing, with and without security investment, and with and without an actual attack. Measures of progress, essential to assessment and adjustment, are inherently uncertain absent an attack.

The public sector thus has a difficult role to plan in infrastructure protection – but an imperative role. If any of these tasks is ignored or badly carried out, a regime to promote infrastructure security that involves extensive private involvement and substantial private discretion will be less effective, more expensive, or both, than it would otherwise be. These governmental tasks are of an entirely different nature from more familiar security regulations, such as writing blanket regulations for nuclear-plant containment vessels, or sending a company of National Guardsmen to patrol a port. They are subtle, complex, and fundamentally analytical. In infrastructure security, perhaps to an even greater extent than other policy domains, collaborative governance implies a role for government that is different from but no less vital than more familiar roles – and a role for which government is, for the most part, not yet well prepared.

NOTES

1. Bureau of Labor Statistics 2003.
2. The airline security issue is discussed at more length in Box 24.1.
3. The thoroughly inadequate and terribly coordinated policies in the few days surrounding Hurricane Katrina show the impossibility of developing effective collaborative arrangements predominantly on the fly. Hurricanes are different, to be sure, than terrorism threats, but in many ways simpler. For example, they give considerable advance warning.
4. Moran et al. 2006.
5. Gerth and Mills 1946.
6. The Pennsylvania Associators were a private force organized by Benjamin Franklin to substitute for the state militia that Quaker Pennsylvania balked at mustering under public authority. The associators figure in Fisher 2004. Their origins and organization are described on pages 26–28.
7. Singer 2002.
8. Office of Management and Budget 2004.
9. Even in the heyday of direct government delivery, important work was delegated to the private sector, including in ways that we would call collaborative. We are grateful to Lewis M. Branscomb for reminding us of the "cooperative agreements" that let federal officials enlist private collaborators on terms of shared investment and shared discretion.
10. Coglianese et al. 2004.
11. For collaboration in park management, see Donahue 2003, and Donahue and Rosegrant 2004. For student loans, see Lundberg 2005. For foreign assistance, see Lundberg 2004.
12. Sometimes the choice of public or private security arrangements is less consequential than it seems. Paul DiMaggio and Walter Powell argue that institutions performing similar tasks tend to conform to similar models of operation, whatever their formal structure. See DiMaggio and Powell 1983.
13. The public's attitudes toward the appropriate provision of security, however, may be strongly shaped by the most recent dramatic failure. Government efforts to deal with Hurricane Katrina, which bring to mind many comparisons with protection against terrorism, may have dampened enthusiasm with the government as the guarantor of security. Failed effectiveness in a dramatic event may promote a "throw the rascals out" attitude.
14. The basic terms of the choice between internal production and contracting-out are described in Donahue 1989, chapter 5.

15. More formally, let x indicate the level of production discretion, with $f(x)$ giving net production benefits (Figure 24.1). Let $g(x)$ be the level of payoff discretion (Figure 24.2), and let $c(g(x))$ be the cost of payoff discretion (Figure 24.3). Similarly, let $h(x)$ be the level of preference discretion, and let $d(h(x))$ be the cost of preference discretion. Our optimality condition is that $f' = c'g' + d'h'$.

16. Lipton 2005.

17. Kent Smetters of Pennsylvania's Wharton School has suggested that under TRIA, private owners of vulnerable assets will under-invest in security when much of the cost of a catastrophic incident falls to government. TRIA's origins, provisions, and incentive effects are discussed in Smetters 2004. The key terms are covered on pages 16–17. But other analysts, including one of the editors of this volume, view TRIA more favorably and predict much less distortion of private motives to minimize risk. See Kunreuther and Michel-Kerjan 2004.

18. This would be the case whether the urban port is owned by a private firm or by a public agency such as New York's Port Authority.

19. For purposes of this illustration, we are assuming, as seems reasonable, that the facility owner would not or could not be forced to fully compensate other parties for the avoidable damage they suffer due to the facility's failure to take security externalities into account.

20. Attempting to achieve the same outcome through regulation will not work. The regulated party, if forced to pay all of the costs, may just drop out of the market, which is likely to be inefficient if others benefit from having its services in the market.

21. The solution was first described in Lindahl 1919.

22. This example posited a private contribution from a second major private party, the neighboring factory. Often, free-riding tendencies would defeat such spending. The government would then be forced to be the sole supplement to spending by (in this instance) the chemical plant. The government could simply say that it will contribute 30 percent to anything the plant spends whether through direct dollars or a tax incentive.

23. Thus, the societal gain from the measure will only be the difference in the expected damages between the two targets, something that is virtually never computed.

25

THE PARIS INITIATIVE, "ANTHRAX AND BEYOND"

Transnational Collaboration Among Interdependent Critical Networks

Patrick Lagadec and Erwann O. Michel-Kerjan

It has been rather misleading and unfortunate that the academic study of crisis management was initiated chiefly by the Cuba missile crisis in 1962. . . . It appeared to approximate to the form of a "two-person game". . . . The episode really did look rather like a diplomatic chess game. . . . If there is a "game" model for crisis, it [is] certainly not chess, but poker for five or six hands in the traditional Wild West saloon, with the participants all wearing guns, and quickness on the draw rather than the fall of the diplomatic cards tending to determine who eventually acquire the jackpot.[1]

> – Coral Bell, *Decisionmaking by Governments in Crisis Situations*, 1978

As previous chapters of this book highlight, organizations face a new web of challenges made of "unconventional" events. They reflect more than mere local incidents and stationary trends in the occurrence of untoward events. Rather, global turbulences, real-time large-scale risks, and out-of-scale domino effects in an increasingly interdependent world demonstrate that the actions of one organization can have a direct or indirect impact on others thousands of miles away. In an editorial we published in the autumn of 2005, we argued that these untoward events frame "a whole new ball game."[2]

Most people can deal with well-known risks that could cause local damage. As a result, most crisis management tools developed over the past 20 years are based on the outdated assumption that risks are always formatted – that is, that it is possible to list all untoward events that could happen, determine their probability based on past experience, and measure the costs and benefits of specific mitigation measures. But the hallmarks of the current brave new world include more and more unthinkable events, new contexts not seen before, and new pressure to react extremely quickly, even under ignorance of the effects such actions will have.

457

The time has come to be creative. A first step is the recognition that the challenges of large-scale risks and crises have become vital strategy and policy issues for major stakeholders (firms, governments, nongovernmental aid organizations, and the media). Then, the key might lie in the ability to imagine and act more collaboratively, as both the official inquiry into mad cow disease in Britain and the 9/11 Commission in the United States made very clear.

This chapter focuses on how a large initiative came to be organized among postal operators and international postal organizations in the aftermath of the anthrax crisis of 2001. Starting with a small team and building on a positive tipping effect, the "Paris Initiative" illustrates the crucial importance of having a core team made of people both from executives inside the partner organizations and participants outside these organizations who can bring a broader perspective on strategic elements and act as catalysts of the operation.[3]

With this initiative, postal operators have been among the very few to launch an innovative process to understand and meet the collective challenges of an increasingly interdependent world confronted by the emergence of a new spectrum of scientifically complex threats.[4] Hence, there is a large benefit in analyzing the postal operators' process and in suggesting a decisive move beyond the postal sector which could be applied to other critical sectors.

Let us be very clear in this introduction and echo the previous chapter by John Donahue and Richard Zeckhauser. Partnership is a brilliant concept. The practice of partnership is another matter. In this chapter, we focus on *how* strategic partnerships can be developed at the senior-executive level, domestically and internationally, to better prepare organizations in managing and financing new types of emerging risks. We do not pretend to solve all problems, but rather we provide leaders with some "how to do it" tips through a concrete example of leadership and collective action. We first discuss key challenges associated with the operation of critical networks today: high level of surprise (even inconceivability) and scientific uncertainty (even ignorance), increasing interdependencies among networks worldwide, and events capable of inflicting severe long-term economic and social consequences. We then discuss intellectual, training, and behavioral barriers, as well as financial issues associated with extreme events. These barriers need to be considered in order to develop an adequate set of actions for top decision makers. We present the Paris Initiative in greater detail, focusing on perspectives from senior executives of postal operators and academic experts in the field of catastrophic risks and crisis management, who played a key role in that project. This case study suggests key lessons that could be taken away from this initiative and be applied to other industries. We conclude the chapter with recommendations for new strategic avenues.

THE NEW ERA OF LARGE-SCALE RISKS AND CRISES

The first and most crucial step is to understand that governments, industry leaders, and citizens now confront a new world of risks. Most of them are of large magnitude and high speed, and they are characterized by non-linearity and discontinuity. A few recent references embody the current challenge:

- Mad cow disease, United Kingdom, 1986–1996: The scientific expertise was seriously challenged as it was just impossible to offer a definitive diagnostic of what was known for sure about the disease and what was not known (the possible transmission from animal to human). As the Bovine Spongiform Encephalopathy (BSE) inquiry states: "By the time that BSE was identified as a new disease, as many as 50,000 cattle were likely to have been infected. Given the practice of pooling and recycling cattle remains in animal feed, this sequence of events flowed inevitably from the first case of BSE."[5] In March 1996, the British government reversed itself after 10 years of denial and announced that young people were dying from the fatal dementia variant called Creutzfeldt-Jakob disease – mad cow disease in humans. The first case of mad cow disease in the United States in December 2003 destabilized the U.S. meat market in just a few days.
- Ice storm, South Quebec, Canada, January 1998: In a few days, the country faced the most devastating natural disaster of its history; ice covered everything; as ice formed and continuously grew around electrical lines, the lines could not resist the weight and broke one after another. Thousands of miles of electrical lines were permanently destroyed. With no electricity for several days (weeks in some locations), cascading effects were severe on the social and economic activities of the country (especially Quebec). Montreal was about to lose water distribution. As a senior executive of Hydro-Quebec told us: "We were prepared for a technical breakdown. We were confronted with a network collapse."
- Wind storms, Europe, December 26–27, 1999: Within 48 hours, two major storms, Lothar and Martin, hit several European countries; the devastation was historical for France, Germany, Switzerland, and the United Kingdom. Many international networks were hit simultaneously: energy, telecommunications, transport, emergency services, and even a nuclear plant were under threat.
- Terrorist attacks, United States, September 11, 2001: As a large portion of this book demonstrates, the global rules were changed forever. The new nature of international terrorism from extremist religious-based groups became apparent.

- SARS crisis, worldwide, 2003: A jet-propelled contamination forced a shift in public health paradigms all over the world. The first major outbreak of SARS (severe acute respiratory syndrome) came to the world's attention in February 2003, when China reported 300 cases and five deaths. The virus quickly spread to Hong Kong and Vietnam, then to 27 other countries in fewer than three months. The first case to hit Toronto was a traveler from Hong Kong, who had no signs of illness when he landed. By July 2003, the outbreak had infected nearly 8,500 people and killed 812.[6] Three years later, the avian flu generated similar global disruption.

- Heat wave, France, August 2003: While most French people and government officials were on vacation, a major heat wave hit several European countries. Alert systems failed to warn the population early enough; 15,000 people died. "We did not receive any specific alert," the French Minister of Health declared at hearings before the French House of Representatives a few weeks after the catastrophe.

- Northeastern United States and Canada power blackout, August 14, 2003: One technical incident in the U.S. power grid led to a series of major disruptions quasi-instantaneously that plunged a quarter of North America into the dark. Fifty million people and hundreds of thousands of businesses were deprived of electivity. "This whole event was essentially a 9-second event, maybe 10," said Michel R. Gent, president and CEO, North American Electric Reliability Council.[7]

- Indian Ocean tsunami, Asia, December 26, 2004: A cataclysmic earthquake of magnitude higher than 9 on the Richter scale lasted close to 10 minutes (when most major earthquakes last no more than a few seconds). It caused the entire planet to vibrate at least a few centimeters. The sudden vertical rise of the seabed by several meters during the earthquake displaced massive volumes of water, resulting in a gigantic tsunami that streaked the coasts of the Indian Ocean. Between 230,000 and 280,000 people were killed. The transnational tsunami became one of the largest-scale natural events ever. As former President George H.W. Bush said, "I don't think there's ever been a tragedy that affected the heartbeat of the American people as much as this tsunami has done. I don't think you can put a limit on it. It's so devastating."[8]

- Hurricanes Katrina and Wilma, United States, 2005: Resulting in vast human tragedy and hundreds of billions of dollars in economic losses, the two hurricanes seriously challenged the reaction capacity of all levels of government and severely threatened the energy infrastructure. For Hurricane Katrina alone, more than one and a half million people were displaced, resulting in a human crisis on a scale unseen in the United States since the Great Depression. "I have been in the business more than 30 years.

This redefined the word 'problem,'" said Dennis Houston, executive vice-president, Exxon Mobil Refining and Supply Company.[9]

Risks and crises have become much more complex over the past years on at least three levels: (1) They have migrated from well-studied risks to those with a high level of surprise and scientific ignorance. (2) Within an increasingly interdependent world, globalization of social and economic activities have led to a globalization of risks among critical networks. (3) Local accidents within a single firm or industry have been replaced by large-scale events or threats that systematically transcend traditional frontiers, firms, industries, and countries, mixing interests from public and private sectors as well as civil society, with potential losses exceeding the capacities of insurance frameworks (see Part V in the book).[10]

HIGH LEVEL OF SURPRISE AND SCIENTIFIC IGNORANCE

"We must be constantly aware of the likelihood of malfunctions and errors. Without a command of probability theory and other instruments of risk management, engineers could never have designed the great bridges that span our widest rivers, homes would still be heated by fireplaces or parlor stoves, electric power utilities would not exist, polio would still be maiming children, no airplanes would fly, and space travel would just be a dream."[11]

These lines from Peter Bernstein's bestseller tell the positive vision of the evolution of risks and risk management. From time to time, however, some errors and malfunctions create real breakdowns, as stated by the author quoting Leibniz (1703): "Nature has established patterns originating in the return of events, but only for the most part." And Bernstein goes on: "Despite the many ingenious tools created, . . . much remains unsolved. Discontinuities, irregularities and volatilities seem to be proliferating, rather than diminishing."[12] These changes raise some key questions. Society was used to anticipate and handle "normal breakdowns," but now it is confronted more regularly with extreme phenomena. People in charge used to rely on the judgments of experts, but now extreme events appear mostly over short periods – not enough time for scientific experts to provide decisionmakers with precise and well-established knowledge. Today the level of scientific uncertainty and even ignorance increases the capacity of catastrophes to destabilize the social, economic, and political continuity of countries. Accordingly, total surprise becomes business as usual.

Moreover, with regard to terrorism or malevolent threats, the nature of the uncertainty also reflects an important difference from other sources of risks (e.g., natural hazards, technological failures). Because attackers adapt their strategy as a function of their resources and their knowledge of the vulnerability of the entity they are attacking, the risk is thus the equilibrium resulting from a complex mix of strategies and counterstrategies developed by a range of stakeholders. The nature of the risk changes over time, and it is continuously evolving – or more precisely, mutating – which leads to dynamic uncertainty.[13]

This dynamic uncertainty also makes efforts to quantitatively model the risk more challenging. One encounters a sort of dynamic game where the actions of the terrorist groups in period t depend on the actions taken by those threatened by the terrorists (i.e., the defenders) in period $t-1$. For example, terrorism risk changes depending on the protective measures adopted by firms at risk and others, as well as actions taken by governments. In that regard, strategy to deal with these risks is a mixed public–private good, which poses real challenges in coordinating actions by the private and public sectors and doing so in several countries at the same time.

AN INCREASINGLY INTERDEPENDENT WORLD: THE NETWORK FACTOR

Increasingly, the dominant features of the new dimension of risks and crises are the set of vulnerabilities associated with the network factor on the global dimension rather than national one. By "network factor" we mean the increasing dependence of social and economic activities on the operation of networks, combined with increasing interdependencies among these networks.

Indeed, there is a paradox. From a technological perspective, important progress has been made in engineering and operation management to obtain better quality and robustness of large infrastructures, as well as just-in-time delivery. In parallel to these improvements, the use of large networks and their interconnections has reduced operating costs, thanks to economies of scale. On the other hand, when these large-scale networks fail, the consequences immediately affect a large number of people and firms, as well as cascading to other networks. It is therefore important to consider not only direct risks that could limit networks' operations (e.g., natural disasters, internal technological failure), but also the interdependencies among networks. In other words, large networks increase quality and robustness but simultaneously induce large risks associated with their potential failure to operate, and large interdependent networks can extend failure far beyond their own spheres.

As remarkably diagnosed as early as 1997 by a U.S. presidential commission, "our national defense, economic, prosperity, and quality of life have long depended on the essential services that underpin our society. These critical infrastructures – energy, banking and finance, transportation, vital human service, and telecommunications – must be viewed in the Information Age. The rapid proliferation and integration of telecommunication and computer systems have connected infrastructures to one another in a complex network of interdependence. This interlinkage has created a new dimension of vulnerability, which, when combined with an emerging constellation of threats, poses unprecedented national risk."[14] Privatization also could have an impact in some cases on the vulnerability of a whole system, as security investments might be reduced to meet competitiveness challenges.

LARGE-SCALE RISKS: REVERSING NETWORK CAPACITY AGAINST POPULATIONS

These large systems of networks are now embedded in a new, violent, and rapidly changing context. Terrorist or malevolent groups seeking to inflict widespread damage can attack by reversing the network capacity against the target population. Terrorists may not even try to physically destroy some elements of a network infrastructure, but rather seek ways to use the huge diffusion capacity of the networks as a weapon.[15]

In that regard, the 9/11 and anthrax attacks in 2001 demonstrated this new kind of vulnerability. In these two cases, attackers used the diffusion capacity of a critical network and turned it against the U.S. population, making each element of the network (e.g., every aircraft, every piece of mail) a potential weapon.

The 9/11 terrorists used the commercial aviation network to attack civil targets outside the system. As the number of hijacked planes on 9/11 was not known and each flying aircraft was a potential danger, the U.S. Federal Aviation Administration ordered all private and commercial flights grounded less than one hour after the first aircraft crashed against the North World Trade Center Tower. The agency had never before shut down the commercial airline system.[16] Other airports had to manage the arrival of so many people at the same time from flights redirected from their initial destinations in the United States. Moreover, because of passenger reluctance to fly in the aftermath of these attacks, as many as 276 commercial passenger aircraft were soon parked in the Mohave Desert because falling demand compelled airlines to curtail their flight schedules. In effect, the 9/11 attacks removed not four, but almost 280 aircraft from service.

Similarly, the anthrax attacks in autumn 2001 were not turned against a specific post office. Rather, the attacker(s) took advantage of the whole U.S. Postal Service network to spread threats and fear throughout the country and abroad by taking advantage of the trusted capacity of the mail to effectively deliver the tainted letters. Any envelope could have been considered contaminated by anthrax, so the whole postal service was at risk.

The question as to whether the postal service itself was contaminated and whether it should be shut down entirely was seriously considered.[17] Shutting down a large-scale network such as the U.S. Postal Service, officials knew, would inflict debilitating impacts on the economic and social continuity of the country, as well as increase stress on the already sensitive psyche of the nation under siege. Because stopping the postal service would not have prevented future contamination if the whole system were already contaminated – one day, it would have been necessary to reopen it. The network was not closed.[18]

MAKING TOP DECISIONS: GETTING OVER MYTHS

This new era has direct implication for the way crises should be addressed in the future. Two related points need to be considered as well. First, the motivations and causes of disasters are increasingly becoming less clear. For example, the city of Toulouse, France, was severely damaged by a colossal industrial explosion ten days after 9/11. Three years after this tragedy, it was still unclear if this event fell into the "industrial disaster" or "terrorist attack" category.[19] In the same vein, it took a long time to clarify the origin and causes of the 2003 U.S.–Canadian power blackout.

As witnessed with SARS or the avian flu, people in charge during a crisis are instantly confronted by a maze of various dimensions of scientific, technical, organizational, economic, diplomatic, cultural, and ethical issues. The business world is spread over several locations: the headquarters in one region, the incident-tracking system in another, the crisis center in a third – with very different actors and frameworks of decision making in each. This limits simple global decision rules during a crisis if not already collectively in place before it occurs. Three crucial lines of challenge must be acknowledged and dealt with to make top decisions in this difficult context: intellectual challenge, training and behavioral challenge, and financial challenge.

AN INTELLECTUAL CHALLENGE: FROM LINEARITY TO DISCONTINUITY

Decision makers have to appreciate how far new types of crises are from their usual references and how their thinking must change to accommodate the types of risk they face. For example, the usual smaller scale of thinking is now outdated. Decision makers need to think globally.

In this new era of potential crisis, decision makers must also face indeterminate output – that is, the impossibility of clarifying the potential seriousness of a suspected threat. One already had to face, as with mad cow disease, situations in which it is impossible to determine whether the case is a "non-event," a medium range problem, a real potential disaster, or a new Great Plague. What level of decision is the right one to fit the level of threat?

Furthermore, typical probability analysis is now often meaningless. The notion of statistical probability loses sense for emerging, novel risks, because no data are available. What is the probability that a terrorist will use weapons of mass destruction next week to attack London, Rome, Philadelphia, or Tokyo?[20]

The sense of timing has also changed. Many people are trained to react swiftly to a situation well specified (in space and time), but most have no experience in successfully responding independently to dramatic speedy events, at international scale, with no scientific consensus available. Compounding the challenge, media outlets are instantly and radically mutating any specific, localized problem into a global, extreme, and instantly emotional issue. Managers are faced with a media force demanding easily digestible yes or no answers, canned emotions, and camera-ready sound bites, especially if the issue is extraordinarily complex and potentially scary.

There is another challenge for decisionmakers: recognizing that when the crisis occurs there will immediately be a very large number of actors who will influence the dynamics of the crisis. Key conventional actors may thus be marginalized by others. These conventional actors will have to collaborate with numerous actors they have never met but who see themselves as legitimate.[21] This may be a particularly serious problem in cyber attacks, where attackers and geographic origins of the threat may never be known.[22] This combination contributes to shattering usual day-to-day references.

Each dimension justifies new intellectual approaches and research, a daunting task as discussed in other parts of this book. The common point to all of these is discontinuity (meaning a fault line, splitting radically different worlds). Society's intellectual tradition poorly incorporates these non-linear jumps, mutations, and snowballing effects. People are trained to expect stability and linearity, with only limited uncertainty at the margin, and to partitioned theaters of operation and optimization under a few well-shared and accepted constraints. Those emerging critical contexts, most of which are unstable by nature, may be far beyond society's capacity to understand. Research has an urgent mission to fulfill. As Hegel said: "If you are confronted with unthinkable challenges, you have to invent unthinkable paradigms."

A TRAINING AND BEHAVIORAL CHALLENGE

Decisionmakers need to begin thinking and be trained to better adapt to surprises. Indeed, it is somewhat surprising how almost all textbooks on strategic management are devoted to that part of the management task which is relatively easy: the running of the organization in as surprise-free a way as possible. As Ralph Stacey already pointed out 10 years ago, "On the contrary, the real management task is that of handling the exceptions, coping with and even using unpredictability, clashing counter-cultures; the task has to do with instability, irregularity, difference and disorder."[23] More generally, even at leading business schools, strategic crisis management is rarely part of the general curriculum of the MBA program. As a result, very few managers receive any training to manage severe loss of references.

Understanding behavioral biases can be useful with regard to important limitations on launching collective initiatives to tackle large-scale risks and crises. First, anticipated catastrophes are not seen as credible events. Most people think "it will not happen to me." Or "if something happens we will be able to deal with it, although our organization has never supported any preparation for it." These are perceptions we need to dispel. In the case of mad cow disease, a few words in the findings and conclusions report of the United Kingdom's inquiry explain the whole dynamics: "In their heart of hearts they felt that it would never happen."[24]

The second behavioral bias is illustrated by experimental studies of ex post responses and consists of (1) over-estimation of the likelihood of a new event similar to one that just happened, and (2) under-estimation, if nothing similar has happened in months or years.[25]

Finally, on several occasions we have observed another important effect: there might very well be deep threats among top-level executives to launch anything new on these issues of emerging risks and crises, whether ahead of or after the fact. When anticipated, emerging risks are not welcomed. It is much more common to treat them as unrealistic, too rare to worry about, or beyond a firm's responsibility. Lack of historical data and the difficulty in measuring these emerging threats with metrics executives are familiar with could make it difficult for them to report to the board of directors on these issues. After disaster strikes, executives rarely take the lead in ordering collective debriefing on a subject that was, by chance or on purpose, ignored until a recent crisis. Even if the crisis directly affected the organization, the first reflex remains often "we don't want to talk about it anymore" or "let's try to forget that episode." For managers in charge in such organizations, they see a hypothetical risk of doing anything afterwards outside of their predefined job description. The short-term incentives facing some managers differ from the long-term incentives facing the firm, industry, or even country. Only a few (usually leaders) consider that the major risk today vis-à-vis extreme risks is to do nothing about them.

A FINANCIAL CHALLENGE

Several key financial challenges are also associated with these large-scale risks and crises related to operation of interdependent networks: Who should pay for the consequences of such events? Who should pay for preventing them? What type of strategy for security investment and collective preparation is more efficient than another? How could one measure such effectiveness?

In situations with global interdependencies, the public sector – or a coalition of private firms – may need to take the leading role with respect to providing protective measures, because private firms individually may have few economic incentives to take these steps on their own. Kunreuther and Heal recently introduced the concept of interdependent security using game-theoretic models as a way of addressing some part of the challenges associated with decisions of investment in security for large-scale interdependent networks.[26] The interdependent security paradigm raises the question of what economic or other competitive incentives firms or governments may have for undertaking protection in a given sector when they are connected to other organizations or groups, and where failures anywhere in the sector may create losses to some or all of the other parties (see Chapter 16).

Specifically, the interdependent security framework has been applied to evaluating investments by firms in operational and systems security related to infrastructure operations. The framework recognizes that any firm's risk strongly depends on the operational behaviors, priorities, and actions of others via interconnected networks and supply chains. The interdependent risks across firms may lead all of them to decide not to invest in security. When the decision is made to invest in new security measures and in preparing their senior executives for managing crises, the universal question as to how to prioritize budget allocation in organization operations is key. In these situations, a general framework for budget allocation could be required, as well as the development of new types of metrics to measure progress over time.

In particular, developing partnerships could allow spreading the costs (and benefits) associated with the implementation of collective preparation and risk mitigation to improve global security over all partners; costs a single organization often cannot afford alone.

Future work should address the appropriate strategies for dealing with situations where there are interdependencies between agents (persons, organizations, countries). An important feature of recent episodes is their potential out-of-scale consequences: the ultimate frameworks are not overtaken at the margin, but appear radically inadequate. The 2001 anthrax attacks demonstrated the asymmetric effect of destabilizing critical networks: a small-scale but carefully targeted attack can cause large-scale reactions because of strong interdependencies and possible cascading fallout. Introducing a pathogenic agent into a nationwide distribution network may require a small financial investment from terrorists compared with the debilitating national damage of such an action to the health and business continuity of the country. In order to prioritize budget allocation, scenario-based simulations, involving senior executives and experts who would be effectively in charge if something happens, can be an important proven way to increase the organization or country's reaction capacity.

THE PARIS INITIATIVE: "ANTHRAX AND BEYOND"

The anthrax crisis during the autumn of 2001 is one of numerous large-scale events that occurred over the past few years that provide the opportunity to discuss a concrete initiative in the context of the framework described in the previous section of this chapter. While in the end, there were only four anthrax-contaminated letters moving through the U.S. Postal Service network, the uncertainty about the real degree of contamination of the system had remained high for several days. The use of the elements of the network as a weapon surprised everyone and turned the U.S. infrastructure into a global threat. Indeed, during the crisis hundreds of false alerts occurred daily in the United States as well as in most postal services worldwide. The decision to shut down the whole U.S. Postal Service was seriously considered. But the service treats about 700 million pieces of mail every day – shutting down the network for a week, just to try to better measure the scale of the contamination, would have implied trying to reopen a system of nearly 5 billion pieces of mail unchecked. Eventually, it was decided not to do so: stopping the whole system would not have allowed determining which pieces were contaminated.

Thus, in essence, the Paris Initiative started only a few weeks after 9/11. The anthrax crisis raised fundamental questions about postal security worldwide. We suggested a response of launching an international debriefing process. Our strategic goal was to help postal operators at the highest executive level meet a double challenge: (1) to understand the new arena of emerging vulnerabilities, and (2) to prepare creative operational breakthroughs that are crucial to the global sustainability and development of postal operations in the future (see Box 25.1).

LAUNCHING AN INTERNATIONAL DEBRIEFING

The determination was strong after the anthrax attacks: "never again." It was seen as unthinkable that the top leaders of postal services could be unable to speak together and share questions and perspectives during a global crisis (notably, this reaction is opposite of the usual denials discussed in the previous section of this chapter).

In April 2002, France's La Poste launched a national debriefing process to learn internally the key lessons of the anthrax attacks (the French network had been challenged by thousands of alerts, but not a single real case). During this debriefing, Patrick Lagadec strongly advised them to go beyond the national process – the crisis had been transnational, and accordingly the debriefing should be transnational. Martin Hagenbourger, special advisor to the President,

BOX 25.1 AN UNCONVENTIONAL EPISODE

The most factual descriptions of the preparation and development of the Paris initiative come from the officials who partnered in it.

A Global Harm: Reversing the Network Factor

"In late September through early October 2001, a series of bio-terror attacks took place on the east coast of the United States. The pathogen used was anthrax and the vector for the attack was the U.S. mail system. The anthrax attack in 2001 was one of the most serious crises ever faced by a postal administration. This event caused the American public to question the very safety and security of their mail. While the level of human tragedy, five deaths, was relatively small, the psychological impact on a large portion of the U.S. population was significant. In the classic sense of a terrorist attack, there was an asymmetric relationship between perception and reality. It caused individual citizens to question a fundamental service provided by their government – the daily delivery of mail" (Thomas Day, Vice President, U.S. Postal Service).

"The anthrax crisis was one of the biggest threats to the worldwide postal service ever because it struck at the very heart of our activity. In other words, it affected the transportation and distribution of mail. It was also an unprecedented crisis since, for the first time in the history of the postal service, the future of our business was at risk" (Jean-Paul Bailly, President, La Poste).

Systemic Dynamics: A Disseminating Capacity Embedded in Systems

"'Cross contamination' was further confirmed through extensive tests conducted by the U.S. Postal Service, in conjunction with the Department of Defense. Simulated anthrax-laden letters were prepared in a manner very similar to the letters used in the actual attack. When run through high-speed automated letter processing equipment in a lab environment, they expelled contaminates in significant quantities. Further, letters that were processed on the same equipment became contaminated, or cross-contaminated" (Thomas Day, Vice President, U.S. Postal Service).

Ignorance and Multi-Actor Theater

"Lack of knowledge and understanding of this new threat were the key features of the first few days. We had to acquire some basic understanding of the science involved, rapidly provided by our medical team; assimilate the U.S. Postal Service experience, which inevitably did not become clear for some weeks; and build new relationships with the emergency services and the National Health Service" (Chris Babbs and Brian O'Connor, Royal Mail).

For anyone to be involved in a crisis situation, a key experience was not to be forgotten: "La Poste's chairman, Mr. Vial at the time, was in New York when he heard the news: According to Agence France Presse (AFP), two persons had been infected with anthrax in Germany, Europe's first confirmed cases in the mail-borne terrorist scare of autumn 2001. He immediately tried to get in touch with his counterpart at Deutsche Post, to no avail. He was also unable to get a hold of the head of Royal Mail. Unfortunately, the news came on November 2, part of a long weekend holiday in much of Europe. Mr. Vial had to settle for a conference call with a few of the staff members at La Poste who were working that day. Tension remained high until 8:30 p.m. that evening, when AFP finally announced that its earlier report had proved false" (Martin Hagenbourger, Advisor to the President, La Poste).

immediately approved the concept, and La Poste's General Postmaster agreed to support the initiative. The decision was rapidly made to launch an international debriefing process, which would lead to a conference in Paris during the following months. Those involved were committed to ensuring that never again would Europe's postal services be at a loss to respond readily to a new crisis, especially one that could paralyze the entire European postal network.

Senior executives were convinced that a swift move was necessary to avoid losing the window of opportunity before an adequate international initiative could be launched. It was decided to act with executives in other countries and PostEurop, which had a membership at the time that encompassed 42 public postal operators across Europe. Experts in public health issues were also included, as well as experts in managing emerging crises.

In June 2002, eight months after the anthrax crisis, La Poste submitted a proposal to PostEurop's management board, suggesting holding a professional meeting on the theme of European postal security. La Poste asserted that a meeting bringing together crisis management and security experts from international postal operators would offer an excellent occasion to exchange experiences and views on what different posts had learned internally from the anthrax crisis as well as what they needed to do to cope better with future large-scale risks and threats. While the anthrax crisis could be viewed as a starting point for discussions, the conference was expected to go much further. The challenge was not anthrax per se, but the emergence of a whole new profile of crises. The objective was to grasp the overall lessons linked to the underlying challenge, not the self-evident tactical difficulties of the specific event. The old dictum "never fight the last war," had to remain in all minds as a key.

Accordingly, participants were invited to share their thoughts on improving the European postal industry's collective ability to respond to future crises. The ultimate goal of the conference was to gather ideas and to serve as the launch-pad for concrete initiatives that would strengthen the ability of postal operators to better handle future contingencies, rather than ordering a shutdown of the whole network again. Three objectives were clarified: (1) learning experiences and lessons of the anthrax crisis from others; (2) sharing ideas and proposals to improve the collective reaction to emerging threats; and (3) establishing Europe–United States crisis management capacity, enabling postal operators to connect with their counterparts and with other international organizations, using a common platform.

LEADERSHIP: PUTTING TOGETHER THE RIGHT TEAM

The conference was not organized simply to provide ready-made crisis management recipes. Rather, La Poste and PostEurop united to launch a collective move to stimulate common efforts in an area where there was no pre-specified answer. The most important components to the successful launch of a "new" initiative were the process itself and the quality of people it brought together. Not only did the initiative involve people at the highest level of organizations (per organization and cross-organizations within a specific sector), but it also included the crucial involvement by external people.

Actually, the risk here is in seeing an idea or plan of action dying internally after several unfruitful meetings. The lack of consensus on what to do, how to do it, and in allocating a sufficient budget for the operation (internal rivalry, competitiveness), could be the only output each organization is likely to end with.

These external stakeholders included a few relevant experts with real capacity for understanding not only the emerging risks and crises but also possible conflicts of interest in the process of launching the partnership. One of the main advantages of having such external people is that they can act as catalysts for launching the process and sustaining it over its lifetime. Such an internal–external cross-organization combination is fundamental for collective thinking, leadership, and innovation. In a competitive world, these neutral catalysts will play a key role in linking the stakeholders involved.

A core team, consisting of Lagadec (Ecole Polytechnique, who had a long experience of debriefing processes in many sectors) and a close advisor to the President of La Poste, constructed the concept of the process and set up an international team. The international team included specialists in managing and financing large-scale risks and crisis management from Wharton, and the European Crisis Management Academy. Their task was to help incorporate what crisis management experts in the field have already learned elsewhere, providing conference participants with a current view of the issues at stake. Michel-Kerjan also took the lead in clarifying the most recent developments in the United States related to protection of critical infrastructure, emerging global crises, and public–private partnerships.

The core team traveled in different countries to meet in advance with European speakers and experts. The team visited people in charge inside postal organizations, listened to them, and suggested that they join the initiative. The team also visited outside organizations and other international experts in the field to persuade them to join the initiative as well. These advance meetings generated trust with perspective participants. They also set in motion a common approach and framework for dealing with the issues that would be central to the conference. Trust was key to sustain the launching process of the Paris Initiative. As with preparedness in crisis management, networking and trust were recognized as vital to the conference, and these aspects were integrated into the planning.

In that spirit, several representatives from European public postal operators were approached, visited, and invited to share their experiences during the anthrax crisis. Operators that sent representatives to the conference included TPG Post (The Netherlands), Post Denmark, Deutsche Post AG (Germany), Royal Mail (United Kingdom), and La Poste (France). These key postal operators helped create a tipping effect, with others following the initiative. In addition, some key operators contributed specific services vital to the success of the conference. For example, PostEurop, via its general secretary, brought support to reach members and to bring in experts and official involvement; La Poste sent out a questionnaire to its European counterparts to find out more about their experiences and expectations, and it provided logistics for the meeting; the U.S. Postal Service, represented by one of its vice presidents, joined to provide a first-hand account of what it was like to deal with the deadly anthrax attacks, and to be part of the international network expected to be launched at the meeting.

NOVEMBER 2002, PARIS: SHARING EXPERIENCES AND LESSONS

Initially the initiative was supposed to be undertaken for just a few postal operators (France, Germany, the Netherlands, the United Kingdom, among others). Eventually it ended up involving nearly 30 countries across Europe and the United States. The conference "Anthrax and Beyond," prepared over the course of six months, took place in Paris in November 2002, one year after the height of the international postal crisis. This two-day meeting involved postal sector representatives sharing their experiences, suggesting new avenues for management, and launching a debate on new operational capabilities. Because emerging crises in interdependent networks would require high-level involvement, international organizations such as the Universal Postal Union and the Comité Européen de Régulation Postale (European Committee for Postal Regulation) sent representatives to the meeting as well.

Many participants shared converging lessons (see Box 25.2). The key was not to search for a miraculous "kit," but rather to develop fundamental values and capacities of people in charge in the organizations. The ultimate message forwarded by attendees of the conference was that "this is a challenge for the whole organization, and especially for top-level decisionmakers, not only for technical specialists, risk managers, and people in charge of public relations."

IMMEDIATE MEASURABLE OUTPUT: STRATEGIC PARTNERSHIP

The Paris Initiative produced more than the sharing of experience and lessons. It constituted the first steps in creating a network to improve the overall reaction capacity among postal networks in case of a new transnational threat. The

BOX 25.2 SHARING EXPERIENCES AND LESSONS: KEYS FROM SENIOR EXECUTIVES WHO MANAGED THE ANTHRAX CRISIS

- Martin Hagenbourger, La Poste (France)

  1. First, we must count on ourselves, which means being proactive. The crisis always comes as a surprise for everyone. It is important to count first and foremost on our own capacity to react.
  2. The crisis shows the need to be modest. We need to be totally transparent in our communication and in our decisions, but it would be a mistake to seek to master everything and to claim to have all the answers right away.
  3. Crisis management begins with the work of multidisciplinary teams. The first act of a crisis manager should be to gather around him all of the experts who can help him master the crisis.
  4. In a crisis, sharing information is a must, as is obtaining and having access to the material resources to distribute this information speedily throughout the company.
  5. Listen attentively to those who manage the crisis out in the field, and always be in a position to respond to their requests.
  6. The capacity to face a crisis largely depends on networks of contacts, which should be set up before the crisis. In the complex world in which we live today, it is impossible to react adequately with the support of only your internal company network.
  7. Where crises are concerned, we should always plan on a "Factor X," which could be referred to as the "unknown crisis scenario." One day, we might need it!

- Thomas Day, U.S. Postal Service (United States)

  1. Effective communication is essential.

     - Reach out to **all** constituencies (e.g., employees, unions, customers).
     - Use multiple forms of communication (e.g., direct talks, written correspondence, the Internet, telephone hotlines, television, radio, newspapers).
     - Tell what you know – don't speculate; don't overstate.
     - You can't communicate too much.

  2. Initial response is critical.

     - Focus must be on the safety of employees and customers.
     - Employees and customers need to see a visible demonstration of action.
     - Use technology or process/procedural changes that work.
     - Tie the response to the communication; decide what to do, tell people why, and do it.

(continued)

BOX 25.2 (*continued*)

3. Technology evaluation requires a rigorous process.

- Find the experts.
- Determine which technologies are proven and validated.
- Understand your own operating environment.
- Combine proven technology with operating environment – figure out what works.

4. Once you have a plan, understand it will change.

- A well-written plan has a limited life; plans must be updated on a regular basis.
- Threat and vulnerability assessments must be continually updated.
- Don't focus on the "last war"; constantly consider future threats.
- Threat and vulnerability assessment must consider biological, chemical, radiological, and explosive threats (and anything else that might be added in the future).

- Chris Babbs and Brian O'Connor, Royal Mail (United Kingdom)

1. The next crisis will never be the same as the last and may well be something the organization has never contemplated.

- Developing processes and relationships is more important than doing detailed planning.
- The processes need to be practiced.
- Not over-planning, as all plans are out of date the moment they are finished, and over-elaborate out-of-date plans can be positively dangerous!
- Try to develop plan "granularity"– small-scale plans that can be fitted together in the framework required by the next crisis.

2. Communications planning requires the same level of effort as operational planning.
3. Managing perceptions can be as important as managing the reality.
4. Concrete gestures, even if not strictly relevant, can have enormous psychological effects.
5. Make sure your crisis management model can accommodate additional specialist input, and make sure you know where to get each kind of expertise.
6. You need people standing back from day-to-day handling of the crisis and seeking to spot the longer-term strategic issues.

initiative also launched an international partnership among postal operators. The partnership included the creation of a global crisis-management network (among other outputs) that includes executive-level instant connecting capability among all the European and U.S. operators. Such a tool was designed to allow them to exchange information about the solutions being implemented by each country and to work out a concerted strategy. This new network had its first test on January 15, 2003 – the day it became operational. Indeed, on that very day, PostEurop had received an advisory from the U.S. Postal Service concerning a possible anthrax contamination in the Washington, D.C. area.[27] The network provided postal services across Europe with accurate and timely information on this potential incident, enabling them to assess the proper scope of the risk involved. The threat proved eventually to be a false alert, but it was a dramatic beginning to the network, which is still operating today. However, in the words of Jean-Paul Bailly, President of La Poste, "we must not allow ourselves to become complacent: from now on we all need to resolutely commit ourselves to making a significant and determined long-term effort to ensure that we are constantly capable of dealing with the complex and ever changing challenges in terms of risks, crises and breakdowns in relations."

In all, the Paris Initiative was ambitious. It offered a breakthrough in practice, an international debriefing, followed by concrete outputs that could be meaningful for the postal industry. Moreover, from the beginning it was mindful of a high level goal of publishing the key features of the process and best results in a leading relevant journal. The organizers did not seek publicity, but rather a real step forward in disseminating the experience among operators of a critical network such as the postal service. As the success of this project was largely due to the commitment of several key decisionmakers within postal organizations, it was crucial to diffuse the knowledge and insights gathered in that effort. This diffusion was the ambition of a special issue of the *Journal of Contingencies and Crisis Management*, published in autumn 2003, just one year after the Paris conference.[28]

MOVING FORWARD

The Guns of August crushed Europe in 1914.[29] The *Planes of September 2001* and other waves of emerging ruptures are setting the scene today, and the stakes are of similar historical importance. The vision is clear: "fiasco is not an option." Society's collective responsibility is to transform emerging global ruptures into emerging global opportunities, and collective answers must be reactive and scaled to the new scene. With the growing globalization of social and economic activities that leads to increasing cross-industry and cross-country interdependencies, as well as large-scale risks associated with a high degree of scientific uncertainty, global actors do not play conventional chess anymore. Events that occurred worldwide over the past five years have shown that today a single event (or threat) can destabilize a whole set of firms or industries, or even several countries, as well as quickly inflict losses of billions of dollars. In that spirit, while boards in industry and governments have begun to consider these issues with a real sense of urgency, budget allocation – prioritization of limited resources – remains one of the most crucial strategic aspects to be decided on.

Related to preparation of executives in charge, it is crucial to train top leaders, as they have the most difficult task in this new environment. Crisis' first target is the key leader. If he or she adopts an inadequate line of action, then the whole organization, as well as others that depend on it, will be in the hand of the crisis. As our involvement in the Paris initiative illustrates, therefore, it is essential to introduce and develop strategic and trusted catalyst teams. These teams, composed of individuals from both inside and outside the organization, can advise top leaders on emerging questions, formulate challenging questions, suggest bold innovations, and engage with multiple bodies outside the organization. And, above all, catalyst teams can take bold initiatives with pilot projects involving unusual circles of people and organizations.

The Paris Initiative illustrates successful collective actions, partly because it was a pragmatic way to produce concrete outputs, and thus to measurable benefits for all stakeholders, whether in terms of better preparation or financial return on investment. Numerous other conferences are now organized on the subject of critical infrastructures and risks associated with globalization. However, conferences are no longer sufficient. What is strongly needed is to go beyond usual borders to develop high-level collective actions across industries and across countries. The entry point of a crisis is not a good time to exchange business cards for the first time. As a very concrete capacity to develop, we advocate the proactive establishment of what we call "Rapid Reflection Forces" (see Box 25.3).

Encouragingly, we have observed an important move over the past few years: Rather than leaving risk managers to tackle issues alone, a number of companies have recognized the strategic aspect of these issues and have now put them on their board agendas. International organizations, such as the Organization for Economic Co-operation and Development in Paris and the World Economic Forum in Geneva, Switzerland, have now also made these large-scale risk issues a priority in their future action plans (see Chapter 26). These new initiatives could lead others to act as well and, eventually, tip a whole new way of managing international crises.

Each critical sector has its own set of key processes, activities, institutional and legal arrangements, and cultures. While the Paris Initiative used postal security as a large-scale pilot initiative, the framework introduced in this chapter would be meaningful for preparing and implementing similar international initiatives in other industries in which activities also are sustained

BOX 25.3 RAPID REFLECTION FORCES

Similar to the military's "Fast Action Forces" to apply strategy on the ground, we suggest the creation of "Rapid Reflection Forces" in every single large corporation and institution, to clarify strategy and to define where to go, from where, with whom, and why, during crisis episodes.

The first priority is to empower a special team that is capable of asking fresh questions, of finding fresh approaches, and of working hard on them very creatively. It must be made of people who have been specially trained: not to have all the answers to predetermined scenarios, but to be balanced (level-headed), creative, and able to work with others when confronted with highly turbulent environments.

The team then needs a methodology for exploring the unknown and for clarifying a way out of the crisis. Experience shows that the team must work on four seminal questions.

1. *What is the true problem?* Generally, people rush into a problem without really understanding the complexities of the situation. For example, in a sense, a class-5 hurricane is not just another hurricane; it is an "outside the box" disaster. The challenge is to clarify what the situation is really about, beyond the initial perception. This question must not be asked just once, but repeatedly throughout the crisis.

2. *What are the key traps?* Generally, fear and stress generate instant collapses and lead to terrible choices and devastating media communication. This is easy to understand but must be avoided. To avoid an instant quagmire, the question "what are the key mistakes to avoid?" must be asked again and again, during the crisis and right until the very end, and in the post-crisis period as well.

3. *Who are the stakeholders?* Unconventional crises cannot be solved solely by and with conventional actors. Commonly, crisis managers tend to work with the very few who are well known to them. During an inconceivable event, decisionmakers must redefine their networks.

4. *Which strategic initiatives are essential?* During a severe and disturbing event, it is essential to restore sense, to re-establish balance, and to initiate powerful new dynamics. The way to do this is to launch some very specific initiatives, with some very specific people, at the right moment. This is perhaps the most difficult challenge: to identify and define two or three specific actions that the team can implement to inject confidence, positive dynamics, and movement.

"Rapid Reflection Forces" must be able to link and interact extremely well with the very top management strata of the organization, which calls for a specific and crucial preparation effort. This process has just been launched in several leading organizations.

BOX 25.4 CHECK-LIST FOR SENIOR EXECUTIVES' BASIC TEST

This check-list is based on our personal experience within a club of senior executives from various critical networks.

You are a senior-executive. You already have a crisis management capacity and good training for well-known untoward events.

Now you can address today's emerging risks.

Just to control your road-map, some guidelines:

Timing

1. When did you organize the latest unconventional simulation exercise in your organization?
2. When did you participate in the latest unconventional simulation exercise in your organization?

If your answer is "never" or "a long time ago," consider the following question:

Why is your organization still among the few ones convinced that "as long as it is unthinkable, there is nothing to think about and prepare?"

Who is in charge, and with whom? (for those who actually participated in an exercise)

1. Did you personally play your role in this exercise? (e.g., as a CEO, did you play a CEO?)
2. Did you involve partners outside of your organization?

What is the rehearsal scenario?

1. Was the simulation effectively anchored in unconventional "out of the box" threats, or did it revolve around old fire evacuation or last-century "media communication" exercises only?
2. Did you organize a debriefing, focusing on the key surprises and reactions to them?

Strategic preparation

1. Are you systematically investigating emerging significant crises at national and international levels? For example, what did you do after 9/11, after the anthrax crisis, the SARS alert, or after the August 2003 blackouts (United States and Italy)?
2. Are you actively involved in an association of executives, presidents, and top-level specialists within leading research institutions and think-tanks to share questions, ideas, answers, as well as face the unthinkable and turn emerging large-scale risks into real opportunities?
3. After reading about the Paris Initiative on Postal Security, do you think other organizations in your sector (for example, your competitors, if any) are better prepared than your organization? What kind of bold initiatives would you be prepared to consider and to launch?
4. In this context, what is your road map for the next two years?

by the continuity of interdependent networks challenged by growing threats. These industries include transportation, telecommunication, defense, energy, banking and finance, insurance, water supply, and hospitals and health systems, among others.

The Paris Initiative has been a watershed. Let it be the first of a long and lively list. Otherwise, the most important risk for society could be distrust in critical services, as well as in those who are in charge of assuring the social and economic continuity of the country. If that distrust were to form, it would likely lead to a growing distrust in the country's governance capacity as well.

It is essential to go from words to work, from visions to actions. We suggest two operational tools as guidelines for moving forward. The first is the basic set of questions to ask for a first step: a very simple check-list to be used to clarify the state of the art in a company or organization (see Box 25.4). The second is a more advanced tool: if the answers to the checklist prove to be successful, the firm might want to address the challenge of a mutating risky global context and sudden large-scale crisis. In that case, the firm must know that more and more innovative multinational firms have begun to adopt a new type of think-tank model by applying the concept of "Rapid Reflection Forces" (see Box 25.3).

Much has to be clarified, but the essential component is to avoid a "wait and see" attitude. New answers to new problems must be searched for and found – they will not "simply fall as a gentle rain from heaven." It is time to get to work to develop through international partnerships more adequate global security strategies. Eventually, this may be the only proven way to re-establish faith in critical infrastructures.

NOTES

1. Bell 1978.
2. Lagadec and Michel-Kerjan 2005.
3. See Chapter 8, which also emphasizes the need for outside as well as inside executive influence.
4. That is not so common. For example, we approached the airline–airport industry after the SARS epidemics to launch a similar initiative. The project, however, never emerged from "great interest but no decisive move."
5. Phillips et al. 2001.
6. World Health Organization 2003a,b.
7. *The New York Times* 2003.
8. Associated Press 2005a.
9. *Wall Street Journal* 2005.
10. Among recent analyses of catastrophe risk coverage, see Godard et al. 2002 and Grace et al. 2003. On terrorism risk coverage, see Kunreuther and Michel-Kerjan 2004, 2005a. See also Part V of this book for a detailed discussion.

11. Bernstein 1996.
12. Bernstein 1996, p. 329.
13. Michel-Kerjan 2003a.
14. President's Commission on Critical Infrastructure Protection 1997, p. ix. As mentioned earlier in the book, the initiative launched by President Clinton in 1996 was the first worldwide initiative to put the issues of protection of critical infrastructures on the top-level agenda of the public and private sectors.
15. Michel-Kerjan 2003b.
16. The terrorists who operated in Madrid on March 11, 2004, followed the same configuration of attack – reversing network capacity against populations – as they probably tried to use the rail network to destroy not some scattered trains but the key station of the Madrid grid (Atocha).
17. Lipton and Johnson 2001.
18. For an analysis of the impact of the anthrax crisis on long-term strategic aspects of the postal service's operation, see Reisner 2002.
19. The distinction does not only affect national security issues but also insurance concerns.
20. The recent development of terrorism models assists in the risk assessment process, but it is difficult to estimate the likelihood of future terrorism attacks given our current state of knowledge. Although none of the terrorist models currently provides well-specified distributions of expected loss (in the statistical sense), they can be helpful in enabling insurers to understand the degree of their exposure under specific attack scenarios. See Kunreuther et al. 2005.
21. After Pan Am Flight 103 crashed on Lockerbie, Scotland, in December 1988, that small city saw in a couple hours its "population" doubled to include, among others, journalists from all over the world, emergency teams, politicians, citizens from other cities coming to see or help. For example, 24 hours after the explosion, 2,500 officials and 1,000 media people were on site.
22. Cukier et al. 2005.
23. Stacey 1996.
24. Phillips et al. 2000, section 1176.
25. See Lagadec 1993; Loch and Kunreuther 2001.
26. Kunreuther and Heal 2003.
27. This was following a positive test result: a piece of mail addressed to the U.S. Federal Reserve and passed through postal facility in the District of Columbia.
28. Lagadec and Rosenthal 2003.
29. Tuchman 1962.

PART VII

Roots of Response

26

LEADERSHIP: WHO WILL ACT?

Integrating Public and Private Interests to Make a Safer World

Philip E. Auerswald, Lewis M. Branscomb, Todd M. La Porte, and Erwann O. Michel-Kerjan

> *"To be courageous ... requires no exceptional qualifications, no magic formulas. ...*
> *It is an opportunity that sooner or later is presented to us all.*
> *The stories of past courage can define that ingredient, –*
> *they can teach, they can offer hope, they can provide inspiration.*
> *But they cannot supply courage itself. For this each man must look into his soul."*
> John F. Kennedy, *Profiles in Courage*, 1956

At the outset of this book, we asserted that the combined efforts of the government and the private sector have not adequately reduced the public's vulnerability to catastrophic terrorist attacks, natural disasters, and other low-probability, high-impact events. Contributors to this volume have discussed five elements of a coherent and complete response: evaluating vulnerabilities, managing organizations, securing networks, creating markets, and building trust. The effectiveness of each depends on the execution of the others. Yet none will develop without a sixth element: sustained commitments carried out through effective leadership.

By "leadership" we do not mean the political image of a charismatic individual able to mobilize action through sheer force of personality (although that is a valuable, albeit rare, attribute). Rather we mean the assumption of responsibility and accountability by individuals with sufficient authority over resources and decisions to effectively address catastrophic events. As many studies document, however, the reality of an immediate response to a disaster is overwhelmingly unplanned, decentralized, and the product of private action – "leadership" on a micro-level, perhaps, but not at the scale of national policy.

Public policy leadership is most essential when decisions involve difficult trade-offs between collective and private interests; it is only *expected* when those trade-offs are widely understood. Leadership, in the absence of such understanding, lacks legitimacy. When disasters do occur and "obviously" important objectives are not achieved (as was the case in New Orleans during and after Hurricane Katrina), it is usually because leadership responsibilities have not been adequately defined or exerted to address these trade-offs.

This book has focused on building awareness about a specific category of trade-off in a complex industrial society: private efficiency versus public vulnerability. This balancing act is well understood in highly industrialized, democratic, market economies. Firms in the private sector are encouraged (by market rewards) to maximize their productivity by cutting costs and increasing efficiency. But their behavior is constrained by an extensive body of government regulations and administrative and legal institutions that interpret and enforce them. Public health for consumers and workers, honest and ethical market behavior, and protection of endangered resources in the natural environment are all values that citizens and consumers seek through collective action by their government. But these protections are usually assembled slowly and through an elaborate give-and-take between public and private political interests.

An acceptable and sustainable set of rules is only achieved when the risks to the public and the requirements of a strong economy are in balance. When the severity or timing of risks are not predictable, the democratic process is unlikely to balance the interests without controversy. An example is the accumulating scientific evidence that dependence on fossil fuels is irreversibly changing the earth's climate. However, neither the pace of change nor its specific consequences in all local regions are yet widely enough accepted to force political acceptance of the economic costs of acting before those consequences have been widely experienced. (On a positive note, see Box 26.1 for a recent example of CEO-level initiative).

The potential for catastrophe, especially as caused by terrorists who may act deliberately and creatively to inflict large-scale damage, poses a challenging dilemma for society: How can the collective interest in reducing risks of high-impact, though low-probability, future events be balanced against the immediate certainty of costs to be incurred by individuals – managers, investors, and consumers – to increase watchfulness, enhance the capacity to manage under extreme stress, and otherwise minimize the consequences of catastrophe?

In this volume, we have used the term "security externalities" to refer to risks in the management of a business enterprise that radiate out to others. Even when taken in sum, the contributions to the volume have not addressed all types of security externalities. We have not considered all categories of catastrophe, notably leaving aside human-induced climate change and other potential seeds of disaster extremely slow in their realization.[1] We also have not considered all sectors of the economy, focusing rather on the provision of those services essential to economic and physical well-being. Private firms bear

BOX 26.1 DAVOS–G8 CLIMATE CHANGE ROUNDTABLE

The World Economic Forum's G8 Climate Change Roundtable was launched at the forum's 2005 annual meeting in Davos, Switzerland, in response to an invitation from U.K. Prime Minister Tony Blair. The group was composed of chief executives from 24 global companies across a diverse set of industry sectors, including energy, air transportation, automotive, banking, metals and mining, and insurance. The roundtable's primary mission was to provide the Prime Minister with the business community's perspective on the climate change agenda for the 2005 G8 summit in Gleneagles, Scotland.

After a series of meetings and workshops between January and June 2005, the group presented Prime Minister Blair with a detailed set of recommendations affirming the importance of the problem – calling for a long-term, globally consistent policy regime involving all major emitters of greenhouse gases, and emphasizing the need to implement performance-based technology incentives. Acknowledging the risks to business posed by future regulation and/or climate-induced damage to assets, the group stressed the need for clear and consistent "price signals" to stimulate businesses to act.

Although the formal discussions of climate change at Gleneagles were disrupted considerably by the terrorist bomb attacks on the London Underground, the roundtable appears to have succeeded in demonstrating widespread support for properly designed mitigation throughout the global business community. The roundtable also helped create a broader context for engaging participation of key developing countries such as China, India, and Brazil in subsequent talks on climate change policy. Most importantly – by demonstrating widespread support for mitigation – the roundtable played an important role in helping shift the debate from "whether climate change is a problem" to "how the problem should be solved."

most of the responsibility for the day-to-day provision of critical infrastructure services. Yet responsibility for the reliability, continuity, and resilience of the infrastructure that provides those services is shared with government.

Chapters 1 and 4 describe the multiple attempts by the U.S. government to define the critical infrastructure challenge. The U.S. government well understands *what* needs to be done, and *why*. Its policy – Homeland Security Presidential Directive 7 (December 17, 2003) – is clear: "The Department of Homeland Security (DHS) is responsible for coordinating the overall national effort to enhance the protection of the critical infrastructure and key resources of the United States [and] leading, integrating, and coordinating efforts to protect critical infrastructure and key resources with an emphasis on those that could be exploited to cause catastrophic health effects or mass casualties."[2] However, the nation will remain unnecessarily vulnerable until deeply divided responsibilities for its protection are reconciled, resulting in a shared understanding of *how* to identify and mitigate vulnerabilities and *who* will assume leadership. If obligations, separate and joint, are not clearly laid out and accepted, then shared responsibility may end up being no responsibility at all.

HOW WELL IS U.S. CRITICAL INFRASTRUCTURE PROTECTED?

What is the state of leadership in the United States with regard to vulnerability reduction and the provision of critical infrastructure services in times of disaster? Most agree that vulnerability is high and action is imperative. Box 1.1 in Chapter 1 provides an illustrative case of tensions between private efficiency and public vulnerability. At issue in that case, involving the District of Columbia and CSX Railroad, were chemical hazards. The magnitude of the challenge posed by this single risk category is enormous: a 2003 report of the U.S. Environmental Protection Agency indicates that there are 123 large chemical facilities in New Jersey alone where a release of chemicals could threaten more than a million people.[3] At the time the report was released, former Senator John Corzine asserted that DHS, the Justice Department, the Environmental Protection Agency, and industry groups such as the Chemical Industry Council were in accord that the issue must be addressed, but could not agree on who should be responsible for what actions.

The chemical industry successfully lobbied against passage of Senator Corzine's bill, the Chemical Security Act of 2003 (S. 157), preferring its own voluntary industry standards for safety and security. Congress, while failing to pass S. 157, did pass unanimously on July 14, 2005, a resolution calling for mandatory federal standards. The standards were not enacted. But in a speech on March 21, 2006, DHS Secretary Michael Chertoff reversed the administration's opposition to mandatory regulation of the chemical industry and supported legislation to require all 15,000 plants that use or store significant quantities of toxic chemicals to prepare security plans and follow up with steps such as fencing, cameras, and identification cards to control access. Thus, the main thrust was to prevent access, not to cause investments to reduce the inherent vulnerability of the plants.

Critics noted that because large firms already comply with most of what the administration proposed, the legislation's main effect is to extend those practices to smaller firms and make them mandatory. Secretary Chertoff also said that the nation should have uniform standards, strongly implying that states should not be allowed to adopt their own rules, as New Jersey did last year, particularly if those rules were more stringent than the federal government's.[4] It is widely understood that the chemical industry has consistently resisted actions that would affect its profitability, which is understandable given that it is a low profit-margin business.

On the other hand, safety records of the largest chemical firms are good. The industry as a whole most likely has the competence to perform much better technically than it lets on. We argue that the safety standards in the chemical industry, including the more general hazard-related issues of chemical substitution, facility siting, transportation routing, and industrial interdependency, should not be determined by the lowest safety performers in the industry, which appears to be the case today. Leadership, both in the private sector and by government, is necessary to orchestrate movement away from the lowest common denominator when it comes to critical infrastructure performance and protection.

Firms will be reluctant to go beyond the proposed legislation and unilaterally invest heavily to reduce their own vulnerability if the industry lobbies effectively against legislation that would require its competitors to do the same thing. A more serious problem arises when the federal government intervenes to prevent state and municipal governments from taking stronger measures to safeguard their own communities against the risk of toxic chemical releases that could kill thousands of people.

If industry itself is not motivated to invest in protection against extreme events, and if the federal government does not take the initiative, who will take responsibility for protecting chemical plants, rail lines, hospitals, telecommunication systems, and other critical services? Who will make it harder for terrorists to magnify the damage of an attack by first attacking the infrastructure on which effective response depends? Who will ensure that these and other elements of the infrastructure are not used as weapons to kill or maim thousands of people in our cities? If they succeed, who will still trust the operation of our own critical services?

The lack of progress toward a well-defined balance of responsibilities between government and industry is illustrated by the proposed second version of the U.S. National Infrastructure Protection Plan (NIPP).[5] The NIPP constitutes a new step in the federal effort to protect the nation's critical infrastructure. This plan has recently been proposed by the government after extensive interagency negotiation led by DHS. The complexity of the task of coordinating roles of federal agencies alone is illustrated by the astonishing number of such agencies involved (see Figure 26.1).

This diagram represents all of the U.S. federal agencies with specific missions in Homeland Security and Homeland Defense.

The U.S. government recognizes that the great majority of the economic assets and the firms providing critical infrastructure services that are likely to

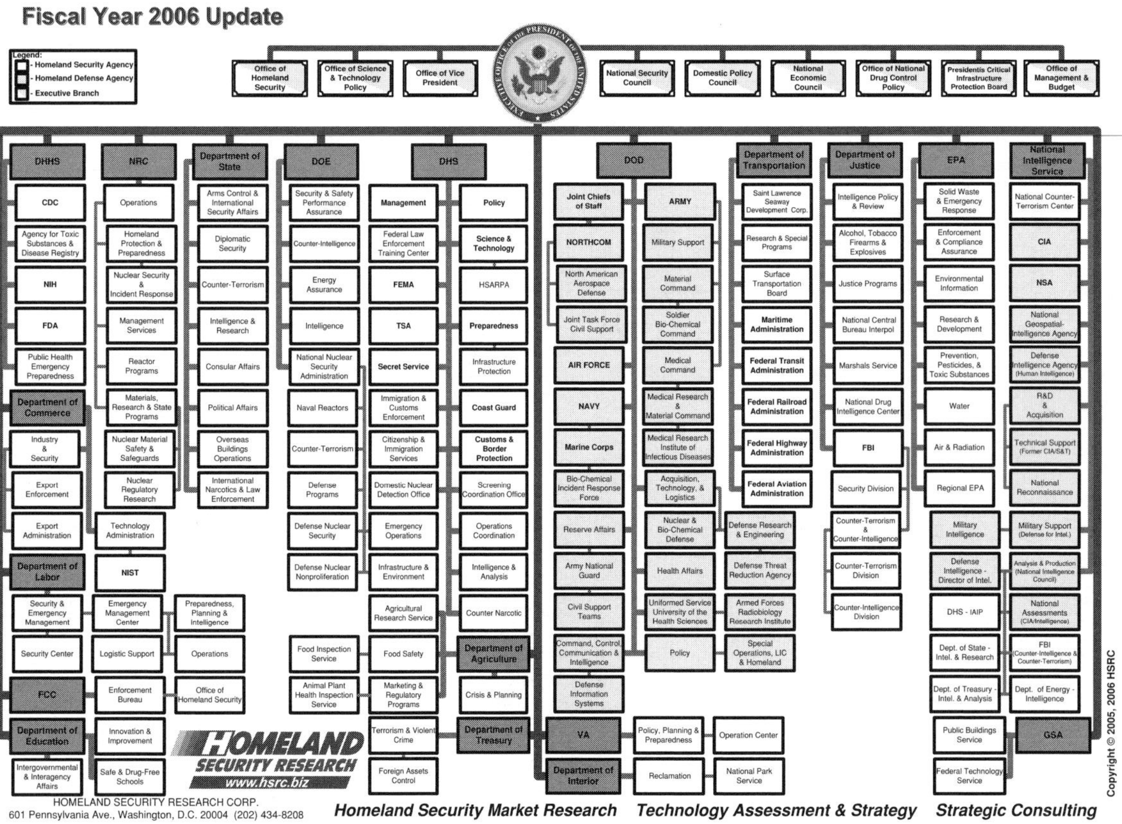

Figure 26.1. U.S. homeland security and homeland defense agencies.

be severely damaged in a disaster are owned by private enterprises. The NIPP document lays out architecture and principles for the many tasks that need to be addressed.[6] But while this plan addresses in detail the roles of all relevant federal agencies, it does not address adequately the critical issues analyzed in this book, including the incentives that would best enhance the willingness of firms to organize and invest in reducing them, while preserving a fair and efficient competitive market for their services.

In fact, the revised NIPP devotes only two pages to the roles and responsibilities of the private sector from the firms' perspective.[7] Nevertheless, the NIPP is replete with emphasis on "security partnerships," implying a broadly understood and accepted set of agreements between government and private firms about how private and public sector institutions will collaborate.[8] In concept, partnership is appealing. The concrete practice of partnership is another matter. Indeed, partnership raises fundamental questions of control, responsibility, coordination, information sharing, liability, trust, and cost sharing, among others, that still need to be addressed by government bodies in charge of protecting the country and by the firms that will bear the financial and managerial burdens of implementing that level of protection. Among the issues that remain to be addressed are:

- How responsibility and accountability are to be apportioned between government and industry;
- What obligations each side will have to share sensitive or proprietary information with each other;
- Who will monitor the performance of each party, and what criteria for evaluation will they use;
- Who will provide the resources required for addressing the security externalities, including organizational reliability, that each side believes the others should cover;
- Who will be held liable after the next disaster, and to what extent;
- How will economic losses be compensated and who will pay for them;
- Up to what extent will taxpayers and consumers (and investors) be willing, over an indefinite period into the future, to pay for increasing public security.

These are challenges that call for a national infrastructure protection plan in which the private sector has a major voice and a major responsibility, and under which critical infrastructure businesses can be held accountable for whatever obligations to partner with government – and with other firms – they undertake. Not only does the first version of the NIPP fail to answer these difficult questions, but also it does not propose a venue within which the negotiation about them can be carried out.

ROOTS OF RESPONSE: SEVEN FINDINGS TO INFORM ACTION

This book describes a complex set of threats to the safety and security of the United States, and indeed of other industrialized democracies. The potential severity of threats to critical infrastructure services is growing. At the same time, the public will demand a higher level of reliability and resilience in infrastructure services as they become more important in the economy. Yet as the requirements for addressing both of these trends grow, solving these problems becomes more difficult. The construction of the institutional relationships that will lead to enlightened decision making and actions will require an unusual degree of forward-looking leadership from both public and private sectors, and a deeper understanding on the part of the public of what is at stake.

Discussions regarding high-impact event preparedness and response almost inevitably feature actions recommended for immediate implementation. A number of these actions have been raised in this book. Equipping private- and public-sector first responders with interoperable communications equipment would at least make it possible for the response to the next major disaster to be more coordinated than was the response to 9/11 and Hurricane Katrina.[9] Issuing universally recognized identification cards to both public-sector and private-sector first responders (notably including infrastructure operators) would allow access to affected areas for all whose actions are required for recovery. Enacting legal provisions in each state to permit governors to suspend temporarily certain statutes if they impede necessary measures to deal with the emergency would reduce routine bureaucratic obstacles to response and recovery. Seeking to distribute federal grants to states and cities in proportion to the risks they face would introduce a minimal level of rationality to the process of public investment in vulnerability reduction.

In the United States in particular, a frustrated public can rightly ask: Why, five years after the September 11, 2001, attacks, and a full year after the Hurricane Katrina calamity, have these simple actions not been undertaken, even when demanded and funded by Congress? How severe does a disaster need to be before it motivates government into action?

The sentiment is a valid one. As Stephen Flynn emphasized in Chapter 3, the need for enhanced preparedness is urgent. Yet, if the many diverse contributions to this volume share one insight, it is that there are no technological quick fixes to the challenge of ensuring the reliable provision of critical services. Without forceful leadership from above and/or exceptional initiative from below, required organizational adaptations will not occur, and needed investment investments will not be made.

We believe that a set of ideas, actions, and policies must be accepted before the United States (and other countries) will respond in a concrete and timely way. This set includes (1) adopting new models for dealing with the new scale of disasters; (2) integrating all-hazard strategies; (3) restructuring management practices and technologies; (4) providing clear incentives, knowledge, experience, and tools; (5) recognizing that perceptions of risk may be as important as their reality; (6) understanding the critical roles of insurance and reinsurance in the recovery process and its capacity to provide incentives for investment in infrastructure protection; and (7) acting with a clear recognition that interdependence is a multinational issue.

Policies and concrete collaborative actions may follow more easily if these seven actions are taken.

1. THE SCALE OF DISASTERS IS GROWING: A NEW ERA CALLS FOR A NEW MODEL

Natural disasters, technological risks, and terrorism threats have always existed in one form or another. But society faces a new scale of these events today and, as we have argued, even more so tomorrow, because of increased aggregation of people and assets exposed to risks, along with the emergence of new forms of threat. As world population grows, people are flocking to cities and to coastal areas; larger numbers of individuals become exposed to a given catastrophic risk. And as incomes rise, the value of assets rises. As the economy grows, firms seek ever-larger aggregations of assets in the quest for economies of scale. With increased global economic integration, disasters reach across national boundaries with increasing frequency. As the scale of damage and death from disaster grows, it becomes necessary to prepare for ever-less-probable but increasingly consequential events.

The Gulf of Mexico has always suffered hurricanes. Hurricane Katrina, a widely predicted Category 3 storm when it made landfall on August 29, 2005, was not, however, just another hurricane. The large-scale hurricane damage, combined with the breach of New Orleans levees, became a major disaster. Preparing to deal with a local and limited event is one thing, but coping with a new dimension of loss and destabilization is another. One cannot simply apply the same evacuation rule for a million and a half people in four states as one would for a city of 50,000. A single event that, on top of several historically devastating years, inflicts insured losses for catastrophe lines equal to one- or even multi-year insured losses worldwide is not the same as numerous small independent events dispersed over 120 countries.

With economic and social activities concentrated in a limited number of areas, this new scale has to be seriously integrated into a new way of making important decisions. These extreme events will not simply require a little more of what we have previously learned, but a radical change in how to tackle them. A new scale calls for a new model.[10]

2. AN INTEGRATED STRATEGY FOR ADDRESSING DELIBERATE, NATURAL, AND TECHNOGENIC DISASTERS IS NEEDED

As discussed in Chapter 1, disasters are essentially of three types: natural, technogenic, and terrorist-caused. These three sources of possible disaster may also be interdependent or occur in combination. While it is critical to recognize the fundamental differences among these disasters and to respond appropriately when need be, the management policies and resources for mitigation and response to dealing with each of them have much in common.

This commonality is particularly apparent in the capabilities and tools of emergency first responders. The mission of the Federal Emergency Management Agency, now a part of DHS, is based on the assumption that this is so. It is widely acknowledged that Hurricane Katrina would have been much less damaging to New Orleans and the Gulf Coast if the destruction had not been compounded by technogenic and poor management amplification (badly engineered levees and barriers, growing populations in hazard-prone areas, poor post-flood response by local, state, and federal governments). In some cases, such as the spread of toxic chemicals in a railroad switchyard, first responders may even be forced to make decisions before they know if the event was accidental or the deliberate act of a terrorist. Thus, strategies intended to address all three – the "all hazard" strategies – need to be addressed by a comprehensive plan that responds to all three types of disasters and their combinations in the most efficient and sustainable way.

Likewise, firms can establish preparedness capacity (evacuation, business interruption issue, liability protection) to be used for all three types of catastrophe. Doing so would show how considering all hazards together spreads costs over a wider range of contingencies, making them more attractive economically than measures devoted to only one.[11]

We support a more sustainable national effort to reduce the danger and consequence of disasters based on the "all hazards" approach, in which investments in vulnerability reduction, continuity of operations, and preparation for recovery for all three types of disasters can, at least to some extent, be shared.

Sustainability of a national effort to reduce infrastructure service vulnerability to high-consequence terrorism may falter if too many years pass without a major catastrophe of a specific type. This is one of the reasons that an "all hazards" approach to infrastructure protection is required. Sustainability may also be threatened if effective protection depends on a level of international cooperation that proves not to be forthcoming.

But the most important element to enhance sustainability of the public commitment to vulnerability reduction is a strategy – industrial, technological, and regulatory – that searches for *dual* benefits (reduced vulnerability *and* better service) from the public and private investments in the effort. Indeed, if one focuses only on the security aspect, it is likely that the short-term return on investment will not be seen as significant enough; but if benefits of better service are included as well (as it should be), then the strategy is immediately viewed as much more appealing. If the public becomes aware of such benefits, and if industry can find and profit from them, a more sustainable effort will be achieved. Some examples of service benefits are improved public health services (for both the normal health needs of communities and faster response to natural threats such as SARS and avian flu), environmental protection, less frequent contamination of the food supply, more reliable electric power and other services, less frequent delays in transportation systems, safer chemical and energy industries, improved defense against hackers and virus attacks, better tracking and billing of goods in transit, and reduced risk to fire, police, and emergency health professionals.

As industry looks for both new technologies and new management methods to reduce the costs of increased reliability and resilience and searches for additional service benefits that can help offset rising costs, the incremental cost to government of preparing for terrorism or unlikely natural disasters may also be reduced. For example, the government investment of $7 billion in preparation for a bird flu pandemic that has yet to occur may also be a valuable step in anticipation of a biological attack, which has not yet occurred either.

3. INCREASINGLY INTERDEPENDENT SERVICES REQUIRES RESTRUCTURED MANAGEMENT PRACTICES AND TECHNOLOGIES TO MAKE THEM MORE RELIABLE AND RESILIENT

High-tech market economies, such as in the United States, are increasingly turning from product manufacturing to integrated provision of services, which in combination with products and services, deliver consumer value most effectively. Given the accelerating rate at which manufactured products are driven to commodity production by competition from high-skilled, "low-ware" firms located abroad (e.g., India and China), the trend toward the increasing share of the economy devoted to provision of services is being driven by economic necessity as well as the quest for greater market satisfaction. The most critical of these services are normally delivered by an increasingly complex web of interdependent infrastructure services operated by the private sector, with highly variable (and generally diminishing) degrees of public regulation or direction.

The government's current list of 13 critical infrastructures is only the tip of the iceberg of interrelated critical services. In fact, as discussed in the early part of the book, the government's list continues to grow. Closer examination of regional economies would show a fractal-like structure of networks of service firms in collaboration and competition with one another, each generating security externalities that require a collective response in the public interest. Thus, sustaining the reliability and resilience of this mesh network of infrastructure services is increasingly vital to economic and social life of the nation.

On the demand side, civil life has become more dependent on increasingly interdependent infrastructure services. As we have noted, because their interdependencies tend to increase the level of consequence when large-scale failures do occur, the public will demand higher levels of reliability, even in the absence of either natural or terrorist-initiated disasters. This demand will certainly be exacerbated in the aftermath of every disaster the country may face in the coming years.

The public's expectations, however, cannot be fully realized without government action in concert with the relevant industries. The public will demand that both private and public institutions make themselves accountable for high levels of service and security. This demand will grow stronger as vulnerability of critical services to both natural and deliberate disasters increases. How this demand will materialize is not clear today. Customers who want more reliable services will have to be willing to pay the price, and both public and private officials will have to be willing to be accountable.

On the supply side, executives of infrastructure service businesses are generally successful in managing to limit the service and financial consequences, in degree and duration, of statistically predictable interruptions in service from natural causes such as hurricanes or floods. They are well organized to deal with the many minor disruptions with which they have experience, and some even offer level-of-service guarantees. But they are increasingly faced with the possibility of less-predictable disasters, not only from terrorism but from decreased resilience of their operations. Firms with experience in providing highly reliable services, such as telephone and financial services, have developed management disciplines that are driven by a long-term commitment to operational goals and that have come to possess the organizational practices, management cultures, and external support needed to sustain them.

The advice in Part III details the essential practices, procedures, and structures that enable firms to manage the unexpected and transform a highly industrialized but loosely coupled economy to one much less vulnerable to high-consequence disasters. But very little attention, except in the most highly regulated industries such as nuclear power, has been given to public policies that might induce more critical infrastructure firms to restructure their management practices, policies, and organization to make them more resilient.

That might not matter if it were not for the fact that, as a general rule, the competitive drive for efficiency results in loss of reliability and resilience in critical services. The urgency associated with public fears of a repeat of 9/11 has induced a very short-term view of critical infrastructure vulnerability. But the threats from nature, terrorists, and human failings will be with us for the indefinite future. Restructuring a highly industrialized economy to reduce not only the threats but the consequences of disaster is likely to be time-consuming and costly. We conclude that the very success of a competitive economy with a strong capacity for innovation may be changing the inherent vulnerability of critical infrastructure systems. Indeed, in many instances, there seems to be a direct but inverse correlation between success at driving business performance to higher productivity and lower cost in "normal times," and resilience in the face of a threat of possible disaster.

As a general rule, firms seeking to become more competitive still seek efficiency gains in economies of both scale and scope, in concentration of activities in a limited number of geographical areas,[12] in reduction of redundancy, in aggregation of resources and services, and in dependence on the services and products provided by other infrastructures. One example of this interdependence of special importance is the advent of just-in-time processes – all of which result in loss of resilience in the face of disasters for which the likelihood and consequences (including ripple affects on those not directly affected by the event) are difficult to quantitatively predict and integrate in day-to-day business decisions.

A key strategic challenge of the new risk era is, that "disaster times" seem to have become much more frequent these past years. If the trend continues and is reinforced, this increase will require a radical change in how demand and supply sides' priorities are established and how resources are allocated between normal and disaster times.

4. KNOWLEDGE, EXPERIENCE, AND TOOLS TO ADDRESS SECURITY EXTERNALITIES ARE REQUIRED TO ALLOW RISKS TO BE ASSESSED AND RESPONSES CREATED

A main objective for senior executives is to reduce the impact of an untoward event on their firm's operations, limit their legal responsibility, and facilitate a back-to-normal crisis management strategy. However, the impacts of executives' actions on other infrastructure services are not often integrated in crisis decision making. The main reason for this lack of integration is the absence of both quantitative information and mechanisms for internalizing these external effects, whether positive or negative. For example, markets do not reward firms for assuring high-reliability service offerings in the event of very low-probability events. This lack of reward inhibits the adoption of high-reliability management methods.

The new dimension of extreme events directly affects the security externality component we define and discuss in the introductory chapter of this book. Beyond the lack of appropriate economic, social, or legal incentives, firms do not tackle the security externality issue adequately for several reasons. While some teams of technical experts in the national labs, in research institutions, and in industry have made progress in methods for evaluating enterprise vulnerability, this knowledge has not been widely tested or diffused. Strengthening the focus of responsibility for critical infrastructure protection in DHS appears a necessary condition, given the diffusion of responsibility in the government today (Figure 26.1). This lack of general knowledge, experience, and tools inhibits market forces from motivating infrastructure service firms to invest in vulnerability reduction to lessen the likelihood of rare, high-consequence events.

The existence of interdependencies that are not well understood may lead organizations to decide not to invest in their own protection because they know that the failure of others to take similar actions can harm them, even if they do make such investments. One valuable way to reduce risks due to interdependencies is to evolve interdependence into mutual support.[13] Moreover, with well-defined risks, it is possible to measure the effective return on investment of specific security/mitigation measures. When it comes to rare disasters, on the other hand, it is very difficult, if not impossible, to define a distribution of probability and to quantify all the direct and indirect effects of such extreme events. What cannot be measured in quantitative terms may be more difficult to support as a private strategy (see Chapter 17).

An appealing way to address the problem is via the establishment of business coalitions. Members of the coalition collaborate to support their decisions aimed at reducing interdependent risks based on the analyses of the whole group.[14] Knowing that all coalition members are acting the same way increases the willingness of each individual member to act as well. When a critical number of participating organizations is reached, others might decide to join, eventually leading to new business practices for all. The key is to find the pivotal few firms that will demonstrate leadership by acting first. The objective should be to find assessment tools for which firms and agencies can have sufficient confidence to justify corporate investments in vulnerability reduction and recovery capabilities, can measure their return, and can be rewarded by specific market mechanisms (e.g., higher prices paid by customers or limited liability).

5. LARGE-SCALE RISK MANAGEMENT MUST REFLECT PERCEPTIONS AND REALITIES OF RISK

As catastrophic risks are difficult to quantify, estimates and decisions are more likely to be based on qualitative factors, and they may even be very subjective.

Although this volume does not specifically address the issue of risk perception, we recognize that it plays a key, if quiet, role. It generally is not effectively integrated in the development of private strategies and public policies to protect critical services. Yet the integration of risk perception is fundamental for the success of any program to deal with catastrophic risk management. Risk perception is concerned with the psychological and emotional aspects of risks, which have been shown to have an enormous impact on individual and group behavior. It is also important to know how this perception and its corresponding behaviors (investments in security, insurance protection, creation of new security-related markets, political behaviors) change over time.[15]

A particularly serious example of a potential difference between perception and reality of risks is the public alarm that seems likely to accompany a terrorist attack with a radiation dispersal weapon, popularly called a "dirty bomb." Such a weapon does not involve the most terrible of weapons of mass destruction, that is, a nuclear explosive, but rather a chemical explosion of radioactive waste material. The general public is poorly informed about the dangers of given types of radiation sources, their rate of dispersion, and common sense ways of reducing one's exposure. Panic is widely predicted in the event of such an attack, and the public may not be willing to reoccupy contaminated areas for generations.

One of the ultimate challenges in protecting critical sectors is the choice of specific allocation of resources, which are by definition limited. Therefore, it is crucial to understand the threats decision makers and the public perceive as being the most important and those that most need to be protected against. The natural tendency to fight the previous war, rather than anticipate and prepare for the next one, must not be underestimated. Focusing for four years on homeland security has led some to forget that the country remains vulnerable to natural disasters as well. A new terrorist attack on U.S. soil would certainly reshape the debate again.

6. THE ROLES OF INSURANCE AND REINSURANCE IN DISASTER RECOVERY AND IN INVESTMENT INCENTIVES IN PROTECTION MUST BE DEFINED AND FACILITATED IN POLICY

Well-defined market mechanisms have a major role to play in assigning responsibility and motivating action to ensure the reliable provision of critical services. Among the market mechanisms, insurance appears to be an appealing candidate. It is well known that, without proper design, the availability of insurance is as likely to blunt incentives for required investments as it is to sharpen them. Yet insurance has potential to be a powerful instrument. The insurance industry is the world's largest when measured in terms of revenues. Insurance diversifies risks nationwide and internationally, and it can play a fundamental role in financially protecting the nation. Insurance constitutes a potential nexus between risk assessment, risk mitigation, and risk financing. Insurers and re-insurers are often seen as experts in understanding risks. They are private-sector players who understand how markets operate, a quality most businesses are often reluctant to attribute to any level of government.

As we demonstrate in Part V, a well-functioning insurance infrastructure is also a critical service itself. The fact that the public sector participates in most disaster insurance programs in the United States and several other industrialized countries shows an implicit recognition by government of the critical role played by the insurance infrastructure. The government has often stepped in when insurers refused to cover such events alone. Because of this importance in managing risks across the whole society, we call for recognizing the insurance industry as a critical sector on its own, rather than including it under a broad banking and finance umbrella. Including the insurance industry as the 14th U.S. critical sector would allow a better understanding by the general public, the government, and other critical services of the strengths and limitations of insurance operations. It would also help society deal with challenges of how best to finance recovery from all types of disasters. Such solutions should encourage the development of better mechanisms to reward investments in security and risk mitigation, thus limiting the need for post-disaster federal aid. Long-term programs also need to take equity issues into account – those who cannot afford insurance should not be left behind.

Large disasters present, however, a set of specific characteristics that challenge insurance and re-insurance operations: difficulty in estimating and pricing risks with confidence, high correlation of risks, and potential for extreme consequences that create solvency problems, among others. On the demand side, one often observes low demand for insurance coverage even in exposed areas (except just after a catastrophe, when demand temporarily increases, often significantly).[16] To make insurance a more effective market-mechanism tool to enhance higher security, one would have to better align demand and supply.

The type of leadership we call for in this book is certainly highly needed in the area of insurance and reinsurance as well. The unprecedented series of extreme events in the past few years have more urgently raised the question of the roles and responsibilities of the public and private sectors in providing adequate protection to catastrophe victims, both people and firms. In fact, between 2001 and 2005, the record of the most costly year ever in the history of catastrophe insurance and reinsurance worldwide has been hit three times; three times due to disasters in the United States. If the country continues to file the vast majority of world insurance and reinsurance claims in the next few years (more than 85 percent in 2005), how long will reinsurers, most of them non-U.S. firms, continue to cover insurers against extreme events in the United States? What maximum capacity will they be able to provide, and at what price? How will insurers react if they cannot increase risk-based prices they would charge in highly exposed states because of strong market regulations such as Florida?

If a major catastrophe were to happen next week, the question of loss sharing and financing the economic and social consequences would likely take center stage. In other words, how best should society finance extreme event losses? This question will not be solved overnight, but it must be addressed as a national priority. However, the current debate on the protection of critical service stays essentially focused on the ex ante aspect (physical and cyber protection), rather than a necessary dual ex ante/ex post perspective (physical, cyber, and financial protection).

Terrorism risk is a perfect illustration. Attacks in Madrid and London, among others, demonstrate that the United States and its allies remain prime targets for some terrorist groups. The American public and business enterprises deserve a robust national debate on a long-term program for dealing with terrorism risk financing. The fact that the Terrorism Risk Insurance Act was renewed on the literal eve of its expiration in 2005 does not signal the type of leadership one might expect from a country that places homeland and national security as a top priority.

7. INTERDEPENDENCE IS MULTINATIONAL: COLLECTIVE INTERNATIONAL ACTIONS MUST FORM AN INTEGRAL PART OF PREVENTION AND RESPONSE STRATEGIES

Finally, as critical services are evolving and their scale of operation is becoming larger and more linked internationally, new collaborative initiatives by the United States need to be undertaken at the international level. In the case of manufacturing supply chains (see Chapter 16), the vulnerability to disruption is rapidly growing as economies become increasingly global. A major incident in the port of Rotterdam, Hong Kong, or Shanghai would have huge impacts worldwide. The challenge of increasing the reliability and resilience of national critical services would be only partially addressed if it is not considered in the context of effective multinational strategies. In today's world, the United States does not have the option of simply closing its borders to protect itself from external threat. The barriers posed by these borders are eroding due to more and more open networks of people and markets in a global interdependent world, resulting in foreign firms operating some of the U.S. critical services and U.S. firms operating these services in other countries.

Ten years ago, with the establishment of the Commission headed by General Robert T. Marsh (author of the foreword to this book), the United States was the first country to put the critical infrastructure challenge on its national policy agenda. Other countries have followed more recently, and their government agencies and businesses are acting to protect their critical services at home as well. For example, the European Council in June 2004 asked the European Commission – representing 25 European countries – to prepare an overall strategy to protect critical infrastructure. In December 2004, the council officially endorsed the commission's initiative to launch its European Programme for Critical Infrastructure Protection, with the release at the end of 2005 of its first official document.[17] As of now, however, the debate on the actions needed in Europe is still in its early stages.

Japan, accustomed to major natural disasters and the victim of domestic terrorist attacks as well (e.g., the Sarin gas attack in the Tokyo subway in 1995), has long had an extensive and well-organized program of response capability. In addition, Japan has now initiated programs of scientific research on means to reduce vulnerabilities, which it is undertaking in collaboration with the U.S. Department of State and other federal agencies.[18] The U.S. government has diligently sought foreign cooperation to make its own protections more effective, for example, in container inspections in foreign ports and new U.S. passport designs with biometric security features. But there are also opportunities for the United States to energize its international collaboration in the broader strategies to make the multinational family of critical service providers more robust, reliable, and resilient. Here again, the private and public sectors need to work hand-in-hand.

One should expect that U.S. partners among market economy democracies would be eager to respond to such initiatives. A major destabilization in the United States could have impacts, direct and indirect, short- and long-term, far from American shores. Interdependencies work both ways. Thus, there is an opportunity for win–win situations in transnational negotiations. In this case also, it requires leadership, indeed, international leadership.

In today's global economy, assuring rapid and transparent exchanges of information and plans for coordinated action must also be international. How is this international collaboration to be achieved? Mechanisms such as were demonstrated by the postal operators of Europe and the United States in response to the crisis created by the 2001 U.S. anthrax attack (see Chapter 25) are a good beginning. They demonstrate that it is possible to learn and act on these issues, and to act at a large scale. These initiatives reinforced trust – a crucial element when collectively preparing to face the unknown. But enhanced international capacity for coordinated real-time operational response is also badly needed in other areas such as information, computer networks, telecommunications, energy, health, and transportation. It is imperative that similar collective actions are launched systematically after each major destabilization and by leading organizations in multiple sectors. Coordination is the only proven way to lay the groundwork for arrangements that enhance each nation's ability to cope the next time. Some encouragement may be drawn from an important move over the past few years.

Economically focused international organizations have started addressing resilience issues from a multinational collaborative perspective as well. The former Secretary General of the Organization for Economic Cooperation and Development (OECD), in a September 2005 address in Beijing, clearly stated the OECD's position (Box 26.2). Recognizing the question of large-scale risks and disasters as a priority of its future action plan, the OECD Directorate for Financial Affairs is now developing a network of reflection, study, and recommendations regarding the new challenges associated with extreme events, both natural and human caused. A multi-year project will be deployed in the coming months and will constitute a natural venue for decisionmakers interested in the critical aspects of dealing with the new scale of disasters.

BOX 26.2 OECD'S SECRETARY GENERAL ADDRESS ON CATASTROPHE RISKS

"The OECD risk management work began four years ago when by making an assessment of OECD countries' capacity to deal with a range of major threats ranging from natural disasters and terrorism to health risks and cyber-attacks. Our conclusion from that wide-ranging study was that, in almost all aspects of risk management – assessment, prevention, response and recovery – our member countries were not well positioned to deal effectively with the scale and complexity of the risks of the twenty-first century, and that considerable efforts would be required to make improvements.

Modern-day societies and economies are complex and sophisticated, often with multiple jurisdictions. In OECD countries there is very rarely a single organization that can legitimately control the operations of all public and private actors in the event of a peace-time disaster. But it is precisely such structural and organizational difficulties that need to be overcome if our capacity for handling disasters effectively is to be significantly improved. In the case of international-scale disasters, coordination is the key. . . .

Governments must address these challenges quickly and comprehensively. Preparing for and managing these risks requires a comprehensive and coordinated approach. A piecemeal response will not work; as the American proverb says "It doesn't work to leap a twenty-foot chasm in two ten-foot jumps."[a]

– Donald Johnston, Secretary-General, Organization for Economic Cooperation and Development

[a] Johnston 2005.

The World Economic Forum (WEF) in Geneva, Switzerland, has also made large-scale risk issues a priority in its future action plans. Indeed, in 2005, it selected for debate one of the most important and intractable threats: anthropogenic climate change induced by greenhouse gases. Box 26.1 illustrates a concrete and detailed initiative launched in 2005 by the forum along with G-8 members and senior executives of a number of multinational firms.

A series of similarly focused initiatives would increase society's common knowledge and be viewed by others as a reason to act. These actions bring the type of leadership we described earlier to the international scene. More broadly, the WEF recently launched its "Global Risks Network." Its aim is to assess key current and emerging systemic risks to global business, to study the links between them for their likely effects on markets and industries, and to advance thinking about mitigation. The network was created in 2004 by the WEF in collaboration with Merrill Lynch. In 2005, Swiss Re and Marsh & McLennan joined, along with several faculty members from the University of Pennsylvania's Wharton School as advisors. The 2006 forum in Davos contributed to increasing the awareness of leaders in businesses, governments, universities, and nongovernmental organizations regarding the network and its activities.

These multinational initiatives could lead to a whole new way of managing large-scale untoward events. Perhaps the most encouraging feature of the OECD and WEF initiatives is their engagement of business leaders in conjunction with international political leaders. While neither of these organizations seems appropriate for the detailed negotiations of responsibilities and accountability that must be agreed to by both business and government in each country, they may serve to stimulate recognition of the high priority of this work.

HOW CAN A NEW CONSENSUS OF PRIVATE AND PUBLIC INTERESTS COME ABOUT? – A CALL FOR COLLABORATIVE LEADERSHIP

The response we seek in this book to risks of extreme events goes well beyond the task of first responders to a disaster underway or to tactical response plans of citizens and local governments. We look to a preventive strategy that avoids the crisis costs and damages that would arise from a society poorly positioned to mitigate disasters before they happen. This crisis avoidance requires more than plans; it requires changes in management structures and practices, in analysis of vulnerabilities and risks, and in some cases changes in technologies. It requires a greater degree of collaboration across critical service sectors and across national boundaries. The current institutional structures needed to undertake this task are not in place – they must be invented. Building these institutions into effective bodies will require a new and different kind of leadership.

Leadership – courage, we may say – will require decision makers in critical industry sectors and in governments to be willing to take a long view of the nation's future, even at the expense of short-term economic gains (industry) and political needs (government). This long-term view must be addressed in a non-partisan, non-ideological way. If dialogue and decisions are to be effective, not only in the short-term but sustained into the future, new institutional mechanisms will be required. The assignment of responsibilities, resources, and accountability requires a venue for addressing public–private collaboration. It cannot be dictated by government, nor will it arise naturally from market forces.

We have argued that the private sector will certainly shoulder the burden of financing most of the capital investment and making most of the institutional improvements that provide high reliability and robustness to their parts of critical service. But the private sector cannot do this alone. It requires incentives beyond those currently existing in critical-sector markets, some perhaps from insurance, others from government. Public–private collaboration with governments at all levels, along with intergovernmental cooperation, will have to rise to a level that businesses and governments do not today enjoy.

Beyond this public–private duality, the triptych of business–government–citizen should be brought together more systematically. Indeed, in an open, democratic society the ultimate decision maker is the citizen, functioning as a consumer and as a voter. Civic engagement and consumer responsibility offer promise for sustainable solutions. On the other hand, consumer negligence and refusal to pay today the price for public peace and security would be a sad alternative. Indeed, public apathy and consumer disengagement from the aggregate impacts of individual decisions create the ideal terrain to nurture the seeds of ever more severe disasters.

Courage "is an opportunity that sooner or later is presented to us all." We can each expect that our moment to assume private responsibility for public vulnerabilities will come in time. The best time to assume that responsibility is now. This book seeks the achievement of a safer, more secure world by guiding the leadership efforts of those who recognize collective action as a proven way to succeed and, most importantly, those of visionaries who share our belief that a better world can be created; for us today, and for our children and grandchildren tomorrow.

NOTES

1. A dramatic if much less likely threat is that of a large asteroid striking Earth. We know this has occurred more than once in Earth's history. Only collective action can be taken to deal with such a threat. See Posner 2005.
2. Flynn 2005a.

3. Stephenson 2005. The GAO quotes DHS estimates that there are 4,000 chemical manufacturing facilities that produce, use, or store more than threshold amounts of chemicals that EPA has estimated pose the greatest risk to human health and the environment (Government Accountability Office 2005d).

4. Lipton 2006.

5. Department of Homeland Security 2006.

6. "Designed to meet the mandates set forth in Homeland Security Presidential Directive 7, the NIPP Base Plan also articulates security partner roles and responsibilities, protective framework milestones, and key implementation actions required to support our national-level critical infrastructures and key resources (CI/KR) protection mission. It establishes the architecture for conducting operational risk assessment and risk management activities and provides processes for coordinating resource priorities and informing the annual federal budget process; strengthening linkages between physical and cyber, domestic and international CI/KR protection efforts; improving information-sharing and public-private-sector coordination; and integrating steady-state protection programs in an all-hazards environment." E-mail communication from the NIPP office at DHS, January 20, 2006.

7. DHS officials expect a series of sector specific plans to be published in the summer of 2006 that will address roles of private firms and government in specific areas of critical infrastructure. Private communication March 15, 2006.

8. In addition, the NIPP lacks guidance for firms concerning operational practices that would improve system resilience and robustness. There are a small but notable number of examples of such systems, most run by some form of public–private partnership involving federal agencies already, which could inform the national policy discussion; some of these have been discussed in this book. The widespread adoption of some of these practices would go a long way to reducing the vulnerability of major disruption from an extreme event.

9. For a discussion of the issues, see National Task Force on Interoperability 2003.

10. Lagadec and Michel-Kerjan 2005.

11. For example, many different insurance solutions exist in the United States to cover against different types of disaster. The National Flood Insurance Program, a public program, covers floods. Storms on the other hand, are covered mainly by the private sector; the distinction between these two types of covering parties in Hurricane Katrina has been the subject of a great deal of conflict between insurance companies and their policyholders. An international terrorism act on U.S. soil would be covered by the Terrorism Risk Insurance Act, a private–public program; but this program does not cover domestic terrorism. Other countries have made a different choice by providing "all hazards" insurance policies. Whether a comprehensive "all hazards" coverage program in the United States would be appropriate economically, socially equitable, and politically sustainable is a question worth studying in more detail. For a discussion on natural hazards, see Kunreuther 2006.

12. In the chemical sector, for instance, there are large concentrations of facilities in several regions (Houston, Texas, the Kanawha Valley in West Virginia, the Delaware Valley, and the Northern New Jersey/New York area). Major disasters in any of these areas could have significant spillovers for the entire economy.

13. See contributions by Brian Lopez in Part II.

14. There might be important anti-trust limitations, however.

15. For recent contributions, see Slovic 1993, 1999, 2000; Horch et al. 2001; Morgan et al. 2002; Pidgeon et al. 2003.

16. There might be several reasons for that: (1) Memories of prior losses tend to fade if no similar events have occurred recently; (2) Insurance is perceived as a bad investment – "I paid this policy for years, and I never suffered any damage, so I'm going to cancel it"; (3) Insurance is only one tool that people and firms can use to protect themselves financially – for example, publicly traded firms can diversify their exposure over all shareholders; (4) The temptation of some to expect the government to step in anyway in the aftermath of a disaster can reduce their willingness to purchase coverage.
17. Commission of European Communities 2005.
18. Branscomb 2004.

REFERENCES

Adamic, L. A. undated. Zipf, Power-laws, and Pareto – A Ranking Tutorial. http://www.hpl.hp.com/research/idl/papers/ranking/ranking.html (accessed June 27, 2006).

Adams, J. 2001. Virtual Defense. *Foreign Affairs* 80: 98–112.

Advisory Panel to Assess Domestic Response Capabilities for Terrorism Involving Weapons of Mass Destruction. 2000. Second Annual Report to the President and Congress of the Advisory Panel to Assess Domestic Response Capabilities for Terrorism Involving Weapons of Mass Destruction, edited by James S. Gilmore et al. Washington, DC.

Albert, R., H. Jeong, and A. Barabasi. 2000. Attack and Error Tolerance of Complex Networks. *Nature* 406: 6794.

Aljazeera. 2004. Full transcript of bin Ladin's speech. November 1. http://english.aljazeera.net/NR/exeres/79C6AF22-98FB-4A1C-B21F-2BC36E87F61F.htm (accessed January 12, 2006).

American Academy of Actuaries. 2005. Statement by American Academy of Actuaries' TRIA Subgroup on Extending or Replacing the Terrorism Risk Insurance Act of 2002 (TRIA) December 1. http://www.actuary.org/pdf/casualty/tria_dec05.pdf (accessed February 25, 2006).

American Enterprise Institute (AEI). 2005. Should the Terrorism Risk Insurance Act of 2002 Be Extended? July 8. http://www.aei.org/events/eventID.1099,filter.all/event_detail.asp (accessed February 25, 2006).

Anonymous. 2003. Communication between a security executive who requested anonymity and the author, April 5.

AON. 2005. Property Terrorism Update: TRIA In The Balance. AON Risk Services October. http://www.aon.com/about/publications/pdf/issues/AonPropertyUpdate-TRIA,Oct2005.pdf (accessed February 25, 2006).

Apt, J., L. B. Lave, S. Talukdar, M. G. Morgan, and M. Ilic. 2004. Electrical Blackouts: A Systemic Problem. *Issues in Science and Technology* 20(4): 55–61.

Apt, Jay, Daniel Hoffman, Howard Kunreuther, and Erwann Michel-Kerjan. 2006. Insurance Industry and Global Warming. Philadelphia, PA: Wharton School, Center for Risk Management.

Associated Press. 2005a. Bush and Clinton, in Thailand, Start Tour of Tsunami Region. *New York Times*. February 20.

Associated Press. 2005b. London Bombings Trigger Surge in Inquiries. AP Online. August 16.

Associated Press. 2006. Report: Telecoms Helped NSA Wiretapping. February 6. http://www.msnbc.msn.com/id/11202938/ (accessed February 28, 2006).

Bak, Per. 1996. *How Nature Works: The Science of Self-Organized Criticality.* New York: Springer-Verlag Telos.

Barabasi A-L., S. V. Buldyrev, H. E. Stanley, and B. Suki. 1996. Avalanches in the Lung: A Statistical Mechanical Model. *Physical Review Letters* 76(12): 2192–2195.

Barabasi, A-L. 2003. *Linked.* New York: Penguin Books.

Bell, Coral M. 1978. Decision-making by governments in crisis situations. In *International Crises and Crisis Management. An East-West Symposium,* edited by D. Frei. New York: Praeger Publishers, 50–58.

Benfield Group Limited. 2005. *Outrageous Fortune: Reinsurance Market and Renewals Review.* January, 13–15.

Benjamin, Daniel, and Steven Simon. 2005. *The Next Attack: The Failure of the War on Terror and a Strategy for Getting it Right.* New York: NY Times Books.

Bennis, W., and B. Nanus. 1997. *Leaders: Strategies for Taking Charge.* New York: Harper & Row.

Bequai, A. 2002. White Collar Crime: A Handmaiden of International Tech Terrorism. *Computers & Security* 21(6): 514–519.

Bergen, Peter. 2002. Al Qaeda's New Tactics. *New York Times,* November 15, A31.

Berinato, S. 2002. The Truth about Cyberterrorism. *CIO Magazine,* March 15. http://www.cio.com/archive/031502/truth.html (accessed May 2, 2003).

Bernstein, Peter L. 1996. *Against the Gods. The Remarkable Story of Risk.* New York: John Wiley & Sons.

Berrick, Cathleen A., Director, Homeland Security and Justice Issues. 2006. Aviation Security: Significant Management Challenges May Adversely Affect Implementation of the Transportation Security Administration's Secure Flight Program. Testimony before the Senate Committee on Commerce, Science, and Transportation. February 9. Government Accountability Office, GAO-06-374T, Washington, DC.

Best's Aggregates & Averages. 2005. AM Best, Olde Wyke, N.J. p. 98.

Biographies in Naval History. 2001. Admiral Hyman G. Rickover. http://www.history. navy.mil/bios/rickover.htm (accessed June 27, 2006).

Block, Robert. 2005. U.S. Finds Ally in Terrorism Fight in FedEx: Since September 11, Firms Cooperate More Often with Officials, Raising Privacy Concerns. *Wall Street Journal Europe.* May 30, A6.

Boardman, Michelle. 2004. *Known Unknowns: The Delusion of Terrorism Insurance.* George Mason University School of Law, Paper 244. http://law.bepress.com/cgi/ viewcontent.cgi?article=1593&context=expresso (accessed February 25, 2006).

Bosk, C. L. 2003. *Forgive and Remember: Managing Medical Failure.* Chicago: University of Chicago Press.

Boulter, J. 1995. Tic-Tac-Toe. http://boulter.com/ttt/ (accessed June 27, 2006).

Bourrier, M. 1996. Organizing Maintenance Work at Two American Nuclear Power Plants. *Journal of Crisis and Contingency Management* 4(2): 104–112.

Brady, Matt. 2006. TRIA Coverage Light, Says Moody's, January 19. National Underwriter Inc.

Braga, G. A., R. Sanchis, T. A. Schieber. 2005. Critical Percolation on a Bethe Lattice Revisited. *SIAM Review* (47)2: 349–365.

Branscomb, Lewis M. 2004. Japanese–American Collaborative Efforts to Counter Terrorism. In *The Bridge: Linking Engineering and Society: National Academy of Engineering* 34(2): 11–16.

Branscomb, Lewis M. 2006. Sustainable Cities: Safety and Security. *Technology in Society* 20(1–2): 225–234.

Brown, J., D. Cummins, C. Lewis, and R. Wei. 2004. An Empirical Analysis of the Economic Impact of Federal Terrorism Reinsurance. *Journal of Monetary Economics* 51: 861–898.

Buchanan, M. 2001. *Ubiquity*. New York: Three Rivers Press.

Bureau of Labor Statistics. 2003. Occupational Employment and Wage Estimates, National NAICS 3-digit Industry Specific Estimates spreadsheet. Occupational Employment Statistics Program. http://www.bls.gov/oes/oes_dl.htm#2003_m (accessed July 2004).

Burns, R. E., J. Wilhelm, J. McGarvey, and T. Lehmann. 2003. Security-Related Cost Recovery in Utility Network Industries. White paper National Regulatory Research Institute, Columbus, OH. http://www.nrri.ohio-state.edu/dspace/bitstream/2068/366/1/05-03.pdf (accessed February 2, 2006).

Bush, George W. 2001. Executive Order 13231. Critical Infrastructure Protection in the Information Age. White House, Washington, DC.

Bush, George W. 2002. Protecting Critical Infrastructure and Key Assets. National Strategy for Homeland Security. White House, Washington, DC. July 16.

Bush, George W. 2003a. Critical Infrastructure Identification, Prioritization, and Protection. *Homeland Security Presidential Directive 7*. White House, Washington, DC. December 17.

Bush, George W. 2003b. *Homeland Security Presidential Directive 8*. White House, Washington, DC. December 17.

Bush, George W. 2003c. Protecting Key Assets. *National Strategy for the Physical Protection of Critical Infrastructure and Key Assets*. White House, Washington, DC. February 2003, p. 2.

Bush, George W. 2004. Press Conference of the President, April 13. http://www.whitehouse.gov/news/releases/2004/04/print/20040413-20.html (accessed February 25, 2006).

Carney, Bill. 2005. TRIA Sunset and it's Impact on Workers' Compensation. *IAIABC Journal*. Fall. 42(2): 167. http://www.iaiabc.org/publications/journal/2005/IAIABC%20Journal%20Fall%202005%20Vol%2042(2)%20cover.pdf (accessed March 4 2006).

Cauley, Leslie, and John Diamond. 2006. Telecoms Let NSA Spy on Calls. *USA Today*, February 5. http://www.usatoday.com/news/washington/2006-02-05-nsa-telecoms_x.htmm (accessed February 28, 2006).

CBS News. 2005. Airline Passenger Privacy Betrayed, CBS News. March 26. http://www.cbsnews.com/stories/2005/03/26/politics/main683296.shtml (accessed November 2005).

Chalk, Peter, Bruce Hoffman, Anna-Britt Kasupski, Robert T. Reville. 2005. *Trends in Terrorism*. June. RAND Corporation, Santa Monica, CA.

Chandler, Alfred. 1977. *The Visible Hand: The Managerial Revolution in American Business*. Cambridge, MA: Belknap Press.

Chertoff, Michael. 2005. Second Stage Review Remarks. Speech at the Ronald Reagan Building, U.S. Department of Homeland Security. July 13. Washington, D.C. http://www.dhs.gov/dhspublic/display?content=4597 (accessed February 28, 2006).

Chisholm, D. 1989. *Coordination without Hierarchy: Informal Structures in Multi-Organizational Systems*. Berkeley, CA: University of California Press.

Clarke, L. 1993. The Disqualification Heuristic: When Do Organizations Misperceive Risk? *Research in Social Problems and Public Policy* 5: 289–312.

Clarke, Richard (ed.). 2004. *Defeating the Jihadists: A Blueprint for Action*. New York: Century Foundation Task Force Report.

Clinton, William J. 1995. U.S. Policy on Counter Terrorism. Washington, DC: White House.

Clinton, William. 1996. Critical Infrastructure Protection. Washington, DC: White House.

Clinton, William. 1998. U.S. Policy on Counter Terrorism. Washington, DC: White House.

Clinton, William. 1999. National Infrastructure Assurance Council. Washington, DC.

CNN. 2002. Official: Voice on Tape is bin Laden's, November 13. http://archives.cnn.com/2002/WORLD/meast/11/12/binladen/statement/ (accessed January 12, 2006).

Coalition for Secure Ports. 2005. Fact sheet. http://www.securereports.org/improving_security/factsheet_screening.html (accessed November 2005).

Coalition to Insure Against Terrorism (CIAT). 2005. Fed Chairman Questions Ability of Private Market Alone To Insure against Terrorism. Press release, February 17. http://www.cmbs.org/Terrorism_Insurance_Files/2_17_05_CIAT_Press_Release.pdf (accessed February 25, 2006).

Coglianese, C., and D. Lazer. 2003. Management-Based Regulation: Prescribing Private Management to Achieve Public Goals. Law & Society Review 37: 691–730.

Coglianese, Cary, Richard J. Zeckhauser, and Edward Parson. 2004. Seeking Truth for Power: Informational Strategy and Regulatory Policymaking. Minnesota Law Review 89(2): 277–341.

Collins, Susan. 2006. Luncheon speech, conference on Protecting Our Future, National Press Club, Washington DC, March 15.

Coluccio, F. 2005. Of Fiber Cuts and Mega RBOC Mergers. http://www.merit.edu/mail.archives/nanog/2005-08/msg00332.html (accessed March 14, 2006).

Columbia Encyclopedia. 2004. Rickover, Hyman George. http://www.bartleby.com/65/ri/Rickover.html.

Comfort, Louise. 2002a. Governance Under Fire: Organizational Fragility in Complex Systems. Paper presented at Symposium on Governance and Public Security, Syracuse, NY, January 18.

Comfort, Louise. 2002b. Institutional Re-orientation and Change: Security as a Learning Strategy. The Forum 1(2).

Commission of European Communities. 2005. Green Paper on a European Programme for Critical Infrastructure Protection. Brussels. November 17.

Commission on National Security. 2001. New World Coming: American Security in the 21st Century. Washington, DC.

Commission on the Intelligence Capabilities of the United States. 2005. Report Regarding Weapons of Mass Destruction. March 3. http://www.wmd.gov/report/report.html#chapter9 (accessed November 2005).

Commission on the Roles and Capabilities of the U.S. Intelligence Community. 1996. Preparing for the 21st Century: An Appraisal of U.S. Intelligence. http://www.gpoaccess.gov/int/report.html (accessed November 2005).

Con Edison. 2005. Con Edison Reports, earnings news release, http://www.coned.com/newsroom/news/pr20060126.asp?from=hc (accessed February 8, 2006).

Congressional Budget Office. 1983. Public Works Infrastructures: Policy Considerations of the 1980s. Washington, DC: U.S. Congress.

Congressional Budget Office. 2004. Homeland Security and the Private Sector. December. Washington, DC.

Congressional Budget Office. 2005. Federal Terrorism Reinsurance: An Update. January. Washington, DC.

Council on Competitiveness. 2002. Creating Opportunity Out of Adversity. Paper presented at National Symposium on Competitiveness and Security, December.

C-SPAN. 2005. Extending the Terrorism Risk Insurance Act of 2002. July 8.

Cukier, Kenneth Neil, Viktor Mayer-Schoenberger, and Lewis Branscomb. 2005. Ensuring (and Insuring?) Critical Information Infrastructure Protection. Working paper number RWP05-055. Cambridge, MA: Kennedy School of Government, Harvard University.

Cummins, D. 2005. Should the Government Provide Insurance for Catastrophes. Paper presented at the 30th Annual Economic Policy Conference, Federal Credit and Insurance Programs, Federal Reserve Bank of St. Louis, October 20–21.

Customs and Border Protection. 2004. Securing the Global Supply Chain: C-TPAT Strategic Plan. Washington, DC: U.S. Government Printing Office, November.

Dacy, Douglas C., and Howard Kunreuther. 1969. *The Economics of Natural Disasters: Implications for Federal Policy*. New York: The Free Press.

Daniels, R., D. Kellt, and H. Kunreuther (eds.). 2006. *On Risk and Disaster: Lessons from Hurricane Katrina*. Philadelphia: University of Pennsylvania Press.

de Bruijne, M., M. van Eeten, E. Roe, and P. Schulman. In press. On Assuring High Reliability of Service Provision in Critical Infrastructures. *International Journal of Critical Infrastructures*.

Dean, J. 2002. Report Stresses Management's Role in Boosting Cybersecurity. http://www.govexec.com/dailyfed/0202/021402j1.htm (accessed May 2, 2003).

Defense Threat Reduction Agency. 2003. Program Review. March 3. Arlington, VA.

Degnan, John. 2003. Statement of John Degnan to the National Commission on Terrorist Attacks Upon The United States. November 19. National Commission on Terrorist Attacks upon the United States. http://www.globalsecurity.org/security/library/congress/9-11_commission/031119-degnan.htm (accessed March 3, 2006).

Dempsey, James. 2004. Moving from "Need to Know" to "Need to Share": A Review of the 9/11 Commission's Recommendations. Testimony to the House Committee on Government Reform. http://www.markle.org/downloadable_assets/james_dempsey_testimony_080304.pdf (accessed November 2005).

Department of Energy. 1993. Earning Public Trust and Confidence: Requisite for Managing Radioactive Waste. Washington, DC: Task Force on Radioactive Waste Management, Secretary of Energy Advisory Board.

Department of Energy. 2003. Causes of the August 14 Blackout in the U.S. and Canada. Washington, D.C. U.S.–Canada Power System Outage Task Force.

Department of Homeland Security. 2004. Survey of the Information Analysis and Infrastructure Protection Directorate. February, OIG 04–13.

Department of Homeland Security. 2006. Personal communication by the NIPP office at DHS to the author, January 20.

Department of Justice. 2001. Press release. http://www.cybercrime.gov/ivanovIndict2.htm (accessed March 14, 2006).

Department of State. 2005. Country Reports on Terrorism. Office of the Coordinator on Counterterrorism. http://www.state.gov/s/ct/rls/45321.htm (accessed January 12, 2006).

Devol, R. C., A. Bedroussian, F. Fogelbach, N. H. Goetz, R. R. Gongalez, and P. Wong. 2002. The Impact of September 11 on U. S. Metropolitan Economies. Milken Institute, Santa Monica, CA. http://www.milkeninstitute.org/pdf/National_Metro_Impact_Report.pdf (accessed February 25, 2006).

DiMaggio, Paul J., and Walter W. Powell. 1983. The Iron Cage Revisited: Institutional Isomorphism and Collective Rationality in Organizational Fields. *American Sociological Review* 48(2): 147–160.

Dixit, A. K. 2003. Clubs with Entrapment. *American Economic Review* 93(5): 1824–1829.

Dixon, Lloyd, and Rachel Kaganoff Stern. 2004. *Compensation for Losses from the 9/11 Attacks*. MG-264-ICJ. Santa Monica, CA: Rand Corporation.

Dixon, Lloyd, and Robert Reville. 2005. National Security and Compensation for Terrorism Losses. Catastrophic Risks and Insurance, Policy Issues in Insurance No. 8, Organization for Economic Co-operation and Development, 59–71.

Dixon, Lloyd, John Arlington, Stephen Carroll, Darius Lakdawalla, Robert Reville, and David Adamson. 2004. *Issues and Options for Government Intervention in the Market for Terrorism Insurance*. OP-135-ICJ. Santa Monica, CA: Rand Corporation.

Doherty, N. 2000. *Integrated Risk Management*. New York: McGraw-Hill.

Donahue, John D. 1989. *The Privatization Decision: Public Ends, Private Means*. New York: Basic Books.

Donahue, John D. 2003. Parks and Partnership in New York City A: Adrian Benepe's Challenge. Cambridge, MA: Kennedy School of Government Case Program.

Donahue, John D., and Susan Rosegrant. 2004. Parks and Partnership in New York City B: The Spectrum of Engagement. Cambridge, MA: Kennedy School of Government Case Program.

Donahue, John D., and Richard J. Zeckhauser: 2006. Public–Private Collaboration. In *The Oxford Handbook of Public Policy*, edited by Michael Moran, Martin Rein, and Robert E. Goodin. New York: Oxford University Press.

Economist. 2003. Fighting the worms of mass destruction. November 27. http://www.economist.co.uk/science/displayStory.cfm?story_id=2246018 (accessed May 2, 2003).

Economist. 2005a. Horrible Business: Terror Insurance. November 19.

Economist. 2005b. In Europe's Midst. July 16.

Electricity Consumers Resource Council (ELCON). 2004. The Economic Impacts of the August 2003 Blackout. Washington, DC: ELCON. http://www.elcon.org/Documents/EconomicImpactsOfAugust2003Blackout.pdf (accessed Feb 8, 2006).

Elias, Bart, W. Krouse, and E. Rappaprot. 2005. Homeland Security: Air Passenger Prescreening and Counterterrorism. RL32802, March 4. Washington, DC: Congressional Research Service.

Ellis III, J. Undated. Terrorism in the Homeland: A Brief Historical Survey of Violent Extremism in the United States. Memorial Institute for the Prevention of Terrorism, Oklahoma City.

Enders, W., and T. Sandler. 2000. Is Transnational Terrorism Becoming More Threatening? *Journal of Conflict Resolution* 44(3): 307–332.

Enders, W., and T. Sandler. 2006. *The Political Economy of Terrorism*. New York: Cambridge University Press.

Energy Advisory Board Task Force on Electric System Reliability. 1998. Final Report of the Secretary of Energy Advisory Board Task Force on Electric System Reliability, September 29. http://www.seab.energy.gov/publications/esrfinal.pdf (accessed February 2, 2006).

Energy Information Agency. 2003. Electricity Transmission Fact Sheet. Department of Energy, August 19. http://www.eia.doe.gov/cneaf/electricity/page/fact_sheets/transmission.html (accessed February 8, 2006).

Energy Information Agency. 2004. Electric Power Annual with data 2004, Table 2.2 Existing Capacity by Energy Source, 2004 (Megawatts). Department of Energy. http://www.eia.doe.gov/cneaf/electricity/epa/epat2p2.html (accessed February 8, 2006).

Etzioni, A. 1965. Organizational Control Structure. In *Handbook of Organizations*, edited by J. G. March. New York: Rand McNally.

Fairly, P. 2004. The Unruly Power Grid. *IEEE Spectrum* 41(8): 22–27.

Farrell, A. E., and H. Zerriffi. 2004. Electric Power: Critical Infrastructure Protection. In *Encyclopedia of Energy*. Amsterdam, Netherlands, Boston: Elsevier.

Farrell, A. E., H. Zerriffi, and H. Dowlatabadi. 2005. Energy Infrastructure and Security. In *Annual Review of Environment and Resources* 29: 421–469.

Farrell, A. E., L. B. Lave, and G. Morgan. 2002. Bolstering the Security of the Electric Power System. *Issues in Science and Technology* 18(3): 49–56.

Farrell, J., and G. Saloner. 1985. Standardization, Compatibility, and Innovation. *The Rand Journal of Economics*. Spring, 16(1): 70–83.

Farson, R., and R. Keyes. 2002. The Failure-Tolerant Leader. *Harvard Business Review* 64–71.

Federal Bureau of Investigation. 2001. E-commerce Vulnerabilities. NIPC Advisory 01-003, March 8. http://www.fbi.gov/pressrel/pressrel01/nipc030801.htm (accessed May 2, 2003).

Federal Bureau of Investigation. 2002. Terrorism 2000/2001. Publication 0328. Washington, DC: Department of Justice, Counterterrorism Division.

Federal Communications Commission. 2001. Network Outage Reporting System. http://ftp.fcc.gov/oet/outage (accessed May 7, 2003).

Federation of American Scientists. 2004. Tracing the Rise and Fall of Intelligence Spending: As Portrayed in Official Government Publications. June 7. http://www.fas.org/irp/budget/ (accessed November 2005).

Feinberg, Kenneth R. 2005. 9/11 Victim Compensation Fund: Successes, Failures, and Lessons for Tort Reform. January 13. Washington, DC: Comments at Manhattan Institute Center for Legal Policy Conference.

Feinberg, Kenneth R., Camille S. Biros, Jordana Harris Feldman, Deborah E. Greenspan, and Jacqueline E. Zins. 2004. Final Report of the Special Master for the September 11th Victim Compensation Fund of 2001. Washington, DC: U.S. Department of Justice. http://www.usdoj.gov/final_report.pdf (accessed January 9, 2006).

Fellman, P. V., and R. Wright. 2003. Modeling Terrorist Networks – Complex Systems at the Mid-Range. Conference on Complexity and Creativity, London School of Economics, UK, September. http://www.psych.lse.ac.uk/complexity/Conference/FellmanWright.pdf (accessed June 27, 2006).

Fellman, P. V., and R. Wright. Undated. Modeling Terrorist Networks – Complex Systems at the Mid-Range. http://www.psych.lse.ac.uk/complexity/Conference/FellmanWright.pdf (accessed March 22, 2006).

FERC. 2001. Statement of Policy on Extraordinary Expenditures Necessary to Safeguard National Energy Supplies. 96 FERC ¶61,299, Docket PL01-6-000. September 14.

Financial Services Sector Coordinating Council. 2005. Protecting the U.S. Critical Financial Infrastructure: An Agenda for 2005. http://www.fsscc.org/reports/FSSCC_2005_Agenda.pdf (accessed March 22, 2006).

Financial Times. 2005. Special Report on Business Continuity. June 27.

Finnegan, W. 2005. *The New Yorker*, July 25.

Finnegan, William. 2005. A Reporter at Large: The Terrorism Beat, *New Yorker*. July 25.

Fisher, David Hackett. 2004. *Washington's Crossing*. New York: Oxford University Press.

Florig, H. Keith. 2002. Is Safe Mail Worth the Price? *Science* 295: 1467–1468.

Flynn, M. F. 2005. Protective Security Division (PSD) Programs and Operations. Department of Homeland Security, March 8. http://www.nrc.gov/public-involve/conference-symposia/ric/past/2005/slides/03-b2-flynn.pdf (accessed March 7, 2006).

Flynn, Stephen E. 2004. The Neglected Home Front. *Foreign Affairs* 83(1): 20–33.

Flynn, Stephen. 2005a. Color Me Scared. *New York Times*. May 25.

Flynn, Stephen. 2005b. U.S. Senate Committee on Homeland Security and Government Affairs. The Security of America's Chemical Facilities: Testimony. 109: 1. April 27.

Fonow, R. C. 2003. Beyond the Mainland: Chinese Telecommunications Expansion. *Defense Horizons* 29: 1–8.

Frank, Thomas. 2004. Terror Warning Surprises Homeland Security Department. *Newsday*. May 28.

Frey, B. S. 2004. *Dealing with Terrorism: Stick or Carrot*. Cheltenham, UK: Edward Elgar Publishing.

Frey, Darcy. 1996. Something's Got to Give. *New York Times Magazine*. March 24, 42-ff.

Furnell, S. M., and M. J. Warren. 1999. Computer Hacking and Cyber Terrorism: The Real Threats in the New Millennium. *Computers & Security* 18(1): 28–34.

Gabrielov, A., V. Keilis-Borok, I. Zaliapin, and W. I. Newman. 2000. Critical Transitions in Colliding Cascades. *Physical Review E* (62) 1, 237–249.

Gerth, H. H., and C. Wright Mills (eds.). 1946. *From Max Weber*. Oxford, UK: Oxford University Press, 78.

Gertz, B. 2001. Al Qaeda Appears To Have Links with Russian Mafia. *Washington Times*. September 27.

Glasser, Susan B. 2005. U.S. Figures Show Sharp Global Rise in Terrorism State Department Will Not put Data in Report. *Washington Post*. April 27, A01.

Glassner, B. 1999. *The Culture of Fear: Why Americans Are Afraid of the Wrong Things*. New York: Basic Books.

Global Intelligence Challenges. 2005. Meeting Long-Term Challenges with a Long-Term Strategy, Testimony of Director of Central Intelligence Porter J. Goss Before the Senate Select Committee on Intelligence. http://www.cia.gov/cia/public_affairs/speeches/2004/Goss_testimony_02162005.html (accessed February 25, 2006).

Godard, Olivier, Claude Henry, Patrick Lagadec, and Erwann Michel-Kerjan. 2002. *Treatise on New Risks. Precaution, Crisis, and Insurance*. Paris: Gallimard, Folio-Actuel.

Goo, Sara Kehaulani. 2004. Confidential Passenger Data Used for Air Security Project. *Washington Post* January 17.

Gorman, Sean P. 2004. Networks, Complexity, and Security: The Role of Public Policy in Critical Infrastructure Protection. Ph.D. dissertation. School of Public Policy, George Mason University, Fairfax, VA.

Government Accountability Office (GAO; formerly General Accounting Office). 2002. Terrorism Insurance: Rising Uninsured Exposure to Attacks Heightens Potential Economic Vulnerabilities. Testimony of Richard J. Hillman before the Subcommittee on Oversight and Investigations, Committee on Financial Services, House of Representatives, February 27.

Government Accountability Office (GAO; formerly General Accounting Office). 2003a. Catastrophe Insurance Risks. Status of Efforts to Securitize Natural Catastrophe and Terrorism Risk. September 24, GAO-03-1033. Washington, DC: U.S. General Accounting Office. http://www.gao.gov/new.items/d031033.pdf (accessed February 25, 2006).

Government Accountability Office (GAO; formerly General Accounting Office). 2003b. Critical Infrastructure Protection: Efforts of the Financial Services Sector To Address Cyber Threats. Report to the Subcommittee on Domestic Monetary Policy, Technology, and Economic Growth, Committee on Financial Services, House of Representatives Washington, DC: U.S. General Accounting Office. http://www.gao.gov/new.items/d03173.pdf (accessed May 7, 2003).

Government Accountability Office (GAO; formerly General Accounting Office). 2003c. Transportation Security: Federal Action Needed to Enhance Security Efforts. September 9, GAO-03-1154T. Washington, DC: U.S. General Accounting Office.

Government Accountability Office (GAO; formerly General Accounting Office). 2004a. Critical Infrastructure Protection: Establishing Effective Information Sharing with Infrastructure Sectors. April 21. GAO-04-699T. Washington, DC: U.S. General Accounting Office.

Government Accountability Office (GAO; formerly General Accounting Office). 2004b. Critical Infrastructure Protection: Improving Information Sharing With Infrastructure Sectors. GAO-04-780, July. Washington, DC: U.S. General Accounting Office.

Government Accountability Office (GAO; formerly General Accounting Office). 2004c. Determining Security Clearance Eligibility for Industry Personnel. May. GAO-04-632, Washington, DC.

Government Accountability Office (GAO; formerly General Accounting Office). 2004d. Security Clearances: FBI Has Enhanced its Process for State and Local Law Enforcement Officials. GAO-04-596, April. Washington, DC: U.S. General Accounting Office.

Government Accountability Office (GAO; formerly General Accounting Office). 2004e. Terrorism Insurance: Effects of the Terrorism Risk Insurance Act of 2002. May 18. GAO-04-806T, Washington, DC: U.S. General Accounting Office.

Government Accountability Office (GAO). 2005a. Aviation Security: Secure Flight Development and Testing Under Way, but Risks Should Be Managed as System Is Further Developed. March. GAO-05-356. Washington, DC: U.S. General Accounting Office.

Government Accountability Office (GAO). 2005b. Aviation Security: Transportation Security Administration Did Not Fully Disclose Uses of Personal Information During Secure Flight Program Testing in Initial Privacy Notices, But Has Recently Taken Steps to More Fully Inform the Public, Government Accountability Office, GAO-05-864R, July 22. Washington, DC: U.S. General Accounting Office.

Government Accountability Office (GAO). 2005c. Catastrophe Risk: U.S. and European Approached to Insure Natural Catastrophes and Terrorism Risks. February. GAO-05-199. Washington, DC: U.S. General Accounting Office. http://www.gao.gov/new.items/d03173.pdf (accessed March 3, 2006).

Government Accountability Office (GAO). 2005d. Protection of Chemical and Water Infrastructure: Federal Requirements, Actions at Selected Facilities, and Remaining Challenges. March, GAO-05-327. Washington, DC: U.S. General Accounting Office.

Grabowski, Martha, and Karlene Roberts. 1997. Risk Mitigation in Large-Scale Systems: Lessons from high Reliability Organizations. *California Management Review* 39(4): 152–162.

Grace, Martin, Robert Klein, Paul Kleindorfer, and Michael Murray. 2003. *Catastrophe Insurance*. Boston: Kluwer.

Graham, J. D., and J. B. Weiner (eds.). 1995. *Risk vs. Risk*. Cambridge, MA: Harvard University Press.

Green, J. 2002. The Myth of Cyberterrorism. November. *Washington Monthly*. http://www.washingtonmonthly.com/features/2001/0211.green.html (accessed May 2, 2003).

Green, R. M. 1980. Inter-Generational Distributive Justice and Environmental Responsibility. In *Responsibilities to Future Generations: Environmental Ethics*, edited by E. D. Partridge. Buffalo, NY: Prometheus Books.

Grid Today. 2003. Grid Technology Used to Hijack PC's? http://www.gridtoday.com/03/0721/101704.html (accessed May 2, 2003).

Grimmett, G. 1999. *Percolation*. Berlin, Germany: Springer-Verlag.

Guttman B., and K. Elburg. 2002. Israel: Cyber terrorism. *Computer und Recht International* 5: 156–157.

Halfele, W. 1990. Energy from Nuclear Power. *Scientific American* 263(3): 136–144.

Halsne, C. 2003. North Sound 911 Service Repeatedly Targeted. KIRO TV http://www.kirotv.com/news/2601577/detail.html (accessed May 7, 2003).

Hamilton, Donald. 2005. Telephone interview with Donald Hamilton, Executive Director, National Memorial Institute for the Prevention of Terrorism. Oklahoma City, OK. March.

Hardin, Garrett. 1968. The Tragedy of the Commons. *Science* 162(1968): 1243–1248.

Harrington, Caitlin. 2005. Former CIA Man Simmons Shoots Again for Unclassified Intelligence Unit at DHS. *CQ Homeland Security*, June 21.

Harris, Shane. 2004. Defense Department Lacks Staff to Tackle Security Clearance Backlog. GovExec.com. May 27. http://www.govexec.com/dailyfed/0504/052704h1.htm (accessed March 1, 2006).

Hartocollis, Anemona. 2005. Port Authority Found Negligent in 1993 Bombing. *New York Times*. October 27. http://select.nytimes.com/search/restricted/article?res=F30616F63A5B0C748EDDA90994DD404482 (accessed March 4, 2006).

Hartwig, Robert P. 2002. Industry Financial and Outlook – 2001 Year-End Results, Insurance Information Institute. http://www.iii.org/media/industry/financials/2001yearend/ (accessed June 23, 2004).

Hartwig, Robert. 2004. The Cost of Terrorism: How Much Can We Afford? National Association of Economics Conference. http://www.iii.org/media/presentations/tria/(accessed February 25, 2006).

Heal, G., and H. Kunreuther. 2005a. You Only Die Once: Interdependent Security in an Uncertain World. In *The Economic Impacts of Terrorist Attacks*,. edited by H. W. Richardson, P. Gordon and J. E. Moore II. Cheltenham, UK: Edward Elgar.

Heal, G., and H. Kunreuther. 2005b. IDS Models of Airline Security. *Journal of Conflict Resolution* 49: 201–217.

Heal, G., and H. Kunreuther. 2006. Security, Supermodularity and Tipping. NBER Working Paper 12281. June.

Heimann, C. F. L. 1993. Understanding the Challenger Disaster: Organizational Structure and the Design of Reliable Systems. *American Political Science Review* 87: 421–435.

Heinrich, C. 2005. *RFID and Beyond*. New York: John Wiley & Sons.

Heller, Miriam. 2001. Interdependencies in Civil Infrastructure Systems. *The Bridge* 31(4).

Hendershot, D. C. 2004. Inherently Safer Design, in *Accident Precursor Analysis and Management: Reducing Technological Risk Through Diligence*, edited by James R. Phimister, Vicki M. Bier, and Howard C. Kunreuther. Washington, DC: National Academy of Engineering, pp. 103–117.

Hendricks, K. B., and V. R. Singhal. 2005. An Empirical Analysis of the Effect of Supply Chain Disruptions on Long-Run Stock Price and Equity Risk of the Firm. *Production and Operations Management* 14(1).

Heymann, Philip, and Juliette Kayyem. 2005. *Protecting Liberty in an Age of Terror*. Cambridge, MA: The MIT Press.

Hobijn, Bart. 2002. What Will Homeland Security Cost? *Economic Policy Review* November, 21–33.

Hoekstra, Peter. 2005. Secrets and Leaks: The Costs and Consequences for National Security. July 29. WebMemo #809, Heritage Foundation. http://new.heritage.org/Research/HomelandDefense/wm809.cfm (accessed November 2005).

Hoffman, B. 1998. *Inside Terrorism*. New York: Columbia University Press.

Horch, Stephen, Howard Kunreuther, and Robert Gunter (eds.). 2001. *Wharton on Making Decisions*. New York: John Wiley & Sons.

Howarth, R. 1991. Inter-Generational Competitive Equilibria under Technological Uncertainty and an Exhaustible Resource Constraint. *Journal of Environmental Economics and Management* 21: 225–243.

http://www.psych.lse.ac.uk/complexity/Conference/FellmanWright.pdf (accessed June 27, 2006).

Hunter, J. Robert. 2004. The Terrorism Risk Insurance Act: Should it Be Renewed? April 19. Washington, DC: Consumer Federation of America. http://www.consumerfed.org/pdfs/terrorism_insurance_report.pdf (accessed February 25, 2006).

Iannaccone G., C. N. Chuah, S. Bhattacharyya, C. Diot. 2003. Feasibility of IP Restoration in a ier-1 backbone. Sprint Atlanta Technical Report TR03-ATL-030666, March. http://www.cambridge.intel-research.net/~gianluca/papers/restoration.pdf (accessed September 14, 2005).

Institute Of Medicine of the National Academies. 2005. Proceedings. Paper read at Protecting Against Foodborne Threats to Health. October 25–26.

Insurance Information Institute. Undated. Facts and Statistics. http://www.iii.org/media/facts/statsbyissue/catastrophes/ (accessed February 15, 2006).

Insurance Journal. 2005. Greenspan: Private Insurers Can't Cover Terror Risk Without Government. July 20. http://www.insurancejournal.com/news/national/2005/07/20/57478.htm (accessed February 25, 2006).

ISAC Council (Information Sharing and Analysis Centers Council). 2004a. A Functional Model for Critical Infrastructure Information Sharing and Analysis: Maturing and Expanding Efforts. ISAC Council white paper, January 31, 2004. http://www.isaccouncil.org/pub/Information_Sharing_and_Analysis_013104.pdf (accessed March 22, 2006).

ISAC Council (Information Sharing and Analysis Centers Council). 2004b. Government–Private Sector Relations. ISAC Council white paper, January 31, 2004. http://www.isaccouncil.org/pub/Government_Private_Sector_Relations_013104.pdf (accessed March 22, 2006).

ISAC Council (Information Sharing and Analysis Centers Council). 2004c. A Policy Framework for the ISAC Community. ISAC Council white paper, January 31. http://www.isaccouncil.org/pub/Policy_Framework_for_ISAC_Community_013104.pdf (accessed March 22, 2006).

Jaffee, D. 2005. The Role of Government in the Coverage of Terrorism Risks. Chapter 7 in *Terrorism Risk Insurance in OECD Countries*. Paris: OECD.

Jaffee, D., and T. Russell. 2005. Should Governments Support the Private Terrorism Insurance Market? WRIEC Conference, Salt Lake City, August.

Johnston, Donald. 2005. Dealing with Disasters and Protecting Critical Services: An International Perspective from the Organization for Economic Cooperation and Development (OECD). Address to the International Risk Governance Council 2005 General Conference, Beijing, September 20–21.

Jones, Donald, and Ronald Skelton. 1999. The Next Generation Threat to Grid Reliability–Data Security. *IEEE Spectrum* June: 46–49.

518 References

Kahneman, D., and A. Tversky. 2000. *Choices, Values and Frames*. New York: Cambridge University Press.

Kane, M. 2002. U.S. Vulnerable to Data Sneak Attack. CNET News.com. August 13. http://news.com.com/2100-1017-949605.html (accessed May 2, 2003).

Kauffman, Stuart. 1993. *The Origins of Self-Organization Selection in Evolution*. New York: Oxford University Press.

Kearns, M. 2005. Economics, Computer Science, and Policy. *Issues in Science and Technology* Winter: 37–47.

Kearns, M., and L. Ortiz. 2004. Algorithms for Interdependent Security Games. In *Advances in Neural Information Processing* Systems 16, edited by S. Thrun, L. Saul, and B. Scholkopf. Cambridge, MA: MIT Press.

Keohane, N., and R. Zeckhauser. 2003. The Ecology of Terror Defense. *Journal of Risk and Uncertainty*, Special Issue on Terrorist Risks, 26(2/3, March/May): 201–229.

Kettl, Donald (ed.). 2004. *The Department of Homeland Security's First Year: A Report Card.* New York: Century Foundation.

King, D., and M. G. Morgan. 2003. Guidance for Drafting State Legislation to Facilitate the Growth of Independent Electric Power Micro-Grids. Carnegie Mellon Electricity Industry Center Working Paper CEIC-03-17. http://wpweb2k.gsia.cmu.edu/ceic/papers/ceic-03-17.asp (accessed February 2, 2006).

Kleindorfer, P. R., and G. H. Saad. 2005. Managing Disruption Risks in Supply Chains. *Production and Operations Management* 14(1).

Kleindorfer, P. R., and L. Van Wassenhove. 2004. Risk Management for Global Supply Chains: An Overview. In *The Alliance on Globalizing*, edited by H. Gatignon and J. Kimberly. Cambridge, UK: Cambridge University Press.

Knake, Robert. 2005. Kennedy School of Government, interview with DHS PCII office, April.

Korten, D. 1980. Community Organization and Rural Development: A Learning Process Approach. *Public Administration Review* 40(5).

Kunreuther, H. 2001. Protective Decisions: Fear or Prudence. In *Wharton on Making Decisions*, edited by S. Hoch and H. Kunreuther. New York: Wiley.

Kunreuther, H. 2002. The Role of Insurance in Managing Extreme Events: Implications for Terrorism Coverage. *Risk Analysis* 22: 427–437.

Kunreuther, Howard. 2006. Has the Time Come for Comprehensive Natural Disaster Insurance? In *On Risk and Disaster Lessons from Hurricane Katrina*, edited by Ronald Daniels, Donald Kettl, and Howard Kunreuther. Philadelphia, PA: University of Pennsylvania Press, 175–202.

Kunreuther, Howard, and Geoffrey Heal. 2003. Interdependent Security. *Journal of Risk and Uncertainty* Special Issue on Terrorist Risk, March/May, 26: 231–249.

Kunreuther, H., and E. Michel-Kerjan. 2004. Challenges for Terrorism Risk Insurance in the United States. *Journal of Economic Perspectives* Fall, 18(4): 201–214.

Kunreuther, H., and E. Michel-Kerjan. 2005a. Insurability of (Mega)-Terrorism, Report for the OECD Task Force on Terrorism Insurance. In *Terrorism Insurance in OECD Countries*, Paris: Organization for Economic Cooperation and Development, July 5.

Kunreuther, H., and Michel-Kerjan, E. 2005b. Terrorism Insurance 2005. Where Do We Go from Here? Regulation. *The Cato Review for Business and Government*, Washington, DC: Cato Institute, Spring, 44–51.

Kunreuther, Howard, and Adam Rose (eds.). 2004. *The Economics of Natural Hazards*, two volumes. International Library of Critical Writings in Economics Series #178. Northampton, MA: Edward Elgar Publishing, Inc.

Kunreuther, Howard, et al. 1978. *Disaster Insurance Protections: Public Policy Lessons.* New York: John Wiley and Sons.

Kunreuther, H., P. McNulty, and Y. Kang. 2002a. Improving Environmental Safety Through Third Party Inspection. *Risk Analysis.* 22: 309–318.

Kunreuther, Howard, Geoffrey Heal, and Peter Orszag. 2002b. Interdependent Security: Implications for Homeland Security Policy and Other Areas. Policy Brief #108, October. Washington, DC: Brookings Institution.

Kunreuther, Howard, Erwann Michel-Kerjan, and Beverly Porter. 2003. Assessing, Managing and Financing Extreme Events: Dealing with Terrorism. November 20. Wharton School and National Bureau of Economic Research. http://opim.wharton.upenn.edu/risk/downloads/03-12.pdf (accessed February 25, 2006).

Kunreuther, Howard, Erwann Michel-Kerjan, and Beverly Porter. 2005. Extending Catastrophe Modeling to Terrorism. In *Catastrophe Modeling: A New Approach to Managing Risk,* edited by Grossi and Kunreuther, with Patel. New York: Springer.

Lagadec, Patrick. 1993. *Preventing Chaos in Crisis.* London: McGraw Hill.

Lagadec, Patrick, and Erwann Michel-Kerjan. 2005. A New Era Calls for a New Model. *International Herald Tribune,* Opinion, November 2.

Lagadec, Patrick, and Uriel Rosenthal (eds.). 2003. Anthrax and Beyond: New Challenges, New Responsibilities. *Journal of Contingencies and Crisis Management* Special Issue 11(3).

Lakdawalla, Darius, and George Zanjani. 2005. Insurance, Self-Protection, and the Economics of Terrorism. *Journal of Public Economics* 89: 1891–1905.

Landau, M. 1969. Redundancy, Rationality, and the Problem of Duplication and Overlap. *Public Administration Review* 27: 346–358.

La Porte, T. 1996. High Reliability Organizations: Unlikely, Demanding, and at Risk. *Journal of Contingencies and Crisis Management* 40: 60–71.

La Porte, T. R. 2003. Institutional Challenges for High-Reliability Systems Across Many Operational Generations – Can Watchfulness be Sustained? Paper presented at AAAS Symposium, Nuclear Waste: File and Forget? February 18, Denver, CO.

La Porte, Todd R. 2004. Challenges of Assuring High Reliability When Facing Suicidal Terrorism. Paper presented at workshop Private Efficiency, Public Vulnerability: Protecting Critical Infrastructure, Cambridge, MA, May 26–28.

La Porte, T. R., and P. M. Consolini. 1991. Working in Practice but Not in Theory: Theoretical Challenges of "High Reliability Organizations." *Journal of Public Administration Research and Theory: J-PART* 1(1): 19–48.

La Porte, T. R., and A. Keller. 1996. Assuring Institutional Constancy: Requisite for Managing Long-Lived Hazards. *Public Administration Review* 56(6): 535–544.

La Porte, T. R., and C. Thomas. 1994. Regulatory Compliance and the Ethos of Quality Enhancement: Surprises in Nuclear Power Plant Operations. *Journal of Public Administration Research and Theory* 5(4): 250–295.

LaPorte, T. R., K. Roberts, and G. I. Rochlin. 1989. High Reliability Organizations: The Research Challenge. Institute of Governmental Studies, University of California, Berkeley, April.

Lawyer, G. 2003. The Battle of the Bug: Government, Industry Move To Protect Internet from Cyber Attacks, Viruses. http://www.xchangemag.com/articles/1B1front4.html (accessed May 2, 2003).

Leavitt, Leonard. 2005. NYPD's Voice Loud and Clear. *Newsday.* October 14. http://www.nynewsday.com/news/local/newyork/ny-nyplaz144468713oct14,0,5267183.column?coll=ny-ny-columnists (accessed November 2005).

Lerner, A. W. 1986. There Is More than One Way to be Redundant: A Comparison of Alternatives for the Design and Use of Redundancy in Organizations. *Administration and Society* 18: 334–359.

Lerten, B. 2003. Tower Saboteur: I Was Only Pointing Out Flaws. *Bend Bugle.* November 23. http://bend.com/news/ar_view^3Far_id^3D12260.htm (accessed May 7, 2003).

Liang Q, Xiangsui. 1999. *Unrestricted Warfare.* Beijing: PLA Literature and Arts Publishing House.

Lindahl, Erik. 1919. Die Gerechtigkeit der Besteuerung Lund: Gleerupska Universitets-Bokhandeln.

Lindstrom, A. 2001. Tunnel Vision? Broadbandweek.com. http://www.broadbandweek.com/news/010806/010806_news_fiber.htm (accessed July 23, 2002).

Lipson, H. F., and D. A. Fisher. 1999. Survivability – A New Technical and Business Perspective on Security. Proceedings of the 1999 New Security Paradigms Workshop, Caledon Hills, Ontario, Association for Computing Machinery.

Lipton, E. and K. Johnson. 2001. Tracking Bioterrorism's Tangled Course. *New York Times Magazine.* December 26, A1.

Lipton, Eric. 2005. Audit Faults U.S. for Its Spending on Port Defense. *New York Times.* February 20, A1.

Lipton, Eric. 2006. Chertoff Seeks a Chemical Security Law, Within Limits. *New York Times,* March 22. http://www.nytimes.com/2006/03/22/politics/22chemical.html (accessed March 27, 2006).

Little, Richard. 2002. Controlling Cascading Failure: Understanding the Vulnerabilities of Interconnected Infrastructures. *Journal of Urban Technology* 9(1): 109–123.

Loch, Stephen, and Howard Kunreuther (eds.). 2001. *Wharton on Making Decisions.* New York: John Wiley & Sons.

Lopez, Brian. 2003a. Critical Assets Workshop Guide: Lawrence Livermore National Laboratory, Vulnerability and Risk Assessment Program.

Lopez, Brian. 2003b. New Approaches Guidance: Lawrence Livermore National Laboratory, Vulnerability and Risk Assessment Program.

Lopez, Brian. 2004. Five Key Pieces on the Board: Lawrence Livermore National Laboratory, Vulnerability and Risk Assessment.

Lundberg, Kristen. 2004. Smarter Foreign Aid? USAID's Global Development Alliance Initiative. Cambridge, MA: Kennedy School of Government Case Program.

Lundberg, Kristen. 2005. Public Service or Gravy Train: The Federal Guaranteed Student Loan Program. Cambridge, MA: Kennedy School of Government Case Program.

Lunev, S. 2001. 'Red Mafia' Operating in the U.S. – Helping Terrorists. http://www.newsmax.com/archives/articles/2001/9/28/90942.shtml (accessed May 2, 2003).

Madigan, Sean. 2005. Shut Out: Overdue Security Clearances Make Fire Officials Smolder. May 2. *CQ Homeland Security,* Congressional Quarterly.

Maine PUC (Public Utility Commission). 2003. Docket Number 2002243. http://www.state.me.us/mpuc/misctranscripts/2002-243%20080503.htm (accessed May 7, 2003).

Mandelbrot, B. B. 1982. *The Fractal Geometry of Nature.* New York: W.H. Freeman and Company.

Marks, Alexandra. 2004. ABCs of the CIA: A To-Do List for Porter Goss. *Christian Science Monitor.* August 13.

Marsh Inc. 2005a. *The Impact of Nature: The Aftermath of Hurricanes Katrina and Rita.* November. http://solutions.marsh.com/hurricane/documents/MarshTheImpactofNature.pdf (accessed March 22, 2006).

Marsh Inc. 2005b. Marketwatch: Terrorism Insurance 2005. Research report. Marsh Inc. Item # 100162 04/05 Compliance # MA5-10185. http://www.marsh.dk/files/Marketwatch_Terrorism_Insurance_2005.pdf (accessed February 25, 2006).

Marsh, R. T. 1997. Critical Foundations. Washington, DC: Commission on Critical Infrastructure.

Mayntz, Renate, and Thomas P. Hughes (eds.). 1988. *Development of Large Technical Systems.* Berlin, Germany: Springer-Verlag.

McCall, William. 2005. City Council Approves Portland's Withdrawal from the JTTF. Associated Press from KATU News. April 28. Portland, Oregon.

McCullagh, Declan, and Anne Broache. 2006. Some Companies Helped the NSA, But Which? February 6. CNET News.com. http://news.com/com/Some+companies+helped+the+NSA,+but+who/2100-1028_3-6035305.html (accessed February 28, 2006).

McDonald, H. 2003. Beijing Spies a Useful Friend in Castro. *The Age.* February 27. http://www.theage.com.au/articles/2003/02/26/1046064102910.html (accessed May 2, 2003).

McWilliams, B. 2003. Cloaking Device Made for Spammers. http://www.wired.com/news/infostructure/0,1377,60747,00.html (accessed May 2, 2003).

Mendeloff, J. 1988. *The Dilemma of Toxic Substance Regulation: How Overregulation Leads to Underregulation.* Cambridge, MA: MIT Press.

Messmer, L. 2003. Navy Marine Corps Intranet hit by Welchia Worm. *Network World Fusion.* http://www.nwfusion.com/news/2003/0819navy.html (accessed November 10, 2003).

Michael, D. 1973. *On Learning to Plan and Planning to Learn.* San Francisco, CA: Jossey-Bass.

Michel-Kerjan, Erwann. 2003a. Large-scale Terrorism: Risk Sharing and Public Policy. *Revue d'Economie Politique* 113(5): 625–648.

Michel-Kerjan, Erwann. 2003b. New Challenges in Critical Infrastructures: A U.S. Perspective. *Journal of Contingencies and Crisis Management* 11(3): 132–141.

Michel-Kerjan, E. 2006. An Unnoticed Paradox: Insurance, the 14th Critical Sector. Working Paper, Center for Risk Management and Decision Processes. Philadelphia, PA: Wharton School.

Michel-Kerjan, E., and B. Pedell. 2005. Terrorism Risk Coverage in the Post- 9/11 Era: A Comparison of New Public–Private Partnerships in France, Germany and the U.S. *The Geneva Papers on Risk and Insurance,* 30(1): 144–170.

Michel-Kerjan, Erwann, and Nathalie de Marcellis-Warin. 2006. Public-Private Programs for Covering Extreme Events: The Impact of Information Sharing on Risk Sharing. *Asia-Pacific Journal of Risk and Insurance* 1(2): 21–49.

Mintz, John, and Susan Schmidt. 2004. Ashcroft Assailed on Terror Warning. *Washington Post.* May 28, A04. http://www.washingtonpost.com/wp-dyn/articles/A61742-2004May27.html (accessed November 2005).

Mintzberg, H. 1979. *The Structuring of Organizations.* Saddle River, NJ: Prentice-Hall.

Moran, Michael, Martin Rein, and Robert E. Goodin (eds.). 2006. *The Oxford Handbook of Public Policy.* New York and Oxford: Oxford University Press.

Morgan, M. G., and H. Zerriffi. 2002. The Regulatory Environment for Small Independent Micro-Grid Companies. *The Electricity Journal* 15(9): 52–57.

Morgan, M. Granger, Baruch Fischhoff, Ann Bostrom, and Cynthia J. Atman. 2002. *Risk Communication: A Mental Models Approach.* Cambridge, UK: Cambridge University Press.

Moteff, John D. 2000. Critical Infrastructures: Background and Early Implementation of PDD-63. Congressional Research Service, Report #RL30153. http://www.ncseonline.org/NLE/CRSreports/Science/st-46.cfm?&CFID=558905&CFTOKEN=30895709 (accessed November 2005).

NARUC/NRRI. 2003. Survey on Critical Infrastructure Protection. http://www.nrri.ohio-state.edu/dspace/bitstream/2068/296/1/04-01.pdf (accessed February 2, 2006).

National Aeronautics and Space Administration. 2003. Final Report of the Columbia Accident Investigation Board, 2003. http://www.caib.us (accessed June 3, 2006).

National Center for Infectious Diseases. 1999. Emerging Infectious Diseases. In *Special Issue on Bioterrorism*. Atlanta, GA: Centers for Disease Control.

National Commission on Terrorism. 2000. Countering the Changing Threat of International Terrorism (Bremer Report). Washington, DC: National Commission on Terrorism.

National Commission on Terrorist Attacks upon the United States. 2004. The 9/11 Commission Report. Washington, DC: Government Printing Office. http://www.9-11commission.gov/report/911Report.pdf (accessed February 25, 2006).

National Council on Public Works Improvement. 1988. Fragile Foundations: A Report on America's public Works. Final Report to the President and Congress. Washington, DC.

National Infrastructure Simulation and Analysis Center. 2003. Defense Treat Reduction Agency Program Review. Arlington, VA.

National Institute of Standards and Technology. 1995. The Impact of the FCC's Open Network Architecture on NS/NP Telecommunications Security Washington DC: National Institute of Standards and Technology. http://csrc.nist.gov/publications/nistpubs/800-11/titleona.html (accessed May 7, 2003).

National Research Council. 2002a. *Cybersecurity Today and Tomorrow: Pay Now or Pay Later*. Washington, DC: National Academies Press.

National Research Council. 2002b. *Making the Nation Safer: The Role of Science and Technology in Countering Terrorism*. Committee On Science and Technology for Countering Terrorism Washington, DC: National Academies Press.

National Security Telecommunications Advisory Committee. 2002. Network Security/Vulnerability Assessments Task Force Report. Washington, DC: President's National Security Telecommunications Advisory Committee. http://www.ncs.gov/nstac/reports/2002/NSVATF-Report-(FINAL).htm (accessed March 6, 2006).

National Task Force on Interoperability. 2003. "Why Can't We Talk? Working Together To Bridge the Communications Gap To Save Lives. National Institute of Justice. http://www.ojp.usdoj.gov/nij/topics/commtech/ntfi_guide.pdf (accessed March 27, 2006).

National Transportation Safety Board. 2006a. Rail Accidents 2006. http://ntsb.gov/Publictn/R_Acc.htm. (accessed March 10, 2006).

National Transportation Safety Board. 2006b. Train Crew Failed to Reline Main Line Switches and Causes Collision and Derailment in South Carolina NTSB Finds. November 29. http://www.ntsb.gov/Pressrel/2005/051129.htm (accessed March 10, 2006).

National Vulnerability Database. 2005. CVE Vulnerability Search Engine. http://nvd.nist.gov/statistics.cfm (accessed February 22, 2006).

Neuman, P. 1991. NY Area Fiber-Optic Telephone Cable Severed; Extensive Effects. *The Risk Digest*. http://catless.ncl.ac.uk/Risks/10.75.html#subj1 (accessed May 7, 2003).

Neuman, P. 2000. Week-long outage after cable cut downs 11,000 phone lines. *The Risk Digest 20:84*. http://catless.ncl.ac.uk/Risks/20.84.html#subj6.1 (accessed May 7, 2003).

New York Times. 2003. Northeastern United States and Canada power blackout, August 14, 2003, p. A1.

Newman, R. 2002. Wall Street Worries. *U.S. News & World Report*, September 23, 46–48.

Nickel, B., and D. Wilkinson. 1983. Invasion Percolation on the Cayley Tree: Exact Solution of a Modified Percolation Model. *Physical Review Letters* 51(2): 71–74.

North American Electric Reliability Council. 2001. System Disturbance Reports. Disturbance Analysis Working Group, review of Selected Electric System Disturbances in North America, 1996, 1998, and 2001. Princeton, NJ: NERC. http://www.nerc.com/~filez/dawg-disturbancereports.html (accessed February 8, 2006).

North American Electric Reliability Council. 2006. System Disturbance Reports. Disturbance Analysis Working Group 2001. http://www.nerc.com/~filez/dawg-disturbancereports.html (accessed February 8, 2006).

Norton, B. 1982. Environmental Ethics and the Rights of Future Generations. *Environmental Ethics* Winter: 319–338.

O'Hanlon, M. E., P. R. Orszag, I. H. Daalder, I. M. Destler, D. L. Gunter, R. E. Litan, and J. B. Steinberg. 2002. Protecting the American Homeland: A Preliminary Analysis. Chapter 6: Principles for Providing and Financing Homeland Security. Washington, DC: Brookings Institution. http://www.brookings.edu/fp/projects/homeland/fullhomeland.pdf (accessed February 2, 2006).

Office of Homeland Security. 2002. National Strategies for Homeland Security. Washington, DC: Office of the President.

Office of Management and Budget. 2004. Budget of the United States Government, Fiscal Year 2004, Historical Table 1–2. http://www.whitehouse.gov/news/usbudget/budget-fy2004/hist.html (accessed March 4, 2006).

Office of the President. 1998. The Clinton Administration's Policy on Critical Infrastructure Protection: Presidential Decision Directive 63. White paper. May 22. http://www.usdoj.gov/criminal/cybercrime/white_pr.htm (accessed November 2005).

Office of the President. 2003. National Strategy for the Physical Protection of Critical Infrastructures and Key Assets. Washington, DC.

Organization for Economic Cooperation and Development. 2005. Terrorism Insurance in OECD Countries. July 5. Paris: OECD.

Ortolani, Alex, and Robert Block. 2005. Keeping Cargo Safe From Terror: Hong Kong Port Project Scans All Containers; U.S. Doesn't See the Need. *Wall Street Journal*, July 29, B1.

Paine, Thomas. 1776. *Common Sense.* http://www.alumni.uchicago.edu/commontext/paine/documents/CommonSense.pdf (accessed February 25, 2006).

Papadakis, I. S., and W. T. Ziemba. 2001. Derivative Effects of the 1999 Earthquake in Taiwan to U.S. Personal Computer Manufacturers. In *Mitigation and Financing of Seismic Risks,* edited by P. R. Kleindorfer and M. R. Sertel. Boston: Kluwer Academic Publishers.

Perrings, C. 1991. Reserved Rationality and the Precautionary Principle: Technological Change, Time and Uncertainty in Environmental Decision Making. In *Ecological Economics: The Science and Management of Sustainability,* edited by R. Costanza. New York: Columbia University Press.

Perrow, C. 1984. *Normal Accidents: Living with High-Risk Technologies.* New York: Basic Books.

Perrow, C. 1999. *Normal Accidents.* Princeton, NJ: Princeton University Press.

Peters, Guy B. 1998. Managing Horizontal Government: The Politics of Coordination: Canadian Centre for Management Development, Minister of Supply and Services.

Peters, Ralph. 1999. *Fighting for the Future: Will America Win?* Mechanicsburg, PA: Stackpole Books.

Philippsohn, S. 2001. Trends in Cybercrime – An Overview of Current Financial Crimes on the Internet. *Computers & Security* 20(1): 53–69.

Phillips, Lord, J. Bridgeman, and M. Ferguson-Smith. 2000. The BSE Inquiry, vol 1. Findings and Conclusions. October, section 1176. London: Stationary Office.

Phimister, James R., Vicki M. Bier, and Howard C. Kunreuther (eds.). 2004. *Accident Precursor Analysis and Management: Reducing Technological Risk Through Diligence.* Washington, DC: National Academy of Engineering.

Pidgeon, Nick, Roger Kasperson, and Paul Slovic (eds.). 2003. *The Social Amplification of Risk.* Cambridge, UK: Cambridge University Press.

Pillar, P. 2001. *Terrorism and U.S. Foreign Policy.* Washington, DC: Brookings Institution Press.

Posner, Gerald. 2003. *Why America Slept.* New York: Random House.

Posner, Richard A. 2004. *Catastrophe: Risk and Response.* New York: Oxford University Press.

Potok, M. 2004. The American Radical Right: The 1990s and Beyond. In *Western Democracies and the New Extreme Right Challenge,* edited by R. Eatwell and C. Mudde. Oxford, UK: Routledge.

President's Commission on Critical Infrastructure Protection. 1997. Critical Foundations, Protecting America's Infrastructures. Washington, DC.

President's Council of Advisors on Science and Technology. 2002. Report on Maximizing the Contribution of Science and Technology Within the new Department of Homeland Security.

President's Council of Science and Technology Advisors. 2003. The Science and Technology of Combating Terrorism.

Pressman, J. L., and A. Wildavsky. 1984. *Implementation.* 2nd ed. Berkeley, CA: University of California Press.

PSERC. 2003. Public Utilities of Commission of Ohio, sequence of events on August 14. http://www.pserc.wisc.edu/Ohio_Only_Sequence_of_Events.pdf (accessed December 7, 2003).

Ralyea, Harold C., and Jeffrey W. Seifert. 2004. Information Sharing for Homeland Security: A Brief Overview. September 30, RL32597. Washington, DC: Congressional Research Service, 22–25.

Reason, J. 1997. *Managing the Risks of Organizational Accidents.* Hampshire, England: Ashgate Publishing Company.

Rees, Joseph. 1996. *Hostages of Each Other: The Transformation of Nuclear Safety since Three Mile Island.* Chicago: University of Chicago Press.

Rees, T. 1994. *Hostages to Each Other.* Chicago: University of Chicago Press.

Regalado, A., and G. Fields. 2003. Blackout a Reminder of Grid's Vulnerability to Terror. *Wall Street Journal,* August 15.

Reisner, Robert. 2002. Homeland Security Brings Ratepayers vs. Taxpayers to Center Stage. In *Postal and Delivery Services. Delivering on Competition,* edited by Crew and Kleindorfer. Boston: Kluwer Academic Publishers.

Renesys. 2003. Blackout Results in Widespread Network Outages. August 14. http://www.renesys.com/news/index.html (accessed December 7, 2003).

Renz, Loren, Elizabeth Cuccaro, and Leslie Marino. 2003. *9/11 Relief and Regranting Funds: A Summary Report on Funds Raised and Assistance Provided.* New York: Foundation Center, December.

Revised Draft National Infrastructure Protection Base Plan. 2006. Version 2.0 January. http://cryptome.org/nipp-v2.zip (accessed March 8, 2006).

Risen, James, and Eris Lichtblau. 2005. Bush Lets U.S. Spy on Callers Without Courts. *New York Times* http://www.nytimes.com/2005/12/16/politics/16program.html?ex= 1292389200&en=e32072d786623ac1&ei=5090&partner=rssuserland&emc=rss (accessed March 14, 2006).

Rittel, Horst, and Melvin Webber. 1973. Dilemmas in a General Theory of Planning. *Policy Sciences* 4: 155–169.

Rivlin, Gary. 2005. New Orleans Utility Struggles To Relight a City of Darkness. *New York Times*, New York City edition, Nov. 19, A1.

Roberts, H. K., and C. Libuser. 1993. From Bhopal to Banking: Organizational Design can Mitigate Risk. *Organizational Dynamics* 21: 15–26.

Roberts, Karlene. 1990a. Managing High Reliability Organizations. *California Management Review* 32, 4: 101–114.

Roberts, K. H. 1990b. Some Characteristics of High Reliability Organizations. *Organization Science* 1(2): 160–177.

Roberts, K. H. 1993. Some Aspects of Organizational Cultures and Strategies to Manage Them in Reliability Enhancing Organizations. *Journal of Managerial Issues* 5: 165–181.

Roberts, K. H., and G. Gargano. 1989. Managing a High Reliability Organization: A Case for Interdependence. In *Managing Complexity in High Technology Industries: Systems and People*, edited by M. A. VonGlinow and S. Mohrmon. New York: Oxford University Press.

Roberts, Nancy. 2001. Coping with Wicked Problems: The Case of Afghanistan. In *Learning from International Public Management Reform*, Vol. 11B. Amsterdam: Elsevier Science Ltd.

Rochlin, G. I. 1993a. Defining High Reliability Organizations in Practice. In *New Challenges to Understanding Organizations*, edited by K. Roberts. New York: Macmillan.

Rochlin, G. I. 1993b. *Trapped in the Net: the Unanticipated Consequences of Computerization*. Princeton, NJ: Princeton University Press.

Rochlin, G. I. 1996. Reliable Organizations: Present Research and Future Directions. *Journal of Crisis and Contingency Management* (Issue on High Reliable Organization Research) 4(2): 55–59.

Rochlin, G. I. 1999. Safe Operations as a Social Construct. *Ergonomics* 42(11): 1549–1560.

Rochlin, G. I. 2001. Highly Reliable Organizations: Exploration and Research Perspectives. In *Organiser la Fiabilite*, edited by M. Bourrie. Paris: L'Harmattan.

Rochlin, G. I., and A. von Meier. 1994. Nuclear Power Operations: A Cross-Cultural Perspective. *Annual Review of Energy and the Environment* 19: 153–187.

Rochlin, G. I., Todd R. LaPorte, and Karlene H. Roberts. 1987. The Self-Designing High-Reliability Organization: Aircraft Carrier Flight Operations at Sea. *Naval War College Review* 76–90.

Roe, E., M. J. G. van Eeten, P. R. Schulman, and M. de Bruijne. 2002. California's Electricity Restructuring: The Challenge to Providing Service and Grid Reliability. Palo Alto, CA: California Energy Commission, Lawrence Berkeley National Laboratory, and the Electrical Power Research Institute.

Roe, E., P. Schulman, M. J. G. van Eeten, and M. deBruijne. 2005. High Reliability Bandwidth Management: Findings and Implications of Two Case Studies. *Journal of Public Administration Research and Theory* 15: 263–280.

Saleh, Mohamad. 2003. Al Qaeda Claims Responsibility for Power Blackout in U.S.! *Dar Al Hayat*, August 18. http://english.daralhayat.com/arab_news/08-2003/Article-20030818-14bdd659-c0a8-01ed-0079-6e1c903b7552/story.html (accessed October 21, 2003).

Sandler, T., and W. Enders. 2004. An Economic Perspective of Transnational Terrorism. *European Journal of Political Economy* 20(2): 301–316.

Sarkar, Dibya. 2004. DOJ Writes to Share. *Federal Computer Week*, October 15. http://www.fcw.com/fcw/articles/2004/1011/web-doj-10-15-04.asp (accessed November 2005).

Scalfane, Susanne. 2006. Unexpected Surplus Climb: Despite Storms, Industry Profits Rise, National Underwriter P&C. January 2/9, 110, 1. http://cms.nationalunderwriter.com/cms/NUPC/Weekly%20Issues/Issues/2006/01/News/P01ISONINE-ss?searchfor=despite%20storms%20january%202006 (accessed March 4, 2006).

Schein, E. H. 1994. Organizational and Managerial Culture as a Facilitator or Inhibitor of Organizational Learning. http://www.solonline.org/res/wp/10004.html.

Schelling, T. 1978. *Micromotives and Macrobehavior*. New York: Norton Interdependent Security.

Schratz, P. R. 1983. Admiral Rickover and the Cult of Personality. *Air University Review*, July–August. http://airpower.maxwell.af.mil/airchronicles/aureview/1983/jul-aug/schratz.html (accessed June 27, 2006).

Schulman, Paul R. 1993a. The Analysis of High Reliability Organizations: A Comparative Framework. In *New Challenges to Organization Research: High Reliability Organization*, edited by K. H. Roberts. New York: Macmillan.

Schulman, P. R. 1993b. A Comparative Framework for the Analysis of High Reliability Organizations. In *New Challenges to Understanding Organizations*, edited by K. Roberts. New York: Macmillan.

Schulman, P. R. 1993c. Negotiated Order of Organizational Reliability. *Administration and Society* 25(3): 356–372.

Schulman, P. R. 2002. Medical Errors: How Reliable Is Reliability Theory? In *Medical Error: 200–216*, edited by M. M. Rosenthal and L. M. Sutcliffe. San Francisco, CA: Jossey-Bass.

Schulman, Paul R., and Emery Roe. 2004. Managing for Reliability in an Age of Terror. Paper presented at Private Efficiency, Public Vulnerability Workshop, Cambridge, MA, May 28.

Schulman, P. R., E. Roe, M. van Eeten, and M. de Bruijne. 2004. High Reliability and the Management of Critical Infrastructures. *Journal of Contingencies and Crisis Management* 12(1): 14–28.

Select Bipartisan Committee to Investigate the Preparation for and Response to Hurricane Katrina. 2006. A Failure of Initiative. U.S. House of Representatives. http://katrina.house.gov/full_katrina_report.htm (accessed March 23, 2006).

Seligman, A. 2000. *The Problem of Trust*. Princeton, NJ: Princeton University Press.

Seltzer, L. 2004. Who Wrote Sobig? eWeek. http://www.eweek.com/article2/0,1759,1716992,00.asp (accessed December 7, 2005).

Selznick, P. 1957. *Leadership in Administration*. New York: Harper & Row.

Sherman, Mark. 2005. Subway Threat Puzzle: When Local Officials, Feds Disagree. *Associated Press*. October 7. http://www.nctimes.com/articles/2005/10/08/news/nation/15_32_5810_7_05.txt (accessed November 2005).

Short, T. 2002. Reliability Indices. Conference report, T&D World Expo 2002, Indianapolis, IN, May 7–9, 2002. http://www.epri-peac.com/td/pdfs/reliability2002.pdf (accessed March 25, 2006).

Shrader, R., and R. J. Woolsey. 2002. Business Has To Be Involved in Security Planning. *Financial Times*, January 16.

Shrader-Frechette, K. 1993. Risk Methodology and Institution Bias. *Research in Social Problems and Public Policy* 5: 207–223.

Simon, Steven, and David Benjamin. 2005. *The Next Attack*. New York: Henry Holt & Company.

Singel, Ryan. 2005a. Passenger Screening, Take 10. Wired News. January 31. http://www.wired.com/news/privacy/0,1848,66433,00.html?tw=wn_story_related (accessed November 2005).

Singel, Ryan. 2005b. Secure Flight Hits Turbulence. *Wired News*. June 15. http://www.wired.com/news/privacy/0,1848,67875,00.html?tw=wn_story_related (accessed November 2005).

Singer, Peter. 2002. *Corporate Warriors*. Washington, DC: Brookings Institution Press.

Slovic, P. 1993. Perceived Risk, Trust, and Democracy. *Risk Analysis* 13(6): 675–682.

Slovic, P. 1999. Trust, Emotion, Sex, Politics, and Science: Surveying the Risk-Assessment Battlefield. *Risk Analysis* 19(4): 689–701.

Slovic, Paul. 2000. *The Perception of Risk*. London: Earthscan Publications.

Smetters, K. 2004. Insuring Against Terrorism: The Policy Challenge. In *Brookings-Wharton Papers on Financial Services*, edited by R. Litan and R. Herring, 139–182.

Sood, Sunil K. 2004. Food Poisoning. eMedicine. http://www.emedicine.com/ped/topic795.htm (accessed March 10, 2006).

Stacey, Ralph. 1996. *Strategic Management & Organizational Dynamics*. London: Pitman.

Starks, Tim, and Martin E. Andersen. 2004. Congress, Industry Both Dismay over Homeland Security's Performance on Critical Infrastructure. *CQ Homeland Security*.

State of New York Public Service Commission. 2005. CASE 04-E-0822 – In the Matter of Staff's Investigation into New York State's Electric Utility Transmission Right-of-Way Management Practices, filed in Case 27605. http://www3.dps.state.ny.us/pscweb/webfileroom.nsf/ArticlesByCategory/BDB52B0CC15BBE74852570260063242B/$File/301.04e0822.pdf?OpenElement (accessed February 9, 2006).

Stauffer, D., and A. Aharony. 1994. *Introduction to Percolation Theory*. London and New York: Routledge.

Stephenson, John B. 2005. Homeland Security: Federal and Industrial Efforts Are Addressing Security Issues at Chemical Facilities, but Additional Action Is Needed. Testimony by John B. Stephenson, U. S. Accountability Office, before the Committee on Homeland Security and Governmental Affairs, U. S. Senate, April 27.

Stern, J. 2003. *Terror in the Name of God: Why Religious Militants Kill*. New York: Harper Collins.

Strohm, Chris. 2004. Threat Warning Creates Confusion Over Homeland Security Roles. GovExec.com. http://www.govexec.com/dailyfed/0504/052804c1.htm (accessed November 2005).

Sturgeon W. 2003. Organized Crime behind Sobig – Virus Expert. http://news.zdnet.co.uk/internet/security/0,39020375,39115886,00.htm (accessed May 24, 2004).

Swiss Re. 2006. Natural Catastrophes and Man-Made Disasters in 2005. Sigma, N2. February.

Talukdar, S., J. Apt , M. Ilic, L. Lave, and M. G. Morgan. 2003. Cascading Failures: Survival vs. Prevention. *Electricity Journal* 16(9): 25–31.

Terrorism Risk Insurance Act of 2002, Pub. Law No. 107–297, 116 Stat. 2322; 31 C.F.R. Part 50. http://www.ustreas.gov/offices/domestic-finance/financial-institution/terrorism-insurance/ (accessed February 25, 2006).

Terrorist Risk Reinsurance Program. 2005. U.S. House of Representatives, July 1.

Thompson, William C. 2002. One Year Later: The Fiscal Impact of 9/11 on New York City. http://comptroller.nyc.gov/bureaus/bud/reports/impact-9-11-year-later.pdf (accessed February 25, 2006).

Tillinghast-Towers Perrin. 2002. September 11, 2001: Implications for the Insurance Industry, Towers Perrin Reinsurance, T193-01, September 21, 2001. New York: Tillinghast-Towers Perrin. http://www.towersperrin.com/tillinghast/publications/reports/Sept_11_Implications_For_Insurance/2002051310.pdf (accessed January 10, 2006).

Time Magazine. 1977. Night of Terror. July 25. 12–26.

Transmission & Distribution World. 2005. AREVA to Build De-Icing and Power-Quality System. http://tdworld.com/mag/power_areva_build_deicing (accessed February 8, 2006).

Transportation of Highly Reliable Organizations: Past Research and Future Explorations. 1999. Paper presented at Workshop on Approaches to Organizational Reliability, October 7–8, at Department Technologies et Sciences de l'Homme, Universite de Technologies de Compiegne, France.

Tuchman, Barbara. 1962. *The Guns of August.* Toronto: Bantam.

Tucker, Jonathan B. 1999. Historical Trends Related to Bioterrorism: An Empirical Analysis. National Symposium on Medical and Public Health Response to Bioterrorism. Emerging Infectious Diseases, July–August, 5(4): 498–504.

Tucker, Jonathan B., and Amy Sands. 1999. An Unlikely Threat. *Bulletin of the Atomic Scientists* 55(4).

Turner, Barry A. 1976. The Organizational and Interorganizational Development of Disasters. *Administrative Science Quarterly* 21(3): 378–397.

Turner, Barry A. 1978. *Man-Made Disasters: The Failure of Foresight.* New York: Crane, Russak.

Turner, Barry A., and Nick F. Pidgeon. 1997. Man-Made Disasters. 2nd ed. Oxford, United Kingdom Butterworth-Heinemann.

U.S. Congress. 2002. Terrorism Risk Insurance Act of 2002. HR 3210 (became Pub. L. 107–297, 116 Stat. 2322). http://frwebgate.access.gpo.gov/cgi-bin/getdoc.cgi?dbname=107_cong_public_laws&docid=f:publ297.107.pdf (accessed March 20, 2006).

U.S. Department of Justice. 1988. The Clinton Administration's Policy on Critical Infrastructure Protection: Presidential Decision Directive 63. White Paper, May 22. http://www.usdoj.gov/criminial/cybercrime/white_pr.htm (accessed November 2005).

U.S. Department of State. 2004. Global Patterns in Terrorism. Washington, DC: Office of the Coordinator for Counterterrorism.

U.S. Department of State. 2005. Country Reports on Terrorism. Released by the Office of the Coordinator on Counterterrorism, April 27. http://www.state.gov/s/ct/rls/45321.htm (accessed January 12, 2006).

U.S. Department of the Treasury. 2005. Assessment: The Terrorism Risk Insurance Act of 2002. Washington, DC: Office of Economic Policy. June 30.

U.S.–Canada Power System Outage Task Force. 2004. Final Report on the August 14, 2003, Blackout in the United States and Canada: Causes and Recommendations. April 5. Washington, DC: U.S. Department of Energy, Office of Electricity Delivery and Energy Reliability.

Van Eeten, M. J. G., E. M. Roe, P. Schulman, and M. L. C. de Bruijne. 2006. The Enemy Within: System Complexity and Organizational Surprises. In *International CIIP Handbook 2006 Vol. II Analyzing Issues, Challenges, and Prospects*, edited by M. Dunn and V. Mayer. Zurich: Center for Security Studies of the ETH Zurich, 89–109.

Vegh, S. 2002. Activists or Cyberterrorists? The Changing Media Discourse on Hacking. *Firstmonday 7:10.* http://www.firstmonday.dk/issues/issue7_10/vegh/ (accessed May 7, 2003).

Verton D. 2003. *Black Ice: The Invisible Threat of Cyber-Terrorism.* New York: McGraw-Hill Osborne Media.

Wall Street Journal. 2005. A Massive Repair Job Begins To Fix Gulf's Broken Oil Network. September 8.

Watts, D. 2003. Security and Vulnerability in Electric Power Systems. Proceedings of the 35th North American Power Symposium, University of Missouri-Rolla, October 20–21, 559–566.

Weber, Max. 1946. Politics as a Vocation. In *From Max Weber: Essays in Sociology,* edited by H. H. Gerth and C. Wright Mills. New York: Oxford University Press.

Wedgwood, R. 2002. Al Qaeda, Terrorism, and Military Commissions. *American Journal of International Law* 96(2): 328–337.

Weick, K. E. 1987. Organizational Culture as a Source of High Reliability. *California Management Review* 29: 112–127.

Weick, Karl, and Kathleen Sutcliffe. 2001. *Managing the Unexpected: Assuring High Performance in an Age of Complexity.* University of Michigan Business School Management Series. San Francisco, CA: Jossey-Bass.

Weick, K. E., K. M. Sutcliffe, and D. Obstfeld. 1999. Organizing for High Reliability: Quantitative and Qualitative Assessment Aboard Nuclear Powered Aircraft Carriers. *Journal of High Technology Management Research* 5(1): 141–161.

Weisstein, Eric W. 1999. Cayley Tree. In *MathWorld – A Wolfram Web Resource.* http://mathworld.wolfram.com/CayleyTree.html (accessed June 27, 2006).

Wenz, P. 1983. Ethics, Energy Policy, and Future Generations. *Environmental Ethics* 5: 195–209.

Western Systems Coordinating Council. 1996. Disturbance Report for the Power System Outage that Occurred on the Western Interconnection, August 10. 1548 PAST, Published October 18, 1996.

Wharton Risk Management and Decision Processes Center. 2005. TRIA and Beyond. Wharton School, University of Pennsylvania, Philadelphia p. 208. http://grace.wharton.upenn.edu/risk/downloads/TRIA%20and%20Beyond.pdf (accessed February 25, 2006).

White House. 1998. Protecting America's Critical Infrastructure: PDD 63 Fact Sheet. Washington, DC.

White House. 2002. National Strategy for Homeland Security. Washington, DC, July.

White House. 2003a. Homeland Security Presidential Directive/HSPD-7. December 17. http://www.whitehouse.gov/news/releases/2003/12/20031217-5.html (accessed November 2005).

White House. 2003b. The National Strategy to Secure Cyberspace Washington, DC: White House Critical Infrastructure Protection Board. http://www.whitehouse.gov/pcipb/cyberspace_strategy.pdf (accessed December 3, 2003).

White House. 2004a. President Bush Celebrates Independence Day, West Virginia Capitol Grounds. http://www.whitehouse.gov/news/releases/2004/07/20040704.html (accessed January 12, 2006).

White House. 2004b. Remarks by the Vice President at the 123rd Coast Guard Academy Commencement. http://www.whitehouse.gov/news/releases/2004/05/20040519-5.html (accessed January 12, 2006).

White House. 2005a. Executive Order: Further Strengthening the Sharing of Terrorism Information to Protect Americans. http://www.whitehouse.gov/news/releases/2005/10/20051025-5.html (accessed November 2005).

White House. 2005b. The National Strategy for Homeland Security. July. http://www.whitehouse.gov/homeland/book/index.html (accessed July 12, 2006).

Wiening, Eric A. 2002. Foundations of Risk Management and Insurance. American Institute for Chartered Property and Casualty Underwriters/Insurance Institute of America, Malvern, PA.

Wiening, Eric A. 2002. *Foundations of Insurance Risk Management and Insurance.* AICPCU/IIA, 1st ed.

Wildavsky, Aaron. 1988. *Searching for Safety.* New Brunswick, NJ: Transaction Books.

Wilson, J. 2003. Blackout: The Conspiracy Theory. *Popular Mechanics* 180(11): 38, 40.

Wilson, J. Q. 1989. *Bureaucracy.* New York: Basic Books.

Wired. 2004. August 11. http://www.wired.com/news/print/0,1294,64168,00.html (accessed July 15, 2004).

World Health Organization. 2003a. SARS Outbreak Contained Worldwide. http://www.who.int/mediacentre/news/releases/2003/pr56/en/ (accessed February 9, 2006).

World Health Organization. 2003b. Update 95 – SARS: Chronology of a Serial Killer. http://www.who.int/csr/don/2003_07_04/en/index.html (accessed February 9, 2006).

Yoran, Amit. 2004a. Locking Your Cyber Front Door – the Challenges facing Home Users and Small Businesses. Statement of the Director, National Cyber Security Division, Office of Infrastructure Protection, U.S. Department of Homeland Security before the Subcommittee on Technology, Information Policy, Intergovernmental Relations, and the Census, Committee on Government Reform, U.S. House of Representatives, June 16.

Yoran, Amit. 2004b. Virtual Threat, Real Terror: Cyberterrorism in the 21st Century. Statement before the Senate Committee on the Judiciary Subcommittee on Terrorism, Technology and Homeland Security, February 24.

Yoshihara, T. 2001. Chinese Information Warfare: A Phantom Menace or Emerging Threat? *Strategic Studies Institute.* http://www.iwar.org.uk/iwar/resources/china/iw/chininfo.pdf (accessed May 7, 2003).

Zerriffi, H. 2004. Electric Power Systems Under Stress: An Evaluation of Centralized versus Distributed System Architectures. PhD Dissertation, Department of Engineering and Public Policy, Carnegie Mellon University, Pittsburgh, PA. http://wpweb2k.gsia.cmu.edu/ceic/theses/Hisham_Zerriffi_PhD_Thesis_2004.pdf.

Zipf, G. K. 1929. Relative frequency as a determinant of phonetic change. *Harvard Studies in Classical Philology* 15: 1–95.

Zipf, G. K. 1965. *Psycho-biology of Languages.* Cambridge, MA: MIT Press.

Zuboff, Shoshana. 1988. *In the Age of the Smart Machine.* New York: Basic Books.

CONTRIBUTORS

Jay Apt is Executive Director of the Carnegie Mellon Electricity Industry Center at Carnegie Mellon University's Tepper School of Business and the university's Department of Engineering and Public Policy, where he is a Distinguished Service Professor. He received an A.B. from Harvard College in 1971 and a Ph.D. in experimental atomic physics from the Massachusetts Institute of Technology in 1976. His research, teaching, and consulting interests are in economics, engineering, and public policy aspects of the electricity industry; economics of technical innovation; management of technical enterprises; risk management in policy and technical decision framing, and engineering systems design.

Recent publication include "Deregulation Has Not Lowered U.S. Industrial Electricity Prices," "Electric Gridlock: A National Solution," "Cascading Failures: Survival vs. Prevention," "Designing an Interdisciplinary Curriculum for the Changing Electric Power Industry," "Managing Soil Carbon," and "Electrical Blackouts: A Systemic Problem." He has co-authored with Lester Lave editorial pieces for the *New York Times* and the *Washington Post*. He received the Metcalf Lifetime Achievement Award for significant contributions to engineering in 2002 and the National Aeronautics and Space Administration's Distinguished Service Medal in 1997.

Philip E. Auerswald, PhD (Editor) is Director of the Center for Science and Technology Policy and an Assistant Professor at the School of Public Policy, George Mason University. Professor Auerswald's work focuses on linked processes of technological and organizational change in the contexts of policy, economics, and strategy. He is the founding co-editor of *Innovations: Technology | Governance | Globalization,* a quarterly journal from MIT Press about people using technology to address global challenges. He was previously a

Research Fellow and Assistant Director of the Science, Technology, and Public Policy Program at the Kennedy School of Government, Harvard University. His published work has addressed entrepreneurial finance, organizational learning, industry dynamics, and innovation policy. He has been a consultant for the National Academies of Science, the National Institute of Standards and Technology, and the Commonwealth of Massachusetts. He holds a PhD in economics from the University of Washington and a BA (political science) from Yale University.

Thomas Bowe is currently PJM Interconnection's Chief Security Officer, responsible for the physical and cyber security of PJM and its business continuity planning. From 2002 to October 2004, he was PJM's Manager of RTO Market Integration, which required the creation of new reliability plans to double PJM's operating area. Additionally, he was the root cause leader in the investigation of the August 14th Power Outage. From 1998 to 2002, he held the position of PJM's Manager of Dispatch, having direct 24/7 responsibility for the operations of the world's third largest centrally dispatched control area. Prior to joining PJM, Mr. Bowe served as a career Infantry Officer in the U.S. Army. He is a graduate of the United States Military Academy, Texas Tech University, and the Harvard Business School.

Lewis M. Branscomb (Editor) is the Aetna Professor of Public Policy and Corporate Management Emeritus and emeritus Director of the Science, Technology, and Public Policy Program in the Center for Science and International Affairs at Harvard University's Kennedy School of Government. Dr. Branscomb graduated from Duke University in 1945, summa cum laude, and was awarded the Ph.D. degree in physics by Harvard University in 1949. A research physicist at the U.S. National Bureau of Standards (now the National Institute of Standards and Technology) from 1951 to 1969, he was Director of NBS from 1969 to 1972. He then became Vice President and Chief Scientist of the IBM Corporation, serving until 1986, when he joined the faculty at Harvard.

President Johnson named him to the President's Science Advisory Committee in 1964, and he chaired the subcommittee on Space Science and Technology during Project Apollo. President Carter appointed him to the National Science Board and he served as Chairman of the NSB during the presidency of Ronald Reagan.

Dr. Branscomb was the co-chairman of the project of the National Academies of Science and of Engineering and the Institute of Medicine, which authored the report *Making the Nation Safer: Science and Technology for Countering Terrorism*, published by the National Academies Press in 2002. He has been actively engaged in promoting bilateral cooperation in counter-terrorism with India, Russia, Japan, and Korea.

Lloyd Dixon is a senior economist at the Rand Corporation, with more than 15 years of experience conducting research on insurance, compensation, and liability issues. In fall 2004, he completed a study of the compensation and assistance received by individuals and businesses affected by the September 11, 2001, terrorist attacks. In a recent paper, he explored issues and options for government intervention in the market for terrorism insurance, and in a paper published by OECD, he examined the links between national security and insurance and compensation policies for terrorism. He is currently conducting two studies on flood insurance – one study examines opportunities and challenges for increasing participation in the National Flood Insurance Program; the other is developing better information on the role played by private insurers in underwriting flood insurance. Dr. Dixon has also examined the standards for admitting expert evidence into state and federal courts. He holds a Ph.D. in economics from the University of California at Berkeley and B.S. and B.A. degrees in engineering and political science, respectively, from Stanford University.

John D. Donahue is the Raymond Vernon Lecturer in Public Policy and Director of the Weil Program in Collaborative Governance at Harvard University. His teaching, writing, and research center on the distribution of public responsibilities across levels of government and sectors of the economy. He has written or edited 11 books, with another – *Leverage: Public Goals, Private Roles* (with Richard J. Zeckhauser) – in progress. Donahue served in the first Clinton administration as an Assistant Secretary and then as Counselor to the Secretary of Labor. He has consulted for business and governmental organizations including the National Economic Council, the World Bank, and the Rand Corporation, and he serves as a trustee or advisor to several nonprofits. A native of Indiana, he holds a B.A. degree from Indiana University and an M.P.P. and Ph.D. from Harvard.

Jacob (Jack) Feinstein is a consultant for the electric power industry. He has more than 38 years of experience in the industry, including 30 years with Consolidated Edison of New York, Inc. Prior to retiring from Con Edison in 1998, he served as Vice President of System and Transmission Operations for seven years. He then joined Cogen Technologies, Inc., as a vice president responsible for new project development before becoming an independent consultant in 1999. His responsibilities at Con Edison included maintaining the operational integrity of the electric bulk power system with an organization that comprised seven operating departments. His organization was also responsible for the purchase and sale of energy and capacity at the wholesale level and the purchase of fuel oil for use in Con Edison's generating stations.

His career at Con Edison began in 1967 as an assistant engineer. Following a two-year rotational training program for entry-level engineers, he was assigned to the Electrical Engineering Department as an engineer designing generation station projects. From there, he was promoted to manager of the system sequence group in the System Operation Department and became the chief system operator in 1977. In 1982, he was promoted to general manager of the System Operation Department and in 1988 to plant manager of the Arthur Kill Generating Station. Mr. Feinstein has presented numerous technical and managerial lectures during his career to various power industry organizations and has collaborated in the preparation of technical papers. While at Con Edison, his experience included developing and delivering both technical and managerial training programs and seminars. He also developed the training program for Con Edison's senior system operators, a position created in 1977 to place experienced graduate engineers in a position to supervise the operation of the power system on a 24/7 watch assignment. He was a member of the New York Power Pool (NYPP) Operating Committee from 1982 until his retirement and is a recognized expert in the reliable and safe operation of the electric power system. He also served on the New York Independent System Operator (NYISO) Transition Steering Committee that was directing the implementation of the restructuring of the wholesale power and energy market in New York State. He has authored operating procedures for both Consolidated Edison and the NYPP. He served as a member of the Reliability Coordinating Committee (RCC) of the Northeast Power Coordinating Council. He also served on the Electrical Systems Division Advisory Committee of the Electric Power Research Institute (EPRI).

Presently, he provides consulting for a developer of power plants and serves as a member of the board of directors of a public company that produces electric energy by using biogas at landfills as the fuel source. He also serves on the New England Power Pool (NEPOOL) Board of Review, an advisory panel to help resolve disputes among participants in the New England wholesale electric power market. A registered Professional Engineer, he holds a B.E.E. degree from the City College of New York.

Stephen E. Flynn is the Jeane J. Kirkpatrick Senior Fellow for National Security Studies at the Council on Foreign Relations, where he specializes in global transportation security, border management, and homeland security. Dr. Flynn's experience includes Commander, U.S. Coast Guard (retired); Member, Marine Board, National Academy of Sciences (current);

Director, Independent Task Force on Homeland Security Imperatives (Gary Hart and Warren Rudman co-chairs, 2002); Consultant on homeland security, U.S. Commission on National Security (Hart-Rudman Commission 2000–2001); Director, Office of Global Issues, National Security Council staff (1997); Associate Professor, U.S. Coast Guard Academy (1994–1999); Guest Scholar and Visiting Fellow, Brookings Institution (1991–1994); and Commanding Officer, U.S. Coast Guard Cutter *Redwood,* 1992–1993, and *Point Arena,* 1984–1986. Selected publications include *America the Vulnerable* (HarperCollins, 2004); "Port Security: Still a House of Cards" in *Far Eastern Economic Review* (Jan/Feb 2006); "U.S. Port Security and the Global War on Terror" in the *American Interest* (Autumn 2005); "The Neglected Homefront" in *Foreign Affairs* (Nov/Dec 2004); and *Defeating the Jihadist: A Blueprint for Action* with Richard A. Clarke et al. (Century Foundation, 2004). Mr. Flynn received his Ph.D. and M.A.L.D. from the Fletcher School of Law and Diplomacy, Tufts University, and his B.S. from the U.S. Coast Guard Academy. Mr. Flynn has received the following honors: Legion of Merit (2001); Coast Guard Academy Distinguished Alumni Achievement Award (1999); Annenberg Scholar-in-Residence, University of Pennsylvania (1993–1994); International Affairs Fellowship, Council on Foreign Relations (1991–1992); and Distinguished Graduate, Fletcher School of Law and Diplomacy, Tufts University (1988).

Robert A. Frosch is a theoretical physicist by education (A.B., Columbia College, 1947; Ph.D., Columbia University, 1952). He conducted research in ocean acoustics at Columbia and later served as Director for Nuclear Test Detection and Deputy Director of the Advanced Research Projects Agency in the Department of Defense, Assistant Secretary of the Navy for Research and Development, Assistant Executive Director of the United Nations Environment Program, Associate Director for Applied Oceanography of the Woods Hole Oceanographic Institution, Administrator of the National Aeronautics and Space Administration, President of the American Association of Engineering Societies, and Vice President of General Motors Corporation (GM) in charge of Research Laboratories. Dr. Frosch retired from GM in 1993 before joining the Kennedy School of Government at Harvard University. He is a member of the National Academy of Engineering, the American Academy of Arts and Sciences, and a Foreign Member of the UK Royal Academy of Engineering.

Sean P. Gorman is the President and CTO of FortiusOne. Prior to founding FortiusOne, Dr. Gorman was a Research Assistant Professor at George Mason University's School of Public Policy. He also served as a vice president of research and development for a telecommunications mapping firm and was Director of Strategy for a Washington, D.C.–based technology incubator. His research focuses on infrastructure security and has been featured in the *Washington Post, Wired, Der Spiegel,* Associated Press, CNN, MSNBC, Fox, CNBC, and NPR. He has published in *Telecommunications Policy, Environment and Planning A & B, Tijdschrift voor Economische Geografie,* and *Journal of Crisis and Contingency Management,* and he authored the book *Networks, Complexity, and Security.* Dr. Gorman also serves as a subject matter expert for the Critical Infrastructure Task Force and Homeland Security Advisory Council. He received his Ph.D. from George Mason University as the Provost's High Potential Research Candidate and Fisher Prize recipient.

Geoffrey Heal, Paul Garrett Professor of Public Policy and Corporate Responsibility at Columbia Business School and Professor of Economics in the School of International and Public Affairs, is noted for contributions to economic theory and environmental economics. Author of 14 books and about 200 articles, he is a Fellow of the Econometric Society, past President of the Association of Environmental and Resource Economists, recipient of its prize for publications of enduring quality, a member of the Scientific Advisory Board of the Environmental Protection Agency, and a Director of the Union of Concerned Scientists. He chaired a committee of the National Academy of Sciences on valuing ecosystem services and was a Commissioner of the Pew Oceans Commission. Recent books include *Nature and the Marketplace,* a review of the scope for market-based approaches to environmental conservation; *Valuing the Future,* a theoretical analysis of sustainability from an economic perspective; and *Valuing Ecosystem Services,* a report of the National Research Council. His current research topics include environmental economics and the social and environmental impacts of business.

Michael Kearns is professor in the Computer and Information Science Department at the University of Pennsylvania, where he holds the National Center Chair in Resource Management and Technology. He is also the co-director of Penn's interdisciplinary Institute for Research in Cognitive Science and has a secondary appointment at the Wharton School. His primary research interests are in artificial intelligence and machine learning, including computational learning theory, reinforcement learning, probabilistic inference, and graphical models. In recent years, he has been mainly working on computational issues in game theory, economics, and finance. In the past, he has worked on a variety of applications of artificial intelligence to human–computer interaction, including spoken dialogue systems and software agents in MUDs (multi-user computer games). He also has interests in cryptography, network security, and theoretical computer science. He currently serves on editorial boards of several journals (*Mathematics of Operations Research, Games and Economic Behavior, Journal of the ACM,* and the MIT Press series on Adaptive Computation and Machine Learning).

He spent the decade 1991–2001 in basic artificial intelligence and machine learning research at AT&T Labs and Bell Labs. During his last four years there, he was the head of the AI department. During his time at AT&T/Bell Labs, he also served as the head of the Machine Learning department and as the head of the Secure Systems Research department. He joined the Penn faculty in January 2002. A graduate from the University of California at Berkeley in math and computer science, he received a Ph.D. in computer science from Harvard University and was a postdoctoral Fellow at the Laboratory for Computer Science at M.I.T. and at the International Computer Science Institute in Berkeley.

Dr. Kearns is also an active member and the vice-chair of DARPA's Information Science and Technology study group and the head of quantitative strategy development in the Equity Strategies department of Lehman Brothers in New York City.

Paul Kleindorfer is the Anheuser Busch Professor of Management Science at the Wharton School of the University of Pennsylvania. Dr. Kleindorfer's primary appointment is in the Department of Operations and Information Management. He is also professor of Business and Public Policy. Dr. Kleindorfer graduated with distinction (B.S.) from the U.S. Naval Academy in 1961. He studied on a Fulbright Fellowship in Mathematics at the University of Tübingen, Germany (1964–1965), followed by doctoral studies at Carnegie Mellon University, from which he received his Ph.D. in 1970 in Systems and Communication Sciences at the Graduate School of Industrial Administration. Dr. Kleindorfer has held university appointments at Carnegie Mellon University (l968–1969), Massachusetts Institute of Technology (1969–1972), The Wharton School (1973–present), and several universities and international research institutes, including the University of Frankfurt, INSEAD, Ulm University, IIASA, and The Science Center (Berlin). He has published more than 25 books and many research papers in the areas of managerial economics and regulation. Dr. Kleindorfer has held a number of editorial and professional positions over the years, including his current positions as President of the Society for Economic Design and Associate Editor of the *Journal of Regulatory Economics*. He has consulted with companies and governmental agencies worldwide on risk management and technology strategy.

Dr. Kleindorfer's early research was concerned with the application of optimal control theory to deterministic and stochastic production planning problems. His later work has been concerned primarily with risk management and with the integration of operations, economics, and finance. His sectoral interests have included a long-standing interest in electric power, in the postal and logistics area, and more recently in capital-intensive sectors such as chemicals and semiconductors. In these areas, he has been concerned with a broad range of risk management activities, ranging from traditional supply chain contracts to hedging and trading arising from derivatives defined on spot markets ancillary to the sector in the question. As part of his ongoing interest in risk management, Dr. Kleindorfer has also developed and maintained a continuing research program in environmental, health, and safety risks, with a primary focus on the chemical and process industries.

Michael Kormos is Vice President of the System Operations Division for PJM Interconnection. He is responsible for ensuring the safe and secure operation of the PJM transmission grid and energy markets. He oversees dispatching, operations development, operations planning, real-time operations, and scheduling functions at PJM. Previously, he was the Operations Coordination Manager of the System Operations Division and was responsible for the oversight of the day-to-day operations and implementation of Locational Marginal Pricing and the new market structures. Mr. Kormos was Acting Manager for the Scheduling Department and as such was responsible for coordination and scheduling of all bilateral energy transactions for the PJM participants, evaluation and scheduling of all PJM spot market transactions, support of the Unit Commitment and generation scheduling functions, load forecasting support, and hydro unit coordination and scheduling. He received a B.S. in Electrical Engineering from Drexel University and a Master of Business Administration from Villanova University.

Howard Kunreuther is the Cecilia Yen Koo Professor of Decision Sciences and Public Policy at the Wharton School, University of Pennsylvania, as well as Co-Director of the Wharton Risk Management and Decision Processes Center. He has a long-standing interest in the ways that society can better manage low-probability–high-consequence events as they relate to technological and natural hazards, and he has published extensively on the topic. He is a Fellow of the American Association for the Advancement of Science and Distinguished Fellow of the Society for Risk Analysis, receiving the Society's Distinguished Achievement Award in 2001. Dr. Kunreuther has written or co-edited a number of papers and books including *On Risk and Disaster: Lessons from Hurricane Katrina* (with Ronald Daniels and Donald Kettl), *Catastrophe Modeling: A New Approach to Managing Risk* (with Patricia Grossi), and *Wharton on Making Decisions* (with Stephen Hoch). He is a recipient of the Elizur

Wright Award for the publication that makes the most significant contribution to the literature of insurance.

Todd M. La Porte (Editor) is an associate professor in the School of Public Policy at George Mason University. His current research interests include public organizations, governance, and the use and impacts of networked information technologies, for which he has received National Science Foundation and Pew Foundation support. He is also working on public attitudes to technology and homeland security, critical infrastructure protection, and organizational responses to extreme events, specifically the attacks of September 11, 2001, and Hurricane Katrina. Dr. La Porte teaches courses on critical infrastructures and extreme events, global Internet public policy, introductory international political economy, technology and institutional change, and culture, organizations, and technology.

Before joining George Mason, La Porte was a member of the Faculty of Technology, Policy and Management at the Delft University of Technology in The Netherlands, where he was Associate Professor. From 1989 to 1995, he was an analyst at the Office of Technology Assessment, a research office of the U.S. Congress, where he worked on the role of wireless telecommunications and the National Information Infrastructure, international trade in telecommunications services and U.S. policy, and international defense industrial cooperation and the arms trade. In addition to his work at OTA, Dr. La Porte has published works on public organizational challenges of the World Wide Web in disaster assistance, on European technology assessment methodologies and practices, and on the social implications of telecommunications mobility. He received his Ph.D. in political science from Yale University in 1989 and his B.A. in sociology and political science from Swarthmore College in 1980. He lives in Washington, D.C.

Todd R. La Porte is Professor of Political Science at the University of California, Berkeley (since 1965), where he was also Associate Director of the Institute of Governmental Studies (1973–1988). He received his B.A. from the University of Dubuque; his M.A. and Ph.D. from Stanford University; and he has held faculty posts at the University of Southern California, Stanford University, and the University of California, Berkeley. He teaches and publishes in the areas of organization theory, technology and politics, and the organizational and decision-making dynamics of large, complex, technologically intensive organizations, as well as public attitudes toward advanced technologies and the challenges of governance in a technological society. He was a principal of the Berkeley High Reliability Organization Project, a multi-disciplinary team that studied the organizational aspects of safety-critical systems such as nuclear power, air traffic control, and nuclear aircraft carriers. His research concerns the evolution of large-scale organizations operating technologies demanding a very high level of operating reliable performance across a number of management generations, and the relationship of large-scale technical systems to political legitimacy. This took him to Los Alamos National Laboratory (1998–2003) to examine the institutional challenges of multi-generation nuclear missions. Most recently, he has taken up questions of crisis management in the face of new types of threats emerging from the United States' sustained engagement with radical Islamic movements.

He was elected to the National Academy of Public Administration in 1985 and was a Fellow with the Woodrow Wilson International Center for Scholars, Smithsonian Institution, and a Research Fellow at Wissenschaftszentrum (Sciences Center) in Berlin and the Max Planck Institute for Social Research, Cologne. Service on editorial boards includes *Policy Sciences, Public Administration Review, Technology Studies, Journal of Contingencies and Crisis Management,* and the Steering Committee, Large Technical Systems International Study Group. He has been a member of the Board on Radioactive Waste Management and has served on panels of the Committee on Human Factors and Transportation Research Board, National Academy of Sciences. He served on the Secretary of Energy Advisory Board, Department of Energy, and chaired its Task Force on Radioactive Waste Management, examining questions of institutional trustworthiness, and he was on the Technical Review Committee, Nuclear Materials Technology Division, Los Alamos National Laboratory. He has also served as a member of the Committee on Long Term Institutional Management of DOE Legacy Waste Sites: Phase Two and the Committee on Principles and Operational Strategies for Staged Repository Systems, both of the Board on Radioactive Waste Management, the National Academies of Science (2001–2003). He is currently a Faculty Affiliate, Decision Science Division, Los Alamos National Laboratory, and has consulted with the U.S. Department of Energy's Defense Nuclear Facilities Safety Board.

Patrick Lagadec is author of 10 books on emerging risks and crises, among which are *States of Emergency* (1990), *Preventing Chaos in a Crisis* (1991), and *Treatise on New Risks* (2002). Director of Research at the Ecole Polytechnique (Paris), he is founding member of the European Crisis Management Academy and a member of its Governing Council. Dr. Lagadec has a long history of direct involvement with critical infrastructure and vital network operators internationally (e.g., space, energy, banks, transport, public health). He developed the theory of Major Technological Risk (1979) and is a specialist in crisis prevention and management.

In the past 10 years, he has broadened his work on governance of organizations and complex systems confronted by global crises and paradigm shifts, in terms of safety, security, and sustainability (e.g., climate, natural disasters, health, social, terrorist threats, and breakdowns). He has extensive experience as a strategic advisor and trainer in the field of major risks, unconventional crises, and global "ruptures" for the past 25 years. His expertise is in preparedness and implementation of new paradigms and innovative operational processes to help public officials, executive committees, and citizen groups to build new frameworks and more sustainable capability to deal with a world in rapid mutation. A member of the French National Academy of Technologies, Dr. Lagadec received the Engelberg Prize in 1999.

Lester B. Lave is University Professor and Higgins Professor of Economics at Carnegie Mellon University, with appointments in the Business School, Engineering School, and the Public Policy School. He has a B.A. from Reed College and a Ph.D. from Harvard University. He was elected to the Institute of Medicine of the National Academy of Sciences and is a past president of the Society for Risk Analysis. He has acted as a consultant to many government agencies and companies. He has received research support from a wide range of federal and state agencies, as well as foundations, nongovernmental organizations, and companies. Dr. Lave is the director of the CMU university-wide Green Design Institute and, with M. Granger Morgan, directs the CMU Electricity Industry Center. His research focuses on applying economics to public policy issues, particularly those related to energy in general and electricity in particular.

Brian Lopez is a computer scientist at Lawrence Livermore National Laboratory (LLNL). For the past eight years, he has led LLNL's Vulnerability and Risk Assessment Program (VRAP), which provides in-depth, multi-disciplinary assessments of threat, vulnerability, and consequence. Past projects include work in 26 U.S. states and internationally across a variety of sectors such as electric power, oil, gas, water, chemical, aviation, rail, maritime, telecommunications, national icons, and classified sites. He assembled and led security teams for the 2002 Winter Olympics, California Energy Crisis, and 9/11 response. Currently he is leading a comprehensive assessment of a 34-city region for the Department of Homeland Security. His previous work has been in the areas of nuclear material tracking, secure systems design, knowledge management, and counterterrorism.

James W. Macdonald is an independent commercial insurance and reinsurance consultant based in Philadelphia. Between 2001 and 2005, he was the Chief Underwriting Officer for ACE USA. He has more than 30 years of insurance industry experience and is an experienced author and public speaker. Prior to joining ACE, he served in a variety of executive, brokerage, consulting, and underwriting roles at CNA Financial, American International

Group, Conning & Company, Marsh & McLennan, and Munich American Reinsurance.

His recent publications and presentations include *The Terrorism Risk Insurance Extension Act of 2005* (International Risk Management Institute); *Risk Report* (February 2006); *Caveat Emptor When Buying Terrorism Insurance* (National Underwriter, February 2006); *Underwriting Discipline in a Softening Market* (John Liner Review, Summer 2005); *Terrorism, TRIA & a Timeline for Market Turmoil?* (RIMS Convention, 2004); *Terrorism, Insurance & TRIA: Are We Asking the Right Questions?* (John Liner Review, Summer 2004); and *Medical Malpractice: A Prescription for Chaos* (Conning & Company, May 2001).

Mr. Macdonald is a former member of the Advisory Board of the Rand Corporation's Institute for Civil Justice and the Rand Corporation Center for Terrorism Risk Management Policy. He is also a former Board member of the National Patient Safety Foundation at the American Medical Association. A graduate of the University of Notre Dame with a B.A. in English Literature, he has completed postgraduate studies in Fine Arts at Montreal's Concordia University and in Philosophy and Finance at the New School for Social Research and New York University.

Prior to his retirement from active duty with the U.S. Air Force in 1984 following a distinguished career, **General Robert T. Marsh** commanded the Air Force Systems Command. After retirement, General Marsh has been employed as an aerospace consultant. He served as the Chairman of Thiokol Corporation from 1989 to 1991, as it transitioned from Morton Thiokol Corporation to independent status. He served as the Executive Director of the Air Force Aid Society from 1995 until April 2001. He was appointed by the President as Chairman of the President's Commission on Critical Infrastructure Protection in 1996 and served in that capacity through 1997. Currently, he serves as a director of Verint Technology, Inc., and SI International, Inc. He is a Trustee Emeritus of the MITRE Corporation.

Erwann O. Michel-Kerjan (Editor) is Managing Director of the Wharton School's Risk Management and Decision Processes Center, a center with 20 years of experience in developing strategies and policies for dealing with catastrophic risks. Dr. Michel-Kerjan joined the Wharton School in 2002, where his research has been focused on managing and financing extreme events, primarily natural disasters and mega-terrorism, and on the consequent strategic crisis management. In particular, his interest is in the creation, implementation, and development of private–public collaboration among top decision makers to deal with emerging large-scale risks. His work also includes several projects on national security and the protection of critical infrastructure in partnership with Lockheed Martin and several federal agencies.

Dr. Michel-Kerjan has been working on these issues in collaboration with industry, governments, academia, and international organizations in North America and in Europe for nearly 10 years. He is invited regularly to bring his dual experience from and to each side of the Atlantic. Michel-Kerjan's work on financing extreme events has appeared in leading media in the United States and aboard. His first book, *Treatise on New Risks* (with O. Godard, C. Henry, and P. Lagadec), was published in 2002.

Between 2003 and 2005, he served on the OECD Task Force on Terrorism Insurance, and in 2005 he co-led, with Howard Kunreuther, the Wharton initiative on the future of terrorism risk financing in the United States *(TRIA and Beyond)*. He is a member of the American Economic Association, the American Risk and Insurance Association, and the Econometric Society, and he is a faculty research associate at the Ecole Polytechnique in Paris. He also serves as an expert for the Division of Financial Affairs of the OECD and he is a member of the Global Risk Network of the World Economic Forum.

M. Granger Morgan currently holds the following positions at Carnegie Mellon University: University and Lord Chair Professor in Engineering; Head, Department of Engineering and Public Policy; Professor, Electrical and Computer Engineering; and in the H. John Heinz III School of Public Policy and Management. Dr. Morgan is interested in a wide range of problems in science, technology, and public policy. Much of his work has involved the development and demonstration of methods to characterize and analyze uncertainty. With colleagues in two NSF-supported climate research centers, he has addressed issues in the integrated assessment of climate change impacts and policy. With colleagues in the Electricity Industry Center, he is exploring problems such as distributed resources, carbon management, and basic technology research to support clean energy. He has worked extensively in risk analysis, communication, and ranking. He chairs the EPA Science Advisory Board, EPRI's Advisory Board, and the S&T Council for the International Risk Governance Council. He received a B.A. (Physics) in 1963 from Harvard College; an M.S. (Astronomy and Space Science) in 1965 from Cornell University; and a Ph.D. (Applied Physics and Information Science) in 1968 from University of California, San Diego.

Franklin W. Nutter has been president of the Reinsurance Association of America (RAA) since May 1991. He held the same position with the RAA from 1981 to 1984. Prior to becoming president of the RAA in 1981, he served as the Association's general counsel from 1978 to 1981. In the interim, he was president of the Alliance of American Insurers and the Property Loss Research Bureau.

Mr. Nutter currently serves on the Board of Trustees of the Bermuda Biological Station for Research; the Board of the International Hurricane Center; the Advisory Board of the Center for Health and the Global Environment, an adjunct to the Harvard University Medical School; and the Advisory Board to the National Center for Atmospheric Research.

Mr. Nutter has chaired the Natural Disaster Coalition, an effort to develop a program to respond to catastrophic earthquakes, hurricanes, and volcanic eruptions in the United States. He served as a trustee to the National Commission Against Drunk Driving and has served as a member of the Board of Directors of the Advocates for Highway and Auto Safety, the Insurance Institute for Highway Safety and the Worker's Compensation Research Institute, and the Board of Overseers of the Institute for Civil Justice, a subsidiary of the Rand Corporation. Mr. Nutter was also a member of the Department of Commerce's Industry Sector Advisory Committee on Services for Trade Policy Matters. He has been active on reinsurance advisory committees and task forces of the American Bar Association and of the National Association of Insurance Commissioners. He served on the faculty of the American Institute's first advanced education program and served on the Brookings Council, an affiliate of the Brookings Institution in Washington, D.C. Mr. Nutter has a Juris Doctorate from the Georgetown University Law Center and a bachelor's degree in economics from the University of Cincinnati. He is a Vietnam veteran and is listed in *Who's Who in America.*

Daniel B. Prieto III is Director of the Homeland Security Center and Senior Fellow at the Reform Institute. Previously, he served as Research Director of the Homeland Security Partnership Initiative and Fellow at the Belfer Center for Science and International Affairs at the Harvard University Kennedy School of Government. He is author, with Stephen Flynn, of *Neglected Defense: Mobilizing the Private Sector to Support Homeland Security,* a special report from the Council on Foreign Relations.

Mr. Prieto has served on the professional staff of the Select Committee on Homeland Security in the U.S. House of Representatives. As a former technology-industry executive and investment banker, he has served as a strategist or advisor on more than $100 billion in transactions. He is an associate member of the Markle Foundation Task Force on National Security in the Information Age and recently chaired the management working group of the Center for Strategic and International Studies/Heritage Foundation Task Force Examining the Roles, Missions, and Organization of the Department of Homeland Security. He is a past recipient of the International Affairs Fellowship from the

Council on Foreign Relations and an honors graduate of Wesleyan University and the Johns Hopkins University School of Advanced International Studies.

Robert Reville is a labor economist who serves as the director of the Rand Institute for Civil Justice and the co-director of the Rand Center for Terrorism Risk Management Policy. His research focuses on compensation and insurance public policy. Dr. Reville has recently written several articles on terrorism insurance. He is a national expert in workplace injury compensation policy and the impact of disability on employment, and he has written extensively on workers' compensation in California, New Mexico, and other states. His publications in this area have been widely cited in the California legislature and have helped bring about new legislation to improve the workers' compensation system in the state. He was recently appointed to the Board of Scientific Counselors of the National Institute for Occupational Safety and Health, Centers for Disease Control and Prevention. He also serves on the Workers' Compensation Steering Committee of the National Academy of Social Insurance. Dr. Reville received his Ph.D. in economics from Brown University.

Emery Roe is a practicing policy analyst working on science, technology, and environmental controversies. He specializes in better understanding of management strategies in large technical systems for the provision of highly critical services, such as electricity and water. He is author or co-author of many publications, including *Narrative Policy Analysis* (1994), *Taking Complexity Seriously* (1998), *Except Africa* (1999), and *Ecology, Engineering and Management* (2002, co-authored with M. J. G. van Eeten). He has also helped design and direct initiatives on, among others, agriculture and urban sprawl in California's Central Valley, indicators of ecosystem health in the San Francisco Bay–Delta region, and campus/community partnerships in underserved urban minority neighborhoods, in addition to research on issues at the intersection of global population growth, natural resource utilization, and the environment.

Paul R. Schulman Professor of Government at Mills College, has also taught at Brown University and the University of California, Berkeley. He has done extensive research on large-scale public policy undertakings and on organizations that attempt to design and manage large and complex technologies. These organizations include NASA, nuclear power plants, air traffic control centers, and, most recently, California's electrical grid management organization, the California Independent System Operator. He is also researching the problem of medical errors in large health care facilities. His writings include *Large-Scale Policy-Making; California's Electricity Restructuring* with Emery Roe, Michel van Eeten, and Mark de Bruijne; as well as numerous articles that have appeared in journals such as the *American Political Science Review; Journal of Politics; Administrative Science Quarterly; Administration and Society; Quality and Safety in Health Care;* and *Journal of Contingencies and Crisis Management.* He has consulted for the Lawrence Livermore National Laboratory and the Atomic Energy Control Board of Canada.

Richard J. Zeckhauser is Frank P. Ramsey Professor of Political Economy, Kennedy School, Harvard University. He pursues a mix of conceptual and applied research. He is among the world's foremost authorities on economic behavior in the context of uncertainty. (In this spirit, he is an avid contract bridge player, and he placed second and third in U.S. national championships in the last three years.) Dr. Zeckhauser is a pioneer in the field of policy analysis and the author of numerous studies applying these methodologies to a range of public policy issues in areas such as health care, the environment, and terrorism. The primary challenge facing society, he believes, is to allocate resources in accordance with the preferences of the citizenry.

Dr. Zeckhauser is a Fellow of the Econometric Society, the Institute of Medicine (National Academy of Sciences), and the American Academy of Arts and Sciences. His current research projects are directed at environmental disasters, deception and reputations, bad apples and bad bets in social policy, trust in Islamic and Western nations, information economics and Italian Renaissance art, and the blending of negotiations and auctions. He is writing a book with John D. Donahue – his co-author in this volume – on collaborative undertakings between the public and private sectors.

AUTHOR INDEX

SUBJECT INDEX